Developing ASP Components

Second Edition

Shelley Powers

O'REILLY®

Beijing · Cambridge · Farnham · Köln · Paris · Sebastopol · Taipei · Tokyo

Developing ASP Components, Second Edition

by Shelley Powers

Copyright © 2001, 1999 O'Reilly & Associates, Inc. All rights reserved.
Printed in the United States of America.

Published by O'Reilly & Associates, Inc., 101 Morris Street, Sebastopol, CA 95472.

Editor: Ron Petrusha

Production Editor: Leanne Clarke Soylemez

Cover Designer: Hanna Dyer

Printing History:

April 1999:	First Edition.
March 2001:	Second Edition.

ISBN: 1-56592-750-8

[M]

Table of Contents

Preface

Developing ASP components requires knowledge not just of one tool or of one technology, but of many. You have to become familiar with one or more development tools, such as Visual Basic or Visual C++ (this book covers both, along with Visual J++, Delphi, and Perl), and of course you also have to become familiar with the tools' underlying language. However, you can't stop there.

ASP components are nothing more than specific types of COM-based components; that is, they're COM components designed to interface with Active Server Pages and, most commonly, with Microsoft's Internet Information Server (IIS). Consequently, you need to develop a certain level of familiarity with COM, the Component Object Model that underlies much of Microsoft's technology. Becoming familiar with COM development in turn requires that you become familiar with threads, so that you can understand how a COM component interacts with a client as well as the performance issues involved with clients and components that are based on different threading models.

Once you've become familiar with working with a tool that supports COM component development and you're aware of some of the issues involved with COM development, you still have other new technologies to learn. As you develop ASP components, you need to become familiar with web-based development in general and with the ASP environment in particular. The way in which your components interact with the "world" they find themselves in—with the web server, the browser, or the web page reader—occurs through built-in objects that Microsoft has provided for ASP development.

Originally, the built-in objects could only be instantiated based on specific event handlers. In IIS 4.0, however, the built-in objects could be accessed from Microsoft Transaction Server (MTS) objects. And now, in IIS 5.0, the ASP built-in objects can be accessed from COM+ objects. In addition, COM+ Services provides a number of features (such as transaction management, just-in-time activation, and object pooling) that are increasingly important for middle-tier components. So you are going to need to become familiar with COM+ as well.

This seems like a very formidable list of tools and technologies, and it is. But we're not finished yet. Most applications—including more and more ASP applications—require some form of data access. If you need to provide support for data access, then you need to become familiar with ActiveX Data Objects (ADO), the data access technology from Microsoft that's built on top of OLE DB. Frequently, the content of an ASP page is assembled from data found in a message store, or conversely the data gathered from the user's interaction with an ASP page is sent in an email or placed in a message store. For applications such as these, you need to become familiar with Collaborative Data Objects for Windows 2000 (CDO). Under Windows 2000 and IIS, a good deal of system information is stored in Active Directory; to retrieve information from and write information to Active Directory, you should know the Active Directory Service Interface (ADSI). Finally, ASP applications, and particularly ASP e-commerce applications, often require communication across systems and involve events that can occur at different times (as, for example, when a user orders products online and a pick list is needed by a system in the warehouse for printing). To take advantage of such loosely coupled events, you should be familiar with Microsoft Message Queue (MSMQ).

Finally, once you know the programming language used for the component, the tool used to build the component, the implications of developing a COM-based component, the functionality available through built-in and COM+–supplied objects, and how you can access data and the other services needed by your application, then and only then you can take on the functionality that your component needs to provide. Then, you add additional functionality such as file input and output, object serialization, access to other Windows functionality, and so on.

So, do you feel tired before you even start? Well, I want to tell you that developing ASP components really isn't all that bad, and in fact, you are about to start having some fun. Not only that, you are also going to learn to work with technology that faces directly on that road racing to the future: the road to distributed and component-based development.

This book introduces you to working with COM development as well as working with threads and those pesky little "not threads, not processes"—apartments. It also provides an overview of the ASP operating environment as well as some things you need to know about COM+ and how to work with it. Finally, to complete this environment overview, the book explores the interaction between the component and the script used to instantiate and invoke the methods of that component.

Following this introduction, the book then covers component development using Visual Basic and Visual C++. In the case of Visual Basic, chapters include accessing the intrinsic ASP objects from a Visual Basic component, accessing data using ADO, incorporating messaging with CDO for Windows 2000, using MSMQ, and using components to generate XML. The Visual C++ chapters discuss some of this same material (accessing ASP intrinsics, data access using ADO, using MSMQ), along with persistence using the Microsoft Foundation Classes (MFC) and the ActiveX Template Library (ATL). But if your organization is like so many others nowadays, your group is probably not using just one tool in its web development efforts. It's just not that unusual for shops to program in Visual C++ and Java, Visual Basic and Delphi, or Visual Basic and Perl. Rather than focus this book on one or two languages, I picked the tools/languages most likely to be used. Consequently, separate chapters examine issues in component development using Java, Delphi, and Perl. Each of these chapters is based on the earlier chapters that cover component development using Visual Basic and explores techniques and issues in component development using that language or tool.

Who This Book Is For

This book is geared to the developer who has worked with one of the target languages/tools but either has not created COM objects before or has not worked with developing ASP components or ASP applications. I hope that the book provides enough of an introduction to COM and threads to make you feel more comfortable with these topics if you haven't worked with them before and to provide a good review if you have. The book does not provide an exhaustive overview of COM+ and developing COM+ components but does provide, again, enough of an overview so you feel comfortable working as a developer in a COM+ environment.

The book also provides a comprehensive overview of the ASP component environment, including using tools and wizards in each language/tool to assist in creating the components, and covering every aspect of accessing the built-in ASP components essential for your development effort. In addition, the book also provides good coverage of data access using ADO, messaging using CDO for Windows 2000, and message queuing using MSMQ.

How This Book Is Structured

Informally, this book is divided into four parts. The first part introduces ASP component development and covers topics that are of concern to all component developers, regardless of the language they use. This part consists of six chapters. Chapter 1, *Writing ASP Components*, examines some of the reasons that you'd want to develop an ASP component rather than rely on a simple ASP script. It also mentions some of the technologies (COM+ services, ActiveX Data Objects, and Active Directory, to name just three) that you can draw on in developing your components. Chapter 2, *Setting Up the ASP Development Environment*, examines how to set up your development environment to insure that you can develop with maximum productivity and that your testing doesn't impact on a production system. In addition, the chapter covers programmatic administration of IIS using Active Directory and the IIS Admin Objects. Chapter 3, *ASP Components and COM*, examines Microsoft's Component Object Model (COM), which provides the basis for developing all types of components. Chapter 4, *ASP Components, Threads, and Contexts*, provides developers with the information that they need to know about threading models when developing ASP components, and particularly when accessing global data from the ASP Application object. It also examines the notion of context (a grouping of objects that share the same requirements), an understanding of which is essential to working successfully with COM+. Chapter 5, *COM+ Services and ASP Components and Applications*, examines the new interfaces supported by COM+, shows how components written to take advantage of COM+'s predecessor, Microsoft Transaction Server (MTS), can be ported to COM+, and examines range of services provided by COM+. Chapter 6, *ASP Interaction: Scripting and ASP Components*, covers an often-neglected component development topic: your component may be accessed by any of a number of scripting languages—VBScript, JScript, PerlScript, Python, Rexx, etc.—and communication between script and component is often not as seamless as you'd like. The chapter looks at what you can do when developing your ASP component to insure that it can work with as many scripting languages as possible.

The second portion of the book, which consists of seven chapters, focuses on component development using Visual Basic. In addition, its chapters serve as a kind of model for how to develop ASP components if you're using a high-level language like Visual Basic that masks much of the complexity of COM and COM+. Chapter 7, *Creating a Simple Visual Basic ASP Component*, introduces Visual Basic as a tool for ASP component development and examines how to access the ASP object model from Visual Basic. Chapter 8, *Creating ASP/ADO Components*, looks at accessing data in heterogeneous sources using ActiveX Data Objects (ADO). Chapter 9, *Creating an ASP Middle Tier with ADO*, discusses component design for multi-tier applications, focusing particularly on the degree of separation between the middle tier and the client tier. The remaining chapters focus on individual technologies that developers frequently use when creating ASP Components. These include the following:

- XML is discussed in Chapter 10, *Server-Side XML Through VB ASP Components*.

- Collaborative Data Objects (CDO) for Windows 2000 is covered in Chapter 11, *Take a Message: Accessing CDO from ASP Components*.

- Active Directory is discussed in Chapter 12, *Working with Active Directory from ASP Applications.*

- Microsoft Message Queue (MSMQ) is examined in Chapter 13, *Working with MSMQ Components.*

The third portion of the book, consisting of six chapters, treats component development using Visual C++. In addition, its chapters serve as a kind of model for ASP component development using a high-level language like Visual C++ that exposes much of the complexity of COM and COM+. Chapter 14, *Creating C++ ASP Components*, introduces Visual C++ as a tool for ASP component development and examines how to access the ASP intrinsic objects from a Visual C++ component. Chapter 15, *Adding Data Access to C++ Components with ADO*, examines accessing data in heterogeneous sources using ADO. The next three chapters cover the following individual technologies that are often used in developing components for IIS 5.0:

- Collaborative Data Objects (CDO) for Windows 2000 is covered in Chapter 16, *The CDO Interfaces from C++ Components.*

- Active Directory is discussed in Chapter 17, *Accessing Active Directory from C++ Components.*

- Microsoft Message Queue (MSMQ) is examined in Chapter 18, *Accessing MSMQ from C++ ASP Components.*

Finally, coverage of Visual C++ and ASP component development ends with Chapter 19, *Persistence with ASP Components Using ATL and MFC*, which discusses ways in which your component can save its data to the filesystem.

The final portion of this book features individual chapters on component development using the following programming languages and environments:

- Java is covered in Chapter 20, *ASP Components Created with Java.*

- Delphi is discussed in Chapter 21, *Creating ASP Components with Delphi.*

- Perl is covered in Chapter 22, *Perl-Based Components Using ActiveState's PDK.*

- Windows Script Components (WSC), a scriptable yet powerful development environment for creating ASP components, is discussed in Chapter 23, *Creating Scripting Language Components.*

Finally, the book includes two appendixes. Appendix A, *ASP Built-in Object Quick Reference*, provides a handy guide to the objects, properties, methods, and events of the ASP object model. Appendix B, *The Weaver Database*, examines the tables contained in the sample Weaver database, which is used in the book's examples. It can be downloaded from *http://vb.oreilly.com.*

Obtaining the Sample Code

All of the example source code from *Developing ASP Components, Second Edition*, along with the sample Weaver database discussed in Appendix A, is freely downloadable from the O'Reilly & Associates web site at *http://vb.oreilly.com*. Just follow the link to the book's title page, then click on the *Examples* link.

Conventions Used in This Book

Throughout this book, we have used the following typographic conventions:

Italic

> Represents intrinsic and application-defined functions, the names of system elements such as directories and files, and Internet resources such as web documents. New terms are also italicized when they are first introduced.

Constant width

> Indicates a language construct such as a language statement, a constant, or an expression. Interface names appear in constant width. Lines of code also appear in constant width, as do function and method prototypes.

Constant width italic

> Indicates replaceable parameter names in prototypes or command syntax and indicates variable and parameter names in body text.

 Indicates a note or tip.

 Indicates a warning.

Comments and Questions

Please address comments and questions concerning this book to the publisher:

> O'Reilly & Associates, Inc.
> 101 Morris Street
> Sebastopol, CA 95472

(800) 998-9938 (in the United States or Canada)
(707) 829-0515 (international or local)
(707) 829-0104 (fax)

We have a web page for this book, where we list errata, examples, or any additional information. You can access this page at:

http://www.oreilly.com/catalog/devaspcom2

To comment or ask technical questions about this book, send email to:

bookquestions@oreilly.com

For more information about our books, conferences, software, Resource Centers, and the O'Reilly Network, see our web site at:

http://www.oreilly.com

For technical information on Visual Basic programming, to participate in VB discussion forums, or to acquaint yourself with O'Reilly's line of Visual Basic books, you can access the O'Reilly Visual Basic web site at:

http://vb.oreilly.com

Acknowledgments

I want to thank the book's tech reviewers, Daniel Creeron and Matt Childs, for their thorough reviews and helpful comments. I also want to thank Bob Herbstman and Tatiana Diaz, members of the O'Reilly editorial staff, for their hard work and dedication to this project.

I also want to thank my long-suffering editor, Ron Petrusha. This is the second edition of this particular book, and he's done a terrific job of editing both of them. I also want to thank my coworkers at Skyfish.com for being a terrific group of people. Specifically, I want to thank a certain group of Australians in the company— guys, the best to you all, and may your dreams find you.

Finally, thanks to my readers—I'm here because you're here.

1

Writing ASP Components

When Microsoft first released Active Server Pages (ASP) with the company's web server, Internet Information Server (IIS), the functionality included with this early release amounted to little more than an ability to handle server-side scripting. If you haven't worked with server-side scripting, it is the inclusion of script, such as VBScript or JScript, in web pages so that the script is processed on the server rather than on the client. This early ASP release soon gave way to the ASP we have now, a sophisticated server-side application-building environment that still supports server-side scripting, but also includes integration with other Microsoft server products such as COM+ Services and allows ASP pages to access COM/COM+ objects.

This book is about writing COM/COM+ objects to work within this ASP environment. Since they are COM/COM+-based, you know that whatever functionality you can implement with COM/COM+ components, you can also implement with ASP components. This means that you can create an instance of an ASP component and use that component instance to do things such as query a database, open a file, or send an email to a client. However, ASP components are created for a specialized environment, and there are certain things you might consider doing with COM objects that you probably wouldn't consider doing with ASP components. For instance, because an ASP component resides on the server, you aren't going to use any message windows to communicate with the user; all communication is handled through IIS.

In addition, by being part of the ASP environment, ASP components have access to built-in objects that contain information not normally available to a "standard" COM object—information such as form field values submitted from an HTML form, the type of browser being used to access the page, or even the language, such as English, preferred by the client.

The information available to an ASP component is also available to ASP scripting blocks, so why use components when you can use scripting, especially since scripting is fairly simple to use and can be learned relatively quickly?

The first and foremost reason to use ASP components instead of in-page ASP scripting blocks is reusability. It's difficult to package an ASP script in such a way that it can be used over and over again in many different pages. Additionally, if you or your company is considering packaging some ASP functionality for resale or distribution, the use of ASP scripting becomes insupportable. You probably won't be in business long if people can both see and modify your source code.

Another reason to use ASP components is that the components themselves can reside virtually anywhere, even on different machines. You can create an ASP application that may update a customer database and that uses one component to update the person's address and another component to update the person's preferences. One or both of these components can reside on the same machine as the web server, but one or both of these components can as easily reside on other machines, with remote COM+ being used to access the component. While you can distribute web pages containing script on various machines, the maintenance and access issues become much more complicated and usually require hardcoding the physical addresses of the pages within the application. With COM+-based functionality, only the operating system COM+ manager needs to know where the ASP components reside. Moving components is a matter of changing the location of a component once on the client machine; all accesses to the component now occur at its new location.

An additional reason to use ASP components is that they can incorporate the fullest range of functionality on the server, including database access, file access, archiving, messaging, and other functionality difficult or impossible to do with script. You can even transcend object systems and access CORBA-based components with the support of products such as Iona's COM-CORBA Bridge and others.

The Role ASP Components Play

As stated earlier, ASP components are COM+-based components that encapsulate a specific functionality and that are invoked either directly from an ASP page or indirectly via some other ASP component. If you have worked with COM+ before, ASP components don't use any additional technology, but they can use additional objects available only within the context of an ASP application. However, if a component does not access the ASP-specific objects provided through the ASP object model, it can be used within a distributed application, from other components (whether or not they're part of an ASP application), or even within a flat one-tier application that has no involvement with ASP, IIS, or the Internet. From this point of view, this book could actually be about writing COM+ components, albeit with a specific focus.

Having said that an ASP component is really no different than any other COM+ component, I want to add that the focus of writing an ASP component can alter how that component is created. First, the component will usually reside on the same server as the client of the component, with the client for ASP being the web server. I say *usually* with some reservation, since there is no requirement that ASP components *must* reside on the same machine as the client application.

In addition, an ASP component is almost always an in-process (ActiveX DLL) component, though you can use out-of-process components if you wish. However, ASP is optimized for in-process access of components.

As in-process COM+ objects, ASP components are usually created using the apartment- or both-threaded model or the new neutral-threaded apartment model. ASP components are not and should not be created using the single-threaded model, since the component locks down all access to a single thread, which causes access problems in a multiuser environment such as the Web and a multiuser application such as a web server. The component shouldn't be created using the free-threaded model either, since all communication between the ASP page and the component must then be *marshaled*, a process that can impact on the ASP application's performance.

There is an additional constraint if you're using a multithreaded model such as the both-threaded model: the ASP components must be thread-safe. What's a thread-safe ASP component? One that does not contain global data, that does not yield control internal to the processing of the component, and that is safely reentrant. Chapter 4, *ASP Components, Threads, and Contexts*, goes into more depth on threads and apartments. That chapter also covers how threads and the new COM+ contexts work together to provide optimized management of the components.

Now that you have a basic idea of what ASP components are, the next section discusses why you would use ASP components instead of creating the ASP application using scripting exclusively.

Why Use ASP Components?

In the beginning of the chapter, I started listing some reasons to use ASP components instead of scripting. In this section, I want to discuss this topic in a little more detail.

An ASP component can be used in place of scripting where scripting is just not workable or efficient. For example, your ASP application may need to make direct calls to the Windows internals through the Win32 API or manage file input and output. These operations cannot be done from within a scripting language such as JScript or VBScript. The IIS scripting engine can be extended to other scripting languages, such as Tcl or PerlScript, which do support direct filesystem access or calls to the Win32 API. However, the use of these scripting languages comes at a cost: the code is a little more difficult to read, a little more difficult to maintain, and a whole lot more difficult to secure against editing from external sources. If the code needs to remain unaltered, perhaps to enforce standards compliance or universal data access, the code should be contained within binary components.

Along with implementing functionality that is either unsupported or not easily supported by scripting languages, ASP components are also developed to be reusable and to wrap routines that are commonly called in ASP applications, something that isn't as easy to implement with script. This means that, if the code needs to change, the change then needs to be propagated to all the pages that use the code. In contrast, reusable code is more easily and efficiently managed through components. All ASP applications can access a single physical component. And when that component needs to be modified or revised, the change needs to be made in just a single place. So for code that needs to be reusable, an ASP component is a better choice than ASP scripting.

ASP components can be used to modularize an application, splitting off discrete, manageable bits of functionality that can then be coded by several people in parallel or even purchased from some other party. An additional advantage to modularization of code in components is that the components can themselves be distributed on different machines, and component access can be handled remotely through DCOM or some other equivalent technology. This approach ensures that the application is more scalable and will be able to handle increasingly larger numbers of accesses. If the ASP components are also configured and coded as COM+ components, transaction management for all of the components can be handled directly by COM+ regardless of where the component resides. Though transactions can be used with scripting and ASP pages can be located on other machines, the management of pages containing straight scripting blocks instead of components under such conditions can become more complicated.

If an organization is considering building an application that is n-tier rather than fitting within the traditional client-server paradigm, ASP components are an excellent tool to use to implement one or more of the application layers. A classic approach is to implement the business layer of an ASP application as one or more ASP components and handle the presentation layer in the web page using HTML and client-side scripting, including the newer Dynamic HTML (DHTML). The data access layer would be contained within the database used in the application.

Finally, ASP components are a handy way of ensuring uniformity of an application. For example, if database queries are formatted for output into HTML tables with a certain look, the data presentation functionality can be maintained within ASP components in a layer between the web pages and the business logic and used for all database queries.

COM+ Services and ASP Components

ASP components within the Windows 2000 environment can use one of several COM+-managed services to enhance the performance of both the component and the component's ASP application.

One popular COM+ service is *just-in-time (JIT) activation.* JIT is used to instantiate the component when the component's methods are called, not when it's instantiated in the ASP script. JIT also deactivates the component when it's no longer active, though the ASP page may still be processing other component method calls. This late instantiation/early release model helps free up scarce system resources such as memory and database connections, as described in more detail in Chapter 5, *COM+ Services and ASP Components and Applications.*

Another COM+ service is *object pooling.* Object pooling is used to create a pool of ASP components that are then used to process component method requests, rather than creating a new component for every request. Object pooling can increase the speed with which components are instantiated. However, only components that meet certain criteria, as described in Chapter 5, can take advantage of object pooling.

Resource Management

Resource pooling recognizes that some resources—such as database connections, threads, and other finite resources—are expensive. By preallocating a pool of resources, access to the resource happens more quickly. Since quick allocation of the resource is assured, the developer will most likely write code that allocates the resource, uses it, and releases it as soon as possible. When the developer uses this type of coding practice, the pool of available resources can be kept as small as possible. By keeping the resource pool as small as possible, the whole system performs better, and the developer receives positive feedback—a nicely performing application or component—encouraging the developer to continue using the sound coding practices that actually assist in the well-behaved application or component. This is just the kind of cycle that should be encouraged with development.

By utilizing resource pooling, expensive and time-consuming resources such as database connections can be created when the application is started and can be used for all resource access, rather than having to create a new reference every time the application wants to create a new connection. Based on resource pooling, the connection happens more quickly, and the system is more scalable, since limited resources are managed finitely and controls are maintained on the number of resources allocated.

Database connections are the most widely known resource that participates in resource pooling, but any resource can be managed in this manner by creating the appropriate resource dispenser. COM+ provides for resource pooling of ASP or other components by providing an object called ObjectControl that actually allows the component to be used within a resource-pooling context. Additionally, for specific resources, developers can actually create resource dispensers that manage allocation of the resource connections for any resource they believe would benefit from this process.

In addition to supporting resource pooling, COM+ also provides for just-in-time activation, which means that when a client makes a connection to a component managed by COM+, it is really getting a connection provided by COM+ and not directly by the component. If the component signals that it is finished with its process using the SetComplete or SetAbort methods on the component's associated ObjectContext object (discussed in the next section), COM+ knows that it can mark the component for release, even while the client still maintains the connection to the component. When the client next accesses a method on the component, COM+ loads a new instance of the component, and the client is never aware that it is no longer using the original "component reference."

COM+ also provides for transaction management, as described in the next section.

Transaction Management

If an ASP component performs a task that begins and finishes within a single function call, transaction management is not that much of an issue. However, ASP components can call other components and perform other actions such as database activity, each of which requires some form of overall transaction support.

One of the problems with a distributed application (and an ASP application can be distributed) is transaction management across several different application components and potentially across several different machines. For instance, one component can update an address in a database, and another component can update an associated name. If the address update fails, the associated name update should also fail in order to maintain consistency of the data. If both the updates occur within the same component, this isn't a problem, since both database transactions can be *rolled back*. Rolling back a change means that the impacted database data exists in the same state as it did before the change was attempted.

If the updates occur with two different components, transaction management becomes more complex. One possibility is to use one database connection for both components, and one of the components—the one making the name update—calls the other component that performs the address updating. The component performing the address update returns a value signifying success or failure of its operation. If the update failed, the first component would not make its update. Though workable, the approach is cumbersome, and neither component is able to work independently of the other.

Another approach is to handle transaction management within an ASP page or by a third component that creates both updating components, tests the return state of both components, and commits or rolls back all of the changes based on the results returned by either component. This is a better solution, since now both components can make their updates without having to worry about what is happening with any other component. However, in a larger application that makes multiple changes of this type, having the application itself maintain consistency between the data updates of all the components can become overwhelming at some point.

The best solution of all is to have some other process manage the transaction state of the components and test to see whether each component has succeeded in its operation or whether one of the components has failed. If any one of the components fails, then the changes made by *all* of the components are rolled back. This is where COM+ comes in.

COM+ provides a two-phase commit transaction management scheme that ensures that, unless all participants in a transaction complete successfully, none of the participant updates are committed. You might say that this first phase of the commit operation consists of a pass made of all participants in a transaction to ask if they are ready to commit their changes. The second pass then checks to make sure all of the components have made updates without errors.

ASP applications can participate in COM+ transactions, and transaction management can occur within an ASP page, an ASP component, or both. A transaction can be created within an ASP page and then used for all of the components created directly from the page or created from within another component accessed in that page. Failure in any one component means all of the updates made by all of the components within the transaction are rolled back. Components themselves do not have to create transactions directly but can be registered with COM+ in such a way as to participate in an existing transaction or have COM+ automatically create a new transaction for the component when the component is created.

To facilitate transaction management from within the component, there are COM+ objects with methods the component can call to signal to COM+ the state of both the component and the transaction. If the component uses the COM+ `IObjectContext` or `IContextState` interface methods, such as SetAbort or Set-Complete, the component is basically providing information to COM+ that it has finished its processing and can be unloaded from memory. The following code is an example of using the ObjectContext SetAbort method from within a Visual Basic component:

```
Dim objContext As ObjectContext
Set objContext = GetObjectContext()
...
objContext.SetAbort
```

By using the ObjectContext object's SetAbort method, COM+ knows that the component has finished its processing but that the processing was not successful. In a two-phase commit paradigm, the object passes the first phase successfully—it is finished with its processing. The second pass of the process would operate on the information that this component failed, which means that the transaction failed and that none of the updates made by any component in the transaction are committed.

Using the SetAbort method also lets COM+ know that it can unload the component from memory even if the client of the component still maintains a pointer to the component. When the client next accesses the component, COM+ loads a new version of it and passes all component references to the new component. This is an example of JIT that was discussed earlier.

Each of the language-specific chapters of the book (Chapters 7, 14, and 20–23) covers the use of transactions from within components.

Transactions are particularly important if your ASP components are making updates to a persistent data source using data objects such as ActiveX Data Objects (ADO), discussed next.

Accessing Data with ASP Components

There are few applications, Internet-based or otherwise, that do not perform data access in one form or another. ASP applications are no exception. There are actually several methodologies that an ASP application and an ASP component can use to manage or query data.

RDO and DAO: Earlier Data Access Techniques

First, an ASP component may access data through a set of APIs provided by the data source engine that allows direct access to the data. Though efficient, the problem with this approach is that the data access is locked into the particular database engine. An additional problem is that there is no guarantee that the API may not change over time, forcing changes to the component using it. An example of using a direct call-level interface is DB Library for SQL Server.

If the data source has an ODBC driver, the ODBC call-level interface could be used instead. The advantage to using ODBC is that the same techniques used to query and manage data for one data source can also be used for another data source, as long as both data sources provide a compliant and compatible ODBC driver. However, this technique requires a fairly in-depth understanding of ODBC.

Microsoft provided Data Access Objects (DAO) for access to the Jet database engine that ships with Visual Basic and Access. The advantages of DAO are that it is optimized for ISAM or Jet database access, and it can support single queries against multiple data sources. The disadvantages to using DAO are that it is not an optimum approach to access data from relational data sources, and it requires more memory than other approaches, such as the Remote Data Objects (RDO) discussed next. Also, before the release of ODBCDirect, DAO could not be used with ODBC data sources. ODBCDirect now provides RDO functionality from DAO objects, though the other limitations remain.

RDO objects are really wrapper objects for the ODBC API that lessen the complexity of using ODBC. RDO provides for powerful functionality, including the use of local cursors and batch operations. RDO is also fast and efficient, but its performance can actually degrade or it can even fail when used with ISAM data sources.

The previous generation of data access techniques tended to support particular types of data access. Some, like DAO, are geared for ISAM data access, and others, like RDO, are geared more toward relational database access. In addition, none of the approaches are designed to access data from text files, email, or any other of the many data sources that we use on a day-to-day basis. To address the gaps in data access, Microsoft proposed the concept of Universal Data Access, discussed next.

Universal Data Access

Universal Data Access is nothing more than a single data access technology that can be used with different types of data, regardless of the format or structure of the data source. This means that the same objects can be used to access an ISAM data source, a relational database, a text file, and even data from an email.

To support the concept of Universal Data Access, Microsoft used COM as an implementation paradigm and created OLE DB. OLE DB is a set of interfaces based on COM that provide for data access through *data providers* that produce and control data and *data consumers* that use the data. In this context, SQL Server is considered a data provider, and an ASP component that uses OLE DB directly is a data consumer.

OLE DB is very fast and efficient, but it is not necessarily simple to understand or use outside of the OLE DB templates for Visual C++. To assist developers in using

OLE DB, Microsoft also provided ActiveX Data Objects (ADO), a set of objects implemented on top of OLE DB that can be used with any programming language or tool that has COM access.

ADO consists of a very small set of objects that can be accessed either hierarchically or directly. One of the disadvantages of both DAO and RDO is that their objects form an enforced hierarchy, and any one object can only be accessed from its parent objects within the hierarchy. With ADO, an object like a result set can be accessed and used directly without having to access it from either a command or a database connection, unless this hierarchical access is what you want.

In Chapter 8, *Creating ASP/ADO Components*, ADO is used to demonstrate basic data access techniques with ASP components created using Visual Basic, though the techniques can apply to ADO access from any language. Chapter 9, *Creating an ASP Middle Tier with ADO*, describes some of the techniques and issues to be aware of when developing a component for the middle tier. In addition, Chapter 15, *Adding Data Access to C++ Components with ADO*, covers the use of ADO from Visual C++, and the other language chapters in the final section of the book each demonstrate how to use ADO with that specific language.

Windows 2000 Technologies Accessible from ASP Components

An ASP component within the Windows 2000 operating system environment has access to a wealth of technologies that can be used to send or read emails, post deferred messages, manage an LDAP directory, and so on.

Microsoft has provided the Active Directory Service Interface (ADSI) to work with Active Directory. Directory services are used to manage users, groups, and system resources, including controlling application access and issues of security. The ADSI is used to manage the IIS environment, as detailed in Chapter 2, *Setting Up the ASP Development Environment*. ADSI can also be used to provide LDAP directory service functionality to an ASP application. Using ADSI is demonstrated using Visual Basic in Chapter 12, *Working with Active Directory from ASP Applications*; using ADSI with Visual C++ is discussed in Chapter 17, *Accessing Active Directory from C++ Components*.

Collaborative Data Objects (CDO) for Windows 2000 can be used from within your ASP components to send and retrieve email messages. The messages can be as simple as a single text string or can include complex hierarchical multipart messages with MIME formatting. Chapter 11, *Take a Message: Accessing CDO from ASP Components*, and Chapter 16, *The CDO Interfaces from C++ Components*, demonstrate the use of CDO from Visual Basic and Visual C++, respectively.

The Microsoft Message Queue (MSMQ) technology is used to create deferred application-specific messages. For instance, a salesperson in the field can get several orders that are stored in his laptop. At some point he can connect to the company's server process and upload the orders as MSMQ messages, to be processed immediately or at a later time.

To work with MSMQ technology, you can use MSMQ COM objects, as described in Chapter 13, *Working with MSMQ Components*, or you can access the MSMQ functions from Visual C++, as described in Chapter 18, *Accessing MSMQ from C++ ASP Components*.

The mechanics of using each of these technologies is covered in the Visual Basic chapters of this book, and demonstrations of how to use them within an environment where more of the COM+ infrastructure is exposed is covered in the chapters devoted to demonstrating C++.

Though much of the Windows 2000 functionality covered in this book is demonstrated with Visual Basic or Visual C++, you can implement the same functionality in your COM-compliant language. Each of the languages covered in the final portion of the book—Delphi's Pascal, Perl, and Java—as well as scripting languages can access any of the functionality just discussed. To do so, read the Visual Basic chapters first in order to get an overview of the technology. Then apply the techniques exposed in either Visual Basic or Visual C++ to your own language.

Each of the language chapters takes one aspect of the Windows 2000 technologies and demonstrates how it can be accessed in the specific language.

A Rose by Any Other Name: Programming Language Choice

In actuality, there is no "right" tool or language to use for writing ASP components. Any tool that is capable of creating COM-compatible objects can be used to create ASP components. This includes C++ (through tools such as Visual C++ or Inprise's C++ Builder), Visual Basic, and Java (through Visual J++ or through the Java SDK, depending on the functionality you include in your component).

This also includes languages considered as "not traditional" ASP programming languages, such as Pascal, through Delphi from Inprise (formerly Borland), and Perl, with the help of the Perl Dev Kit from ActiveState.

As for which language to write the component in, there is no one choice that stands out clearly over the others. Writing ASP components using Visual Basic exposes less of the underlying functionality than writing the same component using Delphi or Visual C++. Because of this, Visual Basic is the easiest tool to use, particularly for a shop that has primarily used tools such as PowerBuilder or Visual Basic for most application development. If a shop is porting a traditional Visual Basic client/server application to an n-tier system, the continued use of Visual Basic also makes sense.

However, for a Delphi or Perl shop, it makes no sense to switch to Visual Basic when you can use either of these languages in your component development. Both provide modules or wizards you can use to facilitate your ASP component development.

For Delphi or Perl developers, the Visual Basic chapters in this book provide overviews of the technology being demonstrated in the chapter, such as CDO, as well as examples of using CDO with VB components. You can benefit from both the overview and the demonstrations in these chapters, even though you program in a different language. Consider Visual Basic as the closest "pseudocode" language we can find when it comes to demonstrating techniques.

If your exposure to development has been primarily with scripting, then you can also use scripting languages such as JavaScript/JScript or VBScript to create your components, by using the Windows Script Components (WSC). How to use the WSC is described in Chapter 23, *Creating Scripting Language Components*.

Visual C++ exposes more of an ASP component's underlying COM architecture and can be used to create efficient and speedy components. However, that same exposure to COM also makes using Visual C++ a more difficult choice. If the shop creating the components has no C++ or Visual C++ experience, this approach becomes prohibitive. However, if a shop has used Visual C++, then Microsoft has provided the ActiveX Template Library (ATL) to assist in implementing ASP components; it handles almost all of the details associated with the implementation of a COM component. Using ATL and accessing the ASP built-in objects are covered in Chapter 14, *Creating C++ ASP Components*. In addition, Chapter 19, *Persistence with ASP Components Using ATL and MFC*, provides coverage of file I/O in addition to serializing information for persistence beyond the life span of an ASP application.

As for concerns about interoperability, considering that ASP components are COM components, they are by their very nature interoperable within a COM environment. Even within an organization that uses CORBA rather than COM+, there are COM/COM+-to-CORBA bridges to handle communication between the two component management/communication approaches.

The underlying language used to create the component does not matter because ASP components are based on a binary interface, not a language-specific interface.

What About ASP.NET?

As you move into the future with your ASP development, you'll eventually start moving your applications over to ASP.NET rather than the existing ASP. How will this new environment and framework impact on your component development?

Actually, you'll find that ASP components work equally well in an ASP.NET environment as in an ASP environment. In fact, the whole concept of ASP.NET is that any language—including those demonstrated in this book—can be used to create ASP.NET applications.

Instead of using separate script blocks using JScript and VBScript, you can use programming languages such as C++, Perl, Visual Basic, or the new C# (pronounced "C sharp") to create functionality within an ASP.NET page or within an externally accessed COM+ component. The underlying infrastructure compiles the language code into a common Intermediate Language (IL) code.

The ASP objects change with ASP.NET, so you'll want to consider using the ASP built-in objects from your component code sparingly, if at all.

Regardless of how fast you move to the ASP.NET environment, Microsoft realizes that it must support components created using classic COM/COM+ functionality—which means that the components you create now will continue to function into the future.

2

Setting Up the ASP Development Environment

ASP is a web development tool and environment and thus requires that a web server be available. Originally, only Microsoft supplied web servers that provided the necessary support to run an ASP application. It wasn't long, though, before companies such as Chili!Soft extended support for ASP to other web servers such as Apache, Netscape's servers, and even O'Reilly's web server, all of which increased the popularity of ASP as a web development tool. However, IIS is still the primary web server used with ASP.

IIS can be installed as an option when you install Windows 2000. If you're upgrading, IIS is installed automatically if the upgrade process detects an existing copy of the web server. You can also install IIS at a later time. Once IIS is installed, though, additional work is necessary to configure the environment to support ASP, depending on whether the web server is a standalone server set up for development or a production machine accessed internally through an intranet or externally through the Internet.

IIS can be configured and administered locally or remotely through the use of tools that Microsoft has provided. In addition, IIS also has a support data structure known as the IIS Metabase, which can be manipulated programmatically using objects provided with IIS or using the Active Directory Services Interface (ADSI).

Once IIS is installed and configured, the next step is to create an ASP application to act as the development test environment. Specifically, there are configuration settings that can help the ASP component developer during the development process. These and all of the other issues just mentioned will be covered in this chapter.

Though this chapter focuses exclusively on IIS, you should be able to install another web server and add support for ASP with Chili!Soft or another comparable ASP support application. The components discussed in this book have been tested only within a Windows 2000 environment, in both Advanced Server and Professional installations. Many of the components use features and facilities that are specific to Windows 2000, such as COM+ support. Because of this, there is no guarantee that the components demonstrated throughout the book will work with any other operating system.

Configuring the IIS Environment

ASP first appeared as an ISAPI extension with Version 3.0 of IIS. Since that time, the capabilities of ASP have grown from a server-side scripting technique to a rich n-tier and web-based application development environment. As ASP has grown in functionality, so has the support environment, and this includes IIS.

IIS 5.0, included with Windows 2000, provides for a high degree of control of the web server environment, including being able to create more than one web site in the same IIS administration context, as well as being able to create one or more *virtual directories*, each of which can emulate a totally separate web environment. In addition, each web site can be configured to handle specific numbers of connections and allow open or restricted access; each virtual directory can have its access constrained; and both the web site and virtual directories can be opened for general or restricted access based on NT roles.

Each of these options and others are discussed in this section, but first, let's make sure IIS is installed correctly.

You will need Administrative privileges to install and set up IIS on a particular machine.

Installing IIS

To develop ASP components, you need to have a test environment, and for Windows 2000 this most likely means having access to an IIS test installation. You could be sharing a test environment with other folks, something that IIS supports quite nicely, or you might have your own version of IIS to use for development.

You're given the choice whether to install IIS when you do a clean Windows 2000 installation. If, however, you install Windows 2000 as an upgrade to an existing system, IIS is installed automatically only if the previous installation also had IIS installed. As such, an automatic installation of IIS occurs only when you're upgrading an NT 4.0 server. Then the Windows 2000 installation tries to match, as closely as possible, the configuration of your existing server. If you're installing Windows 2000 Professional over Windows 95 or 98, you'll need to install IIS as a separate component at a later time.

The procedure to install IIS is, fortunately, relatively simple. First, make sure IIS 5.0 isn't already installed by checking for the Internet Services Manager menu item, located in the Administrative Tools menu folder if you are using Windows 2000 Server. If you are using Windows 2000 Professional or Server, you can access the Internet Services Manager from the Administrative Tools folder contained in the Control Panel.

To install IIS, access the Add/Remove Application option in the Control Panel. Select the option to add or remove Windows components. From the window that opens, click on the checkbox next to Internet Information Services to install the IIS component, or click the Details button to fine-tune your selection. If disk space is at a premium, you might want to skip the installation of FTP, NNTP, and other web applications. You should, though, choose to install the default web server, checked by default.

Once you've made your choice, the Windows Components Wizard installs IIS with default values. You can test your installation by accessing the IIS introduction page using the following URL:

```
http://localhost/localstart.asp
```

This opens a page introducing IIS and also opens a separate window containing IIS documentation. Become familiar with this page and the documentation, since you will be using it throughout this book and in your development efforts.

After IIS is installed and you've had a chance to become familiar with the startup page and documentation, the next step to setting up a development environment is to create a separate development web server. In the Internet Information Services snap-in service component, you should see the name of your IIS server (the machine's name), and below this you should see the default web server and administration web server, which are already defined.

For the purposes of this book, we'll redefine the default web server as the Development server. To do this, you'll rename the server and also point it to your development subdirectory.

First, use Windows Explorer to create a new top-level directory named *development*. Next, you'll set up the web server to point to this new directory.

Right-click on the default web server name and select Properties from the menu that opens. In the Properties window, select the Web Site tab, and type in the new web server name, Development. You can also turn off logging, unless your development effort is dependent on web logs.

After renaming the web server, select the Home Directory tab. Find the Local Path text box in the page and type in or browse for the location of the development directory you created. In addition, rename the Application name to Development. You're now ready to access the development content using the *localhost* IP alias.

 If you are working with Windows 2000 Professional, the version of IIS installed in this environment will not let you create separate Administration and default web servers, nor can you create a new web server—only one server is allowed. However, you can change the location of this server to point to the directory where you will be creating your test ASP pages. Additionally, you can also create multiple virtual directories as detailed in the later section, "Creating Separate ASP Applications with Virtual Directories."

If the default web server is being used for other purposes, you can create a separate development server. To do this, right-click on the Windows 2000 server name—the topmost object in the Console window—and from the pop-up menu, select New, then select Web Site. The Web Site Creation Wizard opens up and will guide you through the server setup.

Stepping through the Wizard pages, you'll enter a description of the web server first—in this case, you'll type in Development. Next, you'll need to specify IP and port settings. Unless the web server needs to be accessed from an intranet, for shared access, or from the Internet (not a good idea for a development test server), you'll want to leave the setting of All Unassigned as is, or use the IP of 127.0.0.1, also known as the *local loopback address*. You'll be able to access your web site using the uniquely defined DNS value of *localhost* with either of these settings.

If you want to support more than one web server using the same IP address but with a different physical location and with different property settings, you can create the new server with a different TCP port number. Then, to access each web server, you specify the port number, as follows:

```
http://localhost:8000/default.asp
```

The only limitation with specifying separate ports is you can't specify one already being used. Checking your installation, you'll find that the default web server is already using port number 80, the default port, and the administration web server uses a port assigned a randomly generated number between 2000 and 9999. If

Domain Names and the HOSTS File

Localhost is predefined in the *HOSTS* file in Windows 2000. You can see this file in the Windows OS directory, under *\system32\drivers\etc. HOSTS* contains the IP-to-name mapping; the first entry will be "localhost," and its IP address will be 127.0.0.1. In a small intranet, you can use the *HOSTS* file to specify domain name aliases and IPs for all members of the intranet, without having to use DNS.

For fun, and if your computer is isolated from a network, rename *localhost* to whatever name you would like to use with your development effort, such as *devaspcomp.com.* Just be forewarned that if you use a name that is available on the Internet, redefining *localhost* on your machine to that name will mean you're going to get your web server, not the site on the Net, when you access the name in a web page.

you're using the separate port approach to create a development web server, use port number 8000 unless it's already assigned to another service.

As an alternative, if you are setting up a site with multiple IP addresses, you can take advantage of site socket pooling implemented with IIS 5.0. With socket pooling, web sites served from different IPs can use the same port, which, in turn, allows each of the sites to use the same socket. This decreases the overhead required for all of the sites. However, if you have only one IP address, such as on a standalone machine, and you want to try different sites, use different ports.

The next setup option is to pick the physical directory where your host will reside. You'll want to type in or browse for the development directory, created earlier. You'll also want to leave the checkbox labeled Allow Anonymous Access checked, unless you're in a shared or exposed environment.

Going on to last setup page, the Web Site Creation Wizard provides you with options to set the Access Permissions for the web site. You'll want to accept the default values of Read and Run Scripts at this time.

 Access permissions and user and role security issues will be discussed a bit later in this chapter, in the section titled "Securing the Development Environment."

Once the web server is created, you can configure it to fit your needs. Since we're setting up a development environment, the next step is to configure the server to run in an isolated environment, discussed next.

Creating an Isolated ASP Development Environment

ASP became very popular primarily because of its ease of use—all a developer needed to do to add server processing was embed a few lines of script within an HTML page. To make the environment even more attractive for developers, Microsoft added support for ASP components in IIS 3.0. By adding in support for components—basically COM server objects—developers could create objects in a variety of programming languages and access these components from more than one web page.

As powerful as ASP components are, folks quickly encountered a problem with them: if a developer loads a web page into a browser that accesses a component and then tries to make a code change and recompile the component, the following error results:

```
Permission Denied
```

The reason is that IIS, in an effort to improve performance, keeps the component loaded, hence locked, even when you are no longer accessing the page that contains the component. In fact, IIS will continue to hold the component until the web service is shut down—notice I say *web service* and not *web server*—or some other event causes the component to be unloaded.

With IIS 3.0, ASP component developers tried shutting down the web server they used to access the component, but the permission problem still remained. The reason is that shutting down the web server won't release the hold on the component; it is the actual web service, IISADMIN, that maintains the lock on the component, and it is this service that must be shut down.

The most common way to stop this service and release the locks on any components was to issue a network stop command, for example:

```
NET STOP IISADMIN /y
NET START W3SVC
```

The **NET STOP** command stops a network service—the IISADMIN service—and the /y option forces a release of all resources the service had when it was stopped. The web service and server are then both started with the second network service command, **NET START**, giving it the overall web server name W3SVC.

Stopping and starting the web service releases the server, but there is a major drawback to this approach: shutting down the web service just to release a lock on a component is equivalent to cutting down a walnut tree in order to get one nut to chop for your hot fudge sundae—it's a bad case of overkill. In a shared environment, with more than one developer developing to the same web server and service, not only is the approach overkill, it's downright rude.

To address this problem, Microsoft added the ability to IIS Version 4.0 to run an ASP application in isolation in order to be able to unload a specific application. Once the application was unloaded, the component accessed by the application was unlocked and could then be recompiled.

With IIS Version 5.0, you have three options to control ASP application isolation:

- You can create a new web server that runs within the shared IIS process environment (through *Inetinfo.exe*).

- You can set your application to run within a pooled environment (through *dllhost.exe*).

- Your application can run as an isolated application (again, through *dllhost.exe*).

By default, the web server is set up to run within a pooled environment, but this can be changed in the server's Properties page. To change the setting for the new development web server, right-click on the server in the Internet Information Services console snap-in, and pick Properties from the menu that opens. Then, select the Home Directory tab from the window that opens, as shown in Figure 2-1. The program isolation setting is an option labeled Application Protection. Set this to High (Isolated) to be able to unload the application and release any locks on components without having to shut down either the web server or the web service.

You can change several other properties for the server, including performance tuning and setting security for the site, from the Properties window. But first, time to try out your test environment. To do this, you'll need a test ASP component.

To test the environment, you'll need an ASP component you can use to make sure the application isolation is set correctly and you can unload the web site without having to shut it down. Then you'll need to create a simple ASP page that accesses the component. For this example, we'll create a component using Visual Basic.

 If you aren't using Visual Basic and are running this test using the component copied from the code examples, you can still test out the application isolation feature. Instead of trying to recompile the component, try deleting it. Without unloading the server application first, you should get a Sharing Violation error and a message about the component being in use. Unload the server application and then try again to delete the component—this time you shouldn't have any problems removing it.

The details of creating a Visual Basic ASP component are covered in Chapter 7, *Creating a Simple Visual Basic ASP Component,* but for now create the component project as an ActiveX DLL, and name the project **asp0201** and the project file

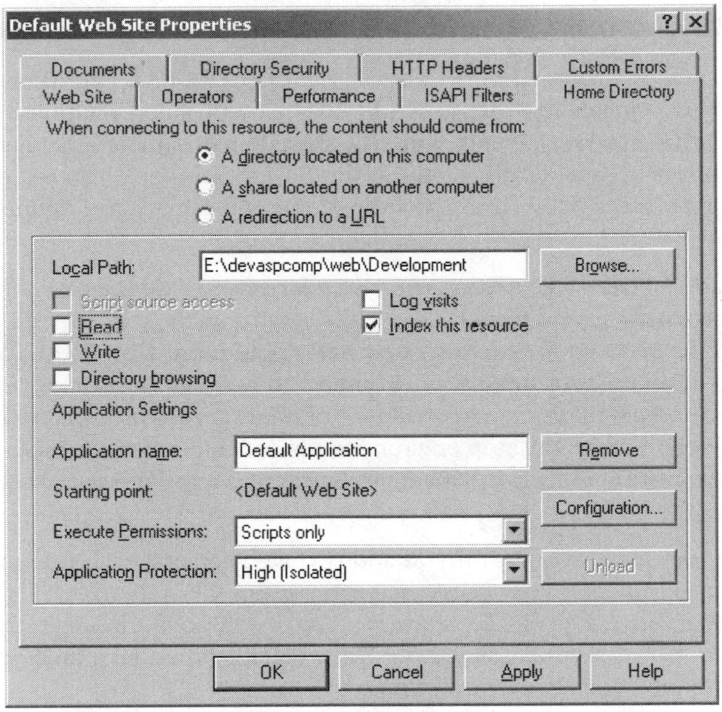

Figure 2-1. Setting the isolation level for the new development web server using the server Properties dialog box

asp0201.vbp. A class is automatically created for a project such as this; rename this class **tstweb** and the class file *tstweb.cls*. Accept all the defaults for the project and the class.

The next step in creating the test component is to add in the class code, in this example a very simple function that returns a very traditional message to the ASP page, as shown in Example 2-1.

Example 2-1. Simple Visual Basic Component to Return a "Hello, World!" Message

```
Option Explicit

' tests new Development Web
Function tstNewWeb() As String

   tstNewWeb = "Hello, World!"

End Function
```

Once you've added the code to the class, compile the component by accessing the File menu and clicking on the "Make asp0201.dll" menu item. A dialog box opens

Performance Issues with Application Isolation

As you'll read in Chapter 3, *ASP Components and COM*, IIS applications require a runtime executable in order to work. An ASP application running in the IIS process environment operates within a shared-environment executable that has been tuned to work efficiently in the IIS environment. Therefore it performs better and has much less overhead then an application defined to be pooled or isolated.

Pooled and isolated web servers use a standard COM/COM+ host, *dllhost.exe*, which provides an individual executable environment, one for all pooled applications and one for each isolated ASP application. However, *dllhost.exe* is not the most efficient runtime environment to work in. In addition, each isolated web server requires its own instance of *dllhost.exe*, which in turn requires a completely separate desktop environment in order to run. This puts a burden on the NT host supporting the IIS environment and requires special configuration to support more than a small number of separate web servers.

You can see this for yourself if you add two web servers, each running as an isolated application. If you access the processes for the system, you should see two different instances of *dllhost.exe* running. Add another instance of an isolated web server or virtual directory, which you'll read about a little later, and you'll add another instance of *dllhost.exe*.

The isolated option is still the best approach to use for the ASP application when developing ASP components. However, for a production environment, you'll want to use the shared or pooled environments for more efficient performance.

Running the web server in isolation allows you to unload the server to recompile components. An additional benefit to this type of web application is that problems within the one application won't impact other applications. Problems within a shared or pooled environment can be propagated to other web servers.

---

that contains a default name for the component (the name of the project with a DLL extension). In this dialog box, you can change the component's name and location and other application options, which we won't go into until Chapter 7. For now, accept everything at its default value and compile the component.

Visual Basic creates the component file and also registers it as a COM object accessible from applications. If you don't have Visual Basic, you can also copy the test component from the downloadable code examples and register in on your machine using the *regsvr32* utility as follows:

```
regsvr32 asp0201.dll
```

Next, create the ASP page that accesses the component, calling it *asp0201.asp*. Without going into too much detail on what is happening, the ASP page creates an instance of the component and invokes the component's one and only method. The text returned from the method is written out using one of the ASP built-in objects, the Response object (discussed in Chapter 7 and detailed in Appendix A, *Quick ASP Built-In Object Reference*). The code for *asp0201.asp* is:

```
<HTML>
<HEAD>
<TITLE>Developing ASP Components - Example 2-1</TITLE>
</HEAD>
<BODY>
<%
Dim obj
Set obj = Server.CreateObject("asp0201.tstweb")

Dim str
str = obj.tstNewWeb
Response.Write str
%>
</BODY>
</HTML>
```

When you access the ASP page through your web server, use syntax similar to the following:

```
http://localhost/asp0201.asp
```

Or if you set up a new web server with a different port number, use this syntax instead:

```
http://localhost:8000/asp0201.asp
```

If the web server is set up correctly, you should see the message, "Hello, World!"

To make sure that the application isolation feature is working properly, try recompiling the ASP component. You should get a Permission Denied error. To release the component, access the Development Web Server Properties dialog box again, go to the Home Directory page, and click the Unload button. Now try to recompile—this time you shouldn't have any problems.

At this point you've set up your development web server and have modified it to run as an isolated application. What's next? Well, in a development environment, you might need to have different versions of an application accessible at any time, or you might have more than one developer sharing the same environment. You could create new web servers for every instance of the ASP application or for every developer, but then you would have to find and assign different IPs and/or port numbers for all of the servers.

An alternative approach to creating separate web servers for more than one ASP application is to create the applications in their own virtual directory. This approach is used throughout the book for all of the code examples and is discussed next.

Creating Separate ASP Applications with Virtual Directories

IIS virtual directories are used to add different directories to a web server, including directories located on other machines. Virtual directories are also a terrific way to create separate ASP applications, each of which lives in its own location, without having to access different IP addresses and port numbers.

A limitation to virtual directories is that they cannot have their own domain name and must be accessed using the domain of the web server.

You'll create a separate virtual directory for every chapter in this book, starting by creating one for the Chapter 2 examples and naming it chap2. To create the virtual directory, right-click on the development web server and select New, then Virtual Directory. The Virtual Directory Creation Wizard pops up and guides you through the directory creation process.

The first page the Wizard displays asks for the alias used for the directory; type in chap2. Next, you'll be asked for a physical location for the directory. For the book examples, you'll most likely want to create a subdirectory to the development web site directory (created earlier) for each chapter. If you use this approach, create a new subdirectory now and name it *chap2*. You'll then specify this new subdirectory as the physical location for the virtual directory.

The wizard then asks for the Access Permissions for the virtual directory—accept the default of Read and Run Scripts (such as ASP Scripts) for now.

At this point, you're done with creating the virtual directory. However, you still have one more task in setting up your separate ASP application environment: you need to change the application isolation for the directory, otherwise you'll continue to have the component locking problem even if you've set the parent web server to run as an isolated application.

Change the application isolation for the virtual directory by right-clicking on the virtual directory name and choosing Properties from the menu. Select the Virtual Directory tab and change the Application Protection value from its default of Medium (Pooled) to High (Isolated), as shown in Figure 2-2.

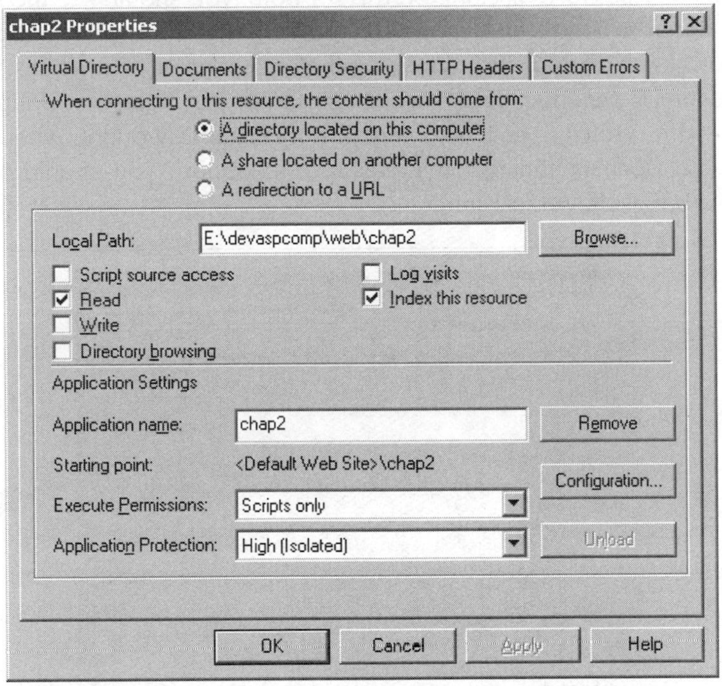

Figure 2-2. Setting the application isolation to High in the directory's properties

Test the application isolation of the new virtual directory by copying *asp0201.asp* from the web server main directory to the new *chap2* subdirectory and running the *chap2* application using syntax similar to the following:

```
http://localhost/chap2/asp0201.asp
```

Again, the page should show as before, with the words "Hello, World!" displayed in the upper-left corner. Also, as before, trying to recompile the component at this point should result in a Permission Denied error. However, accessing the Properties for the *chap2* virtual directory, then accessing the Virtual Directory tab and clicking the Unload button should unload the ASP application; the component can then be recompiled.

So now you have your development web server and your first ASP application virtual directory and have had a chance to test both. The next step you'll take is to fine-tune the security settings for both.

Securing the Development Environment

You probably noticed that the Properties windows for both the development web server and the Chapter 2 virtual directory had several pages, among them a page labeled Directory Security. Clicking on this for both, you should see the same page with three different control areas: one labeled "Anonymous access and authentication control," one labeled "IP address and domain name restrictions," and one labeled "Secure Communications." We won't cover the latter two options, which have to do with restricting access to certain domains and working with server certifications, but opening the "Anonymous access" option, you should see a window similar to that shown in Figure 2-3.

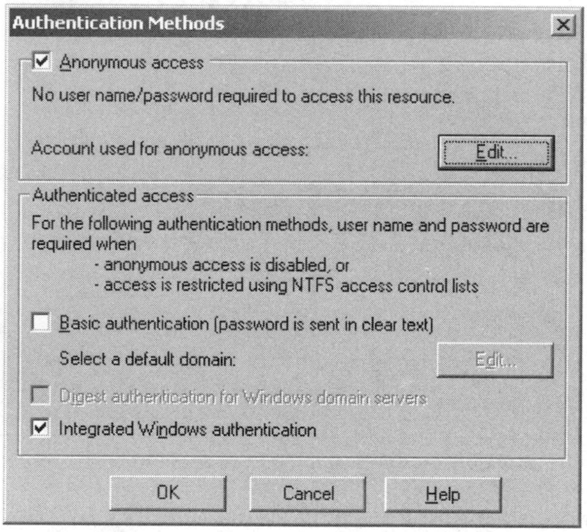

Figure 2-3. Authentication Methods dialog box for the virtual directory

With anonymous access, a default user is created for the machine, consisting of the prefix `IUSR_` and appended with the name of the machine. My machine is named `flame`, so my anonymous user is defined as `IUSR_FLAME`. With this username, folks can access pages and content from my site without having to specify a username and password.

One of the problems with the anonymous user, though, is that you can run into inexplicable and unexpected permission problems when you move your ASP application between machines.

For instance, if you develop on the same machine you test with (using *localhost*), chances are you're logged into the machine under a specific username and set of permissions. When you test pages at your web site on this machine, you don't have any problems with access. However, when you move the pages and the associated resources for the pages, such as ASP components, to a different machine (such as your production box), you can run into permission problems. The reason? Windows is using integrated authentication when you access the page, which means it's using your username and permissions when you test pages locally, and your permissions can be drastically different than those of the anonymous user.

To ensure consistent test results, you'll want either to move your ASP application to a separate test machine or create another user for your machine that has very limited access—equivalent to an anonymous user.

If your development environment is accessible externally, make sure your web server and virtual directories are secured if there is the possibility of access to the site externally, such as through an intranet or through the Internet if you connect to the Net through a modem. Remember that an IP connection is two-way: you can access out, and others can access your machine through the assigned IP.

Finally, you have to ensure that the access permissions are also set for your components. These can be set by accessing the Properties for the component or the component's subdirectory and setting the permissions to Read and Read & Execute for Everyone or for the IUSR account. If you set the permissions on the directory and check the option to allow inheritance of permissions from the parent for all components within the directory, you can assign the same security settings to a group of components in one location, and the permissions propagate to all of the components, as shown in Figure 2-4.

Remote Administration of IIS

You can administer IIS using a variety of techniques. For example, all of the work you've performed in setting up your development web server and the Chapter 2 virtual directory has occurred through the console snap-in designed for IIS. You also could have used the default Administration server installed with IIS on Windows 2000 Server. In addition, on Windows 2000 Professional, you have access to an interface modeled on the interface provided with the Personal Web Server (PWS).

Managing ASP Applications with the Internet Services Manager

You can administer an IIS installation in Windows 2000 servers using the HTML-based Internet Services Manager. This manager is installed as the administration web server within the IIS installation. Access the properties for this site to find the IP address and port number necessary to access the manager, then use these as the URL to pull the site up in a web browser.

For instance, if the IP address is 153.34.34.1, and the port number assigned to the administration web server is 4990, you can access the site with the following URL:

```
http://153.34.34.1:4990
```

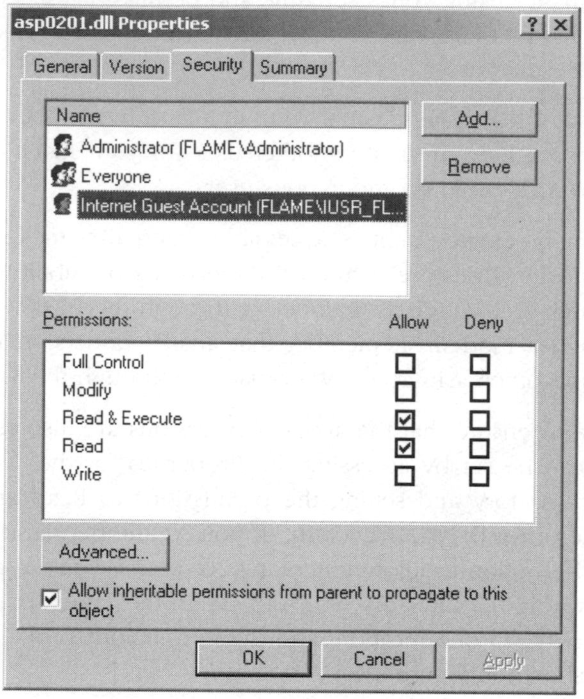

Figure 2-4. Setting the permissions to access the ASP components

You can also access the site using the name assigned through the DNS (Domain Name Service) for the specific IP address. For instance, if the IP address were configured with the alias *myweb.com* through DNS, you would access the site using something such as the following URL:

```
http://www.myweb.com:4990
```

Note that in either case you need to provide a username and valid password to enter the site, and the username must be mapped to the Administrator role. If you've logged in as Administrator, no username and password will be requested.

If more than one domain is mapped to a specific IIS server—if more than one web server on separate IPs is hosted through one installation of IIS—you can administer the site remotely if the IIS installation adds you to the Web Site Operator group for the server. With this group membership, you can then access the administration for the site using an URL such as the following:

```
http://www.myweb.com/iisadmin
```

You can try this with your local installation by using the following URL:

```
http://localhost/iisadmin
```

This should open the administration pages for the default web server.

You can also connect to your site for administration using the Terminal Service. If you're connected through an intranet and your client can support it, you can remotely administer your site using the IIS Console snap-in. Note, though, that your client needs to have Windows Console support through Windows 2000 or NT.

Finally, you can create your own administration programs using ASP pages and ASP components. The tools to do this are your favorite programming and scripting languages, ADSI, and the IIS Admin and Base Admin objects, covered in the next several sections.

Using ADSI to Administer IIS Programmatically

 Use a great deal of caution when altering IIS programmatically. Incorrect settings can damage the Metabase and force a reinstallation of IIS.

There might be times when administrating IIS through the Windows Console IIS snap-in or through the web interface provided by Microsoft does not work for your needs. For instance, you and your organization may need to do a sequence of activities rather than individual ones, and the only way to accomplish this is to create an application that performs the entire sequence.

Microsoft has opened up IIS administration through two sets of objects: the IIS Admin objects (which can be accessed through script using any of the automation support languages or through Visual Basic and other COM-capable languages) and the IIS Base Admin objects (which can be accessed only through C++).

Both sets of objects—the IIS Admin and the IIS Base Admin—are accessed through ADSI, and both work with the IIS Metabase.

Working with the IIS Metabase

Prior to the release of IIS 4.0, administrative information for the web service was stored in the Windows Registry, an online binary database containing name-value pairs accessible via paths. Starting with IIS 4.0 and continuing with IIS 5.0, Microsoft added the IIS Metabase, a memory-resident data store that is quickly accessible and contains configuration and administration information for IIS.

As with the Registry, Metabase entries are found via paths, or keys, similar to those used with file paths. These key paths, also referred to as *ADsPaths*, have the same structure as the paths used within ADSI and comply with the following general structure:

```
IIS://machinename/service/service_instance
```

In this line, *machinename* can be either LocalHost for the local machine or a specific name, *service* can be something such as W3SVC (a web service), and *service_instance* can be a specific instance of that service, such as a web site.

To access the Metabase object associated with the *chap2* web directory created earlier, you would use the following ADsPath:

```
IIS://localhost/W3SVC/1/root/chap2
```

This path breaks down into the virtual directory called *chap2* located off the *root* subdirectory of the first (1) web server instance on the local machine.

Metabase properties are small enough in size that they can be memory resident because they are based on inheritance by default. This means that information about all properties for all objects does not need to be maintained in memory except when the default property value is overridden. As an example, if the top-level web service has a ConnectionTimeout property set to 900 seconds, all child nodes, such as virtual directory sites created from this top-level service, automatically inherit a timeout of 900 seconds unless a different value has been explicitly defined for the node.

The Metabase objects, as well as their properties and methods, can be accessed from within an ASP script or an ASP component using the IIS Admin objects, discussed next.

The demonstrations of the IIS Admin objects are all shown in Visual Basic. However, you can re-create the examples with any programming language and tool that allows you to access COM objects.

The section later in this chapter on the IIS Base Admin objects demonstrates how to access IIS Administration data with C++.

Programmatically Administering IIS with ADSI

The IIS Admin objects support the ADSI interface by implementing the *Name*, *ADSI Path*, *Class*, *GUID*, *Parent*, and *Schema* properties. To demonstrate these properties, we'll create an ASP component project and add several methods to it, each demonstrating one of the properties.

To start, create a new ActiveX DLL project in Visual Basic and call it *asp0202.vbp*. Rename the generated class to tstAdmin. You'll be adding new methods to this new component throughout this section.

If you don't have Visual Basic, you can use the *asp0202.dll* component that comes with the book examples. If you're using a different tool, such as Delphi, Perl, or Java, then you might want to read the chapter based on your language first (Chapter 20, *ASP Components Created with Java*; Chapter 21, *Creating ASP Components with Delphi*; or Chapter 22, *Perl-Based Components Using ActiveState's PDK*), then alter the following examples to work with your tool/language.

Name

The *Name* Admin object is the attribute used to refer to the object within a given namespace. As an example, the name W3SVC refers to the *IISWebService* class, which is the web service. The name is also used to represent specific instances of any particular service, except that *name* in this case represents the number of the instance rather than a user-defined name. For example, if more than one web service is running on a machine, each individual web service can be accessed by a number representing its location within the web service listing, as well as a descriptive name mapped to the instance.

For example, in your development environment, you should now have three web servers defined: the default web server, the development web server, and the administration web server. The default web server is located first, so it is given the label 1. The administration web server is next, and it has a name of 2, followed by the development web server with a name of 3.

If you're using Windows Professional 2000, you should have one default web server. You'll need to adjust the examples shown in the following sections to match your environment.

The Name property can be accessed from ASP components as well as from an ASP scripting block. Example 2-2 shows a method that accesses the IIS Admin object and returns the object's ADSI Name. Try this by creating the method in the tstAdmin class of the asp0202 project, name the method adminName, and define it to return a String value.

Example 2-2. Returning the IISWebService Object's ADSI Name Property

```
Function adminName() As String
    Dim myObject
    Set myObject = GetObject("IIS://localhost/W3SVC")
    adminName = myObject.Name
End Function
```

To use this object, create an ASP page named *asp0202.asp* that instantiates the object and calls the object's methods. Place this ASP page, shown next, in the *chap2* virtual directory location.

```
<HTML>
<HEAD>
<TITLE>Developing ASP Components - Example 2-2</TITLE>
</HEAD>
<BODY>
<%
Dim obj
Set obj = Server.CreateObject("asp0202.tstAdmin")

Dim str
str = obj.adminName
Response.Write str
%>
</BODY>
</HTML>
```

Accessing the test page and the component method should result in a page that displays W3SVC, the name of the IISWebService. Instead, however, a web server error (500) occurs. Why is this?

IIS Admin objects must be accessed from within an administrative environment, and the current location for the test page is *chap2*, which is accessible by everyone. To make this example work, the ASP test page—not the component, the page—must be moved to an administrative location, or the physical directory's security must be changed to administrative access only.

You can move the component to the *IISAdmin* location. Find this by accessing the *IISAdmin* virtual directory or by accessing the administration web server and checking out the location of its home directory. You can also change the security for *chap2* by accessing the Directory Security tag in the Properties dialog box, clicking the "Anonymous access and authentication control" button, and unchecking the Anonymous Access checkbox when the Authentication Methods dialog box opens.

Once you've secured the ASP application, access the test page and component again, and the application should work this time.

The rest of the examples in this chapter involve modifying or accessing IIS Administration properties using the IIS Admin objects or the IIS Admin Base Objects. Based on this, all ASP test pages need to be located within an administration server location. For development purposes, the best approach to take is to modify the security settings for the IIS application—either the development web server or the virtual directory—to restrict access.

ADSI path

Access to IIS Admin objects occurs via the ADSI path, which Microsoft refers to as the ADsPath. This path usually has the configuration of `IIS://` followed by the computer name (or `LocalHost` for the local IIS installation), followed by the specific service, such as `W3SVC` for the web service. To access the first web site on the local machine, the following path would be given:

```
IIS://LocalHost/W3SVC/1
```

The `1` at the end of the path accesses the first web site installed on the local machine, a value of 2 accesses the second, a value of 3 accesses the third, and so on. If you have NNTP or FTP installed, this numbering system may change.

From the specific web instance, extending the path provides access to virtual directories contained within the specific web server, as the following demonstrates for the *chap2* virtual directory:

```
IIS://LocalHost/W3SVC/1/root/chap2
```

The different services, such as W3SVC, are equivalent to the different IIS Admin objects. These services are examined in more detail in the section "The IIS Admin Objects," later in the chapter.

Class

The class is the name of the schema class and is not unique for service instances. For example, each virtual web service, such as *chap2*, has a class name of `IIsWebVirtualDir`; each top-level web service, such as `Development`, has a class name of `IIsWebServer`.

GUID

The globally unique identifier (GUID) is the unique identifier for the specific class. Like the class, the GUID is unique only for the specific schema class, not for each instance. For example, the GUID for the `IIsWebServer` class is:

```
{8B645280-7BA4-11CF-B03D-00AA006E0975}
```

To find the GUID for the web service, add a new method to the `asp0202.tstAdmin` component. The method, shown in Example 2-3 and named adminGUID, accesses this value and returns it to the calling program.

Example 2-3. Accessing the IISWebService Class-Unique GUID

```
Function adminGUID() As String
    Dim myObject
    Set myObject = GetObject("IIS://localhost/W3SVC")
    adminGUID = myObject.Guid
End Function
```

The following test ASP page, named *asp0203.asp*, accesses the new method to get the GUID and then displays it:

```
<HTML>
<HEAD>
<TITLE>Developing ASP Components - Example 2-3</TITLE>
</HEAD>
<BODY>
<%
Dim obj
Set obj = Server.CreateObject("asp0202.tstAdmin")

Dim str
str = obj.adminGUID
Response.Write str
%>
</BODY>
</HTML>
```

Parent

The parent for an administrative object is the ADsPath of the IIS administrative object that contains it. For example, the parent for the local machine `LocalHost` is shown only as `IIS:`. Since the ADsPath for the top-level web service is:

```
IIS://LocalHost/W3SVC
```

the parent for this object would then be:

```
IIS://LocalHost
```

The parent-child relationship is important because the IIS Metabase is based on inheritance. Most properties are inherited from an object at a higher level, and this object can be found by retrieving each object's Parent property.

Schema

The Schema property is the ADsPath of the object representing the schema class for the Admin object. For instance, the value for the Schema property for the top-level web service is:

```
IIS://localhost/schema/IIsWebService
```

The ADSI Object Methods

The ADSI IIS Admin object methods are used to access and set the IIS Admin object properties. The ADSI properties are accessible directly from the ADSI object, but the IIS Admin object properties must be set or accessed using ADSI methods.

Any of the ADSI methods can be used with any IIS Admin object and can be used to access or set any property, as demonstrated in the following sections.

Get

The Get method returns the value for a specific property. The property name is passed as an argument to this ADSI method, and its value is returned in a datatype that is appropriate for the property.

To demonstrate Get, add the adminScriptLanguage method shown in Example 2-4 to the `asp0202.tstAdmin` component. The adminScriptLanguage method displays the value of the AspScriptLanguage property for the *chap2* virtual directory. Currently, this value should be VBScript, which is the default scripting language used for ASP pages.

Example 2-4. Using the ADSI Get Method to Access the AspScriptLanguage Property Value

```
Function adminScriptLanguage() As String
    Dim myObject
    Set myObject = GetObject("IIS://localhost/W3SVC/1/root/chap2")

    adminScriptLanguage = myObject.Get("AspScriptLanguage")
End Function
```

Next, create the test ASP page, named *asp0204.asp*, to display the name of the default scripting language. Since the AspScriptLanguage property has a datatype of String, the return value for the function is defined to be String—other properties will have other datatypes. The ASP test page uses VBScript, which supports only variants; as a result, the processing to display the return value can be the same regardless of the datatype returned.

```
<HTML>
<HEAD>
<TITLE>Developing ASP Components - Example 2-4</TITLE>
</HEAD>
<BODY>
<%
Dim obj
Set obj = Server.CreateObject("asp0202.tstAdmin")

Dim str
str = obj.adminScriptLanguage
Response.Write str
%>
</BODY>
</HTML>
```

With VBScript and Visual Basic, the property can also be accessed with the *object. property* syntax, using something similar to the following:

```
codePageValue = myObject.AspCodepage
```

GetEx

The GetEx method can be used to access single or multivalue properties. An example of a multivalue property is HttpErrors, which returns a list of formatted HTTP error strings. These strings are returned as an array of Variants.

Example 2-5 shows a new method, adminErrors, that uses GetEx to access the HttpErrors property for the *chap2* virtual directory and returns the results as an array of variants to the ASP page.

Example 2-5. Using the ADSI GetEx Method to Access the HttpErrors List

```
Function adminErrors() As Variant
    Dim myObject
    Set myObject = GetObject("IIS://localhost/W3SVC/1/root/chap2")
    adminErrors = myObject.GetEx("HttpErrors")
End Function
```

The ASP test page, shown in the following block of code and named *asp0205.asp*, takes the results returned from calling the adminErrors method and displays each element from the variant array:

```
<HTML>
<HEAD>
<TITLE>Developing ASP Components - Example 2-5</TITLE>
</HEAD>
<BODY>
<%
Dim obj
Dim vAry
Dim l,u
Dim ct

Set obj = Server.CreateObject("asp0202.tstAdmin")
vAry = obj.adminErrors

' set boundaries of array

l = LBound(vAry)
u = UBound(vAry)

' access each list item, print out to page
For ct = l to u
    Response.Write vAry(ct) & "<br>"
Next
%>
</BODY>
</HTML>
```

The results will be shown as separate lines and will have the following format:

- Error number, such as 400 for Not Found

- Error subnumber, such as 3

- A value of FILE or URL to designate whether a file or an URL is returned to the client
- The URL or the filename, depending on whether the URL or file is returned

The following is an example of one of the lines returned:

```
401,3,FILE,E:\WINNT\help\iisHelp\common\401-3.htm
```

If you look at this line and then access the Custom Errors tab of the *chap2* Properties dialog box, you'll see that this line appears in the list box on this tab.

 Other IIS Admin object properties will be discussed in the later section "The IIS Admin Objects."

GetInfo

The GetInfo method refreshes the IIS Admin object by requerying the Metabase and resetting the property values to those found in the Metabase. When you create an IIS Admin object, its properties are initialized to those that existed in the Metabase at the time the object was created. If you hold an object for a time and want to set the properties to those *currently* in the Metabase, you use GetInfo to refresh the object.

GetDataPaths

The GetDataPaths method can be used to traverse a hierarchy of web objects to see which objects have a specific property. It then returns a list of ADsPath values of each of the objects. A developer uses this method to quickly check whether a specific property is set and inherited throughout an entire IIS installation or within a specific web server or Virtual Directory.

The GetDataPaths method can also be used to traverse web objects and retrieve the ADsPath of each object where the property is implemented. Once you have access to an object's ADsPath, you can use this to access that object specifically. To demonstrate this, add two new methods to asp0202.tstAdmin: adminPropAccess and objProperty. The adminPropAccess function has two parameters, the ADsPath for the top-level object and the name of the property for which you are searching. The objProperty function takes an ADsPath and a property name as parameters and returns the property value. Example 2-6 shows both of these new methods.

Example 2-6. Methods to Retrieve a Collection of AdsPaths Whose Objects Implement a Property and to Get the Property Value for an Object Property

```
Function adminPropAccess(ByVal obj As String, ByVal prop As String) _
                              As Variant
```

*Example 2-6. Methods to Retrieve a Collection of AdsPaths Whose Objects Implement a Property
and to Get the Property Value for an Object Property (continued)*

```
    Const IIS_ANY_PROPERTY = 0

    Dim myObject
    Set myObject = GetObject(obj)
    adminPropAccess = myObject.GetDataPaths(prop,IIS_ANY_PROPERTY)
End Function

Function objProperty(ByVal obj As String, ByVal prop As String) _
                                          As Variant
    Dim myObject
    Set myObject = GetObject(obj)
    objProperty = myObject.Get(prop)
End Function
```

The GetDataPaths method takes two parameters: the IIS Admin object and a constant that indicates whether to return a path only if the property is inheritable. The two allowable values for this constant parameter are the following:

Value	Constant
0	IIS_ANY_PROPERTY
1	IIS_INHERITABLE_ONLY

The adminPropAccess method uses the `IIS_ANY_PROPERTY` constant, which means the ADsPath will be returned regardless of whether the property is inheritable. If the constant `IIS_INHERITABLE_ONLY` is specified and the property is not inheritable, an `MD_ERROR_DATA_NOT_FOUND` error is returned.

The ASP test page calls both of these new methods, accessing each item in the collection returned from adminPropAccess and using this item in a call to the objProperty method. The objProperty method returns the value for the specified property. The ADsPath, the property, and the property value are then displayed. In the following page, named *asp0206.asp*, the property we are searching for is Auth-Anonymous, which is set to a value of **TRUE** when anonymous access is allowed for the IIS Admin Object and **FALSE** otherwise:

```
    <HTML>
    <HEAD>
    <TITLE>Developing ASP Components - Example 2-6</TITLE>
    </HEAD>
    <BODY>
    <%
    Dim obj
    Dim cPaths, Path
    Dim prop
    prop = "AuthAnonymous"
    Set obj = Server.CreateObject("asp0202.tstAdmin")
```

```
    cPaths = obj.adminPropAccess("IIS://localhost/W3SVC", prop)

' access each path, print out to page
For each Path in cPaths
    Response.Write Path & " "
    Dim prp
    prp = obj.objProperty(Path, prop)
    Response.Write prop & " value of " & prp & "<br>"
Next
%>
</BODY>
</HTML>
```

The results of running this ASP page with the top-level **IIWebService** object is a listing of several IIS Admin object paths and the value of the AuthAnonymous property for each object. The development web server and the *chap2* virtual directory appear in the list as follows:

```
IIS://localhost/W3SVC/1/Root AuthAnonymous value of True
IIS://localhost/W3SVC/1/Root/chap2 AuthAnonymous value of False
```

GetPropertyAttribObj

The GetPropertyAttribObj method returns a specified IIS Admin object property as an object rather than as a value; that is, it returns a Property object, rather than a property's value. This object can then be used to access information about the property, such as whether the property is inherited or if a partial path is present. The syntax for the method is:

```
Set obj = adminObj.GetPropertyAttribObj("some_property_name")
Var = obj.attribute
```

where *attribute* is one of the following:

Inherit
> Whether the property is inheritable

PartialPath
> Whether a partial path is present

Secure
> Whether the property is secure

Reference
> Whether the property is received by reference

Volatile
> Whether the property is volatile

IsInherited
> Whether the property is inherited

InsertPath

   Whether there is a specific, special character in the property

AllAttributes

   All property attributes, represented by a long value

The ADSI methods implemented for the IIS Admin objects can also set property values as well as retrieve them, as demonstrated with the Put method, described next.

Put and SetInfo

The Put method sets the value for a specific property. As with Get, the property name is passed as the first parameter to the method, and the new value, which must be a datatype that is appropriate for that property, is passed as the second parameter.

To save the results back to the Metabase, you use the ADSI SetInfo method. Without using SetInfo, the properties changed using Put (or using the VBScript and Visual Basic *object.property* method) are not saved.

As an example of using Put to alter an Admin object property and SetInfo to save the property change, Example 2-7 shows a new method, adminAllowAnon, which takes an IIS Admin object ADsPath and a Boolean value to alter the authAnonymous authorization for the specified IIS Admin object. The method uses the *object.property* approach to setting the value rather than using Put specifically. Add this new method to your test ADSI component.

Example 2-7. Using Put and SetInfo to Alter the authAnonymous Property

```
Sub adminAllowAnon(ByVal obj As String, ByVal bl As Boolean)
    Dim myObject
    Set myObject = GetObject(obj)
    myObject.AuthAnonymous = bl
    myObject.SetInfo
End Sub
```

The ASP test page, named *asp0207.asp*, calls the method and passes the ADsPath for the virtual directory *chap2*. Sending a value of **True** turns on anonymous access authorization for the directory, allowing anonymous access to the directory.

```
<HTML>
<HEAD>
<TITLE>Developing ASP Components - Example 2-7</TITLE>
</HEAD>
<BODY>
<%
Dim obj
Set obj = Server.CreateObject("asp0202.tstAdmin")
```

```
On Error Resume Next
Dim adspath
adspath = "IIS://localhost/W3SVC/1/Root/chap2"

obj.adminAllowAnon adspath, True
%>
<H1>Changing Properties with Put</H1>
</BODY>
</HTML>
```

After running this example page, access the ASP page, *asp0206.asp*. You would expect to see that the AuthAnonymous value is now **True** for *chap2*, where before the value was **False**. However, what is most likely to happen is that you'll get an error, especially if you close the browser after running the *asp0207.asp* test page, open the browser again, and then access *asp0206.asp*.

Why the error? By setting the authAnonymous property of *chap2* to **True**, you've removed the security restriction necessary to run an ASP page that accesses the IIS Admin properties. Even if you change the text in *asp0207.asp* to set the authAnonymous property to **False**, you can't run *asp0207.asp* again—it also accesses the IIS Admin objects. You'll need to open the IIS Console or IIS Admin web site to change the property back to **False** before you can run an ASP page that access IIS Admin objects and properties from *chap2* again.

PutEx

The PutEx method is similar to Put, in that you can use the method to alter properties of existing IIS Admin objects. However, unlike Put, PutEx allows you to alter properties that are multivalued in addition to altering single-valued properties.

As a demonstration, we'll combine a previous example, Example 2-5, which returned a list of HTTP error messages for *chap2*, with a new method, adminSetErrors, to write a modified list of error messages back to the Metabase. Then we'll use SetInfo to save any changes to this list. Example 2-8 shows the new method, which updates the Metabase with the new HttpErrors property list.

Example 2-8. Put the HTTP Errors Back to the Metabase, and Use SetInfo to Save the Changes

```
Sub adminSetErrors(ByVal obj As String, ByVal vAry As Variant)
    Const ADS_PROPERTY_UPDATE = 2
    Dim myObject
    Set myObject = GetObject(obj)
    myObject.PutEx ADS_PROPERTY_UPDATE, "HttpErrors", vAry
    myObject.SetInfo
End Sub
```

The second parameter to PutEx is the name of the property being updated, and the third parameter is the Variant array of HTTP error messages that were originally retrieved using the adminErrors method from Example 2-5. The first parameter is a constant value that determines how the property is to be altered. The two possible values that can be used in the first parameter of adminSetErrors are shown in the following table:

Constant	Value	Description
ADS_PROPERTY_CLEAR	1	Clear property values.
ADS_PROPERTY_UPDATE	2	Update property with new value.

The example uses `ADS_PROPERTY_UPDATE` to update the existing list rather than clear it.

The ASP test page that calls this new method is named *asp0208.asp*. Notice that the adminErrors method from Example 2-5 is called first to get the Variant list of HTTP error messages. These values are displayed, and the first three characters of each line are examined for the match to 404. When found, a new entry with a changed filename replaces the existing array entry, and adminSetErrors is called to update the messages. Afterward, the HTTP messages are again accessed with adminErrors to display the "after" values. Make sure you change the page values to reflect your own environment.

```
<HTML>
<HEAD>
<TITLE>Developing ASP Components - Example 2-8</TITLE>
</HEAD>
<BODY>
<%
Response.Write "<h3>Before Changes</H3>"

Dim obj
Dim vAry
Set obj = Server.CreateObject("asp0202.tstAdmin")
vAry = obj.adminErrors

' set boundaries of array
l = LBound(vAry)
u = UBound(vAry)

' access each list item, print out to page
Dim str, val
For ct = l To u
    Response.Write vAry(ct) & "<br>"
    str = Left(vAry(ct),3)
    if str = "404" Then
      vAry(ct) = "404,*,FILE,E:\devaspcomp\web\chap2\asperrors.htm"
    End If
Next

Response.Write "<h3>After Changes</H3>"

' update HTTP error messages
```

```
obj.adminSetErrors "IIS://localhost/W3SVC/1/root/chap2", vAry

' get error messages again
vAry = obj.adminErrors

' set boundaries of array again
l = LBound(vAry)
u = UBound(vAry)

' access each list item, print out to page
For ct = l To u
    Response.Write vAry(ct) & "<br>"
Next
%>
</BODY>
</HTML>
```

In this section you had a chance to access and set various IIS Admin object properties using methods such as Get and Put, GetEx and PutEx. These methods are actually implementations of the primary ADSI interface, **IADs**. However, there are also IIS Admin objects that can contain other objects, and these collection-type objects also implement the **IADsContainer** interface, to provide for collection member access. The methods to work with these collections using ADSI are discussed in the next section.

The ADSI Container Object Properties and Methods

Certain IIS Admin objects can contain other objects, which means that they support the **IADSContainer** interface in addition to the **IADs** interface. Because these objects implement the container interface, they can support certain container functionality, such as a count of contained objects and a method of enumerating these objects.

The ADSI Container object properties are the following:

_NewEnum

> For automation languages such as Visual Basic, this property returns an enumerator that allows the language to retrieve the contained objects. An enumerator in Visual Basic is an object that provides built-in functionality to iterate or enumerate the objects in a collection. Visual Basic Collection objects automatically have this enumerator capability built in through the use of _NewEnum. This means that each object can be accessed using the following syntax:

> ```
> For each obj in ObjectCollection
>     ...do something
> Next
> ```

Count

> Returns a count of contained objects.

The following are the ADSI Container object methods:

CopyHere
> Copies an object into a container and returns a pointer to the object.

Create
> Creates a new object of a given type and name within the container.

Delete
> Removes an object of a given type and name from a container.

GetObject
> Returns the ADSI object of a given class and name.

MoveHere
> Removes an object from its source and places it in the container.

These Container methods and properties allow you to add or remove new virtual web sites, access information about any aspect of an IIS installation, and, most particularly, traverse a hierarchy of IIS objects.

Since you're going to need to create virtual directories for each of the chapters of this book, we'll create the virtual directory you'll use for Chapter 3. Once it's created, we'll list the development web server's virtual directories again to the web page to ensure the new directory has been created.

Example 2-9 modifies the basic characteristics of the development web server, so use it cautiously and only in a development environment—preferably one that's isolated. In addition, you must run these examples from another web server, such as the Administration server, since you cannot modify the characteristics of a web site you're currently using. Just make sure that the server you use has the security configuration necessary to run administration applications. Finally, if you're working with Windows 2000 Professional, you'll want to skip running this example altogether, because you can have only one web server in this operating system version, and this examples requires two.

Since we're using a different set of objects, we'll create a different component. Create a new Visual Basic ActiveX DLL project, and name the project **asp0203** and the class that's generated **tstContainer**. Create a subroutine method in this component and call it createDirectory. This method will access the development web server and then create a new virtual directory on this server using the Create method. Once the new virtual directory is created, its path is assigned to a physical location with a subdirectory named the same as the virtual directory, as shown in Example 2-9.

Example 2-9. Method to Create a New Virtual Directory on the Development Web Server

```
Sub createDirectory(ByVal name As String)
    Dim iisAdminObj
    Dim iisDirObj

    ' Access IIsWebServer object for Development
    Set iisAdminObj = GetObject("IIS://localhost/W3SVC/1/Root")

    ' create virtual directory
    Set iisDirObj = iisAdminObj.Create("IIsWebVirtualDir", name)
    iisAdminObj.SetInfo

    ' set virtual directory's name and access
    iisDirObj.Put "Path", "E:\devaspcomp\web\" & name
    iisDirObj.Put "AccessRead", True
    iisDirObj.Put "AccessScript", True
    iisDirObj.SetInfo

    ' create inproc application
    iisDirObj.AppCreate True
    iisDirObj.SetInfo

    ' set inproc's process isolation and name
    iisDirObj.Put "AppIsolated", 1
    iisDirObj.Put "AppFriendlyName", name
    iisDirObj.SetInfo

End Sub
```

The method will be called once for each virtual directory we're going to create. Notice that the SetInfo ADSI object method is used to update the Metabase after the virtual directory is created, after the path and access permissions are added for the new virtual directory, and after the new in-process application is added to the virtual directory using IIsWeb

The ASP script page that calls this method only creates virtual directories for Chapters 3 through 10, which should be enough to get us through almost half the book. The ASP script page shown in Example 2-10 also displays the contents of the Development Web server, creates the new virtual directories, and then displays the contents of the web server again by using the container implementation of For Each...In that is implemented in both VBScript and Visual Basic. This will create an object for each contained object within the target container and allow us to manipulate this object. In the case of the ASP page, the script displays the object's Name property.

Example 2-10. ASP Page That Prints Out the ADSI Container Object's Name, Calls Method to Create Virtual Directories, and Then Prints the Container Object's Contents Again

```
<HTML>
<HEAD>
<TITLE>Developing ASP Components - Example 2-10</TITLE>
```

Example 2-10. ASP Page That Prints Out the ADSI Container Object's Name, Calls Method to Create Virtual Directories, and Then Prints the Container Object's Contents Again (continued)

```
</HEAD>
<BODY>
<%
Dim obj
Dim ct
On Error Resume Next

Set obj = Server.CreateObject("asp0203.tstContainer")

Dim iisAdminObj

Set iisAdminObj = GetObject("IIS://localhost/W3SVC/1/Root")

Response.Write("<h3>Existing Virtual Directories</H3>")
For Each adminobj In iisAdminObj
  Response.Write adminobj.Class & " " & adminobj.Name & "<br>"
Next

For i = 3 To 10
    obj.createDirectory "chap" & i
Next

Set iisAdminObj = GetObject("IIS://localhost/W3SVC/1/Root")

Response.Write("<h3>New Directories</H3>")
For Each adminobj In iisAdminObj
  Response.Write adminobj.Class & " " & adminobj.Name & "<br>"
Next

%>
</BODY>
</HTML>
```

Before running the ASP page and creating the *chap3* virtual directory and application, the physical location has to be created; otherwise, an error will result when you try to access the directories. Figure 2-5 shows the web page that results from running Example 2-10. Notice that *chap3* is now added to the virtual directories for the development web server.

Throughout this section you've had a chance to work with several IIS Admin objects and properties. The next section lists all of the IIS Admin objects and several of the more interesting properties.

IIS Admin Object Overview

IIS can be administered using IIS Admin objects, which can be accessed the same way any other active ASP object is accessed. The advantage of exposing administration tasks to ASP applications is that organizations can create their own ASP

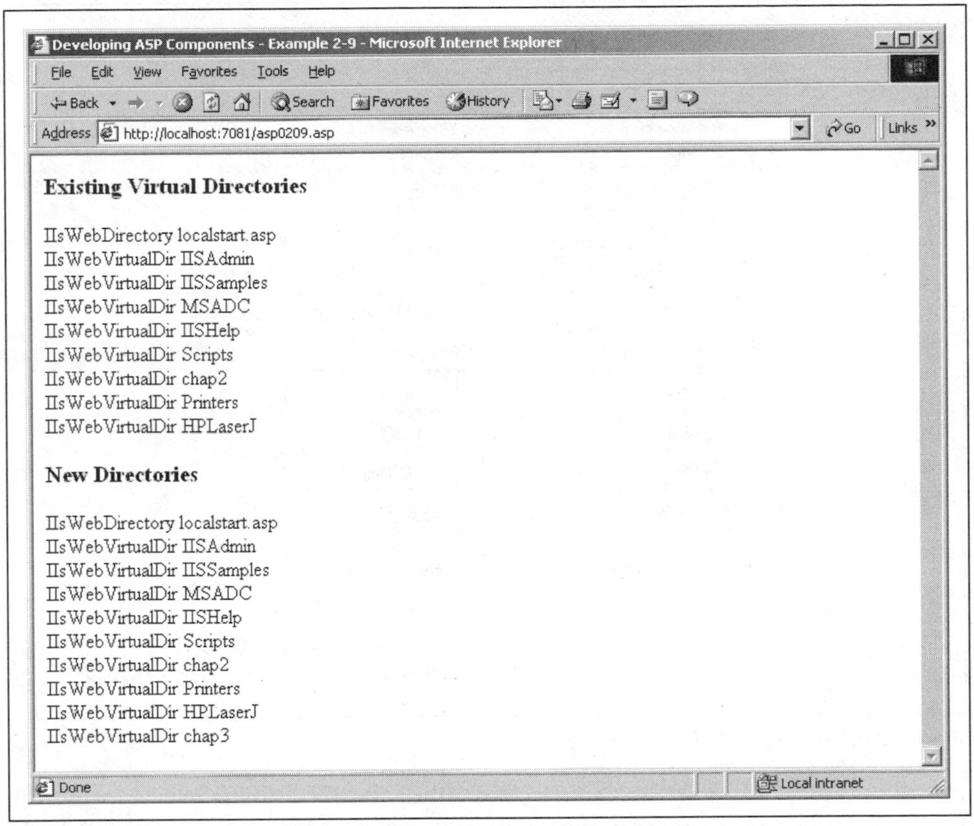

Figure 2-5. Adding a new virtual directory

administration applications, customized to the organization's needs or to a specific application's needs. Another advantage is that the ASP application and the IIS installation can actually be configured and managed remotely.

The biggest disadvantage to using the IIS Admin objects is that they expose IIS administration tasks to remote access, so the objects should be used with care. Microsoft recommends placing the applications accessing the objects in a secure subdirectory and setting the permissions to that subdirectory to NT Challenge/ Response, which means that anonymous access is disallowed and NTFS security is used to verify access to the subdirectory.

The IIS Admin Objects

The IIS Admin objects form a hierarchy, with many objects contained within another object, and so on. You saw this demonstrated in Example 2-9 and Example 2-10 in the last section. The hierarchy of these objects is shown in Figure 2-6.

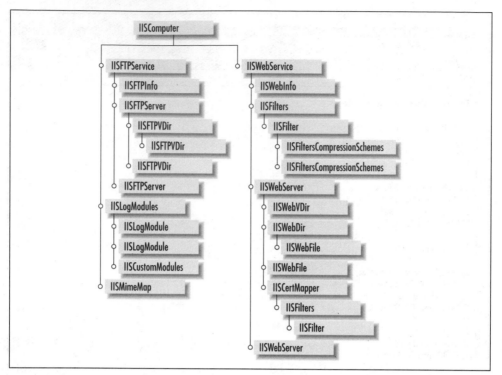

Figure 2-6. Hierarchy of IIS Admin objects

In the interests of brevity, we won't cover all of the IIS Admin objects in the following sections, just those that impact on ASP web development the most: IIsWebService, IIsWebServer, IIsWebInfo, and IIsWebVirtualDirectory. You can check Microsoft's documentation to read more on the ones not covered.

> The ADsPaths in the rest of this book use `localhost` to represent the name of the machine. If you're accessing the IIS Admin objects on your local machine, you can use `localhost`; otherwise, use the machine's name or URL.

IIsWebService

In the previous examples in the book, you accessed the IIsWebService object any time you supplied an ADsPath similar to the following:

```
IIS://localhost/W3SVC
```

The IIsWebService object is the object that contains all of the web servers for an installation, and it is through this object that you can set all inheritable properties for all web servers, virtual directories, and so on. For instance, you can use the following to change the AuthAnonymous property for the web service and have this setting trickle down to all contained objects, unless they override this property:

```
Set iisAdminObj = GetObject("IIS://localhost/W3SVC")
iisAdminObj.Put "AuthAnonymous",True
```

The IIsWebService contains direct references to all of the web servers set up for an IIS installation, and these are discussed next.

IIsWebServer

The IIsWebServer is the object representing a specific web server for a machine. It is accessed through a browser using a unique combination of IP address and port number, such as the following:

```
http://localhost
http://www.someurl.com
http://localhost:90
```

As with IIsWebService, you can set properties for an IIsWebServer object and they'll propagate to all contained elements, or at least to the ones to which the property applies. For instance, you can set the AccessRead property for a web server, and it will apply to all contained virtual directories, web directories, and web files:

```
Set iisAdminObj = GetObject("IIS://localhost/W3SVC/1")
iisAdminObj.Put "AccessRead",True
```

You can also create objects off the IIsWebServer, as demonstrated in Example 2-9, when we created a new virtual directory using the Create method. Other methods unique to IIsWebServer are the following:

Stop
> Stops the web server.

Start
> Restarts the web server.

Status
> Determines the status of the web server.

Pause
> Pauses the web server.

Continue
> Resumes the web server after it has been paused.

In addition to accessing the IIsWebServer objects through the higher-level IIsWeb-Service, you can also access IIsWebInfo.

IIsWebInfo

General information about the web service is contained in the IIsWebInfo object. This can include information such as custom error messages and whether encryption is enabled, and it includes values that are set when the service is first installed.

The IIsWebInfo IIS Admin object implements *IADs* but not *IADsContainer*, which means you can't use any of the container methods, but you can use Get and Put and the other noncontainer methods. For instance, Example 2-11 shows an ASP page, *asp0210.asp*, created using VBScript that uses Get to access one property of the IIsWebInfo object, CustomErrorDescriptions. This property contains a list of custom error messages installed when IIS was installed. In the example, this list of messages is accessed and displayed one at a time, similar to the results shown when accessing the component created in Example 2-8.

Example 2-11. Accessing CustomErrorDescriptions from the IIsWebInfo Object

```
<HTML>
<HEAD>
<TITLE>Developing ASP Components - Example 2-11</TITLE>
</HEAD>
<BODY>
<%
Dim iisAdminObj
Set iisAdminObj = GetObject("IIS://localhost/W3SVC/INFO")

Dim customErrors
customErrors = iisAdminObj.get("CustomErrorDescriptions")

' set boundaries of array
Dim l,u
l = LBound(customErrors)
u = UBound(customErrors)

' access each list item, print out to page
For ct = l To u
   Response.Write customErrors(ct) & "<br>"
Next
%>
</BODY>
</HTML>
```

IIsWebVirtualDirectory

The IIsWebVirtualDirectory object can apply to all virtual directories contained within a web server or to a specific one, depending on how it is accessed. To set or get properties that apply to all virtual directories, access the object using syntax similar to the following:

```
IIS://localhost/1/Root
```

However, to access properties for one specific virtual directory, use the following:

```
IIS://localhost/1/Root/chap2
```

As you saw in Example 2-9, you can add an in-process ("inproc") application to a specific virtual directory with the AppCreate method. Using this method, you can create an application that can exist independently of other applications running from the same virtual directory. You can then manipulate this application using ADSI, or you can manipulate it using Component Services, discussed in more detail in Chapter 5, *COM+ Services and ASP Components and Applications*. Other methods available for use programmatically are the following:

AppCreate2
> Creates an application and marks it as running in-process, out-of-process, or pooled.

AppDelete
> Deletes the application and releases resources if none are currently being accessed.

AppDeleteRecursive
> Deletes the application and all contained object applications; resources are not released.

AppDisable
> Disables an out-of-process application and releases its resources.

AppDisableRecursive
> Disables an out-of-process application and all contained objects.

AppEnable
> Reenables an out-of-process application.

AppEnableRecursive
> Enables an out-of-process application for the object and all contained objects.

AppGetStatus
> Gets the status of an application.

AppUnload
> Unloads the application and releases resources if out-of-process or if in-process and no longer being accessed.

AppUnloadRecursive
> Unloads the application for the object and any contained objects.

AspAppRestart
> Restarts the application.

A very useful method for ASP component developers is the AppUnload method, which unloads the existing ASP application so that the component can be compiled. To demonstrate, Example 2-12 shows an ASP page named *asp0211.asp* that will unload the ASP application that runs in the *chap2* virtual directory.

Example 2-12. Unloading an ASP Application with the AppUnload Method

```
<HTML>
<HEAD>
<TITLE>Developing ASP Components - Example 2-12</TITLE>
</HEAD>
<BODY>
<%
Dim iisAdminObj
Set iisAdminObj = GetObject("IIS://localhost/W3SVC/1/Root/chap2")
Response.Write "<H3>Unloading Application..."
iisAdminObj.AppUnload
%>
<H3> Application Unloaded</H3>
</BODY>
</HTML>
```

To run this ASP page and unload the *chap2* application, access this page from some administrative server other than the *chap2* virtual directory, such as the following URL that accesses the page from a new web site (note the different port number):

```
http://localhost:8000/asp0211.asp
```

The reason this page must be run from some location other than *chap2* is that the application can be unloaded and *all resources released* only if the application is not being accessed directly.

 Remove anonymous access from the web server before accessing *asp0211.asp*, or you'll get a permission error when your page calls *GetObject*.

In addition to several IIS Admin objects, there are also several dozen properties which you can access and set using ADSI methods. Several have been demonstrated in the last sections, and others are covered in the next section.

The IIS Admin Object Properties

An IIS Admin object property can apply to only one IIS Admin object, such as the AdminServer property for IIsWebInfo, or a property can apply to several types of objects, such as AccessRead. Each of the IIS Admin objects and its respective properties is listed in the documentation that comes with IIS. However, the ASP-specific properties of the IIsWebServer/IIsWebService and IIsWebVirtualDir objects can be especially useful when setting up the IIS test environment or when creating ASP components for Internet or intranet development. These properties are discussed and demonstrated in the following sections.

AspAllowOutOfProcComponents

In IIS 4.0, by default, only in-process components could be accessed from within ASP scripting blocks. To access out-of-process components—components compiled into ActiveX executables—you had to set the AspAllowOutOfProcComponents property to **True**.

However, with IIS 5.0, AspAllowOutOfProcComponents is set to **True** by default, which means all in-process IIS web servers or virtual directories—those set to run in low (IIS process) or medium (pooled) application protection—can access executable components. In addition, all high (isolated) IIS applications can also access out-of-process components regardless of how AspAllowOutOfProcComponents is set.

To illustrate the AspAllowOutOfProcComponents property, create a new Visual Basic project, except this time use the Visual Basic ActiveX EXE project type. Name the project *asp0204.vbp* and the generated class *tstProc.cls*.

The tstProc component has a single method, outOfProc, that takes a String parameter and concatenates it to another string to create a personalized variation of the traditional "Hello, World!", as shown in Example 2-13.

Example 2-13. An Out-of-Process Component

```
Function outOfProc(ByVal strName As String) As String
    outOfProc = "Hello, " & strName & "!"
End Function
```

After creating the component, compile it and place the resulting executable in the *chap2* virtual directory. In addition, change the Execute Permissions on this directory to Scripts and Executables.

Next, create an ASP page named *asp0212.asp* and place this page in *chap2*. The page accesses and prints out the value of the AspAllowOutOfProcComponents property and then accesses and runs the out-of-process component *asp0204*, as shown in Example 2-14.

Example 2-14. ASP Page That Accesses an Out-of-Process Component

```
<HTML>
<HEAD>
<TITLE>Developing ASP Components - Example 2-14</TITLE>
</HEAD>
<BODY>
<%

Dim iisAdminObj
```

Example 2-14. ASP Page That Accesses an Out-of-Process Component (continued)

```
Set iisAdminObj = GetObject("IIS://localhost/W3SVC/1/Root/chap2")

Dim val
val = iisAdminObj.Get("AspAllowOutOfProcComponents")
Response.Write("out of proc is " & val & "<br>")

Dim myObject
Set myObject = Server.CreateObject("asp0204.tstProc")

Dim hello
hello = myObject.outOfProc("Shelley")
Response.Write hello
%>
</BODY>
</HTML>
```

The only way to set the value to **False** is to access and change the property. This property can be applied to the IIsWebService, IIsWebServer, IIsWebVirtualDir, and IIsWebDirectory IIS Admin objects.

AspAllowSessionState

When a user accesses a web page from an ASP application for the first time within an Internet session, an ASP Session object is created. This object can be used to store and access session-level information, making this information available while the ASP session is in effect.

The AspAllowSessionState property can be used to enable or disable the session state. If the property is set to the default of **True**, the session state is created, and session information can be maintained. In addition, the Session_OnStart and Session_OnEnd event handlers can be included in *global.asa*, a file that maintains global scripting for an ASP application.

However, if no session-level information needs to be tracked for the application, the AspAllowSessionState property can be set to **False** to stop session state maintenance. This value can also be overridden with the **ENABLESESSIONSTATE** directive:

```
<%@ ENABLESESSIONSTATE = False %>
```

AspBufferingOn

ASP buffering prevents any output from being sent to the client until all the output is collected. This approach can be used to throw away output for an incomplete transaction or to discard or modify output based on application results. ASP buffering can be turned on or off using the Response object, discussed in more detail in Chapter 6, *ASP Interaction: Scripting and ASP Components*; setting the AspBufferingOn Metabase property can also alter it.

The AspBufferingOn property is set to **True** by default, which means buffering is enabled and output is not sent directly to the web client as it is generated. This differs from the property in IIS 4.0, where AspBufferingOn was set to **False** by default.

AspCodepage

Specifying the codepage controls what character language mapping is used within a web page. By default, the value of the codepage for an ASP application is zero (0), which is designated as **CP_ACP, System ANSI**.

Individual ASP applications can alter this by supplying a codepage specification within a scripting block or by setting the CodePage property of the built-in Session object. However, overall control of the codepage for a specific web or virtual web server can be handled through the use of the AspCodepage property. Setting this property overrides any other codepage specification for an ASP application page accessed by the web service, server, or virtual web server.

Setting a property at the web server that overrides local settings within ASP pages can cause a frustrating experience for the ASP developer, especially if the developer is not aware of the global setting. Use global settings with caution, and document and publish the settings when the default values are altered.

This property can be applied to the IIsWebService, IIsWebServer, IIsWebVirtualDir, and IIsWebDirectory IIS Admin objects.

AspEnableParentPaths

By default, relative paths can be used when specifying URL locations relative to a given location. As an example, a web page can be located using the absolute path *http://www. someurl.com/devaspcomp/*.

To access a web page within the scripting subdirectory, a reference can use a relative notation such as *../index.htm*. This is equivalent to providing the full path, *http://www. someurl.com/index.htm*.

However, relative paths can actually cause a security risk, since pages can be accessed outside of the directory defined for the virtual web site. To prevent the use of relative paths, the AspEnableParentPaths property can be set to **False**.

This property can be applied to the IIsWebService, IIsWebServer, IIsWebVirtualDir, and IIsWebDirectory IIS Admin objects.

AspExceptionCatchEnable

To enable the Microsoft Script Debugger, the ASP component developer can turn on debugging from within the IIS administration tools, or the developer can set the AspExceptionCatchEnable property to `True`, the default value. This turns on the script debugger until the property is specifically set to `False`.

This property can be applied to the IIsWebService, IIsWebServer, IIsWebVirtualDir, and IIsWebDirectory IIS Admin objects.

AspLogErrorRequests

In order to track client access errors within an ASP application, error codes can be written to a log file. This logging is enabled by default, but setting the AspLogErrorRequests property to `False` can turn off logging.

This property can be applied to the IIsWebService, IIsWebServer, IIsWebVirtualDir, and IIsWebDirectory IIS Admin objects.

AspQueueTimeout

The AspQueueTimeout property specifies the amount of time an ASP script will wait to be executed in a queue. If you have ever received a message from an ASP-based server that the server is too busy or the request has expired, the time the script waited to run exceeded the time allowed for it to run.

This property can be applied to the IIsWebService, IIsWebServer, IIsWebVirtualDir, and IIsWebDirectory IIS Admin objects.

AspScriptEngineCacheMax

More than one scripting language can be supported for use with ASP. Engines can be loaded and cached in memory for Perl, Tcl, REXX, and other scripting languages. The AspScriptEngineCacheMax property is used to specify the number of scripting engines cached in memory; it is set to 30 by default.

This property can be applied to the IIsWebService, IIsWebServer, IIsWebVirtualDir, and IIsWebDirectory IIS Admin objects.

AspScriptErrorSentToBrowser and AspScriptErrorMessage

When a scripting error occurs, details about the error, such as the error line number, are returned to the browser. If debugging error messages are not sent to the client, a default error message can be set using the AspScriptErrorMessage property. Example 2-15, created in an ASP page named *asp0213.asp*, illustrates setting the AspScriptErrorSentToBrowser property to `False` and providing an error message in AspScriptErrorMessage.

Example 2-15. ASP Script to Override Standard Script Error Message

```
<HTML>
<HEAD>
<TITLE>Developing ASP Components - Example 2-15</TITLE>
</HEAD>
<BODY>
<%

Dim iisAdminObj
Set iisAdminObj = GetObject("IIS://localhost/W3SVC/1/Root/chap2")

iisAdminObj.Put "AspScriptErrorSentToBrowser", FALSE
iisAdminObj.SetInfo

Dim strErrormessage
strErrormessage = "Something broke"
iisAdminObj.Put "AspScriptErrorMessage", strErrormessage
iisAdminObj.SetInfo

Response.Write(iisAdminObj.Get("AspScriptErrorSentToBrowser"))

%>
</BODY>
</HTML>
```

You can trigger the error by doing something like this:

```
    iisAdminObj.Put "SomeProperty", True
    iisAdminObj.SetInfo
```

The AspScriptErrorSentToBrowser and AspScriptErrorMessage properties can be applied to the IIsWebService, IIsWebServer, IIsWebVirtualDir, and IIsWebDirectory IIS Admin objects.

AspScriptFileCacheSize

IIS has the ability to cache ASP scripts. Changing this value can change how much caching occurs. Setting AspScriptFileCacheSize to –1, the default, caches all scripts. Setting the property to 0 turns caching off. A value other than these two will cache that number of scripts. For instance, the VBScript code in Example 2-16, in an ASP page named *asp0214.asp*, lets the cache store 10 scripts only.

Example 2-16. Changing the Script Caching Size

```
<HTML>
<HEAD>
<TITLE>Developing ASP Components - Example 2-16</TITLE>
</HEAD>
<BODY>
<%

Dim iisAdminObj
```

Example 2-16. Changing the Script Caching Size (continued)

```
Set iisAdminObj = GetObject("IIS://localhost/W3SVC/1/Root/chap2")

iisAdminObj.Put "AspScriptFileCacheSize", 10
iisAdminObj.SetInfo

%>
</BODY>
</HTML>
```

Adjusting this value dynamically is an effective technique to fine-tune the performance of a web site based on current usage.

This property can be applied to the IIsWebService, IIsWebServer, IIsWebVirtualDir, and IIsWebDirectory IIS Admin objects.

AspScriptLanguage

VBScript is the default scripting language used for an ASP application. Setting the AspScriptLanguage property can alter this default scripting language. The following code sets the default scripting language to JScript:

```
iisAdminObj.AspScriptLanguage="JScript"
```

This property can be overridden with the use of a directive, such as the following:

```
<%@LANGUAGE = "JScript"%>
```

This property can be applied to the IIsWebService, IIsWebServer, IIsWebVirtualDir, and IIsWebDirectory IIS Admin objects.

AspScriptTimeout

By default, scripts have 90 seconds until a timeout occurs and the script is terminated. This timeout value can be changed either by using the ScriptTimeout method for the built-in Server object or by setting the AspScriptTimeout property to a different value.

If an ASP application has components that can take considerable time, such as components that access a database, the AspScriptTimeout property should be changed to prevent the script accessing the component from timing out.

AspSessionTimeout

Each request to an ASP application from a single web page reader resets the timer for the Session object timeout. If another request from the same reader exceeds this timeout time, an error message is returned to the reader. The Session timeout time can be reset using the AspSessionTimeout property.

This property can be applied to the IIsWebService, IIsWebServer, IIsWebVirtualDir, and IIsWebDirectory IIS Admin objects.

There are several more properties that can be accessed and set within the IIS Admin objects, described in the documentation that comes with IIS 5.0.

The IIS Base Admin Objects

Up to now, we've been programmatically altering IIS using the relatively friendly IIS Admin objects with the help of ADSI. Now it's time to go one step lower into the workings of the Metabase and the IIS administration objects and plunge both hands deep into the IIS Base Admin objects. In other words, it's time to bring out the C++.

The IIS Admin object works directly from an ASP script, or it can be accessed in Visual Basic. However, to administer IIS from a C++ application requires accessing the IMSAdminBase interface. This interface supports several different methods similar to those provided by ADSI for the IIS Admin objects. These methods are listed in Table 2-1.

Table 2-1. IMSAdminBase Methods

Method	Description
AddKey	Adds a key to the Metabase. AddKey is similar to the IIS Admin object Create method, which can add new IIS objects.
Backup	Backs up the entire Metabase to a location you specify.
ChangePermissions	Normally, you obtain a handle to an IIS Base Admin object (a key) and open the handle for read or write permission or both. ChangePermissions allows you to change this permission on an open handle.
CloseKey	Closes an open handle.
CopyData	Copies the data from one Metabase key to another.
CopyKey	Copies the keys from one Metabase key to another.
DeleteAllData	Deletes all data contained in the Metabase key and any subkeys.
DeleteBackup	Deletes a Metabase backup.
DeleteChildKeys	Recursively deletes all keys of the Metabase key.
DeleteData	Deletes all data for the Metabase key.
DeleteKey	Deletes a specific Metabase key.
EnumBackups	Enumerates through the backups at a given location.
EnumData	Enumerates all data for a given key.
EnumKey	Enumerates all subkeys for a given key.
GetAllData	Gets all data associated with key.
GetData	Gets data for a specified key and property.
GetDataPaths	Gets the path associated with a specific data identifier.

Table 2-1. IMSAdminBase Methods (continued)

Method	Description
GetDataSetNumber	Gets the unique numbers associated with a data item in a key..
GetHandleInfo	Gets information about an associated Metabase key handle.
GetLastChangeTime	Gets the time when the key was last changed.
GetSystemChangeNumber	Gets the number of times a key's data was changed.
OpenKey	Obtains a handle to a specific key.
RenameKey	Renames the specified key
Restore	Restores the Metabase from a backup.
SaveData	Saves changes made to Metabase data.
SetData	Changes the value of a data item for a specific key.
SetLastChangeTime	Sets the last time data associated with the key was changed.

To demonstrate how the **IMSAdminBase** interface works, we'll create one last ASP component for this chapter, but this time the component will be created with Visual C++ and not Visual Basic.

Creating Visual C++ ASP components is covered in more extensive detail in Chapter 14, *Creating C++ ASP Components*.

Creating the ASP Component

The component will have two methods, one to set a specific Metabase property and one to retrieve it. The property used in this example is the AspScriptTimeout value, which controls how long a script will process before it times out. The property will be accessed for the *chap2* virtual directory, which is the key we will access using **IMSAdminBase**.

To create the component, you first need to create a new Visual C++ project. Create the project using the ATL COM Wizard and name the project **asp0205**. When the wizard runs, select Dynamic Link Library from Step 1 and do not check any of the options at the end of the page, and click the Finish button.

Once Visual C++ has automatically generated the framework code for the component, you'll next need to add a component class. Select Insert from the main menu and then select New ATL Object. From the dialog box that opens, select Simple Object as the type of component to create. In the next page, select the Names tab and give the component a Short Name of **tstBase**. The other fields will automatically be filled in.

Select the Attributes tab next, make the component both-threaded with a dual interface, and choose to aggregate the component by selecting Yes from the Aggregation radio box. Click on the OK button to generate the component class.

Once the class is created, access the Class View page for the project and right-click on the interface created for the new component, `ItstBase`. From the menu that opens, select Add Method. In the Add Method to Interface dialog box, give the method a name of getTimeout and provide the following for the Parameters field:

```
[out,retval] VARIANT *pvarScriptTimeout
```

The getTimeout method returns a Variant that contains the value of the AspScript-Timeout property. Clicking on the OK button will add the method to the component's IDL file and will add a method signature to the component's C++ file, *tstBase.cpp*.

You need to add support for `IMSAdminBase`, so you'll need to open the component's header file, *tstBase.h*, and include three header files, *iadw.h* and *iisconfig.h* (both necessary to support IMSAdminBase) and *comdef.h*, to add support for COM-based objects. Add these directly below the *resource.h* file:

```
#include "resource.h"      // main symbols

#include <iadmw.h>
#include <iiscnfg.h>
#include <comdef.h>
```

Close *tstBase.h*. Open the component's class file, *tstBase.cpp*, next.

At this time, the *tstBase.cpp* file contains the method signature (method name and parameter and return type), a return value, and the opening and closing method brackets:

```
STDMETHODIMP CtstBase::getTimeout(VARIANT *pvarScriptTimeout)
{
return S_OK;
}
```

To access the AspScriptTimeout property for *chap2*, you first need to obtain a handle to the *chap2* Metabase key and then use GetData to get the property information. However, before you can use the GetData method, there is a structure you need to be aware of: `METADATA_RECORD`.

The METADATA_RECORD Structure

You'll be using the GetData and PutData methods with the `IMSAdminBase` interface to get and set the AspScriptTimeout property value. However, to access a property from the Metabase using `IMSAdminBase`, you need to specify information about the property, such as the size of the variable used to get the data, the datatype, and so on. This exchange of information about datatypes of properties is handled behind the scenes within the IIS Admin object methods, but it is exposed with the IIS Base Admin objects. Based on this exposure, you'll need to pass information with the GetData and PutData methods; the METADATA_RECORD structure is used for this purpose.

METADATA_RECORD has the following structure definition:

```
typedef struct _METADATA_RECORD {
    DWORD dwMDIdentifier;
    DWORD dwMDAttributes;
    DWORD dwMDUserType;
    DWORD dwMDDataType;
    DWORD dwMDDataLen;
    unsigned char *pbMDData;
    DWORD dwMDDataTag;
} METADATA_RECORD;
```

The *dwMDIdentifier* member contains the Metabase identifier for the property. This value can be found in the IIS 5.0 documentation pages, and the value for AspScriptTimeout is MD_ASP_SCRIPTTIMEOUT. *dwMDAttributes* contains additional information about the property, such as whether it is inherited (METADATA_ INHERIT) or whether there are no attributes (METADATA_NO_ATTRIBUTES). For the example, you'll be using METADATA_INHERIT.

A complete listing of values for *dwMDAttributes* and the other METADATA_RECORD fields can be found in the Visual C++ documentation or at Microsoft's web site by looking up METADATA_RECORD.

---

dwMDUserType specifies whether the information is about an ASP application, a file, or a server. Possible values are specified in the IIS 5.0 documentation for the Metabase property. For AspScriptTimeout, the value used is ASP_MD_UT_APP.

dwMDDataType and *dwMDDataLen* specify information specific to the property, such as its datatype and the size of the variable used to set or get the property value. The AspScriptTimeout value is a Long datatype, which equates to the DWORD_METADATA type value, and this is used for the *dwMDDataType* field. In addition, the sizeof operator is used to get the size, in bytes, of the variable used to hold the data, and this size is passed in the *dwMDDataLen* field.

Lastly, the *pbMDData* field is used to hold a reference to the variable that either contains the property value, if SetData is being used, or to get the property value, if GetData is used. Variables of different types can be used to set this field as long as the storage is preallocated for the variable if GetData is being used and the variable is cast to a byte pointer (PBYTE).

Now that you've had a chance to review the METADATA_RECORD structure, you can create the getTimeout method on your new component.

Creating the getTimeout Method

You access the Base Admin objects using a technique similar to the technique you used to access the Admin objects—you specify the ADsPath for the object. However, unlike the Admin objects, you can use a shortcut keyword, LM, to represent IIS://localhost. So, to access the root directory of the development web server, you would use an ADsPath of:

```
/LM/W3SVC/1/Root
```

The first code you'll add to the getTimeout method is to create an instance of IMSAdminBase, using the template CComPtr to wrap the interface pointer. You'll use coCreateInstance to create the IMSAdminBase reference:

```
// get a pointer to the IIS Admin Base Object
hr = CoCreateInstance(CLSID_MSAdminBase, NULL, CLSCTX_ALL,
        IID_IMSAdminBase, (void **) &spAdminBase);
```

Once you have a reference to the IMSAdminBase interface, you'll use this to access the IIS Base Admin object for the development web server, using the Open-Key method:

```
// open key - access IIsWebServer
    hr = spAdminBase->OpenKey(
        METADATA_MASTER_ROOT_HANDLE,
        b,
        METADATA_PERMISSION_READ|METADATA_PERMISSION_WRITE,
        60000,
        &hMetaData
        );
```

The OpenKey method takes a Metabase handle, the ADsPath for the Metabase key, permissions, a method timeout value, and a reference to a Metabase handle for the newly opened key. For the example code, the METADATA_MASTER_ROOT_ HANDLE is used for the first parameter.

The METADATA_MASTER_ROOT_HANDLE is a defined value that represents the master root for the IIS installation. Instead of using this predefined value, you can also specify a previously opened Metabase key handle in OpenKey.

The OpenKey method then returns a handle for the key specified in the ADsPath. Once you've opened the Metabase key for the development web server, you can use this to both set and get data from the key, delete the key, or do any number of other operations. For getTimeout, you'll use the key to get the value of Asp-ScriptTimeout by first defining the **METABASE_RECORD** values and then calling the GetData method. The accessed value is then returned to the ASP application page. The complete code for the getTimeout method is shown in Example 2-17.

Example 2-17. getTimeout Method Using IMSAdminBase

```
STDMETHODIMP CtstBase::getTimeout(VARIANT *pvarScriptTimeout)
{
    HRESULT hr = S_OK;
    CComBSTR b("/LM/W3SVC/1/Root");
    CComBSTR c ("/chap2");
    METADATA_HANDLE hMetaData;
    METADATA_RECORD mdRecord;
    DWORD lnth;
    DWORD dwTime;
    CComPtr <IMSAdminBase> spAdminBase;
    CComVariant vtResponse;

    // get a pointer to the IIS Admin Base Object
    hr = CoCreateInstance(CLSID_MSAdminBase, NULL, CLSCTX_ALL,
            IID_IMSAdminBase, (void **) &spAdminBase);

    if (FAILED(hr))
        return hr;

    // open the key for the Development Web Server
    hr = spAdminBase->OpenKey(
        METADATA_MASTER_ROOT_HANDLE,
        b,
        METADATA_PERMISSION_READ,
        60000,
        &hMetaData
        );

    if (FAILED(hr))
        return hr;

    // define the METABASE_RECORD values for AspScriptTimeout
    mdRecord.dwMDIdentifier = MD_ASP_SCRIPTTIMEOUT;
    mdRecord.dwMDUserType = ASP_MD_UT_APP;
    mdRecord.pbMDData = (PBYTE)&dwTime;
    mdRecord.dwMDDataLen = sizeof(dwTime);
    mdRecord.dwMDDataType = DWORD_METADATA;
    mdRecord.dwMDAttributes = METADATA_INHERIT;

    // get the property value
    hr = spAdminBase->GetData(hMetaData, c, &mdRecord, &lnth);

    if (FAILED(hr))
        return hr;

    // assign the property value to the component return variable
```

Example 2-17. getTimeout Method Using IMSAdminBase (continued)

```
vtResponse = (long)dwTime;
vtResponse.Detach(pvarScriptTimeout);

// close the metabase key
spAdminBase->CloseKey(hMetaData);

return S_OK;
}
```

Notice in the call to GetData that the virtual directory name for *chap2* is passed within the method call. Also notice that the fourth parameter for the method is a pointer to a DWORD variable. This variable is set if the variable used in the METABASE_RECORD structure is not large enough to contain the property value being returned. If this happens, an ERROR_INSUFFICIENT_BUFFER error is returned, and the size of buffer necessary to hold the data is returned in the fourth parameter. Otherwise, this value will be 0.

 Example 2-17 does not show error handling, but you can access error codes from the HRESULT value set with the method call.

Once the code for the asp0205.tstBase component's getTimeout method is finished, it is compiled and accessed within an ASP page. The page, named *asp0215.asp*, creates a reference to asp0205.tstBase and then calls the getTimeout method, which is then displayed to the browser.

```
<HTML>
<HEAD>
<TITLE>Developing ASP Components - Example 2-17</TITLE>
</HEAD>
<BODY>
<%
Dim obj
Set obj = Server.CreateObject("asp0205.tstBase")

Dim timeout
timeout = obj.getTimeout

Response.Write "<H3>Script Timeout is " & timeout & "</H3>"
%>
</BODY>
</HTML>
```

The result of running this ASP script is a web page with the following:

```
Script Timeout is 90
```

You can verify the script timeout value by accessing the Properties page for *chap2*, then clicking on the Configuration button in the Virtual Directory tab. Another dialog box opens containing information about the ASP application associated with the directory. Access the App Options tab in this dialog box, and you can see an ASP Script Timeout field in the page, with a value of 90 seconds.

Now that you've been able to get the ASP script timeout value, you can try changing this with the IIS Base Admin objects. This is covered in the next section, where you'll create the putTimeout method.

Creating the putTimeout Method

To change the AspScriptTimeout value, you'll create a new method called put-Timeout. To create the method, you'll again access the Class View page of the **tstBase** component within the **asp0205** project, and you'll add the new method, named putTimeout, with one parameter, **DWORD** *dwTimeout*:

```
[in] DWORD dwTimeout
```

In the method, you'll still access the **IMSAdminBase** interface and use this to get a handle to the development web server key with OpenKey, but you'll be setting the AspScriptTimeout value with SetData instead of accessing it with GetData. The definition for the **METABASE_RECORD** structure is similar, as is the use of the Open-Key and CloseKey methods. What differs is the use of SetData to set the property value and the use of SaveData to save the changes to the Metabase.

When you make changes to the Metabase, you need to save them. You did this with SetInfo with the IIS Admin objects, and you'll use SaveData to save the changes with the IIS Base Admin objects. However, one important piece of information to keep in mind when working with **IMSAdminBase** is that you must close the Metabase key before you try to save any changes to it. Trying to save to an open key will result in an error. Other than that, the methods for getTimeout and putTimeout are very similar. The code for putTimeout is shown in Example 2-18.

Example 2-18. putTimeout Method That Sets the AspScriptTimeout Property Using the IMSAdminBase Interface

```
STDMETHODIMP CtstBase::setTimeout(DWORD dwTimeout)
{
    HRESULT hr = S_OK;
    CComBSTR b("/LM/W3SVC/1/Root");
    CComBSTR c ("/chap2");
    METADATA_HANDLE hMetaData;
    METADATA_RECORD mdRecord;
    CComPtr <IMSAdminBase> spAdminBase;
    CComVariant vtResponse;

    // get a pointer to the IIS Admin Base Object
```

Example 2-18. putTimeout Method That Sets the AspScriptTimeout Property Using the IMSAdminBase Interface (continued)

```
        hr = CoCreateInstance(CLSID_MSAdminBase, NULL, CLSCTX_ALL,
            IID_IMSAdminBase, (void **) &spAdminBase);

    // open key - access IIsWebServer
    hr = spAdminBase->OpenKey(
        METADATA_MASTER_ROOT_HANDLE,
        b,
        METADATA_PERMISSION_WRITE,
        60000,
        &hMetaData
        );

    if (FAILED(hr))
        return hr;

    // set METADATA_RECORD values
    mdRecord.dwMDIdentifier = MD_ASP_SCRIPTTIMEOUT;
    mdRecord.dwMDUserType = ASP_MD_UT_APP;
    mdRecord.pbMDData = (PBYTE)&dwTimeout;
    mdRecord.dwMDDataLen = sizeof(dwTimeout);
    mdRecord.dwMDDataType = DWORD_METADATA;
    mdRecord.dwMDAttributes = METADATA_INHERIT;

    // set property
    hr = spAdminBase->SetData(hMetaData, c, &mdRecord);

    if (FAILED(hr))
        return hr;

    // close key before saving
    spAdminBase->CloseKey(hMetaData);

    // save change to metabase
    hr = spAdminBase->SaveData();

    return hr;
}
```

Once you add the code for putTimeout to tstBase, recompile the project. To try the new method, create another ASP test page, named *asp0216.asp*, that accesses the `asp0205.tstBase` component and calls the putTimeout method. The value passed to this method will be 180, doubling the current value:

```
<HTML>
<HEAD>
<TITLE>Developing ASP Components - Example 2-18 </TITLE>
</HEAD>
<BODY>
<%
On Error Resume Next
Dim obj
```

```
Set obj = Server.CreateObject("asp0205.tstBase")

Dim timeout
timeout = 180
obj.setTimeout timeout
If Err.Number <> 0 Then
    Response.Write Err.Description
End If
%>
timeout = obj.getTimeout
%>
<H3>Changed Script Timeout to <%= timeout %> seconds</H3>
 </BODY>
</HTML>
```

The ASP page shows that the scripting timeout property has now been set to 180 seconds.

3

ASP Components and COM

ASP components are dependent on an architecture being in place to support component communication, and COM, or the Component Object Model, is the approach Microsoft has taken for this type of communication. With Windows 2000, Microsoft extended the COM architecture to include the services provided by MTS (Microsoft Transaction Server) as well as other services, but the basics of COM are still present.

COM is based on a binary and network standard that transcends any dependence on computer language. By using machine-level communication, a component written in Visual C++ can invoke functions exposed on a component written in Java, for example, and a Java component can invoke a function within a C++ object. All that is required is that the underlying COM implementation be installed for the operating system where the components reside.

This chapter does not provide an in-depth description of how COM works, since entire books have been written about this subject. However, it does cover some of the information that component developers should understand about COM before beginning to write components.

The chapter begins with a brief overview of how COM works and how it is implemented, then progresses into those features of COM that are incorporated into COM-compliant components.

Beginning with Windows 2000, the basic services provided by COM have been extended, and these new services are called COM+. Chapter 4, *ASP Components, Threads, and Contexts*, discusses one architectural change made to COM—the addition of the COM+ context. Now, components not only live within specific threads, they also live within specific contexts. The chapter also discusses the new neutral-apartment threading model. Chapter 5, *COM+ Services and ASP Components and Applications*, discusses other COM+ services, such as role-based security, just-in-time activation, transaction support, pooling, and others.

Overview of COM for ASP Component Developers

One important aspect you should know about COM is that implementation details are hidden, and COM components are usually seen as black boxes with no exposure at all of the component internals. A component exposes its functionality through interfaces, which can be considered "strongly typed semantic contracts between the client and the object," according to the documentation on the COM specification provided by Microsoft. When a COM developer provides an interface, she is saying that the interface will perform in the same manner throughout all time or at least for the life of the component, whichever ends first. What this means is that an application developer can create a client that accesses the component's functionality, and the developer does not need to know how the functionality is implemented. Moreover, by saying that an interface is a "semantic" contract, there is a defined behavior for each interface, a behavior that is guaranteed to exist regardless of future changes to the component.

To ensure that one component's interfaces are unique to that component, regardless of the interface names used, each component is assigned a unique identifier, hence the term *strongly typed*.

The COM specification provides for the following:

- Binary communication between components

- A unique class identifier to represent a unique component

- Functionality accessible through interfaces

- Interfaces that are never changed and are considered immutable

- A method to query for interfaces if a component contains more than one

- A method to track references to an object, to determine when an object is no longer being referenced, and to remove a reference to an object

There are other aspects to COM, but at a minimum this list captures the fundamentals, which are covered in more detail in the following sections.

Binary Communication

The COM specification is a binary and network specification, which means that the components are not language-dependent. They are, however, dependent on the implementation of the COM infrastructure, an implementation that is at this time primarily limited to Microsoft operating systems, such as Windows 2000. However, as IIS is limited to this same environmental constraint, this should not pose a problem unless you want to create a remote component on some operating system other than a Windows 32-bit operating system.

 Companies such as Software AG have provided programmatic support for COM/DCOM within Unix environments. In addition, the company Chili!Soft has provided software support for ASP from web servers such as Netscape's Enterprise Server. Based on these, one can't assume that an ASP application will be running within a Windows 32-bit environment. However, the majority of ASP applications and ASP components are created for Windows NT/2000, so I'll concentrate on the Windows platform in this book.

One of the most powerful features of COM is that, when a client accesses a COM component, the actual location of that component is transparent to the client. This means that the component can exist locally, on the same machine as the client, or remotely, on some other machine. This location independence makes a COM-based application highly scalable, since components can be moved to separate machines to decrease the load on one machine for better performance without requiring changes within the application using the component.

If the component is an in-process component, it runs within the same process as the client; this type of component is created as a dynamic link library, or DLL. An out-of-process component is one that runs in its own process space. COM further specifies two versions of out-of-process components: those that run locally and those that run remotely. A local out-of-process component is created as a separate executable with an EXE extension. A remote component can be created as either an executable or as a DLL. If it is created as a DLL, accessing the component remotely actually creates a surrogate client on the remote machine in order to load the component.

How does the operating system know which component is being accessed? Each component is registered on the machine containing the client and on the machine containing the component if the component is accessed remotely. The most common tool used to register COM components is the *regsvr32.exe* utility. Other tools for viewing component registry information are *oleview.exe*, included with Visual Studio or downloadable from Microsoft, and *dcomcnfg.exe*, used to manage remote components and found in the Windows subdirectory, usually *c:\ windows* or *c:\winnt*.

Since more than one component can be used within an application, and components can have the same interface names, how do the application and the operating system know which specific component is being accessed? The use of class identifiers ensures access to a specific component, and they are discussed next.

Strong Typing Through Unique Identifiers

Each COM component has an identifier, called a *class identifier* (CLSID), also known as a *globally unique identifier* (GUID). Because of this, no two components with the same object or interface names can be mistakenly used for each other, since each is identified by its own unique CLSID. The concept of the unique identifier first arose in the Open Software Foundation (OSF) Distributed Computing Environment (DCE) specification. The DCE has a concept called the *universally unique identifier* (UUID), which is a 128-bit integer guaranteed to be unique (at least virtually guaranteed to be unique) across time and space.

The COM CLSID can be generated using a variety of tools, or it is created as part of building a COM component using Visual C++, Visual Basic, and other tools. In fact, with these tools, you won't have to perform any special activities in order to access and include the CLSID within the component; the tool handles this for you. For objects created with other tools or versions of these tools that don't support automatic handling of the CLSID, the utilities *UUIDGEN.EXE* and *GUIDGEN.EXE* can be run separately to create unique identifiers. These utilities can usually be found in the */bin* subdirectory of one of the Visual Studio tools or can be downloaded from the Microsoft web site.

A real key to the power of COM is the use of interfaces, detailed in the next section.

 If this is your first exposure to working with COM, you should take the time to read at least the first two chapters of the Component Object Model specification, accessible from the Web at *http://www. microsoft.com/com/*, in addition to reading this chapter.

Interfaces

By using interfaces, COM provides support for objects that can be accessed externally, but without having to publish the object's implementation. The interface itself never changes and basically does nothing more than provide a pointer to the actual implementation. However, by providing this layer of separation between the client of the component and the component implementation, the component developer can make changes internally to the component without requiring any changes at all to the client. The client doesn't even need to be recompiled, since all of its access to the component occurs through the interface.

This separation of interface and implementation provides support for true object-oriented encapsulation or implementation hiding, though COM itself is not object-oriented in the purest sense. Based on this, the COM component developer can implement the object using any technique or even any programming language, as long as the technique and language support COM.

In the last paragraph, I stated that COM is not object-oriented in the purest sense. What I meant by this is that COM is not based on code source reusability, with a new object derived by inheritance from an existing object. It is based on binary reusability, with a component or application using the existing functionality of a component by including a reference to the component within code, rather than inheriting from the component.

One aspect of COM that can be difficult to work with at first is the fact that COM interfaces are not mutable, which means that different versions of an interface cannot be created. For example, I can create an interface called `IAddress` with a method called AddAddress. In the beginning, I could have four parameters for the AddAddress method: street address, city, state, and ZIP Code. However, let's say that I open the interface up for international use. In this case, I would want an address to consist of items such as street address, city, region, country, and postal code. I couldn't just modify `IAddress`'s existing AddAddress method and redistribute it as Version 2.0, since this would cause havoc with existing customers using the original address interface. What I would do instead is create a new interface— let's call it `IInternationalAddress`—to support international customers. This new interface inherits from my existing interface and expands on it as needed. By following this approach I "keep the faith" with my existing clients, so to speak, as well as providing the necessary new functionality for my new clients.

When I first worked with COM, I was not used to this concept of multiple interfaces. Like most developers, I had spent considerable time creating different versions of the same software, going from revision 1.0 to revision 2.0 and so on. I was not comfortable at first with the concept of creating a whole new interface whenever a change was needed. However, it is this quality that is absolutely essential for the success of COM.

First, components are not applications, but instead are grouped functions and data created for a specific purpose and having methods that are guaranteed to work in a specified manner. Based on this, whenever an application developer has need of the same behavior in more than one application, the same component can be used again and again. If the component creators decided to support a new set of behaviors and altered the component methods as well as added new methods, the application developers would have to upgrade all applications using the component to use the newer version, even if they want to use only the new functionality for some of the applications.

However, if the component developers add a new interface to the component that contains the new functionality, then the application developer could access the new interface only when needing to use the new functionality. The applications that don't need the new functionality continue to use the same, unchanged interface.

In order to support multiple interfaces, applications need to have some method of querying a component's interfaces to see what it supports and what it doesn't support. A basic COM feature is the ability to return a pointer to an interface based on a request, discussed next.

Referencing an Interface

To return a reference to an interface, each COM object must implement a function that allows the client to query for a specific interface. In the COM system, this function is called *QueryInterface*. *QueryInterface* takes a unique identifier of the interface as the first argument and an interface pointer as the second argument. If the *QueryInterface* call is successful, this second argument will contain the pointer to the interface when the method returns.

Rather than adding to the complexity and size of a component by adding automated garbage collection routines, COM utilizes a manual process of freeing component resources. When a component interface is first accessed, the component is loaded into memory and remains in memory as long as at least one interface is accessed. However, when the last interface is released, the component can then be unloaded.

A component can provide pointers to the same interface to more than one application, so how does COM know when there are no longer any references to any component interfaces so that it can unload the component from memory? The answer is that, in addition to having to implement the *QueryInterface* method, each component must also implement a method to increment some form of a counter when an interface is accessed. When a pointer to an interface is successfully accessed, a counter associated with the interface is incremented by one. This counter is then used by COM to determine when all references to an interface have been released so that the component can be released from memory. So, in addition to the function to query for the interface, another function, *AddRef*, adds to the reference count, and a third function, *Release*, decrements this reference count. When the component's reference count reaches zero (0), the component is marked for removal from memory.

If a COM-based component—ASP or otherwise—supports no other methods, it must support the ability to query for a specific interface, to increment the count when an interface reference is returned, and to decrement the interface reference count when an interface reference is released. However, as you will see in the section on COM implementation, much of this functionality is added to a component automatically, just by inheriting from one specific interface. Other aspects of COM functionality are discussed next.

Additional COM Functionality

In addition to the major COM specifications for immutable interfaces that can be queried and for maintaining reference counts for interfaces, other basic COM functionality has to do with maintaining state for a component, known as persistent storage, as well as the use of monikers. *Persistent storage* is the ability of an object to write state information about itself to storage and later retrieve this state information from storage.

Monikers are an interesting concept. Without going into too much detail, a moniker can be thought of as an intelligent name. By this I mean that not only does a moniker maintain a reference to some object, it also has information about how to access the object. For example, consider an application that accesses a component on a remote server using a moniker to maintain a reference to the pointer to the component interface. While the application was off doing other things, the connection to the server component was lost. However, the moniker would not only know what component interface to access, it would have enough information to reinitialize the reference to the component interface if the interface pointer is no longer valid.

Since a moniker must have enough information about the component interface to re-create the interface pointer, monikers are actually created by the interface instance itself and are made available to clients.

In addition to persistence and monikers, COM also contains processes for dealing with data transfer through its Uniform Data Transfer (UDT) specification. This specification provides for an interface that separates the transfer protocol from the actual data itself and also provides definitions for transfer medium and a mechanism to determine what data is being transferred and whether the data of interest has changed. UDT serves to provide a standard for data transfer regardless of the medium used to make the transfer.

How COM Is Implemented

COM is a specification and an implementation. It consists of interfaces that separate client access from component implementation, a defining language to describe these interfaces in a tool/language-neutral manner, and a predefined set of interfaces that are used to derive all other COM interfaces.

What Is an Interface?

Interfaces are abstract base classes. As such, they are not implemented but instead contain virtual functions that are themselves pointers to the actual functions that implement this functionality. Pointers to the actual functions are contained in what is known as the *virtual function table*, or *vtbl* for short.

The concept of virtual functions arose in C++ object-based programming, not with COM. When a C++ compiler finds a reference to a virtual function, it generates an entry into an array that contains a function pointer for every virtual function. For example, if the C++ compiler finds this definition in a C++ source code file:

```
class someclass {
public:
     virtual void somefunction();
};
```

the compiler creates an entry into the vtbl for *somefunction*. How does a client access the function pointer to invoke the actual implemented function? Each time an instance of the class **someclass** is created, a pointer is also created within the instance that points to the first entry of the vtbl for the class. The C++ compiler implements this pointer for every instance derived from a class that contains virtual functions. The C++ compiler also handles all of the details for the virtual-to-real function call, which makes this type of functionality doubly attractive. Additionally, the overhead for this functionality is equivalent to an indirect function call—in other words, it is minor at most.

So for the example class just shown, if I write client code that calls the function *somefunction*, the C++ compiler generates the code that accesses the pointer to the class vtbl. The C++ compiler also generates the code to access the index for the function—again with no intervention by the C++ class developer—which then returns the function pointer to the *real* function.

This use of virtual functions enables polymorphism within C++, and this same concept of virtual functions is used to separate the interface from the implementation within COM. However, what happens when you use some programming language other than C++ to create the COM component or the client? You can't use C++ programming language datatypes directly, since these might not map cleanly between the client and the component.

What is needed is a language-neutral method to define objects, methods, method parameters, and return types; for this task, Microsoft uses the *Interface Definition Language* (IDL) for COM.

Using IDL to Define the Interfaces

Interfaces are usually, but are not required to be, defined in a separate file using a language called Interface Definition Language (IDL). IDL is itself a subset of the Object Definition Language (ODL) used in OLE, which in turn is derived from the Open Software Foundation's (OSF) Distributed Computing Environment (DCE) Remote Procedure Call (RPC) IDL.

IDL provides a neutral language to describe interfaces, their parameters, and their results. The IDL that Microsoft supports for COM is similar to the IDL that the OMG group supports for CORBA, though not identical. As an example of a fairly neutral IDL, the following is the definition of a method that takes two long values and returns a short value:

```
short somefunction (in long lParamOne,
                     in long lParamTwo);
```

The modifier [in] is used to denote a parameter that is passed by value only. Another modifier is [out], used to denote a parameter passed by reference.

As stated, Microsoft has its own version of IDL that has COM-specific *annotation* or *decoration*. The Microsoft-specific version of the IDL for the function shown previously is:

```
HRESULT somefunction([in] long lParamOne, [in] long lParamTwo,
       [out,retval]short retVal);
```

To explain this example, Microsoft requires that the return type of all COM methods is defined to be HRESULT, a macro for an OLE data value that returns the success or failure of the method call. However, you can actually return, literally, a different datatype to the calling program by using the modifier [retval]. For the method *somefunction*, the parameters are two long values passed in by value and one return value of type short.

Though the IDL defines three parameters, and the function within the COM component would code for three parameters, you would actually code for only two parameters and a short result in the client, as the VBScript in the next block shows:

```
Dim retValue
Dim lParam1, lParam2
lParam1 = 2
lParam2 = 3
retValue = somefunction(lParam1,lParam2)
```

If the method were coded in Visual Basic, the return value parameter would be listed as the actual return value for the method instead of as one of the parameters, as shown in the following Visual Basic code fragment:

```
Public Function somefunction(ByVal lParam1 As Long, ByVal lParam2 As Long) _
                            As Integer
```

How IDL is used to handle parameter typing and method description within COM is discussed later in this chapter, in the section titled "Notable COM Interfaces."

Implementing the Interface

Once an interface is defined, it's implemented using whatever approach works with the language you're currently using. For instance, when you add a new component class to a Visual C++ project, the tool creates an interface for the component. You then add the interface methods and properties to this generated interface.

Figure 3-1 shows an ASP component created in Visual C++ in Chapter 18, *Accessing MSMQ from C++ ASP Components*. Notice the component's interface, Imsgqueue, and all of its defined methods in the left side of Figure 3-1.

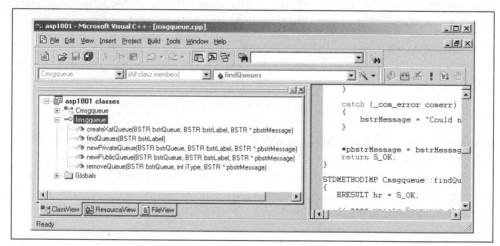

Figure 3-1. C++ interface and its methods

In Visual Basic, you don't have to create the interface directly, since the tool handles this for you. In fact, even if you wanted to modify the IDL for the interface for a Visual Basic component directly, you can't.

In Perl with the Perl Dev Kit (PDK), an interface is created in the same manner as any other Perl module—depending on whether you're using PerlCtrl to wrap the Perl module in a COM DLL or using PerlCOM to access the module's methods and properties. Delphi provides a Type Library Editor that allows you to manipulate the methods and properties of an interface and then export the information to the IDL file. In the actual component code, the only reference made to the interface is within the class definition:

```
TFirst = class(TASPMTSObject, IFirst)
```

Again, the tool determines the level of exposure of the interface to the developer.

Another key to the COM architecture is that components can implement more than one interface.

Multiple Interface Support in Components

If a component could implement only one interface, it would be useful—but the real power of COM comes from a component's ability to implement more than one interface.

In Visual Basic, when you create a VB class, you're implementing the VB interface associated with the class—but the implementation isn't exposed. If you also wanted to implement another interface, such as IObjectControl (discussed in Chapter 5), you can, just by using the following line:

```
Implements IObjectControl
```

The Implements keyword allows you to implement more than one interface within your component in order to "absorb" the behaviors from more than one interface.

In Delphi, this is shown, again, in the class definition statement. For instance, if you want to implement IObjectControl, you would use:

```
IManual = class(TAutoObject, IManual, ObjectControl)
```

In C++ when using ATL, you would add the interface to the class definition:

```
class ATL_NO_VTABLE Cnewguys :
    public CComObjectRootEx<CComMultiThreadModel>,
    public CComCoClass<Cnewguys, &CLSID_newguys>,
    public IObjectControl,
    public IDispatchImpl<Inewguys, &IID_Inewguys, &LIBID_ASP1504Lib>
```

You would also add the interface to the COM map defined for the component:

```
BEGIN_COM_MAP(Cnewguys)
    COM_INTERFACE_ENTRY(Inewguys)
    COM_INTERFACE_ENTRY(IObjectControl)
    COM_INTERFACE_ENTRY(IDispatch)
END_COM_MAP()
```

By providing support for multiple interfaces, your component isn't limited to one set of behaviors, but can incorporate many.

Speaking of interfaces, let's take a look at the key interfaces you'll use when developing the ASP components in this book and in your own ASP applications.

Notable COM Interfaces

There are a great number of COM interfaces—interfaces provided by Microsoft to support the COM architecture. There are even more defined for the support of COM+ (which will be discussed in Chapter 5). However, there are some interfaces that are key to your (and all) component development efforts. This section will take a look at these most important interfaces.

IUnknown

In order to support a multiple immutable interface approach, COM has provided an interface, IUnknown, and all component interfaces must be derived, directly or indirectly, from it. IUnknown has three abstract methods, QueryInterface, AddRef, and Release, which provide references to the necessary functionality for querying for a specific interface, adding a reference to the interface from within an application, and releasing the reference when the interface pointer is no longer needed.

IUnknown is an abstract base class, which means it contains nothing but virtual functions and has no implementation itself. You cannot directly create an instance of IUnknown. In addition, each of the IUnknown functions is a pure virtual function, which means that each of these functions must be implemented within any interface that inherits from IUnknown.

IUnknown provides the methods to access an interface and update the interface reference counter, but a problem with runtime access of an interface and its methods is determining the structure of a particular method call, including the number and types of parameters passed in the call. To address this problem, Microsoft also provided another standard interface, itself derived from IUnknown, that is called IDispatch. IDispatch is also known as the COM automation object.

IDispatch

As mentioned earlier, interfaces can be defined in IDL to provide a language-independent description of the interface. However, IDL doesn't just define the interface and its methods as an esoteric exercise. An IDL file can be used to generate a *type library*. A type library contains information about a COM object, such as the interface object's methods and parameters. This information can then be used whenever an interface method is invoked.

If the client does not have access to the type library, does it mean it can't access the component? No, but extra effort is necessary to allow access to a component's methods. If the client does not have information about the component interface method, it must first call a method to get identifiers for the method and each of the method's parameters, and then pass this information along on each call to the method. The functionality to make this call resides with another basic COM interface, `IDispatch`.

The earliest implementations of `IDispatch` performed two function calls for every method called on the interface that was derived from `IDispatch` (current implementations are discussed in the next section). The first call was to a function called GetIDsOfNames, which returned a special ID, called the `DISPID`, for the method. The `DISPID` is then passed as the first parameter of another `IDispatch` method, Invoke, which used to actually invoke the derived interface method. So if you had a component with a method called getTestScores, calling this method from an application or another component resulted in two method calls on `IDispatch`: one to GetIDsOfNames to get the `DISPID` of getTestScores and one to Invoke with the `DISPID` to actually call the method. In addition to the `DISPID` passed to the `IDispatch` Invoke method, a structure containing the parameters for getTest-Scores is also passed to Invoke. This structure is of type `DISPPARAMS` and is generated by default using a standard proxy/stub implemented by Microsoft specifically for default marshaling.

A Brief Word on Early and Late Binding

As you can imagine, having to call two functions for every interface method call, a process known as *late binding*, could become a bit of a performance issue, particularly if the component exists across a network. In answer to performance concerns, Microsoft provided the type library, discussed earlier. What was not discussed earlier was how the type library can be used in place of the `IDispatch` GetIDsOfNames function.

Instead of having to call GetIDsOfNames to get the `DISPID` of the method, the type library provides the `DISPIDs` for each of the interface methods; `IDispatch` can use these to pass to the Invoke method, rather than having to call GetIDsOfNames. Because the binding information is retrieved early on, it is known as—what else?—*early binding*.

However, using `IDispatch` is not the only technique that can be used to access an interface method. Another technique to invoke a method on an interface is to access the vtbl entry for the method directly, rather than accessing it through `IDispatch`. Accessing the vtbl directly is supported for most programming languages and tools, including Visual Basic, Visual C++, Java (with help from the Microsoft COM Java wrapping), Delphi, and Perl, but it is not supported for scripting languages such as VBScript and JScript. Because of this, vtable binding is not supported in ASP scripting blocks. Since not all COM clients support vtbl binding, most COM-based components, including ones created specifically for use in ASP applications, use a method known as the *dual interface*. A dual interface component is one that has support for vtable binding as well as IDispatch in cases in which vtbl binding is not supported. The components in this book all use the dual interface.

At a minimum, a COM-based component can be created using just IUnknown and, usually, IDispatch, and in a later section, we'll use Visual C++ to create just such a simple component. However, for the client to retrieve a reference to a class instance through an interface, the instance must be created, and this is where IClassFactory enters the picture.

IClassFactory

IUnknown defines a method that can be used to query for an interface, and IDispatch can be used to invoke a method on the interface, but we are missing something here. Something, somewhere has to create the instance of the class associated with the interface.

When a client wants to create an instance of a component and query for an interface on that component, it must do two things. First, it must initialize COM—call it waking COM up—by calling a method named *CoInitialize* or *CoInitializeEx*. *CoInitialize* takes one parameter, a value of NULL, and *CoInitializeEx* takes two parameters, the first again being NULL and the second containing a flag describing the thread's concurrency model. Either of these functions is called only once on a thread and basically initializes the COM library on that thread.

   Threads are discussed in more detail in Chapter 4.

After the function call to kick COM awake, so to speak, the next function the client must call is either *CoCreateInstance* or *CoCreateInstanceEx*. *CoCreateInstance* takes as parameters the CLSID for the object (either a pointer to an object for aggregation or NULL), the context of the component (whether the component is in process or not, or running remotely or locally), the identifier of the interface reference used to communicate with the object, and finally, the pointer to hold this interface reference. The more modern version of *CoCreateInstance*, *CoCreateInstanceEx*, takes the same first three parameters, but then it takes the name of the component server as a fourth parameter (or NULL if the component is local), the number of query interface structures passed in the last parameter, and an array of query interface structures in the last parameter. *CoCreateInstance* can return only one interface on the local machine. *CoCreateInstanceEx* can return an array of interfaces on either the local or a remote machine.

As *CoCreateInstance* implies, the purpose of this method is to create an instance of the object identified by the CLSID. For this to work, the component must have some associated technique to provide for class construction; this technique is implemented through the `IClassFactory` interface. Each method invokes the `IClassFactory` interface method CreateInstance internally, with either *CoCreateInstance* or *CoCreateInstanceEx*.

When a call to *CreateInstance* is made for an interface, it is the component's implementation of the `IClassFactory` interface that generates the new instance of the component, becoming literally the component's class factory, hence the name.

So what happens when a client creates an instance of a COM object and calls one of its methods? The client first of all initializes COM (*CoInitialize*) and then it creates an instance of the component (*CoCreateInstance*), which in turn creates an instance of the component (through `IClassFactory`'s CreateInstance). Next, it queries the component for a specific interface (`IUnknown`'s QueryInterface), and once the interface is returned, it invokes a method on the interface (`IDispatch` Invoke). If the client does not have a type library associated with the interface, COM must obtain the dispatch identifiers for the method (`IDispatch` GetIDs-OfNames). If a dual interface is supported, the client may make a call to get the function pointer for the method directly.

A Brief Word on Containment/Aggregation

If you are just learning about COM and writing COM-based components, you are probably concerned first of all with creating a component that doesn't break and, second, with creating one that actually works. Your component's reusability is probably a distant concern at this time. Eventually, though, you may want to extend an existing component, and reusability is the key to doing this.

COM provides not just one but two mechanisms for reusability. The first is known as containment/delegation; the second is known as aggregation.

Containment/delegation basically wraps one component around another, with the outer component intercepting all of its own interface method calls and those of the contained object. The outer component then uses whatever interfaces of the contained component it needs to create its own implementation.

Aggregation is used when the outer component exposes an inner component's interfaces as if they were its own. The advantage of this approach is that the outer component only implements extended functionality, rather than having to implement its own functionality and that of its contained component. However, problems occur with the handling of IUnknown calls to the inner component interface. IUnknown calls increment or decrement a reference count, and when made by the client, they should go to the outer component, not to the inner component. Yet with exposure of the inner component directly to the client, IUnknown calls are made to the inner component.

To prevent this, COM provides a mechanism so that, when the outer component creates the inner component, it passes its own IUnknown interface to the inner component. If you remember from the section on IClassFactory, the inner component is created with *CoCreateInstance* or *CoCreateInstanceEx*, except instead of passing in NULL as the second parameter, the pointer to the outer component is passed. Sending a non-NULL value serves as a signal to the inner component that it is being aggregated. If the inner component supports this, it then creates two IUnknown interfaces, one that is nondelegating and one that delegating. When the client makes IUnknown calls, these are made on the delegating IUnknown interface and are delegated to the outer component. When the outer component itself, though, makes a request for the IUnknown interface from the inner component, the component knows to return the nondelegating IUnknown interface. With this, the IUnknown calls from the client are correctly routed to the outer component, and the outer component can control the lifetime of the inner component by its own IUnknown calls.

The Enumerator Interfaces: IEnumXXXX

The IEnumXXXX interfaces (the XXXX being replaced by specific datatypes) aren't absolutely essential for your ASP component development, but there is a strong possibility you will be working with them. The main reason is that Microsoft has implemented several collections for many of its technology APIs (such as the ASP built-in objects, the CDO objects, and so on), and enumerators are what you'll use to iterate through these collections.

A *collection* is a related group of like objects along with an associated set of methods that can be used to access specific objects or to iterate through the collection of objects. For instance, if your component is processing the contents of an HTML form, you could access these contents through the Forms collection of the ASP Request object.

Instead of having to find a count of the objects and then manually create a loop to access each item, you can use the built-in enumeration methods to access all of the items sequentially.

Enumeration is implemented in different ways in different languages, but whether the actual details of enumeration are exposed or not, the actual implementation occurs through the IEnumXXXX interfaces.

The IEnum*XXXX* interfaces support a specific set of methods used to enumerate through the collection. For instance, use the Next method to go to the next item in the collection, use Skip to skip over an item, and use Reset to reset the collection back to the beginning.

Though all of these methods are implemented for the IEnum*XXXX* interfaces, the actual implementation details can vary based on the language. In Visual Basic, you enumerate through a collection using the **For Each**...**Next** statement, as the following code example demonstrates with the ASP Request object's ServerVariables collection:

```
For Each x In rqstObject.ServerVariables
    rspnseObject.Write x & " = " & rqstObject.ServerVariables(x)
Next
```

In this code block, each item in the ServerVariables collection is assigned to *rqstObject*, the variable contained within the **For Each**...**Next** statement.

In Delphi and C++, you'll have to access the enumerator from the IUnknown interface. In C++, this looks like:

```
// get ServerVariables
hr = m_piRequest->get_ServerVariables(&piDict);
if (FAILED(hr)) return hr;

// get enumerator
hr = piDict->get__NewEnum(&piUnk);
if (FAILED(hr)) return hr;

hr = piUnk->QueryInterface(IID_IEnumVARIANT, (void **)&piEnum);
if (FAILED(hr)) return hr;

// enumerate through collection, printing out values
_variant_t vtItem, vtValue;
while (S_OK == piEnum->Next(1,&vtItem,&lValue)) {

    m_piResponse->Write(vtItem);

    ...
}
```

Calling the get_ServerVariables method returns the ServerVariables collection. Then you access an IUnknown interface pointer to the collection's enumerator interface and call QueryInterface on it to get the actual IEnum*XXXX* interface, in this case, a pointer to IEnumVARIANT.

For the ASP objects and most other object models, you'll almost always use the IEnumVARIANT enumerator, since the collections contain variant datatypes.

Within Delphi, the sequence of events is almost identical to that within C++, except you can use the Delphi **As** keyword instead of QueryInterface:

```
// get ServerVariables and enum for variables
piReqDict := m_piRequest.Get_ServerVariables;
piIUnknown := piReqDict.Get__NewEnum;
piIEnum := piIUnknown As IEnumVariant;

// while S_OK get name and value, print
while piIEnum.Next(1,ovName,liReturn) = S_OK do
  begin;
    m_piResponse.Write(ovName);
    ...
  end;
```

In Java, the Next method actually returns all elements into an array, and you then traverse the array:

```
iRqstDict = iRequest.getServerVariables();

// get enumerator
IEnumVariant ienum;
ienum = (IEnumVariant) iRqstDict.get_NewEnum();

// set up enumeration
int[] iItems = new int[1];
iItems[0] = 0;

int iCount = iRqstDict.getCount();
Variant[] vt = new Variant[iCount];
ienum.Next(iCount,vt,iItems);
```

ActiveState (the company that provides ActivePerl and the Perl Dev Kit, enabling Perl for ASP and PerlScript) has implemented a Perl Enum package that can be used to traverse the collection:

```
# access ServerVariables collection as a list
@lst = Win32::OLE::Enum->All($request->ServerVariables);

# iterate through each list item, printing out
# item name and its value
foreach my $item(@lst) {
  $response->Write($request->ServerVariables($item)->item);
  ...
}
```

Regardless of how each language implements enumeration, the key to each is that you can access the collection as a group and process each collection element rather than having to access each element individually.

In the examples, the **IEnumVARIANT** interface was used to access the elements in the Request object's ServerVariables collection. The **IEnumVARIANT** interface returns objects as **VARIANT**s, the most commonly used datatype with COM/COM+ components. This and other COM datatypes are discussed in the next section.

COM Datatypes

One of the problems with an interface-based system such as COM is managing datatypes between languages. For instance, the C++ and Java integers are 32-bit values, while the integer is 16 bits in VBScript and Visual Basic. Strings and string allocation are handled differently in all of the languages, as is the implementation of most datatypes.

The way that Microsoft dealt with language issues in the implementation of COM was to define a set of datatypes that are COM-compatible. This means that any language (or any development tool) that supports COM supports at least some of the most basic of the COM-compatible datatypes.

How datatypes are handled internally within a component method isn't important. However, when passing data to and from the component through parameters, your component should use only COM-compatible datatypes.

A further limitation when creating ASP components is that VBScript, the most commonly used ASP scripting language, supports only the COM **VARIANT** datatype. Based on this, all methods that return values as output parameters must be defined to be the **VARIANT** datatype.

 Chapter 6, *ASP Interaction: Scripting and ASP Components*, provides details of the interaction between your components and the scripting environments, including the datatypes of parameters.

The **VARIANT** datatype isn't a scalar value. It's a structure that contains information about the variable as well as the variable value itself. The complete **VARIANT** structure (as defined in C++) is:

```
typedef struct tagVARIANT {
    VARTYPE vt;
    unsigned short wReserved1;
    unsigned short wReserved2;
    unsigned short wReserved3;
    union {
        Byte            bVal;           // VT_UI1.
        Short           iVal;           // VT_I2.
        long            lVal;           // VT_I4.
        float           fltVal;         // VT_R4.
        double          dblVal;         // VT_R8.
        VARIANT_BOOL    boolVal;        // VT_BOOL.
        SCODE           scode;          // VT_ERROR.
        CY              cyVal;          // VT_CY.
        DATE            date;           // VT_DATE.
        BSTR            bstrVal;        // VT_BSTR.
```

```
          DECIMAL                 FAR* pdecVal;            // VT_BYREF|VT_DECIMAL.
          IUnknown                FAR* punkVal;            // VT_UNKNOWN.
          IDispatch               FAR* pdispVal;           // VT_DISPATCH.
          SAFEARRAY               FAR* parray;             // VT_ARRAY|*.
          Byte                    FAR* pbVal;              // VT_BYREF|VT_UI1.
          short                   FAR* piVal;              // VT_BYREF|VT_I2.
          long                    FAR* plVal;              // VT_BYREF|VT_I4.
          float                   FAR* pfltVal;            // VT_BYREF|VT_R4.
          double                  FAR* pdblVal;            // VT_BYREF|VT_R8.
          VARIANT_BOOL            FAR* pboolVal;           // VT_BYREF|VT_BOOL.
          SCODE                   FAR* pscode;             // VT_BYREF|VT_ERROR.
          CY                      FAR* pcyVal;             // VT_BYREF|VT_CY.
          DATE                    FAR* pdate;              // VT_BYREF|VT_DATE.
          BSTR                    FAR* pbstrVal;           // VT_BYREF|VT_BSTR.
          IUnknown                FAR* FAR* ppunkVal;      // VT_BYREF|VT_UNKNOWN.
          IDispatch               FAR* FAR* ppdispVal;     // VT_BYREF|VT_DISPATCH.
          SAFEARRAY               FAR* FAR* pparray;       // VT_ARRAY|*.
          VARIANT                 FAR* pvarVal;            // VT_BYREF|VT_VARIANT.
          void                    FAR* byref;              // Generic ByRef.
          char                    cVal;                    // VT_I1.
          unsigned short          uiVal;                   // VT_UI2.
          unsigned long           ulVal;                   // VT_UI4.
          int                     intVal;                  // VT_INT.
          unsigned int            uintVal;                 // VT_UINT.
          char FAR *              pcVal;                   // VT_BYREF|VT_I1.
          unsigned short FAR *    puiVal;                  // VT_BYREF|VT_UI2.
          unsigned long FAR *     pulVal;                  // VT_BYREF|VT_UI4.
          int FAR *               pintVal;                 // VT_BYREF|VT_INT.
          unsigned int FAR *      puintVal;                // VT_BYREF|VT_UINT.
      };
```

Information about the VARIANT's datatype can be found in the *vt* structure variable. If the VARIANT contains a string, *vt* is set to a value of VT_BSTR. If the VARIANT is an integer, *vt* is set to VT_I2. The setting in *vt* provides information about where the VARIANT's actual value is set. A string value is assigned to the VARIANT structure's *bstrVal* data member or to the *pbstrVal* if the element contains a pointer to a string. Other datatypes, including objects, are assigned to the VARIANT structure member of the appropriate type. As you can see, the VARIANT structure is capable of dealing with all datatypes you could possibly need when writing ASP components.

Some languages handle conversion of data to and from the VARIANT without your having to do anything specific in your code. Visual Basic is a language that handles all conversion automatically, for the most part. However, within Visual Basic, you can use the *VarType* function to test for a specific datatype before processing the VARIANT:

```
' test for variant array
   If VarType(vArray) = (vbVariant + vbArray) Then
```

In other languages, you'll usually have to add code to handle most of your conversions or assignments when working with the VARIANT datatype. In C++, you can assign a string to a **VARIANT** directly when that **VARIANT** is used to output a value to the web page through the Response object:

```
vt = "this is the string";
```

However, for the most part, you'll have to set the **VARIANT**'s data members directly:

```
var.vt = VT_BSTR;
char * s1 = "weaver";
_bstr_t str = s1;
var.bstrVal=str;
```

If you use any of the other COM-compatible datatypes for your input or return value parameters, COM handles all conversion between the value and a **VARIANT** type when the component is called from VBScript. The only conversion COM doesn't handle is converting output parameters (parameters returned by reference), which is why you'll always have to use **VARIANT** as the datatype for method parameters passed by reference.

 What's the cost of the VARIANT datatype in size? It's 16 bytes—the first 8 bytes define the datatype; the second 8 bytes hold the value.

Two of these datatypes are of special note: **BSTR** and **SAFEARRAY**. The **BSTR** datatype is a string type that was originally defined for use with Visual Basic. It not only contains the string value itself, but it also has information about the string, such as the string's length. **BSTR** is defined as a 32-bit character pointer and is defined in C++ as the following:

```
typedef OLECHAR FAR* BSTR;
```

In C++, you can work with **BSTR** datatypes directly, though you'll need to provide memory allocation for the **BSTR** value unless you use the C++ COM helper classes found in the *comdef.h* library. In this library, the **BSTR** datatype is wrapped in a class called **_bstr_t**, which handles all memory allocation and deallocation; all you have to do is use the value:

```
_bstr_t bstrValue;
bstrValue = "this is a string"
```

In Visual Basic, you use the String datatype to work with **BSTR**, and VB handles all memory allocation. In Delphi, you would use the WideString datatype, and in Java, you'd use the Java String type (though String in Java is immutable—see Chapter 20, *ASP Components Created with Java*, for more information on this). In Perl, you can create a **BSTR** value directly using the Win32::OLE::Variant module, or you can use Perl strings.

The SAFEARRAY is a structure that encapsulates arrays, providing not only a reference to the array elements, but also a count of the number of elements. Chapter 6 has more information on SAFEARRAYs and how to pass parameters of this type to and from components.

Other COM datatypes are more basic, such as the integer values (INT, FLOAT, DECIMAL), single character values (CHAR), dates (DATE), and so on. Additionally, pointers to the IUknown and IDispatch interfaces are common within COM methods, as are pointers to other interfaces that aren't defined until runtime (designated by a pointer to a void datatype, as in (void **)).

If you're in doubt about whether a datatype is COM-compatible, check the COM documentation that Microsoft provides at its developer web site (*http://msdn. microsoft.com*).

4

ASP Components, Threads, and Contexts

I first had a chance to really learn about threads and NT when I attended a Boston University WinDev conference outside of Boston years ago. The big story at the conference was Microsoft's brand new operating system, which many of us had not seen yet. The operating system later became NT, and though I didn't necessarily realize it at the time, I was learning about NT from the masters.

I have never attended another conference that had so many well-known Windows development people. I attended one session given by Charles Petzold, probably the undisputed father of Windows API programming, who invited the whole group to join him for beers at the end of the day. I also attended sessions on OLE given by Kraig Brockschmidt. All the sessions were terrific, but one of my favorites was on threads and was given by none other than Jeffrey Richter, author of the well-known book *Advanced Windows NT,* published by Microsoft Press. If you are going to learn about something, there's nothing like learning from the best.

When I mention threads in this chapter, I mean the threads that Richter defines as "units of execution in a process." I don't mean threads of communication between client browser and web server. Multithreaded applications are ones that take advantage of a threaded environment to split off part of their functionality into separate executable chunks. On a multiple-CPU system, these can run simultaneously. On a single-CPU system, the operating system kernel gives each thread a period of time to run, then cycles through each thread in a round-robin fashion.

ASP components are first and foremost COM components. This means that whatever works and doesn't work with COM components will and won't work with ASP components. One aspect of COM that can either speed up performance or bring your application crashing to the ground is the use of threads. Because of this, this chapter provides an overview of threads, threading models, and the impact each of the models has on ASP components.

Beginning with Windows 2000, the model of threads and apartments implemented and controlled by COM/COM+ has been joined by the context. Contexts
group components based on requirements and replaces the thread as the smallest
unit of execution for the component. This chapter introduces the concept of contexts when used with ASP components. First, though, a look at threads.

What Are Threads?

Threads are the smallest unit of execution, and a process (or an application) can
execute its functionality using one thread or many threads executing at the same
time.

Threads can enhance application performance by assigning I/O-intensive operations such as file or database access to one thread while other threads continue
with other processing. These types of operations are ideal for creation on separate
threads because most time in I/O operations is spent waiting and listening for a
response, whether from you or from the printer. While these operations are waiting, other operations can continue with their work.

On 32-bit Windows platforms (9x, NT, 2000), if you run a process in the background, chances are good that the application has been programmed to create a
new thread for the background process. By assigning the process to a background thread, the user can continue to work with the application and do other
tasks while waiting for the background process to complete. For example, if you
are out browsing the Internet using a browser such as IE or Navigator and you
find a file to download, this downloading process is actually performed in the
background on a separate thread. Because the download occurs separately from
the main browser thread, you can continue browsing other pages while the download occurs. As each new page is downloaded to the browser, synchronization
occurs between the thread handling the file download and the thread handling the
download of a page to the browser. The thread performing the file download
shares bandwidth and CPU with the browser thread, and both actions seem to
occur simultaneously. If this didn't happen, you would not be able to see the new
page until the file finished downloading.

You can actually see something like this happening. To demonstrate, go to the
Microsoft web site and select a file for downloading. An excellent place to get
such files is the COM web site at *http://www.microsoft.com/com/*. Pick a larger file.
Once the file starts to download, browse through the rest of the site, but always
bring the download dialog up after clicking on a new URL. You can actually see
the download progress "hesitate" each time the browser page receives content and
vice versa. When the file is finished downloading, depending on the browser, a
message may open that states the download is finished, or the download dialog

may be removed. This is a preemptive action on the part of the new thread to inform you that the action is finished and to perform any cleanup necessary after the action is complete.

On a single-processor system, multiple threads can only work one at a time. The system provides a bit of time for each thread to work and then moves on to the next. This "round-robin" approach of assigning time to each process running on a separate thread in turn prevents one operation from holding up all others. It is this type of process that allows you to continue typing into a Word document while another document is printing or that allows a file to be downloaded from the Internet while you continue to browse. This activity occurs even in a single-processor system and with an operating system such as Windows 9x that allows only single processors.

Using multiple threads in a single-processor system can improve performance with I/O-bound operations, such as printing or opening a document. However, using multiple threads with a single processor for an operation that is CPU-intensive can actually degrade the performance of the operation. This type of thread, also called a *compute-bound thread*, competes for scarce system resources and, unlike I/O operations, does not normally spend periods of time awaiting responses. If the system contains only one CPU, a context switch must occur to allow each compute-bound thread its opportunity at the CPU. This effort adds a small measure of activity to the load on the CPU that would normally be offset by the advantages of using multiple threads. If the compute-bound thread's activities are short and over quickly, the overhead for managing the different threads is not offset by the overall result, and performance can actually degrade in comparison to serial requests to the CPU.

In a multiprocessor system, a thread can be running in the background by actually using a different CPU than the thread currently handling interactive commands. If a system has multiple processors and an application uses threads to take advantage of them, the application can be very fast. That is, up until a point of diminishing returns is reached, and the overhead of maintaining all the different processors and threads actually diminishes performance. Other unexpected results from using multiple threads occurs when threads access the same resource, discussed in the next section.

Of Deadlocks, Odd Results, and Thread Synchronization

When threads access the same resource, their activity must be synchronized. When synchronization is used correctly, the results are definitely an improvement over serial access of the resource. However, the lack of synchronization can lead to problems. When two threads compete for the same resource at the same time, a deadlock condition may result, and both threads can become suspended, each waiting for access to the resource. Or worse, if multiple threads access the same resource and modify the resource in some way, the results may be unwanted.

For instance, imagine that a file contains a string with a value of 10. Two threads access the file at the same time and read the current value.   The first thread increments the value by 5 and writes the results to the file. The second thread increments its value by 10 and then writes the results. But in the meantime, the first thread has already written a value of 15. What is the final value in the file? The file now contains a value of 20, not the value of 25 that you'd expect by incrementing the original value by 5 and then by 10. Why is this? Because the first thread modified the value between the time the second thread accessed the original value of 10 and the time that the second thread wrote the new value of 20. In the process of doing this, the second thread overwrote the value of 15 that the first thread wrote. I know this may sound as clear as mud, but a demonstration of something like this occurring within an ASP application is given later in this chapter.

To ensure reliable and consistent results and to prevent deadlock, certain synchronization mechanisms can be used, some of them beyond the scope of a book on writing ASP components. However, measures can be taken to prevent such problems. They include obtaining an exclusive lock on a file before allowing the contents to be modified and releasing that lock as soon as possible, as well as using caution with global data.

One other consideration with the use of multiple threads, or multiple processes for that matter, is that communication between components that exist on different threads or processes requires some special handling. This is discussed in the next section, which covers marshaling.

Marshaling

A component and a client that reside in the same process and on the same thread share the same address space, which means they share the same address space stack. This means that when a client calls a component's method and passes parameters with the method call, the component can access these values directly from the stack. When the method finishes, if it returns a value or if the parameters are passed by reference, the client can also access the values directly from the stack. This is an efficient and fast way to access parameter data. However, if a client and a component execute on different threads or in different processes, the two no longer share the same address space stack. Instead, the parameters passed to the method and returned from the method must be *marshaled*. Marshaling is the process whereby values passed as parameters are accessed on the client stack, placed into a stream, and pushed onto the component stack.

When a client calls a component method on a different thread or process, it is a client *proxy* that pulls the values for the parameters from the client's address space stack and creates a stream of data that is sent to the component. On the component side, a *stub* function then accesses this stream and pulls the separate parameter values from the stream, pushing these values on the component's stack. The component method then accesses the parameters from the stack.

Marshaling can occur when a client and a component are on different threads, known as *cross-thread marshaling*, or when a client and a component are in different processes, known as *cross-process marshaling*. Even if the component resides on a separate machine, the same type of process occurs; it's just that other players, such as the DCOM runtime and the Service Control Manager (SCM), become involved. In addition, information about the component's methods must be installed on the client, usually by installing the component's type library.

The process of cross-process or cross-thread local communication can be improved with the use of *aggregation*, which uses a free-threaded marshaler to allow direct access to an object, rather than having to go through marshaling. When using the free-threaded marshaler, a pointer to the actual component (rather than a pointer to the proxy) is passed to the client, even if the component resides on a different thread. Aggregation provides the best overall performance because the component can be created on a separate thread but can still be accessed directly. Of course, the cost of using the free-threaded marshaler is that the component must be made thread-safe, something that does add a burden to the component developer.

Threading models in the Windows environments are based on the concept of apartments, conceptual units that determine which thread handles a component's tasks. Threads and apartments are discussed next.

Threads and Apartments

In the next section, we'll take a look at the threading models, but first, let's take a brief look at how the concept of an apartment is implemented. If an in-process component is defined as apartment-threaded (or as a single-threaded apartment), it's instantiated on the same single-threaded apartment (STA) thread as the client, if the client is also STA. What *apartment* means in this context is that the component's methods are always implemented on the thread that created it—it must "live" within the apartment where it was first instantiated. No other threads can call into the apartment because of the threading model. The concept of apartment basically specifies exactly which thread can call into the component. Consider the apartment as being similar to the doorman at a five-star hotel: there is only one door, and you have to meet the doorman's criteria before you can enter. Taking this analogy a bit further, the STA model states that not only does a doorman exist to prevent unauthorized access, but by using STA with your component, you can live only within this same hotel. In other words, if other threads don't have access to your component, the reverse is true—your component's methods can't be processed by any other thread.

If the component is defined as belonging to a multithreaded apartment, specifically a free-threaded component, it can live only within another type of apartment—the multithreaded apartment. This type of apartment means that any thread within this apartment can call into the component, rather than being limited to the thread in which the component is first instantiated. This type of apartment is similar to a hotel with no doorman and no security: anyone can enter at any time. Along with the freedom of access from other threads within the multithreaded apartment (MTA), your component's methods can also be implemented by any one of the threads.

The point is that apartments aren't real constructs. They are, instead, the rules (and the implementation of these rules) that COM follows to determine what thread can or cannot implement your component's methods. More on the threading models in the next section.

The Threading Models

There are five threading models, with the newest model having been released only with Windows 2000:

The single-threaded model
> Each instance of a component is created on a single main thread. This model locks the component down to a specific thread, different from the threads that process the ASP pages. Using this approach, your ASP application will quickly run into performance bottlenecks as your component waits until the main thread is free in order for its methods to be called. Add to this the proxy handling that must occur between the ASP page and the component (the page will be implemented on a different thread), and you can see why this approach is not viable for ASP.

The apartment-threaded model
> In this model, an instance of the component is created in the same thread of the client that created the instance. Thread safety is guaranteed, since all calls to the component are serialized through the client thread. ASP applications accessed directly through IIS or processed through a COM+ application that's defined as a library application can successfully use the STA model, and the thread that processes the ASP page is also the same thread that processes the component.

The free-threaded model

This is the least constrained of all the threading models and is not recommended for ASP. When an instance of a component is created, COM creates the instance on a different thread than the one that created the instance and then marshals all calls to this thread. As ASP pages are implemented as STA, using the free-threaded model means that proxy communication is always used between the ASP page and the component—which is why this threading model is *not* recommended.

The both-threaded model

The component is treated as both apartment-threaded and free-threaded, and, as seen later, it is accessed directly by clients created using either threading model. A component defined as both-threaded can be implemented and accessed on either an STA or an MTA thread—it can be accessed anywhere.

The neutral-apartment model

This is similar to the both-threaded model in that the in-process component can be accessed by a client based in any threading model without the necessity of using proxies—clients can call the component from threads other than the one the component is created in. An additional advantage of the neutral-threading model is that if certain flags are set within the COM+ application that manages it, the component is thread safe but can still be called by multiple threads. MTA threads can be called by multiple threads, but there isn't anything guaranteeing thread safety, putting the burden of thread safety on the component developer.

When a client application such as a browser window is created, the system creates one main thread, which becomes the apartment the process resides in. It may create additional threads to handle other tasks within the process, or, if the application is single-threaded, all tasks of the process are run within this main thread.

Threads work differently depending on whether the component is created as an in-process component or an out-of-process component. An in-process component is created as a DLL and marks the type of threading model it uses in its `InProcServer32` key in the registry. An out-of-process component calls one of the COM initialization methods (*CoInitialize*, *CoInitializeEx*, or *OleInitialize*) in order to initialize the COM library, and all calls to the component occur as cross-process calls and are marshaled.

If the component is in-process, its interaction with the client depends on both the client's and the component's threading models. If both the component and the client are single-threaded, the component is created on the client's main thread. If, however, the client is multithreaded and the component is single-threaded, the component is created on the client's main thread, and all calls to the component from the client occur through the client proxy.

If the client is free-threaded and the component is apartment-threaded, a single apartment thread is created to house the component, and an interface pointer is returned to the client. All calls to the component then occur through this pointer. The same is true, but in an opposite manner, if the client is single-threaded and the component is multithreaded, except that, in this case, a free-threaded apartment thread is created and returned to the client. In all of these cases, calls to methods are marshaled.

If the component and client use the same threading model, the client has direct access to the component and can call the component's methods directly. Based on this, components created as both-threaded can be accessed directly by a client regardless of which threading model the client implements. The reason is that both-threaded components support both the single-threaded and the free-threaded threading models. If the component is accessed from a single-threaded client, it is created in the single-threaded client's thread. If a multithreaded client accesses the component, it is created in the multithreaded client's main thread. However, access to the component must occur within the apartment in which the component is created, even though other threads within the same process may try to access that component.

To speed access to both-threaded components, aggregation can be implemented using a special function (*CoCreateFreeThreadedMarshaler*), which basically allows all threads of one process to access the component directly. This and the results of implementing in-process components using the different threading models are demonstrated in the following sections.

 The components demonstrated in the rest of this chapter are all in-process components. Which threading model is used is particularly significant with in-process components and less significant with out-of-process components. Access to out-of-process components must be marshaled regardless of what type of threading model the component is based on. However, the performance of an in-process component can differ dramatically based on the threading model of the client and the threading model of the component.

With the neutral-threaded model, if the client is apartment-threaded (STA), the component is created on the client's STA. If the client is free-threaded, the component is created within the client's MTA. This behavior is similar to that of a both-threaded model. However, if the client is both-threaded or neutral-threaded, the component is created within the neutral apartment and any thread can then access the component.

Are Single-Threaded or Multithreaded Components Better?

I have one word for you if you are considering creating a single-threaded component: don't. By their very nature, web applications are multiuser, and a single-threaded ASP component basically restricts all access to the component to one main thread, the one started when the first call to *CoInitialize* or *CoInitializeEx* is made. If an application wants to access a COM object, a call must be made to the *CoInitialize* or *CoInitializeEx* method before the application can make use of COM features. With ASP, IIS creates a thread that calls *CoInitialize* and then directs all object calls to this thread. When an application accesses an ASP component, IIS must marshal all calls to the component through this single, main thread. So if one page is accessing the component, another access to the component from within the same page or from another page has to wait until the component is finished processing the earlier page request. All requests to the component are queued, a situation quickly leading to a bottleneck condition.

To demonstrate this, create a new Visual Basic ActiveX DLL component (using techniques discussed in Chapter 7, *Creating a Simple Visual Basic ASP Component*) and name it **asp0401**. Name the generated class **threads**.

 If you don't have Visual Basic, you can use the version of *asp0401.dll* included in the examples. It's been compiled using single-threading.

Add a component method named threadTest that has no parameters; its code is shown in Example 4-1. The component method contains one loop that, in turn, contains another loop. The outer loop cycles 32,000 times, and the inner loop cycles 10,000 times, basically forcing the component to take a visually noticeable amount of time to run.

Example 4-1. Visual Basic Code Testing Queuing of Requests with Single-Threaded Component

```
' test method
Public Sub threadTest()
    Dim count As Integer, count2 As Integer
    count2 = 0

    ' outer loop
    For count = 1 To 32000
        count2 = count2 + 1
        Dim count3 As Integer

        ' inner loop
```

Example 4-1. Visual Basic Code Testing Queuing of Requests with Single-Threaded Component (continued)

```
    For count3 = 1 To 1000
      '
    Next
  Next count
End Sub
```

Compile the component as a single-threaded component by selecting the Single Threaded option from the General tab of the Project Properties dialog.

The following ASP test page, *asp0401.asp*, has script that writes out the system time before and after the component's method is executed:

```
<%
Dim tst
Set tst = Server.CreateObject("asp0401.Threads")
Response.Write Time & "<P>"
tst.threadTest()
Response.Write Time
%>
```

Open two different browser windows and call the test ASP page from both. Open the page first in one browser and then immediately switch over to the second browser and open the test page in it without waiting for the first browser to finish.

Figure 4-1 shows the result of running the same ASP page in both browsers at the same time, with both accessing the same single-threaded component. As you can see from the figure, the process takes 9 seconds to run, and the process in the second browser window does not begin until the first process is finished, no matter how quickly you access the page. The beginning timer is the same because it is called from an apartment-threaded process that handles the ASP page—and the pages are processed on different threads.

No matter how many times the same test is run, the effect is the same: the second ASP page cannot run until the first is finished. The reason for this is that the ASP component created from the code in Example 4-1 is first instantiated by the ASP application based on the call to CreateObject in the page for the first browser, and the component's only method is called. Since the component is single-threaded, all other requests to this component are queued until the current request is finished processing, which does not occur until after the method is finished. This means that the request to create the new object using CreateObject in the same ASP page accessed in the second browser is queued until the ASP page in the first browser is finished being processed. Since the value in the page is written for the first time after the component is created, this value is not accessed and added to the page until the second browser's CreateObject request is finally processed.

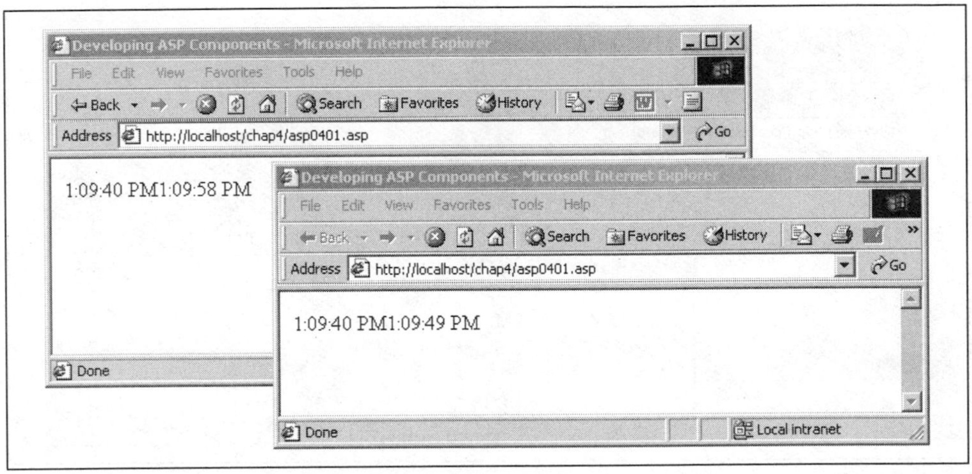

[Figure: two overlapping browser windows titled "Developing ASP Components - Microsoft Internet Explorer" at http://localhost/chap4/asp0401.asp. The first window shows "1:09:40 PM1:09:58 PM"; the second shows "1:09:40 PM1:09:49 PM".]

Figure 4-1. Two separate browser windows accessing the same ASP page and the same single-threaded ASP component

Next, recompile the component, except this time as an apartment-threaded in-process component by using the Apartment Threaded option in the General tab of the Project Properties dialog. This means that the component is created within each thread that creates the object and that each of the two separate browser windows creates a separate instance of the ASP component.

 Again, if you don't have VB, use the precompiled component named *asp1401b.dll*, contained in the examples for this book.

Running the same test by accessing the ASP page that instantiates the component in two separate browser windows at the same time has a different result when the component is based on the apartment-threaded model. Figure 4-2 shows the two browsers with the results of running this new version of the component. Notice from the figure that the first time value in the second browser window appears during the time that the first browser's ASP page is being processed, rather than after the component has finished in the first page. Running the test several times has virtually the same results. The reason is that the component in the second page is created before the first page is finished because the two requests are being handled by two different components on two different threads.

As a comparison of Figure 4-1 and Figure 4-2 shows, the accumulated time for both processes to run is about the same as each running separately, one after the other. That's because, in this case, the machine running the ASP component has only a single processor. However, if the machine had multiple processors, each

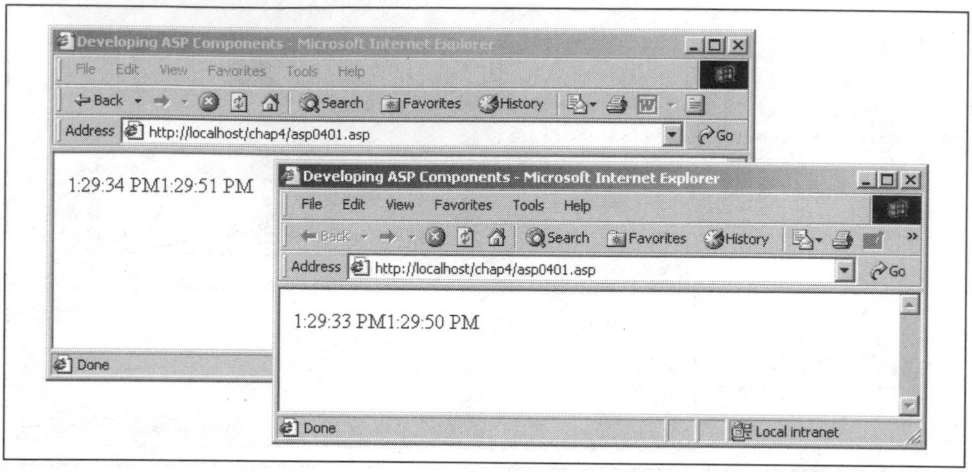

Figure 4-2. Two separate browser windows accessing the same ASP page and the same apartment-threaded ASP component

thread would run on a different processor and the component runtime should be correspondingly less.

Even with a single processor machine, if a component method invoked in one ASP page is involved in an IO intensive operation such as accessing a database, component methods invoked in other ASP pages, even those belonging to the same component object, can be processed while waiting for the IO operation to complete. Additionally, if the component method is itself accessing another component method that resides on a remote machine, the process can continue without waiting for the remote method to finish.

In summary, ASP components should not be created as single-threaded components.

The Single-Threaded and Multithreaded Apartment Schemes

A form of thread classification builds on the concept of apartment threading, and classifies threading into single-threaded apartment (STA) and multithreaded apartment (MTA) schemes. STA is equivalent to the original classification of single-threaded and apartment-threaded models, and MTA contains the free-threaded model. When a combination of STA and MTA models is used, the threading scheme encompasses the threading model known as both-threading or mixed-model threading.

In Windows 2000, a new threading model that is apartment (and thread) neutral is the neutral-apartment threading model (hence the name).

The single-threaded model just demonstrated is considered an STA main thread only, as all instances of the component are created on the same, main thread. As stated in the last section, this type of threading model is not appropriate for use with ASP components. The other threading models are discussed in the next four sections.

The Apartment-Threading Model

The apartment-threading model is the only multiple-threading model that Visual Basic 6.0 supports.

Apartment-threading within an ASP environment is fairly straightforward. When IIS processes an ASP page, an available thread is assigned to that specific page to process any ASP script. When an instance of the apartment-threaded component is created, it's created on this same thread because the thread assigned to the page is also apartment-threaded.

Because the thread processing the ASP page and the component are the same type, all calls to the component on this thread are not marshaled. (Again, marshaling is the process of pulling the parameters for the called function from the client's stack and sending this data to the server, which unmarshals the data and adds these parameters to the component's own stack.)

The STA model is also a relatively safe model to use, since any global data for the component is created in its own global data area within the thread containing it and is protected from corruption by processes running on any other thread. The only potential problem with global data for a component built using the apartment-threading model occurs when a call is made to the component from within the same session, and the component is added to the Session object's collections. Since apartment-threaded components can be accessed only by the thread they are created on, you as the component developer don't have to add code to protect the component from being accessed by more than one thread at a time.

In addition, if the component is added to one of the Session object's collections, the session is locked down to the particular thread where the component was originally created. So, when the client accesses another ASP page, it'll still get the same thread—even if that thread is currently processing another request, and even if other threads are available to handle the page request. Why? Because the Session contents contain an object that was apartment-threaded and was created on that specific thread—apartment-threaded component methods can be accessed only by the same thread that originally created it.

Additionally, you can't attach an apartment-threaded component to an Application object's collections. If you try with IIS 5.0, you'll receive an error.

The Free-Threaded Model

When IIS receives a new ASP request, it creates a new thread to handle the request. If the requested page instantiates an ASP component built based on the free-threaded model, the component is created in the IIS multithreaded apartment. Each application can have, at most, one multithreaded apartment, and free-threaded components must be created within a multithreaded apartment. This means that the component will reside on a different thread than the client thread that created it. Because of this, all calls to the component's methods must be marshaled, reducing the overall performance of the object.

If a free-threaded component is created as an application-level element, all accesses to this object from any ASP page are locked down to this single thread. This also means that all ASP application pages accessing the same component basically share the same global data. A free-threaded component must ensure that its data is safe, since threads accessing any one of the component's methods can change global data, even while one thread is processing one of the method calls. The component can be accessed by multiple threads, and there are no controls about which thread accesses the component or when. Based on this, the component developer must ensure that the component is thread-safe.

To demonstrate the problems that can occur with a free-threaded component that has global data, create a Visual C++ COM Wizard project named `asp0402`. Once the project files are generated, insert a new ATL object using the Simple Object option in the ATL Object Wizard dialog (it appears when you select the New ATL Object option from the Insert menu) and name the object `tstThread` in the Short Name text box. Change the threading model to free-threaded in the Attributes tab, and leave all other options at their default values.

 If you don't have Visual C++, you can use *asp0402.dll*, which is included in the examples for the book, and skip over the next few pages and the code block shown in Example 4-2 if you wish. For more information on creating a Visual C++ component, see Chapter 14, *Creating C++ ASP Components*.

This class has three methods: two of the methods modify a value created as a member of the C++ class, basically creating a data value global to all the components in the class; the third method returns this value to the client. Add the methods from Page View by right clicking on the `ItstThread` interface and selecting the Add Method option from the context menu. The first two methods, named setValue and tstAfterLoop, don't have parameters.

The third method created for the component, getValue, takes one parameter:

```
[out, retval] int * iTstValue
```

Next, add a data member to the class by changing to File View and opening the header file generated for the component, *tstThread.h*, and adding the following to the public members for the new class:

```
int iValue;
```

Finally, add the code for the three component methods shown in Example 4-2 to the generated class prototypes.

Example 4-2. Visual C++ Component Methods, Used for Testing Threading and Global Data

```
STDMETHODIMP CtstThread::setValue()
{
    iValue = 4334;
    return S_OK;
}

STDMETHODIMP CtstThread::tstAfterLoop()
{
    // set tstValue, but after long loop
    int count2;
    iValue = 0;
    count2 = 0;
    while (count2 < 32000) {
      count2++;
      int tst = 0;
      while (tst < 10000)
          tst++;
    }

    // set value - should be 32,000
    iValue=iValue + count2;
    return S_OK;
}

STDMETHODIMP CtstThread::getValue(int *iTstValue)
{
    // return tstValue
    *iTstValue = iValue;
    return S_OK;
}
```

To test the component, create two ASP pages. The first ASP page, *asp0402.asp*, calls the tstAfterLoop method to set the public data variable and then calls the getValue method to output its value:

```
<%
' first page
Dim tst
Set tst = Server.CreateObject("asp0402.tstThread")
```

```
// call looped method
tst.tstAfterLoop

Dim iValue
iValue = tst.getValue
Response.Write CStr(iValue)
%>
```

The second ASP page, *asp0403.asp*, calls the setValue method to set the public data member and then calls getValue to print out the results:

```
<%
' second page
Dim tst
Set tst = Server.CreateObject("asp0402.tstThread")
tst.setValue

Dim iValue
iValue = tst.getValue
Response.Write CStr(iValue)
%>
```

Running both pages at the same time using two separate browsers results in one browser showing the value of 32000 in its page and the second browser showing the value of 4334 in its page. Though the two components ran virtually at the same time, the results are as expected, since each component was created on a new thread, the free-threaded component was created in a separate multithreaded apartment, and the global data area for both component instances was kept separate.

Next, test the components by creating an instance of the component as an application-level element in the first ASP test page, as found in *asp0404.asp*. Call the method's tstAfterLoop and getValue methods and print out the value returned as well as the time before and after the component is accessed:

```
<%
' first page
Response.Write CStr(Time) + "<p>"

Dim tst
Set tst = Server.CreateObject("asp0402.tstThread")

// add to Application
Set Application("tst") = tst

// call looped method
tst.tstAfterLoop

Dim iValue
iValue = tst.getValue
Response.Write CStr(iValue)
Response.Write "<p>" + CStr(Time)
%>
```

The second ASP test page, *asp0405.asp*, accesses the component from the Application object and calls setValue to set the global data and then getValue to get the value to print. It, too, prints out the start and end times:

```
<%
' second page
Response.Write CStr(Time) + "<p>"

Dim tst
Set tst = Application("tst")
tst.setValue

Dim iValue
iValue = tst.getValue

Response.Write CStr(iValue)
Response.Write "<p>" + CStr(Time)
%>
```

By showing beginning and ending times, the time taken for each script block to run is also displayed on the web page.

Open two browsers, each with an independent session, by accessing the browser icon on the desktop for each or by accessing the browser from the Start menu twice. (Using File → New → Window usually opens the browser in the same session, depending on which browser you use.)

The first browser should run the first scripting block, which sets the application-level object and runs the longer method, tstAfterLoop. The second browser runs the page containing the block that accesses the application-level object and then runs the short method, the one that just assigns the global data member a constant value.

Unlike the results when the component was instantiated by two different browsers, the results of this test are definitely unexpected. Instead of a value of 32000 showing in the first browser page, it shows a value of 36334, as shown in Figure 4-3.

The first page shows an "incorrect" value because the components run on totally separate threads, which means that the calls to the component's methods are not serialized and happen asynchronously. However, both browsers are accessing the same instance of the component, which is created as an application-level component. The method calls from both ASP pages are made directly to this application-level component, and methods in both pages share the same global data area. The result is that the component data member *iValue* is set to 0 in the tstAfterLoop method called in the first page, but while the loop is being performed in this method, a second ASP page calls the setValue method on this same component.

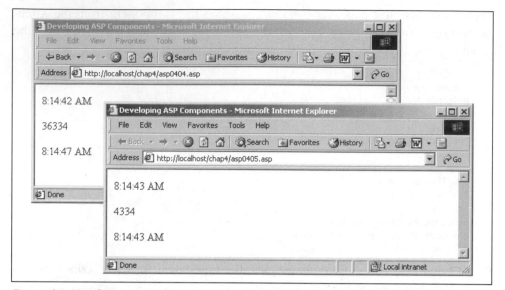

Figure 4-3. Two browser windows accessing methods of the same free-threaded ASP component, at the same time, impacting on the same global data member

This second method sets *iValue* to 4334. As you can see from the timestamps in Figure 4-3, the second ASP page method has a chance to finish before the first ASP page finishes. When the long loop in the first method finally does finish, it sets *tstValue* to the sum of *tstValue* and the counter. Instead of *tstValue* having a beginning value of zero, which it received when the method first started, it has been changed to 4334 based on the results of the method call from the second ASP page.

For a further test, open a browser page and then open a second one using File → New → Window, which effectively places both pages in the same session. This means that both browsers are accessing the same component from the same client thread. Running the first ASP page in the first browser window and the second ASP page in the second browser window does not have any unexpected consequences. The reason is that both browsers run in the same session and effectively on the same thread (unless there is a lot of contention for threads, in which case the pages may use different threads), and method calls to the same component for both browsers are serialized. The method calls to the component for the first ASP page have a chance to finish before the method calls from the second ASP page are run.

Due to problems such as the global data issue just demonstrated, and due to performance and resource considerations, you should avoid adding ASP components to either the Session or the Application object whenever possible. Limit these objects' collections to simple scalar values—or don't use them at all. If you don't use the Session object, you can disable its creation in IIS and actually improve performance when processing the ASP pages.

Any Apartment (Both-Threaded) Model

Another recommended threading model to use with ASP components is the both-threading model. Components created with this threading model actually adapt to the type of thread creating the component. If the client is running as a single-threaded apartment, the component is created in that same apartment, and all accesses to the component from the client are direct. If the client is a free-threaded component, the component is created in the client's multithreaded apartment and can support multiple thread requests from the same client process—all accesses to the component from the same client thread occur directly. The one disadvantage to the both-threaded model, though, is that requests to the component coming from the same client process but from other threads have to be marshaled, which can impact access performance.

However, since ASP components are primarily accessed by apartment-threaded clients (through the ASP pages), you shouldn't have to be concerned about a client with multiple threads trying to access the component.

If there is a possibility of a multithreaded client accessing the component, you can solve the marshaling problem through the use of aggregation, handled through the special function *CoCreateFreeThreadedMarshaler*. Fortunately, when creating a component in C++ using the ATL wizard, the use of aggregation and this function can be added to the component just by checking two boxes.

Note that using the free-threaded marshaling object with a both-threaded component means that the component can respond to calls from more than one thread. Based on this, the component must be thread-safe, with protection provided for the global data.

If you wish to create a component that is poolable, then your component should be marked as both-threaded, and support for aggregation must be included.

However, you can't use the free-threaded marshaler with a component that is pooled, so you can't use this option with these types of components.

In addition, as with the free-threaded component, you have to protect global data if you add the both-threaded component to the Application object.

The Neutral-Apartment-Threading Model

The neutral-apartment-threading model has many of the same characteristics of the both-threaded model in that no marshaling is required for accessing the component's methods, regardless of the threading model of the client. However, instead of creating the component within the client's thread, the component may be created within the process's single neutral apartment, depending on the type of threading model used with the client.

If the client is apartment-threaded, as it would be if the component were accessed directly from an ASP page, the neutral-apartment-threaded component is also created on that client's STA thread. If the client were free-threaded (unlikely within an ASP scenario), the component would be created within the process's MTA thread. However, if the component is accessed from a both-threaded client (as it would be if the component is created within a COM+ application and the application is defined as a Server application), then the component is created within the neutral apartment. The same holds true if the client is also neutral-threaded.

The reason that the component is created within this different apartment is that a neutral-threaded component can avoid the issues of global data corruption and unsynchronized thread access that plagues both-threaded components by having its access synchronized through the use of COM+ services when the component is added to a COM+ application.

 I didn't test the neutral-threaded model, since Visual C++ 6.0 doesn't support this threading option. Technically, it is possible to change the model in the Registry, but there could be issues, especially when using ATL, that make this a particularly risky operation to attempt.

What Are COM+ Contexts?

In Windows NT, contexts were implemented by MTS; the concept of context is not an integral part of COM. However, in Windows 2000, contexts have now been added to the COM/COM+ architecture.

As stated earlier, a context is a grouping of objects based on the same requirements. For instance, if several components support the same transaction through the use of COM+ Services and all other context-specific properties are shareable, the components should share the same context—as long as the threading models (and hence apartments) between the components are compatible.

Each context has a unique object—the object context—that defines it. It is the object context that allows component code to interact with the context through the use of context services. In Windows NT, the object context was created by MTS as a wrapper for a component, and you could access the object context with a method call such as the following:

```
Set obj = GetObjectContext
```

You can still use GetObjectContext to access the object context, but the context the object represents is now a part of the COM architecture. In fact, it's now the smallest unit of execution containment, as you'll see in the next section.

For more information on the COM+ Services, see Chapter 5, *COM+ Services and ASP Components and Applications.*

Relationships Between Contexts and Apartments

Apartments are still supported in the new COM+ environment, except that instead of being the smallest unit of execution containment as they were in Windows NT (or Windows 9x), they may now contain one or more contexts. The context is now the smallest unit of execution.

The new hierarchy of containment with Windows 2000 and COM+ means a process can contain more than one apartment, and an apartment can contain more than one context, as shown in Figure 4-4.

If a component isn't configured (through COM+ Services, discussed in more detail in the next chapter), it is always implemented within the same context as the client that created it. So an ASP component would be implemented within the context created for the ASP page that accesses it.

Each apartment has at least one context, the default context that's created when the apartment is created.

If the component is configured, it is created within the context of the client only if the two—the client and the component—share enough configuration parameters to ensure that they can share a context. When a component isn't configured

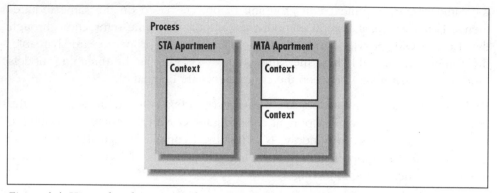

Figure 4-4. Hierarchical structure of process, apartment, and contexts

(through a COM+ application), it's automatically created within the thread's default context.

If the client and the component don't share the same context, then communication between the two must occur through interception, discussed next.

Interception (Cross-Apartment, Cross-Context Calls)

With COM, communication between a client and a component that live in different apartments must occur through proxies, and the component methods must be marshaled.

In Windows 2000, and with COM+, communication between a client and a component that live in different contexts must occur through proxies. If the client and the component live in different apartments, they'll also live in different contexts, and, again, the client/component communication must be marshaled.

However, there is a difference between proxies used to handle cross-thread (apartment) and cross-context method calls. Cross-thread proxies must use thread switching to handle communication between the client and the component. In Windows 2000, cross-context method calls are handled by what is known as *lightweight proxies*—proxies that handle any differences between the two contexts. This process of intercepting method calls and channeling them to a proxy is known as *interception*. Though performance isn't as good as direct raw communication between the component and the client, cross-context communication through proxies isn't as expensive in terms of performance as cross-thread communication.

In the case of ASP components, if the context of the object processing the ASP page satisfies all the runtime requirements of the component that it accesses, the component should be created within the same context as the client object. So how do you know if the ASP page context and the component context are the same?

Well, this depends on how you set up the ASP application and how you configure the ASP component.

> At the time this was written, there was no documentation about how ASP, ASP components, IIS, and COM+ work as an integrated whole. In other words, I'm making a best-guess interpretation of what I'm finding in the environment in this section.

For instance, if you set up the ASP application to run within its own process, an interesting thing happens with Component Services: a default COM+ application is created for the newly isolated process. Contained within the process is a version of the IISWAM component, the object used to process the ASP page script. You'll also find that this component is defined with a free-threading object model. If your component isn't configured in its own COM+ application, or if it is and the application is created as a library application (implemented within the client's process) and the component can be created within the isolated process's MTA thread, then the component should be instantiated within the client's context. Otherwise, the component will be created either in a different apartment (if the threading models are incompatible) or in a different context (if the client context doesn't satisfy the component's runtime requirements).

One thing you can do to force a component to be created within a client's context is to configure the component with this option. Do this by checking the "Must be activated in caller's context" option, found on the Activation tab of the COM+ application component's Properties dialog. However, if you do this and access the component from an ASP page and get the following error:

```
The specified activation could not occur in the client context as specified
```

then you know that the component can't be created within the ASP page's IISWAM component's context, and all communication between the client (the ASP page) and the component occurs through interception.

Regardless of whether your ASP client and the component communicate directly or through the cross-context proxy, your page performance shouldn't be adversely impacted—at least, not as much as cross-thread communication would impact performance.

5

COM+ Services and ASP Components and Applications

You can create your ASP components and use them successfully without directly accessing any of the COM+ services. However, these same services can make the difference between an ASP application that performs OK and one that scales well and can keep up with the demands on it—regardless of what those demands are.

The COM+ services you'll most likely use with your ASP components are transaction management, just-in-time activation, and pooling. In addition, new interfaces have been created to handle much of the functionality of these new services. However, before we take a look at these, we'll first look at using components within an application.

Developing Component-Based Systems

A component-based system is one that separates individual processes into reusable chunks of code and data and then uses one or more of these components to build a complete application. Among the different types of applications that can be built are client/server, distributed, and n-tier systems. A *client/server system* is one in which processing is split between the client and the server, with the client handling all user interaction, display, and client-side validation, and the server handling most database access, server-side validation, and business rule enforcement. A *distributed system* is one in which the application's components can exist on different machines and may exist in different geographical locations. In addition, more than one instance of a component can be created in order to handle multiple requests and provide the same service to multiple clients. An *n-tier system* combines elements of the client/server system and the distributed system; there is a hierarchy of components, as with a client/server system, but the components themselves can be duplicated to distribute processing load and distributed across many machines and locations, as with a distributed system. The traditional n-tier system can consist of the client, which handles all user interaction, client-side validation, and display; the business layer, which enforces all business rules and performs overall transaction management and validation; and the data layer, which handles all the direct data access.

The use of components facilitates distributed systems, primarily because components are small, compact, and portable (as long as the host machine provides the framework the component needs). If an access load on one server begins to impact the machine, and the machine's overall performance starts to degrade, the component or group of components is easily moved to another server with no impact to the code accessing the component. Additionally, because the components are modularized, one or more can be moved to one new server and others moved to other servers until the load processing of all servers is balanced. Applications created without this modularization cannot be split up and cannot be distributed across many machines.

Another advantage of components is that more generic functions can be split into separate components and used throughout the system. Additionally, the use of components facilitates the design and construction of an n-tier system. An example of an n-tier system is one where an interface component accesses and validates address information. The validation is generic and confirms that all the necessary fields, such as city and ZIP Code, are filled in. The business layer can then process the address information for the application based on the type of business. It can do things such as perform lookups based on the address information, such as finding shipping zones for a component used in a shipping application or delivery zones for a online ordering system. The component can then access the data layer to store the address information, retrieve additional information, or even trigger other online business components to perform additional work on the information. The data layer itself can be split over separate machines, separate databases, or even different types of data stores, with some information going into long-term storage and some short-term storage to be used for a specific task and then discarded.

However the components perform their task, the concept is to separate more generic functions, such as accessing and validating address information necessary for many applications, from the more business-specific functions, such as finding shipping zones for a shipping application. In addition, an n-tier application also looks to separate the user interface components, which should contain only enough processing to successfully acquire the information needed, from the business layer, which understands how the information relates to other information in order to perform a business function. The business layer is separate from the data layer, which concerns itself only with having enough information to successfully make a data transaction and does not care how the information is acquired or the purpose of the information being acquired.

ASP components participate in this type of system by providing functionality at either the business level or the data level, with the user interface handled in the browser that is accessing the ASP application.

In Windows 2000, component usage is further facilitated through the use of COM+ services to handle such things as component pooling and transactions. To provide this functionality, new interfaces have been added to the traditional COM interfaces (see Chapter 3, *ASP Components and COM*), discussed next.

The COM+ Interfaces

Most of the important interfaces necessary for COM, such as IUnknown and IDispatch, still perform the same purpose within the new COM+ environment. The major difference between COM and COM+ is that the functionality provided by MTS in Windows NT and Windows 9x is now integrated into the COM architecture with COM+. This integration not only adds new functionality through COM+ services, it also improves the performance of components.

 See Chapter 3 for more on the COM interfaces such as IUnknown and IDispatch.

To support the new COM+ services, several new interfaces have been added to those already provided by the original MTS implementation. The key ones that impact most on your development of ASP components are discussed in the next several sections.

IObjectContext

Chapter 4, *ASP Components, Threads, and Contexts*, discusses the concept of *contexts* as a grouping of objects based on the same requirements. Among some of the shared requirements can be whether a component is pooled or whether a component participates in a transaction with other components.

In Windows 2000, a component's context is a set of runtime properties that can be accessed or changed through the component's associated ObjectContext—an object that manages the context information for the component. The interface you use to access the ObjectContext properties is IObjectContext, and you can access this interface through the COM+ Services type library.

How you access ObjectContext differs a little based on the type of programming language you use. For instance, in Visual Basic, you first import a reference to the

COM+ Services into the project, and then you can create a reference to ObjectContext and call GetObjectContext to instantiate it:

```
Dim objContext As ObjectContext
Set objContext = GetObjectContext
```

In Visual C++ under Windows NT, you would also use GetObjectContext to access ObjectContext:

```
CComPtr<IObjectContext> m_spObjectContext;
hr = GetObjectContext(&m_spObjectContext);
```

However, in Visual C++ under Windows 2000, you use *CoGetObjectContext* instead, passing in the GUID for the interface:

```
hr = CoGetObjectContext(IID_IObjectContextInfo,
                        (void **)&m_spObjectContext);
```

The same behavior results regardless of whether you use GetObjectContext or *CoGetObjectContext*, because GetObjectContext in COM+ wraps a call to *CoGetObjectContext*. In Visual C++, you would also have to add a reference to the COM+ Services header file (*comsvcs.h*) as well as add a reference to the associated object file (*comsvcs.lib*) to the component's library path.

Once you have a reference to **IObjectContext**, you can call its methods, listed in Table 5-1.

Table 5-1. IObjectContext Methods

Method	Description
CreateInstance	Instantiates an object
DisableCommit	Indicates that the component is not ready to commit a transaction
EnableCommit	Indicates that the component is in process still, but transactions can be committed
IsCallerInRole	Indicates whether the caller is within a specified role (role-based security)
IsInTransaction	Indicates whether the component is within a transaction
IsSecurityEnabled	Indicates whether security is enabled
SetAbort	Indicates that the component is finished with its work and the transaction is aborted
SetComplete	Indicates that the component is finished with its work and the transaction is ready to be committed

IObjectContext also has properties, such as the following:

ContextInfo
   Returns a reference to the context information object associated with the component

Count

Indicates the number of named properties for the object

Item

Contains the named properties

Security

Returns a reference to the Security object associated with the ObjectContext

We'll look at the context information interface, `IObjectContextInfo`, in more detail in the next section. The Item collection is used to access the ASP built-in objects. You can access it directly within Visual Basic:

```
Dim oc As ObjectContext
Dim app As Application
Set oc = GetObjectConext
Set app = oc.Item("Application")
```

You can also access the ASP objects via ObjectContext:

```
Set app = oc("Application")
```

In other programming languages, you'll have to access the ASP objects using other techniques. For instance, in C++, you'll need to query for an instance of the `IGetContextProperties` interface in order to access a specific ASP object:

```
CComPtr<IGetContextProperties> pProps; //Context Properties

// get ObjectContext
hr = CoGetObjectContext(IID_IObjectContext,
                        (void **)&m_spObjectContext);
if (FAILED(hr)) return hr;

// get context properties
hr = m_spObjectContext->QueryInterface( IID_IGetContextProperties,
            (void**)&pProps );
if (FAILED(hr)) return hr;

// get Response property
bstrProp = "Response";
hr = pProps->GetProperty( bstrProp, &vt ) ;
if (FAILED(hr)) return hr;

piDispatch = vt. pdispVal;
hr = piDispatch->QueryInterface( IID_IResponse,
                    (void**)&m_piResponse );
```

The documentation for `IGetContextProperties` states that it is valid only within the Windows NT environment, but it can still be used to access the ASP built-in objects within Windows 2000.

Chapter 7, *Creating a Simple Visual Basic ASP Component*, demonstrates how to access ObjectContext within Visual Basic, including using this object to access the ASP built-in objects. Chapter 14, *Creating C++ ASP Components* demonstrates the same for Visual C++, and Chapters 20, 21, and 22 describe how to access ObjectContext within Java, Delphi, and Perl components. Each uses different techniques, but the result is the same—a reference to the component's associated ObjectContext and the ability to use this object to commit or abort transactions, as well as to access the ASP objects.

IObjectContextInfo

The `IObjectContextInfo` interface is used to get transaction, activity, and context information about the current component. With this interface you can access a pointer to the `ITransaction` interface. Table 5-2 shows the `IObjectContextInfo` methods.

Table 5-2. IObjectContextInfo Methods

Method	Description
GetActivityId	Returns the current activity identifier
GetContextId	Returns the current context identifier
GetTransaction	Returns pointer to the `ITransaction` interface
GetTransactionId	Returns the current transaction identifier
IsInTransaction	Indicates whether the component is running within a transaction

If you're using synchronization with your COM+ component (described later), using GetActivityId returns the identifier of the current activity; otherwise, you'll receive a null value.

The GetTransaction method actually returns a reference to the `ITransaction` interface. You can use this interface to commit and abort the transaction, though you should perform these functions through ObjectContext or through the `IContextState` interface, discussed next.

IContextState

`IContextState` gives you finer control of transactions and activation than `IObjectContext`. For instance, with `IObjectContext`, you mark that a component is finished with its processing and wants to commit a transaction using SetComplete; you use SetAbort to mark that a component is finished processing and wants to abort the current transaction.

There are actually two conditional bits that are set when you use SetComplete or SetAbort. The first is the *done* bit, and setting it indicates to COM+ that the component is finished processing. The second is the *consistency* bit. Setting this bit controls whether the component's transaction can be committed or must be aborted.

The `IObjectContext` SetAbort and SetComplete methods set both bits at a time— both set the done bit to `True`, indicating that the component is finished with its processing. However, with `IContextState`, you can mark that a component is finished processing and mark its transaction state separately.

`IContextState` has four methods, shown in Table 5-3.

Table 5-3. IContextState Methods

Method	Description
GetDeactivateOnReturn	Gets the status of the done bit
GetMyTransactionVote	Gets the status of the consistency bit
SetDeactivateOnReturn	Signals that the component is finished
SetMyTransactionVote	Indicates whether the component's transaction can be committed or aborted

You can get and set the done bit using the SetDeactivateOnReturn and GetDeactivateOnReturn methods. If the value of the done bit is `True`, the component deactivates when the component's method finishes; otherwise, the component is not deactivated.

To try this out, you'll create a Visual Basic component that implements `IObject-Control` in order to capture the JIT events (`IObjectControl` is described in detail in the next section). The component will have two methods, both of which call `IContextState`'s SetDeactivateOnReturn method. The first function will call the method, passing in a Boolean value of `False`; the second one will pass in a Boolean value of `True`.

 If you don't have Visual Basic, you can access the component described in this section from the examples included with the book. All you need to do is register the component using *regsvr32.exe* before accessing the ASP test page.

Create a Visual Basic project, name it `asp0501`, and name the generated component class `done`. Attach the COM+ Services and Microsoft Active Server Pages type libraries to the project. Once the type libraries are added as resources, implement the `IObjectControl` JIT methods Activate, Deactivate, and CanBePooled, as shown in Example 5-1.

Example 5-1. Implementing the IObjectControl JIT Functions

```
Implements ObjectControl

Dim objResponse As Response

Private Sub ObjectControl_Activate()
  Set objResponse = GetObjectContext().Item("Response")
  objResponse.Write "<h3>Activated</h3>"
End Sub

Private Sub ObjectControl_Deactivate()
  objResponse.Write "<h3>Deactivated</h3>"
  Set objResponse = Nothing
End Sub

Private Function ObjectControl_CanBePooled() As Boolean
    ObjectControl_CanBePooled = False
End Function
```

In the Activate method, a reference to the ASP built-in Response object is created and used to display a message that the component is activated. In the Deactivate method, a message is written to the web page that the component is deactivated. By examining these messages, we can determine when the component is activated and deactivated.

Next, add the two component functions that are called by the ASP page. The first, named *function1*, accesses `IContextState` and calls its SetDeactivateOnReturn method, passing in a value of **False**. The second function, *function2*, also calls SetDeactivateOnReturn, but this time it passes in a value of **True**. Example 5-2 shows the code for both functions, which you should add to your component.

Example 5-2. Subroutines That Call SetDeactivateOnReturn

```
Sub function1()

Dim iCntxt As IContextState
Set iCntxt = GetObjectContext

iCntxt.SetDeactivateOnReturn False
End Sub

Sub function2()

Dim iCntxt As IContextState
Set iCntxt = GetObjectContext

iCntxt.SetDeactivateOnReturn True
End Sub
```

Once the component project is compiled and added to a COM+ application, test the new component using ASP script similar to the following (found in *asp0501.asp*):

```
<%
Dim obj
Set obj = Server.CreateObject("asp0501.done")

Response.Write "Calling function 2" & "<br>"

obj.function2

Response.Write "Calling function 1" & "<br>"

obj.function1

Response.Write "Calling function 2" & "<br>"

obj.function2
%>
```

The first function called is *function2*, which deactivates the component when the function returns. Because of this, the Activated message should be displayed when the component function is accessed, and the Deactivated message should be displayed when the function returns, before the "Calling function 1" message.

However, when the first function—which doesn't deactivate the component—is called, the Deactivated message should not appear when the function returns.

Finally, when *function2* is called again, both the Activated and Deactivated messages should be displayed, generating a web page that has the following messages:

```
Calling function 2

Activated

Deactivated

Calling function 1

Activated

Calling function 2

Deactivated
```

As you can see, with `IContextState`, you can control component activation without impacting on the component's transaction, whether the component is within a transaction or not.

IObjectControl

The last section demonstrated how the lifetime of a component is manipulated using the `IContextState` interface. The example also used JIT—just-in-time activation—to control the component's instantiation and to write out to the web page when the component is activated and deactivated through the `IObject-Control` interface's Activate and Deactivate methods.

Enabling support of JIT for a component means that the component isn't activated until it's actually needed, rather than when it is first created within an ASP page. In addition, the component isn't deactivated until the component marks that it is ready to be deactivated, the component is destroyed within the ASP page (i.e., set to `Nothing` if you're using VBScript), or the process leaves the page scope.

The process of activation and deactivation is controlled by COM+, with programmatic cues provided by developers, such as the one demonstrated in the last section when `IContextState`'s SetDeactivateOnReturn method is called.

As a component developer, you can capture when the component is activated and deactivated by implementing `IObjectControl`'s Activate and Deactivate methods. By using these, you don't hold on to resources, such as a reference to the Response object shown in Example 5-1, while the component is idle and waiting for its methods to be called.

If you implement `IObjectControl`, you must implement both the Activate and Deactivate methods in addition to the CanBePooled method. This latter method defines whether the component is in a state in which it can be pooled. Later in the chapter, we'll look more closely at component pooling when we look at the COM+ Services.

To take advantage of JIT, your component must be installed in a COM+ application, and JIT must be enabled. However, support for JIT is enabled by default for every component within a COM+ application, as shown in Figure 5-1.

The `IObjectControl` and `IObjectContext` interfaces were implemented in Windows NT and managed through MTS. In fact, except for components that use specific NT services, the ASP components that you created for Windows NT should port without problems to Windows 2000 and COM+, as will be discussed in the next section.

In Windows NT, you had to avoid using the Initialize and Terminate event handlers, since you couldn't access an instance of ObjectContext within these. This limitation has been removed in Windows 2000. However, you should still consider implementing `IObject-Control` and trapping the Activate and Deactivate events in order to access and release globally accessible resources.

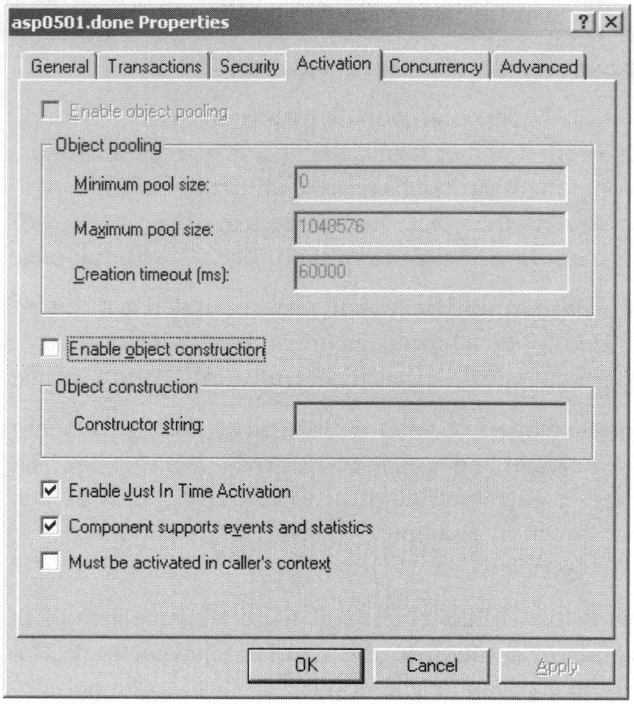

Figure 5-1. Enabling support for JIT

Porting MTS Packages to COM+ Applications

In Windows NT (or Windows 9x), components could be managed as part of MTS packages. By being a part of an MTS package, a component could take advantage of several MTS features, such as the use of transactions and JIT. These same features and more are also available in COM+, and you can access them with existing ASP components just by porting the MTS package, the components, or both to the new environment.

To port an existing MTS package, you first need to export the package into a file with an extension of *.pak* (MTS package file). This option is available to you by right clicking on the existing MTS application and selecting the Export option from the menu. Follow the directions to export the MTS package file, including whether to export roles with the package.

You can port your MTS packages to COM+ relatively simply by creating a new COM+ application (through the Component Services Console) and selecting the Install Pre-built Application(s) option. When the COM Application Install Wizard asks for the name of the existing application, find and select the PAK file that you created earlier.

When you import an existing MTS package into a new COM+ application, the Component Services Manager also imports the roles and tries to match existing MTS functionality with new COM+ Services functionality, including any transaction and JIT settings.

Instead of exporting an MTS package and importing it into a COM+ application, you can instead create the COM+ application as an empty application, then re-create any existing roles and add in any existing components. With this approach, you can make sure that the COM+ application's properties are defined as you would prefer.

Speaking of COM+ applications, the next section discussions some of the COM+ application settings that can impact on an ASP application.

Access Windows 2000 help to get more information about using the Component Services Console (in a topic titled "Using Component Services").

Activating COM+ Applications

COM+ applications add additional activation, transactional, and security support for the components included within the application. In particular, COM+ applications add support for method- as well as component-level security and for in-process and out-of-process activation.

Not all of the possible COM+ services are detailed in this section—just those most pertinent for ASP component development, such as security, transactions, and object pooling. JIT was detailed in the section of the chapter that discussed `IObjectControl`.

Application Security

You can control the security of your ASP application at a page and resource level using NTFS security and the security provided by IIS. You can add another layer of security by using COM+ application role-based security.

When you implement role-based security, you create a role within the COM+ application and add users to that role. Then, when a component or component method is accessed, COM+ checks the security privileges of the role that the user is a member of against the required security for the component or component method and denies access if the user's privileges don't match those required.

Figure 5-2 shows a COM+ application with one role and one component (the done component you created in Examples 5-1 and 5-2). The standard IUSR_ machinename (IUSR_FLAME on my machine) user has been added to the tester role, though any user can be added to a specific role. Role-based security can then be applied to the component or to a specific component method through the Properties dialog.

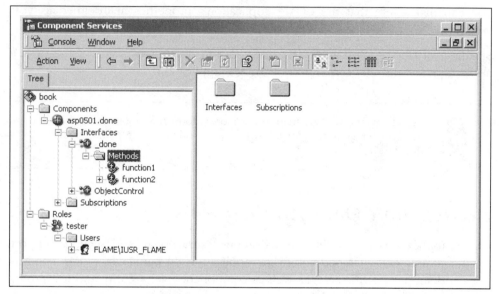

Figure 5-2. Creating a COM+ application role

A COM+ application can be created using two different activation schemas: activation within the client's process or activation as an isolated process.

If you create a COM+ application as a *server application*, accessing a component within an ASP page generates a separate *dllhost.exe* for the component and any other component that is part of the COM+ application. Because the component is in a separate process, all calls from the ASP page to the component must be marshaled. However, if the component generates havoc, the havoc is contained within the *dllhost.exe* and shouldn't adversely impact IIS or other ASP applications.

If you create the COM+ application as a *library application*, when a component is accessed within the ASP page, the component (and any other component within that COM+ application) is instantiated within the same process as the ASP page as long as the component's threading model is compatible. Since COM+ applications allow only apartment-threaded, both-threaded, and neutral-threaded components, the COM+ application component should be instantiated within the ASP page's process, and all calls between the page script and the component occur on the same thread.

COM+ Services

A component that is installed as part of a COM+ application (through the COM+ Services Manager) is known as a *configured component* and can benefit from COM+ services, such as support for transactions and JIT (discussed earlier). A component that isn't installed as part of a COM+ application and is registered using the development tool (such as VB) or using *regsvr32.exe*, is known as an *unconfigured component.* This type of component can be used in ASP applications, but you can't implement IObjectControl or take advantage of JIT, nor can you use ObjectContext for transaction support. You can, however, still access the ASP built-in objects using ObjectContext.

One of the main reasons to add a component to a COM+ application is because you want the component to participate in transactions, discussed next.

Transaction Support

One of the problems with components based on COM/DCOM is that component communication, especially remote communication, is not trivial. Compound that with having to be concerned about tracking whether a component successfully completes its processing and what to do and how to recover if one component fails to accomplish its task while others succeed, and a distributed system can soon become very difficult to create and maintain.

MTS was created to simplify this process by taking care of much of the administration of a distributed system. It ensures that a transaction completes successfully as a whole or fails in its entirety. It also manages processing and threads for an application, something that becomes very critical when one component calls methods on another, which calls methods on another, and so on.

MTS also provides resource managers and dispensers that actually control stored data, such as database data. In fact, any database system that supports OLE transactions, such as SQL Server, can participate in transactions controlled by MTS. This means that if a component that participates in a transaction fails, not only can the action of the component and other components be rolled back (reversed), any database activity can also be rolled back.

The transaction capability of MTS is present in COM+ services and is available for use with configured components. What's different in COM+ (and Windows 2000) is the presence of the IContextState interface, which allows you to separate the activation of a component from the transaction control. With this interface, you can signal whether a component wants to commit or abort a transaction but still keep the component activated, as was demonstrated earlier in Example 5-1.

What Are Transactions?

If you have had experience with commercial database systems such as Oracle, Sybase, and Microsoft SQL Server, you are probably aware of what transactions are. A *transaction* is one or more tasks, grouped in some logical manner, that are meant to succeed together or fail together if any one task within the transaction fails. If a transaction fails, no changes are made to any of the data associated with the transaction. If the transaction succeeds, changes made to the data are committed. An example of a transaction containing more than one task is transferring money from your savings account to your checking account. Though it seems like one transaction, actually two are happening. The first is that the money must be taken from the savings account (or debited to the account). The second is that the money must then be added to your checking account (or credited to your checking account). If the debit operation on your savings account succeeds but the credit to your checking account doesn't, you will want the entire transaction to be reversed and to start over again. Transactions are essential in a system that updates more than one data structure, such as database tables, based on one action, and updates must succeed for all of the data structures in order for the one action to successfully complete.

COM+ expands on this by introducing the concept of transaction management to component development. It also simplifies the process of developing distributed component-based applications by handling most of the transaction success/failure communication.

How Components Participate in Transactions

A component can use COM+ transaction capability if it meets certain criteria. First, the component must be an in-process server (that is, a *.DLL*). Second, the component must not be free-threaded. Further, if the component is implemented in Visual C++, it must implement a class factory and use standard marshaling. A type library must be created for the component.

Once a component meets the minimum requirements, it then needs to be registered with COM+ to get transaction support. During the registration process, the type of transaction the component participates in is set as a property of the component. For instance, Figure 5-3 shows a component that requires a transaction and that overrides the transaction timeout—setting a value of 10 seconds for the transaction to complete.

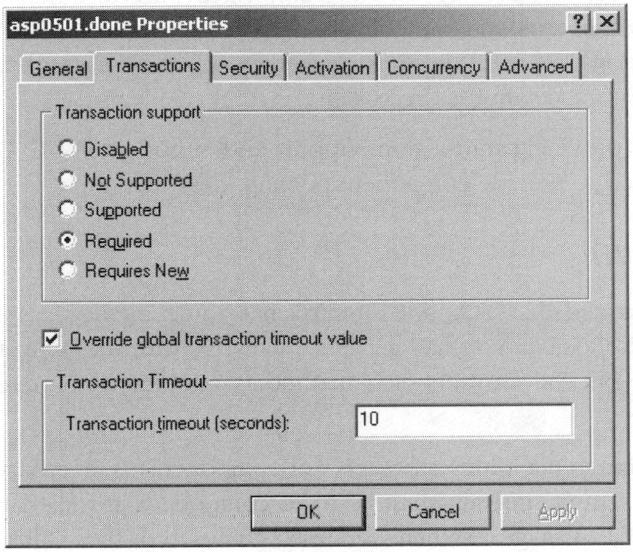

Figure 5-3. Setting a transaction requirement for a component

To start a transaction within the ASP page, use the transaction directive as the first line of the page:

```
<%@ TRANSACTION = required %>
```

To work with transactions, the component must reference an instance of Object-Context (or IObjectContext) or an instance of IContextState. You can mark a component as ready to commit using the ObjectContext object's SetComplete method or using IContextState's SetMyTransactionVote:

```
objContext.SetComplete
```

or:

```
objContext.SetMyTransactionVote adCommit
```

You can mark a transaction for rollback using the same interfaces:

```
objContext.SetAbort
```

or:

```
objContext.SetMyTransactionVote adAbort
```

If you want to see transactions in action, Chapter 9, *Creating an ASP Middle Tier with ADO*, has examples of COM+ transactions used with database updates—the traditional use of transactions. Though you can use database transaction capability (rather than COM+ transaction capability) directly, through the ADO Connection object, examples in this chapter will show how you'll want to use COM+ transaction capability for transactions that span components and database connections.

COM+ transactions can also be used to control activities on other resources, such as messages within a message queue. In Chapter 13, *Working with MSMQ Components*, transactions are used to control whether or not a message is permanently removed from a queue after it's accessed.

In addition to providing transaction support and support for JIT, COM+ Services can also be used to provide component pooling, described next.

Object Pooling

Earlier I mentioned that `IObjectControl` has three methods: Activate, Deactivate, and CanBePooled. You had a chance to work with the Activate and Deactivate methods, but the CanBePooled method is important if you're using object pooling.

In object pooling, a minimum set or *pool* of components is created when a COM+ application is started, and all requests for a component are filled from this pool through a pool manager. When requests come into the manager for more instances of the component than are available within the pool, the manager creates another instance of the component to add to the pool if the maximum pool size has not been met. If the pool is at its maximum, the new request is queued until a component is available.

There is a specific set of criteria that must be met before a component can be pooled. First, the component must not have thread affinity, which means that it must not be apartment-threaded (leaving out VB components at this time). Next, the component must support aggregation, but it can't aggregate the Free-Threaded Marshaller (FTM).

If the component participates in transactions, it must manually enlist resources and manually turn off the resources' autoenlistment (a process that differs from resource management and one that is outside the scope of this book).

If resources are accessed by the component, the component should implement Activate, Deactivate, and CanBePooled, the three `IObjectControl` methods. The resource can be accessed within the Activate method (when the component is created in the client ASP page), and it can be released when the component is released by the client (in the Deactivate method). In addition, the component must test whether its resources are at a state in which they can be pooled when it, the component, is deactivated. If they can, the component's CanBePooled method should return `True`. If not, the component must return a value of `False` to prevent the component from being returned to the component pool.

Finally, the component must be stateless, meaning that no session-specific state should be maintained for it.

You can create a poolable component using Visual C++ (or any language that supports the free- or both-threading models). To demonstrate how to use object pooling, create a new Visual C++ project named **asp0502** using the ATL COM AppWizard. Don't select any of the MTS/MFC or proxy/stub code options when given the choice by the wizard.

If you don't have access to Visual C++, you can use the copy of *asp0502.dll* that comes with the examples in this book.

Once the project files are generated, add a new component using the ATL Object Wizard (how to use the ATL Object Wizard is detailed in Chapter 14), and select the Simple Object type. Name the component **pooledComponent**, and on the Attributes page, select the both-threading model and support for aggregation (but not support for FTM).

To add support for **IObjectControl**, add the following to the component class definitions contained in *pooledComponent.h*:

```
public IObjectControl,
```

Also add a COM entry reference to the COM map:

```
COM_INTERFACE_ENTRY(IObjectControl)
```

You'll be accessing **IObjectContext** and the ASP built-in Response object in the component, so you'll need to add in the COM+ Services and ASP type library header files:

```
#include <comsvcs.h>
#include <asptlb.h>
```

You'll also need to add the **IObjectControl** method prototypes as well as a reference to two private data members of type **IObjectContext** and **IResponse** (the ASP built-in Response object). The complete code for the pooledComponent's class definition header file is shown in Example 5-3.

Example 5-3. Poolable Component Header File

```
// pooledComponent.h : Declaration of the CpooledComponent

#ifndef __POOLEDCOMPONENT_H_
#define __POOLEDCOMPONENT_H_

#include "resource.h"       // main symbols
#include <comsvcs.h>
#include <asptlb.h>
```

Example 5-3. Poolable Component Header File (continued)

```
/////////////////////////////////////////////////////////////////////////////
// CpooledComponent
class ATL_NO_VTABLE CpooledComponent :
    public CComObjectRootEx<CComMultiThreadModel>,
    public CComCoClass<CpooledComponent, &CLSID_pooledComponent>,
    public IObjectControl,
    public IDispatchImpl<IpooledComponent, &IID_IpooledComponent,
                                        &LIBID_ASP0502Lib>
{
public:
    CpooledComponent()
    {
    }

DECLARE_REGISTRY_RESOURCEID(IDR_POOLEDCOMPONENT)

DECLARE_PROTECT_FINAL_CONSTRUCT()

BEGIN_COM_MAP(CpooledComponent)
    COM_INTERFACE_ENTRY(IpooledComponent)
    COM_INTERFACE_ENTRY(IObjectControl)
    COM_INTERFACE_ENTRY(IDispatch)
END_COM_MAP()

// IpooledComponent
public:
    STDMETHOD(Activate)();
    STDMETHOD_(BOOL, CanBePooled)();
    STDMETHOD_(void, Deactivate)();

private:
    CComPtr<IObjectContext> m_spObjectContext;
    CComPtr<IResponse> m_piResponse;

};

#endif //__POOLEDCOMPONENT_H_
```

Next, add the COM+ Services library (*comsvcs.lib*) to the project's linked library list through the Link tab of the Project Settings dialog.

You'll have to implement the three `IObjectControl` methods. In the component's C++ file, add the code shown in Example 5-4 to your component. In this code, instances of `IObjectContext` and `IResponse` are created in the Activate method and released in the Deactivate method. In addition, the component marks that it can be pooled by returning `True` from the CanBePooled method.

Example 5-4. Component's Implementation of IObjectControl's Methods

```
HRESULT CpooledComponent::Activate()
{
    HRESULT hr;
```

Example 5-4. Component's Implementation of IObjectControl's Methods (continued)

```
    CComBSTR bstrProp;
    CComVariant vt;
    CComPtr<IGetContextProperties> pProps; //Context Properties

    IDispatch* piDispatch = NULL;

    // get ObjectContext
      hr = CoGetObjectContext(IID_IObjectContext,
                             (void **)&m_spObjectContext);
    if (FAILED(hr)) return hr;

    // get ContextProperties
    hr = m_spObjectContext->QueryInterface( IID_IGetContextProperties,
                 (void**)&pProps );
    if (FAILED(hr)) return hr;

    // get Response property
    bstrProp = "Response";
    hr = pProps->GetProperty( bstrProp, &vt ) ;
    if (FAILED(hr)) return hr;

    piDispatch = vt. pdispVal;
    hr = piDispatch->QueryInterface( IID_IResponse,
                     (void**)&m_piResponse );

      return hr;
}

void CpooledComponent::Deactivate()
{
    m_piResponse.Release();
     m_spObjectContext.Release();
}

BOOL CpooledComponent::CanBePooled()
{
     return TRUE;
}
```

At this time, compile the component to make sure you've added in the necessary code and library.

Add a method to the new component named *testPooledComponent* through the Class View; the method takes no parameters. The method is simple: it only outputs a message to the web page using the Response object. Add the component method code shown in Example 5-5.

Example 5-5. Pooled Component's Lone Method

```
STDMETHODIMP CpooledComponent::testPooledComponent()
{
    // print message
```

Example 5-5. Pooled Component's Lone Method (continued)

```
CComVariant vt("Hello from pooled component");
m_piResponse->Write(vt);

    return S_OK;
}
```

To use component pooling, the component will need to be added to a COM+ application. Create a new one (using the Component Services Management Console), or use an existing COM+ application and add the component to the application.

Once the component is added to the COM+ application, access its Properties dialog (from its popup menu) and select the Activation tab. In this tab, check the option to pool the component, and set its minimum pool size to 10 and its maximum to 20. Figure 5-4 shows the component's activation settings.

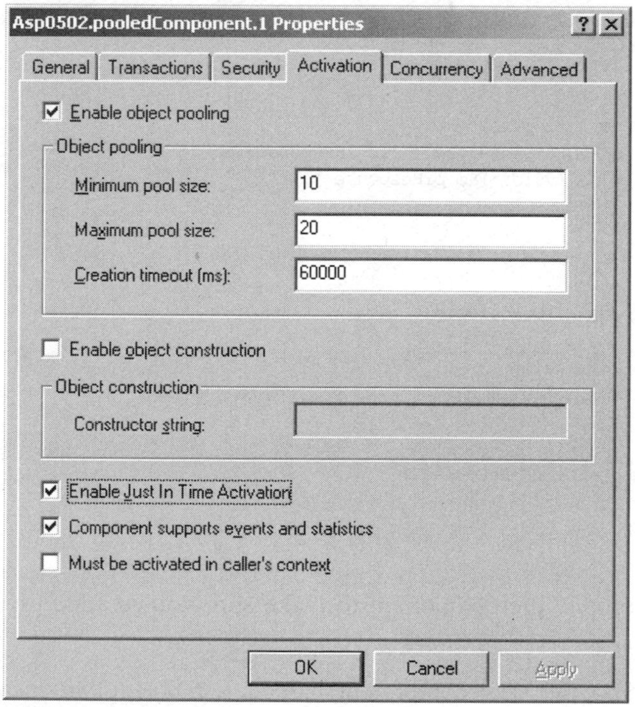

Figure 5-4. Activation settings for pooled component

When the COM+ application is first started, it creates a pool of 10 of the components you just created. As the components are accessed within ASP pages, they're taken from this pool until all of the components are currently activated. At that point, additional requests for the component add additional instances of the component to the pool, until the maximum pool size of 20 is reached.

Test the component using the following ASP test page (found in *asp0502.asp*):

```
<%
Dim obj(20)

For i = 1 to 20
    Set obj(i) = Server.CreateObject("asp0502.pooledComponent")
    obj(i).testPooledComponent
    Response.Write "<br>"
Next
%>
```

In this page, 20 instances of the component are created and the method of each instance is called. The result of accessing this ASP page is a list of messages with the line "Hello from pooled component." The first 10 instances were created when the COM+ application was first started, and the latter 10 were created when the ASP page was accessed.

Now, change the number of instances to 21 and then try the ASP page. Then, the page seems to hang. The page hangs because the pool manager has allocated all of the components from the available pool and has reached its maximum pool size. The request for the 21st component is queued until a component is available. But since no component becomes available until the page is finished, and the request for the component occurs in the same page, the 21st component cannot be instantiated and the page hangs. In fact, the page will continue to hang until the component request timeout is reached. At that point, the ASP page shows the following error:

```
COM+ activation failed because the activation could not be
completed in the specified amount of time.
```

As has been demonstrated, object pooling may be a powerful boost to performance, but it can also limit scalability, as well as drain resources (all of the pooled components are maintained in memory). Use this COM+ service with caution.

6

ASP Interaction: Scripting and ASP Components

An ASP component is technically a server component that can be accessed by any client application. However, there are some challenges associated with ASP components that are unique, not the least of which is an understanding of the environment in which these components operate, including component/script interaction.

When I refer to component/script interaction, I am talking about components as they are accessed within script blocks in ASP pages. The script blocks are usually written in VBScript, but they can also be written in JScript (Microsoft's version of JavaScript), as well as the increasingly popular PerlScript (based on the programming language Perl), in addition to other scripting languages. Having a variety of scripting languages available for use is terrific, but there is a price to this flexibility when it comes to ASP component development, because not all scripting languages provide the same support for component instantiation, component methods, and particularly component method parameters.

For instance, an array passed from VBScript is definitely handled differently in code than an array passed from JScript. In addition, the results of passing certain datatypes to and from components can differ, as can error handling.

Scripting Language Support Within ASP

The default scripting language that's used in ASP pages is VBScript, Microsoft's scriptable version of its popular Visual Basic programming language. However, other scripting languages can be used if support for the Microsoft Windows Script engine interfaces has been provided for the language. Basically, this means that a COM object is created that must implement a set of ActiveX scripting interfaces that provide an interface between the scripting environment and the scripting language implementation.

Microsoft has extended scripting language support to include a variation of Java-Script known as JScript. In addition, third-party developers have added scripting engine support for Perl, implemented as PerlScript, as well as Python and other languages. This section will discuss how to use VBScript, JScript, and PerlScript interchangeably in a web page and how to set up your environment to use JScript or PerlScript as the default scripting language.

Though I don't go into detail on using Python in ASP, you can access the Python web site at *http://www.python.org*, search for ActiveX scripting, and find out how to download and install Python for use in ASP pages. You can also download ActivePython for no charge from the ActiveState web site (*http://www.activestate.com*).

Support for VBScript and JScript is included with the scripting engine that is installed with IIS (and Internet Explorer and the Windows Script Host (WSH)). However, you'll need to install Perl programming support for Windows to use PerlScript. You can do this by downloading ActivePerl from the company ActiveState. ActivePerl is a free, Win32-based Perl package that includes support for traditional Perl packages, as well as packages created specifically for use in a Windows environment—including support for PerlScript.

ActivePerl is available without charge and can be accessed at the ActiveState web site at *http://www.activestate.com*. Make sure you download ActivePerl 617 and up, specifically tested with Windows 2000. Follow the instructions included with ActivePerl to install the package. Once it's installed, you're ready to work with VBScript, JScript, *and* PerlScript in your ASP pages.

Setting Scripting Language Choice

You can set the scripting language used within an ASP page in two different ways. First, you can change the default scripting language for all ASP applications using the Management Console or through the IIS Admin objects. Chapter 2, *Setting Up the ASP Development Environment*, covers setting the scripting language program-matically, but to change the default script language with the Console, open the Internet Services Manager, right-click on the ASP application, and choose Properties from the menu that opens. Then, in the Properties dialog, select the Virtual Directory (or Home Directory) tab. From this page, click on the button labeled Configuration and then select the App Options tab when the Configuration dialog opens. The App Options tab has a text field you can modify to change the default scripting language from VBScript to another language, such as JScript or PerlScript. Figure 6-1 shows the App Options tab after the default scripting language for the default web site has been changed to PerlScript.

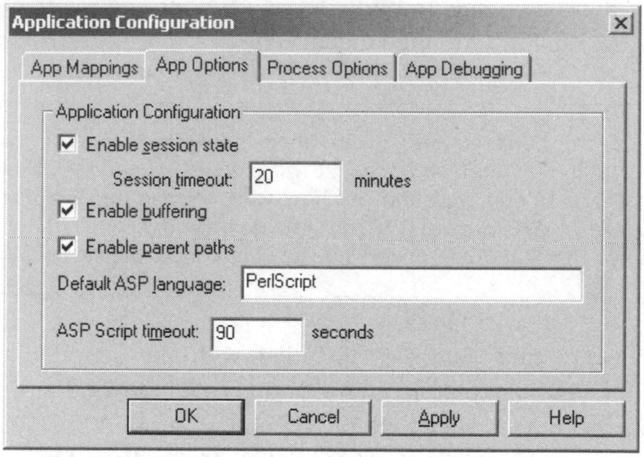

Figure 6-1. Changing the default scripting language for all ASP applications

A second approach to change the scripting language is to define the scripting language directly in an ASP page. To set the scripting language for the page, you include a scripting directive as the first line of the page. Directives begin and end with specific characters and provide information for the operating environment, such as the scripting language (in our current example), the start of a new transaction, the need to maintain session state, or the locale for the page. To change the scripting language for the page to PerlScript, you would use the following ASP directive:

```
<% @LANGUAGE=PerlScript %>
```

The directive starts with the leading characters "<%@" followed by the directive command, LANGUAGE=PerlScript, and then the end directive characters "%>".

Finally, to set the scripting language for just a specific code block, you can use the <SCRIPT> tag and set the language accordingly using its LANGUAGE attribute. If you use the <SCRIPT> tag, make sure to set the RUNAT attribute to Server to ensure that the block is run at the server as ASP rather than at the browser as client-side script. For example:

```
<SCRIPT LANGUAGE=PerlScript RUNAT=Server>
...some script
</SCRIPT>
```

You can mix scripting languages in one ASP page when using the <SCRIPT> tag and specifying different languages for each block, but be aware that there is no guarantee of the order in which the scripting blocks are processed. Scripts delimited by the <SCRIPT> tag with a language specified are processed before those using the more widely used "<%" and "%>" script delimiters and before scripts delimited with the <SCRIPT> tag but using the default scripting language. You may want to use multiple scripting languages in a page only when you are accessing language-specific functions or language-specific functionality and the order of script execution doesn't matter.

Once you've added support for the scripting language of your choice, you can create instances of your ASP components within the ASP blocks using each scripting language's specific techniques. These are discussed in the next section.

Instantiating Components

When Microsoft first released ASP, it didn't include support for accessing externally built components. This kind of support didn't occur until Version 2.0 of ASP, but it quickly made ASP a viable technology to use for Web application development. By adding support for COM and for components created using a variety of programming languages, Microsoft made it possible for developers to create reusable code components that could be accessed from many different ASP pages. Additionally, the code used to build the components is protected from modification and view by all but the component developers—providing higher levels of security and consistency. Precompiled components using languages such as C++ and Visual Basic also tend to be more efficient in execution, increasing the overall performance of the ASP application.

Regardless of the programming languages used to build components, we want to ensure that our components can be instantiated and used regardless of the scripting language. Because a language exposed as an ASP scripting language must implement the required functionality, we are guaranteed that the language supports certain basic functionality such as external component instantiation, though the method of instantiation may differ based on what is supported in the language.

A component can be created or accessed from an ASP script using three different techniques (some of which may be specific to the scripting language):

- The ASP built-in Server object's CreateObject method
- The *CreateObject* or *GetObject* function directly in script
- The <OBJECT> tag in the ASP application's *global.asa* file

Appendix A, *ASP Built-in Object Quick Reference*, provides an over-view of each of the built-in ASP objects (such as the Server object), including its methods, collections, and properties. If you haven't worked with ASP prior to reading this chapter, I suggest you take some time to review Appendix A first—specifically the sections covering the Server and Response objects. These objects are used in the rest of this chapter.

Creating an Object Using CreateObject

The scripting language used most within ASP pages is VBScript, so it's appropriate to take a look at component instantiation using VBScript first.

VBScript supports a built-in function, *CreateObject*, that can be used to instantiate, or to create an instance of, a component. The method takes as its only parameter a string with the component's *programmatic identifier* (ProgID) or component identifier. The typical format of a ProgID is either:

```
LibraryName.ComponentName
```

or:

```
LibraryName.ComponentName.Version
```

as the following illustrates:

```
ADODB.Connection
asp0601.arry.1
```

To create a component using VBScript, you could use code like the following:

```
Dim obj
Set obj = CreateObject("asp0601.arry.1")
```

Once the component is created, you can then access its methods and properties:

```
obj.tstArray        ' call to tstArray method
obj.prp = 1         ' assignment to prp property
```

For ASP, Microsoft added CreateObject as a method to the ASP built-in Server object. When developing ASP applications, instead of calling the VBScript *CreateObject* function directly in ASP script, you would call the CreateObject method from the Server object, as the following demonstrates:

```
Dim obj
Set obj = Server.CreateObject("asp0601.arry")
```

Instantiating the object using the Server object exposes the object's methods and properties for access in your ASP page, just the same as using the VBScript version of *CreateObject*.

If you're writing your scripts in VBScript, you could continue using the VBScript version of *CreateObject*, but this isn't recommended, nor is it favorable for your application's performance. The ASP environment can track instances of your object when you use the Server's CreateObject method, whereas using *CreateObject* directly bypasses this level of integration. Additionally, components created using the VBScript *CreateObject* function can't access the ASP built-in objects themselves nor can they participate in transactions.

 You don't have to use *CreateObject* to instantiate an object. For instance, you can use the function GetObject to use automation to retrieve a COM moniker. This approach can be used to access a Java class within an ASP page without having to wrap the class with COM registration information. See more on this in Chapter 3, *ASP Components and COM*, and Chapter 20, *ASP Components Created with Java*.

Of course, if you're using a scripting language other than VBScript, the *CreateObject* function or some equivalent that supports object instantiation may not be available. But as long as the ASP intrinsic objects are available to the scripting language, you can use the Server object's CreateObject method for object instantiation. For example, you'd instantiate a component in JScript using the Server.CreateObject method as follows:

```
var obj;
obj = Server.CreateObject("asp0601.arry");
```

In PerlScript, you could also create the component using the Server object and its CreateObject method as follows:

```
#use strict;
use vars qw($Server $Response);

my $myobj = $Server->CreateObject("asp0601.arry");
```

Creating a component directly in the script isn't the only way to instantiate a component. For all three scripting languages (and all others), you can also include an <OBJECT> tag in the *global.asa* file for the ASP application.

Using the global.asa File to Instantiate Components

Every ASP application has one *global.asa* file located in the application's root directory. The *global.asa* file can be used to provide event handlers for events such as the start of an ASP application (when an ASP application is first loaded by its first user) or the beginning of a new user session. The file can also provide component instantiation as well as access to type libraries in ASP pages.

COM/COM+ components can sometimes require access to built-in constants and enumerators, such as those used with ADO (e.g., adCmdText). These predefined values are usually bundled into a type library to make them easily accessible to component users. To include a type library within an ASP application, use a statement like the following in the *global.asa* file:

```
<!--METADATA NAME="Microsoft ActiveX Data Objects 2.5
Library" TYPE="TypeLib" UUID="{00000205-0000-0010-8000-
00AA006D2EA4}"-->
```

This type library definition adds the ADO 2.5 constants and enumerators to the current ASP application.

Component instantiation within the *global.asa* file is handled through the use of the <OBJECT> tag. This tag has several parameters that define what the component is and when to create it:

```
<OBJECT RUNAT=Server Scope=scope ID=identifier
{PROGID=progid | CLASSID=classid}>
</OBJECT>
```

The *scope* of the object must be set to **Application** or **Session**, meaning that the object is added to either the built-in ASP Application object's collection or to the Session object's collection. In the former case, this means that the component is accessible within the scope of the entire ASP application, and in the latter case, it means that it is accessible only within a specific user session. The *identifier* is the name given to the component and is used within ASP pages to access the specific component. The class from which the object instance is to be derived is identified by either its *progid* or its *classid*.

To demonstrate how the <OBJECT> tag works in the *global.asa* file, we'll use Visual Basic to create a simple component. Open a new ActiveX DLL project, name the project asp0601, and name the class generated with the component global. The class itself has one method named tstGlobal, which takes a String parameter by value, concatenates a brief message to the string, and returns it to the invoking application. The source code for the method is shown in Example 6-1.

Example 6-1. Simple Method to Concatenate String Message to Name Passed as Parameter

```
Option Explicit
Function tstGlobal(ByVal strName As String) As String
   Dim strReturn As String
   strReturn = "Hello " & strName
   tstGlobal = strReturn
End Function
```

Compile the Visual Basic component. (This also automatically registers it on your system.) The ProgID for the new component is `asp0601.global`, and you can access the class identifier using a utility such as OLEView, a tool that comes with Visual Studio (or can be downloaded from Microsoft's web site). Select the View TypeLib option from its View menu, then navigate to and select the *asp0601.dll* file in the Open dialog. You can determine the CLSID by selecting the `coclass` `Global` item.

If you aren't using Visual Basic, the example code that comes with this book has the Visual Basic *asp0601.dll* included within the code. All you need to do is install the example code for this chapter and register *asp0601.dll* using COM+ services or the older *regsvr32* method, both of which are discussed in Chapter 3.

After you find the CLSID for your new component, access (or create) the *global. asa* file for your ASP web test environment; add the following two <OBJECT> entries to this file:

```
<OBJECT RUNAT=Server Scope=Session ID=test1
    PROGID="asp0601.global">
REM testing global.asa
</OBJECT>

<OBJECT RUNAT=Server Scope=Session ID=test2
    CLASSID="Clsid:7347EB1C-FACA-47EE-BC3E-9D5FFEB402CC">
REM testing global.asa
</OBJECT>
```

Note that, if you've downloaded the `asp0601.global` component, its CLSID is {7347EB1C-FACA-47EE-BC3E-9D5FFEB402CC}; if you've created it yourself, however, it will have a different CLSID.

Once the ASP web server is restarted, the first access to the component identified as *test1* or *test2* results in instantiation of the component for the current user session (each session will get its own reference to the component or components). You can test this by creating a new ASP page, *asp0601.asp*, similar to that shown in Example 6-2. In this page, both identifiers are used to reference the component, resulting in two instances of the same component being created.

Example 6-2. ASP Page Accessing a Component Instantiated in the global.asa File

```
<!DOCTYPE HTML PUBLIC "-//W3C//DTD HTML 4.0//EN">
<HTML>
<HEAD>
<TITLE>global.asa</TITLE>
</HEAD>
<BODY>
```

```
<H1> Testing global.asa</H1>
<%
  Dim strName
  Dim strMessage
  strName = "Shelley"

  ' test component accessed through progid
  strMessage = test1.tstGlobal(strName)
  Response.Write(strMessage & "<p>")

  ' test component access through class ID
  strMessage = test2.tstGlobal(strName)
  Response.Write(strMessage)
%>
</BODY>
</HTML>
```

Since both *test1* and *test2* have been defined as session-level components, they persist until the user's session terminates. This occurs when the session times out or the session is deliberately terminated through some programmatically supplied action, such as the user logging out of the application (and abandoning the session by calling Abandon on the built-in ASP Server object).

There are performance issues that impact on whether you should create a component as an Application, Session, or page-level component (a component that exists only within the scope of execution of the specific page). Components created within an ASP page using CreateObject (through the ASP Server object and the direct VBScript *CreateObject* methods) are created with page-level scope. Based on this the component can be either a both- or apartment-threaded component and performance is not adversely impacted.

However, if you create a component using *global.asa* and the <OBJECT> tag, or if you attach the component created in an ASP page to the Contents collection of the Application or Session object directly at runtime, then the component should be marked as both-threaded. Failing to do so will generate an error with the Application object and can severely impact performance with the Session object. See Chapter 4, *ASP Components, Threads, and Contexts*, for more on thread-based performance issues when working with ASP components.

As you've seen, component instantiation is very similar with the three scripting languages explored in this chapter. Because all three have access to ASP objects, all three use the Server object, and all three can call the Server object's CreateObject method. However, the scripting language used can impact on the design of your component and particularly on the datatypes of the parameters you use. These issues are detailed in the next section.

COM+ Datatypes and Script/Component Interaction

Distributed and component-based systems place some restrictions on how components are created, how methods are defined, and what types of data are supported. Without these restrictions, the infrastructure necessary to support the environment would be too unwieldy and most likely would not be successful.

However, just because there are limitations on the types of data that are supported across component boundaries doesn't mean that a component developer or user can't have all the functionality they need in order to create their applications. For instance, the most common COM datatype is the Variant, which is discussed next; not only can it be used to hold virtually any type of data, but it also provides the means to find information about the data beyond just its value.

The Variant Datatype

Henry Ford, the founder of today's Ford car company, pioneered the mass production of automobiles in this country. He once said, "People can have the Model T in any color—so long as it's black."

VBScript has taken Mr. Ford's concept to heart when it comes to datatypes: you can have any datatype you want to use in VBScript—so long as it's a Variant. The premise for this is that the Variant datatype can hold virtually any kind of data, provide means to access the data safely, and provide methods to query the Variant variable to find out information about the data such as its size or the number of array elements if the variable holds an array. All of this combined makes the Variant datatype the *safest* datatype to use.

As discussed more fully in Chapter 3, the Variant datatype is really a structure that contains fields to hold the actual value being referenced in a variable or parameter. The structure also contains information about the value, such as whether the value is a BSTR or some other datatype, whether it is an array or a scalar value, and whether the variant is passed by reference or value when used with a parameter. Whether or not these fields are exposed depends on the language accessing the variant: Visual Basic and VBScript hide most of the implementation details of the Variant datatype, while C++ exposes the Variant structure for direct access of its members in code.

When a Variant is passed as a parameter to an ASP component method, methods are usually used to extract information about the Variant. For instance, in Visual Basic, you can access the Variant's data subtype using the *VarType* function:

```
' test for variant array
If VarType(vArray) = (vbVariant + vbArray) Then
```

The *VarType* function returns the predefined constant associated with the data subtype, such as **vbLong** for a long value, **vbString** for a string, and so on. Additionally, you can add the constants together and compare this aggregate to the value returned by *VarType* to find out whether the variant contains an array of variants, as the example just displayed demonstrated.

To access the value of the Variant in Visual Basic, you access the variable directly:

```
Dim strName As String
strName = varName
```

Though Visual Basic supports other datatypes, if a variable is declared and not explicitly given a datatype, it is created as a Variant by default:

```
Dim tst     ' created as a Variant
```

Within Visual C++ or other languages that expose more of the underlying COM functionality than Visual Basic, you can also use predefined functions to test the variant subtype, though the functions will be language-specific. For instance, in Visual C++, you would determine the data subtype of a variant using the helper macro V_VT; this macro assigns the variant type to a variable based on the enumeration type, **VARTYPE**. The newly assigned variable can then be used with the bitwise-**AND** operator against any of the predefined COM Variant datatype constants to search for a datatype match:

```
// get variant type
VARTYPE vttype = V_VT(&vtArray);

// if ARRAY, process as SAFEARRAY
if (vttype & VT_ARRAY)
```

Of the scripting languages, only VBScript supports the Variant type; JScript doesn't support the Variant type at all, and PerlScript provides a specialized Perl module for Variants. How all of this impacts the interaction between script and ASP components is discussed in the next section.

Variant Datatypes: From Script to Component

When you create your ASP components in any programming language that supports COM/COM+ datatypes, you can use the Variant datatype for all of your parameters: those passed by value, those passed by reference, and those returned as a result of a method call. This holds true regardless of the scripting language used, though the results may be unexpected, as you'll see in this section.

Of the three scripting languages discussed in this chapter, JScript doesn't support an explicit Variant datatype, though you can treat parameters sent from JScript as Variants in components. As an example, you'll add a second component class to the Visual Basic component *asp0601.dll*, which you created earlier in Example 6-1.

Name the new class **varcmp**, and add a method, tstVariant, as a Visual Basic function. This new function takes a Variant parameter passed by value and returns a Variant. In the function, shown in Example 6-3, the data subtype of the Variant parameter is tested against a subset of the possible Variant subtypes, and the name of the subtype, if found, is assigned to a string variable. This string variable is then returned to the ASP script. If the Variant subtype is not in the list, the words "another type" are returned. Variant coercion, discussed later, handles the conversion of the String datatype to the Variant type returned by the function.

Example 6-3. Testing the Type of a Variant

```
Option Explicit
Function tstVariant(ByVal vrType) As Variant

Dim strType As String

' test type
If varType(vrType) = vbString Then
    strType = "string data type"
ElseIf varType(vrType) = vbDate Then
    strType = "date data type"
ElseIf varType(vrType) = vbLong Then
    strType = "long data type"
ElseIf varType(vrType) = vbDouble Then
    strType = "double data type"
ElseIf varType(vrType) = vbBoolean Then
    strType = "boolean data type"
Else
    strType = "another type"
End If

' assign return value
tstVariant = strType

End Function
```

To test the component, create a new ASP page, *asp0602.asp*, and set the script language to JScript. The page, which is shown in Example 6-4, creates several variables of different types and sends them to the tstVariant method. The types tested are a JScript string, a Date, an integer, a Boolean, and a Number. The datatype is then printed out to the web page.

Example 6-4. JScript to Create Variant Datatype Test Component

```
<%@ Language="jscript" %>
<!DOCTYPE HTML PUBLIC "-//W3C//DTD HTML 4.0//EN">
<HTML>
<HEAD>
<TITLE>Variant Data Type</TITLE>
<BODY>
<H1>Variants</H1>
```

Example 6-4. JScript to Create Variant Datatype Test Component (continued)

```
<%
   var obj = Server.CreateObject("asp0601.varcmp");

   var str = "data type is string";
   var reslt = obj.tstVariant(str);
   Response.Write(reslt + "<p>");

   var dt = new Date(2000,6,18);
   reslt = obj.tstVariant(dt);
   Response.Write(reslt + "<p>");

   var int = 20;
   reslt = obj.tstVariant(int);
   Response.Write(reslt + "<p>");

   var bl = true;
   reslt = obj.tstVariant(bl);
   Response.Write(reslt + "<p>");

   var dec = new Number(30.5);
   reslt = obj.tstVariant(dec);
   Response.Write(reslt);
%>
</BODY>
</HTML>
```

The results might surprise you a bit—the values printed out to the page, in the order they appear in the code in Example 6-4, are:

> string data type
> string data type
> long data type
> boolean data type
> double data type

The first value is what we would expect. We sent a string, which shows up in the Visual Basic component as a string. However, after that the results might be unexpected. For instance, the Date object in JScript (JavaScript) is treated as a string within the ASP script engine, and this is reflected in the Variant datatype within the VB component. The JScript integer value is a Long value in VB—a VB Integer type is 16 bits long, but a JScript integer is really 32 bits long, equivalent to a VB Long datatype. (This is reflected as a Long datatype.) The JScript boolean and the Variant Boolean data subtype agree, and the Number value is handled as a VB Double—a double-precision floating point value.

Unlike JScript, VBScript uses the Variant datatype for all of its variables. To ensure that a data value is treated as a specific type in the component method, conversion functions such as *CLng* are called, to mark the variant subtype as a specific datatype. With this conversion, the datatypes of the variants displayed by *asp0603. asp*, the VBScript page in Example 6-5, should be what we would expect: a string, a date, a long, a boolean, and a double datatype, in that order.

Example 6-5. VBScript to Create Variant Datatype Test Component

```
<!DOCTYPE HTML PUBLIC "-//W3C//DTD HTML 4.0//EN">
<HTML>
<HEAD>
<TITLE>Variant As Parameter</TITLE>
</HEAD>
<BODY>
<H1>Variants</H1>

<%
  ' create ASP component
  Dim cmp
  Set cmp = Server.CreateObject("asp0601.varcmp")

  Dim str
  Dim reslt
  str = "this is string type"

  reslt = cmp.tstVariant(str)
  Response.Write(reslt & "<p>")

  Dim dt
  dt = Date
  dt = CStr(dt)
  reslt = cmp.tstVariant(dt)
  Response.Write(reslt & "<p>")

  Dim i
  i = 20
  i = CLng(i)
  reslt = cmp.tstVariant(i)
  Response.Write(reslt & "<p>")

  Dim bl
  bl = True
  reslt = cmp.tstVariant(bl)
  Response.Write(reslt & "<p>")

  Dim dec
  dec = 35.50
  reslt = cmp.tstVariant(dec)
  Response.Write(reslt)

%>
</BODY>
</HTML>
```

The results returned from accessing this new ASP page are:

> string data type
> date data type
> long data type
> boolean data type
> double data type

Again, the results are what we would expect: the string is defined as a string type, the Date as a date, and so on. If you didn't use *CLng* with the long value, you would receive a result of "another type," because the value would have been passed as an integer subtype—and we're not testing for integers in the component code.

Next, we'll test the VB variant type component from PerlScript to see how datatype conversion fares between this scripting language and the ASP component. The test page, *asp0604.asp*, creates the ASP component and calls the tstVariant method with different datatypes, as shown in Example 6-6. However, there is a problem: there are no explicitly defined Boolean values of true and false in PerlScript. Instead, the Boolean datatype is implicit. Any string is true in PerlScript (or Perl for that matter), except for an empty string or a string containing a zero (0). Additionally, any number is true except for an undefined number or one containing a value of zero (0). For the example, we'll send a value of one (1) to represent the implicit Boolean value of true.

Example 6-6. PerlScript to Create Variant Datatype Test Component

```
<%@ Language="PerlScript" %>
<HTML>
<HEAD>
<TITLE>Testing Variants</TITLE>
</HEAD>
<BODY>
<H1>Variants</H1>
<%

#use strict;
use vars qw($Server $Response);
use Time::localtime;

my $myobj = $Server->CreateObject("asp0601.varcmp");

my $str = 'this is a string';
$reslt = $myobj->tstVariant($str);
$Response->Write($reslt);
$Response->Write('<p>');
```

Example 6-6. PerlScript to Create Variant Datatype Test Component (continued)

```
my $dt = ctime();
$reslt = $myobj->tstVariant($dt);
$Response->Write($reslt);
$Response->Write('<p>');

my $i = 30;
$reslt = $myobj->tstVariant($i);
$Response->Write($reslt);
$Response->Write('<p>');

my $bl = 1;
$reslt = $myobj->tstVariant($bl);
$Response->Write($reslt);
$Response->Write('<p>');

my $dec = 35.50;
$reslt = $myobj->tstVariant($dec);
$Response->Write($reslt);
$Response->Write('<p>');
%>
</BODY>
</HTML>
```

The results produced by this ASP page are:

> string data type
> string data type
> long data type
> long data type
> double data type

Three of the results—the first, third, and last—are more or less as expected. The string datatype shows as a string variant in the component, just as it does with VBScript and JScript. A Perl integer is a 32-bit value, as it is with JScript, so it shows up in the variant as a VB Long in the component. The same holds true for the last value, a double.

Where we are faced with differences is the datatype values for the Date and the value for the Boolean. The *ctime* function in Perl returns a date string, not an actual date value, so the datatype is String—the same as it would be with JScript. Surprisingly though, the Boolean value we're testing shows as long type. Why is this? Because there isn't a true Boolean datatype in Perl or PerlScript; there are only values that result in **true** or **false** if the value is used within a comparison operation. Testing the value of one (1) results in **true**, but the value itself is passed as a Long from PerlScript to the VB component. If we had used the string "1" to emulate **true**, we would then get the String data subtype.

Is there any way to deliberately specify a boolean value from PerlScript? Yes—by using the Win32::OLE::Variant Perl module. Using Variant, we can explicitly create a Boolean Variant in PerlScript:

```
my $bl = Variant(Win32::OLE::Variant::VT_BOOL, 1);
$reslt = $myobj->tstVariant($bl);
$Response->Write($reslt);
$Response->Write('<p>');
```

The script in Example 6-6 is modified to use the Variant Perl module. Example 6-7 shows the page, *asp0605.asp,* after the datatypes of the function arguments have been created using Variant, rather than directly using Perl datatypes.

Example 6-7. Using Win32::OLE::Variant to Coerce Perl Types into COM Variant Subtypes

```
<%
use strict;
use vars qw($Server $Response);
use Time::localtime;
use Win32::OLE::Variant;

my $myobj = $Server->CreateObject("asp0601.varcmp");

my $str = 'this is a string';
my $reslt = $myobj->tstVariant($str);
$Response->Write($reslt);
$Response->Write('<p>');

my $ldt = localtime->mon() . '/' . localtime->mday() . '/' .
          localtime->year() + 1900;
my $dt = Variant(Win32::OLE::Variant::VT_DATE,$ldt );
$reslt = $myobj->tstVariant($dt);
$Response->Write($reslt);
$Response->Write('<p>');

my $i = 30;
$reslt = $myobj->tstVariant($i);
$Response->Write($reslt);
$Response->Write('<p>');

my $bl = Variant(Win32::OLE::Variant::VT_BOOL, 1);
$reslt = $myobj->tstVariant($bl);
$Response->Write($reslt);
$Response->Write('<p>');

my $dec = 35.50;
$reslt = $myobj->tstVariant($dec);
$Response->Write($reslt);
$Response->Write('<p>');
%>
```

With this adjusted script and with the help of Win32::OLE::Variant, the results displayed to the page are:

> string data type
> date data type
> long data type
> boolean data type
> double data type

The Variant Datatype and the LCD

From the last section, it would seem that the use of the Variant datatype could generate unexpected results if your ASP component is used from different scripting languages. However, this doesn't have to be that serious a problem if you remember to code to the ASP Scripting LCD—Lowest Common Denominator.

For instance, the String datatype passes from all three scripting languages without a problem in interpretation within the component, but the same cannot be said for the Date datatype. However, if your component is expecting a date parameter, you can test its datatype and process the parameter accordingly. If the data subtype of the variant shows as a string, verify that it can be converted into a valid date (for example, using the Visual Basic *IsDate* function or an equivalent), parse out the date elements, and create whatever date structure your programming language supports, or use the string to create the Date object directly. If the variant shows as a Date subtype, then use the object directly, or pull values out of the object to again construct your "script-safe" version of the date.

Use the Long datatype to process integer-like parameters from script. This will match the values passed from PerlScript and JScript, and the VBScript Variant integer subtype can be coerced into a Long using the helper function *CLng*. Again, you can test your parameter datatype and perform coercion in your component, or you could direct that users of your component should pass through long values—and use the *CLng* method with integer values in VBScript.

Both JScript and VBScript support a Boolean datatype. PerlScript can also support the Boolean datatype when using the Win32::OLE::Variant module. Again, you could test the datatype of the variant parameter in your component and attempt to coerce the value into a Boolean, but the Boolean value from PerlScript is not like the datatype in JScript: there is more than one way to pass a `true` or `false` value as a component parameter, and your component may not want to test for both a string and a numeric. Instead, you'll most likely want to specify that your component is expecting a Boolean value as the parameter and provide instructions for PerlScript users about how to create a Variant with a data subtype of `VT_BOOL`.

As a rule of thumb, when you create an ASP component that has methods with Variant parameters and that could be used by multiple scripting languages, test the component within each of the scripting languages you plan on supporting. To not do so may lead to surprising results.

Using Other COM Datatypes as Parameters

You can use the Variant datatype for all of your ASP component parameters, but any COM datatype can work—depending on the scripting language you're using and depending on whether the value is passed by reference, passed by value, or returned as a result of a function call. The COM datatypes are detailed in Chapter 3, but some of the most common are the BSTR for strings, the IDispatch or IUnknown interfaces for objects, the Date, and the Short, Long, Double, and other numeric datatypes. Another type of parameter is an array, but this is discussed a little later in the chapter, in the section on passing arrays as parameters.

However, if you don't use Variant parameter types, you can get unexpected results. For instance, you could specify a Date datatype for a parameter, but unless the structures are the same or similar between the scripting language Date type and the type supported for COM, the parameter won't work.

To demonstrate, we'll add a second function to asp0601.varcmp, the component we created in the last section. The function, named *tstDate*, takes a Date by value and returns a copy of the date from the function call, as shown in Example 6-8.

Example 6-8. Assigning Date Passed in by Value to Function Return Call

```
Function tstDate(ByVal dt As Date) As Date

   ' assign date
   tstDate = dt
End Function
```

A new ASP page, *asp0606.asp*, shown in Example 6-9, uses VBScript to test the new function by creating a variant of subtype Date and passing it to the component. The returned date is then displayed to a web page.

Example 6-9. Testing Passing Date as a Parameter

```
<!DOCTYPE HTML PUBLIC "-//W3C//DTD HTML 4.0//EN">
<HTML>
<HEAD>
<TITLE>Dates</TITLE>
</HEAD>
<BODY>
```

Example 6-9. Testing Passing Date as a Parameter (continued)

```
<H1>Dates</H1>
<%
  ' create asp component
  Dim cmp
  Set cmp = Server.CreateObject("asp0601.varcmp")

  Dim dt,dt2
  dt = Date
  dt2 = cmp.tstDate(dt)
  Response.Write(dt2 & "<p>")
%>
</BODY>
</HTML>
```

As expected, the combination of VB component and VBScript works, because the Date datatype is the same with both VB and VBScript. However, if you create a second test page, this time in JScript and named *asp0607.asp*, shown in Example 6-10, passing a JScript Date from the page to the component generates a type mismatch error, because the JScript Date is a string and can't be coerced into a VB Date datatype.

Example 6-10. Passing a JScript Date to a Component Expecting a VB Date

```
<%@ Language="jscript" %>
<!DOCTYPE HTML PUBLIC "-//W3C//DTD HTML 4.0//EN">
<HTML>
<HEAD>
<TITLE>Date</TITLE>
<BODY>
<H1>Date</H1>
<%
  var obj = Server.CreateObject("asp0601.varcmp");

  var dt = new Date(2000,6,18);
  var dt2 = new Date();
  dt2 = obj.tstDate(dt);
  Response.Write(dt2);

%>
</BODY>
</HTML>
```

We have more luck from PerlScript, depending on the approach we use. In Example 6-11, in a new ASP page named *asp0608.asp*, we test the new function using two different PerlScript variables. One is created as a Variant with a Date type, and the other is created using the Perl function *ctime* directly.

Example 6-11. Testing Passing a Date Using a Variant and a PerlScript "date"

```
<%@ Language="PerlScript" %>
<HTML>
<HEAD>
<TITLE>Testing Dates</TITLE>
</HEAD>
<BODY>
<H1>Date</H1>
<%
use strict;
use vars qw($Server $Response);
use Time::localtime;
use Win32::OLE::Variant;

my $myobj = $Server->CreateObject("asp0601.varcmp");

my $year = localtime->year() + 1900;
my $mon = localtime->mon() + 1;
my $day = localtime->mday();

my $ldt = $mon . '/' . $day . '/' . $year;

my $dt = Variant(Win32::OLE::Variant::VT_DATE,$ldt );
my $dt2 = $myobj->tstDate($dt);
$Response->Write($dt2 . '<p>');

my $dt3 = ctime();
$Response->Write($dt3 . '<p>');
my $dt4 = $myobj->tstDate($dt3);
$Response->Write($dt4);
%>
</BODY>
</HTML>
```

This script should print out three data variables, but only two actually show on the page when it's displayed in the browser:

```
9/10/2000
Sun Sep 10 10:23:22 2000
```

In the script, the first time the Visual Basic component is called, we're passing in a value that has been coerced into a Variant Date subtype. This date parameter should work with the Visual Basic component, and it does. The page next displays the *ctime*-derived data string. However, the second time the VB component method is called with the *ctime*-derived data string, nothing happens. We should get a mismatch datatype error, but no error occurs. In fact, the function doesn't return any data—definitely unexpected results.

The Date datatype is a bit esoteric. What happens if we try a simpler datatype, such as a string, instead? Again, we'll create a new method in asp0601.varcmp, calling it *tstString*. As with the date test, we'll pass a string in as a parameter and assign it as a return value. The returned value then is displayed on the web page. The new component function is shown in Example 6-12.

Example 6-12. Test of Passing a String in by Value and Returning It from Function Call

```
Function tstString(ByVal str As String) As String

    ' assign string
    tstString = str

End Function
```

To test this new function, create test pages in VBScript, JScript, and PerlScript, naming them *asp0609.asp*, *asp0610.asp*, and *asp0611.asp*, respectively. The scripting blocks for all three pages are shown in Example 6-13. (Note that you need to add a Language directive for the JScript and PerlScript examples.) When you run the three test pages, you'll see that with all three pages and all three scripting languages, COM automation is able to successfully coerce each scripting language's version of a string into the COM-compatible datatype of BSTR. The COM BSTR value is equivalent to Visual Basic's String datatype, so the parameter coercion was able to work with a datatype such as BSTR.

Example 6-13. Three Scripting Blocks from Three Separate ASP Pages, in VBScript, JScript, and PerlScript

```
VBScript:
<%
  ' create ASP component
  Dim cmp
  Set cmp = Server.CreateObject("asp0601.varcmp")

  Dim str, str2
  str = "this is a test"
  str2 = cmp.tstString(str)
  Response.Write(str2)
%>

JScript:
<%
  var obj = Server.CreateObject("asp0601.varcmp");

  var str, str2
  str = "this is a test"
  str2 = obj.tstString(str);
  Response.Write(str2);
%>

PerlScript:
<%
use strict;
use vars qw($Server $Response);
```

Example 6-13. Three Scripting Blocks from Three Separate ASP Pages, in VBScript, JScript, and PerlScript (continued)

```
my $myobj = $Server->CreateObject("asp0601.varcmp");

my $str = 'this is a test';
my $str2 = $myobj->tstString($str);
$Response->Write($str2);
%>
```

Further testing will show that coercion works with most of the simple types, such as the numeric types.

Up to now all of the examples have shown the arguments being passed from the scripting blocks to the components by value. What happens if the argument is passed by reference?

Arguments passed by reference from VBScript must, and I want to emphasize *must*, be a Variant datatype: any other value results in a mismatched datatype error. Additionally, JScript does not support passing values by reference. You can pass a value successfully, but the changed value is not reflected back to the ASP script.

Based on both of these limitations—by reference arguments must be Variant types, and JScript does not support passing by reference—you should avoid by-reference parameters if your component must be usable by different scripting languages and if you want to process parameters as other datatypes. If you do decide to support passing values by reference, make sure then that the parameter is coded as a Variant in any programming language that you use.

To summarize, then, this section on parameter passing and compatibility of types between ASP script and the ASP component, we have found that:

- COM automation handles variant coercion between script and ASP components, though the results can be unexpected.

- Coding a component for the LCD of scripting languages, JScript, you should process date parameters as strings and treat all integers as VB Longs (32-bit integers).

- Communicate the expected data subtypes of each of a component's parameters—don't just specify that the parameters are Variant. With this information, those using scripting languages such as PerlScript or VBScript can use built-in functions or modules to ensure that the variant datatype matches exactly.

- Use the Variant datatype for all parameters, including returned values. However, if you wish to use another datatype, test the parameter in as many scripting languages as you wish to support, to ensure the parameter will work with the language.

- A rule of thumb is that "simple" datatypes such as strings and numeric types can be passed by value or returned as a return value.

- Avoid passing parameters by reference—this isn't supported by JScript. If you must pass a parameter by reference, make sure you set the parameter datatype to Variant. Not doing so will generate an error in VBScript, the most commonly used of the ASP scripting languages.

If you thought there was a lot to learn about scripting language/ASP component scalar parameters, wait until you see the challenges associated with passing a more complex parameter such as an array, covered next.

Passing Arrays as Parameters

A popular type of parameter to pass from an ASP script to a component and back is an array. However, an array is the data structure most heavily impacted by the scripting language used. As such, when developing ASP components using arrays, you should test the component in all scripting languages your component can be referenced from. At a minimum you should test the component using VBScript, JScript, and PerlScript. Testing in all three of these languages should give you a high degree of confidence that your component array processing will work with the most widely used ASP scripting languages. In addition, the use of the three scripting languages should also drive out any scripting language foibles that can have an impact on using array parameters—helping you design truly COM/COM+-compatible ASP components.

Before looking at examples of array parameters, you should first have a good understanding of how COM/COM+ handles arrays. For this, you need to examine the COM **SAFEARRAY** datatype.

The SAFEARRAY

The problem with arrays as method parameters is that the method doesn't necessarily know anything about the array. For instance, does the array consist of one dimension or more than one dimension? What is the range for the array elements? What is the datatype of the array elements, and, more importantly, what is the size of the datatype? Unlike parameters that contain scalar values (such as integers) with known size and type information, arrays are one big unknown, and that makes working with *raw* arrays a bit dangerous.

To make working with array parameters (or, more accurately, to make working with arrays in general) a bit safer, Microsoft came up with the concept of the Safe-Array. The SafeArray (or **SAFEARRAY**, if you will) is a structure that includes a reference to the original array data, but that also includes additional information about the array, such as the array boundaries and number of dimensions. By providing information about the array, programmers can query for this information and process the array safely; hence the name *SafeArray*.

SafeArrays actually originated with Visual Basic applications, and all arrays within a VB application, ASP-based or not, are stored as SafeArrays. Since VBScript is based on a subset of Visual Basic, VBScript arrays are also treated as SafeArrays, even when the arrays are passed to ASP components written with programming tools other than Visual Basic.

Encapsulating an array within a SafeArray structure might be a problem with ASP components written in Visual J++ or Visual C++ or other languages outside of Visual Basic except for one thing: ASP components are based on COM, and COM can handle the *coercion* between the originating source and the target source as long as the conversion is allowed and the datatypes used to define the method parameters are allowable COM datatypes. So SafeArrays can be passed to any other language and tool as long as support for COM automation is provided.

It is COM automation in general, and the Variant datatype in particular, that are the real keys to passing arrays to ASP components, as you'll see in the examples. The Variant datatype is used to define the parameters containing the array references, and using the Variant helps get the array through the door, so to speak. Once in the component method, you can use language-specific techniques, such as SafeArray functions and methods, to access information about the array and to access the array data.

We'll create components using Visual Basic and Visual C++ to perform array parameter processing as well as to return arrays from functions. First, though, we need to understand the mechanics of array handling with the scripting languages.

Array Handling in ASP Script

VBScript is a variation of Visual Basic, and as such it handles all arrays as SafeArrays. Passing arrays from VBScript to a component and back again is a fairly simple process:

```
Dim arry(3)
arry(0) = "pear"
arry(1) = "orange"
arry(2) = "banana"
arry(3) = "grape"

cmp.tstArray arry

Dim arry2
arry2 = cmp.tstArray2()
```

However, successfully passing array parameters from a script to a component or from a component to a script is not such a simple process in JScript or PerlScript.

In JScript (or JavaScript for that matter), an array parameter appears to COM as a string of concatenated values separated by commas. You can create an array and access and set its elements in JScript using arraylike notation:

```
var arry = new Array(3);
arry[0] = "one";
arry[1] = "two";
arry[3] = "three";
```

However, when you pass the array to an ASP component, the array really appears as a string:

```
"one, two, three"
```

Perl also implements arrays, and you can create and work with arrays in PerlScript. However, to create SafeArrays in PerlScript—arrays that can be passed to and from ASP components—you must use the Variant module to create the array. For instance, the following will create a three-element array of strings in PerlScript:

```
use Win32::OLE::Variant;

my @item = qw(one two three);
my $arry = Variant(VT_ARRAY|VT_BSTR,[0,3]);

$arry->Put(\@item);
```

In PerlScript, you must specify that the new object is an array and specify the type of data stored in the array—in this case the BSTR datatype. You then assign the Perl array to the new Variant array (SafeArray) using the Variant Put method.

When processing VBScript, JScript, or PerlScript (or any other scripting language) arrays within components, you use the Variant datatype as the parameter type, and you should test the datatype of the parameter to see if it is an array or a BSTR. If it is an array, then you can use whatever SafeArray techniques are available in the programming language to process the contents. If it is a string, then you can use string functions to parse the string based on a comma (,) delimiter. This latter processing is necessary when handling arrays from JScript. In Visual Basic, for instance, you can call the *IsArray* function to determine whether the value passed to a component is an array.

If your component supports both VBScript and PerlScript, the SafeArray passed as a parameter should contain Variant datatypes. To ensure that the component can process both the PerlScript array as well as one passed to and from VBScript, in PerlScript declare the array as an array of Variants rather than another datatype, and make sure to pass the array by reference:

```
my $arry = Variant(VT_ARRAY|VT_BYREF|VT_VARIANT,[0,3]);
```

This definition for this SafeArray passed as a parameter from PerlScript to the ASP component matches the characteristics of an array parameter passed from VBScript to the component, and, as a result, the processing of arrays from both scripting languages can be the same.

Now that we understand some of the restrictions of creating arrays in scripting languages, let's take a look at how arrays are processed in ASP components. In the next two sections, we'll look at creating both a Visual Basic and a Visual C++ ASP Component to process the arrays.

Array Parameter Processing in Visual Basic

To test array parameters in Visual Basic, you create a new component in the existing `asp0601` project. This component takes an array parameter and displays the array elements to the web page. Additionally, the component creates an array to return to the ASP script, which in turn processes and displays the array elements.

Name the new component `array` and add two methods to it:

tstArray
> A subroutine that has a Variant parameter

tstArray2
> A function that has no parameters but returns a Variant datatype

Since the new component makes use of the built-in ASP Response object, you also add a reference to the COM+ Services Library and a reference to the Microsoft Active Server Pages Object Library to the project.

 Using the ASP built-in objects and attaching references to necessary type libraries for a Visual Basic component are covered in Chapter 7, *Creating a Simple Visual Basic ASP Component.*

Once the supporting type libraries are added to the project, add code for the two new methods. The first method, tstArray, uses the COM+ *GetObjectContext* function to return a reference to an ObjectContext object. The Item collection of this object contains a reference to each of the built-in ASP objects, so the Response object is retrieved from this collection.

In tstArray, the Variant parameter that contains the array is tested to see if it is an array or if the Variant contains a `BSTR` object. If the Variant contains an array, it is assigned to a new Variant created in the code. However, if the Variant contains a `BSTR` value, the Visual Basic *Split* function is used to split the concatenated values in the comma-delimited string into an array, which is assigned to the new Variant variable. Once the processing to handle the two different parameter types is finished, the resulting Variant array (which has either been assigned directly or generated using *Split*) is traversed, and each of its element's values is displayed using the ASP Response object. The code for tstArray is shown in Example 6-14.

Example 6-14. Visual Basic Method for Processing ASP Array Parameters

```
Sub tstArray(vArray As Variant)

  ' get Response object for output
  Dim objContext As ObjectContext
  Set objContext = GetObjectContext()

  Dim objResponse As Response
  Set objResponse = objContext.Item("Response")

  ' working array
  Dim v As Variant

  ' if vArray is an array, then assign to variant
  ' otherwise treat as string, with values concatenated with commas
  If VarType(vArray) = (vbVariant + vbArray) Then
     v = vArray
  ElseIf VarType(vArray) = vbString Then
     v = Split(CStr(vArray), ",")
  Else
     Err.Raise 5   'E_INVALIDARG error code
  End If

  ' print out array contents
  Dim lLArray As Long
  Dim lUArray As Long
  Dim l As Long

  lLArray = LBound(v)
  lUArray = UBound(v)

  For l = lLArray To lUArray
     objResponse.Write (v(l))
     objResponse.Write "<p>"
  Next l

End Sub
```

If the argument passed to the tstArray method is neither an array nor a String, an invalid argument error is returned. The method also uses the Visual Basic *LBound* and *UBound* functions to find the upper and lower boundaries of the array. These are then used in a For...**Next** loop to output the array element values.

Arrays can also be passed from Visual Basic back to ASP script blocks. The reverse process is fairly simple and basically involves creating a Variant array, which is then returned by the function, as shown in the code for the tstArray2 method in Example 6-15.

Example 6-15. Simple Visual Basic Function That Returns a String Array

```
Function tstArray2() As Variant

  Dim arry(0 To 3) As Variant
  arry(0) = "one"
  arry(1) = "two"
  arry(2) = "three"
  arry(3) = "four"

  tstArray2 = arry
End Function
```

Instead of having the method return an array, the Variant array can also be passed back to the ASP block in a **ByRef** parameter, but then the array values will not be accessible within a JScript block. (JScript, as you may recall, does not support passing parameters by reference.)

To test the two Visual Basic methods, recompile the component, then create three ASP test pages, each using a different scripting language.

The first test page uses VBScript and is called *asp0612.asp*. The script in this page creates an array of four elements, each containing a string with the name of a fruit. In the code, the first component method, tstArray, is called to process the array elements. When the first component method finishes, the script then calls the second component method, which returns an array. The upper boundary for the array is found (VBScript arrays always start with zero), and this is used in a **For...Next** loop to output the new array element values, as shown in Example 6-16.

Example 6-16. ASP Page with VBScript That Implements an Array Parameter to an ASP Component and Processes an Array Returned from the ASP Component

```
<!DOCTYPE HTML PUBLIC "-//W3C//DTD HTML 4.0//EN">
<HTML>
<HEAD>
<TITLE>Arrays</TITLE>
</HEAD>
<BODY>
<H1> Testing Arrays</H1>

<%
  ' create the component instance
  Dim tmp
  Set tmp = Server.CreateObject("asp0601.arry")

  ' create array
  Dim arry(3)
  arry(0) = "pear"
  arry(1) = "orange"
  arry(2) = "banana"
  arry(3) = "grape"
```

Example 6-16. ASP Page with VBScript That Implements an Array Parameter to an ASP Component and Processes an Array Returned from the ASP Component (continued)

```
' process array
tmp.tstArray arry

' call second component to get an array
Dim ubnd
Dim lval
Dim arry2
arry2 = tmp.tstArray2()

' get the second array's boundary and process
' results
ubnd = UBound(arry2)
' cycle through array, print out value
For lval = 0 to ubnd
   Response.Write(arry2(lval))
   Response.Write("<p>")
Next

%>
</BODY>
</HTML>
```

When you run the test page, you'll see that the results are a list of the four fruit names found in the first array, followed by the four numbers found in the second array. Figure 6-2 shows a page that should look similar to the results you'll get with the example.

The JScript ASP test page isn't all that complicated either—except for a slight limitation: JScript doesn't know how to process a SafeArray. Since the second Visual Basic component method you are testing returns a SafeArray, this could be a problem.

To resolve the problem of SafeArrays being passed to JScript, Microsoft enhanced this scripting language by providing the *VBArray* function. VBArray converts a SafeArray into a format that JScript can handle and returns the converted array to the JScript code.

 Unfortunately, there is no reverse function that converts a JScript array into a SafeArray before passing it as an argument.

Example 6-17 shows the script and HTML to create the JScript test page (named *asp0613.asp*). An array is created in the script using the JavaScript *Array* function, and the four elements of the array are set to strings. The code then calls the Visual Basic ASP component tstArray method. Once this method completes, the JScript

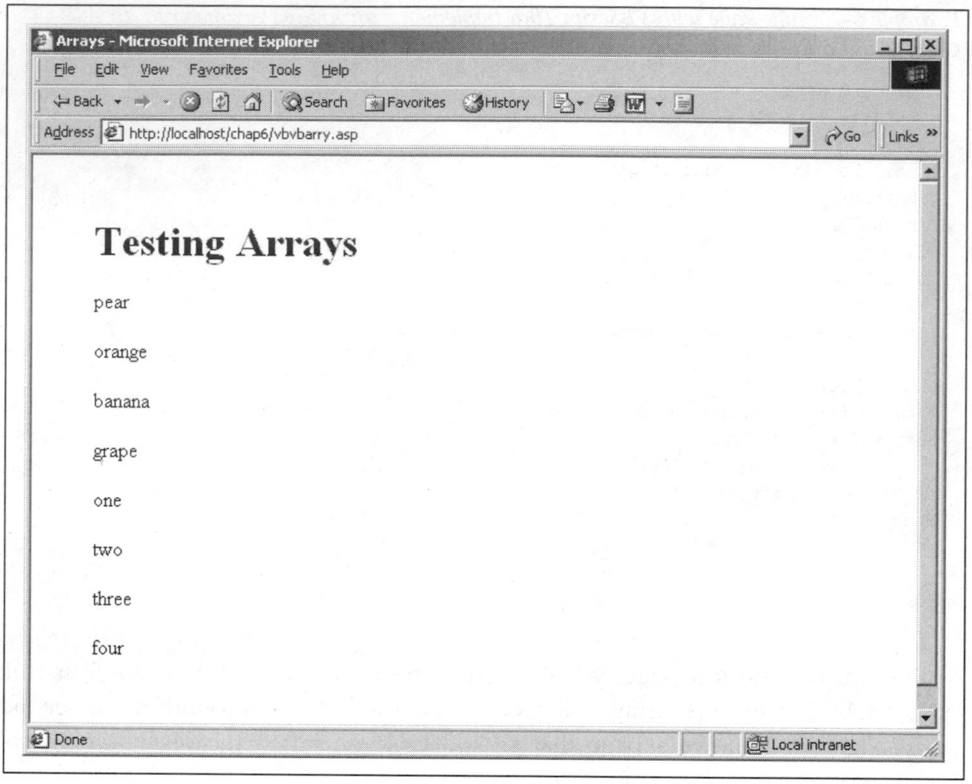

Figure 6-2. Results of running array parameter test with a VB component, invoked from a VBScript page

calls the second method, tstArray2, and gets the SafeArray value back from the function. This is passed to the built-in *VBArray* function, which returns a JScript-compatible array. Finally, the page processes the array results and displays them to the browser.

Example 6-17. ASP Page with JScript That Implements an Array Parameter to an ASP Component and Processes an Array Returned from the ASP Component

```
<%@ Language="jscript" %>
<!DOCTYPE HTML PUBLIC "-//W3C//DTD HTML 4.0//EN">
<HTML>
<HEAD>
<TITLE>Arrays</TITLE>
<STYLE type="text/css">
      BODY { margin: 0.5in }
</STYLE>
<BODY>
<H1> Testing Arrays</H1>

<%
  tmp = Server.CreateObject("asp0601.arry");
```

Example 6-17. ASP Page with JScript That Implements an Array Parameter to an ASP Component and Processes an Array Returned from the ASP Component (continued)

```
// create new array
var arry;
arry = new Array(4);

arry[0] = "apples";
arry[1] = "oranges";
arry[2] = "pear";
arry[3] = "grapes";

// call method to process array
tmp.tstArray(arry);

// call second method
var arry2 = tmp.tstArray2();

// process second array results
// first call VBArray to convert SafeArray to
//     jscript array
var arry3 = new VBArray(arry2);
var arry4 = arry3.toArray();

// process array
for (i =0; i <= arry3.ubound(); i++) {
  Response.Write(arry4[i]);
    Response.Write("<P>");
  }
%>
</BODY>
</HTML>
```

When you run the JScript example, you should get a page formatted identically to the page produced by the VBScript test and shown in Figure 6-2—the only differences being the order and the names of some fruit.

The PerlScript test page, *asp0614.asp*, looks quite a bit different from the VBScript and JScript test pages, primarily because you must explicitly create a Variant array for the array parameter-passing test. Other than that, the basic functionality is the same. An array is created and its elements given string values containing the names of fruit. This array is passed to the ASP component's tstArray method where the results are processed. Then, the second component array method, tstArray2, is called, and the returned array is processed and its element values output. Example 6-18 shows the code for the PerlScript array parameter test page.

Example 6-18. ASP Page with PerlScript That Implements an Array Parameter to an ASP Component, and Processes an Array Returned from the ASP Component

```
<%@ Language="PerlScript" %>
<HTML>
<HEAD>
```

Example 6-18. ASP Page with PerlScript That Implements an Array Parameter to an ASP
Component, and Processes an Array Returned from the ASP Component (continued)

```
<TITLE>Arrays</TITLE>
<STYLE type="text/css">
     BODY { margin: 0.5in }
</STYLE>
</HEAD>
<BODY>
<H1> Testing Arrays</H1>
<%

use strict;
use vars qw($Server $Response);
use Win32::OLE::Variant;

# create array of fruit names
my @item = qw(apple pear peach grapes);

# access component
my $myobj = $Server->CreateObject("asp0601.arry");

# create Variant array and assign array as value
my $arry = Variant(VT_ARRAY|VT_BYREF|VT_VARIANT,[0,4]);
$arry->Put(\@item);

# call function and pass in array
$myobj->tstArray($arry);

# call second function and process array
my $arry2 = $myobj->tstArray2();
my $ct = scalar(@$arry2);

for (my $i = 0; $i < $ct; $i++) {
   $Response->Write($arry2->[$i]);
   $Response->Write("<p>");
}
%>
</BODY>
</HTML>
```

Most of the mechanics in dealing with Variant parameters containing scalar or array
data are hidden with Visual Basic. The same is not necessarily true in C++, though
the steps involved are essentially the same, as you'll see in the next section.

Array Parameter Processing with Visual C++

The basics of processing array parameters with Visual C++ components are very
similar to those with the Visual Basic components, except there is a whole lot
more code. The details of the processing are more exposed with Visual C++, so
we can see a little more of the underlying mechanisms—whether we really want
to or not.

We'll use the ATL COM AppWizard to create a new Visual C++ COM project named `asp0602`, following the procedures outlined in Chapter 14, *Creating C++ ASP Components*.

 If you aren't using Visual C++, the example code that comes with this book has the Visual C++ *asp0602.dll* included. All you need to do is install the example code for this chapter and register *asp0602. dll* using COM+ services or the older regsvr32 method, discussed in Chapter 3 and Chapter 5, *COM+ Services and ASP Components and Applications*.

Once the new project is generated, add a new Simple object using the ATL Object Wizard, name the object `arry`, and change the threading model of the component to be both-threaded. After the C++ class and header files are created, add the two test methods.

Using the Visual C++ Class View, add a method named tstArray, with one input parameter defined as a Variant pointer. The method parameter string should look as follows:

```
[in] VARIANT * pVariantArray
```

Once Visual C++ has generated the method prototype, you next need to add in support for several different C++ libraries, including those for COM+ Services, the ASP built-in objects, string and algorithm processing, as well as COM datatypes. Do this by adding a number of lines to the component header file, *arry.h*, so that the top of the header looks similar to:

```
// arry.h : Declaration of the Carry

#ifndef __ARRY_H_
#define __ARRY_H_

#include "resource.h"       // main symbols
#include <comsvcs.h>
#include <comdef.h>
#include <asptlb.h>
#include <string>
#include <algorithm>
```

To prevent compiler errors because of using the **wstring** class, you'll need to add a namespace definition to the component C++ file, *arry.cpp*:

```
using namespace std;
```

The Visual C++ tstArray method performs the same basic functionality as the Visual Basic component. An instance of the ObjectContext interface is created (`IObjectContext` in Visual C++), and this is used to query for (get) a reference to the Response object (using `IResponse`), a process covered in Chapter 14. Once the reference to `IResponse` is obtained, we can begin to work with the array parameter.

The macro `V_VT` is used to determine the variant type of the parameter and to test whether the parameter is a Variant array or a `BSTR`. If it is an array, then the object is copied to a COM helper datatype, `_variant_t`, which handles all memory allocation for the object. The SafeArray method, SafeArrayCopy, is used to copy the Variant array into a SafeArray structure, and the SafeArray methods SafeArrayGet-LBound and SafeArrayGetUBound are used to get the upper and lower boundaries of the array. Once the boundaries are obtained, these are used to traverse the array, and the array element values are displayed using the `IResponse` object reference.

If the Variant parameter is a `BSTR` value, then the `BSTR` value is assigned to a `BSTR` variable using `_bstr_b`, a COM helper datatype which handles all memory allocation. This is then assigned to a standard template (STL) object, `wstring`. The `wstring` template has methods to find a specific character in the string—in this case the comma (,)—and return a *substring* of all elements up to that character. Using this approach, the parameter string is parsed for all array elements, and their values are then included in the web page returned to the client. The complete code for tstArray is shown in Example 6-19.

Example 6-19. Visual C++ Component Method That Processes an Array Passed from ASP Script

```
// method to parse variant array and print out contents
STDMETHODIMP Carry::tstArray(VARIANT *pVariantArray)
{
    HRESULT hr = S_OK;
    LONG lLBound, lUBound;
    _variant_t vtVal;

    CComVariant vtOut;
    CComPtr<IObjectContext> piObjectContext;
    CComPtr<IResponse> piResponse;
    CComBSTR bstrObj;
    CComVariant vt;
    CComPtr<IGetContextProperties> pProps; //Context Properties

    IDispatch* piDispatch = NULL;

    // get ObjectContext
    hr = CoGetObjectContext(IID_IObjectContext,(void **)&piObjectContext);
    if (FAILED(hr))
      return hr;

    // get Context Properties
    hr = piObjectContext->QueryInterface( IID_IGetContextProperties,
             (void**)&pProps );
```

Example 6-19. Visual C++ Component Method That Processes an Array Passed from ASP Script (continued)

```
if (FAILED(hr))
   return hr;

// get ASP Response property
bstrObj = "Response";
hr = pProps->GetProperty( bstrObj, &vt ) ;
if (FAILED(hr))
   return hr;

piDispatch = vt.pdispVal;
hr = piDispatch->QueryInterface( IID_IResponse,
                (void**)&piResponse );

// wrap variant array with _variant_t for resource allocation and
// deallocation
_variant_t vtArray (pVariantArray);

// get variant type
VARTYPE vttype = V_VT(&vtArray);

// if ARRAY, process as SAFEARRAY
if (vttype & VT_ARRAY)
{
    SAFEARRAY * psa;
    _variant_t vtValue;

  // copy variant array to SAFEARRAY
   hr = SafeArrayCopy(*(vtArray.pparray), &psa);
   if (FAILED(hr)) {
      return hr;
      }

  // get dimensions of array
  // get array bounds
  hr = SafeArrayGetLBound(psa, 1, &lLBound);
  if (FAILED(hr))
     return hr;

  hr = SafeArrayGetUBound(psa, 1, &lUBound);
  if (FAILED(hr))
     return hr;

  // get each value, print out
  vtVal = "<p>";
  for (long l = lLBound; l <= lUBound; l++) {
     SafeArrayGetElement(psa, &l, &vtValue);

     // print out
     piResponse->Write(vtValue);
     piResponse->Write(vtVal);
     }
```

*Example 6-19. Visual C++ Component Method That Processes an Array Passed from ASP Script
(continued)*

```
        // clean up
        SafeArrayDestroy(psa);

    }

    // else, if passed in as BSTR
    //(JScript or other as concatenated string)
    else if (vttype & VT_BSTR) {

        // output variant
        _variant_t vtOut;

        char cFind = ',';
        wstring::size_type iPos;
        wstring strFound;

        // pull out variant, convert to BSTR
        _bstr_t bstrMine (vtArray);

        // assign to STL wstring for manipulation
        wstring wstrVariant = bstrMine;

        // parse string
        iPos = wstrVariant.find(cFind,0);
        vtVal = "<p>";
        while (iPos != wstring::npos) {
           strFound = wstrVariant.substr(0,iPos);
           vtOut = strFound.c_str();
           piResponse->Write(vtOut);
           piResponse->Write(vtVal);
           wstrVariant = wstrVariant.substr(iPos + 1);
           iPos = wstrVariant.find(cFind,0);
           }
        vtOut = wstrVariant.c_str();
        piResponse->Write(vtOut);
        piResponse->Write(vtVal);
        }
    else
        return E_INVALIDARG;

    return S_OK;
}
```

If the Variant parameter does not contain a Variant array or a BSTR, an invalid
argument error is returned.

The second method that creates and returns an array is not as code-intensive as
the one to process the array. First, add a new method named tstArray2 to the class
interface on the Class View page. The method has one parameter, a return parameter of type VARIANT pointer:

```
[out,retval] VARIANT * pVariantArray
```

In the case of COM components, all methods have the same return type, HRESULT. To return a value from a function call, it must be defined as an output, return value ([out,retval]) in the component IDL.

In the component, a new SafeArray is created using the SafeArrayCreate method, and values are added to the array elements. The return parameter is defined to be a Variant array, and the newly created SafeArray is assigned to this parameter and returned. Example 6-20 shows the complete code for this second function.

Example 6-20. Visual C++ Component That Creates an Array and Returns It to the ASP Page

```
STDMETHODIMP Carry::tstArray2(VARIANT *pVariantArray)
{
    HRESULT hr;
    SAFEARRAY * psaiNew;
    SAFEARRAYBOUND aDim[1];
    aDim[0].lLbound = 0;
    aDim[0].cElements = 4;
    long l;
     _variant_t v;

     // equivalent to: Dim aiNew(1 To 8) as integer
    psaiNew = SafeArrayCreate(VT_VARIANT, 1, aDim);
    if (psaiNew != NULL) {
        l = 0;
        v = "one";
        SafeArrayPutElement(psaiNew, &l, &v);
        l = 1;
        v = "two";
        SafeArrayPutElement(psaiNew, &l, &v);
        l = 2;
        v = "three";
        SafeArrayPutElement(psaiNew, &l, &v);
        l = 3;
        v = "four";
        hr = SafeArrayPutElement(psaiNew, &l, &v);
        if (FAILED(hr))
            return hr;
    }
    V_VT(pVariantArray) = VT_ARRAY | VT_VARIANT;
    V_ARRAY(pVariantArray) = psaiNew;

    return S_OK;
}
```

Once you add the code for the two methods to the component, compile it; the DLL is automatically registered for access. To test the page, create three new ASP pages that are *identical* to those used to test the Visual Basic component, except that they create the C++ component (asp0602.arry) rather than the Visual Basic component (asp0601.arry). Name the files *asp0615.asp* (the VBScript ASP page), *asp0616.asp* (the PerlScript ASP page), and *asp0617.asp* (the JScript ASP page).

(The code and HTML for the pages are omitted here because of the similarity to those from the pages that test the Visual Basic `asp0601.arry` component in Examples 6-16 through 6-18.)

Accessing each of the pages, the results returned are identical to those achieved when accessing the Visual Basic component. Splitting the process into string and array manipulation to handle scripting differences is a workable solution in both programming languages and should continue to be workable in all programming languages that can be used to create ASP components.

One thing the script-to-component interaction examples in this chapter have not demonstrated is how to handle errors that occur in the component. This is covered in the next section.

Error Handling Between Component and Script

When error conditions occur in the component, the component should handle them gracefully (or as gracefully as possible). However, the error conditions should also be returned to the ASP page so that the script can handle them. VBScript and JScript both have built-in error-processing capability, though the capability differs between the languages.

In VBScript, you can gracefully handle an error by preceding the call to the component method with the following line:

```
On Error Resume Next
```

This line directs the ASP scripting engine to continue execution of the script on the line following the one on which the error occurred. You can then query the Err object after a method call and test for an error condition:

```
If Err <> 0 Then
```

Once you've trapped the error you can display the error number, or, preferably, you can display the error description.

```
Response.Write Err.Description
```

With JScript, starting with Version 5 of the scripting engine (included with IIS 5.0), you can surround a component method call with `try...catch` statements to trap an error condition. Unlike VBScript, the next line after the component method call won't execute, and control goes immediately to the `catch` block, but you can continue processing the rest of the page following the `catch` block:

```
try {
   ...
}
```

```
catch (exception) {
...
}
```

The **catch** block contains a reference to the new JScript Error object. The JScript Error object, like the VBScript Err object, can be used to retrieve information such as the error description.

To test error handling with both these scripting languages, create a new component named **devaspcomperr** in the Visual Basic **asp0601** project. This component will have three simple methods, each of which generates a particular type of error. The first method, tstError1, will raise an invalid argument error by using the Visual Basic Err.Raise method and giving the invalid argument value (a value of 5). The second method, tstError2, raises error 58, or a "File already exists" error. The third method, tstError, raises error 461, or the method or data member not found error. The code for three methods is shown in Example 6-21.

Example 6-21. Raising Three Different Errors Using Three Different Error Values

```
Sub tstError1()

    err.Raise 5   'E_INVALIDARG error code
End Sub

Sub tstError2()

    err.Raise 58 ' File already exists error

End Sub

Sub tstError()

    err.Raise 461 ' Member not found
End Sub
```

To test the error handling, create an ASP page named *asp0618.asp* that uses VBScript error handling. This page creates the ASP component and also uses the **Resume Next** error handling statement to ensure that the next line of code after an error occurs is processed. The script, as shown in Example 6-22, invokes the first error handling method, the one that raises the invalid argument error. In the script block, the error is accessed and the description is printed out to the page. At the end, the error value is cleared.

Example 6-22. ASP Page That Handles Error Conditions Raised in Visual Basic ASP Component

```
<!DOCTYPE HTML PUBLIC "-//W3C//DTD HTML 4.0//EN">
<HTML>
<HEAD>
<TITLE>Errors</TITLE>
```

Example 6-22. ASP Page That Handles Error Conditions Raised in Visual Basic ASP Component (continued)

```
</HEAD>
<BODY>

<%
  On Error Resume Next

  ' create ASP component
  Dim cmp
  Set cmp = Server.CreateObject("asp0601.devaspcomperr")

  cmp.tstError1
  If Err <> 0 Then
    Response.Write "Result of function call is <strong>"
    Response.Write Err.Description
    Response.Write "</strong><p>"
    Err.Clear
  End If

  Response.Write("After error handling")

%>
</BODY>
</HTML>
```

The result of running the page in Example 6-22 is shown in Figure 6-3, where the error message is displayed along with another message that indicates that the error handler has finished executing. This demonstrates that the error handling does let the rest of the page processing finish, rather than abruptly returning an incomplete and possibly confusing page to the web page reader.

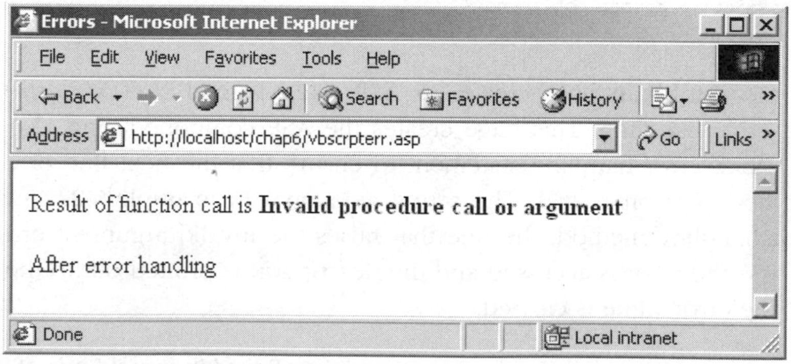

Figure 6-3. Error handling using VBScript to print out error message and continue processing

Next, create a test page named *asp0619.asp* that uses JScript and JScript error handling. The code and HTML for the second test page is shown in Example 6-23.

This page encloses the component method call within a `try...catch` structure and captures the exception after it has been triggered from the component by the call to the tstError2 method. In the exception handler, the error message that the file already exists is displayed.

Example 6-23. ASP Page Handles Error Conditions Raised in Visual Basic ASP Component

```
<%@ Language="jscript" %>
<!DOCTYPE HTML PUBLIC "-//W3C//DTD HTML 4.0//EN">
<HTML>
<HEAD>
<TITLE>Date</TITLE>
<BODY>
<%
  var cmp = Server.CreateObject("asp0601.devaspcomp");

  // first error
  try {
     cmp.tstError2();
   }
  catch (exception) {
     if (exception instanceof Error) {
        Response.Write("Result of function call is <strong>")
        Response.Write(exception.description);
        Response.Write("</strong><p>");

     }
   }
  Response.Write("After error handling");

%>
</BODY>
</HTML>
```

The page resulting from this test page should be similar to that shown in Figure 6-3, but with a different error message, of course.

I've mentioned JScript and VBScript, and you might be wondering if PerlScript has error handling capabilities. It does, but the error handling for this scripting language actually comes from one of the Win32 Perl modules, Win32::OLE.

The Win32::OLE class has a method named LastError that returns a variable of a specific type known as a *dual type*—a value that can be either a numeric or a string, depending on the context in which it is accessed. Additionally, when an error condition is raised in a component invoked in PerlScript, the script processing does not automatically fail at the point where the error occurred. Using a combination of both nonfailing script processing and LastError, we can implement error handling with PerlScript very much like the error handling in JScript and VBScript.

To test error handling with PerlScript, create another ASP test page and name it *asp0620.asp*. Example 6-24 shows the PerlScript error test page. In this page, the tstError component method, which triggers a member not found error, is called. The script then accesses the LastError method and concatenates the result with a string, thereby retrieving the error description rather than the error number. To clear the error, the error number is deliberately set to zero, which also discards the error description associated with it.

Example 6-24. Processing Error Raised in ASP Component, Within PerlScript

```
<%@ Language="PerlScript" %>
<HTML>
<HEAD>
<TITLE>Testing Dates</TITLE>
</HEAD>
<BODY>
<%

use strict;
use vars qw($Server $Response);
use Win32::OLE;

my $myobj = $Server->CreateObject("asp0601.devaspcomperr");

# error
$myobj->tstError();
my $err = 'Result of function call is <strong>' . Win32::OLE->LastError();
$Response->Write($err);
$Response->Write('</strong><p>');

$Response->Write('after error handling');

Win32::OLE->LastError(0);

%>
</BODY>
</HTML>
```

PerlScript error handling is remarkably similar to that in VBScript and JScript, except that the error description string is more verbose. Figure 6-4 shows the result of running this PerlScript ASP.

With error handling, you can provide more meaningful messages for the web page reader, and you can also provide useful information for yourself, the ASP component developer.

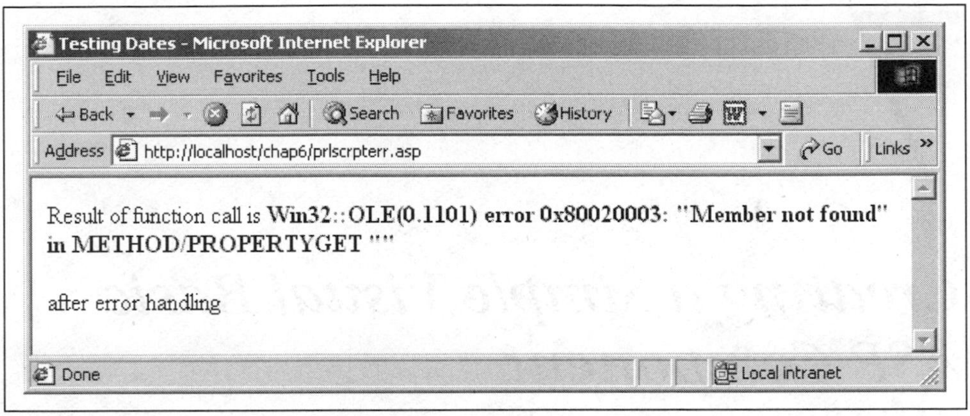

Figure 6-4. Result of PerlScript error handling

7

Creating a Simple Visual Basic ASP Component

Visual Basic offers the simplest approach to creating an ASP component. At a minimum, the ASP component developer only needs to create a new project for the component, add in the class methods and properties, compile the component, and register it either automatically (through *regsvr32.exe*) or within a COM+ application. However, there are a number of decisions that can impact how the component works with the ASP application. Among these are whether the component is an in-process or an out-of-process component; whether the component is multiple- or single-use; whether the component is multithreaded and, if so, how many threads it has and when a new thread is created; and what instancing type is used. Some decisions are made for you based on other decisions. Many you make yourself, and the decision can literally mean the difference between a component that assists in the smooth operation of the ASP application and a component that becomes the worst bottleneck within the application.

By the end of this chapter, you will know the advantages and disadvantages of creating an in-process component compared to an out-of-process component, the advantages and disadvantages of a multiple-use component compared to a single-use and even a global-use component, what Visual Basic does to ensure a thread-safe component, what factors can influence parameter passing when creating component methods, how to register the component, and how to add error handling and debug the component. We'll also take a look at performance issues.

ASP components sometimes need to interact directly with the ASP environment, and this interaction occurs through the use of the ASP built-in objects, such as the Request and Response objects. You'll have a chance to work with the core objects—Application, Session, Response, Request, and Server—in this chapter.

Creating an In-Process or Out-Of-Process Component

An ASP component in Visual Basic is really an ActiveX object, either a dynamic link library (DLL) or an executable. An ActiveX DLL is an in-process component, which means that the component shares the same address space (memory, resources) and threads as the application that creates the component. An ActiveX executable is an out-of-process component, which means that this type of component has its own threads and resources.

The most common and simplest component to create is the ActiveX DLL, the in-process component. This type of component shares the same address space as the client, which can lead to performance gains when the client interacts with the component. For instance, when a client calls a component method and the component and client share the same threading model, as will be discussed, the method's arguments are loaded into the client's own stack. For an out-of-process component, the method arguments are moved between the two processes through a process called *marshaling*—pulling arguments from a stack via a proxy on the client and putting the arguments onto the component's stack through a stub. This extra effort slows the communication process.

Another advantage to in-process components is that if the component is set to use the *apartment-threaded* threading model, it will work safely with any client, including a multithreaded client. The component is created as thread-safe using a technique discussed later in the chapter.

In spite of the problems with out-of-process components, there are also advantages to using these types of ASP components. First, the component itself can assign a different thread to each process begun for each client request. Secondly, out-of-process components do not require the use of the in-process surrogate, *dllhost.exe*, to function.

 An in-process component must be implemented in the address space of a client. If the client is remote from the component, the component must then be instantiated on some form of surrogate application that acts as the component's client. Microsoft provides *dllhost.exe* as the IIS/ASP in-process component surrogate.

The examples using Visual Basic in this and all other chapters are created as in-process components, primarily because this is the most efficient and most commonly used component type.

Component Instancing

A property of ASP components built using Visual Basic is *instancing*. By default, the component is set to an instancing value of 5—MultiUse. This means that each request to the component generates a new instance of the object. This type of instancing enables the component to process more than one request to the object at any one time by providing a different object instance for each object request, a behavior that is essential for any component accessed via a web page, as any ASP component is.

There are six different options for the Instancing property; they may or may not be available, depending on the type of component that the project creates. The six different options are the following:

Private

Access to the class is limited to the component itself; no other application can access the class.

PublicNotCreatable

A class with this instancing type must first be created by the component, usually as a result of calling a method on a publicly creatable object instance and a reference to the instance passed to the client.

MultiUse

Probably the most commonly used instancing type, multiuse means that the component can be instantiated by the client, and it can provide more than one new object instance for a specific client or multiple object instances for multiple clients.

SingleUse

Creates a new instance of the component, which then provides access to a single instance of the component class.

GlobalMultiUse

Creates an object instance whose methods and properties can be accessed by the client without having to create the object and without having to precede the object's properties and methods with an object reference. The methods and properties are treated as if they are global values.

GlobalSingleUse

A new component instance is generated for each component class request, and the properties and methods of the class are treated as if they are globally accessible values.

The type of component can determine which instancing types are available for the component classes. An in-process component (an ActiveX DLL) cannot have a class that uses SingleUse or GlobalSingleUse instancing, because a component must be able to supply multiple instances of its classes to the client the component shares its address space with. Because of this, when assigning a value to the Instancing property in the Properties window, these two instancing types are not even displayed in the dropdown list box when an ActiveX DLL is being created.

You can use the global instance types GlobalMultiUse and GlobalSingleUse with your components to allow for global access to methods and properties. *Global access* means that a new object instance does not need to be expressly created, and the methods and properties are accessed as if they are part of global data. This requires, however, that a reference to the component be added to a client project at design time by accessing the References dialog (Project → References). The component is found within the list of available registered components. Checking the box next to the component adds the component into the project.

Because the client needs a way to attach a reference to a component at design time, in effect accessing the component's *type library*, this also means that the global instance types can be used within a Visual Basic project, but not directly within an ASP page. Based on this latter restriction, using the global instance types is not really an effective approach with components instantiated within ASP applications.

The PublicNotCreatable instancing type can be used to create a *dependent object*. A dependent object is one that is created from within a different object. For example, a component can contain a reference to a collection, and each collection member can actually be another class instance rather than a scalar value. The collection Add method then creates the dependent instance, adds it to the collection, and returns a reference to the collection element. Access to the dependent object's methods and properties occurs through the collection element rather than through direct access to the object.

The Private instance type is used primarily for classes that are created and accessed only internally.

For the examples in this book, the other properties, such as DataBindingBehavior and Persistable, are kept at their default values. This includes the MTSTransactionMode property, which, when the component is used within MTS, controls whether the object runs within an existing transaction, runs in a new transaction, or can't be run within a transaction. This can also be set when the component is registered with COM+, as discussed in Chapter 5, *COM+ Services and ASP Components and Applications*. For now, leave the value at its default of 0—NotAnMTSObject.

Component Execution and Threads

Visual Basic supports single-threaded ActiveX in-process components, but this is not an option you want to choose with an ASP component. Using the single-threaded option means that the ASP component is loaded into IIS's main STA rather than on the specific thread that created it. This means that communication between the component and the page that created it now must occur through a proxy.

If the object cannot be created on the calling application's thread, all arguments passed during method calls must be marshaled. With marshaling, method arguments passed to objects across process or thread (or context) boundaries have to pass from a proxy on the client side to a stub on the component side, and the arguments have to be copied into the address space of the component. If the argument is passed by reference, the argument then has to be sent from the component back to the client and copied on the client's side. This process of passing arguments from proxy to stub and back again can slow the performance of the component.

 Chapter 4, *ASP Components, Threads, and Contexts*, discusses the different threading models.

A preferred choice for ASP in-process components is the STA (single-threaded apartment) apartment-threading model. This model enforces thread safety because each thread has its own global data area, which prevents objects on one thread from contaminating global data for objects on another thread. Additionally, the component can then be created on the same thread as the calling application if the models between the two—the client and component—are compatible. In IIS, the threads that are used to process each page request are based on the STA apartment-threading model, which means that both the page and the component are created within the same thread.

Out-of-process components also support the apartment-threading model. Built-in thread safety, the advantage that in-process components have with apartment threading, is also an advantage of using this threading approach with out-of-process components. However, out-of-process threads are never created within the same thread of the client, so function arguments with out-of-process components are always marshaled.

In addition to the apartment-threading option, the developer can also choose to create the out-of-process component with a fixed thread pool. With this approach, the number of threads available for the component is predetermined at design time rather than at runtime. Creating a fixed pool of threads and setting the thread count to greater than a value of 1 uses a *round-robin* method of assigning the next object created to the next thread up for assignment. This means that if three clients create a total of five objects from a single component and the component has a fixed pool of three threads, the first two threads have two objects each, and the last has one. The next object created goes onto the last thread. Which object was assigned to what thread depends only on the order in which the object was created and which thread was next up for assignment.

An advantage of a fixed thread pool is that the number of threads can be created to equal the number of processors on a system, if the operating system supports multiple processors, as Windows NT does. Assigning a fixed pool of threads can maximize the overall performance of the application utilizing the component. However, there are also two disadvantages to this threading technique. The first is that if one object is processing a call, it blocks the thread of execution from any other object within the thread. If another object also receives a call, it cannot process that call until the first object releases the thread after it has finished its own processing. A second disadvantage to this technique is that load balancing does not occur. In the previous example, with three clients and five objects, if the two objects on the first thread are destroyed, the thread no longer has any objects. However, if a client requests a new object, it is placed on the third thread, which is the next one up for assignment. This then means that the first thread now has no objects, the second and third have two objects, and the process load is not balanced evenly across the threads. Combine that with the blocking nature of multiple objects on one thread, and you have some potential degradation in performance.

A second thread-pooling approach is to assign one thread to each new object created by selecting the "Thread per Object" option in the Project Properties dialog. When the object is destroyed, the thread is also destroyed. This same thread is also used for dependent objects that are created using an instancing type of PublicNotCreatable. Unfortunately, dependent objects using their parents' threads actually is a major disadvantage to using this threading approach. With dependent objects, the thread is not destroyed until all objects with a reference to the thread have released their reference, meaning that the thread is active until all dependent objects are destroyed. Additionally, without any control over the number of threads, more threads can be created than processors exist to handle them, and the performance of the application can actually degrade as the operating system spends too much time trying to handle thread maintenance in addition to application processes.

The explicit use of threads is available only with an ActiveX EXE component. If the machine that the application runs on has only a single processor, creating a fixed pool of one thread is the best approach to take for performance reasons, as well as the most backward-compatible approach.

Setting a DLL to be apartment-threaded doesn't mean it can create its own threads. It just means that when a client creates a component object, that object is created on the same thread used for the client call. Based on this, no cross-thread marshaling is required. If the client has four threads, each creating a component object, four object instances are created on four different threads. The thread on which each object is created is the thread that initiated the object creation. If one client calls a method on an object that exists in another thread, cross-thread marshaling is used to ensure that the data is not corrupted by the external call. If multiple objects are created on the same client thread, the calls to the objects are serialized, which means that one object blocks other objects from receiving and processing calls until it is finished performing its own process and releases the thread of execution.

Note that some actions can force a component to yield control over the thread of execution before the component is finished performing its processing. These actions include using a *DoEvents* function call, invoking a process or method in an object in another thread, and raising an event in another object in another thread. You will want to avoid using *DoEvents* or any other method that passes execution control to an object on another thread.

One final note on threads and object creation: if an object is created publicly and in turn creates a dependent object using the Private instancing type and then provides a reference to the private object to the client, the private object reference becomes invalid when the publicly created object is released by the client. If this invalid reference is accessed, a page fault occurs. To avoid this, use PublicNotCreatable for any dependent objects that have methods accessible by the client.

Additionally, if a component object maintains a global reference to another object, the internally referenced object is not released when the externally referenced object, the object held by the client, is released. This internally held object is no longer accessible, but continues to occupy memory and use resources, effectively creating a memory leak. To avoid this, do not maintain global variable references to any object internally within a component object.

Future versions of Visual Basic could provide support for a new threading model, the neutral-apartment threading model. Read more about this in Chapter 4.

Creating an ASP Project

To create an ASP in-process component, open Visual Basic and select the ActiveX DLL project type, as shown in Figure 7-1. If you were creating an out-of-process component, you would use the ActiveX EXE option instead.

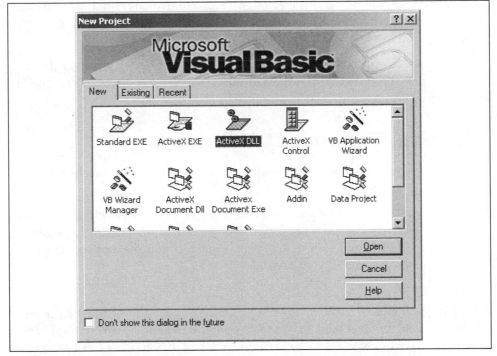

Figure 7-1. Selecting the ActiveX DLL Visual Basic project type

Visual Basic creates the project files and also creates a default class file. The class file is where you'll add your code. The project is named `Project1` by default. For this example, you'll rename it to `asp0701`. Additionally, the default class file is named `Class1`, and you'll rename this to `First`. Rename both the project and the class by clicking on either and changing the name in the Properties window.

From the Project menu, select the asp0701 Properties menu option. The first property page is the General tab, and you'll see that the component is set to apartment-threaded by default. At this point, you can add a description for your project that identifies the component in the Registry; this also is the description used with the object in the VB Object Browser. Accept all the other settings, but check the Unattended Execution option. This option disables all use of user interface functions, such as *MsgBox*. Your component will never interact directly with the client.

The Make tab contains information for making the DLL, and you'll leave this information unchanged. The third tab has compile information. You can adjust the VB component code generation and compilation to optimize your component for your environment. For instance, if your web server is Pentium Pro–based, you could select the Favor Pentium Pro option. Otherwise, though, leave the values unchanged.

The fourth tab has component options, including version compatibility. The examples created for this book are created without compatibility, but you'll usually leave the compatibility setting to Project or Binary compatibility. The fifth tab has debugging options, and you'll leave these alone at this time.

Once you've adjusted the settings for the project, save it by selecting the Save option in the File menu. This will save the VB project as *asp0701.vbp* and the class file as *First.cls*.

Creating Component Methods

Once you've generated the component's project and class, you can begin to add methods to your new component.

In Visual Basic, you don't have to define your variables explicitly before using them. However, not doing so can cause problems that are difficult to debug. To force you to always explicitly define your variables, add the `Option Explicit` statement as the first line of your class file:

```
Option Explicit
```

When this statement is present, any time a variable is used without being defined, an error results. `Option Explicit` affects only the module in which it appears. If you want to require variable declaration in all of the modules of all of your projects (this is highly recommended), select Tools → Options. In the dialog box that appears, select the Editor tab and check the Require Variable Declaration box.

Visual Basic component methods are created as either subroutines or functions. The difference between the two is that subroutines don't have a return value, but functions do. The first method you'll create for your new component is named sayHello and returns a String.

You can apply modifiers to your methods, such as `Public` or `Private`, which define whether the method is accessible externally (from ASP script). You'll use the `Public` modifier for all component methods exposed to access by script, but since routines are public by default, you don't have to add it to your code.

Create the prototype for your component. As you add the prototype header, you'll find that Visual Basic adds the closing statement for the method:

```
Function sayHello(ByVal strName As String) As String
```

There are two optional argument modifiers, `ByVal` and `ByRef`, that indicate whether the argument is passed by value or by reference. If the argument is passed by value, a copy of the argument is made and sent to the function. If the argument is passed by reference, the address to the argument is passed rather than the value. This means that any changes made to the variable in the routine will be reflected in the value of the variable once control returns to the calling code. In contrast, any changes made to a variable passed by value are discarded once control returns to the calling code. By default, all parameters are passed `ByRef` unless explicitly set to `ByVal`.

How arguments are passed to a method can impact the performance of the object method, depending on whether the component created is in-process or out-of-process. For an out-of-process component, any object that is passed as an argument by reference won't work if the client and the component don't share the same address space. To allow this type of functionality, the object is copied into the component's address space and a pointer to it is then sent as the argument. This overhead makes this process much slower than if the object is passed by value. From an opposite perspective, passing an argument by reference can actually improve performance when passing a reference to larger data, such as a large string, rather than passing the data itself. However, this performance "gain" actually degrades in cross-process and cross-thread marshaling, since the data must be copied via the marshaling process *and* a pointer created and sent to the method.

For an in-process method call, passing larger strings and arrays by reference can improve performance, because a pointer for the argument, which is 4 bytes in size, is sent, rather than the actual data, which is larger than 4 bytes. However, for passing data such as an Integer, which is only 2 bytes in size, or a Long, which is 4 bytes in size, it is more efficient to pass the argument by value.

A good rule of thumb to follow to achieve good overall performance is to pass your arguments by value unless you specifically need to modify the parameter within the component.

The data types of the parameters can be any COM-compatible data type, such as the String used with your first method. COM is able to convert the data type from the calling application to the component as long as the conversion is valid. The Visual Basic String data type is equivalent to the COM-compatible `BSTR` data type, so the input and return parameters are created with valid data types.

The most common ASP scripting language used is VBScript. One limitation (or simplification) with VBScript is that it supports only one data type—the Variant. This doesn't impact input or return parameters, since COM can make the necessary conversion between the parameter type and the Variant in the script. However, this does impact any parameter that you pass by reference, using the `ByRef` modifier. If you pass a variable by reference, it must be passed as a Variant.

Once you've created your method prototype, add the code in Example 7-1 to complete the functionality.

Example 7-1. Component Method to Create Hello Message

```
Option Explicit

Function SayHello(ByVal strName As String) As String

' create message
Dim strMessage As String
strMessage = "Hello " & strName

' return from method
SayHello = strMessage

End Function
```

After adding the code, create the component DLL, discussed in the next section.

Generating, Registering, Installing, and Testing the Component

Generating the ActiveX DLL is actually fairly simple. Once you create the class(es) and their associated methods and properties for the component, save the project. After saving the project, selecting the "Make *componentname.dll*" option from the File menu opens the Make Project dialog to generate the DLL. The name shown matches the name given to the project. The dialog can be used to name the DLL that is generated and to find the location where the DLL is placed. The dialog also has a button labeled Options. This opens a tabbed dialog with the Make tab selected; it provides a way to add information to the DLL such as a company name, a title, a version number, and whether there are any command-line arguments or constants for the DLL. Figure 7-2 shows the Make tab with the information entered for asp0701.

Returning to the original Make Project dialog, clicking the OK button generates the DLL. Compiling the component also registers it using the *regsvr32.exe* utility.

That's it for creating and registering the DLL. The next step is to test the component to make sure the object can be safely created and that its method works. Test your component using script such as the following:

```
<%
Dim obj
Set obj = Server.CreateObject("asp0701.First")

Dim msg
msg = obj.sayHello("World!")
```

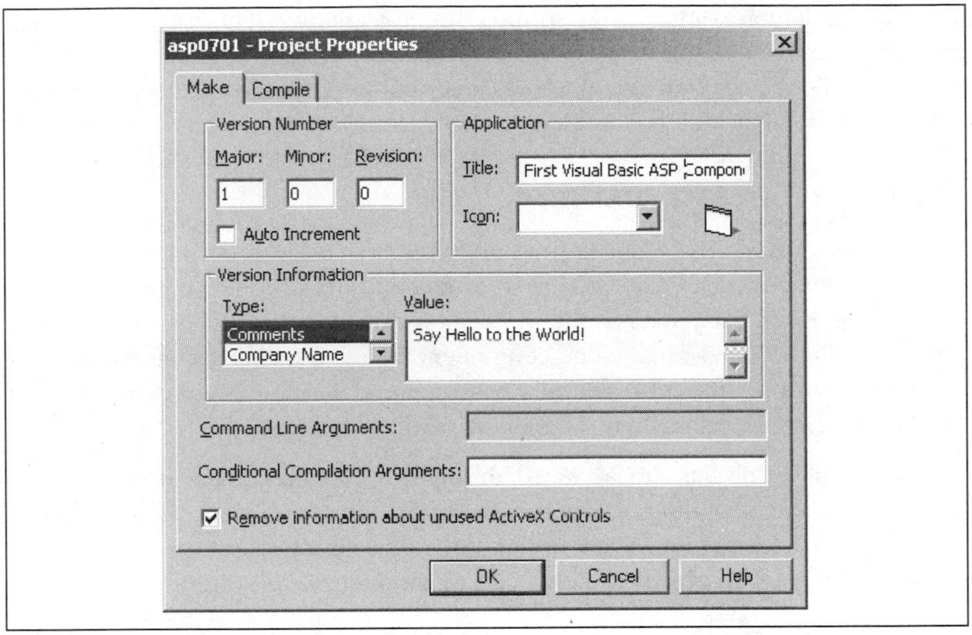

Figure 7-2. The Make tab with the information for your first ASP VB component

```
Response.Write "<h3>" & msg & "</h3>"
Set obj = Nothing
%>
```

In this script, found in *asp0701.asp*, the object is created using the component's ProgID, a combination of the project name and class name, concatenated with a period. The object's method is called and the resulting message is printed out to the web page:

```
Hello World!
```

After accessing a component via a web page, you can make modifications to the code and recompile the object. First, though, you'll have to unload your component.

When you create your test virtual directory or site for working through these examples, make sure to set the site to be isolated—running within its own process. By doing this, you can unload the ASP application by selecting the application's Properties context menu option in the IIS Management Console and clicking the Unload button. If you don't unload the component, you will get a permission error when you try to compile your object again.

Adding Support for COM+ Services

If your ASP component needs transaction support, or if you want to access the ASP built-in objects, you're going to want to access the COM+ Services interfaces.

In addition, if you want to add support for just-in-time (JIT) activation, you're going to want to use the COM+ Services. Specifically, you're going to want to work with the ObjectContext and ObjectControl objects. You could also work with other interfaces, but we'll concentrate on these two for the moment.

The ObjectContext Interface

Adding support for ObjectContext to your component adds in transaction support. When the component is participating in a transaction with other components, all the components participating in the transaction can mark their effort either a success or a failure. Based on any one component failing, the changes all the components made can be rolled back. If all components signal successful completion of their work, then the transaction can be committed as a whole.

The ASP built-in objects are accessed through the ObjectContext object so that they may be created within the existing context and transaction. In addition, by creating these components with the use of ObjectContext, COM+ can control when the ASP built-in object is loaded into memory or released from memory.

 The use of COM+, the COM+ interfaces, and the concepts of object state and just-in-time activation are discussed in Chapter 5.

A constraint to using ObjectContext is that COM+ is multithreaded, which means that the ASP component must be thread-safe and must be created using the apartment-threading model. Since Visual Basic ASP components should be created only with the apartment-threaded option, this isn't going to be a problem.

The COM+ library has a function, GetObjectContext, which returns the ObjectContext object, as shown in the following code:

```
Dim objContext As ObjectContext
Set objContext = GetObjectContext()
```

ObjectContext supports several different methods and properties. Two methods handle transaction support: SetAbort, which aborts the current transaction, and SetComplete, which signals that the transaction can be committed if no other process calls SetAbort. Additional methods are:

Count
    Returns a count of the number of ObjectContext properties

CreateInstance
    Instantiates an object that has been registered with MTS

DisableCommit

   Prevents the transaction from being committed

EnableCommit

   Allows the transaction to be committed

IsCallerInRole

   Determines whether the process calling the server process (that is, a component method) is within a specific role

IsInTransaction

   Indicates whether a component is within a transaction

IsSecurityEnabled

   Indicates whether security is enabled for all components except those running in the client's process

Item

   Returns one of the built-in objects (Request, Response, Application, Session, or Server)

Security

   Returns the Security property for the object

Chapter 9, *Creating an ASP Middle Tier with ADO*, and Chapter 13, *Working with MSMQ Components*, provide examples of how transaction support works with an ASP component. In this section, you'll have a chance to try out some of the other ObjectContext methods.

To work with ObjectContext, create a new Visual Basic project and name it `asp0702`. Name the generated class `objcont`. To add support for COM+ Services to your component, click on Project → References from the main menu. In the list that opens, find and select the COM+ Services type library, as shown in Figure 7-3.

By attaching a reference to the COM+ Services type library, you can access Object-Context (and other COM+ Services interfaces) through early binding. Early binding is used whenever you define a variable as a specific type of object:

```
Dim objContext As ObjectContext
```

rather than defining the object using the more generic Object:

```
Dim objContext As Object
```

You can read more on early binding in Chapter 3, *ASP Components and COM*.

Once you attach the reference to your component, create a new method, a subroutine named testObjContext that has three parameters passed by reference:

```
Sub testObjContext(vtTrans, vtRole, vtSecurity)
```

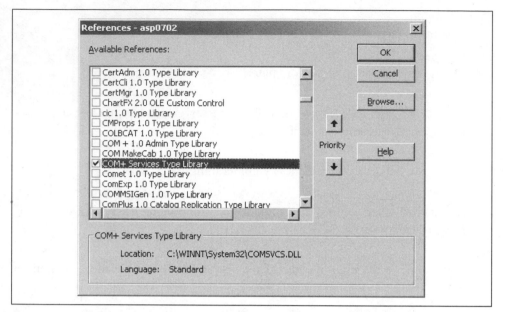

Figure 7-3. Attaching a reference to the COM+ Services type library to your project

Parameters are passed by reference by default, so the `ByRef` modifier isn't necessary. Additionally, parameters are Variants by default, so the data type doesn't need to be specified unless you wish to do so for documentation purposes.

After creating the subroutine header, add the code for the rest of the method, as shown in Example 7-2. In the method, you'll obtain a reference to ObjectContext using the GetObjectContext method. Once you've obtained the object reference, call IsInTransaction to see if the component is contained within a transaction, call IsCallerInRole to see if the user is within a specific role, and call IsSecurityEnabled to see if security is enabled for the component's application.

Example 7-2. Testing the Environment Using ObjectContext

```
Sub testObjContext(vtTrans, vtRole, vtSecurity)

Dim objContext As ObjectContext
Set objContext = GetObjectContext()

' get trans status
vtTrans = objContext.IsInTransaction

' get role status
vtRole = objContext.IsCallerInRole("Developer")

' get security
vtSecurity = objContext.IsSecurityEnabled

End Sub
```

Test your new component by using script such as the following, contained in *asp0702.asp*:

```
<%
Dim obj
Set obj = Server.CreateObject("asp0702.objcont")

Dim blTrans, blRole
obj.testObjContext blTrans, blRole, blSecurity

Set obj = Nothing

' test values
If blTrans Then
    Response.Write "<H3>In Transaction</h3>"
Else
    Response.Write "<H3>Not in Transaction</H3>"
End If

If blRole Then
    Response.Write "<H3>In Role</h3>"
Else
    Response.Write "<H3>Not in Role</H3>"
End If

If blSecurity Then
    Response.Write "<H3>Security Enabled</h3>"
Else
    Response.Write "<H3>Security not enabled</H3>"
End If
%>
```

Accessing the test ASP page should result in messages that the component is not in a transaction, that a user who is a member of the Developer role is accessing it, and that security is not enabled.

To include the component in a transaction, you'll need to add the transaction directive to the ASP page to start a new transaction with the page:

```
<% @ TRANSACTION = required %>
```

Add this to your ASP test page and then access the page again. Now you should see that the component is within a transaction.

ObjectContext returned **True** when you tested for role enrollment even if a person within that role didn't access the component. The reason for this is that IsCallerIn-Role always returns **True** when the component is an in-process component and accessed within a client process. You're accessing the component within the same thread and process as the ASP page, so IsCallerInRole returns **True**. To enforce role-based security, you'll need to add the component to a COM+ application.

Open the Component Services Administrator, and navigate to and open the COM+ Applications folder. Create a new COM+ server application (name it whatever you like), and add `asp0702` as a component in the application. Also, create a new role by right-clicking on the application's Roles folder and selecting New → Role. You'll be asked for the name of the role—give it the name Developer. Next, add users for the role by right clicking on the Users folder contained within the role and selecting New → User. You'll be given a list of users or groups already defined on your system. Select one or more by clicking the Add button to add each user, as shown in Figure 7-4. In the figure, I'm adding the default web user for my system to the Developer role.

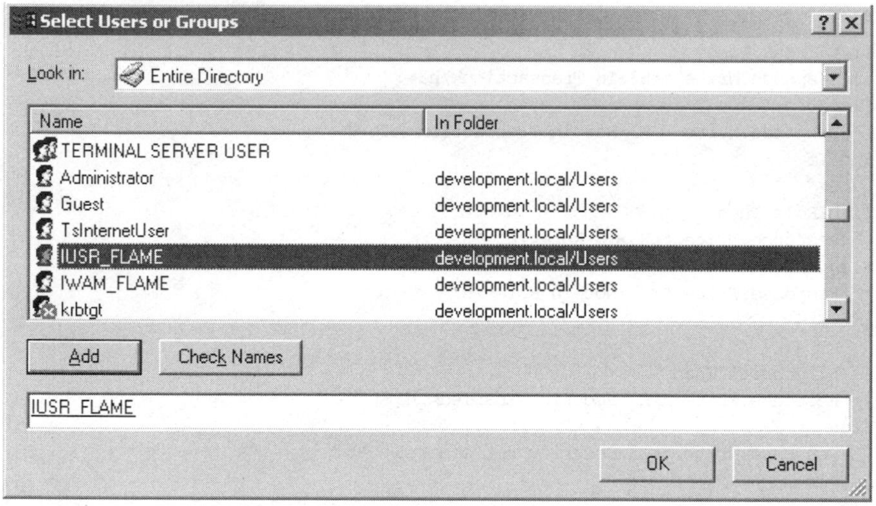

Figure 7-4. Adding the user IUSR_FLAME to the Developer role

To enforce role-based security, access the component properties by right-clicking on the component and selecting Properties from the menu. Switch to the Security tab, check the "Enforce component level access checks" option, and check the box next to the Developer role shown in the bottom of the tab.

> When you create a COM+ application, you can choose whether to run the application as a library or server application. You should pick the Server option in your development environment in order to be able to shut down the application when you want to recompile components. However, when you move your application to test and production, choose the Library option so that your ASP components will run in the same thread as the ASP page.

You'll also need to add security enforcement at the COM+ application level. Access the application's Properties, switch to the Security tab, and check the

"Enforce access checks for this application" option. After making these changes, access the ASP test page again. Now you'll see the following in the web page:

```
In Transaction
In Role
Security Enabled
```

With the current security settings, if you accessed the web page as someone who is not in the Developer role, you would get a security violation error instead.

As I said earlier, ObjectContext can control transactions through the SetAbort and SetComplete method. These methods should always be the last line of code in your component. The SetAbort method call signals that the component is finished and that it didn't succeed in its operation; the SetComplete method also signals that the component method is finished, but this time the method succeeded. The signal that the component method is finished is set in one bit, the done bit; the success of the component is set in another bit. If you want finer control of both bits, you could access a reference to the `IContextState` interface through Get-ObjectContext.

The `IContextState` interface has methods to set and get the flag to deactivate the component when the method returns and to commit or abort the transaction. To set the deactivation for a component, use code similar to the following:

```
Dim iCntxtSt As IContextState
Set iCntxtSt = GetObjectContext()
iCntxtSt.SetDeactivateOnReturn = True
```

When the component method finishes, the done bit is set to **True** and the component can be deactivated. To abort a transaction you could use:

```
iCntxtSt.SetMyTransactionVote (TxAbort)
```

To commit the transaction, use:

```
iCntxtSt.SetMyTransactionVote (TxCommit)
```

If you try to set the done bit to **True**, but the component is not set up with support for JIT, you'll get an error. The next section demonstrates how to add JIT support for your component and how to work with ObjectControl.

To recompile a component added to a COM+ application defined as a Server application, right-click on the application name and select Shut Down from the context menu. To recompile a component that's part of a library-based COM+ application, you'll need to unload the ASP application from the IIS Management Console.

The IObjectControl Interface and JIT

COM+ can control the lifetime of an object based on how the done bit is set when you return from each component's method. If the done bit is set, COM+ can deactivate the component; otherwise, COM+ keeps the component active within the ASP page. With JIT, when the component is deactivated, it isn't marked for removal from memory. Instead, it remains in a deactivated state until it is referenced again. Additionally, when an application such as an ASP application creates an instance of the component, the component isn't actually created until it's used. Both of these actions combined improve the overall performance of the application by minimizing how long an application holds a live reference to the component. The shorter this time, the less memory used by the application.

To take advantage of JIT activation, your component needs to be installed into a COM+ application. Once installed, access the component's Properties dialog, switch to the Activation tab and make sure the Enable Just-In-Time Activation option is checked—the JIT option is checked by default, and cannot be unchecked when transaction support is added.

Normally, global information for a component is set in the Initialize event for the component, but this won't work with a component whose lifetime is being managed with JIT activation. However, you can capture the JIT Activate and Deactivate events by implementing `IObjectControl` within your component. `IObjectControl` exposes three methods: Activate, when your component is activated; Deactivate, when your component is deactivated; and CanBePooled, called when your component is deactivated, to see if it can be pooled.

Beginning with IIS 5.0 in Windows 2000, you can use the Class_Initialize event to access ObjectContext or create global objects for your component, and Class_Terminate for cleanup. These events are now within the COM+ context processing. However, use Activate and Deactivate to catch the JIT events.

To see how JIT and ObjectControl work together, create another Visual Basic project and name it `asp0703`. Name the class file that's generated `jit`. You'll be accessing COM+ Services with this component, so attach the COM+ Services type library to the project. Additionally, you'll be using the ASP built-in Response object, so you'll need to attach a reference to the Microsoft Active Server Pages object library to the project.

To implement an interface within a component, you'll use the **Implements** statement followed by the name of the interface. To implement ObjectControl, add this line to your component class:

```
Implements ObjectControl
```

You'll also have to add the three ObjectControl methods: Activate, Deactivate, and CanBePooled, as shown in Example 7-3. We'll want to provide feedback when the Activate and Deactivate methods are called, so create an instance of the Response object and use it to write out a message in the Activate and Deactivate methods. You'll see the reason why when we start testing the new component.

Finally, as shown in Example 7-3, create another method named sayHello but this time with one String parameter. You'll use the Response object to write out the message rather than returning it to the client script.

Example 7-3. Component That Implements ObjectControl for JIT Processing

```
Implements ObjectControl
Dim objResponse As Response

Private Sub ObjectControl_Activate()
  Set objResponse = GetObjectContext().Item("Response")
  objResponse.Write "<h3>Activated</h3>"
End Sub

Private Sub ObjectControl_Deactivate()
  objResponse.Write "<h3>Deactivated</h3>"
  Set objResponse = Nothing
End Sub

Private Function ObjectControl_CanBePooled() As Boolean
    ObjectControl_CanBePooled = False
End Function

Sub sayHello(ByVal strName As String)
  objResponse.Write "Hello " & strName
End Sub
```

To test the component, you'll need to install it into the COM+ application you created earlier. Access its properties and make sure that the Enable Just-In-Time Activation option is selected. Also make sure that the Developer role is checked in the Security tab. The script that tests the component writes messages to a web page after the component is created, after the method is called, and after setting the component to **Nothing** (releasing it from the application):

```
Dim obj
Set obj = Server.CreateObject("asp0703.jit")

Response.Write "<p>Before call to message, after creating object</p>"

obj.sayHello "World!"

Response.Write "<p>After call to message</p>"
```

```
Set obj = Nothing

Response.Write "<p>After setting object to nothing</p>"
```

The results of accessing the ASP test page, *asp0703.asp*, is:

```
Before call to message, after creating object
Activated
Hello World!
After call to message
Deactivated
After setting object to nothing
```

The messages show that the component is actually activated only when the component's method is called, not when the object is first created. Additionally, the
messages show that the component is deactivated when the object is set to
Nothing, not when the component method is finished. The reason is that there
was no indication to COM+ to deactivate the component.

To indicate to COM+ that the component method is finished, you could create an
instance of ObjectContext or **IContextState** and use either of these interfaces to
signal that the component is done, as the code fragments earlier show. Alternatively, you can enable Auto-Done for the component's externally accessible
method by using Component Services to open the reference to the component
until all of its methods are shown. Right click on the sayHello component DLL and
access its Properties dialog. In the General tab, check the "Automatically deactivate this object when this method returns" option.

By enabling support for Auto-Done, the done bit is set for the method as soon as
it returns. After checking the option, try the ASP test page again. This time, the
results are:

```
Before call to message, after creating object
Activated
Hello World!
Deactivated
After call to message
After setting object to nothing
```

Now, the Deactivate method is called as soon as the component's method returns
control to the ASP script.

The use of transactions and JIT are just two of the services provided by COM+ services, but they are similar to those provided by MTS in Windows NT. If you've
developed ASP components in Windows NT, the next section details how you can
port your MTS components to a COM+ environment.

One other COM+ service, pooling, is not supported with Visual Basic 6.0. The reason is that poolable components must support either the both-threaded or the neutral-apartment threading model. Neither of these are supported in VB 6.0.

Converting MTS Components for Use with COM+

If you've worked with ASP components in Windows NT, you might be curious how they'll migrate to Windows 2000. Actually, they should migrate relatively easily.

In Windows NT, you attached a reference to the Microsoft Transaction Server (MTS) library to access ObjectContext and the ASP built-in objects. You'll find that the MTS services have been subsumed into COM+. Best of all, your component is automatically ported into COM+ because the CLSID for COM+ Services is the same one used with MTS. Open an older NT-based Visual Basic component in Windows 2000, and you'll see that the MTS type library has been replaced by COM+ Services in the project references.

Your use of ObjectContext for transaction and ASP support remains the same. You have new options now, such as `IContextState`, which we just discussed, but ObjectContext is still supported. You can still use ObjectContext to access the ASP built-in objects, but you can also access them through another new interface, `IObjectContextInfo`. Checking out this interface, you'll see it has many (but not all) of the methods and properties of ObjectContext. You create an instance of it using GetObjectContext as you would ObjectContext.

Between them, `IContextState` and `IObjectContextInfo` basically provide all of the same functionality as ObjectContext, and more. Microsoft hasn't officially said that they are replacing Object-Context, but they do seem to be heading this way.

In COM+, CoGetObjectContext has replaced GetObjectContext. However, Get-ObjectContext is a wrapper for this new function, so you can continue to use it. In fact, you have to continue using it, since CoGetObjectContext is not available in Visual Basic.

In Windows NT, you created an object using the ASP Server's CreateObject method or the CreateInstance method in ObjectContext. You didn't use the VBA

CreateObject function directly, since this created the object outside of the current object's context and transaction. In Windows 2000, you can now use *CreateObject* directly to create an instance of an object. In fact, there could be performance gains using this function, as you'll see in the "Performance Issues" section at the end of the chapter. If you used CreateInstance, you won't have to remove this from your code; the ObjectContext CreateInstance method and the *CreateObject* function have exactly the same results in Windows 2000.

Earlier, in Example 7-3, you used the ASP Response object to write out content to the web page. The next section looks at using the ASP built-in objects from within Visual Basic components.

Accessing the ASP Built-in Objects

There are several built-in ASP objects you can use to communicate directly with the environment and with the web page client. Among these are the Application and Session objects, used to store application- or session-specific information, respectively; the Response object, to communicate to the client; the Request object, to get information from the client and the environment; and the Server object, to handle encoding or to create objects. There is also the ASPError object, but this is used primarily within ASP script (to provide custom error handling) and isn't covered in this chapter.

This section takes a look at accessing the ASP objects using ObjectContext and demonstrates how to use each of the objects. You can also get a detailed list of object properties, methods, and collections in Appendix A, *ASP Built-in Object Quick Reference*.

The Application Object Interface

This section provides an overview of the Application object, including demonstrations of some of its methods and properties.

An ASP application begins when the first ASP page for the application is accessed after the web server is started and continues until the web server is shut down or the application times out after the last person to reference the application logs out. The built-in ASP Application object can be used to access objects and values that are defined as application-level objects.

An application-level element can be added to the Application object—specifically the Application object's StaticObjects collection—by using an <OBJECT> tag within the *global.asa* file, by using script, or from within a component. Each ASP application has one *global.asa* file, located in the root directory of the application, which contains definitions for both application- and session-level objects. The following

Separating the Business from the Presentation

Should you use the ASP built-in objects from ASP components? The answer depends on the purpose of the component.

Many of the components in this book use these objects, primarily the Request and Response objects. However, the main reason for this is to include as much of the ASP processing within the component as possible for demonstration purposes. You'll want to include the ASP objects in your components depending on the purpose of the component and whether the component must work in environments other than ASP.

For instance, if you're creating a business component to access a database and perform some form of data update or query, you'll want to restrict the use of the ASP built-in objects, or not use them at all. By limiting the use of these objects, your business object can be easily moved to other server-based environments.

Additionally, you can modify either the business processing or the presentation without impacting on the other. If you decide to have your ASP application output XML instead of HTML, you can make this change without having to change the business component. If your business processing or data access changes, this won't impact your presentation.

However, an advantage of using the ASP objects within your components, especially for database access, is that you can access form values directly from the Request object and not have to create a method with several parameters (or use an array), pull the values from the Request object in your script, and pass them to the component method.

If your components are part of the presentation layer—such as reusable components whose purpose is to generate specific blocks of HTML or XML—then use the built-in ASP objects within the components.

When you're developing a business component, you can temporarily use the ASP built-in objects to assist in the development process. You can then remove them when the business process works to your satisfaction and you're ready to integrate the component into the application environment.

is an example of an entry within *global.asa* which adds a reference to a component to the Application object's StaticObjects collection is:

```
<OBJECT RUNAT=Server SCOPE=Application ID=MyInfo
    ProgID = "testmts.mtstest">
</OBJECT>
```

The object defined in the *global.asa* file can then be accessed from the Application object using the StaticObjects collection:

```
' get objects
Set objContext = GetObjectContext()
Set objApplication = objContext("Application")

' get object from StaticObjects
Set someObj = objApplication.StaticObjects("MyInfo")
```

A COM object stored in the Application object's StaticObjects collection must be both-threaded or neutral-apartment-threaded, or an error occurs.

 Due to memory constraints, avoid adding objects to either the Application or Session objects. Use scalar values if possible.

You can alter the *global.asa* file by removing the definition of an object that uses the <OBJECT> tag and replacing it with a scripting block that traps the Application start event and assigns the object to the Application object, as shown in the following code block:

```
<SCRIPT LANGUAGE=VBScript RUNAT=Server>
' set up application-level constants and variables
Sub Application_OnStart
  Dim value
  value = "some value"
  Application("value") = value
End Sub
</SCRIPT>
```

This scripting block assigns the scalar value to the Application object's Contents collection, rather than the StaticObjects collection. To access the new application-level object, access the object by name from the Contents collection:

```
' get objects
Set objContext = GetObjectContext()
Set objApplication = objContext("Application")

' get object from Contents
value = objApplication.Contents("value")
```

The difference between these last two code blocks is that the first accesses the stored value through the Application object's StaticObjects collection, the second through the Contents collection. You can also access a value from either the StaticObjects or the Contents collection directly from the Application object:

```
Set applApplicationObject = objApplication("MyInfo")
```

This is actually a shorthand form of accessing an application-level variable from the Value collection, which combines the Contents and StaticObjects collections:

```
objApplication.Value("intCounter")
```

This shorthand syntax works because Value is the default property of the Application object.

An application-level variable can be accessed and updated using the Application object. For instance, within the *global.asa* file, a script block can be created that is executed in response to the Application object's OnStart event. Within this block, a variable can be added to the Application object's Contents collection. Then, the variable's value can be accessed within script or by a component.

To demonstrate this, adding the following script block to the *global.asa* file creates an application-level variable called *intCounter*:

```
<SCRIPT LANGUAGE=VBScript RUNAT=Server>
' set up application-level constants and variables
Sub Application_OnStart
  Application("intCounter") = 0
End Sub
</SCRIPT>
```

The variable *intCounter* can be accessed within script, but it can also be accessed from within an ASP component using the Application object and accessing the value from the Contents collection.

To try this yourself, create a new Visual Basic project and name it **asp0704**. Name the generated class file **AppObj**. In the component, attach both the COM+ Services and the Microsoft Active Server Pages type libraries.

Create a method called OnAccessValue and add the code shown in Example 7-4 to it. In this code, a reference to ObjectContext is created and used to obtain references to both the Application and the Response objects. The counter is accessed from the Application object's Contents collection, incremented, and then written back to the collection. The newly incremented value is then displayed.

Example 7-4. ASP Component That Accesses and Increments a Value from the Application Contents Collection

```
Public Sub OnAccessValue()
  Dim intCounter As Integer
  Dim applicationObj As Application
  Dim rspnseObj As Response

  ' access built-in objects
  Dim objContext As ObjectContext
  Set objContext = GetObjectContext()
  Set rspnseObj = objContext("Response")
  Set applicationObj = objContext("Application")
```

Example 7-4. ASP Component That Accesses and Increments a Value from the Application Contents Collection (continued)

```
' access counter and change value
applicationObj.Lock
intCounter = applicationObj.Contents("intCounter")
intCounter = intCounter + 1
applicationObj("intCounter") = intCounter
applicationObj.Unlock

' print out new value
rspnseObj.Write (CStr(intCounter))

' clean up
Set applicationObj = Nothing
Set rspnseObj = Nothing
Set objContext = Nothing

End Sub
```

Note that this code also uses the Application object's Lock and UnLock methods to prevent any changes to the Application object until the object is unlocked. This prevents multiple simultaneous accesses and modifications to the counter object, which could result in unwanted side effects and corrupted data.

Test the component using the following script, found in *asp0704.asp*:

```
<%
Dim obj
Set obj = Server.CreateObject("asp0704.AppObj")

obj.OnAccessValue
%>
```

To summarize, the Application object has three collections (the StaticObject, Contents, and Value collections) and two methods (Lock and UnLock).

The Application object maintains references to elements at the application level, but the Session object maintains references to elements for each user session. The Session object is covered next.

The Session Object Interface

The Session object maintains references to elements for each user session. An ASP session begins when a user accesses an ASP application page for the first time since opening a browser or logging unto the application and continues until the user exits the application (if the application provides this functionality), closes the browser, or times out.

Many of the Session properties—such as CodePage and LCID—are used specifically for internationalization. Others have to do with the Session itself, such as its timeout value and the session identifier used to track the user throughout the current session. In fact, a limitation of the Session object is that the SessionID is actually stored as a cookie, which requires that the client browser must support the use of Netscape-style cookies.

As with the Application object, objects and values can be added to the Session object and accessed throughout all application pages. You can access a value directly from the Session object, or you can enumerate or retrieve a specific value directly from the Contents or StaticObjects collections. To demonstrate this, add a new class to `asp0704` by right-clicking in the Project window and selecting Add → Class Module from the context menu. In the Add Class Module dialog, select the Class Module option. Name the new class `SessnObj`.

Unlike the Application object, you can assign apartment-threaded objects to the Session object's collections, but to do so ties the Session object down to a specific thread—which means that client requests can be processed only by a specific thread, rather than whatever thread is next available. This will severely impact performance.

In the class, add a method called showContents, which is shown in Example 7-5. This method enumerates through the Contents collection, tests to make sure the value being accessed is a string, and, if it is, displays it.

Example 7-5. Enumerating Through the Contents Collection

```
Sub showContents()

Dim objContext As ObjectContext
Dim sesnObj As Session
Dim rspnseObj As Response

' access built-in objects
Set objContext = GetObjectContext()
Set rspnseObj = objContext("Response")
Set sesnObj = objContext("Session")

' enumerate through collection
' print out strings
Dim itm
For Each itm In sesnObj.Contents
    If VarType(itm) = vbString Then
        rspnseObj.Write itm
        rspnseObj.Write "<br>"
    End If
Next

    ' clean up
    Set sesnObj = Nothing
    Set rspnseObj = Nothing
```

Example 7-5. Enumerating Through the Contents Collection (continued)

```
  Set objContext = Nothing

End Sub
```

To test the component, the following ASP script, named *asp0705.asp*, creates five entries in the Contents collection and then calls the components method:

```
<%
Dim obj
Set obj = Server.CreateObject("asp0704.SessnObj")

Session("one") = 1
Session("two") = 2
Session("three") = 3
Session("four") = 4
Session("five") = 5

obj.showContents
%>
```

The Session object can actually be abandoned and the resources it contains released. As an example, the following code abandons the Session object and then accesses the object to invoke the ResponseTest method objWriteHeader:

```
  Set sessnObject = objContext("Session")
  sessnObject.Abandon
  value = sessnObject.Value("value")
```

When the Abandon method is called, the Session object is queued for destruction, but only after the current script is finished. Since the component is invoked within the script, the component method is finished before the object is destroyed.

In addition to abandoning the Session object, a timeout can be set for the session to ensure that a session is not left idle for too long. Maintaining an open session uses server resources, and using a timeout prevents a user from logging onto a session and then leaving his computer and the session running. Using timers can also prevent a breach of security for the session, preventing someone else from accessing the client computer when the user is not present, in turn accessing session information that may be confidential. The timeout is set through the TimeOut property, as follows:

```
  sessnObject.Timeout = 20        ' 20 minute timeout
```

Once the session has timed out, any of the objects contained within the Session object are destroyed. Accessing any of the members of a Session object results in an error, an event that component developers should plan for when creating components that depend on Session variables and constants.

Session information can be used to internationalize the application. A user may select an option to view the ASP application using Russian, and the Session object's LCID and CodePage properties reflect the types of strings used in the application and the type of character set used for the ASP pages, respectively. The LCID property is used to identify specific information, such as how dates and times are formatted, how strings are sorted, and other information. The CodePage property determines how symbols map to a character set. For example, to set the Russian codepage you would do this:

```
sessnObject.CodePage = 866
```

Of course, the client would have to be set up to use the specific CodePage and LCID values; information on this can be found in the operating system help for Windows 2000.

 The Session object also contains a reference to the Session identifier, SessionID, which should never be used directly by the component developer as a database or any other identifier. Its only purpose is to serve as a session identifier between the client browser and the web server application.

The Request Object Interface

The Request object contains information about the user request to the web server, including general browser and client information, as well as specific query string and form data. Of the ASP objects, the Request object has the most collections:

ClientCertificate collection
> Used to retrieve client certificate information

Cookies collection
> Used to retrieve cookie information

Form collection
> Used to retrieve form element data

QueryString collection
> Used to retrieve query string data

ServerVariables collection
> Used to access server and client environment information

Unlike the Session and Application objects, the Request object has a short lifetime. A specific instance of a Request object is valid from the time a web page request is submitted until a response is made from the server back to the browser. Based on this, component developers should store information that should be persisted beyond a specific page request into component-level variables.

As stated, the Form and QueryString collections contain information passed from a web page to the application, usually from an HTML form or by concatenating the information to the URL invoking the ASP application. Which collection is used depends on how the data is sent.

The Form collection contains all values from a form that has been submitted using the POST method. The QueryString collection contains all values from a form that has been submitted using the default GET form posting method or by appending values directly onto the URL that invokes the ASP application. One characteristic of this latter type of data transmittal is that you can actually see the data appended as key-value pairs to the URL.

Regardless of which approach is used and which collection is accessed, the data is transmitted in key-value pairs. The Request information contained within the Form and QueryString collections can be accessed by name or by an index number representing the value's location within the collection.

To demonstrate accessing the Form collection, add a new class to asp0704 and name it ReqObj. Create a method called processForm that accesses the Form collection and lists each name-value pair contained within the form. The code for your new method can be found in Example 7-6.

Example 7-6. Process Form Elements

```
' write out Request Form Value
Public Sub processForm()
  Dim objContext As ObjectContext
  Dim rqstObject As Request
  Dim rspnseObject As Response
  Dim x As Variant

  ' access the built-in components
  Set objContext = GetObjectContext
  Set rqstObject = objContext.Item("Request")
  Set rspnseObject = objContext("Response")

  ' for each collection member, print out name
  ' and value
  For Each x In rqstObject.Form
     rspnseObject.Write (x + "=" + rqstObject.Form(x))
     rspnseObject.Write ("<br>")
  Next

  ' clean up
  Set rqstObject = Nothing
  Set rspnseObject = Nothing
  Set objContext = Nothing

End Sub
```

To test the component, you'll need to create two ASP pages. The first, *asp0706.asp*, contains a form with input text elements and a button to submit the form:

```
<FORM action="asp0707.asp" method=post>
<INPUT type="text" name="field1">
<INPUT type="text" name="field2">
<INPUT type="text" name="field3">
<INPUT type="submit">
</FORM>
```

After the data elements have values added and the form is submitted, a second ASP page, *asp0707.asp*, processes the form results:

```
<%
Dim obj
Set obj = Server.CreateObject("asp0704.ReqObj")

obj.processForm
%>
```

The form posting method is POST rather than the default of GET. Using the POST method results in the field values being added to the Form collection rather than the QueryString collection, as stated earlier.

The values could also have been submitted as attachments to the URL, using syntax similar to the following:

```
<a href="test.asp?test=one&test2=two&test3=three">Test</a>
```

Regardless of which collection is accessed, the approach is the same as that just demonstrated.

Another technique to access the posted data is to use the BinaryRead method, which takes a single parameter, *count*, that represents the number of bytes of the client's posted data to be read, and returns the posted information as raw data assigned to a SafeArray.

 What is a SafeArray? It is a structure that contains the array entries, but also contains information about the array, such as the number of dimensions and bounds for the dimensions.

When BinaryRead returns, *count* is updated to reflect the number of bytes actually read. Note, though, that using this method precludes the use of the Form collection, and accessing the Form collection precludes the use of BinaryRead. If using this method, the TotalBytes method provides the size of the data in bytes. An example of using the BinaryRead function is shown in the following code:

```
Dim binData As Variant
Dim varCount As Variant
```

```
varCount = rqstObject.TotalBytes
binData = rqstObject.BinaryRead(varCount)
```

The BinaryRead method can be used to access non-text-based data, to process the data using some other process or technique, or even to store the raw data for later access.

 When searching through all collections of the Request object using an implicit search, such as **objRequest('somevalue')**, if the Form collection is used within the search, BinaryRead will no longer function and vice versa.

The Request object also maintains collections for client certificate fields and for any cookie information sent with the request. The client certificate properties are defined as key fields; these are:

Certificate
> The complete certificate as a binary stream

Flags
> The certificate's flags

Issuer
> The certificate's issuer

SerialNumber
> The certificate's serial number

Subject
> The certificate's subject

ValidFrom
> The valid beginning date for the certificate

ValidUntil
> The valid ending date for the certificate

To access a client certificate value, use the key name to retrieve the value from the ClientCertificate collection, as shown in the following code fragment:

```
subj = rqstObject.ClientCertificate("Subject")
```

Test to see if the certificate values are present using the *IsEmpty* function.

To find out about the environment, you can access the ServerVariables collection and display its name-value pairs. Among the information you'll see is the raw HTTP request, path information, server information, encodings, the client browser, the IP of the URL, and other information.

To find out this information about your own environment, add a second method to `asp0704.RqstObj` named showEnvVariables. It enumerates through the Server-Variables collection and lists each name-value pair, as shown in Example 7-7.

Example 7-7. Enumerating Through the ServerVariables Collection and Printing the Values

```
Sub showEnvVariables()
Dim objContext As ObjectContext
Dim rqstObject As Request
Dim rspnseObject As Response
Dim x As Variant

Set objContext = GetObjectContext()
Set rspnseObject = objContext("Response")
Set rqstObject = objContext("Request")

' for each collection member, print out name
' and value
For Each x In rqstObject.ServerVariables
  rspnseObject.Write x & " = " & rqstObject.ServerVariables(x)
  rspnseObject.Write "<br>"
Next

' clean up
Set rqstObject = Nothing
Set rspnseObject = Nothing
Set objContext = Nothing

End Sub
```

Test the page using the following script, *asp0708.asp*:

```
<%
Dim obj
Set obj = Server.CreateObject("asp0704.ReqObj")

obj.showEnvVariables
%>
```

Figure 7-5 shows some of the results from running this page in my environment.

The Cookies collection contains individual cookies sent with the request. Each cookie can be a discrete bit of data or can itself contain a hierarchy of cookie information, stored by keys, and known as a *cookie dictionary*. The HasKeys method is used to determine if the cookie information is a single unit (its value is **False**) or a cookie dictionary (its value is **True**).

Cookies are stored on the client and are referenced by the URL of the web page matching the page being accessed in the current request. The browser searches the list of cookies for a matching URL and, if found, returns all cookie name-value pairs as part of the request. These name-value pairs are then stored in the Request object. If there is a cookie reference at *http://www.somecompany.com/first/* and a

```
Developing ASP Components - Microsoft Internet Explorer                          _ □ ×

File   Edit   View   Favorites   Tools   Help

← Back  →    ⊗ ⊕ ⌂    Search   Favorites   History    🖺 🖨 🔟 · 📄 💬

Address  🗐 http://localhost/chap7/asp0708.asp                                    ▼  ∂ Go

REMOTE_HOST = 127.0.0.1
REMOTE_USER =
REQUEST_METHOD = GET
SCRIPT_NAME = /chap7/asp0708.asp
SERVER_NAME = localhost
SERVER_PORT = 80
SERVER_PORT_SECURE = 0
SERVER_PROTOCOL = HTTP/1.1
SERVER_SOFTWARE = Microsoft-IIS/5.0
URL = /chap7/asp0708.asp
HTTP_ACCEPT = */*
HTTP_ACCEPT_LANGUAGE = en-us
HTTP_CONNECTION = Keep-Alive
HTTP_HOST = localhost
HTTP_USER_AGENT = Mozilla/4.0 (compatible; MSIE 5.5; Windows NT 5.0)
HTTP_COOKIE = ASPSESSIONIDQQQQQARK=GCDNONIAGBHLKOCBCGDOGGJJ;
ASPSESSIONIDGQQGQBTC=EDHNDPPAKIMPCGNOHHAHEKGG;
ASPSESSIONIDQQGQQASC=CHGFAEABEFJLLHKAFCDDLMGI
HTTP_ACCEPT_ENCODING = gzip, deflate

🗐 Done                                                    🖳 Local intranet
```

Figure 7-5. Results of accessing and printing out ServerVariables collection items

cookie reference for the relative URL (relative to the main web page) of */first*, the browser returns the cookies that match the lowest level URL, which would be the one at */first/*.

 Complete documentation on cookies can be found at Netscape's site (*http://developer.netscape.com/library/documentation/communicator/ jsguide4/index.htm*).

The Request object contains references to cookies that have already been created. The Response object can (among other things) actually set the values of cookies; it is discussed next.

The Response Object Interface

The Response object has been used throughout this chapter to write output to the web page; it controls the output returned to the browser after a request. Of all the built-in objects, the Response object has the most methods and properties:

AddHeader method
    Adds an HTTP header to the response.

AppendToLog method

Appends a string to the web server log.

BinaryWrite method

Writes the content as raw data without any character conversion.

Buffer property

Defines whether page output is buffered.

CacheControl property

Indicates whether proxy servers can cache output.

Charset property

Appends the character set name to the content type header.

Clear method

Erases buffered output.

ContentType property

Specifies the type of HTTP content; its default is `text/html`.

Cookies collection

The cookies sent with the response.

End method

Forces ASP to stop processing and return any buffered output.

Expires property

The time until the response expires.

ExpiresAbsolute property

The absolute date and time when the response expires.

Flush method

Sends buffered output immediately.

IsClientConnected property

Indicates whether the client is still connected.

PICS property

The PICS rating.

Redirect method

Sends a 302 redirect status to the browser.

Status property

The HTTP status line.

Write method

Writes output with character conversion to the client browser.

The Write method has been used throughout this chapter to output results to a web page. However, the Response object's BinaryWrite method could also have been used to write output without any character conversion.

Buffering can be controlled from within a component. One limitation, though, is that the buffering must be turned on before any other output is sent to the page. Based on this, buffering is usually controlled through scripting by including the following as the first line in an ASP file:

```
<% Response.Buffer = True %>
```

Beginning with IIS 5.0, buffering is now turned on by default. When buffering is enabled, the Response object's End method stops any further buffering and forces an output of the buffer. The Clear method clears the buffer, and the Flush method forces an output of the buffer.

Should buffering be controlled from within an ASP component? Buffering can control whether any other output is sent to an ASP page or whether the output is cleared. The buffering methods and properties should be used sparingly within a component, and their use should be communicated to component users. A better approach is to provide error messages and return values and let the ASP application developer control buffering from the page.

The ContentType property can be used to specify the type of content being returned to the client. One use of this property by a component is to determine whether a person wants to see a web page as it is normally displayed within a browser, or if she wants to see the actual HTML source. The decision would be sent as a parameter to the component method:

```
' write content type
If intDisplayFlag = 1 Then
  rspnseObject.ContentType = "text/HTML"
Else
  rspnseObject.ContentType = "text/plain"
End If
```

The ContentType property can also be used with binary content stored in databases to retrieve the content and display it on the browser in a meaningful format, such as **image/JPEG** for a JPEG image.

Most browsers support page caching in some manner, which means that the next time the page is accessed, the page is pulled from the client cache, not the server, if the server page has not changed. This can cut down on download times as well as decrease the load on the web server. However, if an ASP component makes regular queries to a database and updates a page's contents at a specified interval, the component developer can set the page cache to expire in that same interval to ensure that the most current page is shown to the reader. The Response object has two properties that control page cache expiration: Expires, which sets the expiration to a specific number of minutes, and ExpiresAbsolute, which sets the expiration to a specific date and time.

You can add an absolute expiration for an ASP page from within a component by using a line similar to the following:

```
rspnseObject.ExpiresAbsolute = #12/1/2000 11:00:15 AM#
```

This tells the browser to add an expiration date of December 1, 2000, at a little after eleven in the morning, to the page.

In addition to controlling the cache expiration date for a page, the Response object can set or create a cookie. For example, the following code block adds a cookie named **temp** that has two key values, **one** and **two**:

```
rspnseObject.Cookies("temp")("one") = "one"
rspnseObject.Cookies("temp")("two") = "two"
rspnseObject.Cookies("temp").Expires = #5/1/98#
```

The same string is used for both the key name and key value. In addition, an expiration date is given for the cookie. If a cookie with the name **temp** did not exist, it would be created. Otherwise, a new value and expiration date is assigned to the cookie. Accessing this component from an ASP page displayed by Netscape Navigator generates the following line in Navigator's cookies file, *cookies.txt*:

```
localhostFALSE/FALSE893995200tempTWO=two&ONE=one
```

If no date is used, the cookie is assumed to expire at the end of the session.

 If you try setting a cookie using the Response object and then can't see the cookie in Netscape's *cookies.txt* file, note that the cookie is not actually written until the browser is closed. The cookie is actually maintained in memory until some event forces an output to persist the information.

The AppendToLog method is a great way to record information about the use of an ASP component. One use of this method is to record information about an error if one occurs in the component. Based on this approach, an error handler for a component could have the following code:

```
ErrorHandler:
' write out error to log
rspnseObject.AppendToLog "Error in rspnseTest: " + CStr(Err.Number) + _
                  " " + Err.Description
```

When an error occurs within the component, a line containing the error number and error description is written to the server log.

Another Response object method is AddHeader, which adds to an HTTP header and should be used with caution. This method could be used to ask the client (the browser) to provide additional authentication for the request, but it could also result in the page being undeliverable if the header is malformed as a result of using the AddHeader method. As with other functions that generate header output, the method call must occur before any other page contents are generated, including the opening <HTML> tag.

The Redirect method sends a status code of 302 with the HTTP response and redirects the browser to another specified URL. This is particularly helpful to direct the browser based on information extracted from headers accompanying the browser request, such as the name and version of the browser, and it can be used to prevent older browsers from accessing web pages created with newer technologies.

The Response object's IsClientConnected checks to see if the client is still connected. This can be used to make sure the client is still connected before performing any "expensive" operation, such as running a process-intensive calculation or accessing a database. Don't put the server through work no one will be receiving.

The Server Object Interface

The built-in Server object is used to create instances of components, as demonstrated throughout the test scripts in this chapter. In addition, it has methods that can perform HTML and URL encoding, as well as map a logical location to a physical location. Beginning with IIS 5.0, the object also has the Transfer method, which transfers execution to a different web page but still maintains state information, including any form or query string information, from the original page.

The Server encoding methods provide ways to convert a string for passing as part of an URL or for displaying as part of an HTML page. The URLEncode method uses URL encoding on the string; this does things such as redefining a space as a plus sign (+). The HTMLEncode method uses HTML encoding on the string passed to it; this redefines angle brackets such as the left angle bracket (<) into an HTML-safe string (<), which allows the actual display of the value. The URLPathEncode method uses URL path encoding to convert characters, unlike the URLEncode method, which is primarily used for converting a query string. The MapPath method maps the logical path of the ASP page to its physical location in the filesystem.

To try out the encoding methods, add a new class to `asp0704` and name it `ServObj`. In the class, create a method named encodeStrings that has three input String parameters. These parameters are used in calls to the encoding methods, and the results are printed out. Add the code in Example 7-8 to your component.

Example 7-8. Using the Server Encoding Methods to Encode Strings

```
Sub encodeStrings(ByVal strHTML As String, _
                  ByVal strURL As String, _
                  ByVal strPath As String)

Dim objContext As ObjectContext
Dim srvrObject As Server
Dim rspnseObject As Response

' create objects
Set objContext = GetObjectContext()
Set srvrObject = objContext("Server")
Set rspnseObject = objContext("Response")

rspnseObject.Write srvrObject.HTMLEncode(strHTML) & "<br>"
rspnseObject.Write srvrObject.URLEncode(strURL) & "<br>"
rspnseObject.Write srvrObject.MapPath(strPath) & "<br>"

'clean up
Set rspnseObject = Nothing
Set srvrObject = Nothing
Set objContext = Nothing

End Sub
```

Test the page by passing in three strings to use with each of the encoding methods, as shown in the following ASP page, *asp0709.asp*:

```
<%
Dim obj
Set obj = Server.CreateObject("asp0704.ServObj")

Dim strHTML, strURL, strMap
strHTML = "<H1>This is a test</H1>"
strURL = "% this is a test % ++"
strMap = "/test/test2/"

obj.encodeStrings strHTML, strURL, strMap
%>
```

The new Transfer method can be used to send a different page to the client based on some decision. Best of all, this method also preserves the existing state, including transactions, cookies, and query string or form information, so that this information is available with the new page. Additionally, unlike the Response Redirect method, the new page is loaded without a round-trip to the client. For example:

```
Server.Transfer "asp0708.asp"
```

transfers control from the current page to *asp0708.asp*.

You should not use Response.Redirect when transferring page control but should instead use the new Server.Transfer method.

The only Server property is ScriptTimeout, which can be set to the number of seconds the script containing the component can run before the script times out. This is primarily used to cancel processing that is taking too long.

Error Handling

The primary purpose of formal error handling using techniques such as raising errors is to prevent ASP applications from having fatal errors and, if errors occur, to provide information that can be used to prevent or fix the error.

You and I *know* that we never create bugs, and errors can *never* occur with any code we create, but the powers that be need reassurance to that effect, so this section mentions how to provide error handling for the ASP component.

Handling errors within the component follows standard Visual Basic practices of trapping errors that are raised (also known as *exception handling*) or using inline techniques to test return values for errors. The same two techniques can be used to return error information to the clients that access the component object's methods. As a good general practice, the technique of raising an error is preferred, especially since returning error information as a result of a function call means that the function result now has to be created as a parameter passed by reference.

 Microsoft also now provides exception handling for JavaScript, based on the ECMAScript third edition inclusion of `try...catch` exception handling. Chapter 6, *ASP Interaction: Scripting and ASP Components*, covers error handling within VBScript, JScript, and PerlScript.

Raising errors uses an error data structure, Err, with members such as Number, Source, and Description. The error numbers and descriptive text are created by the component developer(s), and the error numbers are communicated to the users who will use the components within ASP pages. Usually, error-handling codes are included with whatever documentation is included with the component.

For component-class-to-Visual-Basic-application communication, the base for all error numbers is a Public constant. This constant is called **vbObjectError**, and it returns the correct error number to the class that traps the error, as shown in the following:

```
Err.Raise Number:=MY_ERROR + vbObjectError, _
        Description:="custom error"
```

The code to provide the error handling for the component can be similar to this:

```
Option Explicit

Const MY_ERROR = 1
```

```
...

Err.Raise Number:=MY_ERROR + vbObjectError, "custom error"
End Function
```

In the ASP page, this particular error can be trapped, and an error message displayed, as shown in the following VBScript code:

```
Const MY_ERROR = 1

strng = tmp.functionCall()
If Err.Number = INVALID_BROWSER + vbObjectError  Then
   Response.write("//Error Number: " & Err.Number)
   Response.write("; Error Source: " & Err.Source)
   Response.write("; Error Description: " & Err.Description)
   Err.Clear
Else
   ...
End If
```

Based on what action should be taken and who should be informed of an error, the error message can be generated for the page developer as comments, or it can be displayed as an external message to the person accessing the page. The Clear method of the Err object is called to clear the error.

Error handling can also occur within the component by using an error handler, or the error can be passed through to the client without any error handling. To use an error handler within the component, add in a handler using an **On Error Goto** statement similar to the following:

```
On Error Goto HandleError
```

The error handler can then handle the error itself, pass the error through to the client, or raise a different error number:

```
HandleError:
   If Err.Number = 11 Then
    ' division by zero
    Err.Raise Number := Err.Number, Description := "some text"
   ...
```

In this example, the same error number is returned, but the descriptive text can expand on the error and why it occurred (such as "A division by zero occurred within an ASP component used . . . ") so that it's more descriptive then just "Divide by zero."

Error handling can also be especially helpful when debugging complex ASP applications that include more than one component or include components that themselves create other objects, as discussed in the next section.

Debugging

There is more than one approach to debug a Visual Basic ASP component, but the most common is to use the Visual Basic Debugger.

To debug a component, you first have to isolate the server where the ASP test page will call the ASP component and then turn off anonymous access. Without this, you'll get permission errors because the anonymous user does not have permission to access the DCOM server, used for debugging.

The easiest approach to set up your environment for debugging is to run the server in isolation (set the ASP application's isolation level to High) and then remove the anonymous user by accessing the Security tab of the server's properties and unchecking the anonymous user access.

Once you've set your environment, compile your Visual Basic component and add breakpoints to your code (breakpoints are stopping points in your code—the debugger will stop at these when the component code is run). The Visual Basic documentation describes how to add breakpoints.

Next, check that your Project Properties Debug setting (within the Properties Debugging tab) is set to "Wait for component to be created," and then click the Run menu option to load the component into memory, waiting to be accessed.

Microsoft has provided an article on debugging ASP components titled "Debugging ASP Applications, Part 2" and located at *http://msdn.microsoft.com/workshop/server/asp/server04242000-2.asp* when this book was written. Note, though, that most documentation on debugging is geared to components written for the NT 4.0 environment, and you may have problems getting debugging to work in your environment.

Performance Issues

The best performance measure you can take with your Visual Basic ASP component is to use good coding practices. These include:

- Access expensive resources such as database connections late, and release them as soon as possible.

- When implementing your component, avoid using multiple component properties that the ASP page developer has to set; instead, pass all information to the component as method parameters. This eliminates the time needed to access and set each property value individually from the scripted page.

- Don't access functions within loops. If you're accessing a property value such as a collection's Count property, access the value in a variable and use the variable in the loop.

- For the ASP environment, avoid using the Session and Application objects except for key scalar values. Particularly avoid adding objects to either of these collections. Adding objects takes memory or can fail if you attempt to add an apartment-threaded object to the Application object. If you add an apartment-threaded object to the Session object, you won't get an error, but the client's session is now locked to that particular thread. This means that the client's requests can be processed only by that thread, rather than by the next available thread.

- Use early binding to access external objects by attaching a reference to the object's type library to your VB project and accessing the object by name rather than using the generic Object type. For example:

```
Dim objConnection As Connection
Set objConnection = CreateObject("ADODB.Connection")
```

Early binding provides application information ahead of time, eliminating the need to find this information out at runtime. (See more on early binding in Chapter 3.)

- In NT, if you created a component that was part of a transaction, you used the **New** keyword or the ObjectContext object's CreateInstance method to instantiate the object to ensure the object would be created within the same context (and transaction) as the containing object. For example:

```
Dim someObj As New obj
```

or:

```
Dim someObj As obj
Set someObj = New obj
```

or:

```
Set someObj = ObjContext.CreateInstance("some.object")
```

You couldn't use the VBA *CreateObject* function, since the component was created outside of the current context.

In Windows 2000, this has changed. You can now use the VBA *CreateObject* function to create the new object within the current context. Not only that, but you'll find that using *CreateObject* can actually be a performance boost over using the **New** keyword. The reason is that when you create an object in the definition line:

```
Dim someObj As New obj
```

each time the object is accessed in the code, COM+ does a quick check to make sure the object's been created first. If not, it's created when it's used. To avoid this check, use *CreateObject* or separate the instantiation of the object and the definition of the object into two lines:

```
Dim someObj As obj
Set someObj = New obj
```

If you use CreateInstance, you're still okay; in Windows 2000, CreateInstance and *CreateObject* result in exactly the same behavior.

8

Creating ASP/ADO Components

Ask most people interested in building Internet or intranet applications what they consider to be the main use for these applications, and chances are they'll respond that they want some form of data access. The type of data access can change, encompassing such applications as online catalogs, transaction systems, or most forms of information lookup. The key component, however, is that the system must provide some form of data access on the server.

Microsoft supports a couple of different techniques to access data, including Remote Data Service (RDS) to access data directly from a client page, as well as the more traditional Data Access Objects (DAO) to connect to a data source on the server using the Jet database engine. However, to increase the ease with which data is accessed from any application, including an ASP one, Microsoft provides OLE DB, a set of COM interfaces that supports any type of data format as long as the data source implements an OLE DB provider. To support OLE DB with existing applications, Microsoft has already provided an OLE DB provider for ODBC, which means any data source accessed via an ODBC driver can be accessed using OLE DB.

One of the problems with OLE DB is that it is a relatively complicated technology to use to access data. To facilitate the use of OLE DB, Microsoft also created ActiveX Data Objects (ADO), a set of objects built on OLE DB, but hiding most of the complexity of OLE DB. ADO can be used to access data in multiple formats, including relational as well as ISAM databases and even plain text.

As for ASP applications, ADO was created originally for use from Internet applications and can be used directly in server-side scripts as well as within ASP components. ADO is used throughout this chapter, and the first section of this chapter provides a quick overview.

Using ADO, data can be accessed directly within the ASP pages, but if the structure of the data changes—for example, if a column is renamed or removed from a table, or if a column data type changes—each and every instance of the data item has to be altered. One very useful implementation of ASP components is to build a database access layer between the ASP pages and an actual database. So instead of having several ASP pages making the same direct database access to perform a recurring operation, such as a customer search, create an ASP component and have it perform the search and return the results. With this approach, changes to the underlying data structure, such as the customer table, result in changes to just the component, rather than to all the pages that use this functionality.

An additional reason to encapsulate data access within ASP components is that each component can be used many times from many different ASP pages without having to recode the same data access mechanics each and every time. This increases the maintainability of the application, as well as making it easier to alter the access characteristics for the data.

This chapter covers the use of ADO from within Visual Basic ASP components in order to encapsulate data actions to be used from different ASP pages.

 The examples in this chapter use the Weaver database, included with the examples for the book and described in detail in Appendix B, *The Weaver Database*. The examples work with both Access as well as SQL Server, unless otherwise noted. Note, though, that the OLE DB providers used—OLE DB Provider for SQL Server and the OLE DB Provider for ODBC—can generate results different from yours if you use a different OLE DB Provider.

Accessing ADO from a VB Component

ADO is based on COM, which means you can create the ADO objects directly in your component using code similar to the following:

```
Dim objConnection As Object
Set objConnection = CreateObject("ADODB.Connection")
```

This technique uses late binding to access the ADO Connection object. However, you're going to want to take advantage of early binding whenever you can in your ASP component. Early binding with ADO is implemented within a Visual Basic component by attaching the ADO type library to the project's references and then defining the object as a specific ADO object type, rather than as the more generic Object datatype:

```
Dim objConnection As New Connection
```

As discussed in Chapter 3, *ASP Components and COM*, early binding can provide performance benefits, since information about the object, its properties, and its methods are known at compile time. If late binding is used instead, this information isn't known and the underlying component implementation must make COM method calls to find out the information in addition to invoking the object methods or setting or accessing the object's properties.

Another reason you're going to want to attach the ADO type library reference to your project is to have access to the large number of ADO enumerations provided by Microsoft in the type library. For instance, to create a forward-only scrolling Recordset object that uses client-side cursors, you can use the following code:

```
Dim rs As New Recordset
rs.CursorType = adOpenForwardOnly
rs.CursorLocation = adUseClient
```

The values used to set the CursorType and CursorLocation properties are enumerated values defined in the ADO type library. Using enumerations is preferable to hardcoding the actual values because the enumerated values are easier to remember (since they are mnemonic in nature) and because there is no guarantee that the underlying values will not change in future versions of ADO (though you'll most likely have to recompile your component if the underlying values do change in the future).

 Another indirect benefit of using enumerated values in your code is that these values are self-documenting, making the code easier to read as well as maintain.

Based on these two reasons—taking advantage of early binding and access to the ADO enumerations—you'll want to add support for the ADO type library to your ASP components that use ADO.

To add the ADO type library to your component, check the Microsoft ActiveX Data Objects Library box in the References dialog for the component project. Figure 8-1 shows the included references for an ASP component that uses the COM+ Services, Active Server Pages, and ActiveX Data Objects type libraries.

Creating a Simple ADO Component

Before getting into a detailed overview of ADO and looking more closely at the individual objects in the ADO model, let's try out a simple ASP component that connects to a database, performs a query, and processes the results.

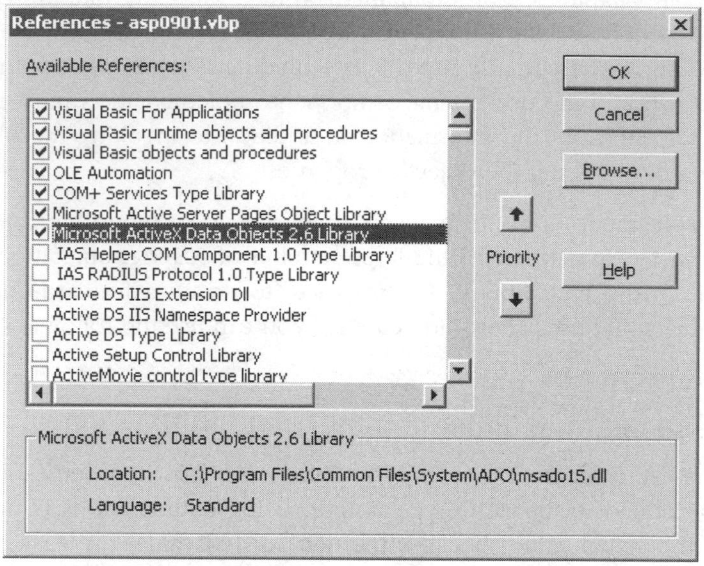

Figure 8-1. *Project references after adding in ADO, ASP, and COM+ type libraries*

Details of using the ADO objects mentioned in this section are provided later in this chapter, in the section, "The ADO Model."

Start by creating a new Visual Basic ActiveX DLL project, naming the project asp0801 and the generated class simple. Next, add in support for COM+ Services, the ASP built-in objects, and ADO by adding in the type libraries as shown in Figure 8-1.

Once you've added in support for ADO, you're ready to start writing your ASP component.

Creating a Data Source Connection

Regardless of what type of activity you're performing against a data source, you're going to need to connect to it first. You can connect to a data source using a couple of different methods. You can use the ADO Connection object to make a data source connection, then perform your data activity on the connection or use one of the other ADO objects to perform the data activity:

```
Dim cn As Connection
cn.ConnectionString = "Provider=SQLOLEDB;server=FLAME;database=weaver;
                       uid=sa;pwd="
cn.Open
```

The connection string just shown breaks down as follows:

Provider
> OLE DB provider (the SQL Server OLE DB Provider in this code)

Server
> The machine server name

Database
> The database name

UID
> The user ID of a valid database user

PWD
> The user's password, if any

This connection string specifies all of the connection information necessary to connect to the data source. Other connection strings can reference a DSN (Data Source Name), configured using your system's ODBC Data Source Administrator applet (as is demonstrated with the Access database later in this chapter).

A second technique you can use is to make the connection directly on the Recordset or Command object, depending on which you'll need to perform your data activity. If you're performing a data source query, then you'll want to use the Recordset object, since a recordset is required to process the results.

For our simple component, we'll connect to the data source using the Recordset object. In `asp0801.simple`, define a subroutine named showWebpages and add the code shown in Example 8-1. In addition to creating the recordset and setting its ActiveConnection property, the code also creates an instance of ObjectContext in order to access the ASP built-in Response object. Response is used later to output the results of running the data source query.

Example 8-1. Creating Objects in a Simple Component

```
Sub showWebpages()

' get ObjectContext
Dim objContext As ObjectContext
Set objContext = GetObjectContext()

' get Respones
Dim objResponse As Response
Set objResponse = objContext("Response")

' create Recordset
Dim rs As New Recordset

' set connection string
```

Example 8-1. Creating Objects in a Simple Component (continued)

```
rs.ActiveConnection = "DSN=weaver;uid=sa;pwd="

End Sub
```

In the example code, we're accessing the Weaver database in Access. To work against the SQL Server version of Weaver, change the ActiveConnection property:

```
rs.ActiveConnection = "Provider=SQLOLEDB;server=FLAME;database=weaver;
                       uid=sa;pwd="
```

With this code, you still don't have a connection to the data source because the recordset has not been opened yet. First, we'll need to add the text for the query that generates the recordset.

Building a Simple Query

Connecting to a data source isn't useful unless you do something once you have the connection.

The majority of accesses to a data source such as a database usually are based on queries rather than updates. In your applications, people will create a record (a unique grouping of data) once, maybe update it a couple of times, and delete it once. However, during the lifetime of the record, it will probably be involved in queries more than once, and frequently it will be queried hundreds of times, depending on the application and the data.

If printing out the words "Hello, World!" is the traditional first test of working with a new technology, language, or application, then querying data is the traditional first use of working with data sources.

In `asp0801.simple`, you'll modify the existing subroutine to add text for a simple query against the Weaver database, specifically the WebPage database. The query text accesses the name, filename, file_size, and page_type_cd columns of the WebPage table and orders the results by page_type_cd and then by name, as shown in Example 8-2. (New code that is not found in Example 8-1 appears in bold.) The query text is assigned to the Recordset object's Source property, and the Recordset object's Open method is called to both make the database connection and perform the query.

Example 8-2. Component Modified to Include Query and Connection to Database

```
Sub showWebpages()

' get ObjectContext
Dim objContext As ObjectContext
Set objContext = GetObjectContext()

' get Respones
```

Example 8-2. Component Modified to Include Query and Connection to Database (continued)

```
Dim objResponse As Response
Set objResponse = objContext("Response")

' create Recordset
Dim rs As New Recordset

' set connction string
rs.ActiveConnection = "DSN=weaver;uid=sa;pwd="

' set query
rs.Source = "SELECT name, filename, page_type_cd, file_size " & _
            "from WebPage " & _
            "order by page_type_cd, name"

' perform query
rs.Open

End Sub
```

You now have a working ASP/ADO component that connects to the Weaver database and queries the WebPage table. However, your component still isn't useful until you process the data that's returned.

 As a quick aside, ordering the result set sorts the records, either alphabetically, numerically, or both, on the specified columns. You can order the result set using SQL, as shown in Example 8-2, or you can use the Sort method on the Recordset object, as will be demonstrated later in this chapter.

Processing the Returned Result Set

Once the query has been run against the database, your component can now process the result. You can process the data directly in the component, return the data to the client application, or do a little of both by partially processing the result set and then returning the processed data to the client application.

For `asp0801.simple`, you'll process the data directly in the component by traversing the records returned from the query, pulling out the data in all of the record fields, and then outputting this data to the client in an HTML table. Because you output the data directly in the component, you need to add support for the ASP Response object.

Finish the component by modifying the component's method to add in the query processing code. As shown in Example 8-3, a `While` loop is created and the contents are processed until the recordset's EOF property returns a value of `True`, meaning that the last record in the result set has been reached. The data is pulled from the recordset's Fields array by column name. You'll also add in error handling that traps an error condition and directs the application flow to the code contained in the error handler. In the handler, the error description is displayed.

Example 8-3. Completed ASP/ADO Component That Performs Query and Processes Results

```
Sub showWebpages()

' add in error handling
On Error GoTo ErrorHandler

' get ObjectContext
Dim objContext As ObjectContext
Set objContext = GetObjectContext()

' get Respones
Dim objResponse As Response
Set objResponse = objContext("Response")

' create Recordset
Dim rs As New Recordset

' set connction string
rs.ActiveConnection = "DSN=weaver;uid=sa;pwd="

' set query
rs.Source = "SELECT name, filename, page_type_cd, file_size " & _
            "from WebPage " & _
            "order by page_type_cd, name"

' perform query
rs.Open

objResponse.Write "<table>"
While rs.EOF <> True
    objResponse.Write "<tr><td>"
    objResponse.Write rs.Fields("name") & "</td><td>"
    objResponse.Write rs.Fields("filename") & "</td><td>"
    objResponse.Write rs.Fields("file_size") & "</td><td>"
    objResponse.Write rs.Fields("page_type_cd")
    objResponse.Write "</td></tr>"
    rs.MoveNext
Wend
objResponse.Write "</table>"

' clean up
rs.Close
Set rs = Nothing
Exit Sub

ErrorHandler:
    objResponse.Write "While querying against Web Page: " & Err.Description

End Sub
```

Once the component is compiled, all that's left is to access the component and call its method, as shown in *asp0801.asp*:

```
<%
Dim obj
Set obj = Server.CreateObject("asp0801.simple")

obj.showWebpages
%>
```

As you can see from this simple component, accessing a data source and processing the results using ADO is not a complex process.

Data Processing Within ASP Components

The simple ASP/ADO component created in Examples 8-1 through 8-3 processed the records resulting from the query directly in the component method, outputting the results to an HTML table. This is a handy technique to use to test queries while you're building the component, but it isn't one you're going to want to consider using in your production applications.

One of the primary reasons to create ASP components is to build a layer of separation between the business processes and the presentation. By enclosing all accesses to the data source within the component, changes to the ASP application code that access the components are lessened. Additionally, if the presentation changes—perhaps XML is used instead of HTML for building the web pages—there is little or no impact on the components.

However, when the lines between the presentation layer and the business layer are blurred, as they were in Example 8-3, then changes in either the data or the presentation impact both the page that creates the component and on the component itself.

The bottom line is, while you're learning how to work with ADO or are testing out queries or other types of data access, it's OK to process the results directly in the ASP component. However, once you start moving your component into the application environment, pull the presentation code out of the component.

The ADO Model

As was demonstrated in the last section, two key characteristics of ADO are that the objects are simple to use and that there is no hierarchical dependency of the objects on each other.

ADO contains only a small number of objects, and therefore it is a relatively easy technology to begin to use. As an example, you can connect to a database and perform a SQL command using only a few lines of code, such as the following:

```
Dim cn As New Connection
cn.Open "DSN=weaver;uid=sa;pwd="
cn.Execute "insert into PageType values('" & _
            UCase(strCode) & "','" & strDesc & "')"
```

Additionally, ADO has been restricted to handle specific types of data access, such as data queries and updates to business data. There are no defined objects within ADO to handle metadata manipulation, and there are no objects to handle more complex multidimensional queries. Instead, Microsoft created additional, companion data models to handle both of these (ADOMD for multidimensional data access, and ADOX for metadata access and updates), keeping ADO itself focused on the objects necessary to work with business data.

As for the lack of enforced hierarchy of the objects, in ADO there is no requirement that you must create one object before you can create another, as there is with technologies such as DAO. For instance, you can both connect to a data source and retrieve a result set using just the Recordset object with ADO. DAO, on the other hand, enforces a hierarchy by allowing access to some objects, such as a Recordset, to occur only through other objects, such as a Database object. By not enforcing a hierarchy with ADO, the amount of code is kept to a minimum—containing only that which is necessary to perform the data operation.

ADO consists of a small set of interrelated objects, each designed to perform specific functionality. Originally, the set of ADO objects—or *model*—consisted of seven objects: Connection, Command, Recordset, Field, Parameter, Property, and Error. Starting with ADO 2.5, two additional objects have been added to the model: the Record and Stream objects.

 Two other objects, DataControl and DataFactory, won't be covered in this book. These objects are used to facilitate the use of Remote Data Service (RDS), a technology that supports remote access of data from a client facilitated by an intermediary such as IIS. RDS is outside the scope of this book.

The Connection Object

Earlier I mentioned that you could connect to a data source directly with a Recordset object. However, if you're making more than one access to the same data store from within a block of code, you should use the ADO Connection object to manage the connection. Additionally, if you need to control other aspects of the connection such as timeouts, you'll want to use the Connection object.

The Connection object has several methods and properties, but the most commonly used are the ConnectionString property and the Open method. Setting the ConnectionString property and calling the Open method are used to create a connection to a data source. Alternately, you can simply call the Open method and pass it a valid connection string as an argument.

The connection string is made up of argument-value pairs, some of which are handled by the Connection object and some of which are passed directly to the OLE DB provider. Of these, the **Provider** argument is used to specify a particular OLE DB provider. To demonstrate, you can create a connection to a SQL Server database by specifying the SQL Server OLE DB Provider and then naming the server, database, username, and password:

```
cn.ConnectionString = "Provider=SQLOLEDB;server=FLAME;database=weaver;
                       uid=sa;pwd="
```

In this example, the SQL Server OLE DB Provider, **SQLOLEDB**, is specified. The other arguments—server, database, username, and password—are then passed to the provider directly.

The username used in the examples throughout this chapter is *sa*, created as a default user for a SQL Server database. If you're creating an application to be used in an intranet or on the Internet, the first thing you're going to want to do is remove the default *sa* user— it is a known security hole, and hackers have been known to access data from Internet sites merely by using the *sa* username.

Instead of specifying an OLE DB provider in the ConnectionString, you can reference a DSN, or Data Source Name, of a data source configured through the ODBC Data Administrator. Using a DSN, as the following demonstrates when connecting to a DSN named **weaver**, doesn't require that you code information about the server and the database name directly in your components:

```
Cn.ConnectionString = "DSN=weaver;uid=sa;pwd="
```

By using a DSN, you can change the underlying server and database without having to change the component code. However, the downside to this approach is that you are locked into using ODBC through the generic and less efficient OLE DB provider for ODBC, rather than an OLE DB provider designed specifically for the data source and therefore more optimized. You'll also reference the OLE DB provider for ODBC when you create a data source connection string that references a specific ODBC provider, as the following demonstrates:

```
cn.ConnectionString = "driver={SQL Server};server=FLAME;uid=sa;
                       pwd=;database=weaver"
```

Instead of specifying the provider in the ConnectionString property, you can set it directly with the Provider property:

```
cn.Provider = "sqloledb"
```

In addition to setting a connection string or an OLE DB provider, you can also access or change other Connection object properties.

Several Connection properties (as well as properties of the other ADO objects) are set with values contained in predefined enumerations. By attaching the ADO type library to your VB component projects, you can use these enumerations when setting property values. For instance, you can change the CursorLocation for an ADO connection to use client-side cursors by setting the property to adUseClient before the connection is opened:

```
cn.CursorLocation = adUseClient
```

Instead of specifying connection information in properties, you can also specify a data source connection string directly as a parameter to the Connection object's Open method:

```
cn.Open "DSN=weaver", "sa"
```

The Open method has optional parameters for the connection string, the username, the password associated with the username, and an enumerated value, ConnectOptionEnum, which determines whether the connection method returns before the connection is made (i.e., it executes asynchronously) or after the connection is made (synchronously). By default, the Open method runs synchronously—the rest of the component code is not executed until after the connection has been made.

Embedded SQL (SQL hardcoded directly in the component code) or a stored procedure can be called using the Connection object's Execute method. The command or query is passed as a string in the first parameter and an optional long value to hold the number of affected records when the method call returns can be passed as the second parameter.

Additionally, a third optional (though recommended) parameter can hold either a CommandTypeEnum value or an ExecuteOptionEnum value that defines what and how the command is to be executed. If your component is calling a stored procedure or performing some other action that doesn't return a recordset, you can improve its performance by setting the *Options* argument to adExecuteNo-Records to signal that a returned recordset is not expected:

```
cn.Execute sqlString, , adExecuteNoRecords
```

One type of SQL statement that doesn't return records is a database update. To insert a record, you could use the following with the Connection object:

```
' perform database operation
cn.Execute "insert into PageType values('" & _
      UCase(strCode) & "','" & strDesc & "')", ,adExecuteNoRecords
```

The Connection object's Execute method always returns a Recordset object unless adExecuteRecords is specified, though the value can be ignored when processing SQL that doesn't result in returned data. The returned recordset is defined to have a forward-only, read-only cursor, which means that you can only scroll forward in the set, and you can only read each record's field values—they can't be changed.

The CommandTypeEnum enumerated value can also be used in the *Options* parameter to define what type of command is being executed. By default, the Connection object is set to a CommandTypeEnum of adCmdUnknown, but you can change this when you invoke the method:

```
Set rs = cn.Execute("WebPage", ,adCmdTable)
```

This Connection query returns a recordset consisting of all of the records from the Weaver database's WebPage table. Only the table name needs to be provided because the adCmdTable value used as the *Options* argument indicates that *CommandText* is to be interpreted as a table name.

If you're accessing a data source that doesn't support transactions as they are defined with COM+ (see Chapter 5, *COM+ Services and ASP Components and Applications*), you can still control transactions for a connection using the Connection object's BeginTrans, CommitTrans, and RollbackTrans methods. They have the following syntax:

```
ConnectionObject.BeginTrans
ConnectionObject.CommitTrans
ConnectionObject.RollbackTrans
```

To begin a specific transaction, you call BeginTrans, and all activities that then occur against the connection maintained by the Connection object are added to the pending transaction. At the end of the transaction, you can then call Commit-Trans to commit all data updates, as follows:

```
cn.BeginTrans
... data updates
cn.CommitTrans
```

Asynchronous Commands in ASP Components

ASP is a server-side technology that processes one or more commands on the server and returns the results of running the commands to the client. Based on this, the use of asynchronous commands is not usually effective and in fact can be counterproductive.

For instance, if you execute a database query that returns data that must then be output to the client in some way, you're not going to want to execute this query asynchronously —how will you pass the results of the query to the client once the query is finished? The ASP page that started the database process has already returned to the client.

On the other hand, if you have a command that updates data rather than performs a query, and you don't care about providing any feedback to the client that the command executed correctly, you can execute the command asynchronously and return the ASP page before the command is finished executing. However, use caution with this approach—most people want to know if the results of their effort have bombed or not.

However, not all data source driver providers support all uses of `Command-TypeEnum`. The Execute code just shown to access the WebPage table generates an error if you try the code with Access using the OLE DB Provider for ODBC but works without a problem with SQL Server.

Alternately, if one of the operations fails, you can call RollbackTrans to roll back changes.

The transaction methods won't work with all data sources. One way to check to see if transactions are supported for a provider is to access the Connection object's Properties collection and see if it contains a name-value pair for "Transaction DDL". The Properties collection contains information about the object, in this case the Connection object, *as a provider implements it.* Check the documentation included with your OLE DB provider to see what it supports. Or you can output the entire contents of the Properties collection and see what's supported directly.

 Use the Connection object's transaction methods to control transactions with Access, which doesn't have COM+ transaction support. For SQL Server, though, you'll want to use ObjectContext and the transaction methods supported with COM+.

To output the Properties collection, create a new Visual Basic ActiveX DLL project, name it `asp0802`, and name the generated class `Conn`. In the class, you'll add a method that traverses the Connection object's Properties collection, displaying values using the built-in ASP Response object. To support this code, you'll need to add in three type libraries: the COM+ Services library to access ObjectContext, the Microsoft Active Server Pages Object library to access the built-in ASP objects, and the Microsoft ActiveX Data Objects library.

Next, add the code for the component's method. The method, showProperties, creates an instance of the Connection object and connects to an Access 2000 database version of the Weaver database. The method, which is shown in Example 8-4, also uses ObjectContext to instantiate the Response object to list each element in the Connection object's Properties collection.

Example 8-4. Iterating Through Connection Properties Collection for Weaver Database Implemented in Access

```
Sub showProperties()

' get ObjectContext
Dim objContext As ObjectContext
Set objContext = GetObjectContext()

' get Respones
Dim objResponse As Response
Set objResponse = objContext("Response")

' connect to database
Dim cn As New Connection
cn.ConnectionString = "DSN=weaver;uid=sa;pwd="
cn.Open

' traverse collection, print out values
Dim prp
For Each prp In cn.Properties
  objResponse.Write prp.Name & " = " & prp.Value
  objResponse.Write "<br>"
Next

cn.Close
Set cn = Nothing

End Sub
```

Once compiled, when the component is accessed from the following ASP page, *asp0802.asp*, the Connection object's Properties collection is displayed to the client:

```
<%
Dim obj
Set obj = Server.CreateObject("asp0802.Conn")

obj.showProperties
%>
```

Not all providers have the same entries in the Properties collection. If you modify the showProperties code to access Weaver from SQL Server, using the SQL Server OLE DB Provider:

```
' connect to database
Dim cn As New Connection
cn.Provider = "SQLOLEDB"
cn.ConnectionString = "server=FLAME;uid=sa;pwd"
cn.Open

' set default database
cn.DefaultDatabase = "weaver"
```

and run the example, you'll get a different list of properties, as well as different values for the same properties. For instance, the value defined for the property "Maximum tables in select" is 256 tables for SQL Server but only 16 tables for Access using the OLE DB Provider for ODBC.

Another Connection object collection is the Errors collection, which contains any data source errors or warnings generated as a result of running one or more database statements. These aren't ADO-specific errors and therefore don't *always* trigger the ADO error handling that can be trapped using **On Error** exception handling. However, errors that occur with the data source *usually* generate a trappable error, which can be processed in VB using error handling:

```
On Error GoTo ErrorHandler
...
ErrorHandler:

    Err.Raise Err.Number, Err.Source, "Accessing PageTypes: " &
                                      Err.Description
```

I've covered the Connection properties and collections and several of the object's methods in this section, but there is one more method of the Connection object that merits discussion: the OpenSchema method. If you're creating an application that uses ad hoc reporting, or if you need to get information about the data source at a metadata level, than the OpenSchema method should be of particular interest to you. With this method, you can actually query for information about the data source itself, such as table or column names, access privileges, indexes, and so on.

 What is metadata? Metadata is data about data. In other words, it is information about the data source itself, usually stored in a database catalog or administration tables.

OpenSchema takes three parameters, the second two being optional. The first parameter takes one of the **SchemaEnum** values, which specify what type of metadata information to return. For instance, to get information about tables in the database, you would specify the `adSchemaTables` value when calling Open-Schema:

```
Set rs = cn.OpenSchema(adSchemaTables)
```

The result of this method call is a recordset containing information about the database tables, including table name, its type (i.e., view or table), when it was created or last modified, and so on.

The next parameter in OpenSchema is an array containing query criteria that are applied to the returned data. The number of entries in the array is determined by which `SchemaEnum` value is used for the first parameter. For instance, to specify that OpenSchema return only information about tables associated with the Weaver database in SQL Server, you would use the following OpenSchema command:

```
Set rs = cn.OpenSchema(adSchemaTables, Array("weaver", Empty, Empty, Empty))
```

The final parameter for the method is a schema identifier, if the provider supports schemas. Usually, this isn't provided.

To demonstrate the use of OpenSchema, we'll create a third component, naming the VB project `asp0803` and the generated class `schema`. After creating the project, add the type libraries for COM+ Services, ASP, and ADO.

Example 8-5 shows the code used for the component's method, showColumns. In it, a connection is made to the SQL Server version of the Weaver database, and the OpenSchema method is called, passing in the `adSchemaColumns SchemaEnum` value. We're only interested in looking at the columns for the Weaver database, so `weaver` is passed as the table catalog name in the first array element of the second parameter. When the recordset is returned from the method call, it's traversed, and the table name, column name, and data type identifier are displayed. To prevent the repetition of the table name, a string containing the previous table name is kept, and it's compared with the table name of the current record—if the two are the same, the table name is not displayed.

Example 8-5. Component Method That Uses OpenSchema to Pull in Weaver Database Table and Column Names

```
Sub showColumns()
' get ObjectContext
Dim objContext As ObjectContext
Set objContext = GetObjectContext()

' get Respones
Dim objResponse As Response
Set objResponse = objContext("Response")

' connect to database
```

Example 8-5. Component Method That Uses OpenSchema to Pull in Weaver Database Table and Column Names (continued)

```
Dim cn As New Connection
cn.Provider = "SQLOLEDB"
cn.ConnectionString = "server=FLAME;database=weaver;uid=sa;pwd="
cn.Open

' query schema
Dim rs As Recordset
Set rs = cn.OpenSchema(adSchemaColumns, Array("weaver",
                                        Empty, Empty, Empty))

' process schema results
objResponse.Write "<table border=2>"
Dim strTable As String
Dim curTable As String
Do While Not rs.EOF <> True
  objResponse.Write "<tr><td>"
  curTable = rs("TABLE_NAME")
  If curTable <> strTable Then
     strTable = curTable
     objResponse.Write strTable
  End If
  objResponse.Write "</td><td>"
  objResponse.Write rs("COLUMN_NAME") & "</td><td>"
  objResponse.Write rs("DATA_TYPE") & "</td></tr>"
  rs.MoveNext

Loop

End Sub
```

The component is created in an ASP page and the method is called by *asp0803. asp*, as follows:

```
<%
Dim obj
Set obj = Server.CreateObject("asp0803.schema")

obj.showColumns
%>
```

The result of calling showColumns is a web page with a listing of the Weaver tables and columns.

The Recordset Object

As you found in the last section, you can connect to a data source with or without using the Connection object. Unlike the Connection object, though, the Recordset object is required if you're expecting returned data that you want to process.

A recordset can be created directly, or it can be created as the result of running a query with the Command or Connection object. For instance, to perform a simple query with a recordset, you could use code similar to the following:

```
rs.Open "select * from WebPage", "DSN=weaver;uid=sa;pwd="
```

The first parameter in this code is the SQL query, and the second is the connection string for the database connection.

Alternatively, you can execute the same database query with the Connection object:

```
cn.Open "DSN=weaver;uid=sa;pwd="
Set rs = cn.Execute "select * from WebPage"
```

The end result of either query is the same—a returned result set containing all WebPage records in the Access version of the Weaver database

The Recordset object has more properties and methods than any of the other ADO objects. You've seen the use of the Source property to define the source used to build the Recordset object. You've also seen the database connection coded directly into the Recordset object's Open method. Instead, you can also set the ActiveConnection property of the Recordset object to an open Connection object:

```
Set rs.ActiveConnection = cn
```

Notice that the **Set** statement was used when setting the ActiveConnection property. If **Set** had been omitted, the Connection object's connection string would be assigned the ActiveConnection property (since ConnectionString is the default property of the Connection object), and another connection would be opened when the Recordset object's Open method was called:

```
rs.ActiveConnection = cn
rs.Open
```

In the recordset examples, no properties other than Source and ActiveConnection were used when creating the result set. This means that the other properties that could impact on the behavior and type of recordset returned are set to their default values.

Two of these other properties control the result set cursor. *Cursors* are used to control navigation through the result set, as well as the visibility of the result set to other applications. The type of cursor can be set through the CursorType property. By default this property is set to **adOpenForwardOnly**, which means that you can only scroll forward through the recordset. However, you can set this to a different value before the recordset is opened. For example, to create a dynamic cursor through which your application can scroll forward and backward and one in which all updates, deletions, and insertions into the result set are visible, use the **adOpenDynamic** cursor type:

```
rs.CursorType = adOpenDynamic
```

The CursorLocation property determines which cursor service is used and is set to `adUseServer`, a server-side cursor, by default. You can change this to client-side cursors using the following syntax:

```
rs.CursorLocation = adUseClient
```

Client-side cursors are used with disconnected recordsets.

By default, the records in the result set can only be read—they can't be modified. Recordset locking is controlled by the LockType property, which is set to `adLockReadOnly` by default. If you're working with disconnected recordsets, which use a client-side cursor, the only LockType settings supported are `adLock-BatchOptimistic` or `adLockReadOnly`. If you're using a server-side cursor, the `adLockOptimistic` setting should be sufficient for your ASP applications, unless there's a high likelihood of two users trying to update the same record at the same time. If this is possible, then you'll want to use the `adLockPessimistic` setting so that the application that makes the first modification to the record locks out other modifications until the modifications are committed to the database.

An online store offers an example of a potentially contentious database update. Consider the possibility of two people ordering the same product at the same time when only one of that product is in stock. The first person to submit the order for processing also has several other items in his shopping cart that he wants to buy. In the meantime, a second person also submits an order, but she has only one item in her cart, so her entire order is processed more quickly.

During order processing, the inventory for the product is updated, and only orders for in-stock items are processed. In fact, triggers on the database won't allow the inventory for any item to fall below a count of zero (no items).

If optimistic locking were used, then the second person's order could access, modify, and more importantly *update* the inventory record for the product while the first person's order was still being processed. When the inventory record is updated (that is, when the record is actually being modified), a lock is set on the record that prohibits other changes. When the order is finished and the record modifications are committed, then the inventory count is reduced to zero. The second person gets the product. When the first person tries to update the inventory record, even if the second person's order processing no longer has a lock on the record, his update is rejected because the inventory is now at zero and no more orders of the product will be accepted. This means that the first person in this scenario would not get the item, since his order took longer to process because it included more items. This is not the behavior we want to encourage from our ASP applications.

However, if pessimistic locking were used, as soon as the order processing for the first person's order made an edit to the inventory record for the item (actually made a change to a value in the Recordset's Field collection for that record), the record would be locked, even though the rest of the order may take some time to finish (our shopper has a lot of money to spend). The second shopper's order processing couldn't update the inventory until the first shopper's order was finished. Based on this, the first person to submit the order for the item would get the item—and the later shopper would then be out of luck.

 Of course, a downside to pessimistic locking is that locks are maintained on records for a longer time than would occur with optimistic locking—and processing record updates could take longer.

There are also several Recordset properties that have to do with how a result set is retrieved for the Recordset object. However, many of these aren't effective in a web-based application. For instance, you can set a cache size for the recordset through the CacheSize property, but if your application processes an entire recordset on the server before returning the web page to the client, you've not gained anything by setting this property. (Caching controls the number of records maintained on the client at one time for a query.)

The same applies to paging—paging isn't effective when you process the entire result set before returning to the client. However, you can use paging with an ASP application—the key is to persist the dataset.

To demonstrate working with paging, create a new Visual Basic component and call the project asp0804. Rename the generated class to page. Add references to the ADO, ASP, and COM+ Services type libraries to the project. Also add the Microsoft Scripting Runtime library to the project for access to the FileSystemObject object.

This example has two methods: one to create a recordset that is then saved to a file, and one to use the ASP Response object to list the records for a specific recordset page. Both methods are called from the same ASP page.

Add the code for the first method, createRecordset, which is shown in Example 8-6. This method opens a recordset with an embedded SQL query—a join on the WebPage and Directory tables—and then persists the recordset to a file using the Recordset object's Save method. The Save method persists a recordset in either an XML (Extensible Markup Language) or ADTG (Advanced Data Tablegram) format to a file or to an ADO Stream (discussed later). Before the query is made, though, the FileSystemObject object is used to test to see if the file already exists. If it does, the method exits.

Example 8-6. Create Recordset and Persist to File

```
Sub createRecordset()

' make sure file doesn't exist first
Dim fsObject As New FileSystemObject
If fsObject.FileExists("c:\datasets\set.adtg") Then
   Exit Sub
End If

Dim rs As New Recordset

' set up recordset
rs.Source="select WebPage.name, filename,page_type_cd, web_location " & _
          "from WebPage, Directory " & _
          "where directory_id = Directory.id"
rs.CursorLocation = adUseClient
rs.ActiveConnection="Provider=SQLOLEDB;server=FLAME;database=weaver;" & _
                    "uid=sa;pwd="
rs.Open

' save recordset
rs.Save "c:\datasets\set.adtg"

End Sub
```

The second method is called showPage and is shown in Example 8-7. This method takes two parameters—the page size and the page to make current. It opens the persisted recordset, sets the Recordset object's PageSize property to generate the record pages, and then sets the AbsolutePage property to the page selected for viewing. The WebPage names are pulled from the recordset and listed, embedded within a hypertext link created by concatenating the page's directory location and the page's filename. Add this code to your own component.

Example 8-7. Show All Records for a Specific Recordset Page

```
Function showPage(ByVal iPageSize As Integer, _
         ByVal iCurrentPage As Integer) _
         As Integer

On Error GoTo ErrorHandler

Dim objContext As ObjectContext
Dim objResponse As Response

' get object content, response
Set objContext = GetObjectContext()
Set objResponse = objContext("Response")

' get persisted recordset
Dim rs As New Recordset

rs.Open "c:\datasets\set.adtg"
```

Example 8-7. Show All Records for a Specific Recordset Page (continued)

```
' set page size, current page
rs.PageSize = iPageSize
rs.AbsolutePage = iCurrentPage

Dim i As Integer
i = 1
While i <= iPageSize
   objResponse.Write "<p><a href='http://" & rs("web_location") & _
                                   "/" & rs("filename")
   objResponse.Write "'>" & rs(0) & "</a></p>"
   rs.MoveNext
   If rs.EOF Then
       i = iPageSize + 1
   Else
       i = i + 1
   End If
Wend
showPage = rs.PageCount

ErrorHandler:
   objResponse.Write Err.Description
End Function
```

Once you've compiled the component, you can test it by accessing the *asp0804.*
asp test page included with the examples and shown in Example 8-8. In the page,
a current page value is taken from the Request object's QueryString collection. If
this value exists, the records for the current recordset page are shown; otherwise,
the recordset is created and the first page is shown.

Example 8-8. Using Absolute Page Component to Page Through WebPage Records

```
<%
On Error Resume Next
Dim obj
Set obj = Server.CreateObject("asp0804.page")

' get current page, if any
Dim currPage, pageCount
currPage = CInt(Request.QueryString("currPage"))

' if first time accessing page
If currPage <= 0 Then
   currPage = 1
   obj.createRecordset
End IF

' show pages
pageCount = obj.showPage(5,currPage)

' show page index
Response.Write "<hr> Page: "
For i = 1 to pageCount
```

Example 8-8. Using Absolute Page Component to Page Through WebPage Records (continued)

```
   If i <> currPage Then
      Response.Write "<a href='asp0804.asp?currPage=" & i & "'>" & _
                                                        i & "</a>"
   Else
      Response.Write currPage
   End If
   Response.Write " "
Next
%>
```

This page and the associated components allow a person to scroll through the web pages currently in the Weaver database and access the page through the browser if they wish. They can access each individual page by clicking on the hypertext link associated with each page. Each link has the page number appended to the link's query string.

One limitation with the example as written is that all web pages in the Weaver database will be displayed, including those such as JavaScript files and XML DTD files—files that shouldn't be accessed directly from the browser. A better approach would be to show only those web pages meant to be accessed directly, such as HTML or ASP application pages.

A second limitation with the application is that the web pages are presented in the order in which they're found in the database, rather than an order that might be friendlier to the application user, such as sorting and displaying the pages alphabetically.

Both of these limitations can be fixed with modifications to the original query. The returned dataset could be refined by using the page type code in the WHERE clause and returning only HTML or ASP pages. Additionally, an ORDER BY clause could be appended to the query to sort the pages by name.

However, in the example, we'll modify the result set directly by using the Recordset object's Filter and Sort properties.

The Filter property can fine-tune the result set without permanently changing it. You can restrict the set based on any criteria, and to all intents and purposes, the recordset acts as if the only records in it are those that match the filter. However, you can change or remove the filter to work with a different recordset or to work with all of the records returned from a query.

The Sort property sorts the records on one or more fields, in ascending or descending order, without physically rearranging the recordset. Instead, temporary indexes are created and used for the sort.

To demonstrate both properties, create a new method on the asp0804.page component, showSpecificPage, shown in Example 8-9. This method is exactly the same as that shown in Example 8-7, except that the records are filtered so only those web pages that have the HTM or APP page types are shown. Additionally, the records are sorted on the WebPage name, in ascending order. Add the code for the new method to the component and then recompile the project.

Example 8-9. Filtering and Sorting a Recordset Before Access

```
Function showSpecificPage(ByVal iPageSize As Integer, _
            ByVal iCurrentPage As Integer) _
            As Integer

On Error GoTo ErrorHandler

Dim objContext As ObjectContext
Dim objResponse As Response

' get object content, response
Set objContext = GetObjectContext()
Set objResponse = objContext("Response")

' get persisted recordset
Dim rs As New Recordset

rs.Open "c:\datasets\set.adtg"

' set page size, filter, sort
rs.Filter = "page_type_cd = 'HTM' or page_type_cd = 'APP'"
rs.Sort = "name ASC"
rs.PageSize = iPageSize

' current page
rs.AbsolutePage = iCurrentPage

' scroll through records, print out info
Dim i As Integer
i = 1
While i <= iPageSize
    objResponse.Write "<p><a href='http://" & rs("web_location") & _
                                    "/" & rs("filename")
    objResponse.Write "'>" & rs(0) & "</a></p>"
    rs.MoveNext
    If rs.EOF Then
        i = iPageSize + 1
    Else
        i = i + 1
    End If
Wend
showSpecificPage = rs.PageCount

rs.Close

ErrorHandler:
    objResponse.Write Err.Description
End Function
```

Test the component with the *asp0805.asp* test page. This page has the same script as that shown in Example 8-8, except that the new method is called instead of showPage:

```
pageCount = obj.showSpecificPage(5,currPage)
```

Depending on the number of records you have in the Weaver database, you'll notice that the number of pages you can view has decreased from the first example.

As demonstrated, recordsets can be created either through the Connection object or directly. A third technique to create a Recordset object is to use the Command object, discussed next.

The Command Object

You can execute SQL directly using the Connection object, and you can query a data source either using the Connection object in conjunction with the Recordset object or using the Recordset object alone. However, neither of these objects has facilities for passing parameters with SQL other than to embed the parameter values directly in the SQL command or query. To use mutable parameters—ones that can change without having to rebuild the SQL query—you'll need to use the Command object.

The Command object has properties such as ActiveConnection, used to set the connection, and CommandText, used to define the text for the command. Additionally, you can define the type of command you're making with the CommandType property. For instance, to call a stored procedure, you could use code similar to the following:

```
Dim cmdObject As New Command
Set cmdObject.ActiveConnection = cn
cmdObject.CommandText = "sp_someprocedure"
cmdObject.CommandType = adCmdStoredProc
cmdObject.Execute
```

This block of code invokes a stored procedure that takes no input parameters, returns no recordset, and uses an existing open Connection.

Both the Connection and Recordset objects can invoke stored procedures, but the strength of the Command object is that it has a Parameters collection used to change the parameters passed with the command. Additionally, setting the Command object's Prepared property to **True** compiles the command the first time it's executed and saves the compiled form for subsequent usage, increasing the overall performance of using the command.

To explore the strengths of the Command object within an ASP component, create a new Visual Basic project named **asp0805**, and name the generated class **cmnd**. This component has two methods: showPages, which takes a variant array as its parameter, and showPageInfo, which takes a recordset and a variant for its two parameters.

The showPages method queries the Weaver database for the WebPage records matching the page type codes passed as entries in the Variant array. To do this more efficiently, a Command object is used and a parameter is created for the page type code. Additionally, the command itself is compiled when first executed, and the compiled version is then used each time the Execute method is called.

Each returned Recordset object is passed to the second component method, show-PageInfo, for further processing. Add the showPages method code, shown in Example 8-10, to your component.

Example 8-10. Using a Parameterized Command to Retrieve Several Recordsets

```
Sub showPages(ByVal varTypes As Variant)

Dim cmndObject As New Command
Dim parm As Parameter
Dim rs As Recordset

' set command properties
cmndObject.ActiveConnection = "Provider=SQLOLEDB;server=FLAME;" & _
                              "database=weaver;" & _
                              "uid=sa;pwd="
cmndObject.Prepared = True
cmndObject.CommandType = adCmdText
cmndObject.CommandText = "select name, filename from WebPage where " & _
                         "page_type_cd = ?"

'set parameter
Set parm = cmndObject.CreateParameter("page_type_cd", _
                                      adChar, adParamInput, 3)
cmndObject.Parameters.Append parm

' get array boundaries
Dim lLow, lHigh, l
Dim val As Variant
lLow = LBound(varTypes)
lHigh = UBound(varTypes)

' for each entry in array
' set parm value, and execute command
For l = lLow To lHigh

   ' get parameter
   val = varTypes(l)

   ' set parameter and execute
   parm.Value = val
   Set rs = cmndObject.Execute

   ' process results
```

Example 8-10. Using a Parameterized Command to Retrieve Several Recordsets (continued)

```
  showPageInfo rs, val
Next

Set cmndObject = Nothing

End Sub
```

The second method, showPageInfo, processes the recordset by printing out the record's file and filename values using the ASP Response object. Add this second method, shown in Example 8-11, to your new component.

Example 8-11. Process Recordset by Printing Out Its Fields Using Response

```
' display records
Private Sub showPageInfo(rs As Recordset, ByVal val)

Dim objContext As ObjectContext
Dim objResponse As Response

Set objContext = GetObjectContext()
Set objResponse = objContext("Response")

' process and display records
objResponse.Write "<h3>" & val & "</h3>"
objResponse.Write "<TABLE border='1' cellpadding='5' cellspacing='0'>"

While rs.EOF <> True
    objResponse.Write "<TR><TD>"
    objResponse.Write rs("name") & "</TD><TD>" & rs("filename")
    objResponse.Write "</TD></TR>"
    rs.MoveNext
Wend

objResponse.Write "</TABLE>"

End Sub
```

Once the component is compiled, testing it is relatively simple: create an array containing page type codes and call the publicly exposed showPages method, as shown in *asp0806.asp*:

```
<%
Dim obj
Set obj = Server.CreateObject("asp0805.cmnd")

Dim ary(2)
ary(0) = "APP"
ary(1) = "HTM"
ary(2) = "STY"

obj.showPages (ary)
%>
```

The array variable in the VBScript code is surrounded by parentheses so that it can be passed by value to the component method. Removing the parentheses results in an error.

Find out more about passing arrays to components in Chapter 6, *ASP Interaction: Scripting and ASP Components.*

Running this example against the Weaver test data generates a web page containing three HTML tables, each with WebPage records reflected by the associated page type codes—HTML pages with the HTM type code, ASP pages with the APP type code, and CSS/XSL type pages with the STY type code.

One of the considerations in using the Prepared property effectively is that the extra effort to compile the command should be justified by the Command object being executed more than once. The same could also be said of the Parameters collection: its effectiveness is directly proportional to the ability to change the parameters and execute the command more than once.

Instead of using the Parameters collection and the Prepared property, we could achieve the same effect from this application by accessing all records with type codes matching those in the array:

```
where page_type_cd IN ('APP','STY','HTM')
```

and then sorting and filtering the recordset to display HTML tables with each page type code.

The Prepared property and the Parameters collection are more effectively used in an interactive environment such as a more traditional client-server application. In this environment, the command can be created, the parameters updated, and the results displayed based directly on the action of the user. In a server environment, such as ASP, you won't want to keep the Command object active between user actions. In fact, you'll want to create it, use it, and remove the Command object as soon as possible to free up data source resources.

The Command object is especially effective when used with stored procedures. Unlike the Connection or Recordset objects, the Command object and its associated parameters collection can process input and output parameters, as well as stored procedure return values.

To demonstrate working with both input and output parameters, create a stored procedure on the SQL Server Weaver database. Example 8-12 contains the code for the procedure that returns the file and filename from the WebPage table based on the **page_type_cd** passed in as a parameter. The procedure also gets the count of rows found with the query and returns a value indicating whether rows were found or not.

Example 8-12. Stored Procedure with Input, Output, and Return Parameters

```
CREATE PROCEDURE [sp_getpages]
(@output integer OUTPUT,
@page_type CHAR(3))
AS
BEGIN
SELECT name, filename FROM WebPage WHERE page_type_cd = @page_type
SELECT @output = COUNT(*) FROM WebPage WHERE page_type_cd = @page_type
IF (@output > 0)
  RETURN 0
ELSE
  RETURN 99
END
GO
```

Next, add a new method to **asp0805.cmnd** named showPagesWithParms; it is shown in Example 8-13. This method takes a single page type code as a parameter and returns a string with the count of rows found in the query, if any. The new method is similar to the one shown in Example 8-10, except that three parameters are defined within the Parameters collection: the page type code input parameter, a return value, and an output parameter. The return and output parameter are created directly in the Parameters collection, and the input parameter is created as an individual Parameter object. The command test is set to the stored procedure name, and the command type is set to **adCmdStoredProc**.

Once the command is executed, the recordset is passed to the showPageInfo method to again output a table with the pages found. Your code can't access the output and return parameters until the recordset is fully traversed or is closed. As the recordset is traversed in another method, and the recordset is passed by value, it needs to be closed before accessing the return and output parameters. The value of the return parameter determines which string is returned from the new method.

Example 8-13. Command Object with Input, Output, and Return Parameters

```
Function showPagesWithParms(ByVal varType As String) As String

Dim cmndObject As New Command
Dim parm As Parameter
Dim rs As Recordset

' set command properties
cmndObject.ActiveConnection = "Provider=SQLOLEDB;server=FLAME;" & _
                              "database=weaver;" & _
                              "uid=sa;pwd="
```

Example 8-13. Command Object with Input, Output, and Return Parameters (continued)

```
cmndObject.CommandType = adCmdStoredProc
cmndObject.CommandText = "sp_getpages"

'set parameters
cmndObject.Parameters.Append cmndObject.CreateParameter("return", _
                                    adInteger, adParamReturnValue)
cmndObject.Parameters.Append cmndObject.CreateParameter("output", _
                                    adInteger, adParamOutput)
Set parm = cmndObject.CreateParameter("page_type_code", _
                                    adChar, adParamInput, 3)
cmndObject.Parameters.Append parm
parm.Value = varType

' execute stored procedure
' process results
Set rs = cmndObject.Execute
showPageInfo rs, varType
rs.Close

' get return value
Dim lReturn, lRows As Long
Dim strReturn As String
lReturn = cmndObject(0)
lRows = cmndObject(1)

' create return string
If lReturn > 0 Then
    strReturn = "No rows were found for the page type code"
Else
    strReturn = "Number of rows found was " & CStr(lRows)
End If

' clean up
Set cmndObject = Nothing
showPagesWithParms = strReturn

End Function
```

Once the component is recompiled, test it by passing to the method an existing and a nonexistent page type code:

```
On Error Resume Next
Dim obj
Set obj = Server.CreateObject("asp0805.cmnd")

Dim code, return

' existing code
code = "SCR"
return = obj.showPagesWithParms(code)
Response.Write "<P>"
Response.Write return & "</p>"
```

```
' nonexistent code
code = "BRB"
return = obj.showPagesWithParms(code)
Response.Write "<P>"
Response.Write return & "</p>"
```

The returned web page contains a table with pages for the first page type code, as well as the number of rows found and a message that no rows were found for the second page type code. Figure 8-2 shows the result of running the ASP test page, *asp0807.asp.*

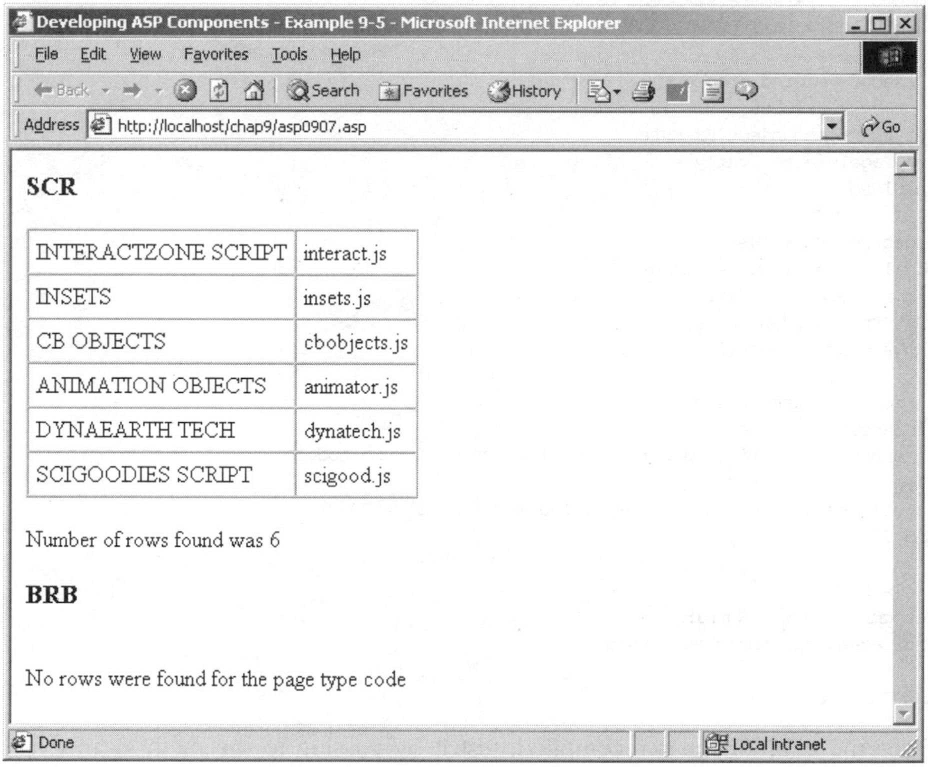

Figure 8-2. WebPage record file and filename fields for two page code types

File and Directory Access with ADO Streams and the Record Object

So far, we've been looking at ADO objects that have existed since ActiveX Data Objects was released. However, recent releases of ADO have introduced some new objects; we'll take a quick look at these in this section and see how they relate to one another and to the older objects.

Both the Stream and Record objects were created to deal with data that doesn't exist in traditional database tables, such as files within a directory system. The Record object can be used to access files and directories or email messages in an email system. The Stream object is used to work with a specific file or email message stream. With the use of a specialized OLE DB provider—the OLE DB Provider for Internet Publishing—the Record object can even access and manipulate objects through a URL.

The Record and Recordset objects can be used together. For instance, you can open a Record object with the contents of a specific recordset row. Additionally, you can open a filesystem directory with the Record object and then access each directory element (file) using the Recordset object.

To demonstrate using the Record and Recordset objects together in order to access the files within a directory, create a new Visual Basic component, name the project asp0806, and name the generated class newguys—for the new ADO objects. Add a method to the component called displayFileNames, which is shown in Example 8-14. This method has a string parameter containing the URL of the web site you wish to access. You'll be listing the filenames for this web site using the ASP Response object, so attach the ASP and COM+ Services type libraries with the ADO library to the project.

In the component method, open the web site by using the Record object's Open method and setting the connection string to a value similar to:

```
URL=http://localhost/weaver/
```

If you don't specify the OLE DB Provider for Internet Publishing, MSDAIPP.DSO, directly in the connection string, you have to use the URL= prefix or you'll get an OLE DB error. Conversely, if you do specify the OLE DB provider directly and use the URL= prefix, you'll also get an error.

Once the directory is opened with the Record object, the files collection contained in the directory is assigned to a Recordset object for traversal. The recordset rows are then traversed and the filename (the first field in the row) is listed to the web page.

Example 8-14. Using the Record Object to Access a Web Site and the Recordset Object to Print Out the Filenames

```
Sub displayFileNames(ByVal strURL As String)

Dim objContext As ObjectContext
Dim objResponse As Response

Set objContext = GetObjectContext()
Set objResponse = objContext("Response")
```

Example 8-14. Using the Record Object to Access a Web Site and the Recordset Object to Print Out the Filenames (continued)

```
On Error GoTo ErrorHandler

Dim grec As New Record
Dim grs As New Recordset

' open directory, get files
strURL = "URL=" & strURL
grec.Open "", strURL
Set grs = grec.GetChildren()

' print out filenames
While Not grs.EOF
    objResponse.Write grs(0) & "<br>"
    grs.MoveNext
Wend

grec.Close
grs.Close

Exit Sub
ErrorHandler:
   objResponse.Write Err.Description
End Sub
```

To access a web site, the site's (or virtual directory's) permissions must be altered to allow access with the OLE DB Provider for Internet Publishing. For instance, to access the files of the directory, in IIS set the site or virtual directory's access permissions to allow for Directory Browsing and Script. To create a new file or directory, turn on Write access for the site.

Use caution when allowing Write access to an externally exposed web site—be sure to use authentication to ensure that only the appropriate people can write to the site.

To test the component, the ASP test page, *asp0808.asp*, passes a valid URL to the method. For the test case, we'll pass in the Weaver administration application web site, installed locally:

```
<%
Dim obj
Set obj = Server.CreateObject("asp0806.newguys")
Dim url
url = "http://localhost/weaver/"
obj.displayFileNames url
%>
```

Before running this example, adjust the Weaver application's permissions, as shown in Figure 8-3. Once the permissions are set correctly, the example component and ASP page list the Weaver application files to the page.

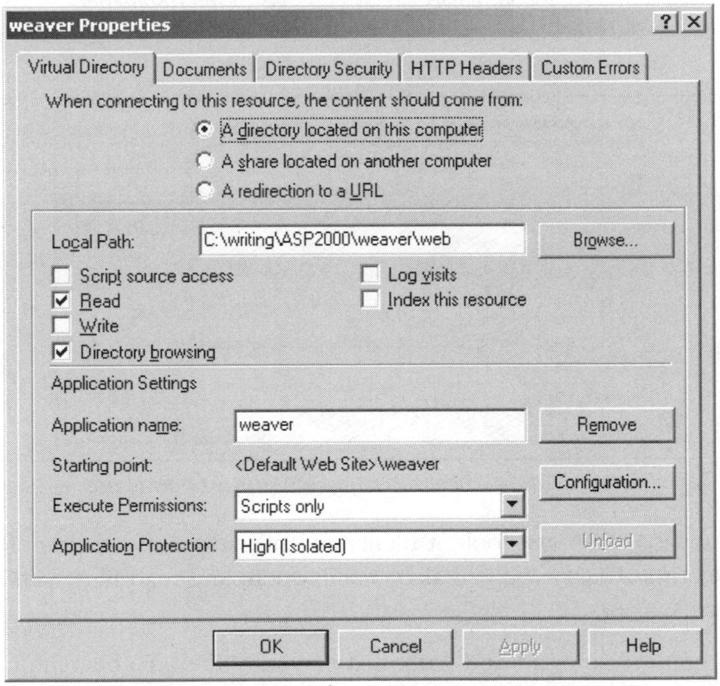

Figure 8-3. Setting the Weaver application's permissions

If the web site is Frontpage-enabled or accessible through web folders via the WebDAV protocol, the site should already be configured for using OLE DB Provider for Internet Publishing. If you change the URL for this example to point to a site external to your machine that has this type of setup, you'll get an authentication login to sign in with your valid username and password.

So, if I access one of my web sites as the standard Internet user (IUSR_ MACHINENAME):

```
Dim obj
Set obj = Server.CreateObject("asp0806.newguys")
Dim url
url = "http://www.yasdbooks.com/devaspcomp/"
obj.displayFileNames url
```

I'll get a login box similar to that shown in Figure 8-4. After typing in my username and password, the list of files and directories located in the provided URL is then displayed.

For more information on using Frontpage, see the documentation provided by Microsoft for this tool. You can read more about web folders in the help documentation that's installed with Windows 2000 or at the Microsoft MSDN site at *http://msdn.microsoft.com.*

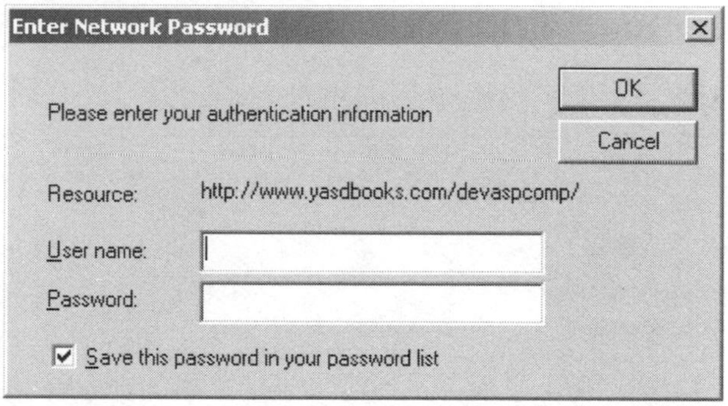

Figure 8-4. Login authentication when accessing web site as Internet user

You can do more than just look at filenames and view the contents of a directory with the Record object—you can also create, open, and read files with a little help from the Stream object.

The Stream object can read and write text or binary files. To become familiar with this object, you'll add a new method to the `asp0806.newguys` component. The method is named copyFile, and it takes three string parameters: the URL of an existing file, the filename, and the name of a new file. The method will contain code that opens the existing file, reads in the contents, and then writes them out to the new file.

Add the code shown in Example 8-15 to the component. Notice that in the call to the Record object's Open method, the *CreateOptions* argument (the third argument) is set to `adOpenIfExists Or adCreateStructDoc` because you're now opening a file rather than a directory. After the record is opened, it's passed as the source for the Stream object's Open method. Other options specified with the method set the file access to read-only (`adModeRead`) and create the stream from a record (`adOpenStreamFromRecord`). Once the Stream object is created, the contents of the source file are read into a local variable.

Both the Stream and Record objects are closed for reuse. Then the new file is created through the Record object's Open method and passed as a parameter to the Stream object, where the contents from the previously opened file are written to it.

Example 8-15. Copy File Using Record and Stream Objects

```
Sub copyFile(ByVal strURL As String, _
             ByVal strFile As String, _
             ByVal strNewFile As String)


Dim recObject As New Record
Dim strmObject As New Stream

' open directory, get file
Dim strModURL As String
strModURL = "URL=" & strURL
recObject.Open strFile, strModURL, adModeRead, _
                                   adOpenIfExists Or adCreateStructDoc

' open stream, read contents
strmObject.Open recObject, adModeRead, adOpenStreamFromRecord
strmObject.Charset = "ascii"
strmObject.Type = adTypeText

Dim str As String
str = strmObject.ReadText(adReadAll)

' close Record and Stream to reuse
recObject.Close
strmObject.Close

' copy file
recObject.Open strNewFile, strModURL, adModeWrite, _
                           adCreateStructDoc Or adCreateOverwrite
strmObject.Open recObject, adModeWrite, adOpenStreamFromRecord
strmObject.WriteText str

' clean up
recObject.Close
strmObject.Close
Set recObject = Nothing
Set strmObject = Nothing

End Sub
```

When the target file is opened, the record creation option for the Record object's Open method is set to **adCreateStructDoc Or adCreateOverwrite**. With this setting, if the file had existed, it would be overwritten with the new contents.

The ASP test page to try out the new method, named *asp0809.asp*, copies a file from the Weaver ASP application to the local Chapter 8 working directory. Once the file has been copied, the Server.Transfer method is used to transfer the web page to the new file:

```
Dim obj
Set obj = Server.CreateObject("asp0806.newguys")
```

```
Dim url, file, newfile
url = "http://localhost/chap8/"
file = "asp0808.asp"
newfile = "listfiles.asp"
obj.copyFile url, file, newfile

Server.Transfer "listfiles.asp"
```

Because the file being opened is a "script" file (with the ASP extension), you'll
need to modify the Access permissions for the Weaver application to allow for
script source access. In addition, as you're creating the copy of the source file in
the Chapter 8 directory, you'll need to set the Chapter 8 virtual directory access
permissions to allow for write access.

Instead of using the Record object to open a new file and then writing the contents of the first file to it, you could have used the Stream object's SaveToFile
method:

```
strmObject.SaveToFile strNewFile, adSaveCreateOverwrite
```

The Stream object can be used with the Recordset object as well as the Record
object to persist data to a stream. This and other persistence techniques are discussed next.

Persisting Data

For most of your ASP applications you'll access data from a data source, process
the data in some way, and then discard your reference to it. However, there are
times when it's more effective to persist the data for a period of time, rather than
retrieving it again and again from the data source. To support this application
need, ADO has techniques you can use to persist a recordset's data to either a file
or to a Stream object.

When you persist data to a file or stream, you are actually persisting the Recordset
object itself. However, before you do this, you have to make sure that your
Recordset object is defined correctly to support persistence. Recordsets that are
going to be persisted must be disconnected from the data source. A requirement
for disconnected recordsets is they must be defined to use client-side cursors:

```
rs.CursorLocation = adUseClient
```

Once the recordset has been opened, to disconnect it you'll need to set the Active-
Connection to Nothing:

```
Set rs.ActiveConnection = Nothing
```

At this point, you can then close the connection if it was created with a Connection object. If it was created specifically with the recordset, setting the ActiveConnection to Nothing closes the connection.

Once you have a disconnected recordset, you can then persist it to either a file or a stream.

The Recordset object's Save method is used to save the data to either a file or a stream, and the Open method is then used to retrieve the data from the file or stream. Earlier, in Example 8-6, you used the Save method to save data to a specific file. In Example 8-7, you then used the Open method to retrieve the disconnected recordset from the file. These two examples saved the data in the ADTG format. Instead, you could have saved the data using an XML format.

To demonstrate saving a recordset formatted as XML, create a new Visual Basic project and call it *asp0807.asp*. Name the generated class `persist`. Add references to both the ActiveX Data Objects library and the Microsoft Scripting Runtime library. The component has one method, saveRsAsXml, with one parameter, a string containing the absolute location and filename of a file.

In your new method, add the code shown in Example 8-16. First, the FileSystemObject is used to test for the existence of the file and delete it if it does exist. Next, a Connection object pointing to the SQL Server version of the Weaver database is opened. The Recordset object is created using the existing connection. For the example, all of the columns and rows from the WebPage table are returned in the result set. Once the data is retrieved, the recordset is disconnected from the connection and persisted to the file in an XML format.

Example 8-16. Saving a Recordset in XML Format

```
Sub saveRsAsXml(ByVal strLoc As String)

' if file exists, delete
Dim fsObject As New FileSystemObject
If fsObject.FileExists(strLoc) Then
    fsObject.DeleteFile strLoc, True
End If

Dim rs As New Recordset
Dim cn As New Connection

' connect to database
cn.ConnectionString = "Provider=SQLOLEDB;server=FLAME;" & _
                      "database=weaver;" & _
                      "uid=sa;pwd="
cn.Open

' set up and open Recordset
rs.CursorLocation = adUseClient
rs.Open "WebPage", cn, adOpenForwardOnly, _
                      adLockReadOnly, adCmdTableDirect

' disconnect/save recordset
Set rs.ActiveConnection = Nothing
```

Example 8-16. Saving a Recordset in XML Format (continued)

```
cn.Close
rs.Save strLoc, adPersistXML

' clean up
rs.Close
Set cn = Nothing
Set rs = Nothing

End Sub
```

To test the component, use ASP script similar to the following, but with your own XML filename and location:

```
<%
Dim obj
Set obj = Server.CreateObject("asp0807.persist")
Dim file
file = "c:\datasets\webpages.xml"
obj.saveRsAsXml file
%>
```

You can find this script in the ASP test page, *asp0810.asp*.

Why save recordset data in an XML format? XML has wide industry acceptance, which translates into a plethora of tools that can work with data in this format. By saving your data as an XML file, you can then access the individual data elements using Microsoft's XML parser (MSXML) or any other XML parser. Additionally, you could add presentation information with XSL (Extensible Stylesheet Language) or CSS (Cascading Style Sheets) and display the data directly to the client via an XML-capable browser.

See more on working with XML and ASP components in Chapter 10, *Server-Side XML Through VB ASP Components.*

As with recordsets persisted as ADTG, you can also reopen the file and reload it into a recordset as well as work with the data in its XML format.

In addition to persisting data to a file, you can also persist it to an ADO Stream object. Once contained in this object, the data can be manipulated, copied to other Stream objects, or saved to a file.

To persist a Recordset to a Stream object, the only difference from the code shown in Example 8-16 would be the following:

```
' create Stream object
Dim strmObject As New Stream
```

```
' save recordset
rs.Save strmObject, adPersistXML
```

As with saving the data to a file, you can accept the default formatting for the data (ADTG) or save the data in XML format.

To access the data from the stream, use the following:

```
rs.Open strmObject
```

Instead of a filename or SQL statement, pass the Stream object that contains the data as the first parameter in the Recordset object's Open method.

9

Creating an ASP Middle Tier with ADO

For years, the most commonly used implementation model for new systems was either the mainframe "dumb terminal" model, with its whisper-thin client, or the client/server model, usually containing fat and chunky clients. With these approaches, the processing tended to congregate totally in the backend of the application with the mainframe application or on the presentation layer with the client/server model. The problem with both approaches is that presentation, data, and business processes become so intertwined that it is virtually impossible to separate the layers in order to modernize or replace any one of them.

Another approach that is gaining popularity, especially with applications making use of the Internet/intranet, is the multitier or n-tier application model. This model, usually implemented in three tiers, splits the business processing from the presentation and data layers. The advantage to this is that the presentation can be changed or even moved to a new medium without having an impact on the business layer. Additionally, the data access can itself be moved to a different database, database model, or machine, again with no impact on the business layer. The business layer itself can also be replaced without necessarily impacting either the presentation or data layers.

One of the most common uses of ASP components is to create a middle tier that separates the presentation layer, which is returned as HTML to the client, and the database or other data source. Components are ideal for this use because they isolate both the data source connectivity (such as user IDs and passwords) as well as hide the details of the database (which can change over time).

The use of ADO to access the data source is ideal—it simplifies data source access and provides all of the power and functionality a developer needs.

This chapter takes a look at some specific issues of using components as an ASP middle tier, including data wrappers, using stored procedures, and others. First, though, we'll take a closer look at what is meant when folks say *separation of data from presentation*.

 Though this chapter uses Visual Basic to create the components in the examples, the concepts that are discussed can be applied to components written in any programming language.

How Separate Should the Layers Be?

If your business is like most, its most consistent aspect is the data, and the most stable component of any development environment is the database schema. The most changeable aspect of your system, on the other hand, is the presentation layer. This can change based on new technologies, new focus within the company, or half a dozen other reasons. Because of this, you'll want to separate the processing that supports the database schema—the business processing—from that of the presentation.

Separation of the business data from the presentation can be as extensive as you wish and depends highly on your type of environment. You can create objects that update specific database tables, then wrap these in other objects that call these objects based on business processes and which are, in turn, invoked from within ASP pages—the presentation layer.

For instance, the administration application included with the Weaver database (see Appendix B, *The Weaver Database*, for more information) is highly separated from not only the presentation but also the environment. However, the presentation isn't as highly separated from the data.

In the Weaver administration application, the components used to manage the data of the database don't access any part of the ASP environment. Instead of using the ASP Application object (and the *global.asa* file) to access the connection string for the database, the connection string is included directly within the components. This means that the connection string needs to be changed if the environment changes—but there isn't any direct access to the environment from the component.

Instead of using the ASP Response object to display any values, the values are returned as disconnected recordsets, arrays, or single values. Instead of using the ASP Request object to pull in HTML form values, the values are passed as parameters to the component methods.

Using this approach with the Weaver data components means that these components could just as easily be accessed from a Visual Basic frontend application as from an ASP page.

However, the same level of isolation doesn't exist between the data and the presentation layer. By returning disconnected recordsets, there is an assumption that the client (in this case the ASP page) must know enough about the recordset to extract the values it, the page, needs from the recordset. Still, the level of isolation is pretty high—even if you have to pull specific values from the recordset, you still don't know how the recordset was created or what the underlying structure of the database is.

Another approach to separation takes it a bit further. A set of components is created to provide direct access to a data source, such as connect to a database, run a query, call a stored procedure, and so on. However, another layer of components that implements the actual business rules and processes accesses this set of data components. Instead of ASP pages directly accessing the data components, they access the business components, which in turn access the data components.

With this, there really is a true level of separation between the presentation layer (and the environment, such as the ASP environment) and the data. This approach is particularly effective if you're unsure of your data source access or if the database may change or does change frequently (something to avoid, by the way).

That components are used to process business rules and access the business data doesn't mean that all presentation issues are handled by ASP pages. Components can be used to provide presentation layer processing, but these components are then considered part of the presentation layer. For instance, you can have presentation *helper* components that do such things as place all HTML form values into an array that is then returned to the ASP page and passed to the business components. Another component can do the same with recordsets—retrieving recordsets into an array or displaying the recordsets using HTML or XML.

However, for the most part, your ADO components form part of the business/data layer, and it is this layer that we'll look at in the rest of this chapter, starting with the concept of component data wrappers.

Creating ADO Data Wrappers

What's a data wrapper? A *data wrapper* is a piece of code wrapped around a specific data entity—such as a database table—providing access to the entity's data through code, without having to use SQL directly to get or set values. They're called wrappers rather than business entities because they don't perform business processes per se; business processes usually impact on more than one entity at a time.

The advantage to a data wrapper component is that other applications can access the underlying data entity without having to know how to access the data source directly. In a larger shop, the people doing the application development may be somewhat isolated from the database schema and may not have a good idea of how the database is accessed, or even what tables exist in the database. By providing data wrappers, the application developers don't have to know all about the database schema—they only have to know about the objects they're accessing in the specific application they're creating. An additional advantage to data wrappers is that the underlying database schema can change, and unless the change impacts the data wrapper component's interface, the applications using that component aren't impacted.

However, data wrappers can degrade performance. For instance, if your application is updating three data entities at once and doing these updates directly on data wrapper objects, there will be at least three calls made to the database. However, if the updates to all three entities were contained in one stored procedure, then the only communication from the application to the database would be the one stored procedure call, which results in better performance and less stress on valuable database connections and resources.

Still, wrapping a table with a component can be handy at times, particularly if the table is usually accessed individually.

Java-based EJB (Enterprise JavaBeans) can be considered the ultimate data wrapper. These Java-based components wrap one database table with code that handles all creation, destruction, access, and updates of that table. Additionally, the EJB environment handles all management of the bean, including transaction, security, and life cycle management. You can emulate this in your environment by providing this same functionality for your significant business tables.

An example of a good use of a data wrapper is to wrap a code table. A code table usually has two columns: a code and a description. For instance, a table holding state abbreviations (such as MA or OR) and their associated descriptions (Massachusetts or Oregon) is an example of a code table. The description is the value that's shown to the client, but the code is the value that's stored in any related tables, such as an address table.

Code tables can also be lookup tables—used to look up and display a predefined set of values, usually in dropdown or other forms of list boxes.

When you access the higher-level business object, such as the address, you'll pull the code table into the query and return the full description rather then the code (usually). However, if you're adding a new address and you want to display a list box with associated states, you'll need to access the lookup table independently to get a listing of states (both code and description). You'll also update and manage the code table independently of any other table—making it a good candidate for a data wrapper.

To demonstrate creating a data wrapper, you'll wrap the MediaType table included in the Weaver database (see Appendix B for more information on this database). The MediaType table has a listing of codes representing the multimedia files used at a particular web site. Currently, the database has the following code/description values:

Code	Description
GIF	GIF89a format
JPG	JPEG image file

There are other multimedia types that can be used at the web site, so you'll need to create a component that can maintain this table.

To create the MediaType data wrapper, create a new Visual Basic project and name it `asp0901`. Name the generated class **MediaType**. Attach the COM+ Services type library (for transaction support) and the latest Microsoft ActiveX Data Objects type library to your project.

The examples in this chapter use the Access version of the Weaver database. You can instead use the SQL Server version just by changing the connection string. See Chapter 8, *Creating ASP/ADO Components*, for an example of the SQL Server OLE DB Provider connection string I use in my own development environment.

Adding a New Media Type

The first method you'll create for the data wrapper is the subroutine to create a new MediaType object as a row within the table. This table has two columns, so the subroutine, newMediaType, will have two parameters, one for each column. Both parameters are of the String data type.

Within the subroutine, which is shown in Example 9-1, some data validation occurs, primarily to make sure that the code is three characters long and the description isn't longer than the column length. A connection is made to the database, and the new row is inserted, with both operations using the Connection object. If no problem occurs, the ObjectContext object's SetComplete method is called to signal that the insertion was successful; otherwise, SetAbort is called.

Example 9-1. Data Wrapper Create Method

```
Sub newMediaType(ByVal strCd As String, _
                 ByVal strDesc As String)

' get object context
Dim objContext As ObjectContext
Set objContext = GetObjectContext

On Error GoTo ErrorHandler

' validate data
If Len(strCd) <> 3 Or Len(strDesc) > 50 Then
   Err.Raise E_INVALIDARG
   Return
End If

' create connection
Dim cn As Connection
Set cn = New Connection

' open conn to database
cn.ConnectionString = "DSN=weaver;uid=sa;pwd="
cn.Open

' insert row
cn.Execute "insert into MediaType values('" _
         + strCd + "','" + strDesc + "')"

'commit
objContext.SetComplete
cn.Close

Exit Sub
ErrorHandler:
   objContext.SetAbort
   Err.Raise Err.Number, Err.Source, Err.Description

End Sub
```

To test the wrapper's method, create two ASP pages: one with a form to add the new media type and one that processes the form and creates the data wrapper component. Both of the test pages (*asp0901.asp* and *asp0902.asp*) can be found in the examples that come with the book, the ASP script in the second page looks like the following:

```
<%
On Error Resume Next

Dim obj
```

```
Set obj = Server.CreateObject("asp0901.MediaType")

Dim cd, desc
cd = Request("cd")
desc = Request("desc")
obj.newMediaType cd,desc
If Err.Number <> 0 Then
    Response.Write "<h3>" & Err.Description & "</h3>"
Else
    Response.Write "<h3>Media Type added</h3>"
End If
%>
```

To test, access the form in *asp0901.asp*, and add the following new media type:

```
PNG     Portable Network Graphics
```

When you submit the form, if no error occurs, a page with the string "Media Type added" is output to the page, and the new type should be in the MediaType table.

Maintaining the Media Types

Other maintenance subroutines performed on the MediaType table and accounted for in the data wrapper delete or update a specific MediaType entry.

To delete a MediaType row, the type's code value is passed into a new data wrapper subroutine called deleteMediaType. As with the method shown in Example 9-1, the Connection object is again used to execute the SQL directly to perform the MediaType maintenance operation, as shown in Example 9-2. After adding the deleteMediaType method, recompile `asp0901.MediaType`.

Example 9-2. Deleting a Specific Media Type

```
Sub deleteMediaType(ByVal strCd As String)

' get object context
Dim objContext As ObjectContext
Set objContext = GetObjectContext

On Error GoTo ErrorHandler

' validate data
If Len(strCd) <> 3 Then
    Err.Raise E_INVALIDARG
    Return
End If

' create connection
Dim cn As Connection
Set cn = New Connection

' open conn to database
cn.ConnectionString = "DSN=weaver;uid=sa;pwd="
```

Example 9-2. Deleting a Specific Media Type (continued)

```
cn.Open

' delete row
cn.Execute "delete from MediaType where cd = '" _
        + strCd + "'"

'commit
objContext.SetComplete
cn.Close

Exit Sub
ErrorHandler:
  objContext.SetAbort
  Err.Raise Err.Number, Err.Source, Err.Description

End Sub
```

The component code to delete the code value is easy, but the referential integrity of the underlying database can add complexity to the process of deleting the row. Depending on your database and the type of referential constraints defined for the database tables, you may or may not be able to delete a code table row until other data that references the deleted data is also deleted. For instance, the Weaver MediaObject table contains a foreign key reference to the MediaType table, and if you were to delete a MediaType currently used within MediaObject, the table's referential integrity would be violated.

 What is referential integrity? It is the rules that govern how tables relate to one another and is usually enforced through foreign key relationships between the tables. The purpose of referential integrity is to ensure consistent and reliable data within the database.

Referential integrity rules in both the SQL Server and the Access versions of the Weaver database will prevent you from deleting any of the MediaType records that are associated with rows in the MediaObject table. To see what happens when you try, access the ASP test page, *asp0903.asp*:

```
<head>
<title>Weaver: Add new MediaType</title>

<script type="text/javascript" language="javascript">

function check_values() {
var frm = document.forms[0];

if (frm.cd.value.length <= 0) {
    alert("Please Enter Media Type Code");
```

```
            return;
        }


    frm.submit();

    }
    </SCRIPT>
    </head>
    <body style="margin-left: 20px; margin-top: 20px">
    <h1> Delete Media Type</h1>
    <form method="POST" action="asp0904.asp">
    <p>
    <input type="text" size="10" name="cd" />   
    </p>
    <p>
    <input type="button" value="Delete MediaType" onClick="check_values()" />
    <input type="reset" value="Clear Form">
    </p>
    </form>
    </body>
```

This page contains a form in which you can enter a specific MediaType code to delete. Enter the code value of GIF and submit the form.

The *asp0903.asp* test page invokes another ASP test page, *asp0904.asp*, containing the following script:

```
<%
On Error Resume Next

Dim obj
Set obj = Server.CreateObject("asp0901.MediaType")

Dim cd, desc
cd = Request("cd")
obj.deleteMediaType cd
If Err.Number <> 0 Then
    Response.Write "<h3>" & Err.Description & "</h3>"
Else
    Response.Write "<h3>Media Type deleted</h3>"
End If
%>
```

If an error occurs, the error message is output to the return page. When you try to delete the GIF MediaType, you'll get the following error (if you pointed your ASP component at the Access version of Weaver):

```
[Microsoft][ODBC Microsoft Access Driver]
The record cannot be deleted or changed because table
'MediaObject' includes related records.
```

This type of behavior is exactly what you would want to maintain the integrity of the MediaObject and MediaType tables. If you try *asp0903.asp* again, but this time type in the new PNG media type you just created, you won't get any errors—there are no records in MediaObject using this media type.

The same constraints that apply to deleting a media type code that's used elsewhere in the database also apply to updating the media type's code column value, though you can update the description without a problem. In fact, for small code tables such as MediaType, an "update" can be nothing more than a deletion of the existing record followed by an insertion of the new values.

To demonstrate this, add a third subroutine, named updateMediaType, to the MediaType data wrapper (asp0902.MediaType); its source code is shown in Example 9-3. The updateMediaType method has two parameters: the code and the description. In the method, instead of accessing the database directly, the code calls the component's own deleteMediaType method (to delete the existing code row). Then the code calls the newMediaType method to insert the new row. (Although the objContext object has been instantiated elsewhere—see Chapter 7, *Creating a Simple Visual Basic ASP Component*, for more information about creating an instance of objContext—the code included in the examples has instantiated this object.)

Example 9-3. Updating Code Table Row by Deletion and Then Insertion

```
Sub updateMediaType(ByVal strCd As String, _
                ByVal strDesc As String)

On Error GoTo ErrorHandler

deleteMediaType strCd
newMediaType strCd, strDesc

Exit Sub
ErrorHandler:
  objContext.SetAbort
  Err.Raise Err.Number, Err.Source, Err.Description

End Sub
```

Doing a deletion followed by an insertion is a valid technique—but not necessarily for a parent or a code table. Even without testing the component, you can see a problem occurring with the referential integrity that won't allow you to delete a MediaType row that's referenced in the MediaObject table. So if you try to update the GIF row using this component method, your update will fail.

Instead of using the delete/insert method of updating, add the code shown in Example 9-4 to the asp0901.MediaType component. It contains a new version of updateMediaType, called updateMediaType2, that uses SQL to perform an explicit update of the description for the row containing the target code.

Example 9-4. Updating the Description for a Specific MediaType Code

```
Sub updateMediaType2(ByVal strCd As String, _
                ByVal strDesc As String)

' get object context
Dim objContext As ObjectContext
Set objContext = GetObjectContext

On Error GoTo ErrorHandler

' validate data
If Len(strDesc) > 50 Then
   Err.Raise E_INVALIDARG
   Return
End If

' create connection
Dim cn As Connection
Set cn = New Connection

' open conn to database
cn.ConnectionString = "DSN=weaver;uid=sa;pwd="
cn.Open

' insert row
cn.Execute "update MediaType set description = '" _
        & strDesc & "' where cd = '" & strCd & "'"

'commit
objContext.SetComplete
cn.Close

Exit Sub
ErrorHandler:
  objContext.SetAbort
  Err.Raise Err.Number, Err.Source, Err.Description

End Sub
```

An assumption is made with this second update method: the description and not
the code is the value to be updated. If the client wanted to update the code and
not the description, the update would fail, since no row would be found in the
MediaType table matching the new code.

To best way prevent a user from trying to update the code itself is to provide a list
of codes for the user to select from. The next section finishes the MediaType data
wrapper by creating functions that return information from the MediaType table.
At that time, you'll also have a chance to test your new update method.

MediaType Data Wrapper Queries

With a code and/or a lookup table, most operations on the data will be queries rather than updates. In fact, once a code table has initially been populated, modifications to the table will be rare.

With a code table, the most common queries are to return a description given a specific code and to return all code and description values. In this section, you'll create component methods in `asp0901.MediaType` for each of these queries.

The first query to implement is one that returns all codes and descriptions from the MediaType table, which can then be used to populate dropdown list boxes. Add a new method to `asp0901.MediaType` called getCodes, as shown in Example 9-5. There are no parameters, but the method is a function, returning a Variant data type. You're accessing a result set, so you'll use the ADO Recordset object within this function. In the code, query for all MediaType codes and descriptions, and assign the values to a Variant array, which is then returned from the function. You'll use the Recordset object's GetRows function to assign the rows to a two-dimensional array—the first dimension has the field name, the second the associated value for that field.

Example 9-5. Getting Codes and Descriptions from MediaType Code Table

```
Function getCodes() As Variant

' create recordset
Dim rs As Recordset
Set rs = New Recordset

' Recordset properties
rs.ActiveConnection = "DSN=weaver;uid=sa;pwd="
rs.Source = "select cd,description from MediaType"

' query
rs.Open

' process result
getCodes = rs.GetRows

End Function
```

One thing about code or other lookup tables is that the number of rows contained in the table is usually small (less than 100). If the table starts to become large, chances are your database design is mixing code types—the table contains more than one set of code values. For instance, you wouldn't combine "states" and "counties" into the same table. Instead, you'd create your state table and then create a county table, with state being part of the county identifier (one county name can be in more than one state). With this approach, you can access the state values separate from the county, and the two distinctly different types of data aren't mixed into the same code table.

To try out getCodes, the following ASP page, *asp0905.asp*, contains a <SELECT> form element containing the codes returned by the getCodes method:

```
<form method="POST" action="asp0906.asp">
<p>
<select name="cd">
<%

Dim obj
Set obj = Server.CreateObject("asp0901.MediaType")

Dim ary, i, ct
ary = obj.getCodes

ct = UBound(ary,2)

For i = 0 to ct
   Response.Write "<option value='"
   Response.Write ary(0,i) & "'>" & ary(0,i)
   Response.Write "</option>"
Next
%>
</select>
  <input type="text" name="description" size="80"></p>
<p>
<input type="submit">
</p>
</form>
```

In this form, the description values aren't used, but client-side scripting could be used to display the current description for the associated code value whenever the client selects a different code. Select the GIF value from the list, and change the description to:

```
A popular form of image used in Web pages
```

When you submit the form with the changed description, the following ASP page, *asp0906.asp*, processes the form and calls updateMediaType2, passing it the existing code and the new description:

```
<%
On Error Resume Next

Dim obj
Set obj = Server.CreateObject("asp0901.MediaType")

Dim cd, desc
cd = Request("cd")
desc = Request("description")
obj.updateMediaType2 cd,desc
```

```
If Err.Number <> 0 Then
    Response.Write "<h3>" & Err.Description & "</h3>"
Else
    Response.Write "<h3>Media Type updated</h3>"
End If
%>
```

If you access the data directly in the database manager (using either Access or SQL Server, or using the Weaver administration application), you'll see that the description is changed for the GIF code.

Instead of displaying the code values, you could display the descriptions. In the Weaver administration application, the description for the media types is shown when adding a new Media object.

The Weaver administration application components return disconnected recordsets when populating dropdown list boxes. Both approaches—the two-dimensional array or the disconnected recordset—are feasible to use.

In the next query you'll implement, a description is returned for a specific code value. Add the method named getDescription, which is shown in Example 9-6, to the `asp0901.MediaType` component. The getDescription method has one input parameter and a string return value. If a row is found that has a matching code value, the description is returned; otherwise, an empty string is returned.

Example 9-6. Getting Description for Specific Code from MediaType

```
Function getDescription(ByVal strCode As String) As String

' create recordset
Dim rs As Recordset
Set rs = New Recordset

' Recordset properties
rs.ActiveConnection = "DSN=weaver;uid=sa;pwd="
rs.Source = "select description from MediaType where cd = '" _
            & strCode & "'"

' query
rs.Open

getDescription = rs("description")

rs.Close

End Function
```

To test the new component code, the following ASP test page, *asp0907.asp*, lists the MediaType codes in a list box, using code identical to that shown earlier in the *asp0906.asp* ASP test page:

```
<head>
<title>Weaver: Add new MediaType</title>
</head>
<body style="margin-left: 20px; margin-top: 20px">
<form method="POST" action="asp0908.asp">
<p>
<select name="cd">
<%

Dim obj
Set obj = Server.CreateObject("asp0901.MediaType")

Dim ary, i, ct
ary = obj.getCodes

ct = UBound(ary,2)

For i = 0 to ct
    Response.Write "<option value='"
    Response.Write ary(0,i) & "'>" & ary(0,i)
    Response.Write "</option>"
Next
%>
</select>
<p>
<input type="submit">
</p>
</form>
</body>
```

Select one of the media types and click the Submit button. This requests the second ASP test page, *asp0908.asp*, which calls getDescription, passing it the code value and displaying the returned string. This is the *asp0908.asp* test page:

```
<%
On Error Resume Next

Dim obj
Set obj = Server.CreateObject("asp0901.MediaType")

Dim cd, desc
cd = Request("cd")
desc = obj.getDescription(cd)
If Err.Number <> 0 Then
    Response.Write "<h3>" & Err.Description & "</h3>"
Else
    Response.Write "<h3>" & desc & "</h3>"
End If
%>
```

The getDescription method shown in Example 9-6 doesn't test for the existence of the description, because the code used to find it is taken from the same table. However, in an environment in which updates are frequently made to the code or lookup tables, you'll want to test to make sure that the description is found before accessing it—the row could have been deleted (unlikely as that is) between the time the dropdown was populated with the code values and the time the query for the description was made.

Data wrappers are useful for code or other lookup tables, but for the most part you'll create business object components to maintain and query your data source. A business object differs from a data wrapper because more than one table is impacted.

Defining Business Objects

Instead of using data wrappers, most applications define components that represent business objects. These objects can update more than one table. For instance, if you have customers, you might have a customer table, an address table, an order table, and so on, each of which is managed or impacted by the Customer business object.

With business objects, queries are likely based on table joins, with two or more tables providing information. Updates can be made to two or more tables, with child or dependent tables updated first and master tables updated only when all other updates succeed.

In the Weaver database, an HTML web page entity actually references the following Weaver tables:

WebPage
> The main web page table

Directory
> The directory where the page is located

HTMLWebPage
> Additional information unique to HTML pages only

PageType
> The code for the type of web page

AssistingTool
> A tool used with the WebPage

Other tables can be impacted, such as the PageMedia table, containing the WebPage/MediaObject associations, and PageStyle, with the WebPage/StyleWebPage associations.

In the Weaver Administration application, when you add an HTML web page, you'll be supplying information that updates both the WebPage and the HTML-WebPage tables at once, since HTMLWebPage is a category of WebPage with associated information specific to HTML web pages. In fact, you'll update the HTMLPage table only if the update to the WebPage table was successful, since the same identifier used with WebPage is used with the HTMLWebPage table.

The WebPage table has a *category* relationship with several other tables, such as HTMLWebPage, AppWebPage, and StyleWebPage. Each of the child tables has the same identifier as the parent WebPage table, and the category code that determines which child table is populated is the `page_type_cd`.

Category relationships always have one column in the parent that determines which of the child tables is populated.

To query for information about a specific HTML web page, you'll retrieve information from the WebPage and HTMLPage tables, as you would expect. However, you'll also access Directory, to get the description for the directory where the page is located, as well as AssistingTool, to get the description for any tools, such as validation tools, used with WebPage. The relationships between all of these tables are shown in Figure 9-1 using the IDEF1 data-modeling format.

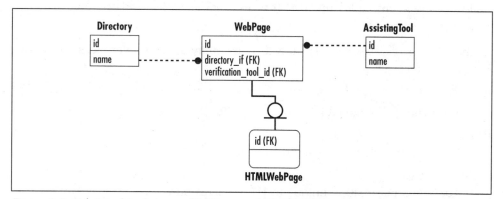

Figure 9-1. Relationships between WebPage and HTMLWebPage, Directory, and AssistingTool

If you open the WebPage component in the administration application and then access the HTML class, you'll see that when a new HTML web page is added to the database, both the WebPage and the HTMLWebPage tables are updated, as shown in Example 9-7. In this component method, the insertion in the WebPage table is made, and then the insertion into the HTMLWebPage table is made only if the insertion into WebPage was successful.

Example 9-7. Maintaining Parent/Child Dependencies in an HTML Web Page

```
' create page
Sub createHtmlPage(ByVal varIdentifier As Variant, _
                   ByVal strName As String, _
                   ByVal strFile As String, _
                   ByVal strExt As String, _
                   ByVal varDirectoryId As Variant, _
                   ByVal strPageType As String, _
                   ByVal varFileSize As Variant, _
                   ByVal varToolId As Variant, _
                   ByVal varVerificationDt As Variant, _
                   ByVal varPulledDt As Variant, _
                   ByVal strVersion As String)


Dim objCntxt As ObjectContext

On Error GoTo ErrorHandler

Set objCntxt = GetObjectContext()

' open connection
Dim cn As New Connection
cn.ConnectionString = m_connString

cn.Open

' possible null values
If Len(varVerificationDt) = 0 Then
    varVerificationDt = "null"
Else
    varVerificationDt = "'" & varVerificationDt & "'"
End If
If Len(varToolId) = 0 Then
    varToolId = "null"
End If
If Len(varPulledDt) = 0 Then
    varPulledDt = "null"
Else
    varPulledDt = "'" & varPulledDt & "'"
End If

' truncate strings if necessary
strName = UCase(Left(strName, 20))
strFile = Left(strFile, 20)
strVersion = Left(strVersion, 20)

' build insert
Dim str As String
str = "insert into WebPage (id, name, filename, ext, directory_id, " & _
  "page_type_cd, file_size, verification_tool_id, verification_date, " & _
  "pulled_date)" & _
  " values(" & varIdentifier & ",'" & strName & "','" & _
  strFile & "','" & UCase(strExt) & "'," & varDirectoryId & _
  ",'" & strPageType & "'," & varFileSize & "," & varToolId & "," & _
```

Example 9-7. Maintaining Parent/Child Dependencies in an HTML Web Page (continued)

```
varVerificationDt & "," & varPulledDt & ")"

' execute SQL
cn.Execute str

' associated table insert
str = "insert into HtmlWebPage (webpage_id, html_version) " & _
      "values(" & varIdentifier & ", '" & strVersion & "')"

cn.Execute str

cn.Close

' commit and deactivate object
objCntxt.SetComplete

Exit Sub

ErrorHandler:

    ' abort and raise error and deactivate object
    objCntxt.SetAbort
    Err.Raise Err.Number, Err.Source, str & "Creating Page: " & _
                    Err.Description

End Sub
```

To delete the HTML web page data, the row associated with the HTMLWebPage is deleted first, or the referential integrity associated with the tables' association wouldn't allow the WebPage row to be deleted. The deletions from both tables are committed only if both deletions succeed.

Another approach to maintain referential integrity in a parent/child relationship is to use functionality provided by the database: cascaded deletes. This approach is discussed in the next section.

Maintaining the Integrity of the Data

Earlier, you had a chance to test referential integrity when you tried to delete a MediaType row that still had associated records in the MediaObject table. Since MediaType is a code table, this action was appropriate. However, in a parent/child or dependent table relationship, another approach that you can use (if it's supported by the database engine) is *cascaded deletes*.

In cascaded deletes, a parent table row is deleted, and any associated child or dependent table rows are also deleted in one operation. You don't have to do anything in the code to enforce cascaded deletes—they're handled by the database. Because the operation is handled by the database, referential integrity is guaranteed, and you make only one call to the database—the call to delete the parent table record.

To try this out for yourself, create a new Visual Basic project and name it asp0902. Name the generated class **HTMLPage**. Attach both the COM+ Services and Microsoft ActiveX Data Object type libraries to the project.

In the new component, create a method named deletePage that takes the page identifier as its only parameter; its source code is shown in Example 9-8. The method deletes the record in WebPage that matches the page ID.

Example 9-8. Using Cascaded Deletes to Maintain Referential Integrity

```
Sub deletePage(ByVal iPage As Variant)

' get object context
Dim objContext As ObjectContext
Set objContext = GetObjectContext()

On Error GoTo ErrorHandler

' create connection
Dim cn As Connection
Set cn = New Connection

' open conn to database
cn.ConnectionString = "DSN=weaver;uid=sa;pwd="
cn.Open

' delete page
cn.Execute "delete from WebPage where id = " & iPage

'commit
objContext.SetComplete
cn.Close

Exit Sub
ErrorHandler:
   objContext.SetAbort
   Err.Raise Err.Number, Err.Source, Err.Description

End Sub
```

As you can see from the code with the component, you don't have to add any special code to get the benefits of cascaded deletes. You do, however, have to adjust the database to enforce referential integrity by using cascaded deletes for the component.

Of course, the parent table could have more than one dependent relationship. For instance, if you delete a web page that has associated entries in PageComponent or PageMedia (other tables dependent on WebPage), you'll still get a referential integrity error. You would have to modify the relationship with all of the dependent tables to support cascaded deletes.

Each database engine has different techniques you'll need to follow to add support for cascaded deletes. For the Access version of the Weaver database, you'll access the Relationships dialog of the database (available on the toolbar or from the Tools menu), and then double-click on the relationship between WebPage and HTMLWebPage. In the Edit Relationships dialog, check the Cascade Delete Related Records option, as shown in Figure 9-2, and save the change.

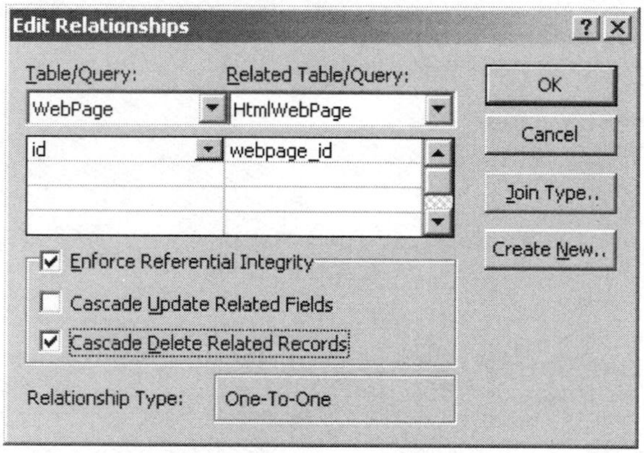

Figure 9-2. Adding cascade delete referential integrity enforcement

To test both the new referential integrity enforcement and the new component, access the following ASP test page, *asp0909.asp*, which prints out a line of information about each HTML web page using the Weaver administration `WebPage.HTML` component:

```
<head>
<title>Weaver: Display HTML Pages</title>
</head>
<body style="margin-left: 20px; margin-top: 20px">
<h1>Current HTML Pages</h1>
<table width="95%" align="center" border="1" cellpadding="10" cellspacing="0">
<tr style="background-color: #009900">
<th>Page Name</th>
<th>Filename</th>
<th>Directory</th>
<th colspan=3>Action</th>
```

```
</tr>
<%
On Error Resume Next

Dim obj
Dim rs

Set obj = Server.CreateObject("WebPage.HTML")
set rs = obj.getPartialPages()
If Err.Number <> 0 Then
   Response.Write Err.Description
Else
   Dim i, ct
   ct = rs.RecordCount
   For i = 0 to ct
      Response.Write "<tr>"
      Response.Write "<td>" & rs.Fields(1) & "</td>"
      Response.Write "<td>" & rs.Fields(2) & "</td>"
      Response.Write "<td>" & rs.Fields(4) & "</td>"
      Response.Write "<td><a href='asp0910.asp?id=" & rs.Fields(0)
                     & "'>Delete Page</a>"
      Response.Write "</TR>"
      rs.MoveNext
   Next
End If
Response.Write ("</table>")

%>
</body>
```

Pick one of the pages to delete, and click on the link labeled Delete Page. Clicking on the link calls another ASP test page, *asp0910.asp*, that calls the new component's deletePage method; the source for *asp0910.asp* is as follows:

```
<%
On Error Resume Next

Dim obj
Set obj = Server.CreateObject("asp0902.HTMLPage")

Dim id
id = Request.QueryString("id")

obj.deletePage id

If Err.Number <> 0 Then
   Response.Write "<h1 style='color: darkgreen'>Error with Data</h1>"
   Response.Write Err.Description
Else
   Response.Write "<h1 style='color: darkgreen'>
                                  HTML Page has been deleted</h1>"
End If
%>
```

When this page is called, if you hadn't adjusted the referential integrity from prevent (the default) to cascaded delete, you would receive an error when you delete the page using `asp0902.HTMLPage`—the child table row would still be in the database, so you couldn't delete the parent or master table row. However, with cascaded deletes, both associated rows are deleted.

Using the database integrity enforcement rules is an exceptionally good idea, as long as you're aware of the structure of the database. If you have a sequence of tables that are related to one another in a parent/child relationship, one deletion on the highest-level master table is all you'll need to ensure that all of the tables are kept in sync with one another. However, you must be sure that there is a parent/child relationship and not a relationship that exists from something such as a code lookup table and another table. This latter type of hierarchical table relationship should never be maintained with cascaded deletions—the use of this technique would be inappropriate.

You can also use cascaded updates to update parent/child tables based on the change of the identifier in the parent. However, parental identifiers should *not* change, and cascaded updates should be used rarely, if at all.

Integrity rules can be enforced by the database engine or by database triggers. For more complex relationships, you can code the rules enforcement directly within the component. However, this isn't the best approach to use, since one database change can mean changing several components. Instead, you should consider handling anything beyond the simplest database accesses (update or query) with stored procedures, discussed next.

Using Stored Procedures

Stored procedures are functions created and stored in a precompiled form in the database. Instead of embedding a SQL statement such as a query directly in your ASP component code, you call the procedure instead, passing in any parameters it might require. Stored procedures can be used for any type of data access, including updates to the database.

There are several advantages to using stored procedures. First, developers who are more familiar with the database organization, as well as more familiar with efficient database access, can create the stored procedures. Component developers may not have this same level of familiarity with either the database schema or with database access techniques. Secondly, stored procedures hide much of the physical implementation of the database schema, making it simpler to make changes to the schema at a later time, if needed, without necessarily impacting the applications that access the data. A third reason that stored procedures are efficient is that they're stored in a compiled form within the database itself, increasing the speed with which the database access request is processed. Embedded SQL must go through the database engine's SQL engine first before the SQL can be processed.

One downside to stored procedures is that not all databases support them. For instance, the application I provided to administer the Weaver database included with this book does not use stored procedures because one version of the database was created in Access. Still, if your organization is using a database that supports stored procedures, such as Oracle or SQL Server, and has the expertise to create these procedures, consider using them for anything but the simplest database access.

To demonstrate how to call a stored procedure from an ASP component, create a new stored procedure, *sp_getPageAssocs*, shown in Example 9-9, in the SQL Server version of the Weaver database. This procedure queries for and returns rows containing component, script, image, and stylesheet usage information for a specific HTML, ASP, or XML web page. If you have access to the SQL Server version of the Weaver database, create this stored procedure in that database.

Example 9-9. Stored Procedure Returning Multiple Recordsets

```
CREATE PROCEDURE sp_getPageAssocs
 @pageid int
 AS
BEGIN

/* get component information */
select "Page Components",  name, filename,
comp_type_cd, comp_language from
component, PageComponent where page_id = @pageid and
component.id = PageComponent.component_id

/* get script information */
select "Page Scripts", name, filename, script_language from
WebPage, ScrptWebPage, PageScript where
PageScript.page_id = @pageid and
WebPage.id = PageScript.script_page_id and
ScrptWebPage.webpage_id = PageScript.script_page_id

/* get image info */
select "Page Images", name, filename, description from
MediaObject, MediaType, PageMedia where
page_id = @pageid and
MediaObject.id = PageMedia.media_id and
MediaType.cd = MediaObject.media_type_cd

/* get style information */
select "Page Stylesheets", name, filename, description from
```

Example 9-9. Stored Procedure Returning Multiple Recordsets (continued)

```
WebPage, StyleWebPage, StyleType, PageStyle where
PageStyle.page_id = @pageid and
WebPage.id = PageStyle.style_page_id and
StyleWebPage.webpage_id = PageStyle.style_page_id and
StyleType.cd = StyleWebPage.style_code

END
```

In the stored procedure, the type of the object being returned is created as the first field in the recordset. This will be used to create a title for the display of the objects, as you'll see next.

Create a new Visual Basic component and name it **asp0903**. Name the generated class **strproc**. Attach the ADO, ASP, and COM+ Services type libraries to the project.

Add a method to the new component named getPageAssociations that has one parameter, an integer representing a specific web page; its source code is shown in Example 9-10. The method creates a connection to the SQL Server Weaver database and calls the stored procedure by using the Connection object's Execute method. A Recordset object is returned from the method call. The component code will access each recordset from the stored procedure call and display the field values using an HTML table. Each recordset is accessed in turn until the Recordset object is set to **Nothing**, which means that the last stored procedure result set has been processed.

Example 9-10. Calling a Stored Procedure and Printing the Result Sets

```
Sub getPageAssociations(ByVal iPageId As Integer)

Dim cn As Connection
Dim rs As Recordset
Dim connString As String

' connect to database
connString = "Provider=SQLOLEDB;server=FLAME;database=weaver;uid=sa;pwd="
Set cn = New Connection
cn.ConnectionString = connString
cn.Open

' call stored procedure
Dim cmndString As String
cmndString = "exec sp_getPageAssocs " & CStr(iPageId)
Set rs = cn.Execute(cmndString)

' create Response object
' process Results
Dim objResponse As Response
Set objResponse = GetObjectContext().Item("Response")
```

Example 9-10. Calling a Stored Procedure and Printing the Result Sets (continued)

```
Dim fld As Field
With objResponse

  Do Until rs Is Nothing

    ' get caption
    .Write "<h3>" & rs(0) & "</h3>"
    .Write "<table border='0' cellpadding='10'>"

    ' get next set of objects
    Do While Not rs.EOF
      .Write "<tr>"

      ' get object fields
      For Each fld In rs.Fields
        .Write "<TD>" & fld.Value & "</TD>"
      Next fld
      .Write "</TR>"
      rs.MoveNext
    Loop
    .Write "</TABLE>"

    ' next recordset
    Set rs = rs.NextRecordset
  Loop
End With

cn.Close

End Sub
```

To test the new component and the stored procedure, use the Weaver Administration tool (in the Weaver subdirectory of the examples for the book) to create several page/component, page/style, page/media object, and page/script associations for one of the ASP application web pages, such as the page named *Articles Main*. Once you've staged your test data, access `asp0903.strproc` with the following ASP script, contained in *asp0911.asp*:

```
<%
On Error Resume Next

Dim obj
Set obj = Server.CreateObject("asp0903.strproc")

obj.getPageAssociations 15
If Err.Number <> 0 Then
    Response.Write "<h1 style='color: darkgreen'>Error with Stored Procedure Call</
h1>"
    Response.Write Err.Description
End If
%>
```

The results should look similar to those shown in Figure 9-3: the results or each page association are printed out to the web page with a separate header and in a separate HTML table.

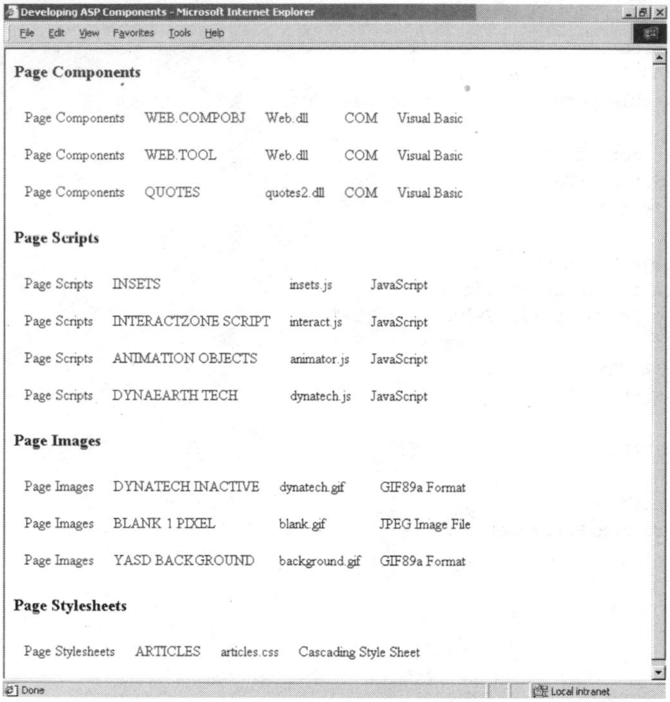

Figure 9-3. Accessing a stored procedure with multiple recordsets from an ASP component

Instead of embedding each query within the component, you called one stored procedure that in turn created each query. With this approach, you've simplified your ASP component code, and you've increased the performance of the application. Instead of several calls made to the database, you made only one, and that to a precompiled stored procedure.

Earlier in the chapter, you created a component that used cascaded deletes to maintain the referential integrity between WebPage and HtmlWebPage. You can use this approach to ensure that the referential integrity is handled correctly for all WebPage associations, such as those with PageComponent, PageMedia, PageStyle, and PageScript, as well as with HtmlWebPage. Alternatively, use a stored procedure to handle the referential integrity when you delete a specific page.

You might prefer to handle referential integrity yourself, in order to perform actions other than just deleting the child dependent rows. For instance, you might want to update other data based on the deletion.

To test using a stored procedure to maintain referential integrity when you delete an HTML page, create a new SQL Server stored procedure named *sp_deleteHtml-PageAssocs*, as shown in Example 9-11. In the procedure, individual deletions are made of each table dependent on WebPage: PageComponent, PageScript, PageMedia, PageStyle, and HtmlWebPage. Lastly, the WebPage table row itself is deleted.

Example 9-11. Stored Procedure to Delete Dependent Table Rows

```
CREATE PROCEDURE sp_deleteHtmlPageAssocs
 @pageid int
 AS
BEGIN

/* delete page/component associations */
delete from PageComponent where page_id = @pageid

/* delete page/media object associations */
delete from PageMedia where page_id = @pageid

/* delete page/script association */
delete from PageScript where page_id = @pageid

/* delete from page/style association */
delete from PageStyle where page_id = @pageid

/* delete HTML page */
delete from HtmlWebPage where webpage_id = @pageid

/* finally, delete the web page */
delete from WebPage where id = @pageid

END
```

Add a new method to **asp0903.strproc** called deleteHtmlPage. Add the code shown in Example 9-12 to your component method. This method, like the first for the component, takes a page identifier as its only parameter. As with the first component method call, the new stored procedure is called, but this time, there is no recordset returned from the procedure call.

Actually, there is a Recordset object returned anytime you call the Connection or Command object's Execute method—but it is set to Nothing if no result sets are returned.

Example 9-12. Calling Procedure to Delete an HTML Page and Maintain Referential Integrity

```
Sub deleteHtmlPage(ByVal iPageid As Integer)

Dim cn As Connection
Dim connString As String

' connect to database
connString = "Provider=SQLOLEDB;server=FLAME;database=weaver;uid=sa;pwd="
Set cn = New Connection
cn.ConnectionString = connString
cn.Open

' call stored procedure
Dim cmndString As String
cmndString = "exec sp_deleteHtmlPageAssocs " & CStr(iPageid)
cn.Execute (cmndString)

cn.Close

End Sub
```

Since you're making database updates, you'll need to use transactions with the component, so add **asp0903.strproc** to an existing (or new) COM+ application, and set its transaction property to Required. Also add the following **Transaction** directive to the ASP page:

```
<%@ TRANSACTION = required %>
```

Next call the component in this ASP test page, *asp0912.asp*, making sure to call ObjectContent's SetAbort if you don't want the table deletions to be permanent:

```
<%
On Error Resume Next

Dim obj
Set obj = Server.CreateObject("asp0903.strproc")

obj.deleteHtmlPage 1
ObjectContext.SetAbort
If Err.Number <> 0 Then
    Response.Write "<h1 style='color: darkgreen'>Error with Stored Procedure Call</
h1>"
    Response.Write Err.Description
Else
    Response.Write "<h1 style='color: darkgreen'>HTML Page deleted</h1>"
End If
%>
```

If you want to make sure that the stored procedure is working, you can change the ObjectContext call to SetComplete—but make sure you use a test page that you won't mind deleting, such as the one you created earlier when you tested queries from stored procedures.

Other Data Integrity Issues

In the last section, you used a stored procedure and cascading deletes to maintain referential integrity, but there are other types of data integrity that you'll most likely have to enforce within application code—but not necessarily within your component or only within your component.

For instance, you might have a parent/child table dependency that is further refined to allow only five children table rows. If you have a purchase order form that only allows five purchase order items, you might enforce this in your component code as the items are added to the purchase order item table.

Other types of data integrity are those that test whether a data value provided fits within a specific format. A Social Security number must consist of numbers only and be exactly 9 characters wide without the hyphens. This type of data checking, however, should be performed on the client using script when the data is input, and an error message should be provided before the data is even sent to the ASP page for processing.

You'll also usually check the data again within the component just to ensure that it's the proper format and data type. This protects data integrity in the event of a deliberate attempt to bypass client-side data validation.

Another form of data validation is range checking. For instance, if you're getting someone's age, you might safely test to make sure that the value entered is more than 0 and less than 150 years. At this time, I'm unaware of anyone falling outside this age group. Again, this type of check can be made on the client first, or it may be made on the server based on data pulled from the database.

If you need data from the database in order to validate new data, your best approach is to attach pre-update or pre-insert triggers on the target field and use database processing to test the validity of the data. This should prevent extra network calls for all cases except when the data validation fails.

What About ACID?

You've probably heard the term *ACID* referred to when it comes to data operations. This acronym stands for atomicity, consistency, isolation, and durability, and it refers to transaction management rather than data integrity—though integrity of the data is the end result of the successful application of ACID with transactions.

A data source transaction is *atomic* if every operation to every data source contained within one transaction succeeds as a unit or fails as a unit. The use of COM+ services transaction management has been used in this chapter and throughout the book to ensure the atomicity of the data source updates.

A data source transaction is *consistent* if all component methods call SetAbort or SetComplete at the end of the method to ensure that the transaction is aborted or committed, respectively. In the last section, in Example 9-12, the SetAbort or Set-Complete method was called in the ASP script rather than in the component to allow you to change whether the stored procedure deletion occurred. However, in a production system, you should always call the SetAbort or SetComplete (or Set-MyTransactionVote if you're using `IContextState`) within the method, rather than within the ASP script.

A data source transaction is *isolated* to ensure that two transactions running at the same time don't impact each other's results, in order to make sure that each can complete with a consistent state.

Finally, a transaction is *durable* if all updates that occur with a successful transaction are permanent (can no longer be rolled back or undone).

How can you ensure that your components operate according to the principles of ACID? Make sure that your components are added to a COM+ application, they support transactions, and you call ObjectContext's SetComplete or SetAbort or `IContextState`'s SetMyTransactionVote method within your component's methods. If your data source can participate in a COM+ transaction, the COM+ transaction (and COM+ services) will take care of the rest.

Historical or Archival Data

I want to discuss one other update technique before ending this chapter.

Today, most companies want to keep track of data, even after it's been "deleted" from the system. One way to do this is to have database backups that can be accessed if needed, but this approach is cumbersome and should be reserved for database recovery. Another approach, and one commonly used with many database applications, is to do what is known as *end dating* the table records.

End dating involves creating an end date column for each table whose data you want to maintain. When you "delete" the table row, what you're really doing is adding a date to the end date column, effectively marking that record as no longer active in the system.

When rows are accessed from the table based on searches, these inactive rows are excluded from the results, usually by testing to see if the row's end date column is null:

```
select * from target_table where end_date is null
```

If your database tables are getting large, then another approach is to have a batch process access the database tables periodically, look for records that have been end dated, and move these records to a separate archived database. You'll still have easy access to the data without having these pseudo-deleted rows within your active database.

To enforce referential integrity with end dating, you'll want to use a stored procedure or post-update database triggers to update the end date column of all dependent tables when a parent table row is end dated.

10

Server-Side XML Through VB ASP Components

There are few technologies that have excited developers as much as XML—Extensible Markup Language. I've heard people talk about XML as a replacement for everything from HTML to SQL. If you view available jobs on the Internet, you'll find few having anything to do with web applications that don't also mention the use of XML in some capacity.

ASP application developers are not immune to the lure of XML, yet there is confusion about how XML can be used with a server-side technology such as ASP, especially when writing ASP components.

This chapter provides an overview of XML, as well as XML formatting techniques, because it's necessary to have an understanding of XML before working on the examples in the second part of the chapter. These examples and their related discussions cover working with XML in ASP components written in Visual Basic. Some of the examples we'll look at include accessing and creating XML through the Microsoft XML parser (MSXML), working with XML through ADO, and mixing ASP processing with XML content.

 XML is a recommended specification from the World Wide Web Consortium, otherwise known as the W3C. You can access the specification at the W3C web site at *http://www.w3.org*.

XML Basics

XML is a simple-to-use basic markup language that is a subset of the more complex SGML—or Standard Generalized Markup Language. The specification was created primarily due to insufficiencies of the HTML standard and particularly the difficulties inherent in introducing a new element into the HTML standard.

For instance, mathematicians have a unique professional grammar and syntax that they use to describe their work, but there are no tags within the HTML specification that could be used for this effort. However, to expand HTML just for mathematicians—or musicians, physicists, and so on—isn't efficient.

This problem became very apparent when Netscape began to introduce elements into its rendering of HTML—elements such as FONT for defining font characteristics. By introducing new elements outside of the HTML specification, pages that were created to work with Netscape Navigator didn't work well with Internet Explorer or other browsers.

Another limitation of HTML is that there is an assumed presentation and layout associated with the elements in an HTML document, but not all rendering engines (browsers) provide identical element presentations. The HTML standard just doesn't provide a means of defining every aspect of how an element is shown on the page. A problem associated with combining presentation as well as content within the same specification is that the specification can either become overly large and complex, or pages created using the specification don't always look the same across different browsers, different operating systems, or both.

XML was created as a solution to both of these HTML limitations.

First, XML is a way of creating a document that can contain an arbitrary set of elements—defined with unique element tags—but still be accessible to document parsers that weren't created specifically to work with the page's elements. The reason that parsers can process the page is that the page and the elements follow a specific set of rules.

Secondly, there is no presentation or layout associated with XML elements. This is provided, instead, by separate standards, specifically by Cascading Style Sheets (CSS) or Extensible Stylesheet language (XSL). Separating presentation from content enables anyone to create their own set of XML elements, provide their own presentation with CSS or XSL, and have the page appear the same regardless of what browser parsed the page.

 This chapter barely touches on the subjects of the XML, CSS, and XSLT specifications—just enough to introduce the examples. For more detailed information, check the XML SDK that's available at the Microsoft web site at *http://msdn.microsoft.com/xml/*.

A Well-Formed XML Document

One reason XML has become so popular is that it's relatively easy to understand the rules governing this markup language. By following the rules, a web developer creates a "well-formed" document that can be parsed by any XML parser, including those built into browsers such as IE, Mozilla, and Navigator 6.0. When the rules aren't followed, the parser can't process the document, and an error results—the parser does not attempt to recover from the error.

 Another problem with HTML parsers is that they can be very forgiving at times, and web page developers have developed some bad habits as a consequence. A case in point is people using opening tags such as the paragraph (<P>) or list (<LI>) tag in their document but without providing a closing tag for the content.

The first line of an XML document can contain the XML declaration, though this isn't required:

```
<? xml version='1.0' ?>
```

This line consists of the XML document tag, in addition to the version of XML used in the document. At this time, there is only one version of XML, but you should use the 1.0 version number to differentiate the XML used in the document from future versions of XML.

The XML declaration can also include the character encoding used in the document, such as UTF-8 or EUC-JP. Not all XML processors can process all encodings, and an error results if you use an encoding the processor doesn't recognize.

All XML elements must either be empty tags or have both beginning and closing tags. For instance, if your XML document has an element such as the following, with attributes but no content, then the element must be defined as an empty tag and have a forward slash at the end of the element:

```
<template attribute="process" />
```

If your element defines content, then you'll need to use both a beginning and an ending element tag:

```
<city>Boston</city>
```

Not providing either the forward slash for an empty tag or the closing tag results in an XML processor error.

Another XML rule is that any Document Type Definition (DTD) files or rules must be specified before any other element in the document. DTDs provide grammar or additional application-specific rules that can be applied to the XML document.

Though not required, providing a DTD file makes the XML document *valid* as well as well-formed:

```
<!DOCTYPE template SYSTEM "template.dtd">
```

An additional rule for the XML document is that the elements contained in it must not overlap. This means that you can nest elements, but a nested element must be closed with the appropriate closing tag (or be an empty tag) before the closing tag of the outer element is reached:

```
<template>
<inner>
</inner>
</template>
```

Overlapping elements result in an XML processor error.

XML is case-sensitive, so the case used for the opening tag of an element must match the case used for the closing tag. Otherwise, again, an XML processor error results.

Additionally, there are certain characters that should not be used within attribute values or content, characters such as angle brackets (< and >) or the ampersand (&). These characters have special meaning in XML, just as they do in HTML documents.

Other rules are that element attributes must not repeat within a tag, and they must not reference external entities.

A Valid XML Document

Earlier I mentioned that an XML document with an associated DTD file is considered a valid document. The reason for this is that the DTD file provides the grammar and rules to validate the XML used in the document.

For instance, if an element can contain data, a rule could be added to the DTD file for the XML document, similar to the following:

```
<! ELEMENT template (#PCDATA)>
```

As efficient as DTD files are, a problem with them is that the syntax used to define the document grammar differs from the syntax for the XML documents, forcing a person to become familiar with two syntaxes. Efforts are underway to define XML schemas to provide for XML entity and attribute descriptions. XML schemas, unlike DTD files, use XML to describe the XML data.

XML Namespaces

XML is first and foremost extensible. This means that more than one set of XML elements for more than one purpose could be included within the same XML document. However, if the same element name is used with two differing components, you have element collision. To prevent something like this from happening, the W3C provided the XML Namespaces specification in 1999.

Namespaces are identified with URIs and are then used as an alias for elements and element attributes within that namespace. With this approach, a document can contain elements from several difference namespaces, and though the names of the elements are the same, the namespaces prevent collision.

For instance, a namespace could be defined with the following:

```
xmlns:mine='http://www.somecompany.com/namespc'
```

And used as is shown in the following:

```
<mine:book>
...
</mine:book>
```

No document needs exist at the namespace URI—the URI itself is the key to defining the namespace.

Formatting XML

XML by itself has no presentation or formatting information associated with it. It's used to define elements and their relationships with each other (as in container and contained). Other W3C-recommended specifications are then used to provide formatting, layout, and presentation information about the XML document elements.

Using CSS to Format Content

CSS can be used to provide both layout and presentation information to an XML processor to define how an XML document is presented. CSS has been used with HTML documents to provide additional formatting information. However, unlike using CSS with HTML, there is no built-in display information for any XML element—you have to provide all display characteristics.

To add CSS to an XML document, add the stylesheet using the following syntax:

```
<?xml-stylesheet type="text/css" href="asp1001.css" ?>
```

To demonstrate using XML with CSS, create a new XML document, name it *asp1001.xml*, and add the contents of Example 10-1 to it. The document contains the XML declaration and a statement to include a CSS file. An outer element with a default namespace is defined to hold the document's contents.

Example 10-1. XML Document

```
<?xml version='1.0'?>
<?xml-stylesheet type="text/css" href="asp1001.css" ?>
<doc xmlns='http://www.yasd.com/doc' >
```

Example 10-1. XML Document (continued)

```
<p>
Example of "paragraph", as formatted with CSS.
</p>

<UL>
<LI>one</LI>
<LI>two</LI>
</UL>

<table>
<tr>
<td>first cell</td>
<td>second cell</td>
</tr>
</table>
</doc>
```

The elements in this example resemble those found in HTML, such as `<p>` for paragraph and `<table>` for table. However, unlike HTML, there is no built-in formatting for these elements; you have to provide it all in the CSS file.

Create the CSS file next, and name it *asp1001.css*; Example 10-2 has the complete contents for the CSS file. The file provides CSS style definitions for all of the elements, including providing a `display` attribute setting for each. The `display` attribute is used to define whether the element is displayed inline or in block format or is displayed as a list item, table element, or other. Several other style settings are set to provide borders, margins, and padding.

Example 10-2. CSS File Providing Formatting/Layout Info for an XML Document

```
p {
    display: block;
    border-style: groove;
    border-width: 2px;
    border-color: red;
    width: 90%;
    margin-left: 20px;
    margin-top: 10px;
    padding: 10px;
 }
UL {

    display: block;
    margin-left: 30px;
    margin-top: 30px;
}
LI {
    display: list-item;
    list-style-type: circle
}
table {
    display: table;
```

Example 10-2. CSS File Providing Formatting/Layout Info for an XML Document (continued)

```
    border-width: 1px;
    border-style: solid;
    border-color: #CCCCCC;
    margin: 50px
    }
tr {
  display: table-row;
  }
td {
  display: table-cell;
  padding: 5px;
  border-style: solid;
  border-width: 1px;
  border-color: #CCCCCC;
  }
```

You can open the XML document directly into a browser. However, if you use Internet Explorer 5.x to open the file, you'll find that most of the CSS settings have no impact on the elements. The reason is that Microsoft has not implemented much of the CSS functionality for XML contents at this time (the company focuses more on XSL, discussed in the next section).

However, if you open the document with something that has broader CSS support for XML, like Mozilla or Navigator 6.0, you'll find that the CSS style settings do work with the elements, as shown in Figure 10-1.

By the time you read this book, Microsoft may have improved the support of CSS in XML documents in Internet Explorer, and the Mozilla browser may have a different look than that shown in Figure 10-1. Such is life in the web fast lane.

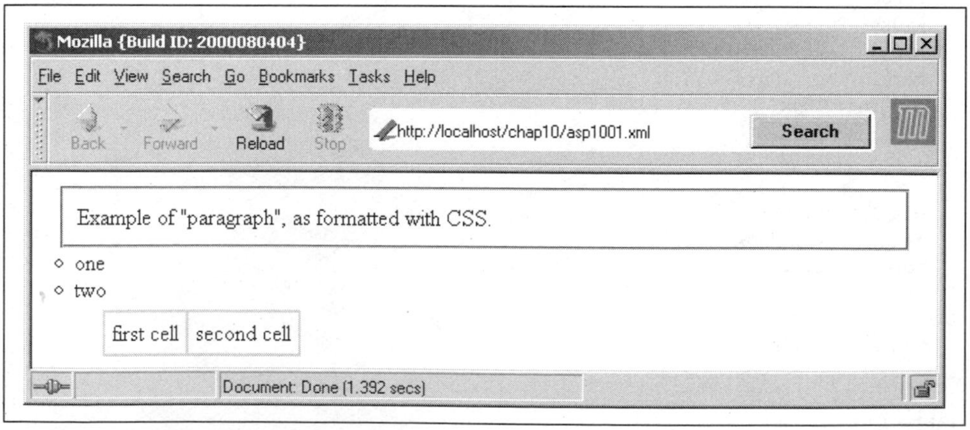

![Screenshot of Mozilla browser displaying CSS-formatted XML. The address bar shows http://localhost/chap10/asp1001.xml. The content shows a box with "Example of "paragraph", as formatted with CSS." followed by a bulleted list "one" and "two", and a table with cells "first cell" and "second cell". The status bar reads "Document: Done (1.392 secs)".]

Figure 10-1. CSS-formatted XML, displayed in the Mozilla browser

Using XSLT to Transform XML

A second technique to format XML documents is XSL—Extensible Stylesheet Language. XSL consists of several specifications; we'll take a look at one of them, Extensible Stylesheet Language Transformations (XSLT).

Unlike using CSS with XML, XSLT is a template-based specification. You create an XML document, which is used to provide the data, and then you create the XSLT document that provides the template to process the data. The template uses HTML elements to provide data layout information, but the format of the XSLT document is XML.

The XSLT document begins with the XML declaration line, followed by the namespace definition for XSLT:

```
<?xml version='1.0'?>
<xsl:stylesheet xmlns:xsl="http://www.w3.org/TR/WD-xsl">
```

To begin processing the contents, a root element is defined for the entire document. This root element references content with a forward slash:

```
<xsl:template match="/">
```

There are specific elements with associated behaviors defined in XSLT. To process every occurrence of an element in the XML document, you can use the **for-each** element:

```
<xsl:for-each select="element">
```

The **for-each** element processes every occurrence of the target element in the page. To access the value of an element, you can use the **value-of** element:

```
<xsl:value-of select="element">
```

The **value-of** element differs from the **for-each** element in that the former returns only the first occurrence of an element within a given content.

Other XSLT elements can be used to provide decision support as well as processing instructions.

To add an XSLT template to an XML document, use the following line, adjusted for the name of your own XSLT file:

```
<?xml-stylesheet type="text/xsl" href="asp1002.xsl"?>
```

To demonstrate how XML and XSLT work together, create a new XML document, and name this one *asp1002.xml*. In the document, add the XML shown in Example 10-3. Note that the contents are very similar to those shown in Example 10-1, except that **<span>** tags surround the contents of the list and table cell elements, and the CSS stylesheet reference has been replaced by one for the XSLT document.

Example 10-3. An XML Document That Uses an XSLT Document for Presentation

```
<?xml version='1.0'?>
<?xml-stylesheet type="text/xsl" href="asp1002.xsl"?>
<doc xmlns='http://www.yasd.com/doc' >

<P>
Example of "paragraph", as formatted with XSL.
</P>

<UL>
<LI><span>one</span></LI>
<LI><span>two</span></LI>
</UL>

<table>
<tr>
<td><span>first cell</span></td>
<td><span>second cell</span></td>
</tr>
</table>
</doc>
```

Create a second document and name it *asp1002.xsl*. This document contains the XSLT to process the page contents, providing a visual display similar to that shown in Figure 10-1; Example 10-4 has the complete contents of the XSLT file.

In the template, the HTML tags to create a document and attach a stylesheet block are added to the page, just as they would be added to an HTML document. The differences occur where the XML contents are referenced.

First, the single paragraph element's value is accessed using an XSLT **value-of** element. Since there is only one paragraph element in the page, the **value-of** element processes this. If there were more, the additional paragraph elements would be discarded.

Both the **<LI>** and the table elements repeat, so a **for-each** XSLT element is used for them. As the elements that repeat are processed in the external **for-each** statement, the actual value of the list item or the table cell is output by accessing the content's **<span>** tag. This is why the contents had to be enclosed in another element, though the **<span>** element didn't have to be used—you could make one of your own.

Example 10-4. An XSLT Document

```
<?xml version='1.0'?>
<xsl:stylesheet xmlns:xsl="http://www.w3.org/TR/WD-xsl">
 <xsl:template match="/">
  <HTML>
   <BODY>
    <STYLE type="text/css">
```

Example 10-4. An XSLT Document (continued)

```
        P { border-style: groove;
              border-width: 2px;
              border-color: red;
              width: 90%;
              margin-left: 20px;
              margin-top: 10px;
              padding: 10px;
          }
      UL { margins: 20px }
      LI { list-style-type: circle }
      TABLE { margin: 50px }
    </STYLE>

      <P><xsl:value-of select="doc/P" /></P>
      <UL>
      <xsl:for-each select="doc/UL/LI" >
          <LI><xsl:value-of select="span" /></LI>
      </xsl:for-each>
      </UL>

      <table border="1px" cellspacing="0" cellpadding="5px">
      <xsl:for-each select="doc/table/tr">
        <TR>
        <xsl:for-each select="td">
          <td><xsl:value-of select="span" /></td>
        </xsl:for-each>
        </TR>
      </xsl:for-each>
      </table>

    </BODY>
   </HTML>
 </xsl:template>
</xsl:stylesheet>
```

In an XSLT-capable browser, when the XML document is accessed, the XSLT template is used to process the contents and the results are returned as a web page. Figure 10-2 shows the results of accessing the XML page shown in Example 10-3 within IE 5.x.

This is a very brief introduction to some of the XML-based technologies, which you will need as we look at working with XML in ASP applications, next.

Working with XML in ASP Applications

Microsoft has an XML parser, MSXML, that you can access in your ASP components or script. With MSXML, you can open and work with existing XML documents or create new XML content.

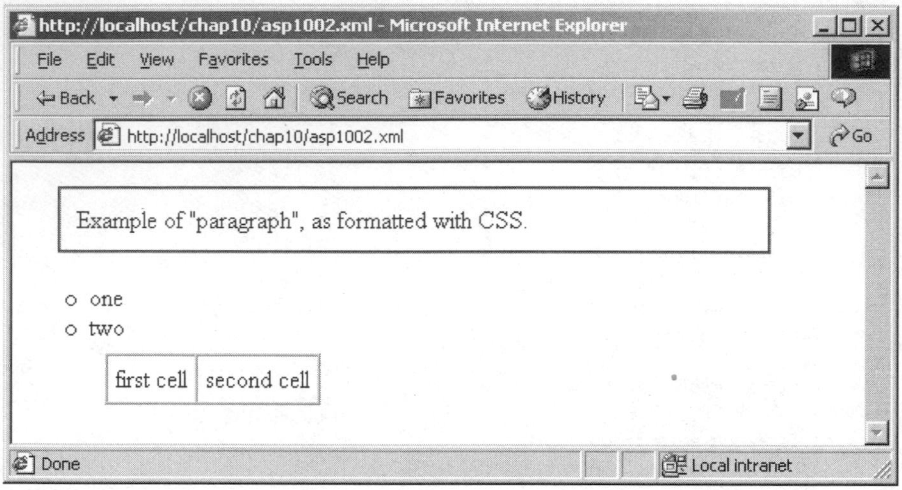

Figure 10-2. XML document formatted with XSLT template file

The MSXML parser is based on the W3C's DOM (Document Object Model) specification, though Microsoft has extended the DOM to provide additional methods, properties, and objects to support XML processing efforts.

You can access the objects defined in MSXML by attaching the Microsoft XML type library to your VB component project. The following are some of the key objects:

XMLDOMDocument
    The top-level XML source object

XMLDOMNode
    Represents a single node in the document tree

XMLDOMNodeList
    A collection of nodes

XMLDOMAttribute
    An element attribute

XMLDOMText
    The text content of either an element or an element attribute

XMLDOMCDataSection
    XML CDATA sections (text that is not processed as markup)

XMLDOMComment
    An XML comment

XMLDOMDocumentFragment
    Represents part of a document tree

You can load an external XML file with the XMLDOMDocument object and then process the contents using one or more of the other objects.

To demonstrate working with XML using MSXML from Visual Basic components, we'll take a different approach to working with XML. Instead of treating XML as a data source, we'll use XML to actually define a database query.

The document root is a query object that can contain several other elements, each defined for a specific purpose. For instance, the tables for the query are contained within `tablename` elements, and the `WHERE` clause column-value pairs are defined within the `where` element: the column is identified by `queryfield`, and the value is identified by `queryvalue`. The columns returned from the query are contained within `fieldname` elements. Example 10-5 contains an XML file defining a query against the WebPage table, returning the name and filename columns for all records where the page type code is set to `HTM`. This XML file is found in the file *asp1003.xml*, located with the examples.

Example 10-5. XML File Containing a Database Query

```
<?xml version='1.0'?>
<doc >
  <query>
    <fields>
      <fieldname>name</fieldname>
      <fieldname>filename</fieldname>
    </fields>
    <tablename>WebPage</tablename>
    <where>
      <queryfield>page_type_cd</queryfield>
      <queryvalue>'HTM'</queryvalue>
    </where>
  </query>
</doc>
```

To process the XML, create a Visual Basic component and name it `asp1001`. Name the generated class **xml**. This component has one method, processXMLQuery, shown in Example 10-6, that generates a database query string from the contents of a preexisting XML document. The string is then used to open an ADO recordset that's returned to the ASP page.

To support XML and ADO in the new component, attach the Microsoft XML and Microsoft ADO type libraries to the new project. Since the example uses the ASP built-in Response object, also attach the COM+ Services and the Microsoft Active Server Page Object type libraries. The processXMLQuery method takes as its only parameter a string containing the name and physical location of the XML file.

There are certain assumptions in the code shown in Example 10-6, such as all WHERE clause conditions are joined by the AND keyword, and all conditions are tests of equality.

The code creates an instance of the DOMDocument object (the XMLDOMDocument object) and calls its load method to load the XML file. Once the file is loaded, the getElementsByTagName method pulls in the elements of the query. The XMLDOMNode object's selectSingleNode method accesses the queryvalue and queryfield elements' values—the selectSingleNode method takes an XSL pattern query, which specifies a node name within the context of the node. The contents of the elements are used to generate the query string to open the ADO Recordset.

Example 10-6. Opening an XML File and Generating a Query from Its Contents

```
Function processXMLQuery(ByVal strFile As String) _
                                  As Recordset

Dim strSelect As String
Dim strFrom As String
Dim strWhere As String
Dim strSQL As String
Dim i As Integer
Dim iCt As Integer

' XML objects
Dim MSXML As New DOMDocument
Dim mslist As IXMLDOMNodeList

' ADO
Dim rs As New Recordset

' load XML file
MSXML.Load (strFile)

' get select fields
Set mslist = MSXML.getElementsByTagName("fieldname")
strSelect = ""
iCt = mslist.length
For i = 0 To iCt - 1
    If strSelect <> "" Then
        strSelect = strSelect & ", "
    Else
        strSelect = "select "
    End If
    strSelect = strSelect & mslist(i).Text
Next

' get tables
Set mslist = MSXML.getElementsByTagName("tablename")
```

Example 10-6. Opening an XML File and Generating a Query from Its Contents (continued)

```
strFrom = ""
iCt = mslist.length
For i = 0 To iCt - 1
   If strFrom <> "" Then
       strFrom = strFrom & ", "
   Else
       strFrom = " from "
   End If
   strFrom = strFrom & mslist(i).Text
Next

' get where clause
Set mslist = MSXML.getElementsByTagName("where")

Dim strField As String
Dim strValue As String
strWhere = ""
iCt = mslist.length
For i = 0 To iCt - 1
   If strWhere <> "" Then
       strWhere = strWhere & " AND "
   Else
       strWhere = " where "
   End If
   strField = mslist.Item(i).selectSingleNode("queryfield").Text
   strValue = mslist.Item(i).selectSingleNode("queryvalue").Text

   strWhere = strWhere & strField & "=" & strValue
Next

' perform query
strSQL = strSelect & strFrom & strWhere
rs.CursorLocation = adUseClient
rs.Open strSQL, "Provider=SQLOLEDB;server=FLAME;database=weaver;uid=sa;pwd="

' disconnect recordset
Set rs.ActiveConnection = Nothing

Set processXMLQuery = rs

End Function
```

To test the example, the ASP test page, *asp1001.asp*, calls the component's method, passing in the name of the XML file. The file is in the same location as the ASP page, so the script uses the Server object's MapPath method to map the relative location of the file to an actual physical location:

```
<%
Dim obj
Set obj = Server.CreateObject("asp1001.xml")

Dim rs
```

```
Set rs = obj.processXMLQuery(Server.MapPath("asp1003.xml"))

' process records
Dim iCt, i
iCt = rs.Fields.Count

Response.Write "<TABLE>"
While rs.EOF <> True
    Response.Write "<TR>"
    For i = 0 to iCt - 1
      Response.Write "<TD>" & rs.Fields(i) & "</TD>"
    Next
    Response.Write "</TR>"
    rs.MoveNext
Wend
Response.Write "</TABLE>"
%>
```

Accessing the page results in the recordset contents being displayed within an HTML table.

By defining the query in an XML document and processing the XML elements for the query, you can create more than one query in more than one XML file. Example 10-7 shows a more complex XML file, *asp1004.xml*, that the `asp1001.xml` component can process without modification. Notice in this example that more than one table is joined in the query, and there is more than one condition in the WHERE clause.

Example 10-7. Second Database Query, Defined Using XML

```
<?xml version='1.0'?>
<doc>
  <query>
    <fields>
      <fieldname>MediaObject.name</fieldname>
      <fieldname>filename</fieldname>
      <fieldname>file_size</fieldname>
      <fieldname>directory.name</fieldname>
    </fields>
    <tablename>MediaObject</tablename>
    <tablename>directory</tablename>
    <where>
      <queryfield>directory.id</queryfield>
      <queryvalue>18</queryvalue>
    </where>
    <where>
      <queryfield>directory_id</queryfield>
      <queryvalue>directory.id</queryvalue>
    </where>
    <where>
      <queryfield>media_type_cd</queryfield>
      <queryvalue>'GIF'</queryvalue>
    </where>
```

Example 10-7. Second Database Query, Defined Using XML (continued)

```
  </query>
</doc>
```

Try `asp1001.xml` with the new XML file, as shown in the following ASP test page, *asp1002.asp*:

```
Dim obj
Set obj = Server.CreateObject("asp1001.xml")

Dim rs
Set rs = obj.processXMLQuery(Server.MapPath("asp1004.xml"))

' process records
Dim iCt, i
iCt = rs.Fields.Count

Response.Write "<TABLE>"
While rs.EOF <> True
    Response.Write "<TR>"
    For i = 0 to iCt - 1
      Response.Write "<TD>" & rs.Fields(i) & "</TD>"
    Next
    Response.Write "</TR>"
    rs.MoveNext
Wend
Response.Write "</TABLE>"
```

The results of the more complex table join XML are displayed in the returned page.

You can also modify XML by replacing or modifying existing contents or creating new contents. As an example, consider the XML document shown in Example 10-5. This XML generates a query that returns the WebPage name and filename columns. You can modify this file and add a new column to the query using MSXML.

To demonstrate, add a second method to the `asp1001.xml` component and call it addXML. This method takes two strings, the name of the XML file and the new field to add to the document's fieldnames list.

Add the code for the method, which is shown in Example 10-8. The addXML method first accesses the `fieldname` element's parent element, `fields`. Next, it creates a new node object using the createNode method and passing in the node type NODE_TYPE (an enumerated value) as the first parameter and the name of the node, `fieldname`, as the second parameter. Passing an empty string as the third parameter defines the element within the default namespace.

Once the node is created, the method inserts it into the XML document using the insertBefore method on the `fields` node. The first parameter of this method is the new node, and the second parameter is the child node in front of which the

new node is placed, or NULL, which means that the new mode is placed at the
end of the child list. Finally, the method saves the modified XML to the existing
XML document.

Example 10-8. Modify Query by Adding New Fieldname to Query XML

```
' add field
Sub addXML(ByVal strFileName As String, _
          ByVal strFieldName As String)

' XML objects
Dim msxml As New DOMDocument
Dim mselement As IXMLDOMNode
Dim msnode As IXMLDOMNode
Dim currnode As IXMLDOMNode
Dim mslist As IXMLDOMNodeList

' load XML file
msxml.Load (strFileName)

' get fields element
Set mslist = msxml.getElementsByTagName("fields")
Set mselement = mslist.Item(0)

' create node, assign node text
' insert into end of fieldname list
Set msnode = msxml.createNode(NODE_ELEMENT, "fieldname", "")
msnode.Text = strFieldName
Set currnode = mselement.insertBefore(msnode, Null)

' save XML file
msxml.save (strFileName)

End Sub
```

After saving and compiling the component, test it using the *asp1003.asp* file. The
query XML file is called *asp1005.xml* and is a direct copy of *asp1003.xml* (shown
in Example 10-7). The script in the test ASP file adds the file_size column name to
the selection list of the query and then calls the processXMLQuery to process the
query:

```
<%
Dim obj
Set obj = Server.CreateObject("asp1001.xml")

Dim file
file = Server.MapPath("asp1005.xml")

' add new field
obj.addXML file, "file_size"

' do query
```

```
    Dim rs
    Set rs = obj.processXMLQuery(file)

    ' process records
    Dim iCt, i
    iCt = rs.Fields.Count

    Response.Write "<TABLE>"
    While rs.EOF <> True
        Response.Write "<TR>"
        For i = 0 to iCt - 1
            Response.Write "<TD>" & rs.Fields(i) & "</TD>"
        Next
        Response.Write "</TR>"
        rs.MoveNext
    Wend
    Response.Write "</TABLE>"
    %>
```

When you access the ASP test page, the results of running the query are shown to the page. If you open the modified *asp1005.xml* file, you should see something similar to the following:

```
    <?xml version="1.0"?>
    <doc>
        <query>
            <fields>
                <fieldname>name</fieldname>
                <fieldname>filename</fieldname>
                <fieldname>file_size</fieldname></fields>
            <tablename>WebPage</tablename>
            <where>
                <queryfield>page_type_cd</queryfield>
                <queryvalue>'HTM'</queryvalue>
            </where>
        </query>
    </doc>
```

Compare this XML with that shown in Example 10-5, and you'll see the addition of the new fieldname element, with the file_size contents. MSXML also nicely formats the output, indenting the elements.

Instead of generating XML by using MSXML, you can also use a new feature in ADO to save the contents of a recordset as XML. This is discussed next.

XML and ADO: Saving Recordsets as XML

Converting database data into XML files quickly becomes pretty cumbersome whether you use MSXML or create the files manually. However, saving an ADO recordset as XML is as easy as calling one method—the Save method.

ADO recordsets could be persisted for sometime now, usually in ADTG (Microsoft Advanced Data Tablegram) format. However, you can also persist a recordset in XML format. Not only that, but when you persist the recordset as XML, you can save it to a file, an existing XML document, or even directly to the ASP built-in Response object.

To demonstrate the three ways in which you can persist the data in XML, you'll create three new methods for `asp1001.xml`.

Add the code for the first method, which is shown in Example 10-9, to your `asp1001.xml` class. This method, saveXMLToDocument, saves the XML-formatted data directly to an XML document. The saveXMLToDocument method creates new MSXML DOMDocument and ADO Recordset objects and sets the Recordset object's CursorLocation property to `adUseClient`. The SQL used with the query is passed as a parameter to saveXMLToDocument, as is the name of the XML document the XML document tree will be saved to. Once the recordset is opened, the data is saved using the Recordset object's Save method. The first parameter is the DOMDocument object, and the second is the format type of the data. A value of `adPersistXML` is used for this parameter, as well as for the next two component methods you'll create later. Once the XML has been added to the document tree, it's saved to an XML file using the DOMDocument Save method.

 You can use server-side cursors with these examples. However, not all OLE DB providers support the same functionality—using the client-side cursor ensures that these examples work regardless of the OLE DB provider used.

Example 10-9. Saving Recordset Data as XML Directly to an XML Document Tree

```
' save to XML document
Sub saveXMLToDocument(ByVal strQuery As String, _
                      ByVal strFile As String)

Dim msxml As New DOMDocument
Dim rs As New Recordset

' perform query
rs.CursorLocation = adUseClient
rs.Open strQuery, "Provider=SQLOLEDB;server=FLAME;database=weaver;uid=sa;pwd="

' disconnect recordset
Set rs.ActiveConnection = Nothing

' save RS to DOM tree
rs.save msxml, adPersistXML
```

Example 10-9. Saving Recordset Data as XML Directly to an XML Document Tree (continued)

```
' save MSXML
msxml.save strFile
End Sub
```

Save the component and recompile it. To test your new method, use the following ASP page, *asp1004.asp*, which instantiates your component and calls saveXML-ToDocument, passing in a query string and the name of the XML document to which the results are to be written:

```
<%
Dim obj
Set obj = Server.CreateObject("asp1001.xml")

' save using XML document
 obj.saveXMLToDocument "select * from directory", _
                       Server.MapPath("asp1006.xml")
%>
```

Notice that the method uses Server.MapPath to map the relative filename to the physical location. Once the *asp1006.xml* document is created, open it with Internet Explorer. You should have a result similar to that shown in Figure 10-3.

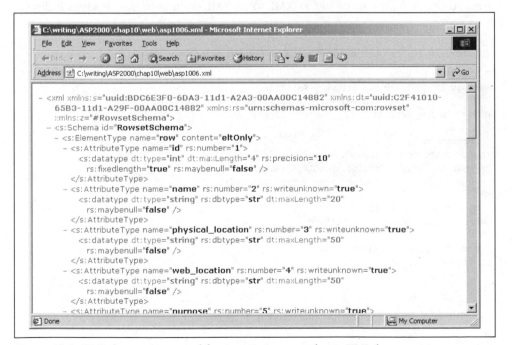

Figure 10-3. XML document created from persisting recordset to XML document tree

Looking at the XML document, you'll notice that not only is the recordset data persisted as XML, but so is the definition of the Recordset object itself. When you persist the Recordset object, you're persisting the entire object—not just the data. You could, if you wished, reopen the recordset from the file into an ADO recordset in another component or in script. If you just want the data, you can copy this directly from the XML document, or you can remove the recordset schema information using MSXML.

 Ever notice how nicely XML documents that don't have associated stylesheets look with Internet Explorer? That's because IE has a built-in default stylesheet used with all XML documents that don't have either an XSL or CSS stylesheet attached.

Next, you'll persist the recordset directly to a file. Create a new method, as shown in Example 10-10, called saveXMLToFile. The method takes two parameters: a query string and the name of the output file. Like SaveXMLToDocument, the saveXMLToFile method again opens the recordset with the provided query, but instead of saving the recordset as XML to an XML document tree, it saves it directly to a file.

Example 10-10. Saving a Recordset as XML Directly to a File

```
' save XML to file
Sub saveXMLToFile(ByVal strQuery As String, _
                  ByVal strFile As String)
Dim rs As New Recordset

' perform query
rs.CursorLocation = adUseClient
rs.Open strQuery, "Provider=SQLOLEDB;server=FLAME;" _
                & "database=weaver;uid=sa;pwd="

' disconnect recordset
Set rs.ActiveConnection = Nothing

' save RS in XML format to file
rs.save strFile, adPersistXML

End Sub
```

Try this component with the following ASP test script, found in *asp1005.asp*:

```
<%
Dim obj
Set obj = Server.CreateObject("asp1001.xml")

' save using file
```

```
obj.saveXMLToFile "select * from MediaObject", _
                                "c:\datasets\mediaobject.xml"
%>
```

The result of running this script is an XML file, created in the specified location (adjust the file location for your own environment). Opening the new file, you'll see that the XML in it is the same as that created with the SaveXMLToDocument method in Example 10-9 and shown in Figure 10-3.

 If the file that the recordset is being saved to already exists, you'll get an error. See more on persisting recordsets in Chapter 8, *Creating ASP/ADO Components*.

Also, be aware of privileges whenever you do any form of file I/O. If your web user doesn't have permission to write or read a file from a given location, an error will occur.

The last component method you'll create for this chapter actually persists the recordset directly to the built-in ASP Response object. This is possible because the Response object supports the OLE DB `IStream` interface, required of any object that serves as the destination for the Recordset object's Save method.

Create a new method called saveXMLToResponse, shown in Example 10-11. The method has one parameter, the query string. It instantiates the Response object and then creates and opens the recordset with the given query string. Finally, it writes out the XML declaration using the Response object and then saves the recordset directly to the Response object.

Example 10-11. The saveXMLToResponse Method

```
' save XML directly to response (stream)
Sub saveXMLToResponse(ByVal strQuery As String)

Dim objContext As ObjectContext
Dim objResponse As Response

Set objContext = GetObjectContext()
Set objResponse = objContext("Response")

Dim rs As New Recordset

' perform query
rs.CursorLocation = adUseClient
rs.Open strQuery, "Provider=SQLOLEDB;server=FLAME;" _
                & "database=weaver;uid=sa;pwd="

' disconnect recordset
Set rs.ActiveConnection = Nothing
```

Example 10-11. The saveXMLToResponse Method (continued)

```
' save RS to DOM tree
objResponse.Write "<?xml version='1.0' ?>" & vbCrLf
rs.save objResponse, adPersistXML

End Sub
```

The method must write out the XML declaration first, or the XML returned by the Response object won't be treated as XML. Setting the Response object's Content-Type property won't work when you persist the Recordset object directly to the object.

The ASP test page, *asp1006.asp*, for this last method is pretty simple—it consists of the ASP script to create **asp1001.devaspcompxml** and call saveXMLToResponse:

```
<%
Dim obj
Set obj = Server.CreateObject("asp1001.xml")
' save to response
obj.saveXMLToResponse "select * from WebPage"
%>
```

The result is a web page with XML defining the recordset and its data.

The end result of persisting the recordset as XML is the same with all three of the techniques used in this section—all that differs is the end location of the recordset and the queries used.

Persisting the recordset by saving it to an XML document, which can then be saved, or by saving it directly to a file provides access to the recordset for other server-side components. Your ASP server-side applications won't be able to access the recordset saved to the Response object, but this approach can be used to pass a recordset to the client when using something such as Remote Data Services (RDS).

 See the documentation provided with the Data SDK from Microsoft on working with RDS.

11

Take a Message: Accessing CDO from ASP Components

I don't know of any Microsoft object-based technology that gives so much in return for so little effort as does Collaboration Data Objects, or CDO. This technology provides the functionality that developers can use to add messaging capabilities to their applications, including ASP applications. With CDO, messages can easily be sent to and read from either an email or a newsgroup server.

Messaging capability is a very useful added functionality for ASP applications. For instance, if you've shopped at an online store, chances are you've received an email with a copy of your order just after you've submitted it. Additionally, some sites have "send this article to a friend" functionality—something that you can create for your own sites with just a few lines of code. You can email confirmation notices, passwords for forgetful folks (such as myself), and even a message thanking someone for expressing an interest in hearing more about a product, idea, or concept.

This chapter looks at using the CDO objects to send and read messages through an SMTP server from within ASP components created using Visual Basic.

 This chapter references the version of CDO created for Windows 2000. Note that this can differ from CDO used with Exchange Server and CDO 1.2 for NTS.

A Brief Overview of CDO

CDO isn't a complicated technology. Basically, you create a message by building each of the message's component parts, and then you send it when finished.

A CDO message can include attachments, and the message body can be formatted in different ways, such as in HTML or as plain text. You can even send messages that are formatted with multiple formats, such as a message that has both plain text and HTML portions. You've most likely received messages of this type, particularly if you use Microsoft Outlook. Messages can also be in more complex document formats, such as a Microsoft Word document.

Messages can be sent and forwarded, read and replied to. You can persist a message using ADO streams. Though not demonstrated in this chapter, you can even create transport event sinks to receive notification when certain message events occur, such as a message arriving at a particular destination.

ASP applications are interactive, and the use of event sinks directly within ASP components is not an effective use of CDO technology. However, you can create external applications that "listen" for specific events and do such things as write logging information to a persistent store. Then you can create ASP applications that read the logs.

To use CDO from within Visual Basic, you'll need to attach the Microsoft CDO for Windows 2000 type library. Additionally, you'll need to attach the Microsoft ActiveX Data Objects library, as shown in Figure 11-1, to work with CDO data.

The CDO Object Model

The CDO object model isn't very large. We'll take a brief look at the objects in the model that we're most interested in and then demonstrate each of the objects mentioned in the sections to follow.

Messages can be accessed from the SMTP service or any folder with the appropriate permissions through the DropDirectory object. This object has one method, GetMessages, used to return a collection of messages through the **IMessages** interface object.

Once you have access to an **IMessages** interface collection, you can enumerate through it to access specific messages. Each message is defined as a Message object that exposes several properties corresponding to message components, such as the message's Subject, the From and To address fields, and the message body itself.

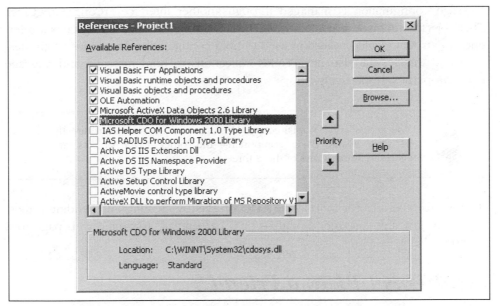

Figure 11-1. References for a VB project after attaching the ADO and CDO type libraries

The Message object also has several methods used to do such tasks as creating an MHTML-formatted message (CreateMHTMLBody) or adding an attachment to a message (AddAttachment). For the latter, the function returns an instance of IBodyPart that you can then manipulate. You can set IBodyPart properties for elements such as the content type (ContentMediaType) or the name of the file forming the attachment (FileName). There are also methods you can use to save the body part's contents to a file (SaveToFile), as well as to attach another IBodyPart object for creating a hierarchy of body parts within the message.

 "A hierarchy of body parts" . . . sounds gruesome, doesn't it?

You can access a Message object's body part through the BodyPart property. To access all of the body parts in the hierarchy, access the BodyParts property in IBodyPart. This property contains a collection of body parts in the message's main IBodyPart object, within a collection accessible through the IBodyParts interface. You can then enumerate through the collection as you would any other, using a statement such as:

```
For Each iBdyPrt in iBdyPrts
```

Message configuration is managed through another interface, `IConfiguration`. This object, which you access in Visual Basic as `Configuration`, contains a reference to an ADO Fields collection used to hold configuration properties. Both Message and `IBodyPart` also have Fields collections to hold message and message body properties, respectively.

You access only DropDirectory, Message, and Configuration directly in your Visual Basic component—the other CDO objects are accessed through one of these three.

It's time to take a closer look at the CDO objects by creating and sending a message. Not just any message, though—you'll be sending a specific web page to a friend.

Send This URL to a Friend

Your first ASP/CDO application is a variation of the "Send this URL to a friend" example I mentioned earlier. To start, create a new Visual Basic ActiveX DLL project and name it `asp1101`. Name the generated class file `msg`. Next, attach a reference to the CDO and ADO type libraries you'll need for this project.

Create a new subroutine named sendURL; its source code is shown in Example 11-1. It takes the following `ByVal` parameters:

strTo
   A string to hold the email address of recipient

strFrom
   A string to hold the sender's email address

strSubject
   A string to hold the subject of the message

strURL
   A string with the URL of the page that's being sent in the message

The msg method creates an instance of the Message and the Configuration objects and defines a variable to hold an ADO Fields object that'll get set to the Configuration object's Fields collection.

Two of the configuration properties set in the code are the SMTP send method and message authentication. Both the values and the property names for these items are enumerated constants provided in the CDO type library. The `cdoSend`-`Using` enumeration contains two values you can use with the cdoSendUsing-Method property: `cdoSendUsingPort` to send the message over the network and `cdoSendUsingPickup` to send the message using the local SMTP pickup directory. In the example, you'll use the `cdoSendUsingPort` value.

 Applications that don't have direct SMTP access can create emails and save them as files within the pickup directory. SMTP then automatically moves these files into the queue for emailing.

The enumerator `cdoProtocolsAuthentication` has three values used to determine what type of authentication is used with the SMTP service when it receives the message. The values are `cdoAnonymous` for no authentication, `cdoBasic` for clear text authentication, and `cdoNTLM` for NTLM authentication. You'll use `cdoBasic` for the example.

The remaining property names are also enumerated constants, but their values should be set for your own specific environment. After you've added the code from Example 11-1 to your component, modify it to use values pertinent to your own SMTP setup. The code contains settings for the SMTP connection timeout, the name of the SMTP server, and the username and login that allows the component access to the service. Once these values are set, the configuration object is attached to the message's Configuration property. Then the method sets the Message object's To, From, and Subject properties with the values passed in as parameters.

 You can find the SMTP properties from your own email setup. If you use Outlook, access Tools → Accounts → Mail → Properties. The Servers tag has the SMTP server name, the account name, and password, though the actual password value is hidden.

Finally, the code calls the createMHTMLBody method with the URL passed as a parameter to the component. The createMHTMLBody method converts the page identified by the URL into an MHTML (MIME Encapsulation of Aggregate HTML documents) document that is then attached to the message body. Once this is finished, the message is sent with the Message object's Send method.

Example 11-1. Send a Friend This URL Component Method

```
Sub sendURL(ByVal strTo As String, _
            ByVal strFrom As String, _
            ByVal strSubject As String, _
            ByVal strURL As String)

Dim iMsg As New CDO.Message
Dim iConf As New CDO.Configuration
```

Example 11-1. Send a Friend This URL Component Method (continued)

```
Dim flds As ADODB.Fields
Set flds = iConf.Fields

' set configuration properties
flds.Item(cdoSendUsingMethod) = cdoSendUsingPort
flds.Item(cdoSMTPAuthenticate) = cdoBasic
flds.Item(cdoSMTPConnectionTimeout) = 20

flds.Item(cdoSMTPServer) = "mail.company.com"
flds.Item(cdoSendUserName) = "person@company.com"
flds.Item(cdoSendPassword) = "password"
flds.Update

Set iMsg.Configuration = iConf

' set rest of message properties
iMsg.To = strTo
iMsg.From = strFrom
iMsg.Subject = strSubject
iMsg.CreateMHTMLBody strURL

' send the message
iMsg.Send

End Sub
```

After compiling the object, create the ASP test pages. There are actually three ASP pages used to test the new component. You can create your own or you can use the ones contained in the book examples. The first page, *asp1101.asp*, has a hypertext link that attaches the URL and the subject for the current page to the query string of another ASP page:

```
<p>
<a href="asp1102.asp?Subject=Test Page&
URL=http://localhost<% = Request.ServerVariables("URL") %>">Send</a>
this page to a friend
</p>
```

The URL for the current page is based on a combination of the friendly name for the site (*http://localhost* for our test environment) and the base URL pulled from the Request object's ServerVariables collection. By not hardcoding the actual page location, you can move the page easily around your site without having to change the query string reference.

The second ASP test page, *asp1102.asp*, which is shown in Example 11-2, has a script that pulls the subject and URL from the Request object's QueryString collection and sets them into hidden fields within a page form. Other form fields take the sender's and the receiver's email addresses.

Example 11-2. ASP Test Page That Has a Form for Sending an URL as an Email

```
<HTML>
<HEAD>
<%
Dim strSubject, strTo, strFrom, strURL
strSubject = Request.QueryString("Subject")
strURL = Request.QueryString("URL")
%>
<TITLE>Send <% = strSubject %> to a friend</TITLE>
</HEAD>
<BODY>
<H3>Please enter your email and your friend's email addresses</h3>
<form method="POST" action="asp1103.asp">
<input type="hidden" name="subject" value="<% = strSubject %>">
<input type="hidden" name="url" value="<% = strURL %>">
<p>
Your email: <input type="text" name="from">
</p>
<p>
Your friend's email: <input type="text" name="to">
</p>
<p>
<input type="submit" value="Send the URL">
</p>
</form>
</BODY>
</HTML>
```

Note that the subject is used to set the page title and the form's hidden field.

When the email addresses are entered and the form's submit button is pressed, the third and final ASP test page, *asp1103.asp*, is opened. This page creates an instance of the new component, `asp1101.msg`, and passes the form values as arguments to the sendURL method:

```
<%
On Error Resume Next
Dim obj
Set obj = Server.CreateObject("asp1101.msg")

' get values
Dim strSubject, strURL, strTo, strFrom
strSubject = Request.Form("subject")
strURL = Request.Form("url")
strTo = Request.Form("to")
strFrom = Request.Form("from")

' send url
obj.sendURL strTo, strFrom, strSubject, strURL
If Err.Number <> 0 Then
    Response.Write "<h3>The URL could not be emailed</h3>"
    Response.Write "<p>" & Err.Description & "</p>"
Else
```

```
    Response.Write "<h3>The page is off and running</h3>"
End If

Set obj = Nothing
%>
```

If everything works, the following message is displayed and the email is sent to your recipient:

```
The page is off and running
```

Otherwise, an error is displayed.

Try the example yourself by using the ASP test pages included with the examples, or add the hypertext link to some of your existing web pages. Fun and useful functionality at the cost of only a few lines of code—now you know why I like CDO.

 A little Net-friendly advice: don't go crazy attaching "Send this page to a friend" links to all of your web pages. You can quickly overwhelm your SMTP service. Instead, use the functionality sparingly, mainly with pages that have a lot of content but few graphics. Also provide warnings that only HTML-capable email readers will be able to process the email message.

Working with the Message Body

In the last section, your message body was pretty easy to create. Basically you had to call one method, passing in an URL. This section goes into how to create other content for your messages.

The simplest approach to sending message content is to attach text to the Message object's TextBody property:

```
iMsg.TextBody = "some string"
```

You can also send a message formatted as HTML by setting the Message object's HTMLBody property:

```
iMsg.HTMLBody = "<p>Some HTML String</p>"
```

Messages can also be sent with both formats: an HTML and a plain text body. These types of messages are called *multipart messages.*

Sending Multipart Messages

There are two techniques you can use to send multipart email messages.

One approach is to set the message object's AutoGenerateTextBody and MimeFormatted properties to **True**, and then assign the HTML content to the HTMLBody property. Setting the AutoGenerateTextBody property to **True** automatically generates a plain text version of whatever contents are set in the message object's HTMLBody property. Setting MimeFormatted to **True** signals that the email is a multipart message containing HTML.

Try this for yourself by creating a new Visual Basic project and naming it **asp1102**. Name the generated class **msgbody**. Attach the CDO and ADO type libraries. Add a method to the new component called sendMultiPart, which is shown in Example 11-3. This method takes four String parameters: the email address of the recipient, the email address of the sender, the subject line, and an HTML-formatted message string. Make sure that you set the SMTP server, username, and password to values that work for your own email setup.

After the sendMultiPart method creates instances of both the CDO Message and Configuration objects and sets the Configuration properties, it sets the Message object's AutoGenerateTextBody and MimeFormatted properties to **True** and then assigns the *strMessage* parameter to the Message object's HTMLBody property. Finally, it sends the message.

Example 11-3. Sending a Multipart Email Message

```
Sub sendMultiPart(ByVal strTo As String, _
                  ByVal strFrom As String, _
                  ByVal strSubject As String, _
                  ByVal strMessage As String)

Dim iMsg As New CDO.Message
Dim iConf As New CDO.Configuration

Dim flds As ADODB.Fields
Set flds = iConf.Fields

' set configuration properties
flds.Item(cdoSendUsingMethod) = cdoSendUsingPort
flds.Item(cdoSMTPAuthenticate) = cdoBasic
flds.Item(cdoSMTPConnectionTimeout) = 20

flds.Item(cdoSMTPServer) = "mail.company.com"
flds.Item(cdoSendUserName) = strFrom
flds.Item(cdoSendPassword) = "somepassword"
flds.Update

Set iMsg.Configuration = iConf

' set rest of message properties
iMsg.To = strTo
iMsg.From = strFrom
iMsg.Subject = strSubject

' set message to generate both
```

Example 11-3. Sending a Multipart Email Message (continued)

```
' HTML and plain text messages
iMsg.AutoGenerateTextBody = True
iMsg.MimeFormatted = True
iMsg.HTMLBody = strMessage

' send the message
iMsg.Send

End Sub
```

To test the new component, the following ASP test script creates an instance of the object and also creates an HTML-formatted string to act as the message body. This and the other parameters are set in the call to sendMultiPart:

```
<%
On Error Resume Next
Dim obj
Set obj = Server.CreateObject("asp1102.msgbody")

Dim str
str ="<h1>Howdy!</h1><p>I hope this finds you <strong>well</strong>!</p>"

obj.sendMultiPart "otheruser@company.com", "someuser@company.com", _
                  "testing multipart", str
If Err.Number <> 0 Then
   Response.Write Err.Description
Else
   Response.Write "<h3>Message sent</h3>"
End If

Set obj = Nothing
%>
```

Test this yourself using the ASP test page *asp1104.asp*, after changing the email addresses. If you use Outlook as your email program, your email should look the same as that shown in Figure 11-2. Notice in the message that HTML header formatting makes the greeting larger and bolder than the rest of the text. The use of the <strong> tag also highlights the word *well.*

By sending the email message in two formats, if the email reader cannot process the HTML content, the person receiving the email should have access to the plain text version of the message. The plain text version is always presented first and then the HTML content is presented next. If the viewer can't process MIME content, the plain text version is shown. However, MIME-compatible readers such as Outlook always present the most complex format of the message that they can process, which is why the HTML formatted version of the message is the one shown by Outlook in Figure 11-2.

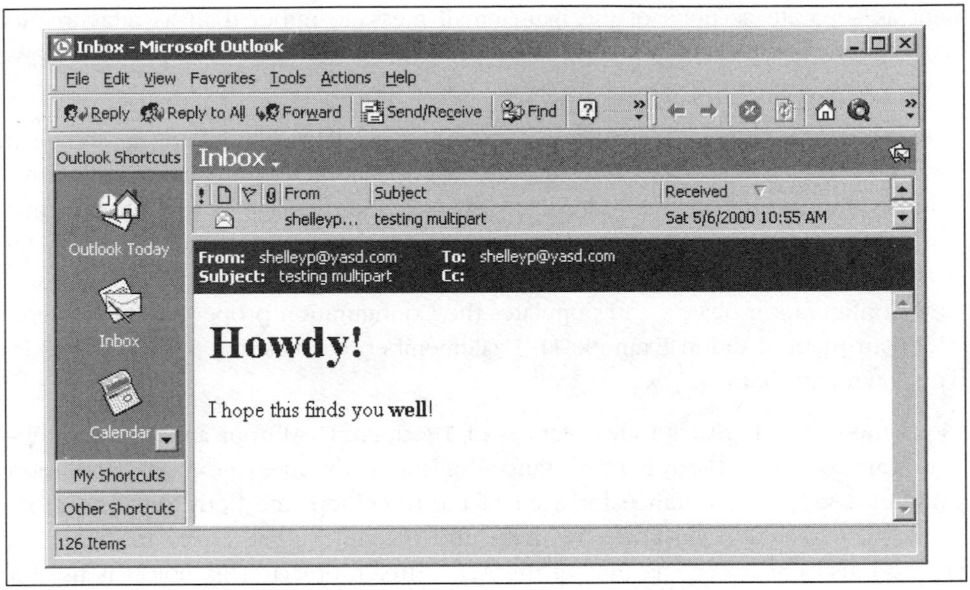

Figure 11-2. The effect of sending a multipart email with HTML-formatted text

Another technique to create multipart messages is to use the IBodyPart interface. By using IBodyPart, you can create messages that consist of several formatting versions of the content, as well as create more complex message body structures.

The IBodyPart Interface

For most uses, directly setting the message using the Message object's properties should meet your needs. However, there could be times when you want more finite control of how the message body is created, and that's where IBodyPart comes in.

There is one instance of IBodyPart, the main IBodyPart representing the main message body, associated as a property of the Message object. However, you can attach multiple instances of IBodyPart to the Message's main IBodyPart object by using the AddBodyPart method. This is the approach you can use to create complex, hierarchical email message bodies.

In the last section, you created a multipart email message consisting of a plain text message and an HTML-formatted message. To do the same using IBodyPart is a bit more complex. It also requires the use of ADO streams.

To demonstrate this second technique for sending a multipart email message, create a new Visual Basic project, name it asp1103, and name the generated class bodypart. Attach the CDO and ADO type libraries. This new example will create an email that has a text message, an HTML-formatted message, and a graphic, all sent as separate sections of the main email message rather than as attachments. You can view the complete code for the finished method in Example 11-4 as we walk through each section of the code.

Add a method to your new component called sendMixedMultiPart, as shown in Example 11-4. It takes the following six String parameters: the recipient's email address, the sender's email address, the subject, the message in plain text format, the message formatted in HTML, and the physical location of a GIF file on the local machine. The sendMixedMultiPart method creates instances of the Message and Configuration objects and populates the Configuration properties, as the send-MultiPart method did in Example 11-3. (Remember to adjust the SMTP settings for your own environment.)

Next, the method creates four instances of IBodyPart. All four aren't necessary—you can use one IBodyPart instance for the main message body and reuse another IBodyPart instance for each of the three separate body sections. However, we'll use four instances to make the example a bit easier to read. The method also creates an instance of the ADO Stream object. This object is used to set the data for each email message body part.

The first IBodyPart instance, iBPMain, is set to the Message object's BodyPart property. iBPMain's ContentMediaType property is set to multipart/mixed, since the email message has three different types of media attached. Then the method creates the first body part section, iBPText, by calling iBPMain's AddBodyPart method. The AddBodyPart method adds the new body part to iBPMain's contents and returns a reference to the newly created object.

The iBPText instance's ContentMediaType property is set to text/plain, and the ContentTransferEncoding property, which controls the type of encoding used for the body part's content, is set to 8bit. To set the actual message text, calling the iBPText object's GetDecodedContentStream method retrieves the Stream object set to the decoded contents of the body part. Text is then added using the Stream object's WriteText method, followed by calling Flush, which forces the Stream contents to be set to the associated object, in this case the iBPText body part.

Once the text body part is finished, the same process is used to add the HTML and GIF body parts. As Example 11-4 shows, each section has different ContentMedia-Type values, as well as different ContentTransferEncoding values. Additionally, the Stream object's LoadFromFile method is used to load the GIF image for the last body part section. After all three body parts have been set, the message is sent.

Example 11-4. Sending a Multipart Message Created Using IBodyPart

```
Sub sendMixedMultiPart(ByVal strTo As String, _
                ByVal strFrom As String, _
                ByVal strSubject As String, _
```

Example 11-4. Sending a Multipart Message Created Using IBodyPart (continued)

```
                        ByVal strMessage As String, _
                        ByVal strHTMLMsg As String, _
                        ByVal strGIF As String)

Dim iMsg As New CDO.Message
Dim iConf As New CDO.Configuration

Dim flds As ADODB.Fields
Set flds = iConf.Fields

' set configuration properties
flds.Item(cdoSendUsingMethod) = cdoSendUsingPort
flds.Item(cdoSMTPAuthenticate) = cdoBasic
flds.Item(cdoSMTPConnectionTimeout) = 20

flds.Item(cdoSMTPServer) = "mail.company.com"
flds.Item(cdoSendUserName) = "person@company.com"
flds.Item(cdoSendPassword) = "somepassword"
flds.Update

Set iMsg.Configuration = iConf

' set rest of message properties
iMsg.To = strTo
iMsg.From = strFrom
iMsg.Subject = strSubject

' ************** Multipart **************
Dim iBPMain As IBodyPart
Dim iBPText As IBodyPart
Dim iBPHTML As IBodyPart
Dim iBPGif As IBodyPart
Dim stmObject As Stream

' get message body part
Set iBPMain = iMsg.bodypart

' set message type
iBPMain.ContentMediaType = "multipart/mixed"

' add text message
Set iBPText = iBPMain.AddBodyPart
With iBPText
   .ContentMediaType = "text/plain"
   .ContentTransferEncoding = "8bit"
   Set stmObject = .GetDecodedContentStream
   stmObject.WriteText strMessage
   stmObject.Flush
End With

' add HTML message
Set iBPHTML = iBPMain.AddBodyPart
```

Example 11-4. Sending a Multipart Message Created Using IBodyPart (continued)

```
With iBPHTML
   .ContentMediaType = "text/html"
   .ContentTransferEncoding = "quoted-printable"
   Set stmObject = .GetDecodedContentStream
   stmObject.WriteText strHTMLMsg
   stmObject.Flush
End With

' add image
Set iBPGif = iBPMain.AddBodyPart
With iBPGif
   .ContentMediaType = "image/gif"
   .ContentTransferEncoding = "base64"
   Set stmObject = .GetDecodedContentStream
   stmObject.LoadFromFile strGIF
   stmObject.Flush
End With

' send the message
iMsg.Send

End Sub
```

To test the new component, create an instance of it in an ASP script and set all of its parameters, as shown in the following ASP page, *asp1105.asp*:

```
<%
On Error Resume Next
Dim obj
Set obj = Server.CreateObject("asp1103.bodypart")

Dim strHTML, strMsg, strGif
strHTML="<h1>Howdy!</h1><p>I hope this finds you <em>well</em>!</p>"
strMsg = "Howdy! I hope this finds you well!"
strGif = "c:\yasd\mm\yasd.gif"

obj.sendMixedMultiPart "person@company.com", "other@company.com", _
                       "testing multipart using IBodyPart", _
                       strMsg, strHTML, strGif

If Err.Number <> 0 Then
   Response.Write Err.Description
Else
   Response.Write "<h3>Message sent</h3>"
End If

Set obj = Nothing
%>
```

Notice in this example that you have to provide the plain text as well as the HTML-formatted version of the message.

When the recipient gets the email, he'll most likely have a text-based email message with two other messages to optionally look at, especially if he is using Outlook as his email reader. As shown in Figure 11-3, any one of the message parts can be accessed and displayed. Clicking on the HTML message part opens the HTML in the default browser. Clicking on the image opens the GIF in whatever tool is defined to be the default image viewer for the recipient's system.

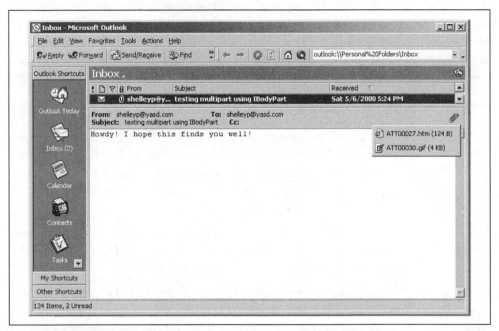

Figure 11-3. Multipart message with text, HTML, and graphic body parts

Though a bit more complicated, one advantage of using `IBodyPart` is that you have more finite control of how the body part is created, and you can specify other types of content media.

You can also choose to attach the content rather than embedding it directly in the message, a topic discussed in the following section.

Attachments

As with creating the message body, you can use either of two techniques to add an attachment to email messages.

The first is very simple: call the Message object's AddAttachment method with the URL of the attachment and optionally include a username and password if the content should be protected:

```
Set iBPMain = iMsg.AddAttachment("http://www.company.com/mm/some.gif")
```

Calling AddAttachment adds the attachment to **IBodyPart**'s Attachments collection. The message's body part is returned from calling AddAttachment and can be used to further refine how the attachment is processed:

```
iBPMain.ContentMediaType = "image/gif"
```

However, you can leave the properties at their defaults.

If you wish more finite control of how the attachment is set, you can create an instance of the message's body part and then create a separate instance of **IBodyPart** specifically for the attachment. Using this approach, you can do such things as set the attachment's content type or assign the name shown for the content when the receiver accesses the attachment from the attachment list.

To work with these two attachment techniques, create a new Visual Basic project, and name it **asp1104** and the generated class **attachment**. Attach both the CDO and ADO type libraries to the project. Create a method called sendAttachments, which is shown in Example 11-5. The method has parameters for the to and from email addresses, the subject, a text message, and two attachment URLs. The second URL also has an associated filename which is passed as an additional parameter, for a total count of seven String parameters.

The sendAttachments method creates instances of the Message and Configuration objects and sets the same properties as the previous examples. It also attaches the message string to the Message object's TextBody property.

The first attachment is added by calling the Message object's AddAttachment method and passing in the first attachment URL string. This method returns a reference to the message's **IBodyPart** property, which the method uses to create a new body part reference by calling the AddBodyPart method. This new body part will contain the second attachment.

As the code in Example 11-5 shows, sendAttachments sets the second body part's properties using techniques similar to those used in Example 11-4, except that it also accesses the body part's Fields collection, which is used to set the **urn: schemas:mailheader:content-disposition** property to **attachment** and with a given filename. Next, it uses an ADO stream to load the attachment, in this case a GIF image, and push the content to the body part object. All that's left then is to send the message.

Example 11-5. Sending Attachments with an Email

```
Sub sendAttachments(ByVal strTo As String, _
                ByVal strFrom As String, _
                ByVal strSubject As String, _
                ByVal strMessage As String, _
                ByVal strAttachment1 As String, _
                ByVal strFile As String, _
                ByVal strAttachment2 As String)
```

Example 11-5. Sending Attachments with an Email (continued)

```
Dim iMsg As New CDO.Message
Dim iConf As New CDO.Configuration

Dim Flds As ADODB.Fields
Set Flds = iConf.Fields

' set configuration properties
Flds.Item(cdoSendUsingMethod) = cdoSendUsingPort
Flds.Item(cdoSMTPAuthenticate) = cdoBasic
Flds.Item(cdoSMTPConnectionTimeout) = 20

Flds.Item(cdoSMTPServer) = "mail.somecompany.com"
Flds.Item(cdoSendUserName) = "person@somecompany.com"
Flds.Item(cdoSendPassword) = "somepassword"
Flds.Update

Set iMsg.Configuration = iConf

' set rest of message properties
iMsg.To = strTo
iMsg.From = strFrom
iMsg.Subject = strSubject
iMsg.TextBody = strMessage

' ************** Multipart **************
Dim iBPMain As IBodyPart
Dim iBPAttach As IBodyPart
Dim stmObject As Stream

' get message body part
Set iBPMain = iMsg.AddAttachment(strAttachment1)

' get attachment body part
Set iBPAttach = iBPMain.AddBodyPart
With iBPAttach
   .ContentMediaType = "image/gif"
   .ContentTransferEncoding = "base64"
   Set Flds = iBPAttach.Fields
   Flds("urn:schemas:mailheader:content-disposition") = _
        "attachment; filename=""" & strFile & """"
   Flds.Update
   Set stmObject = .GetDecodedContentStream
   stmObject.LoadFromFile strAttachment2
   stmObject.Flush
End With

' send message
iMsg.Send

End Sub
```

Test the new component with the following ASP script, which you can find in *asp1106.asp*:

```
<%
On Error Resume Next
Dim obj
Set obj = Server.CreateObject("asp1104.attachment")

Dim strMsg, strAttachment1, strAttachment2, strFile
strMsg = "Howdy! I hope this finds you well!"
strAttachment1 = "http://www.company.com/file.htm"
strAttachment2 = "c:\company\mm\image.gif"
strFile = "image.gif"

obj.sendAttachments "toperson@somecompany.com", "from@company.com", _
                    "testing attachments", _
                    strMsg, strAttachment1, strFile, strAttachment2

If Err.Number <> 0 Then
    Response.Write Err.Description
Else
    Response.Write "<h3>Message sent</h3>"
End If

Set obj = Nothing
%>
```

You can add more than one attachment using either AddAttachment or **IBodyPart**. If you use AddAttachment, the same main body part object keeps getting returned. The second approach is more complicated, but it has the advantage of giving you more control over what recipients see when they get the message. For instance, instead of an attachment with a name such as:

```
ATT000008.gif
```

they'll see the following instead:

```
yasd.gif
```

You've had some fun sending messages; now it's time to talk about reading them.

Retrieving and Reading Messages

Reading email messages consists of creating an object to reference the messages as a group from the folder where they're contained, and then accessing each message one at a time. Once an email message is "read"—accessed from the folder—it can be deleted automatically or cleaned up manually at a later time.

Accessing a DropDirectory

Each SMTP service is given a default drop mail folder on the machine where the SMTP virtual server is installed. By default, this is usually located at the following physical location:

```
C:\Inetpub\mailroot\Drop
```

To access emails from this drop location, you'll need to create a DropDirectory object to reference the folder:

```
Dim iDropDir As New CDO.DropDirectory
Dim iMsgs As CDO.IMessages
Set iMsgs = iDropDir.getMessages("c:\\inetpub\\mailroot\\drop")
```

After creating an instance of DropDirectory, calling its only method, GetMessages, and providing a physical folder location as the parameter opens the folder and gets all the emails it contains. These emails are then added to the **IMessages** collection that the method returns.

Accessing SMTP

Curious about how you can test reading emails on your local machine? If you installed IIS with SMTP, you can send emails to this local installation and read them using the code in this section. To see how to address the emails, open the IIS Manager Console and then click on the Default SMTP Virtual Server. Click on Domains, and find the name of the domain used for your machine. This is what you use following the at sign (@) for your email messages.

The domain I use, *flame.development.local*, was created automatically when I installed Active Directory (see Chapter 12, *Working with Active Directory from ASP Applications*).

Displaying a Message to the Web Page

Once you have access to the **IMessages** collection, there are two techniques you can use to iterate through the collection. You can use the **For Each...Next** construct to enumerate through the objects:

```
For Each iMsg in iMsgs
...
Next iMsg
```

You can also access the IMessages.Count property to see how many messages are in the collection and iterate through it as follows:

```
iCt = iMsgs.Count
For i = 1 to iCt
```

```
       Set iMsg = iMsgs.Index(i)
       ...
   Next
```

I prefer the latter approach if I want to keep track of the index of the message I'm currently reading—either to get more information about the message or to delete it from the collection and the folder.

To demonstrate reading—and cleaning up—messages in a drop folder, create a new Visual Basic project and call it **asp1105**. Name the generated class **drop**. Attach the ADO and CDO libraries, as well as the COM+ Services and the Microsoft Active Server Pages type libraries, since you'll be using the ASP Response object in this example.

The new component will have two methods. The first is getMessages. This method accesses the local machine's drop folder through the DropDirectory object, gets the messages contained in the folder, and then displays the message sender and subject in an HTML table. In addition to this information pulled from the Message object associated with each message, the sender's name is enclosed within a hypertext link that has the message's index number attached as part of the link's query string. Add the code shown in Example 11-6 to your new component.

Example 11-6. Displaying the Sender and Subject of All Email Messages

```
' display all messages
Sub getMessages()

Dim objContext As ObjectContext
Dim objResponse As Response

Set objContext = GetObjectContext()
Set objResponse = objContext("Response")

' create instance of drop directory
Dim iDropDir As New CDO.DropDirectory
Dim iMsgs As CDO.IMessages

' get messages
Set iMsgs = iDropDir.getMessages("c:\\inetpub\\mailroot\\drop")
Dim iMsg As CDO.Message

Dim i, iCt As Integer
iCt = iMsgs.Count

' set up table
objResponse.Write "<table border=2 width='80%' align='center' " _
                & "cellpadding=10>"
objResponse.Write "<TR><TH>From</TH><TH>Subject</TH></TR>"

' for each message, print out msg number,
' from, and subject
```

Example 11-6. Displaying the Sender and Subject of All Email Messages (continued)

```
For i = 1 To iCt
  Set iMsg = iMsgs.Item(i)
  objResponse.Write "<TR><TD>"
  With iMsg

    ' link for message info
    objResponse.Write "<a href='asp1108.asp?ct=" & _
                      CStr(i) & "'>"
    objResponse.Write .From & "</A></TD><TD>"
    objResponse.Write .Subject & "</TD></TR>"
  End With
Next
objResponse.Write "</TABLE>"

End Sub
```

Test this component by creating the following ASP script, *asp1107.asp*, that creates the component and calls getMessages:

```
<%
On Error Resume Next
Dim obj
Set obj = Server.CreateObject("asp1105.drop")

obj.getMessages
If Err.Number <> 0 Then
   Response.Write Err.Description
End If
%>
```

The page displays all email messages contained within the drop folder in an HTML table and allows the user to click on a specific message to read the message body. Figure 11-4 shows an example of a page run on my system.

When one of the emails is clicked, a second page opens that retrieves the message's index from the Request object's QueryString collection and uses this as a parameter for the second method in **asp1105.drop**: getMessage.

The getMessage method also accesses the drop folder of all the messages. This time, though, the code specifically accesses the email that matches the index sent as the parameter to the method and displays its sender, subject, and text. At the end, the email is deleted. Add the code for this second method, shown in Example 11-7, to **asp1105.drop**.

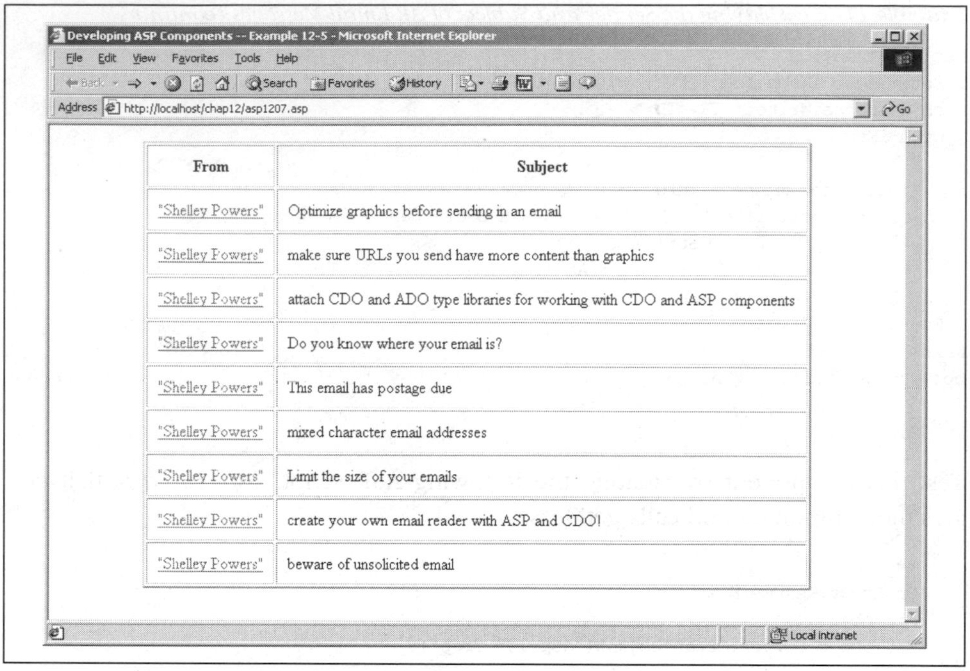

Figure 11-4. List of senders and subjects for existing emails

Example 11-7. Printing the Contents of an Email and Deleting It from the Collection and Folder

```
' get one specific message
Sub getMessage(ByVal iCt As Integer)

Dim objContext As ObjectContext
Dim objResponse As Response

Set objContext = GetObjectContext()
Set objResponse = objContext("Response")

' create drop directory
Dim iDropDir As New CDO.DropDirectory
Dim iMsgs As CDO.IMessages

' get messages
Set iMsgs = iDropDir.getMessages("c:\\inetpub\\mailroot\\drop")

' get specific message
Dim iMsg As CDO.Message
Set iMsg = iMsgs.Item(iCt)

' print message info
With iMsg
  objResponse.Write "<p>From: " & .From & "</p>"
  objResponse.Write "<p>Subject: " & .Subject & "</p>"
```

Example 11-7. Printing the Contents of an Email and Deleting It from the Collection and Folder (continued)

```
  objResponse.Write "<p>" & .TextBody & "</P>"
End With

' delete message
iMsgs.Delete (iCt)

End Sub
```

The ASP script to call this method, *asp1108.asp*, is as follows:

```
<%
On Error Resume Next
Dim obj
Set obj = Server.CreateObject("asp1105.drop")

Dim imsg
imsg = Request.QueryString("ct")

obj.getMessage imsg
%>
```

Try both of the methods on your own system.

You're now well on the way to creating your own ASP-based email applications, including your own online email viewer.

12

Working with Active Directory from ASP Applications

At first glance, it might seem as if you, as an ASP component developer, wouldn't be that interested in working with Active Directory. After all, Active Directory is mainly for administrators, and they have access to the tools they need to perform their functions.

However, Active Directory isn't just for administrators—it can be useful for anyone needing access to system information that's maintained in a directory service. By providing support for Active Directory through an intranet, or even through a carefully guarded Internet application, you can enable your system users to control more of their own information. This empowers them and decreases the burden on your system administrators.

Additionally, you can also provide reporting applications that management can use to find out which people in what departments have access to what functionality. Again, by empowering your managers, you decrease the workload on your system administrators and provide just-in-time information to the folks who need it the most: your bosses.

The examples in this chapter demonstrate accessing Active Directory via ASP components using the Active Directory Service Interfaces (ADSI). ASP applications using ADSI should be enclosed within the strictest security, and access should be restricted to those on a need-to-have basis only.

A Brief Overview of Active Directory in Windows 2000

Active Directory provides a way to work with administrative services, such as managing users and groups, and system resources, such as printers, without having to know the physical location of the items. Additionally, Active Directory provides a structured hierarchical data storage that can be manipulated either through a set of exposed interfaces (ADSI) or through OLE DB and ADO.

Within Windows 2000, Active Directory uses LDAP—Lightweight Directory Access Protocol—for object access. LDAP is a directory service protocol running on TCP/IP that currently has wide industry support (and not just in the Windows environment). The use of LDAP within Windows 2000 should lead to easier integration of Windows 2000 with other platforms, such as Unix systems.

Setting Up an Isolated Active Directory Environment

As a developer, your development machine may or may not be connected to a LAN. If it is, chances are that one machine is set up to be the Active Directory domain controller, and the other machines access the services of this machine through the LAN. However, you might also have a development machine that's isolated or for some other reason doesn't have access to Active Directory, but you still want to work with this technology.

You also might want to be able to freely work with Active Directory without doing damage to an environment that's shared by several people.

In this section, I'll show you how to set up Active Directory on a Windows 2000 development machine that isn't connected to a LAN and, in fact, doesn't even have a Network Interface Card (NIC) installed. For other configurations, check the documentation provided by Microsoft to see about installing Active Directory.

First, Active Directory can be installed only on Windows 2000 servers—you can't install it in a Windows 2000 Professional installation. Once you've installed Windows 2000 Server on your machine, the first thing you'll want to do is set up your network card. If you don't have a network card, then you'll want to install the MS Loopback Adapter.

Active Directory doesn't need the Microsoft Loopback Adapter per se in order to work, but it does need to be able to access a DNS server, and the DNS lookup occurs through the adapter. If you try to install Active Directory without the Loopback Adapter installed (in an isolated environment), halfway through the installation process, you'll get an error that states, "The wizard cannot contact the DNS server that handles the name *(domain name)* to determine if it supports dynamic update. Confirm your DNS configuration, or install and configure a DNS server on this computer."

The Microsoft Loopback Adapter is used where a network installation isn't available or isn't feasible. Additionally, the Loopback Adapter can be used when a problem such as a conflict occurs with your current network connection. When this happens, you switch your network bindings to the adapter to prevent their loss until you can clear up the network problems.

To install the adapter, access the Control Panel and then double-click on the Add/ Remove Hardware option. When the hardware wizard opens, select the Add/Troubleshoot a Device option and then the Add a New Device option after the wizard has finished looking for plug-and-play devices.

From the next window, pick the option that allows you to select hardware from a list. From the page that opens, select the Network Adapter option. From the list of manufacturers that opens in the next page, select Microsoft, and then select Microsoft's only entry, the Microsoft Loopback Adapter, as shown in Figure 12-1. Clicking on the Next button selects this adapter, and in the next page, clicking on the Finish button installs the adapter with the default settings.

You won't need to configure the Loopback Adapter's properties once it's installed. The DHCP server on the machine configures the adapter settings automatically.

Microsoft has provided a Knowledge Base article on installing the MS Loopback Adapter in Windows 2000. The Knowledge Base article number is Q236869, and you can find this article by searching for it at the Microsoft MSDN web site (*http://msdn.microsoft.com*).

Once the adapter has been installed, you're ready to install Active Directory as a domain controller in your isolated environment. Access the Configure Your Server wizard from the Administrative Tools and select the Active Directory option. This starts the Active Directory installation wizard, which will promote your box from being a member server of the domain (the default Windows 2000 installation) to being a domain controller.

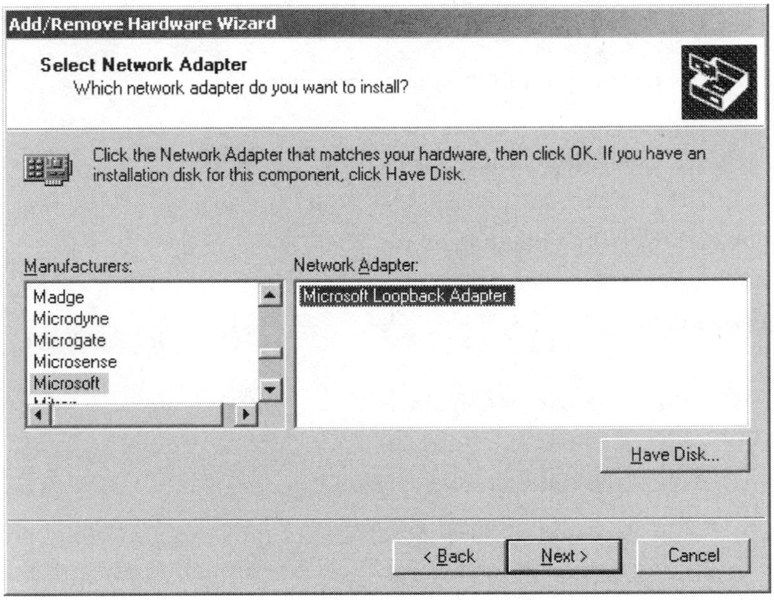

Figure 12-1. Adding the Microsoft Loopback Adapter through the hardware wizard

In the page that opens, provide a NetBIOS name and a domain. Since your installation is isolated, provide *local* as the new domain name of the server. Provide whatever name you wish as the NetBIOS domain name. For example, in my isolated machine, I used *development* as the NetBIOS name and *local* as the domain. When combined, these create an Active Directory domain controller identified by the domain *development.local*.

The installation triggered by Configure Your Server operates without intervention to install Active Directory.

A Refresher on ADSI

You can work with Active Directory using ADO as well as using ADSI (Active Directory Service Interfaces). You had a chance to work with ADSI already in Chapter 2, *Setting Up the ASP Development Environment*, when you worked with the IIS Metabase. In this chapter, you can continue to use ADSI to work with Active Directory.

All ADSI objects (except Namespaces and Container, discussed in the next section on binding) implement the IADs interface, which means all share the same core set of properties and methods. These were covered in Chapter 2 when we used ADSI to work with the IIS Metabase, but I'll repeat them here as a refresher.

The IADs interface properties are the following:

ADsPath
> The object's unique path in the directory service

Class
> The schema class name of the object

GUID
> The object's globally unique identifier (GUID)

Name
> The object name

Parent
> The ADsPath of the parent container

Schema
> The ADsPath of the object's schema class

Objects are usually accessed by their ADsPath, but they can also be found by their GUID. Accessing an Active Directory object occurs through binding to that object, a process I'll discuss in greater detail in the next section. For now, know that in binding, you can specify an Active Directory provider (such as **IIS** for IIS, and **LDAP** for the LDAP provider) and the path for the object, as in the following:

```
IIS://localhost/W3SVC/1/ROOT/test
```

or:

```
LDAP://development.local
```

After the object is bound, you can access its properties. For instance, you can access the IADs properties that all Active Directory objects share, such as Name, Class, ADsPath, or Schema, with code like the following:

```
Set myDomain = GetObject("LDAP://development.local")
prop = myDomain.Name
```

Or you can access the object's own unique set of properties through the use of the IADs interface's Get method:

```
Set myDomain = GetObject("LDAP://development.local")
prop = myDomain.Get("dc")
```

The following are the IADs methods:

Get
> Gets the ADSI object's property value

Put
> Changes the ADSI object's property value

GetInfo

Refreshes the local cache copy of all of the ADSI object's properties

SetInfo

Saves all changes to the ADSI object's properties to the Directory Service (i.e., persists the changes)

Get and Put retrieve and update one property at a time. When an object's properties are first accessed directly or with Get, all the object's property values are copied to a local cache. This prevents unnecessary network traffic to get the properties one at a time. However, you can manually refresh this cache by calling the Get-Info method:

```
myDomain.GetInfo
```

Additionally, if you change any of the ADSI object's properties, the change won't be saved until you call the SetInfo method:

```
myDomain.SetInfo
```

Binding to Active Directory Objects

Before you can work with an Active Directory object, you have to bind to it. Active Directory objects have already been created for the objects in your directory service, so you don't use *CreateObject* with a ProgID (programmatic identifier) to create a new instance. Instead, you call the *GetObject* function and pass in the ADsPath binding string to obtain a reference to the object.

 Use *GetObject* to access Active Directory objects with Visual Basic and ASP script. Use the Win32::OLE Perl Module's *GetObject* method with Perl. With Visual C++ and Java, use ADsGetObject.

For instance, my development machine has an Active Directory domain (or hostname) of *development.local*, so I could use the following to bind to the topmost domain:

```
Set myDomain = GetObject("LDAP://development.local")
```

In this line of code, I'm using the Active Directory LDAP provider to bind to my domain. I could also have used the following syntax, which references the hostname as the domain controller for my environment:

```
Set myDomain = GetObject("LDAP://DC=development,DC=local")
```

Both strings used with *GetObject* return the same Active Directory object: the topmost domain in the Active Directory tree structure. The value specified is also the *defaultNamingContext* for the tree root, as you'll see in the next section.

Alternative Binding Techniques

The core functionality of ADSI is based on four interfaces: `IADs`, `IADsContainer`, `IADsNamespaces`, and `IADsOpenDSObject`.

The `IADsOpenDSObject` interface is used when binding to an Active Directory object using a security context other than the one of the person currently accessing the application doing the binding. It has one method, OpenDSObject. Visual Basic developers can access OpenDSObject through the `IADsOpenDSObject` interface by attaching the Active DS type library to the project. The method has the following signature:

```
obj = OpenDSObject(DN name as BSTR, user name as BSTR, password as BSTR,
    authentication flags from ADS_AUTHENTICATION_ENUM)
```

You'll need to create a reference to `IADsOpenDSObject`, and you do this with *GetObject*, just as you do with an `IADs` interface. Once you have the reference, you can then call OpenDSObject, passing in the username, password, and the authentication flag. To demonstrate, if you want to access a particular user, but using the security context of that same user, you could use the following in Visual Basic:

```
Dim objDS As IADsOpenDSObject
Set objDS = GetObject("LDAP:")
Dim obj As IADs
Set obj = objDS.OpenDSObject("LDAP://CN=Mark Bond,CN=Users,
        DC=development,DC=local", "mark@development.local", "mytest",
                        ADS_SECURE_AUTHENTICATION)
```

The last parameter in the method call is an enumerated value from **ADS_AUTHENTICATION_ENUM**, which determines which authentication process is used with the method call. In this code fragment, secure authentication is used, and Active Directory uses Kerberos and/or NTLM to authenticate the client.

 Windows 2000 has implemented both the Kerberos and the NTLM authentication protocols. With both, a client's identity consists of a domain, a username, and a password (or a token for NTLM). See the Windows 2000 documentation for more on these protocols.

The Namespaces container implements the `IADsNamespaces` interface and provides access to all domains regardless of provider. So if you want to access directory services across IIS and WinNT, as well as LDAP and the other providers, you would first bind to the Namespaces container, and then access the services from there.

The following code contains script from an ASP page that binds to the Namespaces container and then lists the names of the providers available in the current environment:

```
<%
Dim obj
Dim item

Set obj = GetObject("ADs:")
For Each item In obj
    Response.Write item.name & "<br>"
Next
%>
```

In a default Windows 2000 installation, the result should be:

```
WinNT:
NWCOMPAT:
NDS:
LDAP:
IIS:
```

The LDAP provider listed is actually the ProgID of the provider used with an LDAP server. This is the provider you use to access Active Directory services within Windows 2000 and with Exchange 2000. We used the ProgID of IIS to access the IIS Metabase in Chapter 2, and you might use the ProgID of WinNT to access Windows NT Primary Domain Controllers (PDCs) if you work with ADSI in NT. The other two providers support communication with Novell Directory Services (NDS) and Novell Network servers (NWCOMPAT).

Every Active Directory object has a *distinguishedName* (DN) property, which provides a unique name for the object. This name is a string consisting of the object's relative unique name concatenated with the names of the object's ancestors all the way back to the root.

For instance, the DN for the IUSR_FLAME user object on my system is:

```
CN=IUSR_FLAME,CN=Users,DC=development,DC=local
```

The object IUSR_FLAME is contained in the USERS container, within the default domain, identified by DC=development,DC=local.

In case you didn't recognize it, IUSR_FLAME is the IIS default user for the machine named *flame*.

You can access an object by its DN, through the ADsPath, when using *GetObject*:

```
Set user = GetObject("LDAP://CN=IUSR_FLAME,CN=Users,DC=development,
                                                      DC=local")
```

The problem with using a DN is that objects can be moved or renamed. If the object is moved or renamed, than the ADsPath is no longer valid.

Instead of using the DN, you can also bind to an object using the object's GUID, one of the properties supported with the IADs interface. To access IUSR_FLAME with its GUID, you would use the following:

```
Set user = GetObject("LDAP://<GUID=01981092b28e50459c10085ff009b0f7>")
```

The GUID remains the same in the current environment, regardless of whether the object is moved or renamed. Of course, you'll have a problem with hardcoding a GUID if the code's moving to a different environment.

In previous examples of binding to an LDAP domain, I've hardcoded the domain controller (DC) for my environment (LDAP://DC=development,DC=local) directly into the connection string. A better approach is to extract this information from the rootDSE instead.

The *rootDSE* is the root of the directory tree on a directory server; its purpose is to provide information about the directory, such as the name of the domain on the server. Using rootDSE, I can access the default domain using the following code and avoid hardcoding a reference to the domain controller directly:

```
Set myRoot = GetObject("LDAP://rootDSE")
name = "LDAP://" & myRoot.Get("defaultNamingContext")
Set myDomain = GetObject(name)
```

Now, the naming used within the environment should be transparent to my code, and I should be able to move the code (and the component using the code) to a different environment without modification. Microsoft refers to this concept as *serverless binding*.

Binding to Objects Through Collections

Active Directory is a hierarchical structure, which means that objects can have children. Additionally, Active Directory also has several objects that are containers—groupings of similar objects, all based on the same class. All of the collections (parents with children or container objects) are accessible from one or more other ADSI interfaces, and all collection members can be enumerated using standard enumeration techniques.

Unlike the individual ADSI objects, which implement the IADs interface, containers implement the IADsContainer interface. This interface has methods that developers can use to enumerate through the container's collection of objects. Additionally, the `IADsContainer` interface also has its own implementation of the GetObject method to create a reference to an Active Directory object from its container.

There are two special cases of `IADsContainer`: `IADsMembers` and `IADs-Collection`. The `IADsMembers` interface is used to access members of a group and is accessed through the `IADsGroup` interface. A group is physically located within the same path in the Active Directory directory structure.

The `IADsCollection` interface allows access to a named group of objects regardless of where the objects are located. For instance, you can access the print jobs on a printer queue as a collection by calling the IADsPrintQueueOperations.PrintJobs method. This method returns an instance of the `IADsCollection`.

The key difference between a collection and a group is that the objects in the collection must be the same type. The objects in the group can be different types.

To demonstrate the nature of containers, create a new Visual Basic ActiveX DLL project, naming it **asp1201** and the generated class container. You'll need to add three type libraries to the project: COM+ Services, Microsoft Active Server Pages to access the Response object, and the Active DS Type library to access ADSI objects.

In the component class, create a method called enumObjects, as shown in Example 12-1. enumObjects has one parameter, a string containing the distinguishedName for a specific container. The component method retrieves a reference to the container's IADsGroup interface by prepending the Active Directory provider (`LDAP://`) to the distinguishedName value passed to it as a parameter and the passing that string as an argument to GetObject. It then traverses the Members collection of the container, listing each object's unique identifying name (the cn property for the object).

Example 12-1. Component Method to Iterate Through a Container's Objects and Print Out the cn Property of Each Contained Object

```
Sub enumObjects(ByVal strContainer As String)

On Error GoTo ErrorHandler

    ' get ObjectContext
    Dim objContext As ObjectContext
    Set objContext = GetObjectContext()

    ' get Response
    Dim objResponse As Response
    Set objResponse = objContext("Response")

    ' get container
    Dim icontObject As IADsGroup
```

Example 12-1. Component Method to Iterate Through a Container's Objects and Print Out the cn Property of Each Contained Object (continued)

```
Dim strADsPath As String
strADsPath = "LDAP://" & strContainer
Set icontObject = GetObject(strADsPath)

' traverse container
' printing out unique identifier
' of each member
Dim iObj As IADs
For Each iObj In icontObject.Members
  objResponse.Write iObj.Get("cn") & "<br>"
Next
```

```
Exit Sub
```

```
ErrorHandler:
```

```
    objResponse.Write Err.Description
```

```
End Sub
```

To test the component, create a simple ASP page that passes an Active Directory group object's distinguishedName as the parameter. For instance, to call the component method with the test group, use an ASP script similar to the following:

```
Dim obj
Set obj = Server.CreateObject("asp1201.container")
obj.enumObjects "CN=test,CN=Users,DC=development,DC=local"
```

The file *asp1201.asp* contains this test script. You'll want to change the script to reflect your environment.

The previous example accessed a group of items through the **IADsMembers** interface, accessible by a specific method on the **IADsGroup** interface. You can also access a collection directly.

For example, an object that collects elements based on location in the Active Directory is the Users object, identified by the following distinguished name on my box:

```
CN=Users,DC=development,DC=local
```

The Users object contains both *user* and *group* elements. These objects can be accessed directly through **IADsContainer** using code such as this:

```
Dim icontObject As IADsContainer
Set icontObject = GetObject(strADsPath)
Dim iObj As IADs
For Each iObj In icontObject
    ...
Next
```

The IADsContainer is used to access the Users object, and its contained elements are accessed directly from the object rather than from an object's Members property. We'll take a closer look at working with users in the section on working with containers, later in this chapter.

You can test the component shown in Example 12-1 with other groups, but that leads to the question of how to find the distinguishedNames for groups in your Active Directory environment to test this new component. If you have the Microsoft Platform SDK installed, you can use the Active Directory Services Viewer (ADSVW), a utility provided at no charge from Microsoft, to look up these values.

Using the Active Directory Services Viewer

When you start working with Active Directory, the most important tool you can use to help you get started is the Active Directory Services Viewer (ADSVW), also called the Active Directory Browser. This utility is installed as part of the platform SDK installation and can be found as a file named *adsvw.exe*, located in the *bin* subdirectory of the installation. To use it, you should be logged in as the Administrator for the machine where you're running the tool.

The Platform SDK can be downloaded from the Microsoft Developer Network site (*http://msdn.microsoft.com*).

When you start the tool, you're given a dialog with choices to create an Object-Viewer or a Query. To browse through the directory structure, choose the Object-Viewer option. A new dialog opens with fields for the ADsPath. Type in the domain ADsPath and click the OK button.

On my box, I would type in the following:

```
LDAP://DC=development,DC=local
```

as shown in Figure 12-2.

ADSVW then opens a tree structure showing the existing Active Directory objects within your environment. As you click on objects in the structure, information about the object is displayed in the right side of the tool's window. If the object is a higher-level object, more objects display beneath it in the left directory tree structure.

Figure 12-3 shows ADSVW with an expanded Users container displaying all of the users defined in my environment. Notice on the right side of Figure 12-3 the

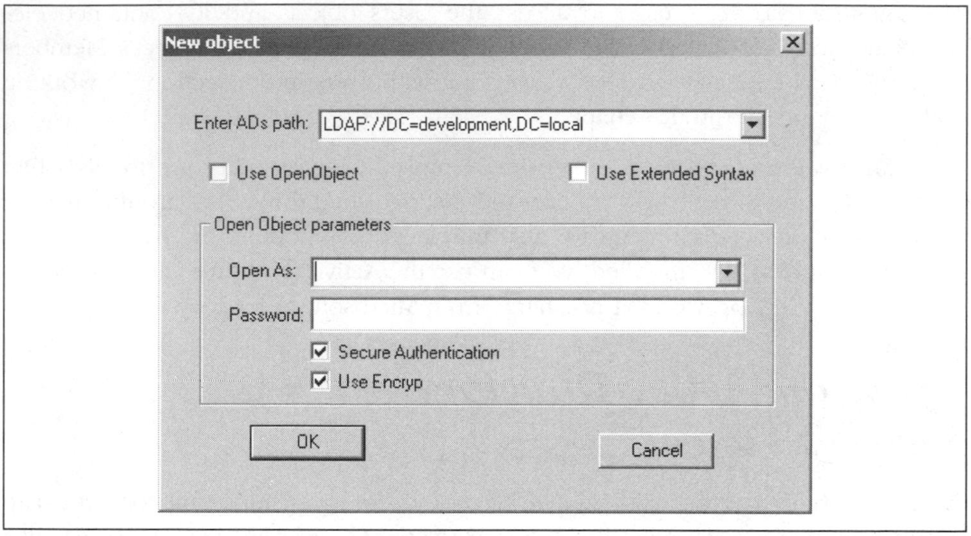

Figure 12-2. Accessing the Active Directory object for the default domain using ADSVW

information about Users, including its ADsPath and the fact that it is a container class. There is also a dropdown list box containing all of the possible object properties in the middle of the page. Picking one of these properties displays the associated value in the text box next to the list box, as shown with distinguishedName.

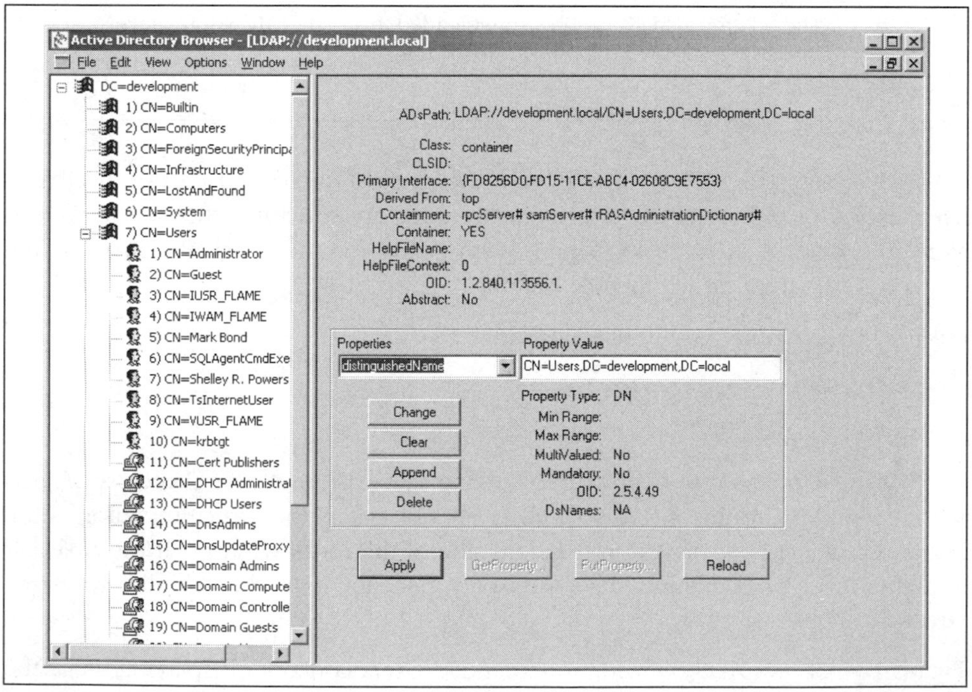

Figure 12-3. Expanded Users in directory tree within ADSVW

You can do more than just view Active Directory information with ADSVW—you can also change it. If you try to change or remove information critical to the object, such as the distinguishedName shown in Figure 12-3, you'll get a constraint error.

You can also manipulate Active Directory objects and information using the ADSI administrative tools, but the rest of this chapter is devoted to working with Active Directory objects via ASP components written in Visual Basic.

Manipulating Containers

As you've seen in the section on binding, you can access an object directly from its container. The **IADsContainer** interface supports other properties and methods of interest, and we'll look at all of these in this section.

You can access an object from a container by enumerating through the Members collection. You can also access a specific object by using the container's GetObject method:

```
Set obj = GetObject(relative name of object as BSTR, DN of object as BSTR)
```

The parameters for GetObject are the object's class name (**user**), and the relative name (**CN=IUSR_NAME**). These are identical to the **IADs** Class and Name properties.

You can also filter the members within the container using the Filter property. Referring to Figure 12-3 again, you'll see in the list under the higher-level Users object that there are two classes of objects in the list: users and groups. Each object class has its own icon in the tree structure. If your code traversed the contained elements in Users, both the group and user class objects would be displayed in the web page. However, if you wanted to restrict the display to only group items, you'd adjust the code to filter the container first before iterating through the collection.

To try out Filter, create a second Visual Basic project, naming the project **asp1202** and the generated class **users**. The component has one method that you'll call enumObjectsByFilter; it is shown in Example 12-2. The method has a single parameter, a Variant array passed from the ASP page that contains the class names of the objects to be filtered with the container.

Again, the component uses the ASP Response object to output results to the web page, so add references to the COM+ Services and Microsoft Active Server Pages type libraries, as well as the Active DS type library to work with Active Directory.

The code for enumObjectsByFilter is similar to the code for enumObjects, shown previously in Example 12-1, except this time, the **IADsContainer** object is used to obtain a reference to the Users object, and the object's children are accessed directly from the object rather than from an object property. Additionally, the *varFilter* parameter array is first assigned to the container's Filter property to filter the children to a specific class.

Example 12-2. Filtering a Parent Object's Children to a Specific Class

```
Sub enumObjectsByFilter(ByVal varFilter As Variant)

On Error GoTo ErrorHandler

    ' get ObjectContext
    Dim objContext As ObjectContext
    Set objContext = GetObjectContext()

    ' get Response
    Dim objResponse As Response
    Set objResponse = objContext("Response")

    ' get container
    Dim icontObject As IADsContainer
    Dim strADsPath As String
    Set icontObject = GetObject("LDAP://CN=Users,DC=development,DC=local")

    ' filter container
    icontObject.Filter = varFilter

    ' iterate through container
    ' printing out cn of each element
    Dim iObj As IADs
    Dim str As String
    For Each iObj In icontObject
        str = iObj.Get("cn") & "<br>"
        objResponse.Write str
    Next

Exit Sub

ErrorHandler:

    objResponse.Write Err.Description

End Sub
```

Make sure to modify the ADsPath for Users to match your current environment.

To test this component, create an array that contains one of the two classes defining the User's children objects. In the following case, the display is restricted to objects with a **group** class:

```
<% Dim obj
Set obj = Server.CreateObject("asp1202.users")

' create array of classes
```

```
Dim vary
vary = Array("group")

obj.enumObjectsByFilter vary %>
```

You can try this yourself by accessing the *asp1202.asp* page included with the examples. Vary the results by changing the **group** in the script to **user** and accessing the page again.

In addition to listing container elements, you can also add and remove members from a container. Note that this does not remove a member from Active Directory; it only removes the object's container membership. To actually create or delete an element from Active Directory, you'll want to access the containing parent object and create or delete the element from this object.

 A demonstration of adding and removing users to and from a group is given in the last section of this chapter.

To demonstrate the distinction between these two actions, you'll create another component, naming its VB project **asp1203** and the generated class **group**. This component has two methods: one to create a new group and one to delete the group. Unlike the previous components, this one doesn't need a reference to the Response object, so you need to add only the Active DS type library to the project.

Add the createGroup method shown in Example 12-3 first. The name of the new group to be created is passed as the method's only parameter. In the code, this name is adjusted to the Active Directory relative name by adding **CN=** before the name. Then, the Users object is accessed through **IADsContainer**, and the new group is created by calling the interface's Create method. A reference to the new object is returned, and then key group properties are set on the object.

Group elements must have the following properties set before the object can be saved to the directory service:

- The CN property, set to the group name.

- The GroupType property, in this case set to a global, secure group.

- The SAMAccountName property, set with the name used by Windows clients to reference the specific item. For this example, this value is the same as the group name.

The GroupType property is set with values from an enumeration, **ADS_GROUP_ TYPE_ENUM**. In Example 12-3, two of the enumerated values, **ADS_GROUP_TYPE_ GLOBAL_GROUP** and **ADS_GROUP_TYPE_SECURITY_ENABLED** are ORed together to create a combined group that can be global (can be exported to other domains) and secure (can apply an access-control list on an object).

 The bitwise OR operator does a bit-by-bit comparison between the two numeric values, setting the resulting bit to 1 if either or both bits have a value of 1.

Only when all of the required properties have been set is the new group saved to the directory service. If the required properties are not set before the object is saved (using SetInfo), a constraint violation occurs.

Example 12-3. Creating a Group Under Users in Active Directory

```
' create a group in the Users container
Sub createGroup(ByVal strGrpName As String)

On Error GoTo ErrorHandler

    ' container and group objects
    Dim iObj As IADsContainer
    Dim iGrp As IADsGroup
    Dim strRNname As String

    ' change group name to relative group name
    strRNname = "CN=" & strGrpName

    ' obtain reference to Users
    ' create new group
    Set iObj = GetObject("LDAP://CN=Users,DC=development,DC=local")
    Set iGrp = iObj.Create("group", strRNname)

    ' required properties
    iGrp.Put "cn", strGrpName
    iGrp.Put "groupType", _
        ADS_GROUP_TYPE_GLOBAL_GROUP Or ADS_GROUP_TYPE_SECURITY_ENABLED
    iGrp.Put "sAMAccountName", strGrpName

    ' save change back to directory service
    iGrp.SetInfo

Exit Sub
ErrorHandler:

    Err.Raise Err.Number, Err.Source, Err.Description

End Sub
```

To test the new component method, create an ASP script that creates the `asp1203.group` object and calls its method, passing in the name of the new group, as shown in *asp1203.asp*:

```
<% On Error Resume Next
Dim obj
Set obj = Server.CreateObject("asp1203.group")

Dim grp
grp = "devaspcomps"

obj.createGroup grp
If Err.Number <> 0 Then
    Response.Write Err.Description
Else
    Response.Write "Group " & grp & " has been added"
End If %>
```

When you try this yourself using the *asp1203.asp* test page, use your own group name—just make sure it's not the same as an existing group, or you'll receive an error.

 It's absolutely essential to specify the relative name for the group or other object you're adding when using the Create method. If you don't, you'll get an "Automation error: The server is unwilling to process the request" error. Since this error is not all that intuitive, be aware that its most likely cause is not specifying the relative name when creating a new object.

You can also remove a group programmatically. Add removeGroup, the second method for the `asp1203.group` component, as shown in Example 12-4. Use the `IADsContainer`'s Delete method to remove a group. Unlike CreateGroup, no call to SetInfo is needed; the group is removed immediately. In the code for remove-Group, the Users object is again referenced with *GetObject* and the Delete method is called, passing in the group's relative name.

Example 12-4. Removing a Named Group from the Users Collection

```
' remove group
Sub removeGroup(ByVal strGrpName As String)

On Error GoTo ErrorHandler

    ' get container
    Dim iGrpObj As IADsContainer
    Set iGrpObj = GetObject("LDAP://CN=Users,DC=development,DC=local")

    Dim strRNname As String
```

Example 12-4. Removing a Named Group from the Users Collection (continued)

```
' change group name to relative group name
strRNname = "CN=" & strGrpName

' delete group
iGrpObj.Delete "group", strRNname
```

```
Exit Sub
ErrorHandler:

    Err.Raise Err.Number, Err.Source, Err.Description

End Sub
```

You can try out the second method by removing the group you added earlier. For instance, the following ASP script results in the **devaspcomps** group being removed from the directory service:

```
<% On Error Resume Next
Dim obj
Set obj = Server.CreateObject("asp1203.group")

Dim grp
grp = "devaspcomps"

obj.removeGroup grp
If Err.Number <> 0 Then
    Response.Write Err.Description
Else
    Response.Write "Group " & grp & " has been removed"
End If %>
```

Again, try this for yourself, using the ASP test page *asp1204.asp*. First, though, modify the code to use the group name you used earlier to create the group.

Earlier examples in this chapter listed all members of a collection or those members that met a specific class filter. You can also search among the contents of an Active Directory installation. The next section discusses how to search Active Directory using an old friend: ADO.

Searching Active Directory with ADO

There are two ways to search through the Active Directory. The first is to use the **IDirectorySearch** object; this approach is covered in Chapter 17, *Accessing Active Directory from C++ Components*. A second approach is to use OLE DB or ADO to search the Active Directory contents. For this section, we'll take a look at using ADO.

Instead of connecting to a database using a database provider, you connect to Active Directory using the Active Directory provider, **ADsDSOObject**. You don't have to provide a username or password; not doing so sets the security context to the current user:

```
Dim cn As Connection
cn.Provider = "ADsDSOObject"
cn.Open
```

You use the ADO Recordset object to work with the returned results. However, how you get those results can vary. You can execute a query against the Active Directory in a similar manner to what you've used to query other data sources. For instance, you could perform the query using the Connection object's Execute method:

```
Set rs = cn.Execute "select cn from 'LDAP://DC=development, DC=local'" & _
                "WHERE objectCategory = 'group'"
```

You could also perform the query with the Recordset object itself:

```
str = "select cn from 'LDAP://DC=development, DC=local'" & _
                " WHERE objectCategory = 'group'"
Set rs.ActiveConnection = con
rs.Open str
```

Or you could create a Command object and use it to execute the query:

```
str = "select cn from 'LDAP://DC=development, DC=local'" & _
                "WHERE objectCategory = 'group'"
Set com.ActiveConnection = con
com.CommandText = str
Set rs = com.Execute
```

Use the technique you're most comfortable with or that fits your application purposes.

 You can get a more in-depth review of ADO in Chapter 8, *Creating ASP/ADO Components.*

Notice in the code fragments that instead of querying against a table or calling a stored procedure, the selection is made against a specific Active Directory object identified by the object's distinguishedName. Instead of referencing columns in the **WHERE** clause of the query, object properties are used for the search criteria. The query just shown in the three code fragments returns a result set containing the cn property of each element that has an objectCategory of type **group**—all of the group elements in the specified domain.

The query starts at the object defined as the "source" of the query (the domain) and then searches all contained elements (all Active Directory elements contained in the domain). The elements must have a schema class of group to match the objectCategory search criteria.

Instead of searching on objectCategory, I could also have searched on object-Class. Either can be used to find specific instances of a schema class. However, the objectClass property contains more than one value—the object's schema class, plus all the inherited or superclasses of the object—whereas the objectCategory property can have at most one value—the class of the object itself. Based on this, objectCategory searches are more selective.

Another reason to use objectCategory is that this property is indexed. To ensure the most efficient searches with Active Directory, you'll want to use indexed properties as much as possible in the search criteria. Which properties are indexed can be determined by examining the schema definition for the property—if the SearchFlags property is set to 1, the attribute is indexed.

Check the documentation that Microsoft provides on Active Directory to see which properties are indexed.

To demonstrate searching Active Directory using ADO, create a new component, and name the VB project asp1204 and the generated class search. Attach a reference to the Active DS type library to the project. To support ADO, you'll also attach a reference to the ADO type library.

In the new component, create a method named doQuery shown in Example 12-5 that connects to the Active Directory through a Connection object and searches for all elements matching specific search criteria. The resulting recordset is then disconnected from the connection and returned to the ASP page for processing. As shown in Example 12-5, the search parameter and its associated values are passed as parameters to the method.

Example 12-5. Using ADO to Find Active Directory Objects

```
Function doQuery(ByVal strSrchProperty As String, _
            ByVal strSrcValue As String) As Recordset

On Error GoTo ErrorHandler

    ' connect to Active Directory
    Dim cn As New Connection
    cn.CursorLocation = adUseClient
    cn.Provider = "ADsDSOObject"
    cn.Open

    ' perform query
    Dim rs As New Recordset
```

Example 12-5. Using ADO to Find Active Directory Objects (continued)

```
    Set rs.ActiveConnection = cn
    rs.Source = "select cn, sAMAccountName, distinguishedName,  ADsPath from " & _
                "'LDAP://DC=development, DC=local' where " & _
                strSrchProperty & " = '" & strSrcValue & "'"

    rs.Open

    ' disconnect recordset
    Set rs.ActiveConnection = Nothing
    cn.Close

    Set doQuery = rs

Exit Function
ErrorHandler:

    cn.Close
    Err.Raise Err.Number, Err.Source, Err.Description
End Function
```

The ADsPath used in the search is the default current domain of **development. local** in my environment. You'll want to change this to match your topmost domain in your environment.

In the ASP test script *asp1205.asp*, the new component is instantiated and doQuery is called with the arguments "objectCategory" and "user". Based on this, all users in Active Directory under the specified domain in the component should be returned in the result set. The results are then displayed to the web page:

```
<%
On Error Resume Next
Dim obj
Set obj = Server.CreateObject("asp1204.search")

Dim rs
Set rs = obj.doQuery("objectCategory", "user")
If Err.Number <> 0 Then
    Response.Write Err.Description
Else
    While rs.EOF <> True
        Response.Write "cn = " & rs.Fields("cn") & "<br>"
        Response.Write "sAMAccountName = " & _
                                rs.Fields("sAMAccountName") & "<br>"
        Response.Write "distinguishedName = " & _
                                rs.Fields("distinguishedName") & "<br>"
        Response.Write "<p>"
        rs.MoveNext
    Wend
End If
%>
```

Try the example first with an objectCategory of user, and then try it out with other schema classes such as group, container, and domainPolicy.

ASP Example: Add and Manage Users Through the Web

So far in this chapter, you've had a chance to list Active Directory entries, either through containers or object parents or using ADO to query the directory service. You've also had a chance to create and remove groups from the Active Directory.

In this last section of the chapter, we'll combine all of the functionality we've demonstrated to create a small ASP application that allows people to create themselves as users and then associate themselves with a predefined group, one with extremely limited function. An application administrator then views all users within the group and determines if they should be moved to a group with more extensive permissions. The administrator can also remove a user from the system. Finally, users can update certain fields in their own records, such as their addresses and contact information.

Creating a New User

For this example, you'll create a new User component within a Visual Basic project named **adsiapp**, with one class named user. Attach a reference to the Active DS type library to the project.

Create a new subroutine, createUser, on the new component. This method, which is shown in Example 12-6, obtains a reference to the Users container object and then uses this object's Create method to create the new user. After the object is created, its properties are set and the object is saved.

As shown in Example 12-6, only a small subset of properties is set for the new object: the user's name, login, company, title, and phone number. The cn and SAMAccountName properties are required values—all others are optional for Active Directory or are set to a default value automatically. The cn property is derived from the user's name. Notice also from the code that some of the properties are set using the IADs Put method; others are properties exposed directly on the IADsUser interface.

Example 12-6. Component Method to Add a New User for the Default Domain

```
' create a new user in Active Directory
Sub createUser(ByVal strFirstname As String, _
              ByVal strLastname As String, _
              ByVal strLogin As String, _
              ByVal strCompany As String, _
```

Example 12-6. Component Method to Add a New User for the Default Domain (continued)

```
            ByVal strTitle As String, _
            ByVal strPhone As String)


On Error GoTo ErrorHandler

    Dim iUsers As IADsContainer
    Dim iUser As IADsUser

    ' get container
    Set iUsers = GetObject("LDAP://CN=Users,DC=development,DC=local")

    ' modify name to relative name
    Dim strRelative As String
    strRelative = "CN=" & strFirstname & " " & strLastname

    ' create user object
    Set iUser = iUsers.Create("user", strRelative)

    ' modify properties
    iUser.Put "cn", strFirstname & " " & strLastname
    iUser.Put "sAMAccountName", strLogin
    iUser.FirstName = strFirstname
    iUser.LastName = strLastname
    iUser.Put "company", strCompany
    iUser.Title = strTitle
    iUser.TelephoneNumber = strPhone


    ' save to directory service
    iUser.SetInfo

Exit Sub
ErrorHandler:

    Err.Raise Err.Number, Err.Source, "Creating User: " & Err.Description

End Sub
```

You can try the new method immediately. There's a web form page, *newuser.asp* (too large to list in this chapter but included with the book examples), that collects the new user information and then submits the form contents to a second web page, *adduser.asp*. This page creates the new component and passes the form information to the createUser method; it is shown in Example 12-7.

Example 12-7. ASP Script to Create Application User Component and the New User

```
<%
On Error Resume Next

Dim obj
Set obj = Server.CreateObject("adsiapp.user")
```

Example 12-7. ASP Script to Create Application User Component and the New User (continued)

```
' get form values
Dim firstname, lastname, login
Dim company, title, phone

firstname = Request("firstname")
lastname = Request("lastname")
login = Request("login")
company = Request("company")
title = Request("title")
phone = Request("phone")

' create user
obj.createUser firstname, lastname, login, company, title, phone
If Err.Number <> 0 Then
   Response.Write Err.Description
Else
   Response.Write "User " & firstname & " " & lastname & " has been added"
End If
%>
```

Access the *newuser.asp* page, adding in a user with a name unlike other users currently in the directory.

Adding a User to a Group

When users are added, they aren't automatically added to a group. Group membership confers or restricts user privileges. We want our new users to be added to what I call the **nopower** group—a group with only limited functionality.

To add a user to a group, modify the group component created earlier in Examples 12-3 and 12-4. Open the **asp1203** Visual Basic project, and add a new method to the **group** class: addUserToGroup. The method, which is shown in Example 12-8, takes two parameters: the group distinguishedName property and the user's CN property (the user's name). The method uses *GetObject* to create a reference to both the user and the group, then calls the **IADsGroup** interface's Add method to add the user to the group.

Example 12-8. Method to Add a User to a Specific Group

```
' add user to a group
Sub addUserToGroup(ByVal strGrpName As String, _
          ByVal strUserName As String)

On Error GoTo ErrorHandler

   ' create group
   Dim iGrp As IADsGroup
   Dim strGroup, strUser As String
```

Example 12-8. Method to Add a User to a Specific Group (continued)

```
    ' create ADsPath for user
    strUser = "LDAP://CN=" & strUserName & _
                                   ",CN=Users,DC=development,DC=local"

    ' create ADsPath for group, given distinguishedName
    strGroup = "LDAP://" & strGrpName

    ' get group object
    Set iGrp = GetObject(strGroup)

    ' add user to group
    iGrp.Add (strUser)

Exit Sub
ErrorHandler:

    Err.Raise Err.Number, Err.Source, "Adding User to Group " & _
           Err.Description
End Sub
```

Modify the *adduser.asp* page to add the user to the **nopower** group after the user object has been successfully added. Example 12-9 shows the modified ASP page script calling the addUserToGroup method.

Example 12-9. Creating a New User and Adding the User to the nopower Group

```
<%
On Error Resume Next

Dim obj
Set obj = Server.CreateObject("adsiapp.user")

' get form values
Dim firstname, lastname, login
Dim company, title, phone

firstname = Request("firstname")
lastname = Request("lastname")
login = Request("login")
company = Request("company")
title = Request("title")
phone = Request("phone")

' create user
obj.createUser firstname, lastname, login, company, title, phone
If Err.Number <> 0 Then
   Response.Write Err.Description
Else
   Dim grpObj
   Set grpObj = Server.CreateObject("asp1203.group")
   Dim name
   name = firstname & " " & lastname
```

Example 12-9. Creating a New User and Adding the User to the nopower Group (continued)

```
    grpObj.addUserToGroup "CN=nopower,CN=Users,DC=development,DC=local", _
                                                                name
    If Err.Number <> 0 Then
        Response.Write Err.Description
    Else
        Response.Write "User " & firstname & " " & lastname & _
                                                " has been added"
    End If
End If
%>
```

The distinguishedName for the group is used because, unlike the Users, which all end up in the Users container in my environment, groups can occur all over the system. To ensure that the appropriate group is used, its distinguishedName (including its relative location) must be used.

One of the problems with this approach of adding a user to a group by default is that the user might successfully be installed in the directory services, but something may prevent the user from being added to the group. Ideally, we want either action—adding a user and then adding the user to a default group—to either succeed as a unit or fail as a unit.

Unfortunately, we can't use COM+ transaction services when working with Active Directory (there is no transaction support built into ADSI), so you'll need to add code to ensure that the two transactions are completed in sync. To accomplish this, add code to remove the user if something occurs to prevent the user from being added to the **nopower** group.

Open the **adsiapp** VB project, and add the removeUser method, which is shown in Example 12-10, to the user class. This method takes the user's CN property (the user's name) as its only parameter and then removes the person from the system using the **IADsContainer** Delete method.

Example 12-10. Method That Removes User from Directory Service

```
' remove specific user
Sub removeUser(ByVal strName As String)

On Error GoTo ErrorHandler

    Dim iUsers As IADsContainer
    Dim iUser As IADsUser

    ' get container
    Set iUsers = GetObject("LDAP://CN=Users,DC=development,DC=local")

    ' modify name to relative name
    Dim strRelative As String
    strRelative = "CN=" & strName
```

Example 12-10. Method That Removes User from Directory Service (continued)

```
' remove user
iUsers.Delete "user", strRelative
```

```
Exit Sub
ErrorHandler:
```

```
  Err.Raise Err.Number, Err.Source, "Removing User: " & Err.Description
```

```
End Sub
```

Modify the *adduser.asp* page to add in a call to this new removeUser method if
the call to `asp1203.group`'s addUserToGroup method call fails:

```
grpObj.addUserToGroup "CN=nopower,CN=Users,DC=development,DC=local", name
If Err.Number <> 0 Then
    Response.Write Err.Description
    obj.removeUser name
```

At this point, if no error has occurred, the new user is added to the directory service to the **nopower** group. Next, you'll create the functionality necessary to look
at all users within this group and to display the available information for a specific
user.

Active Directory Reporting: Displaying User-Specific Information

The administrators for the system need to be able to look at all of the users for a
particular group and then get more detailed information about any one of the users.
To support this functionality, you'll add a new method to the `asp1203.group`
component to list all users for a particular group. Then, you'll add a method to
`adsiapp.user` to return detailed information about a specific user.

First, open the `asp1203` Visual Basic project, and add a new method, getUsers, to
the **group** class; it is shown in Example 12-11. This method returns a Variant array
consisting of the names of users within a group whose name is passed as a parameter to the method. The method gets the group from Active Directory as an
IADsGroup object and then traverses the Members collection to get the **cn** values
for each user. The cn property is the first and last name for the user, concatenated
together with a space between.

Example 12-11. Getting CN Property from Group Members

```
' show users for given group
Function getUsers(ByVal strGrpName As String) As Variant
```

```
On Error GoTo ErrorHandler
```

```
  ' create group
```

Example 12-11. Getting CN Property from Group Members (continued)

```
    Dim iGrp As IADsGroup
    Dim strGroup As String

    ' create ADsPaths for group and user
    strGroup = "LDAP://CN=" & strGrpName & _
                                    ",CN=Users,DC=development,DC=local"

    Set iGrp = GetObject(strGroup)
    Dim varArray() As Variant
    ReDim varArray(iGrp.Members.Count)
    Dim oMember As IADs
    Dim i As Integer
    i = 0
    For Each oMember In iGrp.Members
        varArray(0) = oMember.Get("cn")
        i = i + 1
      Next

    getUsers = varArray
Exit Function
ErrorHandler:

    Err.Raise Err.Number, Err.Source, "Getting Users: " & Err.Description

End Function
```

When the component method is called, the ASP script passes in the **nopower** group name, as shown in this code fragment from the *users.asp* test page:

```
    Dim grp
    grp = "nopower"
    users = obj.getUsers(grp)
```

When the array is returned from the component, the contents are displayed to the web page. Each name is enclosed within a hypertext link associated with another ASP page, *showuser.asp.* Included within the URI is the username added as a query string to the page reference:

```
    Response.Write "<A HREF='showuser.asp?cn=" & users(i) & "'>" & users(i)
                                                    & "</A><p>"
```

Clicking on the name then calls *showuser.asp* with the CN passed via the query string. To try *users.asp* for yourself, modify the group name to match the one you've chosen to represent the **nopower** group and access the page through your development web server.

We'll use ADO to get specific information about one user, so you'll also need to attach the ADO type library to the **adsiapp.user** project. Afterward, add a new method to the user class named getUser, which is shown in Example 12-12. This method takes one parameter—the CN property for the user—and returns an ADO Recordset object with information about the user. The method creates an instance of the ADO Connection object and opens it using the Active Directory `ADsDSObject` provider. It create a new recordset and assigns the active connection to it, then selects specific information about the user from the directory service. The recordset is then disconnected from its connection and returned by the function.

Example 12-12. Getting User Information from Directory Service Using ADO

```
' get user identified by CN
Function getUser(ByVal strCnName As String) As Recordset

On Error GoTo ErrorHandler

    ' connect to Active Directory
    Dim cn As New Connection
    cn.CursorLocation = adUseClient
    cn.Provider = "ADsDSOObject"
    cn.Open

    ' set recordset
    Dim rs As New Recordset
    Set rs.ActiveConnection = cn

    ' perform query
    Dim str As String
    str = "select cn, sAMAccountName, company, title, telephoneNumber" & _
    " from 'LDAP://CN=" & strCnName & ",CN=Users,DC=development, DC=local'"
    rs.Source = str
    rs.Open

    ' disconnect recordset
    Set rs.ActiveConnection = Nothing
    cn.Close

    ' return record
    Set getUser = rs

Exit Function
ErrorHandler:

    cn.Close
    Err.Raise Err.Number, Err.Source, str & Err.Description

End Function
```

In the ASP page that shows the user information, *showuser.asp*, the CN property value is pulled from the ASP Request object's QueryString collection and passed as a parameter to the **adsiapp.user** component's new getUser method. When the method returns the recordset, its information is printed out to the web page:

```
<%
On Error Resume Next
Dim obj
```

```
Set obj = Server.CreateObject("adsiapp.user")

Dim cn
cn = Request.QueryString("cn")

Dim rs
Set rs = obj.getUser(cn)
If Err.Number <> 0 Then
    Response.Write Err.Description
Else
    Response.Write "<tr><td align='right'> User name: </td><td> " & _
                                      rs.Fields("cn") & "</td></tr>"
    Response.Write "<tr><td align='right'> Login:</td><td>  " & _
                             rs.Fields("sAMAccountName") & "</td></tr>"
    Response.Write "<tr><td align='right'> Company: </td><td> " & _
                                   rs.Fields("company") & "</td></tr>"
    Response.Write "<tr><td align='right'> Title: </td><td> " & _
                                     rs.Fields("title") & "</td></tr>"
    Response.Write "<tr><td align='right'> Phone: </td><td> " & _
                           rs.Fields("telephoneNumber") & "</td></tr>"
End If
%>
```

Moving a User to a Different Group

The administrator, after reviewing the information about the user, can do one of four things: leave the user in the **nopower** group, remove the user from the system, remove the user from the **nopower** group but leave the user in the system, or add the user to a different group.

The **adsiapp.user** component already has the functionality, with the removeUser method, to remove a user from the system. Additionally, the **asp1203.group** component has the functionality with addUserToGroup to add a user to a specific group. What's still needed is a method to remove a user from a given group.

Add a new method, removeUserFromGroup, to the **asp1203.group** component; it is shown in Example 12-13. This method takes a group's distinguishedName and the user's CN property and removes the user from the given group but leaves the user in the system. In this method, the **IADsGroup** Remove method is called and removes the user from the group's Members collection.

Example 12-13. The removeUserFromGroup Method

```
Sub removeUserFromGroup(ByVal strGrpName As String, _
                        ByVal strUserName As String)

On Error GoTo ErrorHandler

    ' create group
    Dim iGrp As IADsGroup
    Dim strGroup, strUser As String
```

Example 12-13. The removeUserFromGroup Method (continued)

```
' create ADsPath for user
strUser = "LDAP://CN=" & strUserName & _
                              ",CN=Users,DC=development,DC=local"

' create ADsPath for group, given distinguishedName
strGroup = "LDAP://" & strGrpName

' get group object
Set iGrp = GetObject(strGroup)

' add user to group
iGrp.Remove (strUser)

Exit Sub
ErrorHandler:

   Err.Raise Err.Number, Err.Source, "Adding User " & Err.Description

End Sub
```

To allow the administrator to act on her decision, add menu options to the *showuser.asp* page to allow the administrator to remove the user from the system or from the **nopower** group, as follows:

```
<p><LI><a href="removeuser.asp?CN=<% = cn %>">Remove</a> <% = cn %>
                                             from the system</LI></p>
<P><LI><a href="rmusrgrp.asp?CN=<% = cn %>
&GRP=CN=nopower,CN=Users,DC=development,DC=local">Remove</a>
from nopower group</p>
```

Two new ASP pages are used to perform the actions of removing a user from the system or from the specific group: *removeuser.asp* and *rmusrgrp.asp*.

In *removeuser.asp*, the user's cn property is accessed from the query string and used in a call to the **adsiapp.user**'s removeUser method:

```
<%
On Error Resume Next
Dim obj
Set obj = Server.CreateObject("adsiapp.user")

Dim user
user = Request.QueryString("cn")

obj.removeUser user
If Err.Number <> 0 Then
   Response.Write Err.Description
Else
   Response.Write "User " & cn & " has been removed"
End If
%>
```

In *rmusrgrp.asp*, the user's cn and the group's distinguishedName properties are pulled from the query string and used in a call to the `asp1203.group`'s removeUserFromGroup method:

```
<%
On Error Resume Next
Dim obj
Set obj = Server.CreateObject("asp1203.group")

Dim user
user = Request.QueryString("cn")
Dim grp
grp = Request.QueryString("GRP")

obj.removeUserFromGroup grp, user
If Err.Number <> 0 Then
    Response.Write Err.Description
Else
    Response.Write "User " & cn & " has been removed from group"
End If
%>
```

One last component change needs to be made to support the administrator's decision to add a user to a new group: we need to list the available groups for the administrator to choose from. To support this, you'll add one more method to the `asp1203.group` component to access all of the groups in the directory service and add these groups to a form selection list box. Open the `asp1203` VB project and add a new method, getGroups, to the **group** class; its source code is shown in Example 12-14. This method takes no parameters and returns an ADO Recordset object to the calling ASP page. Since ADO is used, make sure that a reference to the ADO type library has been added to the project.

The getGroups method creates a connection using the Active Directory OLE DB Provider and then creates a query that finds all groups in the directory service and returns each group's cn and distinguishedName properties. The ADO recordset is then disconnected before it's returned by the method.

Example 12-14. Method to Return the cn and distinguishedName Properties for All Groups in the Directory Service

```
' show all groups
Function getGroups() As Recordset

On Error GoTo ErrorHandler

    ' connect to Active Directory
    Dim cn As New Connection
    cn.CursorLocation = adUseClient
    cn.Provider = "ADsDSOObject"
    cn.Open
```

Example 12-14. Method to Return the cn and distinguishedName Properties for All Groups in the Directory Service (continued)

```
    ' set recordset
    Dim rs As New Recordset
    Set rs.ActiveConnection = cn

    ' perform query
    Dim str As String
    str = "select cn, distinguishedName " & _
        "from 'LDAP://DC=development, DC=local' where " & _
        "objectCategory = 'group'"

    rs.Source = str
    rs.Open

    ' disconnect recordset
    Set rs.ActiveConnection = Nothing
    cn.Close

    ' return record
    Set getGroups = rs

Exit Function
ErrorHandler:

    cn.Close
    Err.Raise Err.Number, Err.Source, Err.Description

End Function
```

Now, in the *showuser.asp* page, the groups are accessed by calling `asp1203.group`'s getGroups method and are used to build an HTML form selection list. The form contents from this ASP page are the following:

```
<form method="POST" action="addgrp.asp">
<INPUT type="hidden" name="user" value="<% = cn %>">
<SELECT name="group">
<%
On Error Resume Next

Dim objGrp
Set objGrp = Server.CreateObject("asp1203.group")

Dim rsGrp
Set rsGrp = objGrp.getGroups()
If Err.Number <> 0 Then
    Response.Write Err.Description
Else
    While rsGrp.EOF <> True
        Response.Write "<OPTION value='" & rsGrp("distinguishedName") &
                                            "'>" & rsGrp("cn")
        Response.Write "</OPTION>"
        rsGrp.MoveNext
```

```
    Wend
End If
%>
</SELECT>
```

When the administrator picks a group and clicks on the submit button for the form, a new ASP page, *addgrp.asp*, is called. The page contains ASP script that calls the addUserToGroup method to add the user to the specific group:

```
<% On Error Resume Next
Dim obj
Set obj = Server.CreateObject("asp1203.group")

Dim grp, user
grp = Request.Form("group")
user = Request.Form("user")

obj.addUserToGroup grp, user
If Err.Number <> 0 Then
    Response.Write Err.Description
Else
    Response.Write "User " & user & " has been added to " & grp
End If %>
```

At this point, our little Active Directory services application is complete.

Active Directory Application Summary

To try the Active Directory application yourself, follow this sequence:

1. Add users with the *newuser.asp* page. Submitting this page calls *adduser.asp*, which uses the **adsiapp.user** component's createUser method to create the user, and the **asp1203.group** component's addUserToGroup method to add the user to the **nopower** group. If this latter action fails, then the **adsiapp. user**'s removeUser method is used to remove the newly added user from the system.

2. View a list of users in the **nopower** group by accessing *users.asp*. This page uses the **asp1203.group**'s getUsers method to pull in all users for a specific group, in this case the **nopower** group.

3. Click on any of the users to open the *showuser.asp* page. This page uses the **adsiapp.user** component's getUser method to pull in detailed information about the user to display to the page.

4. In *showuser.asp*, you can remove the user by clicking on the associated link, which results in a call to the *removeuser.asp* page. This page uses the **adsiapp.user** component's removeUser method to remove the user from the system.

5. In *showuser.asp*, you can also remove the user from the **nopower** group by clicking the associated link. This results in a call to *rmusrgrp.asp*, which uses the `asp1203.group` component's removeUserFromGroup method to remove the user from a specific group, in this case the **nopower** group.

6. Finally, in *showuser.asp*, you can view a list of directory service groups, which are displayed using the `asp1203.group` component's getGroups method. Picking one of these and clicking the Add User to Group button calls the *addgrp.asp* page. This page uses the `asp1203.group` component's addUser-ToGroup method to add the user to the new group.

Remember, if you're exposing Active Directory functionality to web access, make sure that access to the ASP application is restricted, or you might find all of your groups and users missing, whether by intent or by accident.

13

Working with MSMQ Components

One of the most interesting new technologies that Microsoft has come up with is MSMQ—Microsoft Message Queues. This technology was created so that applications distributed across different machines could communicate with one another at different times. In an ASP environment, messages can be sent from the application to queues for processing at a later time, allowing quicker page returns to the client. Additionally, the applications processing the messages could access more restricted resources such as databases, thereby removing direct contact between the externally accessed ASP application and the database—messages could be sent from an Internet application but actually processed on an intranet or from restricted pages on the Internet.

This chapter looks at using MSMQ with ASP components. It's not an in-depth review of MSMQ, but it does cover the most commonly used aspects of the technology: creating queues and sending and reading messages. On the way, we'll also take a look at journaling and transactional messages, as well as a brief look at MSMQ security techniques.

MSMQ/ASP Basics

Though MSMQ is geared toward exchanging messages across heterogeneous environments, it's still an effective tool to use with ASP. ASP applications can use MSMQ to send messages to local or remote queues.

For instance, a shopper could order several items from an online store, and the order would go into a message queue, perhaps on another machine. At a later time, the message is pulled from the queue and the order is processed—without the shopper (or others) having direct access to the database. The database is protected from direct outside contact, and the shopper doesn't have to wait for the database processing to occur.

A message queue can also be used in an administrative intranet to schedule system activities or to communicate requests for information between diverse groups.

MSMQ functionality can be accessed directly through a set of functions in languages such as C++, or it can be accessed through a set of COM objects. Developers working with a tool that supports COM objects (all the tools mentioned in this book support COM objects) will usually use the COM implementation of MSMQ.

The MSMQ COM object model consists of 10 objects:

MSMQApplication
> Used to find the machine name or identifier of a specific machine, or to register a security certificate for authenticated messages

MSMQCoordinatedTransactionDispenser
> Provides an MSMQ transaction object for creating transacted messages

MSMQEvent
> Handles events associated with a particular MSMQ queue

MSMQMessage
> Used to create, send, or read a message

MSMQQuery
> Searches for a specific queue or group of queues based on some criteria

MSMQQueue
> Represents an MSMQ message queue

MSMQQueueInfo
> Used to manage and maintain message queues

MSMQQueueInfos
> A collection of queues returned from using MSMQQuery

MSMQTransaction
> Commits or aborts a transaction

MSMQTransactionDispenser
> Creates an MSMQTransaction object

Due to the nature of ASP components, we won't be working with the MSMQ-Event object in this chapter. Our component methods should perform a specific task and return the results as soon as possible. They won't be sitting in the background waiting for a specific event to occur.

The other objects are covered in the chapter, beginning with using MSMQ-QueueInfo to create and remove queues, discussed next.

Working with Queues

The central component of MSMQ is the queue. Applications send messages to queues and read messages from queues. Messages can generate activity, such as performing some administrative task (administrative queue) or responding to a request (response queue).

Applications can track a message using the report queue, which is similar in approach to tracking a package shipped using UPS or FedEx. There's a queue that contains messages based on activities in other MSMQ queues (the journal queue) and a queue that contains messages that just couldn't be delivered for some reason (the dead-letter queue).

Some queues—such as the message, administrative, and response queues—can be created by applications; others, such as the journal and dead-letter queues, are created by the MSMQ system.

In this section we'll take a look at message queues, the most commonly used queues. Later in the chapter, we'll take a look at some other types of queues that can be manipulated by ASP components.

Creating and Deleting Message Queues

Applications can create two types of message queues: public and private. *Public queues* are registered with the directory service (through ADSI in Windows 2000) and are accessible by any MSMQ application. A *private queue*, on the other hand, is local to the machine on which it's created and is not accessible by any application other than the one that created it. Public queues are managed by the directory services, while private queues are managed by the application. Private queues are faster to work with, since there is no directory service overhead when accessing the queue. Public queues are more robust, since they are managed by directory services.

> If you're working with MSMQ on a machine that doesn't have Active Directory installed or doesn't have access to a machine with an Active Directory domain controller, you can create only private queues. See Chapter 12, *Working with Active Directory from ASP Applications*, for instructions on how to set up a standalone Active Directory installation.

To create either a public or a private queue, you need to create an instance of the MSMQ Information object (MSMQQueueInfo), which you use to define the queue properties and then create the queue. If the queue already exists when you try to create the queue, you'll get an error.

To demonstrate working with queues, create a new Visual Basic ActiveX DLL project. Name it `asp1301` and the generated class `msgqueue`. Attach a reference to the MSMQ type library to the project. You'll find it listed as Microsoft Message Queue 2.0 Object Library in your project's References dialog.

Once you've attached the type library, create a new method named newPublic-Queue. This small method, which is shown in Example 13-1, creates an instance of the MSMQQueueInfo object used to create the new public queue. The MSMQ-QueueInfo's PathName property is set to a location and a name relative to the machine. The name of the queue and the queue's label are passed as parameters to the subroutine.

Example 13-1. Creating a Public MSMQ Message Queue

```
Sub newPublicQueue(ByVal strQueueName As String, _
                   ByVal strQueueLabel As String)

' create a public message queue
Dim qPublic As New MSMQQueueInfo

qPublic.PathName = ".\" & strQueueName
qPublic.Label = strQueueLabel

qPublic.Create

End Sub
```

Accessing the component from the following ASP page, *asp1301.asp*, results in the public queue being created:

```
<%
Dim obj
Set obj = Server.CreateObject("asp1301.msgqueue")
obj.newPublicQueue "first", "First Public Queue"
%>
```

On a machine that has access to directory services, the queue is created as a public queue, accessible by all MSMQ applications. However, if you invoke the new-PublicQueue method on a machine on which directory services are not set up, you'll get an error—the machine must have access to directory services to create public MSMQ queues.

You can check that the new message queue has been added by using the Active Directory Browser, a utility that comes with the Platform SDK from Microsoft. Chapter 12, *Working with Active Directory from ASP Applications*, discusses how to use this utility. The new message queue is found under the Domain Controllers collection, under the computer name where the queue was created, and then under the MSMQ object.

If you access the ASP test page twice, an error results. The default error handling provided by IIS 5.0 displays the following error message to the page:

```
Error Type:
MSMQQueueInfo (0xC00E0005)
A queue with the same pathname already exists
```

In fact, the only way to check to see if a queue already exists is to try and create it, handling the error of the queue already existing within the code.

To create a private message queue, add a new method to `asp1301.msgqueue`, and call it newPrivateQueue. This method takes the name of the queue and its label as String parameters. In fact, the code to create the private queue is the same as for the public one, except for the "`PRIVATE$`" modifier in the path name, as shown in Example 13-2.

Example 13-2. Creating a Private MSMQ Message Queue

```
' create a private message queue
Sub newPrivateQueue(ByVal strQueueName As String, _
                    ByVal strQueueLabel As String)

Dim qPrivate As New MSMQQueueInfo

qPrivate.PathName = ".\PRIVATE$\" & strQueueName
qPrivate.Label = strQueueLabel

qPrivate.Create

End Sub
```

Access this new method from an the following ASP test page, *asp1302.asp*, to create a private queue:

```
<%
Dim obj
Set obj = Server.CreateObject("asp1301.msgqueue")
obj.newPrivateQueue "second", "First Private Queue"
%>
```

Unlike the public queue, you won't see the new private queue in directory services.

The PathName specified with both examples creates the queue relative to MSMQ on the machine where the component is created. You can specify any valid DNS or UNC path for the queue location, such as the following, which locates the queue on a machine named *testMachine*:

```
testMachine\testQueue
```

Remember that only public queues can be created on machines other than the local machine.

In the two example methods, the use of the dot (.) in the pathname means that the queue is located on the local machine. Private queues must be located on the local machine. To find out what the pathname is when using the dot notation, you can access the MSMQQueueInfo object's Refresh method.

The queue is placed in the target machine's Windows subdirectory at *\system32\msmq\STORAGE\LQS*. The filenames are encoded. An example of an encoded filename is:

2215ede960bf44d184f52c862f62a680.06ba8b46

Once a queue's been created, you'll want to access it. Again, you'll use the MSMQ-QueueInfo object to access and open a queue that's already been created.

You'll open the queue for access later in the chapter when you send messages to it and read messages from it. For now, though, you'll need the ability to remove a queue once it's been created.

For example, to delete the queues created in Example 13-1 and Example 13-2, add a new method, removeQueue, to the **asp1301.msgqueue** component, as shown in Example 13-3. This method takes two parameters, the queue name and whether the queue is public or private. As with the earlier methods, removeQueue uses the default dot notation to represent the local machine when adding and removing the queue. A value of 1 for the *varType* parameter signals that the queue is private; with any other value, the method treats the queue as public.

Example 13-3. Removing a Public or a Private MSMQ Message Queue

```
' remove a queue
Sub removeQueue(ByVal strQueueName As String, _
               ByVal varType As Variant)

Dim qObj As New MSMQQueueInfo
Dim strPath As String

' check for public or private queue
If varType = 1 Then
```

Example 13-3. Removing a Public or a Private MSMQ Message Queue (continued)

```
    strPath = ".\PRIVATE$\" & strQueueName
Else
    strPath = ".\" & strQueueName
End If

' delete queue
qObj.PathName = strPath
qObj.Delete

End Sub
```

To remove both the public and private queues created with the earlier examples, access this component method twice, once for the public and once for the private queue, as the following page, *asp1303.asp*, illustrates:

```
<%
Dim obj
Set obj = Server.CreateObject("asp1301.msgqueue")

' remove public queue
obj.removeQueue "first", 0

'remove private queue
obj.removeQueue "second", 1
%>
```

Searching for a Specific Queue

In the last section, you used a queue name to find a specific message queue. Sometimes, though, an application doesn't have access to the name of a queue. In those cases, you have to search through the available queues to find the one you want.

The MSMQQuery object is an MSMQ COM object used explicitly for searching the directory services for a specific public queue or a group of public queues. This object has one method, LookupQueue, that takes several parameters used to find the queue (or group of queues) and that returns a collection of matched queue objects. A second MSMQ COM object, MSMQQueueInfos, is then used to traverse the set of queues to find the particular one you're looking for.

To search for a queue, use the **asp1301.msgqueue** object to create several public queues using the newPublicQueue method from Example 13-1, as shown in the following ASP page, *asp1304.asp*, which creates five queues, named one, two, three, four, and five:

```
<%
Dim obj
Set obj = Server.CreateObject("asp1301.msgqueue")

obj.newPublicQueue "one", "Developing ASP Components"
```

```
obj.newPublicQueue "two", "Developing ASP Components"
obj.newPublicQueue "three", "Developing ASP Components"
obj.newPublicQueue "four", "Developing ASP Components"
obj.newPublicQueue "five", "Developing ASP Components"
%>
```

Each queue name is unique, but the same label, "Developing ASP Components," is repeated for each queue.

Next, add a new method named findQueue to the `asp1301.msgqueue` component. The method has one parameter, the label used as a search parameter.

The findQueue method uses MSMQQuery's LookupQueue method to search among the existing queues. There are several different values that you can query on, including the label, the time the queue was created or last modified, and the queue's GUID. The findQueue method uses the label passed to it as a parameter.

In Example 13-4, once the query has been made, the objects returned in the MSMQQueueInfos collection are traversed. Each is accessed as an MSMQQueueInfo object, and the method uses the built-in ASP Response object to list the queue's FormatName and PathName properties.

 Normally, you'll want to avoid accessing the built-in ASP objects from your components in order to maintain a separation of the user interface (the ASP functionality) from the business processes. I use the built-in objects in this book primarily for demonstration purposes.

Since `asp1301.msgqueue` is now using the built-in ASP objects, you'll need to add references to both the COM+ Services and the ASP type libraries to the Visual Basic project.

Example 13-4. Finding Queues Based on Matching Against Queue Label

```
Sub findQueues(ByVal strLabel As String)

Dim qQuery As New MSMQQuery
Dim qInfoObjs As MSMQQueueInfos
Dim qInfo As MSMQQueueInfo

' get object content and set response
Dim objContext As ObjectContext
Dim objResponse As Response

Set objContext = GetObjectContext()
Set objResponse = objContext("Response")

' perform lookup
Set qInfoObjs = qQuery.LookupQueue(Label:=strLabel)
```

Example 13-4. Finding Queues Based on Matching Against Queue Label (continued)

```
' start at first info object
qInfoObjs.Reset

' traverse objects, print out properties
Set qInfo = qInfoObjs.Next
While Not qInfo Is Nothing
   objResponse.Write qInfo.FormatName & "<br>"
   objResponse.Write qInfo.PathNameDNS & "<br>"
   objResponse.Write qInfo.PathName & "<p>"
   Set qInfo = qInfoObjs.Next
Wend

End Sub
```

The new component method is accessed in this ASP test page, *asp1305.asp*:

```
<%
Dim obj
Set obj = Server.CreateObject("asp1301.msgqueue")

obj.findQueues "Developing ASP Components"
%>
```

The result of calling this component method is a web page with values similar to the following, depending on your own machine's name:

```
PUBLIC=ee0d7be5-ba07-483c-8349-2d9803d028cf
flame.development.local\one
flame\one

PUBLIC=de2fa534-038c-4e58-96d9-a5a85654280e
flame.development.local\two
flame\two

PUBLIC=56001290-9795-4e48-8d7e-c499e26c6a15
flame.development.local\three
flame\three

PUBLIC=671a13ab-1921-4822-a427-9a66d5101dda
flame.development.local\four
flame\four

PUBLIC=2215ede9-60bf-44d1-84f5-2c862f62a680
flame.development.local\five
flame\five
```

As you can see, the FormatName property for a queue is equivalent to the part of the encrypted name given to the queue file.

Now that you've had a chance to create and remove message queues and to search for specific queues, let's take a look at sending and retrieving messages from these queues.

Working with MSMQ Messages

MSMQ messages can contain virtually any type of information and any type of object. Messages can contain Word documents and other files, ADO recordsets, scalar values such as integers and strings, and more complex data structures such as arrays.

The message body is defined as a Variant data type, which means that any COM-compatible value can be assigned to the message body and information about the object is available on the receiving end of the message.

The MSMQMessage object is used to create an MSMQ message. When the message object fields have been set, it can then be sent to a message queue. The message queue itself needs to be opened first; the MSMQQueueInfo and MSMQQueue objects are used to find the queue, open it, and then use it.

To jump right in, create a new Visual Basic project. Name it `asp1302` and the generated class `message`. Attach a reference to the Microsoft Message Queue 2.0 type library to the project.

Create a method in `asp1302.message` called sendStringMessage, as shown in Example 13-5. This method takes as parameters the name of a queue, a queue label, and a string to use as the message body. The method opens the queue, assigns the message string to the message's body, and sends the message to the queue.

Example 13-5. Sending a String Message to a Queue

```
Sub sendStringMessage(ByVal strQueue As String, _
                ByVal strLabel As String, _
                ByVal strMessage As String)

Dim qInfo As New MSMQQueueInfo
Dim qQueue As MSMQQueue
Dim qMessage As New MSMQMessage


' open queue for sending
qInfo.PathName = ".\" & strQueue
qInfo.Label = strLabel
Set qQueue = qInfo.Open(MQ_SEND_ACCESS, MQ_DENY_NONE)

If qQueue.IsOpen = 1 Then
  ' define message
  qMessage.Body = strMessage

  ' now send it
  qMessage.Send qQueue

  ' close queue
```

Example 13-5. Sending a String Message to a Queue (continued)

```
  qQueue.Close
End If

End Sub
```

To test the new component and the sendStringMessage method, send three different messages to queue `five`, created in the last section. The following ASP script, *asp1306.asp*, does this:

```
<%
Dim obj
Set obj = Server.CreateObject("asp1302.message")

obj.sendStringMessage "five", "Developing ASP Components", _
                              "This is the first message"
obj.sendStringMessage "five", "Developing ASP Components", _
                              "This is the second message"
obj.sendStringMessage "five", "Developing ASP Components", _
                              "This is the third message"
%>
```

To receive the messages, create a second method in `asp1302.message` called readStringMessage, as shown in Example 13-6. It takes two parameters: the queue name and its label. Since you'll be using the ASP Response object to write out results to the client, also attach references to the COM+ Services and the Microsoft Active Server Pages type libraries to the project.

In the method code, the queue is opened and the MSMQQueue Receive method both retrieves the message and removes it from the queue. Its parameters are:

- An optional transaction object or transaction constant
- A Boolean specifying whether you also want queue information
- A Boolean specifying whether you want the body of the message
- The ReceiveTimeout value

This process of reading and removing the message continues in a loop until the Receive method returns a null message, indicating that no more messages are found in the queue and the Receive method has timed out.

This last statement is absolutely critical for you to understand before beginning to work with MSMQ. When you use the Receive or Peek method to access messages from a queue, if you don't specify a *ReceiveTimeout* value, the application is blocked and sits there listening to the queue until another message comes in. This results in your web page hanging. Not only that, but you won't be able to unload the web server or even shut down the process that's running the MSMQ ASP component.

Always set the *ReceiveTimeout* parameter when accessing messages from a queue.

The *ReceiveTimeout* parameter accepts a numeric value representing the number of milliseconds to wait to time out. In readStringMessage, the timeout value is set to 500 milliseconds.

Example 13-6. Component Method to Get All Messages on a Specific Queue and Print the Message If It's a String Type

```
Sub readStringMessage(ByVal strQueue As String, _
                      ByVal strLabel As String)

' get response object from object context
Dim objContext As ObjectContext
Dim objResponse As Response

Set objContext = GetObjectContext()
Set objResponse = objContext("Response")

Dim qInfo As New MSMQQueueInfo
Dim qQueue As MSMQQueue
Dim qMessage As MSMQMessage
Dim varObject As Variant

' open queue for reading
qInfo.PathName = ".\" & strQueue
qInfo.Label = strLabel
Set qQueue = qInfo.Open(MQ_RECEIVE_ACCESS, MQ_DENY_RECEIVE_SHARE)

' check to see if queue is open
' if it is, receive first message which removes message from queue
If qQueue.IsOpen = 1 Then
   Set qMessage = qQueue.Receive(ReceiveTimeout:=500)

   ' loop through messages
   While Not (qMessage Is Nothing)
      varObject = qMessage.Body
      If TypeName(varObject) = "String" Then
          objResponse.Write varObject
      End If
      objResponse.Write "<br>"
      Set qMessage = qQueue.Receive(ReceiveTimeout:=500)
   Wend

   ' close queue
   qQueue.Close
End If

End Sub
```

In the readStringMessage component method, as each message is accessed, its Body property is checked to make sure it's a string, the datatype we're expecting in the code. It's up to any application—or component—to test the datatype of the message before working with it. The readStringMessage uses the VBA *TypeName* function to test for a string value. You can also use *TypeOf* to test for objects.

In Example 13-6, you used the MQ_RECEIVE_ACCESS enumerated value as the first parameter in the MSMQQueueInfo's Open method. The Open method's parameters are the following:

- *Access* constant specifying how the queue is opened. This value is used if the code is going to read the message using the Receive or Peek method. If you had used Peek, you could have also used the MQ_PEEK_ACCESS value. (The other possible enumerated value for the *Access* parameter is MQ_SEND_ACCESS to open a message queue in order to send a message.)

- Share mode constant, specifying how access to the queue is shared. This parameter controls how locking occurs with the queue. In the example, you used MQ_DENY_RECEIVE_SHARE, which basically denies access to the queue until the component method closes the queue and releases the queue lock. Another browser accessing the ASP page would receive the following error when trying to access the same queue:

  ```
  There is a sharing violation. The queue is already open for an
  exclusive receive.
  ```

In an ASP application, you'll want to use MQ_DENY_RECEIVE_SHARE when it's essential that only one instance of the ASP component have exclusive access to the queue at a time. Otherwise, you might consider using MQ_DENY_NONE, which allows multiple accesses to the queue at one time.

MSMQ and Your ASP Application Audience

The audience that accesses the ASP component to send the MSMQ message can be very different from the one that receives the message.

For instance, if your ASP application is using MSMQ to manage orders for an online store, customers can place many orders, resulting in many messages being sent, each with an individual order. However, sending messages doesn't lock down the queue, so these customers can access the same queue at the same time without running into any conflicts. However, only a select group of people will access the orders from the queue to process them. Additionally, it's essential that the messages with the orders are processed one at a time. For this audience, you definitely want to use MQ_DENY_RECEIVE_SHARE, since you don't want two people trying to access the same order at the same time.

To test the new component, the following example file, *asp1307.asp*, accesses the `asp1302.message` component and calls readStringMessage:

```
<%
Dim obj
Set obj = Server.CreateObject("asp1302.message")

obj.readStringMessage "five", "Developing ASP Components"
%>
```

The messages contained in message queue `five` are listed to the web page in the order that they were received in the queue:

```
This is the first message
This is the second message
This is the third message
```

In Example 13-6, you removed the messages from the queue as they were read. If you wanted them left on the queue, you would use the Peek method instead. Peek has the same syntax as Receive, except that the messages aren't removed (and there is no transaction parameter):

```
Set qMessage = qQueue.Peek(ReceiveTimeout:=500)
```

To loop through all messages using Peek, though, you'll want to use the Peek-Next method to get each message in the queue until the end of the queue is reached. The PeekNext parameters are the same as Peek's:

- A Boolean specifying whether you also want queue information

- A Boolean specifying whether you want the body of the message

- The ReceiveTimeout value

You can also get the queue's current message by using either the ReceiveCurrent or PeekCurrent methods. ReceiveCurrent's parameters are the following:

- An optional transaction object or transaction constant

- A Boolean specifying whether you also want queue information

- A Boolean specifying whether you want the body of the message

- The ReceiveTimeout value

- WantConnectorType (not documented in Microsoft's MSMQ documentation)

The parameters to the PeekCurrent method are the same as those for Receive-Current.

MSMQ messages can contain objects as well as scalar values such as strings. We'll take a look at sending and reading an ADO recordset in the next section, where I'll introduce the use of transactions in working with MSMQ.

Using Transactions

MSMQ messages can be sent or received as transactional messages, which means that sending or receiving the message doesn't occur until the transaction is committed. Using transactional messages is particularly helpful when performing updates to other data stores, such as a database, at the same time as the message activity: you'll want the database and message activity to complete as a unit or be rolled back as a unit.

To use transactions with messages, create the queue as a transactional queue by setting the optional *IsTransactional* parameter in the MSMQQueueInfo object's Create method to True:

```
qInfo.Create IsTransactional:=True
```

Now messages to this queue can be transactional or not, depending on the message activity.

If the queue is remote (located other than on the local machine), then you can't use a transactional receive against the queue. Additionally, you can't use a transactional receive against a nontransactional queue. You can, however, use a nontransactional receive against either a transactional queue or a nontransactional queue, even if the queue is remote.

You can perform a transactional send against a remote transactional queue, but you can't perform a transactional send against a nontransactional queue, regardless of its location. Neither can you send a nontransactional message against a transactional queue.

Two types of transactions can be used with MSMQ:

- *Internal transactions* using MSMQ as the resource manager
- *External transactions* using the MS DTC (Distributed Transaction Coordinator) as the resource manager

If only the messages are impacted by the success or failure of the activity, you can consider using internal transactions. However, if other resources are involved, such as database resources, use external transactions.

Transactional messages must have an **MSMQTransaction** object attached to the message operation. How the transaction object is created differs based on whether the transaction is an internal MSMQ transaction or an external one.

Referencing the BeginTransaction method on the **MSMQTransactionDispenser** object creates an internal transaction. To demonstrate working with internal transactions, you'll create a new ASP component that supports this type of transactional messages. First, though, you have to create a transactional queue.

Create a new Visual Basic project and name it **asp1303**. Name the generated class **queue**, and attach the Microsoft Message Queue type library to the project. This component has only one method, createXatQueue, shown in Example 13-7, that takes a queue name and a queue label as parameters. All the method does is create the transactional queue.

Example 13-7. Creating a Transactional Public Queue

```
Sub createXatQueue(ByVal strQueueName, ByVal strQueueLabel)

' create a public message queue
Dim qPublic As New MSMQQueueInfo

qPublic.PathName = ".\" & strQueueName
qPublic.Label = strQueueLabel

qPublic.Create IsTransactional:=True

End Sub
```

After compiling the component, create the queue used for testing transactional messaging by loading the following ASP page, *asp1308.asp*, that contains the following script:

```
<%
Dim obj
Set obj = Server.CreateObject("asp1303.queue")

obj.createXatQueue "transaction", "XatQueue"
%>
```

This script creates a transactional queue with the label **XatQueue** and the name **transaction**.

Internal Transactions

To demonstrate how to work with MSMQ internal transactions, add a new class module to **asp1303** by right-clicking in the Project Explorer window and selecting Add → Class Module from the popup menu. Name this new class **internal**.

This new component has two methods, sendIntrnlXactMsg and getIntrnlXactMsg, which are shown in Examples 13-8 and 13-9, respectively. Both use internal transactions when they perform their MSMQ activities. The sendIntrnlXactMsg method, shown in Example 13-8, has two parameters: the queue name and the message body (sent as a string). In the method, the process of sending the message is similar to that shown in Example 13-5, except that an instance of MSMQTransaction-Dispenser is created and is, in turn, used to create an instance of the MSMQTransaction object. Note that when the message is sent, the instance of the transaction object is sent with the message. Calling Commit on the transaction at the end of the method commits the message to the queue. By default, if an explicit commit is not given, the message's send operation is aborted and the message is *not* committed to the queue.

Example 13-8. Sending a Transactional Message

```
Sub sendIntrnlXactMsg(ByVal strQueueName As String, _
                      ByVal strMessage As String)

Dim qInfo As New MSMQQueueInfo
Dim qQueue As MSMQQueue
Dim qMessage As New MSMQMessage
Dim qDispenser As New MSMQTransactionDispenser
Dim qXact As MSMQTransaction

' open queue for sending
qInfo.PathName = ".\" & strQueueName
Set qQueue = qInfo.Open(MQ_SEND_ACCESS, MQ_DENY_NONE)

If qQueue.IsOpen = 1 Then
  ' create transaction
  Set qXact = qDispenser.BeginTransaction

  ' define message
  qMessage.Body = strMessage

  ' now send it
  qMessage.Send qQueue, qXact

  ' commit transaction
  qXact.Commit

  ' close queue
  qQueue.Close
End If

End Sub
```

As the transaction is committed, the message is sent to the queue. To test this, the following ASP script, *asp1309.asp*, creates an instance of `asp1303.internal` and calls the sendIntrnlXactMsg method. To verify that the message is in the queue, the script also creates an instance of the `asp1302.message` component, created earlier, to read the message:

```
<%
' create transactional message
Dim obj
Set obj = Server.CreateObject("asp1303.internal")

obj.sendIntrnlXactMsg "transaction", _
                      "This is message to queue"

' now read message
```

```
Dim objMsg
Set objMsg = Server.CreateObject("asp1302.message")

objMsg.readStringMessage "transaction", "XatQueue"
%>
```

Since a nontransactional receive can be performed against a transactional queue, the result of accessing this page script is that the message is displayed to the web page.

What happens if the transaction is aborted? You can see what happens yourself by modifying sendIntrnlXactMsg to abort the message rather than commit it:

```
qXact.Abort
```

Then when you access *asp1309.asp*, no message is displayed, since no message is found on the queue.

You can also use transactional receives to retrieve the message from the queue. The second method we'll add to `asp1303.internal` is called getIntrnlXactMsg and is shown in Example 13-9. Because the method displays each message it finds to the web page using the ASP Response object, you'll need to attach references to the COM+ Services and the Microsoft Active Server Pages type libraries to the project. The getIntrnlXactMsg method takes one parameter, the queue name. Once the queue is open, the method retrieves all messages from it, similar to Example 13-6, except that the operation is attached to a transaction.

 You don't have to specify the queue's label as well as pathname when opening the queue. Examples 13-5 and 13-6 use a label; Examples 13-8 and 13-9 don't.

Labels are used mainly when you want to group several queues together for query purposes.

Example 13-9. Retrieving Messages from a Queue Using Transactional Receives

```
Sub getIntrnlXactMsg(ByVal strQueueName As String)

' get response object from
' ObjectContext
Dim objContext As ObjectContext
Dim objResponse As Response

Set objContext = GetObjectContext()
Set objResponse = objContext("Response")

Dim qInfo As New MSMQQueueInfo
Dim qQueue As MSMQQueue
Dim qMessage As MSMQMessage
Dim varObject As Variant
```

Example 13-9. Retrieving Messages from a Queue Using Transactional Receives (continued)

```
Dim qDispenser As New MSMQTransactionDispenser
Dim qXact As MSMQTransaction

' open queue for reading
qInfo.PathName = ".\" & strQueueName
Set qQueue = qInfo.Open(MQ_RECEIVE_ACCESS, MQ_DENY_RECEIVE_SHARE)

' check to see if queue is open
' if it is, receive first message
'    which removes message from queue
If qQueue.IsOpen = 1 Then
   ' create transaction
  Set qXact = qDispenser.BeginTransaction

  Set qMessage = qQueue.Receive(qXact, ReceiveTimeout:=500)

   ' loop through messages
  While Not (qMessage Is Nothing)
     varObject = qMessage.Body
     If TypeName(varObject) = "String" Then
         objResponse.Write varObject
     End If
     objResponse.Write "<br>"
     Set qMessage = qQueue.Receive(qXact, ReceiveTimeout:=500)
  Wend

   ' commit
  qXact.Commit

   ' close queue
  qQueue.Close
End If
End Sub
```

Notice in the code that the transaction object is passed as the first parameter to the Receive method, but the transaction isn't committed until all of the messages in the queue have been received.

The following ASP test page, *asp1310.asp*, tests the new component method:

```
<%
' create transactional message
Dim obj
Set obj = Server.CreateObject("asp1303.internal")

obj.sendIntrnlXactMsg "transaction", _
                      "This is transactional message to queue"

' now read message
obj.getIntrnlXactMsg "transaction"
%>
```

Again, as before, if the MSMQ transaction weren't committed, the message activity would be aborted by default. You can try this in the example by removing the following line from getIntrnlXactMsg:

```
qXact.Commit
```

Accessing *asp1310.asp* several times just adds messages to the queue (that are displayed), but the message never is removed from the queue because the Receive method's removal activity is aborted.

Internal transactions are an effective tool when the only resource you have to manage is MSMQ. However, if you're using another resource, such as database access, you'll want to use external transactions, discussed in the next section.

Multiresource Transaction Management

Multiple-resource transactions are managed through the Distributed Transaction Controller (DTC). This is the transaction management that was used with MTS and now with COM+. In MSMQ, you can take advantage of external transactions using two techniques: through the MSMQ MSMQCoordinatedTransaction object or by using the component's ObjectContext.

To demonstrate using the two techniques to control external transactions, we'll create a new component that has two methods. The first method adds messages to a queue, but this time, the messages have disconnected ADO recordsets instead of string messages attached. The second method pulls these messages from the queue and accesses the recordset to update the database.

Create the component's Visual Basic project and name it asp1304. Name the class that's generated external. This project will use ADO, the ASP objects, and ObjectContext, as well as the MSMQ objects, so attach the following type libraries to the project: COM+ Services Type Library, Microsoft Active Server Pages Object Library, Microsoft Message Queue 2.0 Object Library, and Microsoft ActiveX Data Objects.

Add the first method, addDirectoryToQueue, shown in Example 13-10, to the new component. This method takes five parameters, all of type String:

strName
    The directory's name

strLoc
    The directory's physical location

strWebLoc
    The directory's web location (URL)

strPurpose

> The purpose of the directory

strQueueName

> The MSMQ queue name

This method creates a record to add a new Directory table in the Weaver database. In the component, an ADO recordset is created and opened without a connection to the database. Then a new record is added to the object, and the record's fields are set to the parameter values. Since there is no information from the database about what the fields look like, the method adds the field descriptions to the recordset's Fields collection first.

 The Weaver database is described in Appendix B.

After the record is created, it's attached to the MSMQ message, and the message is sent. To commit the sending activity, an instance of **MSMQCoordinatedTransactionDispenser** is used to create a new **MSMQTransaction** object. This object is sent with the message, and its Commit method is called at the end of the method to commit the action.

Example 13-10. Creating a Recordset and Attaching It to an MSMQ Message

```
Sub addDirectoryToQueue(ByVal strName As String,ByVal strLoc As String, _
            ByVal strWebLoc As String, ByVal strPurpose As String, _
            ByVal strQueueName As String)

On Error GoTo ErrorHandler

' create Recordset
Dim rs As New Recordset
rs.CursorLocation = adUseClient

rs.Fields.Append "name", adVarChar, 50
rs.Fields.Append "physical_location", adVarChar, 50
rs.Fields.Append "web_location", adVarChar, 50
rs.Fields.Append "purpose", adVarChar, 50

' open recordset
rs.Open , , adOpenStatic, adLockBatchOptimistic

' add new record
rs.AddNew
rs("name") = strName
rs("physical_location") = strLoc
rs("web_location") = strWebLoc
```

Example 13-10. Creating a Recordset and Attaching It to an MSMQ Message (continued)

```
rs("purpose") = strPurpose

' open queue for sending
Dim qInfo As New MSMQQueueInfo
Dim qQueue As MSMQQueue
Dim qMessage As New MSMQMessage
Dim qTransDTC As New MSMQCoordinatedTransactionDispenser
Dim qTrans As MSMQTransaction

qInfo.PathName = ".\" & strQueueName
Set qQueue = qInfo.Open(MQ_SEND_ACCESS, MQ_DENY_NONE)

If qQueue.IsOpen = 1 Then

  ' get transaction
  Set qTrans = qTransDTC.BeginTransaction

  ' define message
  qMessage.Body = rs

  ' now send it
  qMessage.Send qQueue, qTrans

  ' close queue
  qQueue.Close
End If

' commit trans
qTrans.Commit

Exit Sub
ErrorHandler:
    Err.Raise Err.Number, Err.Source, Err.Description
End Sub
```

The next component method, which is shown in Example 13-11, is named get-DirectoryFrmQueue. It takes the queue name as its single parameter. In the method, instances of ObjectContext as well as Response are created, in addition to the MSMQQueueInfo object to open the queue. Also, an ADO Connection object is created that points to the SQL Server version of the Weaver database. (You could also use the Access version of Weaver for this demonstration.) A new recordset is created and set to the Directory table and then opened.

For each message pulled from the queue, the Recordset object's AddNew method is called to add a new record. Then the Recordset object attached to the message is accessed, and its values are used to set the fields within the method's existing Recordset object.

When all messages in the queue have been processed, the UpdateBatch method is called on the method's active recordset, and ObjectContext's SetComplete method is called to signal that the transaction can safely be committed from this method.

Example 13-11. Getting a Recordset from a Message and Using It to Make a Database Update

```
Sub getDirectoryFrmQueue(ByVal strQueueName As String)

On Error GoTo ErrorHandler

' get object context
Dim objContext As ObjectContext
Set objContext = GetObjectContext()

Dim objResponse As Response
Set objResponse = objContext("Response")

Dim qInfo As New MSMQQueueInfo
Dim qQueue As MSMQQueue
Dim qMessage As MSMQMessage
Dim varObject As Variant

' open queue for reading
qInfo.PathName = ".\" & strQueueName
Set qQueue = qInfo.Open(MQ_RECEIVE_ACCESS, MQ_DENY_RECEIVE_SHARE)

' check to see if queue is open
' if it is, receive first message
'     which removes message from queue
If qQueue.IsOpen = 1 Then

  ' connect to database
  Dim cn As New Connection
  Dim rs As New Recordset
  Dim rsnew As Recordset

  cn.ConnectionString = "Provider=SQLOLEDB;server=FLAME;" & _
                        "database=weaver;uid=sa;pwd="
  cn.CursorLocation = adUseClient
  cn.Open

  ' open recordset
  rs.Open "Directory", cn, adOpenKeyset, adLockBatchOptimistic, _
                                                    adCmdTable

  Set qMessage = qQueue.Receive(ReceiveTimeout:=500)

  ' loop through messages
  While Not (qMessage Is Nothing)
     If TypeOf qMessage.Body Is ADODB.Recordset Then
        Set rsnew = qMessage.Body
        rs.AddNew
        rs("name") = rsnew("name")
        rs("web_location") = rsnew("web_location")
        rs("physical_location") = rsnew("physical_location")
        rs("purpose") = rsnew("purpose")
     End If
```

Example 13-11. Getting a Recordset from a Message and Using It to Make a Database Update (continued)

```
                objResponse.Write "Added " & rsnew("name") & "<br>"
                Set qMessage = qQueue.Receive(ReceiveTimeout:=500)
           Wend

           ' close queue and connection
           qQueue.Close
           cn.Close

     End If

     ' signal to commit trans
     rs.UpdateBatch
     objContext.SetComplete

     Exit Sub
     ErrorHandler:
           ' abort transaction, clean up
           objContext.SetAbort
           qQueue.Close
           cn.Close

           Err.Raise Err.Number, Err.Source, Err.Description
     End Sub
```

As you'll notice in Example 13-11, transactions controlled by ObjectContext don't have to be attached to the message, since the *Transaction* parameter for the MSMQQueue object's Receive method is set to MQ_MTS_TRANSACTION by default. In Windows 2000, this translates into transactions controlled by COM+.

 We couldn't use the recordset attached to the MSMQ message to make the database update directly, since this recordset does not have any table or base database information, and therefore trying to update it to the database results in a failure.

To test both methods, first create a new transactional queue using the component created in Example 13-7, asp1303.queue. Call this queue adddir. The following ASP page does this:

```
<%
Dim obj
Set obj = Server.CreateObject("asp1303.queue")

obj.createXatQueue "adddir", "Add Directory"
%>
```

Create a page containing a form that adds a new directory to the Weaver database. The page, named *asp1311.asp*, has no server-side script but does have client-side validation, as shown in Example 13-12.

Example 13-12. Form to Capture New Directory Information

```
<!DOCTYPE HTML PUBLIC "-//W3C//DTD HTML 4.0//EN">
<head>
<title>Developing ASP Components</title>

<script type="text/javascript" language="javascript">

function check_values() {
var frm = document.forms[0];

if (frm.name.value.length <= 0) {
    alert("Please Enter Directory Name");
    return;
    }

if (frm.physical_location.value.length <= 0) {
    alert("Please Enter Physical Location");
    return;
    }

if (frm.purpose.value.length <= 0) {
    alert("Please Enter Directory Purpose");
    return;
    }

frm.submit();

}
</SCRIPT>
</head>
<body style="margin-left: 20px; margin-top: 20px">
<h1>Add a new Directory</h1>
<p style="color: red; margin-left: 30px">
* Required Fields
</p>
<form method="POST" action="asp1312.asp">
<table cellpadding="10" border="0" style="background-color: yellow">
<tr>
<td align="right">
<h5>*Directory Name:</h5>
</td>
<td valign="top">
<input type="text" name="name" size="80" />
</td>
</tr>
<tr>
<td align="right">
<h5>*Physical Location:</h5>
</td>
```

Example 13-12. Form to Capture New Directory Information (continued)

```
<td valign="top">
<input type="text" name="physical_location" size="80" />
</td>
</tr>
<tr>
<td align="right">
<h5>Web Location:</h5>
</td>
<td valign="top">
<input type="text" name="web_location" size="80" />
</td>
</tr>
<tr>
<td align="right">
<h5>*Purpose:</h5>
</td>
<td valign="top">
<input type="text" name="purpose" size="80" />
</td>
</tr>
<tr>
<td colspan=2 align="center">
<input type="button" value="Add new Directory" onClick="check_values()" />
   
<input type="reset" value="Clear Form">
</td>
</tr>
</table>
</form>
</body>
```

You'll also need to create a second ASP page, named *asp1312.asp*, that takes the first page's form contents and passes them as parameters to the `asp1304.external` component's addDirectoryToQueue method, as shown in Example 13-13.

Example 13-13. Page to Process Form Contents

```
<!DOCTYPE HTML PUBLIC "-//W3C//DTD HTML 4.1//EN">
<head>
<TITLE>Developing ASP Components</TITLE>
</head>
<body>
<%

On Error Resume Next

Dim obj
Set obj = Server.CreateObject("asp1304.external")

Dim name, loc, webloc, purpose

name = Request.Form("name")
```

Example 13-13. Page to Process Form Contents (continued)

```
loc = Request.Form("physical_location")
webloc = Request.Form("web_location")
purpose = Request.Form("purpose")

obj.addDirectoryToQueue name, loc, webloc, purpose, "adddir"

If Err.Number <> 0 Then
   Response.Write "<h1 style='color: gold'>Error with Data</h1>"
   Response.Write Err.Description
Else
   Response.Write "<h1 style='color: gold'>Directory has been added to queue</h1>"
   Response.Write "<p><a href='asp1413.asp'>Add Directory to database</a></p>"
End If
%>


</body>
```

Finally, create a third ASP page, *asp1313.asp*, to process the queue contents and add the new directory records. This page has script that creates an instance of **asp1304.external** and calls getDirectoryFrmQueue with the queue's name:

```
<%@ TRANSACTION = required %>
<!DOCTYPE HTML PUBLIC "-//W3C//DTD HTML 4.1//EN">
<head>
<TITLE>Developing ASP Components</TITLE>
</head>
<body>
<%

On Error Resume Next

Dim obj
Set obj = Server.CreateObject("asp1304.external")

obj.getDirectoryFrmQueue "adddir"
If Err.Number <> 0 Then
   Response.Write "<h3 style='color: gold'>Error with getting data from message
queue</h3>"
   Response.Write Err.Description
Else
   Response.Write "<h3 styl='color: gold'>Directory or Directories have been
added</h3>"
End If
%>


</body>
```

The page that calls getDirectoryFrmQueue must start a transaction. It does this by using the **TRANSACTION** directive as the first line in the ASP file. The transaction directive isn't required when using the MSMQ transaction technique.

To test the use of external transactions with MSMQ, add directories to the MSMQ queue using the form in *asp1311.asp*, submitting the form after each. When you're finished, process the queue by accessing *asp1313.asp*, which invokes getDirectoryFrmQueue to pull the directory entries from the queue and add them to the database. You can add several directories to the queue before processing them, if you wish. The getDirectoryFrmQueue method prints out the name of each directory as it is added to the updateable recordset. Figure 13-1 shows the results from adding two directories to the database.

Figure 13-1. Adding two directories to the database

Journaling

There are three types of journaling that you can use with MSMQ, and each is fairly simple to implement.

 Journaling tracks events that occur, such as a message queue receiving a message.

The first technique is to apply journaling to a specific queue. This is accomplished by setting the Journal property in MSMQQueueInfo to `MQ_JOURNAL` before the queue is created:

```
qInfo.Journal = MQ_JOURNAL
...
qInfo.Create
```

You can also add journaling to an existing queue by setting the Journal property and then calling the MSMQQueueInfo's Update method.

Journaling of the queue is called *target journaling*; each message that is received
from the queue (using the Queue Receive method) is added to the journal.

To access the journal messages, you create an instance of the queue's MSMQ-
QueueInfo object and then use its FormatName property to set the FormatName
property of a second MSMQQueueInfo object. Opening this opens access to the
journal:

```
Dim qInfo As New MSMQQueueInfo
Dim qInfoJournal As New MSMQQueueInfo
Dim qQueue As MSMQQueue
qInfo.PathName = ".\adddir"
qInfo.Refresh
qInfoJournal.FormatName = qInfo.FormatName & ";JOURNAL"
Set qQueue = qInfoJournal.Open(MQ_RECEIVE_ACCESS, MQ_DENY_NONE)
... process journal queue's messages as you would any other queue's
```

The MSMQQueueInfo object's Refresh method is called to retrieve the values for
the object from the directory service. This updates the FormatName property.

The second technique is to apply journaling to an entire computer. This type of
journaling, known as *source journaling*, is actually applied by setting the MSMQ-
Message object's Journal property before sending the message:

```
qMessage.Journal = MQMSG_JOURNAL
qMessage.Send qQueue
```

If the message is sent to a remote machine, an entry is made in the originating
machine's journal when the message is successfully sent. If the message is local in
nature, an entry is made in the machine's journal only when the message has been
successfully retrieved from the queue.

To demonstrate source journaling, create a new component that has a method to
send a message using journaling and a method to read the messages from the
journal. Create a new Visual Basic project and name it **asp1305**. Name the generated class **journal**. Attach the Microsoft Message Queue, the COM+ Services, and
the Microsoft Active Server Pages type libraries to the project.

Add the first method, sendJournalMsg, which is shown in Example 13-14. It takes
two parameters: the queue name and the message, both of type string. The
method is identical to others we've looked at that send a message, except that the
MSMQMessage object's Journal property is set.

Example 13-14. Sending a Message with Journaling

```
Sub sendJournalMsg(ByVal strQueueName As String, _
                   ByVal strMessage As String)

Dim qInfo As New MSMQQueueInfo
Dim qQueue As MSMQQueue
```

Example 13-14. Sending a Message with Journaling (continued)

```
Dim qMessage As New MSMQMessage

' open queue for sending
qInfo.PathName = ".\" & strQueueName
Set qQueue = qInfo.Open(MQ_SEND_ACCESS, MQ_DENY_NONE)

If qQueue.IsOpen = 1 Then

  ' define message
  qMessage.Body = strMessage

  ' turn on journaling
  qMessage.journal = MQMSG_JOURNAL

  ' now send it
  qMessage.Send qQueue

  ' close queue
  qQueue.Close
End If

End Sub
```

To read messages from the machine's journal, create `asp1305.journal`'s second method, readJournal, which is shown in Example 13-15 and which doesn't have any parameters. This method doesn't set the PathName property for the MSMQ-QueueInfo object. Instead, the FormatName property is set with the machine's identifier, and the word JOURNAL appended. The machine identifier is found using the MSMQApplication object's MachineIdOfMachineName method, passing it the machine name (in this case **flame**). The journal queue is opened into a regular MSMQQueue object, and the messages in the queue are pulled and processed in the same manner as you've used with other message processing examples in this chapter.

Example 13-15. Reading the Machine's Journal Queue

```
Sub readJournal()

' get response object from objectcontext
Dim objContext As ObjectContext
Dim objResponse As Response

Set objContext = GetObjectContext()
Set objResponse = objContext("Response")

Dim qInfoJournal As New MSMQQueueInfo
Dim qQueue As MSMQQueue
Dim qMessage As MSMQMessage
Dim varObject As Variant
Dim strMachine As String
```

Example 13-15. Reading the Machine's Journal Queue (continued)

```
' get machine ID
strMachine = MachineIdOfMachineName("flame")

qInfoJournal.FormatName = "MACHINE=" & strMachine & ";JOURNAL"

Set qQueue = qInfoJournal.Open(MQ_RECEIVE_ACCESS, MQ_DENY_NONE)

' check to see if queue is open
' if it is, receive first message
'    which removes message from queue
If qQueue.IsOpen = 1 Then

  Set qMessage = qQueue.Receive(ReceiveTimeout:=500)

   ' loop through messages
   While Not (qMessage Is Nothing)
      varObject = qMessage.Body
      If TypeName(varObject) = "String" Then
         objResponse.Write varObject
      End If
      objResponse.Write "<br>"
      Set qMessage = qQueue.Receive(ReceiveTimeout:=500)
   Wend

   ' close queue
   qQueue.Close
End If
End Sub
```

The ASP test page required to test this component is fairly complex. In the script, as shown in Example 13-16 and found in *asp1314.asp*, a new queue is created by creating an instance of **asp1301.msgqueue** and calling its newPublicQueue method. Then, several messages are sent to it using **asp1305.journal**'s send-JournalMsg method. The messages are then retrieved from the queue by creating an instance of **asp1302.message** and calling the readStringMessage method. Finally, the machine's journal messages are read by calling readJournal on **asp1305.journal**. Figure 13-2 shows the result of running this page.

Example 13-16. Creating a Queue, Sending Journaled Messages to It, Reading the Messages, and Then Reading the Machine's Journal Entries

```
<%
' create queue
Response.Write ("<h3>Creating Queue</h3>")
Dim objQueue
Set objQueue = Server.CreateObject("asp1301.msgqueue")
objQueue.newPublicQueue "jrnl", "Testing Journaling"

' send messages
Response.Write ("<h3>Sending Journaled messages</h3>")
Dim objJournal
```

Example 13-16. Creating a Queue, Sending Journaled Messages to It, Reading the Messages, and Then Reading the Machine's Journal Entries (continued)

```
Set objJournal = Server.CreateObject("asp1305.journal")
objJournal.sendJournalMsg "jrnl", "This is the first message"
objJournal.sendJournalMsg "jrnl", "This is the second message"
objJournal.sendJournalMsg "jrnl", "This is the third message"

' get messages from queue
Response.Write ("<h3>Reading messages from queue</h3>")
Dim objMessage
Set objMessage = Server.CreateObject("asp1302.message")
objMessage.readStringMessage "jrnl", "Testing Journaling"

' now get messages from machine journal
Response.Write ("<h3>Reading messages from machine journal</h3>")
objJournal.readJournal
%>
```

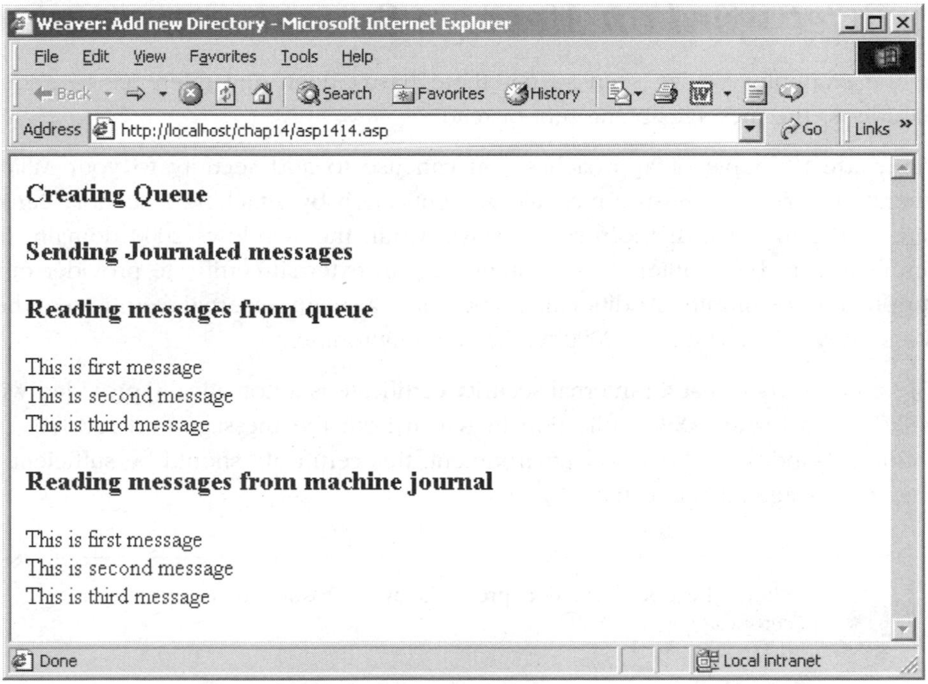

Figure 13-2. Running a page that prints messages and the machine's journal message

If you're interested in whether any messages being sent aren't reaching a queue, you can also target the message to go to the machine's dead-letter queue if it doesn't reach its destination. To do this, change the Journal property from MQMSG_JOURNAL to MQMSG_DEADLETTER:

```
qMessage.Journal = MQMSG_DEADLETTER
```

Two dead-letter queues are created for each machine. One holds transactional messages, and one holds nontransactional messages that don't reach their target destination. To read a dead-letter queue, change the FormatName property from:

```
qInfoJournal.FormatName = "MACHINE=" & strMachine & ";JOURNAL"
```

to:

```
qInfoJournal.FormatName = "MACHINE=" & strMachine & ";DEADLETTER"
```

You can try this yourself by modifying `asp1305.journal` to reflect these new values, changing *asp1314.asp* to send tracked emails to a nonexistent queue, and then reading them from the dead-letter queue entries. The messages aren't transactional, so you'll be reading the non-transactional dead-letter queue.

Needless to say, if you use journaling, make sure to receive the messages in the queues frequently, to keep the queues from becoming excessively large.

A Brief Word on Message Security

In the examples you've seen so far, there hasn't been any reference to adding security to the messages being sent or read.

There are a couple of approaches you can use to add security to your MSMQ operations. You can ensure message authentication by attaching a security certificate to the message. If the message stays within the Windows 2000 domain, the certificate can be an internal one; otherwise, an external certificate provider must supply the certificate. Additionally, you must use an external certificate when working within a Windows 2000 workgroup environment.

The good news is that an internal security certificate is automatically provided with MSMQ, and for an ASP application in which both the message and receiver fall within a Windows 2000 server environment, this certificate should be sufficient to ensure message authentication.

Check the documentation provided by Microsoft on using external certificates with MSMQ.

To ensure that authentication is used properly, you can specify that a queue accept only authenticated messages by setting the MSMQQueueInfo object's Authenticate property before creating the new queue:

```
qInfo.Authenticate = MQ_AUTHENTICATE
```

To authenticate the message, set the AuthLevel property on the message:

```
qMessage.AuthLevel = MQMSG_AUTH_LEVEL_ALWAYS
```

Other values you can use with AuthLevel are **MQMSG_AUTH_LEVEL_MSMQ10** and **MSMSG_AUTH_LEVEL_MSMQ20**. These two settings sign the message with the respective signature and ignore any attached certificate. Make sure, though, that if the computer receiving the message is using MSMQ 1.0, you use the MSMQ 1.0 security setting when sending the message, or the message will be rejected. If the receiving computer is using MSMQ 2.0 (Windows 2000), then you can send either 1.0 or 2.0 signatures.

You can also send your messages encrypted, using either 40-bit or 128-bit encryption. To use encryption, you must create a message queue that supports encryption, otherwise known as a *private message queue*. This type of queue is of particular importance if the messages it contains might have sensitive information, such as credit card account numbers.

To create a private message queue, all you need to do is set the PrivLevel property of the MSMQQueueInfo object before creating the queue:

```
qInfo.PrivLevel = MQ_PRIV_LEVEL_BODY
```

Once the queue's created, send encrypted messages by setting the PrivLevel property on the message object:

```
qMessage.PrivLevel = MQMSG_PRIV_LEVEL_BODY
```

This enforces 40-bit encryption. To use 128-bit encryption, use the **MQMSG_PRIV_LEVEL_BODY_ENHANCED** value for PrivLevel.

Your application can also provide its own encryption. Read the MSMQ documentation for more on application-supplied encryption.

14

Creating C++ ASP Components

C++ opens the door for efficiency tweaks and more finite control over a component, but at the cost of greater complexity in writing and maintaining the component. For instance, a tool such as Visual Basic allows you to create a component that supports apartment threading or single threading, but C++ allows you to specify the both-threaded model, and even to include access to the free-threaded marshaler to improve performance. The downside to using Visual C++ is that other tools, such as Visual Basic, can cut development time, because virtually all of the COM/COM+ implementation details are hidden. With Visual C++, the use of COM/COM+ is much more exposed.

That isn't to say that C++ for ASP development has to be difficult. If you and your group are used to working with C++ and particularly with Visual C++, the use of this language for ASP component development is a natural choice. Additionally, Microsoft has provided a template library known as the Active Template Library (ATL) to help with most of the implementation details. ATL contains templates that handle much of the default processing necessary for maintaining an ASP component, or for that matter any COM-based component. To make the use of ATL even more attractive, there are other advantages to using it, such as the light footprint it adds to any component created using it, detailed in the first section of this chapter.

For using ATL to create a component, Microsoft has provided two ATL wizards to assist in the process. The first is the ATL AppWizard, which generates the project files to maintain an ASP component DLL or EXE, whichever is created. The second is the ATL Object Wizard, used to add an object class (component) and associated interface to a project.

This chapter discusses some of the issues surrounding the use of Visual C++ for creating ASP components, including using the ATL wizards—issues related to threading and aggregation, creating poolable components, and accessing the ASP built-in objects from C++ code. The chapter also looks at error handling and debugging—the latter being of especial interest when developing your first ASP components in C++.

> The examples in this chapter were implemented using ATL 3.0, Visual C++ 6.0 with Service Pack 3.0, and the Platform SDK dated April 2000 or later. The Platform SDK can be downloaded from Microsoft's web site at *http://msdn.microsoft.com*. Make sure to install Visual C++ first, then the Service Pack, and then the Platform SDK. Always use the Platform SDK version of any header and library files, unless Microsoft comes out with a Service Pack for Visual C++ designed specifically for Windows 2000.

ATL or MFC

Creating COM-based ASP components can be accomplished using any C++ library that exposes the necessary COM interfaces, such as **IUnknown** and **IDispatch**. Microsoft has provided two different libraries that can be used: the Microsoft Foundation Classes (MFC) and the Active Template Library (ATL).

The MFC classes have been around for some time and are used for most Visual C++ application building, component-based or otherwise. The classes provide C++ wrappers for most common datatypes and C++ classes to handle many aspects of an application. However, useful as MFC is, it isn't the best library to use for ASP or other component development.

MFC provides a complete framework, essential when building a standalone application. The framework includes document and view objects and an associated frame to "hold" all of the application sections together. The document objects provide support for application data, and the view objects are used to provide one or more views/accesses to the application data. All of this framework support adds considerably to the size of a component.

ATL, on the other hand, does not provide a complete framework; instead, it provides a lightweight, template-based architecture designed specifically for creating COM objects. ATL provides access to all COM implementation objects but little else. This results in the creation of small components that aren't carrying around support for a framework neither used nor needed. Small, optimized components also operate more efficiently, as well as more quickly. The one major disadvantage to ATL is that it doesn't provide COM transparency—that is, it doesn't hide the COM implementation—as much as the MFC classes do.

ATL is not a replacement for MFC. In fact, you can use both MFC and ATL for a project, particularly a project created as a DLL. Chapter 19, *Persistence with ASP Components Using ATL and MFC*, demonstrates using both libraries to create ASP components that read and write to files and use serialization.

It's not very difficult to use MFC and ATL together. For instance, to add an ATL object to an MFC object within the Visual C++ IDE, choose Insert → ATL Object from the menu. Visual C++ then asks whether you want to support ATL within the MFC application. Choosing Yes enables you to add an ATL object and all ATL support templates to the MFC application. Conversely, when you create an ATL application, one of the options you can check is whether to add support for MFC.

For the most part, though, ASP components are created using ATL and not MFC, as are the components created in this chapter and most of the C++ examples in the book.

Using ATL AppWizard to Generate the Basic ASP Component Project

Visual C++ has several wizards to assist in building the basic framework of files and code for certain types of objects, and ATL has its own wizard, the ATL App-Wizard. The AppWizard generates the basic files for the ASP component, leaving us free to write code specific to the component itself. This section describes the steps involved in using the ATL AppWizard and provides a brief overview of the code and files it generates.

Using the ATL AppWizard to Generate the Project Files

The best way to demonstrate ATL is to create a simple C++ ASP component and review the steps necessary to create the basic component files. The component is a Dynamic HTML generator that generates the JavaScript necessary to implement client-side functions that will move a web page object based on whether the page is accessed via a Microsoft Internet Explorer browser or a Netscape Navigator browser.

To use ATL, select the ATL COM AppWizard project type when creating a new project. Use any name you prefer, such as `asp1401`, the first project you'll create for this chapter. Choose the server type of Dynamic Link Library (DLL) in the second dialog page that opens, and don't check the options to add support for MFC or MTS or to allow merging of the proxy/stub code, as shown in Figure 14-1. When you click the Finish button, Visual C++ generates the project files.

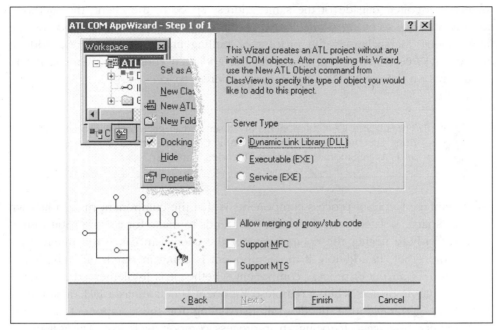

Figure 14-1. Using the ATL AppWizard to generate a default ATL C++ ASP Component project

Before proceeding further with the example, some explanation of the options shown in the ATL AppWizard dialog in Figure 14-1 is in order.

Creating an ASP Component as a DLL, EXE, or Service

The first option listed in the ATL AppWizard dialog shown in Figure 14-1 is whether to create the component as a DLL, EXE, or service, and you'll usually choose DLL when creating ASP components. Components created as DLLs are known as in-process components, and components created as EXEs are known as out-of-process components. There are advantages and disadvantages to creating a component using one or the other of these approaches, and these are detailed in the section "Creating an In-Process or Out-Of-Process Component" in Chapter 7, *Creating a Simple Visual Basic ASP Component.* To recap that discussion, an ASP component created as a DLL runs in the same process as the client that invokes the component, and it shares the same address space depending on thread compatibility. An out-of-process ASP component runs as its own process with its own address space.

The advantage to the in-process component is that communication between the client and the component is much faster, primarily because the same stack is used to pass arguments between the client and the server. Whenever a method of an object is invoked outside of the same address space of the client, the method's arguments have to be *marshaled* between the client invoking the method and the component. Marshaling is the process of pulling arguments from one address space stack, converting them into a stream, and then converting them back into arguments on the stack in the component's address space.

 Threads and C++ components are discussed in greater detail in sections later in this chapter titled "ASP Components and Threading" and "Aggregation and the Free-Threaded Marshaler."

An advantage to out-of-process components is that the component runs in its own address space, isolated from the client. This tends to make for a more robust environment, where neither the component nor the client can cause too much damage to the other. In addition, if the component is being invoked remotely, it will be treated as an out-of-process component whether it is implemented as a separate executable or not. When a remote component is created as a DLL, a stub executable is generated that handles all marshaling for the component, and any performance advantage to being an in-process component is lost. The advantage to an out-of-process component in this case is that it can be developed to handle remote invocation more efficiently.

By default, IIS 5.0 supports both in-process and out-of-process components.

A third option in step 1 of the ATL COM AppWizard is the service component option. A service component is one installed as an NT service, a server that runs in the background when NT starts. Since ASP components should be controlled from IIS (or from COM+, if the component is implemented as part of a COM+ application), this option should never be selected.

The Other ATL AppWizard Project Options

Other options listed in the dialog shown in Figure 14-1 are for merging the proxy/ stub code directly into the DLL and for adding in support for MFC and MTS. Support for MFC is not necessary for the simple ASP component created in this chapter, so do not check this option.

When a component is accessed across threads, across processes, or remotely, marshaling must occur to pass the method arguments from the client to the object. Marshaling is the process of pulling the arguments from the client stack, converting these arguments into a data stream using a proxy on the client side, and reconverting these arguments back into arguments on the stack via a stub on the server side. Normally when a component is accessed remotely, you would not want to install the component's implementation DLL on the client, only a separate proxy/ stub DLL used to access the remote component. The ATL AppWizard supports this by allowing you to choose whether to include the proxy/stub code in the same DLL as the implementation DLL. If the component were being accessed across threads or processes—such as a component created as a separate executable—you would want to include the proxy/stub code as part of the implementation DLL.

If you plan on accessing the component remotely, you would not want to include the proxy/stub code within the DLL but instead would want to compile this code into a separate DLL to install on the client. Since most ASP components are designed to run on the same machine as their client, and in fact are usually designed to run in the address space of their client, proxy/stub code does not need to be added to the DLL.

The final checkbox option in the ATL AppWizard dialog determines whether to add support for Microsoft Transaction Server (MTS). Adding support for MTS to the project adds in an import to the MTS API and builds in support to launch the MTS runtime, *mtxex.dll*, when the project application is launched. For Windows 2000 and IIS 5.0, you'll want to add support for COM+ Services instead. This support is added manually, so the MTS option is not used with any of the Visual C++ components created in this book.

The files that are generated from the ATL COM AppWizard are discussed next.

The ATL AppWizard–Generated Files

Several files are generated based on the options chosen when using the ATL App-Wizard dialog. This section discusses the files that are generated when the simplest ASP component—one that is a DLL, does not include MFC or MTS support, and does not merge in the proxy/stub code—is created.

One of the advantages of using a tool such as Visual C++ to create an ASP component is that the tool generates much of the code to support the DLL, leaving us free to write the code specific to the component itself. As an example of this, the ATL AppWizard generates the C++ code to handle loading and unloading the DLL from memory.

To handle DLL loading/unloading, the DLL's initialization and termination code, which is contained in the *DllMain* function shown in Example 14-1, is generated for the component. Since *DllMain* serves as an entry point for the DLL, when the component is started and is loaded into a process address space, the *dwReason* code is set to DLL_PROCESS_ATTACH, and the initialization code is run. When the client frees the component, the *dwReason* code is set to DLL_PROCESS_DETACH, and the DLL termination code is run.

Example 14-1. The DllMain Function

```
extern "C"
BOOL WINAPI DllMain(HINSTANCE hInstance, DWORD dwReason,
                       LPVOID /*lpReserved*/)
{
    if (dwReason == DLL_PROCESS_ATTACH)
    {
        _Module.Init(ObjectMap, hInstance, &LIBID_SSPLib);
        DisableThreadLibraryCalls(hInstance);
    }
    else if (dwReason == DLL_PROCESS_DETACH)
        _Module.Term();
    return TRUE;     // ok
}
```

Other code generated by the AppWizard is the *DllCanUnloadNow* function, to determine if the DLL can be removed from memory, the *DllGetClassObject* function, which returns the class factory to create the object, *DllRegisterServer* to register the server, and *DllUnregisterServer* to remove the server from the registry.

In addition to generating the .CPP file (containing the C++ code to maintain the DLL) and the .DEF file (to define which functions are exported from the DLL), the AppWizard also generates the .IDL—or Interface Definition Language—file. The IDL defines how other COM applications communicate with the component and serves as the placeholder for the component's GUID.

The C++ code to support the DLL is loaded into a file with the same name as the project and can be viewed from the File View tab. The IDL file is also assigned the same name as the project and is initially created with just a few lines of code. Example 14-2 shows the IDL code generated for the example project by VC++ Version 6.0.

Example 14-2. IDL Code Generated by the ATL AppWizard

```
import "oaidl.idl";
import "ocidl.idl";

[
    uuid(92918FE8-F323-11D1-ABBC-204C4F4F5020),
    version(1.0),
    helpstring("dhtml2 1.0 Type Library")
]
library DHTML2Lib
{
    importlib("stdole32.tlb");
    importlib("stdole2.tlb");
};
```

First, the **import** section lists two imported IDL files that contain the interface definitions to handle several data structures, such as **SAFEARRAY**, as well as the

IUnknown interface. You can actually open and view the contents of these files, but be careful not to make any changes. Following the imports is the interface attribute list. This list includes the UUID (the universally unique identifier), the version number of the interface, and a help string used to describe the object. The latter appears in the Visual Basic Project References dialog.

Following the interface attribute list is a definition of the type library, including import statements (**importlib**) for two type libraries that have already been compiled. These two type libraries are standard OLE 2.0 type libraries.

In addition to the DEF, IDL, and DLL files, the ATL AppWizard also attaches standard C++ and header files, *StdAfx.cpp* and *StdAfx.h*, which are added by all Visual C++ wizards and are used to create the precompiled header for the project, as well as the precompiled object file.

After reviewing the AppWizard-generated code and files, the next step to creating an ASP component is to add a new ATL object to the project, detailed in the next section.

Adding an ATL Object

In addition to generating support code and files, the ATL AppWizard also adds an option to the Visual C++ Insert menu that is used to add a new ATL object. Clicking on this option opens a dialog that lists categories of objects on the left and types of objects associated with each category on the right. For ASP components, the category to use is Objects. This provides several different objects you can choose from for creating the object, including ones for a Simple object, an ASP object, and an MTS object.

The ASP object type adds support for accessing the ASP built-in objects, based on a now deprecated technique of accessing a ScriptingContext object from the component's start page event (ComponentName::OnStartPage) and using this object to access the ASP objects. This ATL object type still works in Windows 2000/IIS 5.0, but you shouldn't use it—the support for this functionality could be removed in future versions of IIS.

The MTS object creates a component that can be used within MTS packages or COM+ applications. This object type generates support for features such as just-in-time activation by adding in support for **IObjectControl** and also providing code to implement **IObjectContext**. However, there are some incompatibilities between MTS and COM+ components, not the least of which is support for aggregation, so the MTS option is not the best choice for an ASP component in Windows 2000.

MTS components can be modified to provide better COM+ support; this is described in more detail later, in the section "Converting MTS Components for Use with COM+."

The option you'll pick for your first Visual C++ component is the Simple Object option, as shown in Figure 14-2.

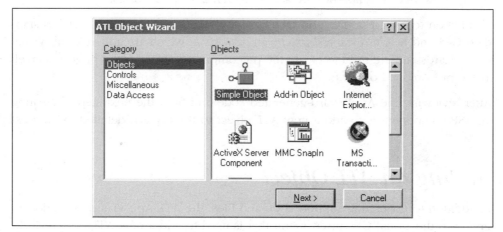

Figure 14-2. Creating a new ATL object using the Simple Object option

After clicking on the Next button, the Names tab of the ATL Object Wizard Properties dialog opens; this provides a place to enter the name of the component. The rest of the fields are automatically generated based on this name as it is typed, though any of the names can be altered manually. Name your first component **First**. After the name is typed into the Short Name field, the values in Table 14-1 are generated for the other fields in the dialog.

Table 14-1. Names of the Objects Generated for the Component

Item	Name
Class	CFirst
.H File	*First.h*
.CPP File	*First.cpp*
CoClass	First
Interface	IFirst
Type	First Class
Prog ID	ASP1401.First

Note that the Prog ID field will contain the name used to access the component from within an ASP page or from another ASP component. If you don't care for this ProgID, you can override the generated value and type in your own.

ATL Object Wizard Properties Attributes Page

Once you complete the Names tab, the next step is to click on the dialog's Attributes tab, which defines the component's attributes. These include the threading model used for the component, the interface, and the aggregation, in addition to options to support `ISupportErrorInfo`, `IConnectionPoints`, and the free-threaded marshaler.

The interface option should be set to Dual (its default), which means the component supports late binding with the `IDispatch` interface, as well as design-time vtable binding. Your component must support the Dual interface to be accessible by script in an ASP page.

The Support ISupportErrorInfo option lets the component communicate to client applications that it provides support for error reporting. If you use `IErrorInfo` to provide error messages to the client, you must implement `ISupportErrorInfo`. You're not using `IErrorInfo` within your first component, so leave this option unchecked. The support for connection points is necessary only if the component is providing outbound interface connections, so this option should also not be checked.

 Would you ever want to support connection points within an ASP component? You wouldn't want to do so for components accessed directly by an ASP page, but you could for components that access a database such as SQL Server or that are accessed by other components. Using connection points, a client can then be notified of events that occur within the server.

The next section details the remaining options and their impact.

ASP Components and Threading

Threading is discussed in more detail in Chapter 4, *ASP Components, Threads, and Contexts*, but since Visual C++ allows a more finite control of threading than a language such as Visual Basic, it's worth taking the time to discuss this expanded functionality here.

You can use Visual C++ to create an ASP component that is single-, apartment-, both-, free-, or neutral-threaded. Apartment-threading is really single-threaded apartment threading, and the both- and free-threading options are treated as multiple-threaded apartment options from the perspective of COM/COM+.

You shouldn't select the single-threaded model, since this model forces serialized access of the component, meaning that the component handles only one web page access request at a time. However, each of the other threading models— apartment, both, or free—has its own advantages and disadvantages.

In the apartment-threaded model, the component is created in an apartment on the thread that instantiates the component. This means that all calls to the component from that thread are direct and don't have to be marshaled. This approach is also inherently thread-safe, since all global data is isolated, and calls from other client threads are serialized to the thread that created the components, ensuring that all messages to the component are queued and processed one at a time. A downside to the apartment-threaded model is that if the component is created from a multithreaded apartment, discussed next, a new single-threaded apartment thread is created to house the component, and all calls between the client and the component must be marshaled.

For the free-threaded component, the opposite problem can occur. Applications have at most only one multiple-threaded apartment. Any free-threaded components would then be placed within this apartment. The free-threaded component is created in the multithreaded apartment for the application, and thread safety becomes the responsibility of the component developer, since calls to the component are no longer serialized. Additionally, if the client invoking the component is single-threaded, the two threading models are not compatible, and a multihreaded apartment would need to be created just to house the component. Because the client thread and the component thread are contained in different apartments, all calls from the client to the component would have to be marshaled.

One way to avoid the problems associated with a free-threaded or single-threaded apartment component is to define the ASP component as both-threaded. This means that the component is always created in the same thread of the client, regardless of which threading model the client uses and as long as the client and the component live in the same host environment. When the client is STA, the component is created on the client's main STA thread. When the client is MTA, the component is created in the client's only MTA thread. In both cases, no marshaling is necessary, since the client and the component share the same address space and the same stack for method parameters.

A new threading option for Windows 2000 is the neutral-threaded option. Neutral-threaded components live in the neutral apartment, regardless of the client's thread. There is no thread switching with this option, so marshaling isn't needed, and the object maintains its own context rather than taking on the client's context.

There is no support for neutral-threading with Visual C++ 6.0, though there will be with Visual Studio 7.0. Technically, you could change the Registry to set a component's threading model to neutral-threaded, using something such as `ThreadingModel=Neutral`. However, the component isn't created with this model, and the results could be unexpected.

Visual C++ 6.0 has no support for the neutral-threaded option, so select the Both threading model option for now.

Aggregation and the Free-Threaded Marshaler

If the component is multiple-threaded, which can occur when it is created as a free-threaded component or as a both-threaded component with a multithreaded client, performance issues arise if the component is accessed by the same process but from different threads. In this case, the component's methods must be marshaled, generating a performance hit. To compensate for this, aggregation and the free-threaded marshaler can be used.

Aggregation is a containment implementation, in that one interface contains another. In order to synchronize the two, the outer object provides for specific implementation of the inner object's `IUnknown` interface and then provides for delegation of all other interface methods to the outer object. With this, the client does not need to know that a method is not being handled directly by the object that is called.

If the client can access the component from more than one thread, the free-threaded marshaler enables direct communication with the component rather than having all method calls occur through a proxy/stub pair.

You can select aggregation without the use of the free-threaded marshaler, and in fact this is the preferred option for creating poolable objects, discussed later in the chapter in the section titled "Adding Support for COM+ Services."

If a component is accessible by only one client and is implemented on one thread within the client process, as is usually the case with ASP components, and the component is not poolable, the use of aggregation and the free-threaded marshaler is not necessary, and the options should not be checked. Make sure these options are unchecked for the first example.

Once you've selected your options for the new component, ATL generates the necessary component files and supporting code, discussed next.

Code Changes Based on Adding a New Object

The ATL Object Wizard creates a new class, CFirst, and an associated interface, IFirst. Both can be seen from the Class View. In addition, the following new entry is made in the IDL file to define the interface for the new component:

```
[
    object,
    uuid(B2CD8DA6-A38E-4684-8F14-71677A3586EE),
    dual,
    helpstring("IFirst Interface"),
    pointer_default(unique)
]
interface IFirst : IDispatch
{
};
```

Note that one of the IDL attributes is **dual**, which declares that the interface supports both IDispatch and vtable interface access. Below the interface attributes, a forward declaration for the interface is listed, again showing that the interface implements the IDispatch base interface.

 Support for both IDispatch and vtable means that the component can be accessed using early binding or late binding. Read more about binding and the advantages of early binding in Chapter 3, *ASP Components and COM*.

In the class header file *First.h*, the class is defined to implement three COM interfaces:

CComObjectRootEx
:   Implements the *QueryInterface* functionality for the component

CComCoClass
:   Adds support for obtaining an object's CLSID and for error support

IDispatchImp
:   Provides support for IDispatch

Each of these is a template, and combined they define a component that is multi-threaded, with a GUID of IID_IFirst and a CLSID of CLSID_First. ATL also generates the default empty constructor for the object:

```
class ATL_NO_VTABLE CFirst :
    public CComObjectRootEx<CComMultiThreadModel>,
    public CComCoClass<CFirst, &CLSID_First>,
```

```
        public  <IFirst, &IID_IFirst, &LIBID_ASP1401Lib>
    {
    public:
        CFirst()
        {
        }
```

In addition to the change in the IDL file and the class definition, a COM object map is generated to expose those interfaces accessible by clients using *QueryInterface*:

```
    BEGIN_COM_MAP(CFirst)
        COM_INTERFACE_ENTRY(IFirst)
        COM_INTERFACE_ENTRY(IDispatch)
    END_COM_MAP()
```

Through this code, clients can access both the component and the IDispatch interfaces externally.

Two other ATL macros are defined: DECLARE_REGISTRY_RESOURCEID, adding registration support for the component, and DECLARE_PROTECT_FINAL_ CONSTRUCT, preventing the object from being deleted when the reference count for the object reaches zero (more on object references can be found in Chapter 3).

Once the object has been created, methods can be added, as you'll see in the next section.

Adding Methods to the Interface

You can add methods and properties to a component once the component files are generated by ATL. You add these methods and properties using the Class View.

To add a new method, right click on the interface, IFirst, in Class View, and select Add Method from the context menu. A dialog opens to add the new method's name and parameters. For your new component, add a new method called sayHello that takes an input BSTR value and returns a pointer to another BSTR value. Figure 14-3 shows the Add Method dialog when this component is defined.

In Figure 14-3, notice that the parameters are defined with MIDL (Microsoft Interface Definition Language) attributes that specify the direction of the parameters. The input parameter has an attribute of [in], and the return value has an attribute of [out,retval]. There can only be one return value for the method, but there can be more than one input or output parameter. A particular MIDL attribute needs to be specified only once, before all parameters of the same direction. For instance, to specify three input BSTR values, use something such as the following:

```
    [in] BSTR bstrOne, BSTR bstrTwo, BSTR bstrThree
```

Add Method to Interface   ? X

Return Type:
[HRESULT   ▼]   [OK   ]

                                                         [Cancel]
Method Name:
[sayHello   ]   [Attributes...]

Parameters:
[[in] BSTR bstrName, [out,retval] BSTR* pbstrMes]

Implementation:
[id(2), helpstring("method sayHello")]
        HRESULT sayHello([in] BSTR bstrName, [out,retval] BSTR*
pbstrMessage);

Figure 14-3. Generating the component's sayHello method prototype

Though the prototype for the sayHello method in Figure 14-3 shows that a **BSTR** is returned from the method, in actuality the method's defined return type is **HRESULT**. All methods exposed through a dual interface implemented in C++ have this same **HRESULT** return datatype. However, the actual value returned to the client as the result of the function call is a string. The **HRESULT** value is accessed through error handling, such as through the Err object from within a VBScript ASP block.

Clicking on the Attributes button in the Add Method dialog opens a second dialog containing attributes for the method. By default, the method is given an identifier, in this case a value of one (1), and a help string. The default help string is "method sayHello". For the example, change this to "Say hello to the world". The help string is displayed in object browsers such as Visual Basic's, and providing a more comprehensive help string ensures the method is used correctly.

There are other attributes that can be used with the method, but they aren't used with this ASP component. The documentation that comes with Visual C++ contains more details on these other attributes.

Close the Add Method dialog, which saves the changes and generates the following IDL for the method:

```
[id(1), helpstring("Say hello to the world")] HRESULT
sayHello([in] BSTR bstrName, [out,retval] BSTR* pbstrMessage);
```

The datatype for both the input and output values is a **BSTR**, though the return value must be defined as a pointer for C++ components. The **BSTR** datatype is a COM-specific datatype. This and other COM datatypes are discussed next.

ATL Method Interface Datatypes

There are several simple datatypes that are used when defining an interface method:

boolean
> Used to set a value to TRUE or FALSE

char
> Single character, one byte (8 bits) in size

double
> A 64-bit floating point number

float
> A 32-bit floating point number

int
> For 32-bit environments, a 32-bit integer; for 16-bit environments, accompanies another keyword, such as small, a 16-bit number

int64
> A 64-bit integer

long
> A 32-bit integer

pointer
> A pointer to type

short
> A 16-bit integer

void
> Void

Earlier I mentioned that two IDL files are imported into the newly generated IDL file for the project. One of these files, *ocidl.idl*, contains the definitions for the standard interfaces, such as IUnknown. The other, *oaidl.idl*, contains the definitions for complex datatypes used in the interface methods. These complex datatypes are the following:

BSTR
> A length-prefixed string; for C++, BSTR types are wrapped in a COM class, CComBSTR.

CURRENCY
> A structure; for C++, currency types are wrapped in an OLE class, COleCurrency.

HRESULT

An integer.

SAFEARRAY

An array that includes an array element count.

VARIANT

Used for any variable/parameter that is not defined as any other type; for C++, they are wrapped in the **CComVariant** COM class.

SCODE

A status code; the same as **HRESULT** in a 32-bit environment, or used to derive **HRESULT** in a 16-bit environment.

IUnknown

An interface pointer to **IUnknown**.

IDispatch

An interface pointer to **IDispatch**.

Any of the COM-compatible datatypes can be used for input ([in]) and return ([retval]) parameters, but only the **VARIANT** datatype should be used for ASP components. The reason is that most ASP script is created using VBScript, and this scripting language only supports the **VARIANT** datatype. COM/COM+ can convert the **VARIANT** to the input parameter datatypes and can successfully convert the return value, but the output parameters (defined with [out]) must be of type **VARIANT*** (pointer to **VARIANT**), or an error will occur when your component is accessed by VBScript.

You'll add code to implement your component's method in the next section.

Adding Code for the Method

As stated earlier, instead of adding code for a method directly to the C++ file, the method is defined for the interface. Visual C++, in turn, generates the skeleton C++ code consisting of the function call, the opening and closing function brackets, and a default **HRESULT** return type of **S_OK**. This skeleton code is added to the interface's implementation class. The developer then manually adds the rest of the code necessary to implement the method.

Open the *First.cpp* file to find the method prototype. You'll add code to append the string passed to the component to a statically created message, which is then returned from the component. Add the code shown in Example 14-3 to sayHello.

Example 14-3. The MoveLeft Component Interface Method

```
STDMETHODIMP CFirst::sayHello(BSTR bstrName, BSTR *pbstrMessage)
{
    CComBSTR bstrMessage = "Hello ";
    bstrMessage.Append(bstrName);

    *pbstrMessage = bstrMessage.Detach();

    return S_OK;
}
```

At the end, a status of S_OK is returned to show that no errors have occurred. This value is one of the standard, predefined HRESULT code values. Other standard return types, such as E_OUTOFMEMORY, are usually used to denote an error and are discussed more fully in the "Error Handling" section at the end of this chapter.

After adding the code for the method, compile the DLL. As it compiles, the ASP component is also registered as a COM component, a process that occurs automatically based on flags and application settings generated by the ATL AppWizard. Once the DLL has been compiled and registered, access the component from the following ASP script, *asp1401.asp*, which creates an instance of the component using the ASP Server object and calls the sayHello method, passing in a string for the greeting message:

```
<%
Dim obj
Set obj = Server.CreateObject("asp1401.First")

Dim msg
msg = obj.sayHello("World!")
Response.Write "<h3>" & msg & "</h3>"
Set obj = Nothing
%>
```

The method returns the greeting, which is displayed to the returned web page:

```
Hello World!
```

That's it for your first C++ ASP component. In this example, the component is registered directly during the compilation process. You could also register a component using the *regsvr32.exe* utility:

```
regsvr32.exe asp1401.dll
```

The component is also registered automatically when it is added to a COM+ application. You can also add additional functionality to your component using COM+ Services, discussed next.

Adding Support for COM+ Services

COM+ Services were added to Windows 2000. These services combine the services provided by COM and MTS (Microsoft Transaction Server) in Windows NT 4.0.

You can add support for COM+ services to your component in order to add transaction support or to access the ASP built-in objects (discussed later in the chapter). You can also add your component to a COM+ application in order to take advantage of some COM+ services, such as just-in-time (JIT) activation and poolable objects.

Object Context

Access to an object's context and transaction support was implemented with the **IObjectContext** interface and MTS in NT 4.0. Both are now accessed through COM+ Services.

The **IObjectContext** object is used to provide access to the ASP built-in objects. However, support for the built-in objects is actually a secondary feature of **IObjectContext**. Its primary purpose is for transaction support.

The principal methods that **IObjectContext** exposes are SetAbort and SetComplete, used to mark a transaction as unsuccessful or successful, respectively. The DisableCommit method prevents a transaction from being committed, and Enable-Commit turns the transaction commitment capability back on. These latter two methods are useful for preventing a transaction from completing until certain operations have finished or certain conditions have been met. The IsInTransaction method returns information about whether the component is within a transaction, the IsSecurityEnabled method returns a Boolean indicating if security is enabled for the component, and the IsCallerInRole method returns a Boolean to indicate whether the process calling the component is within a specific role. Finally, the CreateInstance method instantiates a COM object in the same transaction as the existing object.

You can read more about **IObjectContext** and **IObjectContext-Info** in Chapter 5, *COM+ Services and ASP Components and Applications.*

To include support for **IObjectContext** in your project, add the COM+ Services header file, *comsvcs.h*, to your component's header file. For instance, to add **IObjectContext** support to your existing component, add *comsvcs.h* to *First.h*:

```
#include <comsvcs.h>
```

The method will also use a COM helper class, **_variant_t**, to handle all VARI-ANT object instantiation and cleanup. Add support for the COM helper classes by adding the *comdef.h* header file:

```
#include <comdef.h>
```

To add the COM+ Services library, select the Project → Settings option from the menu, and then select the Link tab. Select General from the Category dropdown list, and add the following to the list of libraries and objects models:

```
comsvcs.lib
```

Figure 14-4 shows the library setting after adding in the COM+ Services library.

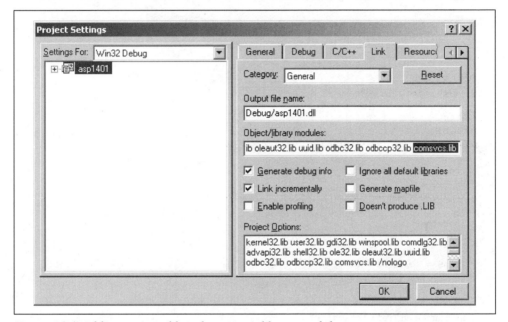

Figure 14-4. Adding comsvcs.lib to the project's library modules

You'll use the *CoGetObjectContext* function to obtain a reference to **IObject-Context** within your component code. This function takes two parameters, the GUID for the interface and a reference to the object to receive the interface:

```
IObjectContext* pObjectContext = NULL;
hr = CoGetObjectContext(IID_IObjectContext, (void **)&pObjectContext);
```

To try out the **IObjectContext** interface, create a new method for your existing component, testObjContext, that uses some of the **IObjectContext** methods. Specifically, the method uses the **IObjectContext** IsCallerInRole, IsSecurityEn-abled, and IsInTransaction methods. Add the method to *First.cpp* through Class View. It takes three output parameters, all of type pointer to **VARIANT**:

```
[out] VARIANT* varTrans, VARIANT* varRole, VARIANT* varSecurity
```

Add the code shown in Example 14-4 to the component method. The method calls each of the **IObjectContext** methods just mentioned after first creating an instance of **IObjectContext**. The results of calling each of the methods are returned in the **VARIANT** parameters.

Example 14-4. CUsing IObjectContext Security and Transaction Support Methods

```
STDMETHODIMP CFirst::testObjContext(VARIANT *varTrans,
                                    VARIANT *varRole,
                                    VARIANT *varSecurity)
{
   HRESULT hr;
   CComPtr<IObjectContext> pObjectContext;

   hr = CoGetObjectContext(IID_IObjectContext, (void **)&pObjectContext);
   if (FAILED(hr)) return hr;

   // test to see if in transaction
   BOOL blTrans;
   blTrans = pObjectContext->IsInTransaction();

   // test to see if in role
   BOOL blRole;
   pObjectContext->IsCallerInRole(L"Developer",&blRole);

   // test to see if security enabled
   BOOL blSecurity;
   blSecurity = pObjectContext->IsSecurityEnabled();

   // return values
   _variant_t vtTrans, vtSecurity, vtRole;

   vtTrans = (blTrans !=0);
   vtSecurity = (blSecurity != 0);
   vtRole = (blRole != 0);

   *varTrans = vtTrans.Detach();
   *varRole = vtRole.Detach();
   *varSecurity = vtSecurity.Detach();

   return S_OK;
}
```

The IsInTransaction method returns **TRUE** if the component is executing within a COM+ transaction. Both IsSecurityEnabled and IsCallerInRole test the security of the environment the component is operating within.

Compile the component and test it using the following ASP script (also found in *asp1402.asp*):

```
<%
Dim obj
Set obj = Server.CreateObject("asp1401.First")
```

```
Dim blTrans, blRole
obj.testObjContext blTrans, blRole, blSecurity

Set obj = Nothing

' test values
If blTrans Then
    Response.Write "<H3>In Transaction</h3>"
Else
    Response.Write "<H3>Not in Transaction</H3>"
End If

If blRole Then
    Response.Write "<H3>In Role</h3>"
Else
    Response.Write "<H3>Not in Role</H3>"
End If

If blSecurity Then
    Response.Write "<H3>Security Enabled</h3>"
Else
    Response.Write "<H3>Security not enabled</H3>"
End If
%>
```

When you access the ASP test page, you'll get messages that the component is not within a transaction, that it is in the specific role, and that security is not enabled.

The reason the component is not within a transaction is that a transaction was not started before the component was accessed. You can change this by adding the **TRANSACTION** directive as the first line of the ASP test page:

```
<% @ TRANSACTION = required %>
```

Now when you access the test page, it reports that the component is within a transaction.

You might be wondering how the IsCallerInRole method returns **True** when the caller is not within the Developer role (or registered at all). The reason is that this method always returns **True** when the component is accessed from a client process. The component is running within the same process as the ASP application, so IsCallerInRole returns **True**.

To test our role-based security, create a new COM+ application (name it anything you like) and add **asp1401.First** to it. Within the application, create a new role by right-clicking on the application's Roles folder and selecting New Role from the pop-up menu. When asked for the role name, type in **Developer**. After the role is created, add users to it by right clicking on the Users folder contained within the role and picking several users from the list that opens, including *IUSR_MACHINE*, the default ASP application user (change *MACHINE* to your machine name).

Next, access the properties for the component by right-clicking on the component and selecting Properties from the menu. Switch to the Transactions tab, and select the Required Transaction support option. Switch next to the Security tab, check the "Enforce the component level access checks" option, and check the Developer role that shows in the second window, as shown in Figure 14-5.

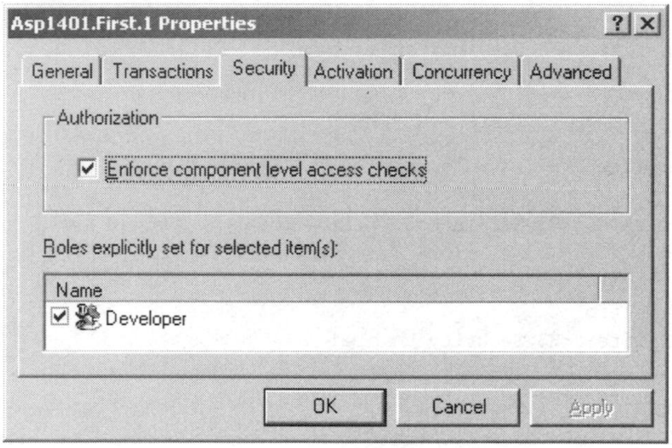

Figure 14-5. Setting component role-based security

Finally, access the Properties dialog for the COM+ application and make sure its security is set to "Enforce access checks for this application."

Now when you access the component using the ASP test page, all three tests (transaction, role, and security) return a value of **True**.

The **IObjectContext** interface also has two methods, SetAbort and SetComplete, that can be used to roll back or commit transactions, respectively. The transactions could encompass database activities as well as other activities where the state of data changes based on the activity, such as with MSMQ (Microsoft Message Queue). Using the SetAbort method informs COM+ that this component is finished processing and that its processing has failed. Using the SetComplete method informs COM+ that this component has finished processing and that its processing has completed successfully. The success or failure of this component will impact on whether the transaction is committed or rolled back for all components that are operating in the same transaction.

Chapter 9, *Creating an ASP Middle Tier with ADO*, demonstrates using COM+ transactions with database updates. Chapter 18, *Accessing MSMQ from C++ ASP Components*, has an example of using transactions with MSMQ messages.

Transactions are really based on two decisions: is the component done, and were the component's actions successful? The SetComplete and SetAbort methods both provide information that the component is finished. They differ in reporting the success of the function. With the introduction of COM+ Services, there is another interface that allows you to have more finite control of transactions—the `IContextState` interface.

`IContextState` can be referenced using *CoGetObjectContext*, passing in the GUID for `IContextState`:

```
CComPtr<IContextState> pContextState;
hr = CoGetObjectContext(IID_IContextState, (void **)&pContextState);
```

To signal that the component is done, the SetDeactivateOnReturn method is called, passing in a Boolean value indicating whether the component is done or not:

```
hr=pContextState->SetDeactivateOnReturn(true);
if (FAILED(hr)) return hr;
```

To signal the success or failure of the transaction, you would use the SetMyTransactionVote method, passing in a value of **TxCommit** or **TxAbort**:

```
hr=pState->SetMyTransactionVote(TxCommit);
```

TxCommit and **TxAbort** are enumerated constants.

The `IContextState` interface is particularly useful when used in conjunction with just-in-time activation, discussed next.

The IObjectControl Interface and JIT

The `IObjectControl` interface was created to add support for just-in-time activation. JIT optimizes the performance of an application by not actually instantiating a component until it's used, regardless of when the component is created in code. Additionally, when the component is discarded in code, the reference—but not necessarily the component—is discarded. Depending on resources, the component may be kept in an instantiated, deactivated state that decreases the time needed to access the component again from the application.

To enable JIT for your component, you *must* install it within a COM+ application and then check the "Enable just-in-time activation" option in the Activation tab of the component's Properties dialog.

 If you implement `IObjectControl` in your component and don't install the component into a COM+ application, the ASP page that accesses your component doesn't respond and the ASP application hangs.

To take full advantage of JIT, you'll want to access your component's resources when the component is activated and discard them when the component is deactivated. To trap the activation and deactivation events, you'll need to implement the `IObjectControl` interface.

Unlike the `IContextState` and the `IObjectContext` interfaces, you'll need to modify your component's class definition to include a reference to `IObject-Control`—`IObjectControl` must be implemented. In addition, you must add three methods—Activate, Deactivate, and CanBePooled—to your class.

To view the changes to your code that you'll need to make to implement `IObjectControl`, add a new ATL object to **asp1401**, again using the Simple Object template and adding in support for the Both-Threaded Model, the Dual Interface, and Aggregation. Name the component **JustInTime**.

Once the component files are created, modify the component's class. First, modify the class definition in *JustInTime.h* to include a reference to `IObjectControl`:

```
class ATL_NO_VTABLE CJustInTime :
    public CComObjectRootEx<CComMultiThreadModel>,
    public CComCoClass<CJustInTime, &CLSID_JustInTime>,
    public IObjectControl,
    public IDispatchImpl<IJustInTime, &IID_IJustInTime, &LIBID_ASP1401Lib>
```

Next, add an entry for `IObjectControl` to the COM Map in *JustInTime.h*:

```
BEGIN_COM_MAP(CJustInTime)
    COM_INTERFACE_ENTRY(IJustInTime)
    COM_INTERFACE_ENTRY(IObjectControl)
    COM_INTERFACE_ENTRY(IDispatch)
END_COM_MAP()
```

Add the two ASP and COM Services libraries to the header file:

```
#include <comsvcs.h>
#include <asptlb.h>
```

Finally add the publicly accessible method prototypes for the `IObjectControl` methods to *JustInTime.h*:

```
// IJustInTime
public:
    STDMETHOD(Activate)();
    STDMETHOD_(BOOL, CanBePooled)();
    STDMETHOD_(void, Deactivate)();
```

Before you compile the component, you'll also need to add the methods to the component's C++ file, *JustInTime.cpp*. At this time, the methods are prototypes only (you'll add code for this component in later sections of this chapter):

```
HRESULT CJustInTime::Activate()
{
    return S_OK;
}
```

```
BOOL CJustInTime::CanBePooled()
{
    return FALSE;
}

void CJustInTime::Deactivate()
{
}
```

The JIT methods aren't doing anything specific at this point, but you can success-fully compile it if you want to test that you've added the code correctly. Now, when the component is activated, the Activate method is called; when the compo-nent is deactivated, the Deactivate method is called.

Use the Activate method to create references to objects that you want to use in all of your component's methods. For instance, with ASP components, it's not unusual to obtain a reference to one or more of the ASP built-in objects in the Activate method and to release these references in the Deactivate method. Later in the chapter, this technique is demonstrated when you have a chance to work with the ASP objects.

You might be tempted to also deactivate your database connections in the Deacti-vate method. However, database connections are expensive resources. A better approach is to create the ADO connection objects in the Activate method but to not actually open the connection until it's used within the component's own meth-ods. Then you could release the Connection object in the Deactivate method.

The overhead to create the Connection object is so slight that I never manage its existence in the JIT methods. Instead, I create the Con-nection object just before I open the connection and then release it as soon as possible. However, I've obtained a reference to the Con-nection string from the ASP Application object in the Activate method.

JIT isn't the only activation setting you can use with your ASP components—you can also pool the object.

Creating Poolable Objects

If you specify that a component can be pooled, COM+ keeps an instantiated ver-sion of it within a pool. When a request for the component is made within ASP script, COM+ pulls the instantiated version of the component from the pool, decreasing the amount of time necessary to activate the component.

When an application, such as an ASP application, that accesses your component is started, instances of your component are created in order to meet the minimum number specified using the Component Services Manager. If you specify a minimum pool of 10 for a specific component, when the ASP application starts, 10 instances of the component are created. COM+ then creates new instances of the component each time an access is made and all of the existing components have already been allocated, up to the maximum pool size set with Component Services.

Pooling is an especially attractive performance enhancement for an ASP component that can be accessed many times within a short time period. The main disadvantage is that the component holds any resources unless you specifically release them using JIT and `IObjectControl`'s Deactivate method.

There are some specific requirements that must be met before your component can be considered poolable. First, the component must be neutral- or both-threaded. Second, the component must support Aggregation but must not support the free-threaded marshaler.

If your component participates in transactions, you must implement `IObject-Control` in order to handle resources within the Activate, Deactivate, and CanBe-Pooled methods. Regardless of your use of `IObjectControl`, your component should not hold a transactional resource such as an open database connection when it is pooled. Instead, activate the resource in the Activate method, and release the resource in the Deactivate method.

If you must hold the transactional resource when the component is pooled, your code will have to handle resource management, which may not be a trivial coding effort, depending on the resource. (Check the documentation provided by the resource manager, such as OLE DB, to see how to manually enlist resources if you want to hold the resources within a pooled component.)

To enable pooling for your new `JustInTime` component, add the component to your existing COM+ application, and then access its Properties dialog. Switch to the Activation page and check the Enable Object Pooling option. Change the minimum pool size to 5 and the maximum pool size to 20, as shown in Figure 14-6.

You'll have a chance to work with both JIT and object pooling in the section of this chapter that covers the ASP built-in objects. First, though, we'll take a look at how you can convert your existing NT 4.0 MTS components to the new COM+ environment.

Converting MTS Components for Use with COM+

To access `IObjectContext` in a C++ component in NT 4.0, you'd attach the MTS header and library files to the project. The MTS header file is *mtx.h*, and the libraries are *mtx.lib* and *mtxguid.lib*. Choosing the MTS option when creating the

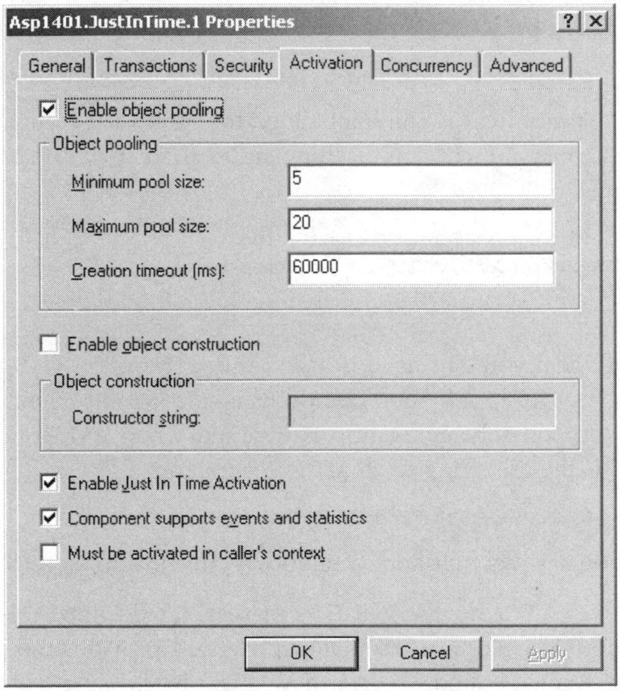

Figure 14-6. Enabling object pooling for the JustInTime component

project automatically adds the MTS libraries to the project. Picking the MS Transaction Server option when using the ATL Object Wizard to create the component automatically adds the MTS header file to the component's header file. Finally, checking the `IObjectControl` option when generating the option automatically adds in support for the `IObjectControl` methods and also creates an instance of `IObjectContext` in the Activate method.

Components created using the MTS options should work without problems in Windows 2000. In fact, the MTS files installed as part of the Platform SDK for Windows 2000 wrap the COM+ Services within the previously used MTS files. For instance, if you open the MTS header file, *mtx.h*, you'll find that it is nothing more than a wrapper for the COM+ Services header file:

```
#define __MTxSpm_LIBRARY_DEFINED__
#include "comsvcs.h"
```

In addition to the COM+ versus MTS support changes, there are new COM/COM+ interfaces to work with and a new function to use to access these interfaces. Previously, you accessed a copy of `IObjectContext` with the function GetObjectContext, passing in a reference to the interface:

```
hr = GetObjectContext(&pObjectContext);
```

In Windows 2000 you'll use *CoGetObjectContext*, passing in the GUID for the interface as well as a pointer to a reference to hold the instance created:

```
hr = CoGetObjectContext(IID_IObjectContext, (void **)&pObjectContext);
```

However, GetObjectContext is still maintained for backward compatibility. In Windows 2000, this older function is nothing more than a wrapper for the newer *CoGetObjectContext*:

```
HRESULT GetObjectContext(IObjectContext **ppoc) {
    return CoGetObjectContext(IID_IObjectContext,
        (void**)ppoc);
}
```

There is one problem you can have in using the MTS option with the ATL Object Wizard if you wish to pool your component—MTS components could not be aggregated, so support for aggregation is disabled when ATL generates the component. ATL adds the following to all MTS components:

```
DECLARE_NOT_AGGREGATABLE(CMtsObject)
```

If you attempt to pool a component created with this macro, an error will occur.

To demonstrate, create a new Visual C++ project named **asp1402**, but this time, add support for MTS when the ATL COM AppWizard provides the project options. When the project is generated, insert a new ATL object using the MS Transaction Server option. Name the component **MtsObject**. While still in the ATL Object Wizard, switch to the MTS page and add support for **IObjectControl**, but don't select the Can Be Pooled option.

When the object is generated, open the *MtsObject.h* file. You'll see that **IObject-Control** has been added to the class definition, as have the COM mapping and the three **IObjectControl** methods. The ATL Object Wizard also added a reference to **IObjectContext** as a class member and included a reference to the *mtx.h* header file.

Opening the *MtsObject.cpp* file, you'll find the three **IObjectControl** methods. The ATL Object Wizard also added the following code to create **IObjectContext** to the Activate method:

```
HRESULT hr = GetObjectContext(&m_spObjectContext);
if (SUCCEEDED(hr))
    return S_OK;
return hr;
```

It also added the following code to release the class member to the Deactivate method:

```
m_spObjectContext.Release();
```

Finally, the CanBePooled method returns **FALSE**.

Use Class View to add a new method to the component called addNumbers that takes two input parameters and a return value, all integers:

```
[in] int iFirst, int iSecond, [out,retval] int* iResult
```

Add the code for the method next. As you can see in Example 14-5, the code is pretty simple—adding two numbers and returning the result.

Example 14-5. Method to Add Two Numbers and Return Results

```
STDMETHODIMP CMtsObject::addNumbers(int iFirst,
                                    int iSecond,
                                    int *iResult)
{
    *iResult = iFirst + iSecond;
    return S_OK;
}
```

Add the component to the COM+ application you created earlier, and don't change any of the default settings for the component. Once you've done this, test the component using *asp1403.asp*, which contains the following ASP test script:

```
<%
Dim obj
Set obj = Server.CreateObject("asp1402.MtsObject")

Dim result
result = obj.addNumbers(35,35)

Response.Write "<h3>" & CStr(result) & "</h3>"
%>
```

The number 70 shows in the page that's returned.

Open the COM+ application again and access the Properties dialog for `asp1402.MtsObject`. Switch to the Activation page and check the option to add object pooling. Access the ASP test page again and see what happens. What you'll get is the following error:

```
Server object, ASP 0177 (0x80040110)
Class does not support aggregation (or class object is remote)
/chap14/asp1403.asp, line 10
```

You've tried to pool a component that doesn't have support for aggregation, and the script failed.

If you wish, you can alter your existing MTS components to work within the COM+ environment more closely by making a few modifications:

1. Change the MTS header reference from *mtx.h* to *comsvcs.h*.

2. Remove the references to the *mtx.lib* and *mtxguid.lib* libraries, and add in *comsvcs.lib*.

3. Change the GetObjectContext method to CoGetObjectContext.

4. If you want to support pooling, remove the reference to `DECLARE_NOT_`
   `AGGREGATABLE(CMtsObject)` after first checking to make sure your resource
   use won't be compromised if the component is pooled.

5. Recompile the component.

Of course, you may have to change code that uses any NT-specific functionality,
depending on how much of the functionality has migrated to Windows 2000. But
most of your existing components that use ADO should work as is in the new
Windows 2000 environment (and using ADO 2.5 and up).

 If you port your components from NT to Windows 2000, make sure
to test thoroughly. The variations between the two environments can
be subtle at times, but they are there, and they can make the difference between an ASP application that works and one that doesn't.

Another ATL Object Wizard option used in NT was the ASP option, to create components with built-in support for the ASP objects. This approach used the older,
and deprecated, `IScriptingContext` interface. These components should be
modernized to COM+, though they will work as is within Windows 2000. Instead
of using ScriptingContext to access the objects, you can use either `IObject-`
`Context` or `IObjectContextInfo`, as discussed in the next section.

Accessing the ASP Built-in Objects

Many of the example components in this book include access to the ASP built-in
objects. The ASP built-in objects provide an interface between the ASP application
(and the application component) and the ASP environment. These objects are the
following:

Application
    Provides ASP application-wide information

Session
    Provides ASP session information

Request
    Contains information provided by the user or client application

Response
    Returns information to the client

Server

Performs some transformations and creates instances of new objects within the context of the ASP application

ASPError

Provides error information

 Appendix A, *ASP Built-in Object Quick Reference*, has a complete reference of all of the ASP objects, their properties, collections, and methods.

In your ASP code, you get information provided by the user—such as form or query string data—through the ASP Request object. You can return information to the web page through the Response object. ASP components are created in ASP script through the use of the Server object's CreateObject method.

The next section outlines how to access the built-in ASP objects from a Visual C++ component.

Accessing the Objects Using ObjectContext

Starting with IIS 4.0 and continuing with IIS 5.0, access to the ASP built-in objects occurs through `IObjectContext`. Within the Windows 2000 environment, you can also access the ASP built-in objects from the `IObjectContextInfo` interface.

To access the ASP objects in C++, add a reference to the ASP header file to your component:

```
#include <asptlb.h>
```

Then you can create instances of any of the objects through `IObjectContext` or `IObjectContextInfo`, using the QueryInterface method to obtain a reference to the `IGetContextProperties` interface:

```
CComPtr<IGetContextProperties> pProps; //context properties
CComPtr<IObjectContext> pObjContext;   //context object
// get ObjectContext
    hr = CoGetObjectContext(IID_IObjectContext,
                            (void **)&pObjContext);
if (FAILED(hr)) return hr;

// get context properties
hr = pObjContext->QueryInterface( IID_IGetContextProperties,
             (void**)&pProps );
if (FAILED(hr)) return hr;
```

Separating the Business from the Presentation

Should you use the ASP built-in objects from ASP components? The answer depends on the purpose of the component.

Many of the examples in this book do use these objects, primarily the Request and Response objects. However, the main reason for this is to include as much of the ASP processing within the component as possible, for demonstration purposes. You'll want to include the ASP objects in your components depending on the purpose of the component and whether the component must work in environments other than ASP.

For instance, if you're creating a business component to access a database and perform some form of data update or query, you'll want to restrict the use of, or not use at all, the ASP built-in objects. By limiting the use of these objects, your business object can be easily moved to other server-based environments. Additionally, you can modify either the business processing or the presentation without impacting either. If you decide to have your ASP application output XML instead of HTML, you can make this change without having to change the business component. If your business processing or data access changes, this won't impact your presentation.

However, an advantage of using the ASP objects within your components, especially for database access, is that you can access form values directly from the Request object and not have to create a method with several parameters (or use an array), retrieve the values from the Request object in your script, and pass them to the method.

If your components are part of the presentation layer—such as reusable components whose purpose is to generate specific blocks of HTML or XML—then use the built-in ASP objects within the components.

When you're in the process of developing a business component, you can temporarily use the ASP built-in objects to assist in the development process and then remove them after the business process works to your satisfaction and you're ready to integrate the component into the application environment.

You then use the QueryInterface method on **IGetContextProperties** to obtain a reference to any of the ASP built-in objects:

```
IDispatch* piDispatch = NULL;
CComPtr<IResponse> piResponse;          //Response object

// get Response property
hr = pProps->GetProperty( L"Response", &vt ) ;
if (FAILED(hr)) return hr;
```

```
piDispatch = vt. pdispVal;
hr = piDispatch->QueryInterface( IID_IResponse,
                    (void**)&piResponse );
```

The Response object is accessed as a **VARIANT** from `IGetContextProperties` using the GetProperty method. The `IDispatch` value is accessed from this variant and used to query for the `IResponse` interface.

Once you're done with the object, release the reference to it:

```
piResponse.Release();
```

References to the ASP objects can be created directly in your component methods, or they can be created within the context of JIT. The latter approach can be best if you have several component methods that use the same ASP object.

Once you've obtained a reference to an ASP built-in object, you have access to all of its properties, methods, and collections.

The IResponse Interface

The ASP Response object handles all communication from the ASP application back to the client web page. This ASP object has more methods than any of the other objects, and one of these, Write, is the primary method used to output information to a web page. You'll work directly with the `IResponse` interface when accessing Response in your C++ component.

To try out `IResponse`, open your **asp1401** project, and add two new private class members to the `JustInTime` component (in *JustInTime.h*):

```
private:
    CComPtr<IObjectContext> m_spObjectContext;
    CComPtr<IResponse> m_piResponse;
```

Also add the *asptlb.h* header file to add support for the ASP objects and *comdef.h* to get access to the COM helper classes.

Add code to instantiate the class member in your component's Activate method, and release the member in Deactivate. After modifying the code, these two methods should look similar to those shown in Example 14-6.

Example 14-6. Instantiating and Releasing the IResponse Class Member

```
HRESULT CJustInTime::Activate()
{
    HRESULT hr;
    CComBSTR bstrProp;
    CComVariant vt;
    CComPtr<IGetContextProperties> pProps; //Context Properties

    IDispatch* piDispatch - NULL;
```

Example 14-6. Instantiating and Releasing the IResponse Class Member (continued)

```
   // get ObjectContext
   hr = CoGetObjectContext(IID_IObjectContext,
                           (void **)&m_spObjectContext);
   if (FAILED(hr)) return hr;

   // get context properties
   hr = m_spObjectContext->QueryInterface( IID_IGetContextProperties,
               (void**)&pProps );
   if (FAILED(hr)) return hr;

   // get Response property
   bstrProp = "Response";
   hr = pProps->GetProperty( bstrProp, &vt ) ;
   if (FAILED(hr)) return hr;

   piDispatch = vt.pdispVal;
   hr = piDispatch->QueryInterface( IID_IResponse,
                     (void**)&m_piResponse );

    return hr;
}
void CJustInTime::Deactivate()
{
   m_piResponse.Release();
   m_spObjectContext.Release();
}
```

Once you've created the **IResponse** class member, you can use it in any of your component's methods. Add a new method to **asp1401.JustInTime** and name it sayHello. The method has one input parameter, of type **BSTR**:

```
[in] BSTR bstrName
```

Like the method shown earlier in Example 14-3, this method also creates a message string to display to the web page. Unlike the earlier example, though, the string is output directly from the component using the Response object's Write method. Add the code shown in Example 14-6 to your component:

```
STDMETHODIMP CJustInTime::sayHello(BSTR bstrName)
{
    CComBSTR bstrMessage = "Hello ";
    bstrMessage.Append(bstrName);

    m_piResponse->Write(_variant_t(bstrMessage.Detach()));

    return S_OK;
}
```

Add **asp1401.JustInTime** to an existing COM+ application (or create a new application). Once you've done that, you can test the component's new method with the following ASP page, *asp1404.asp*:

```
<%
Dim obj
Set obj = Server.CreateObject("asp1401.JustInTime")

obj.sayHello "World!"
%>
```

The "Hello World!" message is displayed in the web page.

In addition to creating output, the Response object and its associated C++ interface can control how and when the output is returned. This control occurs through the Buffer property. Setting this property to a Boolean value of **FALSE** turns page buffering off, which means that content is returned to the page as it is generated. The default value is **TRUE**, meaning that content is buffered and not returned to the page until it's all generated. The Buffer property can be set using the put_Buffer method and retrieved using get_Buffer. Note, though, that the code that sets the property must be accessed before any HTML is generated; otherwise it is ignored.

Other methods that can determine when content is returned to the page are the Clear, End, and Flush methods. The Clear method is used to clear out the buffer contents in case of an error. This is helpful if a problem has occurred and you don't want any content returned to the web page reader, as the following code fragment illustrates:

```
CComVariant vtOut;
vtOut = "some contents";
m_piResponse->Write(vtOut);

    // other activity occurs, and an error results
// clear buffer
m_piResponse->Clear();
```

The End method stops page buffering and returns the page contents directly at that point, while the Flush method returns output but does not turn buffering off. All three of these methods will return an error if buffering is not enabled.

The **IResponse** interface can also control caching. For instance, the put_Expires or put_ExpiresAbsolute methods control when the page expires from the cache. The former method takes a long value representing the number of minutes before the page expires, and the latter takes an actual date. To change the cache expiration date from your **asp1401.JustInTime** component, add a new method called setCacheDate, which is shown in Example 14-7. The method has the following three parameters:

```
[in] int iYear, int iMonth, int iDay
```

The **SYSTEMTIME** structure is used to create the date/time value. It's used as the first parameter in a call to the *SystemTimeToVariant* function. The second parameter in this function is a reference to a double value containing a specific time. This double value is then used in the call to put_ExpiresAbsolute to change the absolute expiration date/time of the cache. Add the code shown in Example 14-7 to your component.

Example 14-7. Setting the Expiration from Cache for the ASP Page

```
STDMETHODIMP CJustInTime::setCacheDate(int iYear, int iMonth, int iDay)
{
    HRESULT hr;
    SYSTEMTIME st;
    double dtTime;

    // initialize memory
    ZeroMemory (&st, sizeof(st)) ;

    // set date
    st.wYear = iYear;
    st.wMonth = iMonth;
    st.wDay = iDay;

    // set time
    st.wHour = 13;
    st.wMinute = 13;

    SystemTimeToVariantTime(&st,&dtTime);

    hr=m_piResponse->put_ExpiresAbsolute(dtTime);

    return hr;
}
```

To test the new method, use the following script, *asp1405.asp*:

```
<%
Dim obj
Set obj = Server.CreateObject("asp1401.JustInTime")

obj.setCacheDate 2002, 12, 12

Response.Write Response.ExpiresAbsolute
%>
```

The result of running this script is a page with a date of 12/12/2002 1:13:00 P.M.

Other methods to control caching include two to get and set the CacheControl property. This property is used to control whether proxy servers can cache the ASP page contents. Passing a **BSTR** value equal to **Public** to the put_CacheControl method enables proxy caching.

The page's return status code can be accessed and controlled using the put_Status and get_Status methods. For instance, the following results in a dialog requesting a username and password when the page is accessed:

```
CComBSTR bstrObj("401 Unauthorized");

m_piResponse->put_Status(bstrObj);
```

Entering a valid network username and password will allow entry to the page.

Another **IResponse** method, AppendToLog, appends to the IIS log file. This is a useful method to output information for debugging and tracking purposes. The Response object's CharSet property can be set using the put_CharSet method. Writing to the web page without any Unicode-to-ANSI conversion is accomplished using the BinaryWrite method.

The **IResponse** interface's only collection is the write-only Cookies collection. You access the collection through the **IRequestDictionary** collection, and you work with an individual item using the **IWriteCookie** interface:

```
hr = m_piResponse->get_Cookies(&piRequestVariables);
if (FAILED(hr)) return hr;

hr = m_piResponse->get_Cookies(&pDict);
if (FAILED(hr)) return hr;

hr = pDict->get_Item(vtCookieName, &vtCookieDict);
if (FAILED(hr)) return hr;

pWriteCookie = (IWriteCookie*)(vtCookieDict.pdispVal);
if (FAILED(hr)) return hr;

hr = pWriteCookie->put_Item(vtCookieKey, bstrCookieVal);
```

The IApplication Interface

The Application object interface, **IApplicationObject**, can be used to store and retrieve information shared across all sessions. The information stored can be a single value or it can be a reference to an object. The values are stored either in the Application object's Contents collection, which includes all values added dynamically to the Application object, or in the Application object's StaticObjects collection, which includes all items added using the <OBJECT> tag in the *global.asa* file.

Appendix A covers the use of the *global.asa* file.

There are two methods you can use to get the Application object collections: get_Contents to get the contents and get_StaticObjects for the static objects. Both of these methods return another interface object, the **IVariantDictionary**, which you can use to enumerate through the collection or to access a specific item.

You can also use the get_Value method directly on **IApplicationObject** to get an item from either collection, and you can call the put_Value method to set an entry into the Contents collection. (You cannot add a member to the StaticObjects collection.)

To demonstrate getting and setting a value using the Contents collection, as well as using **IApplicationObject**'s get_Value, add a new method to the **asp1401**. JustInTime component named getContentValue that gets a value using get_Value and get_Item on the **IVariantDictionary** object, and then displays these values using the Response object. The method also removes all Application contents, one at a time, using the **IVariantDictionary**'s Remove method.

First, add a reference to **IApplicationObject** as a private class data member to *JustInTime.h*:

```
CComPtr<IApplicationObject> m_piApplication;
```

Next, add the code to instantiate the element within the Activate method:

```
// get Application
bstrProp = "Application";
hr = pProps->GetProperty( bstrProp, &vt ) ;
if (FAILED(hr)) return hr;

piDispatch = vt. pdispVal;
hr = piDispatch->QueryInterface( IID_IApplicationObject,
                (void**)&m_piApplication );
```

Add a line to release the **IApplicationObject** reference in the Deactivate method:

```
m_piApplication.Release();
```

Use Class View to add a new method named getContentValue that takes one **BSTR** input parameter, the name of the content item to display. Then add the code shown in Example 14-8. The method calls get_Value to retrieve the value of the item from the Application object and then calls get_Item to retrieve it directly from the Contents collection. Finally, the method removes the item from the Application object's collections.

Example 14-8. Getting Element from the Application Object's Contents Collection
```
STDMETHODIMP CJustInTime::getContentValue(BSTR bstrName)
{
   HRESULT hr = S_OK;
   _variant_t vtValue;

   // get specific item
   hr = m_piApplication->get_Value(bstrName, &vtValue);
   if (FAILED(hr)) return hr;

   // write value out
```

Example 14-8. Getting Element from the Application Object's Contents Collection (continued)

```
    m_piResponse->Write(vtValue);
    m_piResponse->Write(_variant_t("<p>"));


    // get the Contents collection
    IVariantDictionary* piVariantVariables;
    hr = m_piApplication->get_Contents(&piVariantVariables);
    if (FAILED(hr)) return hr;

    // get the item from the Contents collection
    hr = piVariantVariables->get_Item(_variant_t(bstrName),&vtValue);
    if (FAILED(hr)) return hr;

    // write value out
    m_piResponse->Write(vtValue);
    m_piResponse->Write(_variant_t("<p>"));

    // remove the item
    piVariantVariables->Remove(_variant_t(bstrName));

    return S_OK;
}
```

Test the component method with the following ASP test page (in *asp1406.asp*):

```
    <HTML>
    <HEAD>
    <TITLE>Developing ASP Components</TITLE>
    </HEAD>
    <BODY>
    <%
    'On Error Resume Next
    Dim obj
    Set obj = Server.CreateObject("asp1401.JustInTime")

    Application("pie") = "apple"

    obj.getContentValue "pie"

    %>
    </BODY>
    </HTML>
```

Storing information at the level of the Application object is especially helpful for such things as maintaining counts of items in stock for an online catalog system or perhaps maintaining a count of the number of people currently logged into the system. For information specific to the session, which is defined as the time a specific user logs into the application until they log out, the Session object must be accessed through the **ISessionObject** interface, discussed next.

You can add objects to the Application Contents collection, but use caution: if the object isn't both- or neutral-threaded, you'll receive an error. For best performance purposes, assign only nonobject, scalar data to the Contents collection.

The ISession Interface

In C++, Session object information and methods are accessed using the ISessionObject interface. The Session object is similar to the Application object in that variables and other objects can be stored within the object's Contents and StaticObjects collections and can be accessed or altered as long as the Session object is in scope. The primary difference between the Application and Session objects is that the Session object lasts from the time a user accesses the first web page of an ASP application until the user's session times out or she logs out of the application.

To work with the Session contents, use the get_Contents or get_StaticObjects method to access an IVariantDictionary interface, and then use it to enumerate through the collection. Or access an individual item using the ISessionObject get_Value or the IVariantDictionary get_Item method.

 You can assign apartment-threaded objects to the Session object's collections, but to do so ties the Session down to a specific thread—which means that client requests can be processed only by a specific thread, rather than whatever thread is next available. This will severely impact performance.

When working with the Application object, you accessed data from its collection individually when you called the example getContentValue method. In this section, you'll try out the enumeration capability provided by IVariantDictionary by traversing the Session object's Contents collection.

First, add a new private class member of type ISession to the JustInTime component's header file:

```
CComPtr<ISessionObject> m_piSession;
```

Next, instantiate this new member in the component's Activate method:

```
// get Session
bstrProp = "Session";
hr = pProps->GetProperty( bstrProp, &vt ) ;
if (FAILED(hr)) return hr;
```

```
piDispatch = vt. pdispVal;
hr = piDispatch->QueryInterface( IID_ISessionObject,
                     (void**)&m_piSession );
```

Then release the member in the Deactivate method:

```
m_piSession.Release();
```

Add a new method named listContents using Class View. It takes no parameters. Then use Class View to add the source code shown in Example 14-9. The method obtains a reference to an **IVariantDictionary** interface using the Session object's get_Contents method. It then calls get_NewEnum on the interface to return a pointer to an **IUnknown** interface and calls QueryInterface to obtain a reference to an **IEnumVARIANT** interface. The **IEnumVARIANT** interface is used to enumerate through the collection, and the Response object is used to display the name/value pairs.

Example 14-9. Enumerating Through the Session's Contents Collection

```
STDMETHODIMP CJustInTime::listContents()
{
    HRESULT hr;
     IEnumVARIANT* piEnum;
    IUnknown* piUnk;
    IVariantDictionary* piVariant;

    hr = m_piSession->get_Contents(&piVariant);
    if (FAILED(hr)) return hr;

    hr = piVariant->get__NewEnum(&piUnk);
    if (FAILED(hr)) return hr;

    hr = piUnk->QueryInterface(IID_IEnumVARIANT, (void **)&piEnum);
    if (FAILED(hr)) return hr;

    piUnk->Release();

    _variant_t vtItem, vtValue;
    while (S_OK == piEnum->Next(1,&vtItem,NULL)) {

        m_piResponse->Write(vtItem);
        m_piResponse->Write(_variant_t("="));

        // get value
        m_piSession->get_Value(_bstr_t(vtItem), &vtValue);
        m_piResponse->Write(vtValue);
        m_piResponse->Write(variant_t("<p>"));
    }

    piEnum->Release();

     return S_OK;
}
```

Test the component method using the following ASP page, *asp1407.asp*, which contains script that creates five entries in the Session's Contents collection before calling the method:

```
<%
Dim obj
Set obj = Server.CreateObject("asp1401.JustInTime")

Session("one") = 1
Session("two") = 2
Session("three") = 3
Session("four") = 4
Session("five") = 5

obj.listContents
%>
```

The result of accessing this test page is a listing of all five elements in the Contents collection and their respective values.

The Session object also has information about the user session, such as what code page is used to display characters, a value that can be accessed and altered using the get_CodePage and put_CodePage methods, respectively, and what locale is in use, a setting that can be modified and accessed with the get_LCID and put_LCID methods, respectively. The last two methods are especially important if your component must support an international clientele.

The session timeout can be changed or read by using the get_Timeout and set_ Timeout methods. You can also access the specific session ID with get_SessionID, but this should not be used directly by ASP developers. Session identifiers may not be unique across application runs.

The session can be abandoned using the Abandon method, which releases all resources currently held by the Session object.

The IRequest Interface

The Request object and its associated C++ interface, **IRequest**, contain information about the client, such as what browser is being used, client certificate information, the protocol, the server port, and so on. It can also be used to access information provided by the user, either attached as data to the page URL or from HTML forms.

Most of the **IRequest** information is stored in collections, which are accessible by using the **IRequestDictionary** helper interface. The **IRequestDictionary** object works similarly to **IVariantDictionary** in that you can access elements individually, or you can obtain an enumerator from the object and enumerate all values in the collection.

One of the `IRequest` collections is the Form collection, containing name/value pairs from HTML forms that use the `POST` method. You can obtain a reference to this collection using the get_Form method and then either access each element by the form element name or access all form elements using enumeration.

Another collection is the QueryString collection, containing name/value pairs from forms posted using the default `GET` method or attached to the page's URL. An example of an "entry" within the QueryString collection is the following:

```
<a href="test.asp?test=one&test2=two&test3=three">Test</a>
```

The individual collection elements are:

```
test=one
test2=two
test3=three
```

However, if all three name-value pairs had the same name, as with:

```
<a href="test.asp?test=one&test=two&test=three">Test</a>
```

the collection element would be:

```
test=one,two,three
```

Assigning different values to the same named element causes a list of values to be assigned to that named element.

If your site supports digital certificates for security and you need to access information about the client certificate, you can use the get_ClientCertificate method and access the certificate fields directly or again use enumeration.

Your code can access cookies from the Cookies collection using the get_Cookies method. In this case, you might actually want to access each cookie individually. The following code demonstrates how simple it can be to access one specific cookie:

```
CComVariant vt(OLESTR("cookie_name")), vtValue;
CComPtr<IRequestDictionary> piRequestVariables;
hr = m_piRequest->get_Cookies(&piRequestVariables);

// if failure, return
if (!FAILED(hr))

piRequestVariables->get_Item(vt, &vtValue);
```

Another `IRequest` object collection is the ServerVariables collection, which has several server environment variables. A useful component for an ASP developer is one that will return all of the server environment variable names and associated values, if any. With this, you can check out the communication between client and server, how data is returned when accessed from `IRequestDictionary`, what the identifying string for a specific browser looks like, and so on.

To see what the environment variables look like in your own setup, use Class View to add a new method (with no parameters) called showVariables to asp1401.JustInTime. You'll also need to add IRequest as a new private component class member to *JustInTime.h*:

```
CComPtr<IRequest> m_piRequest;
```

Then add the code to instantiate the class member in Activate:

```
// get Request
bstrProp = "Request";
hr = pProps->GetProperty( bstrProp, &vt ) ;
if (FAILED(hr)) return hr;

piDispatch = vt. pdispVal;
hr = piDispatch->QueryInterface( IID_IRequest,
                    (void**)&m_piRequest );
```

and release the member in the Deactivate method:

```
m_piRequest.Release();
```

Finally, add the code shown in Example 14-10. The method code is very similar to that shown in Example 14-9, except that it obtains a reference to the IRequest-Dictionary interface by calling the IRequest object's get_ServerVariables method. Once it has a reference to IRequestDictionary, it obtains an enumerator from the object and enumerates through the server variables.

Example 14-10. Enumerating Through the ServerVariables Collection

```
STDMETHODIMP CJustInTime::showVariables()
{
    HRESULT hr;
    IEnumVARIANT* piEnum;
    IUnknown* piUnk;
    IRequestDictionary* piDict;
    ULONG lValue;

    // get server variables
    hr = m_piRequest->get_ServerVariables(&piDict);
    if (FAILED(hr)) return hr;

    // get enumerator
    hr = piDict->get__NewEnum(&piUnk);
    if (FAILED(hr)) return hr;

    hr = piUnk->QueryInterface(IID_IEnumVARIANT, (void **)&piEnum);
    if (FAILED(hr)) return hr;

    // enumerate through collection, printing out values
    _variant_t vtItem, vtValue;
    while (S_OK == piEnum->Next(1,&vtItem,&lValue)) {

        m_piResponse->Write(vtItem);
```

Example 14-10. Enumerating Through the ServerVariables Collection (continued)

```
        m_piResponse->Write(_variant_t("="));

        // get value
        piDict->get_Item(vtItem, &vtValue);
        m_piResponse->Write(vtValue);
        m_piResponse->Write(variant_t("<br>"));
    }

    // clean up
    piEnum->Release();
    piUnk->Release();

    return S_OK;
}
```

Test the component method using *asp1408.asp*, containing the following script:

```
<%
Dim obj
Set obj = Server.CreateObject("asp1401.JustInTime")

obj.showVariables
%>
```

Figure 14-7 shows some of the results of using this component method in my own environment.

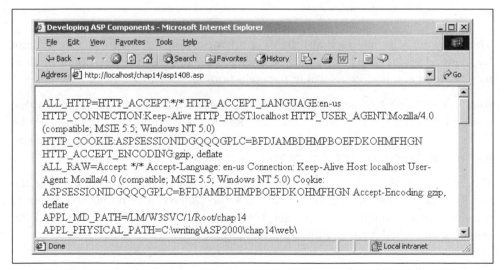

Figure 14-7. Server variables in my environment

If any of the ServerVariables, QueryString, or Form collection elements contain multiple items, such as the QueryString value mentioned earlier, the individual values can be accessed using the IStringList interface. As an example, assume that you want to retrieve the values of the item named `test` from the `IRequest` object. This item happens to be contained within the QueryString collection and contains an array of three values: 1, 2, and 3. The code to access these values using enumeration is:

```
IDispatch* pDispatch;
IStringList* pList;
CComVariant vt;
IUnknown* pUnknown = NULL;
IEnumVARIANT* pEnum = NULL;
ULONG lValue;

    m_piRequest->get_Item(bstrName, &pDispatch);
    hr = pDispatch->QueryInterface( IID_IStringList,
                (void**)&pList );

    // get the item from the Contents collection
    hr = pList->get__NewEnum(&pUnknown);
    if (FAILED(hr)) return hr

    hr = pUnknown->QueryInterface( IID_IEnumVARIANT,
                (void**)&pEnum );
    if (FAILED(hr)) return hr;

    // return the server variable and associated value
    while(S_OK == (pEnum->Next(1,&vt,&lValue))) {
       CComVariant vtValue;
       m_piResponse->Write(vt);
    }
```

The `IStringList` interface also has a get_Item method to access a specific item by name. As with all enumerator type interfaces, it also has the get_Count method to return the count of items within the collection.

Just as the `IRequest` get_Item method is used to obtain a reference to a value contained in the Cookies collection, the `IReadCookies` interface provides similar access to the values associated with the specific name. For the ClientCertificate collection, the `IRequestDictionary` interface is used to obtain the values.

You can read all of the information for the current request at once using the BinaryRead method, storing the results in a **SAFEARRAY**. The number of bytes to retrieve can be found using the get_TotalBytes method. You can also read the contents into a Variant using the Read method.

The IServer Interface

The last ASP built-in object to be discussed is the Server object and its associated interface, `IServer`. This interface has few methods and no collections. It is mainly used to handle URL or HTML encoding, to create a new server object instance, or to set or get the script timeout value.

For encoding, the URLEncode and HTMLEncode methods each takes a string from the server and applies its own encoding method, converting specific characters to special conversion values. As an example, URL encoding replaces spaces with the plus sign (+) and the percent sign with a hexadecimal value of %25. HTML encoding replaces the left and right angle brackets with &lt and &gt, respectively. Additional encoding methods exposed with the `IServer` interface are the URLPathEncode method, which applies URL encoding to all characters except those representing the path, such as the slash (/), and the MapPath method, which generates a physical file location given a relative path and the current server location. This latter method is particularly useful for accessing resources and opening files.

To try out encoding in your `JustInTime` component, add a reference to `IServer` as a private class member to the component in *JustInTime.h*:

```
CComPtr<IServer> m_piServer;
```

Next, instantiate it within Activate:

```
// get Server
bstrProp = "Server";
hr = pProps->GetProperty( bstrProp, &vt ) ;
if (FAILED(hr)) return hr;

piDispatch = vt. pdispVal;
hr = piDispatch->QueryInterface( IID_IServer,
                (void**)&m_piServer );
```

and release it within Deactivate:

```
m_piServer.Release();
```

Use Class View to add a new method called encodeValues. This method takes several `BSTR` input parameters, defined as:

```
[in] BSTR bstrHTML, BSTR bstrURL, BSTR bstrPath, BSTR bstrMap
```

Add the code shown in Example 14-11 to your component. In the code, one of the parameter strings is passed to each of the Server encode methods in turn, and the results are output to the web page using the Response object.

Example 14-11. Using the Server Encode Methods

```
STDMETHODIMP CJustInTime::encodeValues(BSTR bstrHTML, BSTR bstrURL,
                                BSTR bstrPath, BSTR bstrMap)
{
    _variant_t vtOut;
    CComBSTR bstrOut;
    _variant_t vtSeparator = "<p>";

    // HTML encoding
    m_piServer->HTMLEncode(bstrHTML, &bstrOut);
```

Example 14-11. Using the Server Encode Methods (continued)

```
    vtOut = bstrOut;
    m_piResponse->Write(vtOut);
    m_piResponse->Write(vtSeparator);

    // URL encoding
    m_piServer->URLEncode(bstrURL, &bstrOut);
    vtOut = bstrOut;
    m_piResponse->Write(vtOut);
    m_piResponse->Write(vtSeparator);

    // path encoding
    m_piServer->URLPathEncode(bstrPath, &bstrOut);
    vtOut = bstrOut;
    m_piResponse->Write(vtOut);
    m_piResponse->Write(vtSeparator);

    // path mapping
    m_piServer->MapPath(bstrMap, &bstrOut);
    vtOut = bstrOut;
    m_piResponse->Write(vtOut);


    return S_OK;
}
```

The Server object methods are pretty simple, with each taking an input string as a BSTR datatype and producing an output BSTR variable containing the encoded value. Error checking after each method call was omitted for brevity.

Test the page with the following script, *asp1409.asp*, which passes different strings for each encode method:

```
<%
Dim obj
Set obj = Server.CreateObject("asp1401.JustInTime")

Dim strHTML, strURL, strPath, strMap
strHTML = "<H1>This is a test</H1>"
strURL = "% this is a test % ++"
strPath = "test/test2/this is a test"
strMap = "/test/test2/"

obj.encodeValues strHTML, strURL, strPath, strMap
%>
```

The test page generates results similar to the following:

```
<H1>This is a test</H1>

%25+this+is+a+test+%25+%2B%2B

test/test2/this%20is%20a%20test

E:\Inetpub\wwwroot\New Folder\test2
```

Note that the first line, which contains the HTML-encoded string, actually prints out the HTML <H1> tags without producing HTML formatting.

The `IServer` object also can set the ASP script block timeout value. This controls how long a specific scripting block can take for processing. The two methods to access and set this value are get_ScriptTimeOut and put_ScriptTimeOut.

A method used more commonly in ASP script than in ASP components is CreateObject. This can be used to create an instance of an object given a specific programmatic identifier and is used in your ASP test pages to instantiate the ASP components you're creating. In Visual C++, this method can be used in a similar manner, as follows:

```
HRESULT hr = S_OK;
IDispatch* pDispatch = NULL;
ISomeObject* pObj;

hr = m_piServer->CreateObject(L"some.progid",&pDispatch);
if (FAILED(hr)) return hr;

// cast to interface object
hr = pDispatch->QueryInterface( IID_ISomeObject,
               (void**)&pObj );
if (FAILED(hr)) return hr;

// work with the new object
...
```

Instead of accessing identification information using the object's interface ID (IID) and class ID (CLSID) to create a new object using *CoCreateInstance* or the Object-Context CreateInstance method, you can use the program identifier (such as `asp1401.JustInTime`) to obtain a reference to this object. This returns a pointer to an `IDispatch` interface pointer, and its QueryInterface method is used to retrieve a pointer to the server component's interface pointer. At that point, all of the server component's methods and public properties are available for access. The object does not have to be released, since its lifetime ends when the ASP script containing the enclosing component is finished.

Error Handling

In the examples, most of the ObjectContext or ASP object methods return an `HRESULT` value. This value can be checked to see if the method call was successful (returning a value of `S_OK`) or if it failed in some way. The `FAILED` macro is used to test for failure, and if this macro returns a `true`, component processing is terminated and control of the process is returned to the calling ASP page. The failure also generates an error for the ASP page that is automatically handled by IIS 5. 0. Within IIS 5.0, error handling is passed to a special page that retrieves ASP error information and outputs this information to the page.

If you use something such as **On Error Resume Next** in VBScript or exception handling in JavaScript or PerlScript, the default error processing won't occur, and you have to provide your own error handling. One way of doing this is to use **HRESULT** and terminate the component when an error occurs.

The reason you have to test the results of accessing each object's method is that exception handling is not automatically enabled for components created using ATL. This is the case because the C runtime library required for exception handling is not automatically included as part of the code-generation process, since this can increase the size of the component. However, exception handling can be manually turned on, especially when using MFC or the **import** directive, discussed later in this section.

Add exception handling to a project by accessing Project → Settings, switching to the C/C++ tab, selecting C++ Language from the Category dropdown, and then checking the Enable Exception Handling option.

When you create an instance of a new object, if you don't provide exception handling and the object cannot be instantiated, its reference is set to a value of **NULL**. You can check to see if any new object is **NULL** before using it.

A technique you can use to create an object safely, regardless of whether exception handling is implemented, is to use the ATL **ATLTRY** macro. **ATLTRY** can be used with a **new** method and actually surrounds the object creation expression. It can also be used when creating a new CComBSTR object:

```
ATLTRY(CComBSTR bstrHeader(""));
```

The macro is defined within *ATLBASE.H* as:

```
#if defined (_CPPUNWIND) &
    (defined(_ATL_EXCEPTIONS) | defined(_AFX))
#define ATLTRY(x) try{x;} catch(...) {}
#else
#define ATLTRY(x) x;
#endif
```

Basically, if ATL exception handling is enabled, the macro wraps the code within a **try**...**catch** block. Otherwise, it just processes the code as is. Regardless of which approach is taken, a failure in instantiation results in the attribute being set to **NULL**, which can then be tested in the code.

As we saw when discussing basic ATL component creation options, choosing the option that adds support for the **ISupportErrorInfo** interface enables error handling. This option adds the following method to the component:

```
STDMETHODIMP CClass:InterfaceSupportsErrorInfo(REFIID riid)
{
    static const IID* arr[] =
    {
        &IID_Icssp,
    };
    for (int i=0;i<sizeof(arr)/sizeof(arr[0]);i++)
    {
        if (InlineIsEqualGUID(*arr[i],riid))
            return S_OK;
    }
    return S_FALSE;
}
```

The InterfaceSupportsErrorInfo method is invoked from the client to check if the component supports the **IErrorInfo** interface. This interface, in turn, supports passing error information from the component to the client. In the case of the Visual C++ component being invoked from within a VBScript block in an ASP page, the error information is accessed from the Err object. However, to create the error information, the ATL AtlReportError method is used.

The AtlReportError method basically adds information to the Error object using the methods exposed for the **IErrorInfo** interface. It is an overloaded function, which means that there are variations of the same function call, each accepting different sets of parameters. However, for creating an ASP object, the function prototype used most often is the following:

```
HRESULT WINAPI AtlReportError( const CLSID& clsid, LPCOLESTR lpszDesc,
                        const IID& iid = GUID_NULL, HRESULT hRes = 0 );
```

The following are the parameters passed to the function:

clsid
    The component's class identifier, which can be found in the component's header file

lpszDesc
    The description of the error

iid
    The component's interface identifier, which can be found in the component's header file

hRes
    The **HRESULT** for the error

The *clsid* and *iid* values can be pulled from the object's header file. For the example component created earlier in this chapter, the values are **CLSID_First** and **IID_IFirst**, respectively. *lpszDesc* is a string used to provide a meaningful error message to the ASP developer.

The HRESULT value is the result returned from the component. This is set to S_OK if no error occurs, and to a predefined error code for a specific error when an error occurs. The ASP application can access this value and provide different handling routines for different types of errors.

To demonstrate how to use error handling with your components, create a new Visual C++ project and name it **asp1403**. Don't add support for MTS or MFC. When the project files are generated, create a new ATL object using the Simple Object option and name this **test**. In the object's Attributes tab, change the threading model to Both, and make sure Dual and Aggregation Support are checked. Also check the Support ISupportErrorInfo option.

When the new component is generated, add the *comdef.h* header file to the header file in order to use the COM support objects:

```
#include <comdef.h>
```

Add a new method named sayHello that takes two parameters:

```
[in] BSTR bstrName, [out,retval] BSTR* pbstrMessage
```

This method is like the ones named sayHello that you've done before—it takes a name as a string, concatenates it with a greeting, and returns the greeting to the calling ASP script. What's different is that it uses error handling to provide a custom error message. Add the code shown in Example 14-12 to your new component.

Example 14-12. Using Custom Error Handling

```
STDMETHODIMP CTest::sayHello(BSTR bstrName, BSTR* pbstrMessage)
{
    HRESULT hr = S_OK;

   _bstr_t bstrNm = bstrName;
    // to work with header
   if (bstrNm.length() == 0) {
      hr = CTL_E_ILLEGALFUNCTIONCALL;
      LPCOLESTR lpError = L"You must provide a name for the message";
      AtlReportError(CLSID_Test,lpError,IID_ITest,hr);
      return hr;
   }
   else {
       CComBSTR bstrHeader = "Hello ";
      if (!bstrHeader)
           return CTL_E_OUTOFMEMORY;

      bstrHeader.Append(bstrName);

      *pbstrMessage = bstrHeader.Detach();
   }
   return S_OK;
}
```

The method checks the name and if its length is zero (no name provided), an illegal function call error is created. However, instead of using the default error message (which isn't too meaningful), the method creates an error message and calls *AtlReportError* with the new message. In addition, the method also uses the **CTL_E_OUTOFMEMORY** error when the new message object couldn't be created (is set to **NULL**). This value is equivalent to the out-of-memory error used in VBScript.

Test your new component with the following script, contained in *asp1410.asp*:

```
<%
On Error Resume Next
Dim obj
Set obj = Server.CreateObject("asp1403.test")

Dim str
Dim name

str = obj.sayHello(name)
If Err.Number <> 0 Then
    Response.Write Err.Description
Else
    Response.Write str
End If
%>
```

Notice the **On Error Resume Next** error-handling statement. This tells IIS to continue processing with the next statement after the statement that generated the error. The ASP page generates an error because the name string is empty. Changing the string to contain some name results in the message being displayed.

Error handling using the Error object isn't the only approach you can take in your ASP components. In several of the chapters following this one, external libraries to provide support for certain technologies such as MSMQ for messaging and ADO for data access are imported into the component, using the **#import** directive.

The **#import** directive not only provides support for the objects and constants within the ASP component, it also wraps all objects in containers known as *smart pointers*. Smart pointers simplify access to the interfaces supported in the library. Smart pointers also wrap COM exception handling around most of the interface methods. With this, you can use exception handling in your component to process an error in a controlled manner. For demonstrations of this, see the next chapter on using ADO with your C++ components.

15

Adding Data Access to C++ Components with ADO

The introduction of ActiveX Data Objects (ADO) greatly simplified data access from within applications, including access from within ASP application components. ADO provides a small set of easy-to-use objects for the most common data access operations, such as connecting to a data source, issuing a data command, and processing data returned from a query.

This book has presented numerous examples of using ADO within a Visual Basic environment, but this technology is just as easily accessible from Visual C++— especially with the help of smart pointers through the use of the Visual C++ import directive. This chapter looks at examples of working with ADO from Visual C++ using smart pointers.

This chapter does not provide a detailed review of ADO or of the concepts of using ADO from ASP components. You'll want to read Chapter 8, *Creating ASP/ADO Components*, first to get an understanding of how ASP components can work with ADO. Then you can apply this understanding to C++ components by trying out the examples in this chapter. After working with these examples, you'll have the background necessary to implement the data access techniques discussed in Chapter 9, *Creating an ASP Middle Tier with ADO*, using Visual C++.

ADO Access in Visual C++

ADO consists of a set of interfaces you can access directly in your C++ components. However, if you're using Visual C++, you'll want to take advantage of Microsoft's *import directive*, which imports the objects' type library and wraps each interface in *smart pointers*, making access to the interfaces almost as easy as accessing the same objects in Visual Basic.

To import the ADO type library, add the following to your C++ components, usually in the component's C++ file:

```
#import "C:\Program Files\Common Files\System\ADO\msado15.dll" \
    no_namespace rename("EOF", "EndOfFile")
```

This statement imports the type library included within the ADO component's dynamic link library (*msado15.dll*) into the C++ component. The ADO namespace is not used, which means that none of the ADO functionality has to be preceded with the ADO namespace alias. Additionally, the EOF symbol in ADO is renamed to EndOfFile. The EOF symbol is usually designated as a –1 value in most C++ applications, and not renaming the value results in compiler errors.

When using the import statement, you can get a warning message similar to the following::

```
warning C4146: unary minus operator applied to unsigned type,
result still unsigned
```

You can disregard this, since it has no impact on your component.

The **import** directive takes the type library and generates a set of header files based on the library contents. One effect of this process is that you can access properties using a set of generated Get- and Put- methods, such as PutConnectionTimeout to set a connection timeout. You can also set and get the properties directly, in a manner similar to that in VBScript or in Visual Basic. So, to set the Connection object's timeout property value, you can use the following:

```
pConnection->ConnectionTimeout = 30;
```

The **import** directive also wraps the object method calls in COM error exception handling so that an error is thrown, and you don't have to test the results after making each method call. To enable exception handling for the component project, select Project/Settings from the menu and then select the C/C++ tab. Change the Category to C++ Language and check the option labeled Enable Exception Handling.

The ADO Object Model

A few years back, Microsoft came up with the concept of Universal Data Access— using the same data access methods to process data from files, databases, email systems, and other sources. To implement the concept, Microsoft created OLE DB—techniques to work with any data source that can be queried or updated.

To work with a new type of data source, such as a database or a file system, an OLE DB provider is implemented. The underlying mechanism to work directly with the data is hidden from application developers. Instead, they can access a standard set of interfaces that provide consistent data access regardless of the type of data source.

OLE DB is powerful, but not necessarily trivial to use. So Microsoft provided a set of COM objects that are simple to use and that provide a layer of functionality above OLE DB. Best of all, these COM objects, known as ActiveX Data Objects, or ADO, can be accessed in different programming languages, including automation-only languages such as VBScript.

The ADO object model is a small set of objects that has only recently been extended by adding two new objects. The basic ADO objects are the Connection object, used to control the connection to a data source; the Command object, used for executing a data command, including ones with parameters; and the Recordset object, used to process the data returned from a data query.

To support these main objects, the Field object is used to hold field information related to data returned in a Recordset, and the Parameter object is used to support input or output parameters to a parameterized command. Data source errors are reported in the Error object.

Not all OLE DB providers implement the same functional support. To get OLE DB provider-specific implementation details, each ADO object has a Properties collection consisting of Property objects, each of which contains a property name-value pair with values specific to the provider being used.

Starting with ADO 2.5, two new objects have been added to the ADO model: the Record and Stream objects. The Record object is used to work with folder-based data, such as files in a filesystem, and email messages. The Stream object is used to work with the binary stream associated with a file or a message.

Other ADO objects, DataControl and DataFactory, are associated with Remote Data Service (RDS) and are not covered in this book.

This chapter demonstrates how you can access the Connection, Command, Recordset, Record, and Stream objects from Visual C++ components.

The Connection Object

The Connection object is used to obtain a connection to a data source that can be used throughout the lifetime of the component. Technically you don't need to create a Connection object—the Command, Record, and Recordset objects can connect to the data source directly. However, the Connection object can be used when more than one object is connecting to the data source, to use the same connection for all data access. The Connection object can also be used to provide more finite control of the connection, such as changing the default connection timeout value.

 The database used in these examples is the Weaver database, described in Appendix B, *The Weaver Database*.

The Connection object has several properties and methods. For instance, to change the timeout for a connection, you can set this value using:

```
pConnection->PutConnectionTimeout(30);
```

The most commonly accessed Connection property is the ConnectionString, and the most commonly accessed method is Open, to open up a new data source connection. You could also add the connection string into the Open method:

```
pConnection->Open(L"DSN=weaver;uid=sa;pwd=","","",NULL);
```

The four parameters of the Open method are the connection string, the user ID, the password, and an open connection option—all of which are optional. However, if you don't provide the connection information in the Open method, you'll have to specify it by setting the ConnectionString property:

```
pConnection->PutConnectionString(L"DSN=weaver;uid=sa;pwd=");
```

The connection string just shown uses a DSN, defined using the ODBC Administrator, to identify the data source. ODBC data sources, such as an Access database, are accessed through the OLE DB Provider for ODBC Drivers. You can specify an OLE DB provider directly in the connection string, such as the following, using the OLE DB Provider for SQL Server:

```
pConnection->PutConnectionString(L"Provider=SQLOLEDB;server=FLAME;
                                 database=weaver;uid=sa;pwd");
```

You can execute a data command through the Connection object directly using the Execute method. Or you can use the Connection object to establish a connection for a Recordset or Command object, as will be demonstrated later in the chapter.

Earlier I mentioned that all ADO objects have a Properties collection containing OLE DB provider information. In your first example for this chapter, you'll create an ASP component that creates an instance of the Connection object and accesses its Properties collection. The component then enumerates through this collection, listing the property name-value pairs by using the built-in ASP Response object. This object is created as a component data member and is instantiated through just-in-time (JIT) activation, implemented through the IObjectControl interface.

The database connection string is taken from the ASP Application object's collections. The value is set within the *global.asa* file for the ASP application, as follows:

```
<SCRIPT LANGUAGE=VBScript RUNAT=Server>
Sub Application_OnStart

Application("connection") = "Provider=SQLOLEDB;server=FLAME;
                                    database=weaver;uid=sa;pwd"
'Application("connection") = "DSN=weaver;uid=sa;pwd="

End Sub
</SCRIPT>
```

This script has both the Access and the SQL Server connection strings, but the SQL Server connection is the one currently active. You'll need to adjust the appropriate connection string to reflect your own environment.

Create a new Visual C++ project using the ATL COM AppWizard. Name the project **asp1501**, and don't check the MTS or MFC options. When the project is generated, create a new ATL object using the MTS object template, and name it **connection**. Choose the support for **IObjectControl** but not the option to support pooling.

 You can also use the Simple Object option to create the component. See Chapter 14, *Creating C++ ASP Components*, for information about adding in support for **IObjectControl** manually.

Open the generated *connection.h* header file, move the generated object member m_spObjectContext to the **private** section, and add two other members—one for the ASP Response object, and one for a connection string:

```
private:
    CComPtr<IObjectContext> m_spObjectContext;
    CComPtr<IResponse>m_piResponse;
    _bstr_t m_bstrConnection;
```

The Response object is used to output the results of the component in your example. You'll also need to add in support for both COM+ Services and the ASP type libraries by adding the following include files to *connection.h*:

```
#include <comsvcs.h>
#include <asptlb.h>
#include <comdef.h>
```

The last include file adds support for the COM helper objects such as **_variant_t** and **_bstr_t**.

Also add the COM+ Services library module to the project by accessing Project →
Settings from the menu, selecting the Link tab, and adding *comsvcs.lib* to the end
of the Library/Object Modules list.

To complete adding in support for JIT, modify the generated `IObjectControl`
methods to include the code shown in Example 15-1. In the code, the ASP
Response and Application objects are created, and the database connection string
retrieved from the Application object's collections and assigned to the object's data
member.

*Example 15-1. JIT Implementation, Setting Response Object and Data Source Connection
String*

```
HRESULT Cconnection::Activate()
{
   HRESULT hr = S_OK;
   CComVariant vt;
   CComPtr<IGetContextProperties> pProps; //Context Properties

   IDispatch* piDispatch = NULL;

   // get ObjectContext
    hr = CoGetObjectContext(IID_IObjectContext,
                                (void **)&m_spObjectContext);

   if (FAILED(hr)) return hr;

   // get Context Properties
   hr = m_spObjectContext->QueryInterface( IID_IGetContextProperties,
             (void**)&pProps );
   if (FAILED(hr)) return hr;

   // get Response property
   hr = pProps->GetProperty( _bstr_t("Response"), &vt ) ;
   if (FAILED(hr)) return hr;

   piDispatch = vt. pdispVal;
   hr = piDispatch->QueryInterface( IID_IResponse,
                    (void**)&m_piResponse );
   if (FAILED(hr)) return hr;

   // get connection string
   CComPtr<IApplicationObject> pApplication;

   hr = pProps->GetProperty(_bstr_t("Application"),&vt);
   if (FAILED(hr)) return hr;

   piDispatch = vt. pdispVal;
   hr = piDispatch->QueryInterface( IID_IApplicationObject,
                    (void**)&pApplication );
   if (FAILED(hr)) return hr;
```

Example 15-1. JIT Implementation, Setting Response Object and Data Source Connection String (continued)

```
    CComVariant vtConn;
    CComBSTR bstrName("connection");
    hr = pApplication->get_Value(bstrName,&vtConn);

    if (FAILED(hr)) return hr;

    m_bstrConnection = vtConn;

    return S_OK;
}

BOOL Cconnection::CanBePooled()
{
    return TRUE;
}

void Cconnection::Deactivate()
{
    m_piResponse.Release();
    m_spObjectContext.Release();
}
```

Since you're using JIT, you'll need to add your new component to a COM+ application before you access it from an ASP application. In fact, since all of the components in this chapter use JIT, you might want to create a COM+ application for use for this chapter. (See Chapter 5, *COM+ Services and ASP Components and Applications*, for information about creating a COM+ application.)

Next, add a new parameterless method to the component using Class View, and name it showProperties. Once the method prototype has been generated, add the code shown in Example 15-2 to implement the method. The method creates an instance of the Connection smart pointer, sets its connection string, and opens the data source connection. Next, it calls the Connection object's GetProperties method to get the Properties collection. It gets the count of properties in the collection and uses this to control a loop, in which the code accesses each property from the collection and displays the property name and value.

Example 15-2. Show All the Connection Properties

```
// print out contents
// of Connection's Properties collection
STDMETHODIMP Cconnection::showProperties()
{
    _ConnectionPtr pConnection = NULL;
    PropertiesPtr props;
    PropertyPtr prop;
    _bstr_t bstrName;
    _variant_t varValue;
```

Example 15-2. Show All the Connection Properties (continued)

```
try {
   pConnection.CreateInstance(__uuidof(Connection));

   // open connection
   pConnection->PutConnectionString(m_bstrConnection);
   pConnection->Open("","","",NULL);

   // get properties and print out values
   props = pConnection->GetProperties();
   long ct;
   ct=props->GetCount();
   for (long l = 0; l < ct; l++) {

      // get Property
      prop =props->GetItem(l);
      bstrName = prop->GetName();
      varValue = prop->GetValue();

      // write out values
      m_piResponse->Write(_variant_t(bstrName + L" = "));
      m_piResponse->Write(varValue);
      m_piResponse->Write(variant_t("<br>"));
   }
   // close connection
   pConnection->Close();
}

// exception handling
catch (_com_error e) {
    m_piResponse->Write(_variant_t(e.Description()));
}

return S_OK;
}
```

As Example 15-2 shows, to create the instance of the Connection smart pointer, pass the name of the object to the __uuidof keyword. This gets the GUID of the object, which is then passed to the *CreateInstance* function. The CreateInstance method associated with the smart pointer internally calls the *CoCreateInstance* function and queries for the interface, which is then wrapped within the smart pointer.

If an error is thrown by any of the ADO methods, it is caught within the exception-handling catch block, and the error description is written out to the ASP page.

The following ASP test page, *asp1501.asp*, has script to create the component and call the showProperties method:

```
<%
Dim obj
Set obj = Server.CreateObject("asp1501.connection")
```

```
obj.showProperties
Set obj = Nothing
%>
```

The result of accessing this ASP page is a list of the property name-value pairs for the OLE DB provider. If you have support for both Access and SQL Server within your system, change the connection string from one to the other in *global.asa* to see how the property values change based on the OLE DB provider.

Aside from being able to connect to a data source or execute a specific command against a data source, you can also use the Connection object to access schema information about the data source from the OLE DB provider. You use the Open-Schema method to receive a Recordset object with whatever information you're seeking.

The first parameter to OpenSchema is a specific `SchemaEnum` value representing the type of query you're making. Allowable values can be `adSchemaColumns` to get columns, `adSchemaIndexes` to get index information, `adSchemaProcedures` to get stored procedure information, and so on. There are several values defined in `SchemaEnum` you can use.

The second parameter to OpenSchema is an array that represents constraints on the query and whose dimensions are predefined. The first array element represents the catalog name, the second the schema name, the third the table name, and so on, based on the type of query performed. For instance, if you specify a value of `adSchemaTables` in the first parameter, the array must have the following four elements: catalog, schema, table name, and type.

To demonstrate how OpenSchema works, add a new method to `asp1501.connection`, and name it showColumns. It does not take any parameters. In this method, add code to use the OpenSchema method to return the columns for all of the tables in the Weaver database and the numeric representation of their datatypes; the source code appears in Example 15-3. The method outputs this information in an HTML table.

For the example, showColumns accesses all of the table columns in the Weaver database, so it uses the `adSchemaColumns` value as the first parameter to Open-Schema, and a four-element array as the second parameter—all values but the first are set to null. The first array element is the table catalog name, in this case `weaver`. A `SAFEARRAY` is used to create the array, which is then assigned to a `VARIANT` to pass as a parameter. The recordset returned from OpenSchema is processed, and all table and column names and the column datatype are displayed in an HTML table. A running check is kept of the table name to suppress its repetition for each column.

Example 15-3. Show All Table Columnswith the Connection OpenSchema Method

```
STDMETHODIMP Cconnection::showColumns()
{
  _ConnectionPtr pConnection = NULL;
  _RecordsetPtr pRecs;

  _bstr_t bstrName;
  _variant_t varValue;

  try {

    // open connection
    pConnection.CreateInstance(__uuidof(Connection));
    pConnection->PutProvider(L"SQLOLEDB");
    pConnection->PutConnectionString(m_bstrConnection);
    pConnection->Open("","","",NULL);

    SAFEARRAY FAR* psa = NULL;
    SAFEARRAYBOUND rgsabound;
    _variant_t  var;
    _variant_t Array;

    // create safearray
    rgsabound.lLbound = 0;
    rgsabound.cElements = 4;
    psa = SafeArrayCreate(VT_VARIANT, 1, &rgsabound);

    // add array items
    var.vt = VT_EMPTY;
    long ix;
    ix = 1;
    SafeArrayPutElement(psa, &ix, &var);
    ix= 2;
    SafeArrayPutElement(psa, &ix, &var);
    ix = 3;
    SafeArrayPutElement(psa, &ix, &var);
    ix= 0;
    var.vt = VT_BSTR;
    char * s1 = "weaver";
    _bstr_t str = s1;
    var.bstrVal=str;
    SafeArrayPutElement(psa, &ix, &var);
    Array.vt = VT_ARRAY|VT_VARIANT;
    Array.parray = psa;

    // get records
    _variant_t table_name;
    _variant_t curr_table = "";
    _variant_t column_name;
    _variant_t data_type;
    pRecs = pConnection->OpenSchema(adSchemaColumns,&Array);

    // set up output table
```

Example 15-3. Show All Table Columnswith the Connection OpenSchema Method (continued)

```
m_piResponse->Write(_variant_t("<table border=2>"));
while(!(pRecs->EndOfFile)) {

    // get values
    table_name = pRecs->Fields->GetItem("TABLE_NAME")->GetValue();
    column_name = pRecs->Fields->GetItem("COLUMN_NAME")->GetValue();
    data_type = pRecs->Fields->GetItem("DATA_TYPE")->GetValue();

    // output results
    m_piResponse->Write(_variant_t("<TR><TD>"));
    if (table_name != curr_table) {
        curr_table = table_name;
        m_piResponse->Write(table_name);
    }
    m_piResponse->Write(_variant_t("</TD><TD>"));
    m_piResponse->Write(column_name);
    m_piResponse->Write(_variant_t("</TD><TD>"));
    m_piResponse->Write(data_type);
    m_piResponse->Write(_variant_t("</TD></TR>"));

    pRecs->MoveNext();
}
m_piResponse->Write(_variant_t("</table>"));

// close connection
pRecs->Close();
pConnection->Close();

}
catch (_com_error e) {
    m_piResponse->Write(_variant_t(e.Description()));
}

    return S_OK;
}
```

Regardless of what database you connect to (Access or SQL Server), the output from this new component method should be the same. Try this for yourself by accessing the following ASP test page, *asp1502.asp*:

```
<%
Dim obj
Set obj = Server.CreateObject("asp1501.connection")

obj.showColumns
Set obj = Nothing
%>
```

This last example used the Recordset object to process the results of the Open-Schema method call. You can try more Recordset functionality in the next section.

The Recordset Object

If your operation on the data source results in data being returned, you'll use the Recordset object to process this data. The Recordset object can be created by calling the Execute method of either the Connection or the Command object, or the object can be instantiated directly and the query can be executed in the Recordset object's Open method.

The Recordset object has several methods and properties, mostly having to do with defining the type of query being performed and how the data is processed. Some of the recordset properties must be set before a recordset is opened, and others can be set afterward. For instance, the CursorLocation and CursorType properties, as well as the ActiveConnection and LockType properties, must be set before the recordset is opened. The CursorLocation property determines whether the OLE DB client cursor is used with the result set or whether the cursor is provided by the driver or data source. The CursorType property sets the type of cursor used and determines the visibility of changes to the result set to other application users. The ActiveConnection property is either a Connection object or a connection string, and the LockType property sets the record locking.

Other properties can be, or must be, set after the result set is retrieved. The Filter and Sort properties filter and sort the records, respectively; the PageSize property sets the number of records showing per page; and the AbsolutePage property sets (or returns) the current page.

Most of the Recordset object's properties can be both read and modified, but some, such as State (whether the recordset is open or closed) are set by the OLE DB provider.

To demonstrate properties that are set before and after a recordset is opened, create a new Visual C++ project and name it **asp1502**. Use the ATL COM AppWizard to create the project, and don't check the MTS or MFC options.

Create a new ATL object using the MTS (or Simple) object option, as you did with **asp1501**. Name this object **page**, and add in support for **IObjectControl** (but not for pooling).

 If you use the MTS option, your component can't support pooling because this technology requires that the component support aggregation, and MTS components are created without support for aggregation. See Chapter 14 for more on creating poolable components.

Once the new component files are generated, modify the *page.h* and *page.cpp* files to add support for JIT, as discussed in the last section and shown in Example 15-1.

This includes adding the *comsvcs.lib* file to the project's library module list, adding include statements to the class header file, and creating the private class data members (m_spObjectContext, m_piResponse, and m_bstrConnection).

Add the import directive for ADO to the C++ file, just after the include file section:

```
#import "C:\Program Files\Common Files\System\ADO\msado15.dll" \
    no_namespace rename("EOF", "EndOfFile")
```

This new component accesses the WebPage table and displays the table's entries as hypertext links for the user to click on and open the specific page. Instead of listing all of the records within a specific web page, though, the Recordset object's page properties are used to create a multipage application containing groups of WebPage entries.

To improve performance and prevent unnecessary hits against the database, the recordset containing the WebPage rows is accessed once and persisted to a file. This file is then used when each page of the set is accessed, rather than having to go back to the database each time.

To create the persisted recordset, add a method to your new component named createRecordset. This method has no parameters. Add the code shown in Example 15-4 to query the WebPage table for all entries and to save the resulting set of data to a file using the Recordset object's Save method. The data is saved in the ADTG (Microsoft Advanced Data Tablegram) format.

To ensure that the database query isn't made if the persisted recordset file already exists, the createRecordset method uses standard I/O to test if the file exists. If it exists, the method exits before querying the database. To add support for standard I/O, add the following include statements just after the ADO **import** directive in *page.cpp*:

```
#include <stdio.h>
#include <share.h>
```

The query used with the Recordset object joins the WebPage and Dictionary tables to access data from both tables. The recordset is disconnected before it is persisted, so the CursorLocation property must be set to **adUseClient** in order to disconnect the recordset. Not doing so will result in an error when the recordset's ActiveConnection property is set to **NULL** (disconnected) after the query has been made.

You don't have to disconnect the recordset before saving the data. Normally, you would only disconnect a recordset that's being kept active for a time, such as one that's returned to an ASP script from a component method. This way, the active connection isn't held longer than necessary.

Example 15-4. Persisting a Recordset to a File

```
STDMETHODIMP Cpage::createRecordset()
{
    _RecordsetPtr pRecordset = NULL;
    _ConnectionPtr pConn = NULL;

    // test to see if file exists
    // if it does, exit method
    FILE *stream;
    if( (stream = _fsopen( "c:\\datasets\\set.adtg", "rt", _SH_DENYWR ))
                                                    != NULL ) {
        fclose(stream);
        return S_OK;
    }

    try {
        pConn.CreateInstance(__uuidof(Connection));
        pRecordset.CreateInstance(__uuidof(Recordset));

        // open connection
        pConn->Open(m_bstrConnection,"","",NULL);

        // open recordset
        _bstr_t bstrSource ="select WebPage.name, filename, page_type_cd, " +
                        _bstr_t("web_location from WebPage, Directory ") +
                        _bstr_t("where directory_id = Directory.id");

        pRecordset->PutCursorLocation(adUseClient);
        pRecordset->Open(_variant_t(bstrSource),pConn.GetInterfacePtr(),
                        adOpenForwardOnly, adLockReadOnly,adCmdText);

        // disconnect recordset
        pRecordset->PutRefActiveConnection(NULL);

        // close connection
        pConn->Close();

        // save to file
        pRecordset->Save(_variant_t("c:\\datasets\\set.adtg"),adPersistADTG);
        pRecordset->Close();

    }
    catch (_com_error e) {
        m_piResponse->Write(_variant_t(e.Description()));
    }

    return S_OK;
}
```

To disconnect the recordset, the Recordset object's PutRefActiveConnection method is used with a **NULL** parameter. PutRefActiveConnection sets the ActiveConnection property with a pointer to the Connection object rather than a variant. Using **NULL** disconnects the recordset from the connection.

To use the persisted recordset, create a second method called showPage, passing in the page size and current page as input parameters and the page count as an output parameter, as follows:

```
[in] int iPageSize, int iCurrentPage, [out,retval] int* iPageCount
```

This method, which is shown in Example 15-5, accesses the persisted recordset and sets the PageSize property to *iPageSize*, the page size value passed in as a parameter. Doing this sets the number of records that are contained within a dataset page. (A page is a numbered grouping of records that can be handled as a unit.) Setting the AbsolutePage property to *iCurrentPage*, the value of the current page parameter, determines which page is currently being processed in the method.

In the method, the recordset is opened, the page properties are set, and the records in the current page are traversed. The data within the records is written out to an HTML table, with each web page enclosed within a hypertext link to access the web page. The page count is returned from the method.

Example 15-5. Display WebPages Contained in a Persisted Recordset

```
STDMETHODIMP Cpage::showPage(int iPageSize, int iCurrentPage, int* iPageCount)
{
  _RecordsetPtr pRecordset = NULL;

  try {
    pRecordset.CreateInstance(__uuidof(Recordset));

    // open recordset
    pRecordset->Open(OLESTR("c:\\datasets\\set.adtg"),vtMissing,
                   adOpenForwardOnly, adLockReadOnly,adCmdUnknown);

    // adjust paging
    pRecordset->PutPageSize(iPageSize);
    pRecordset->PutAbsolutePage((PositionEnum)iCurrentPage);

    int iCt = 1;

    // cycle through page accessing rows
    while(iCt <= iPageSize) {
      m_piResponse->Write(_variant_t("<p><a href='http://"));
      m_piResponse->Write(pRecordset->Fields->GetItem(
                            _variant_t("web_location"))->GetValue());
      m_piResponse->Write(_variant_t("/"));
      m_piResponse->Write(pRecordset->Fields->GetItem(
                            _variant_t("filename"))->GetValue());
      m_piResponse->Write(_variant_t("'>"));
      m_piResponse->Write(pRecordset->Fields->GetItem(
                            _variant_t("name"))->GetValue());
      m_piResponse->Write(_variant_t("</a></p>"));

      pRecordset->MoveNext();
```

Example 15-5. Display WebPages Contained in a Persisted Recordset (continued)

```
        iCt++;
        if (pRecordset->EndOfFile)
            iCt = iPageSize + 1;
    }
    // return count of pages
    *iPageCount = pRecordset->GetPageCount();

    // close
    pRecordset->Close();
    }
    catch (_com_error e) {
        m_piResponse->Write(_variant_t(e.Description()));
    }

    return S_OK;

}
```

The data in the recordset's rows are accessed directly from the Fields collection by calling GetItem on Fields and then GetValue to get the actual value of the data. The Recordset object's MoveNext method traverses the rows, and the EndOfFile property tests whether the recordset is at the end of the rowset.

To test these two new methods, the ASP test script shown in Example 15-6, *asp1503.asp*, creates an instance of the new component and checks to see if a current page value is stored in the Request object's QueryString collection. If it isn't, the current page is set to 1—the first page—and the component's createRecordset method is called. Then the showPage method is called and is passed the current page and the page size (a value of 5, or five records per page). After the Recordset's data is displayed, a menu is created at the bottom of the page with links to other pages of data. Clicking on one of these links calls the ASP test page again, but this time the current page value is set.

Example 15-6. ASP Script to Display WebPage Entries

```
<%
Dim obj
Set obj = Server.CreateObject("asp1502.page")

' get current page, if any
Dim currPage, pageCount
currPage = CInt(Request.QueryString("currPage"))

' if first time accessing page
If currPage <= 0 Then
    currPage = 1
    obj.createRecordset
End IF
' show pages
pageCount = obj.showPage(5,currPage)
```

Example 15-6. ASP Script to Display WebPage Entries (continued)

```
' show page index
Response.Write "<hr> Page: "
For i = 1 to pageCount
   If i <> currPage Then
      Response.Write "<a href='asp1503.asp?currPage=" & _
                        i & "'>" & i & "</a>"
   Else
      Response.Write currPage
   End If
   Response.Write " "
Next
%>
```

As you can see in Figure 15-1, each of the WebPage records is created as a link, accessible directly from the page.

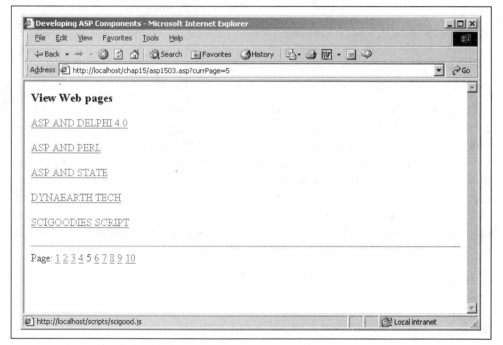

Figure 15-1. Displaying web page contents in an accessible, multipage format

The one problem with this example is that all of the WebPage records are accessible, including those normally not opened in a browser window, such as a JavaScript or CSS file. In addition, the pages are out of order and are listed by their entry in the database rather than alphabetically by the page name.

To fine-tune this application, you'll want to display only those files that can be opened within the browser, such as ASP, XML, or HTML pages. This fine-tuning can occur within the SQL query, by specifying a WHERE clause that accesses only pages with a certain type or types of page codes. The pages can also be ordered in the SQL through the use of the ORDER BY clause. However, you can also fine-tune the recordset after the results are returned by using the Recordset Filter and Sort properties.

Create a new method on `asp1502.page` and name it showSpecificPage. Like showPage, it has three parameters:

```
[in] int iPageSize, int iCurrentPage, [out,retval] int* iPageCount
```

This new method, which is shown in Example 15-7, is identical to that shown in Example 15-5, except that the recordset is both filtered and sorted before the records are processed. In the code, the rows are filtered on the **page_type_cd** field (accepting only HTM, APP, or XML pages) and then are sorted on the page names.

Example 15-7. Displaying Records After First Filtering and Sorting Them

```
STDMETHODIMP Cpage::showSpecificPage(int iPageSize, int iCurrentPage, int *iPageCount)
{
  _RecordsetPtr pRecordset = NULL;

  try {
    pRecordset.CreateInstance(__uuidof(Recordset));

    // open recordset
    pRecordset->Open(_variant_t("c:\\datasets\\set.adtg"),vtMissing,
                     adOpenForwardOnly, adLockReadOnly,adCmdUnknown);

    // set sort and filter
    pRecordset->PutFilter(OLESTR("page_type_cd = 'HTM'
                                 or page_type_cd = 'APP'
                                 or page_type_cd = 'XML'"));
    pRecordset->PutSort(L"name ASC");

    // paging properties
    pRecordset->PutPageSize(iPageSize);
    pRecordset->PutAbsolutePage((PositionEnum)iCurrentPage);

    int iCt = 1;

    // cycle through page processing rows
    while(iCt <= iPageSize) {
      m_piResponse->Write(_variant_t("<p><a href='http://"));
      m_piResponse->Write(pRecordset->Fields->GetItem(
                            _variant_t("web_location"))->GetValue());
      m_piResponse->Write(_variant_t("/"));
      m_piResponse->Write(pRecordset->Fields->GetItem(
                            _variant_t("filename"))->GetValue());
      m_piResponse->Write(_variant_t("'>"));
      m_piResponse->Write(pRecordset->Fields->GetItem(
                            variant_t("name"))->GetValue());
```

Example 15-7. Displaying Records After First Filtering and Sorting Them (continued)

```
    m_piResponse->Write(_variant_t("</a></p>"));

    pRecordset->MoveNext();
    iCt++;
    if (pRecordset->EndOfFile)
        iCt = iPageSize + 1;
    }

    // return page count
    *iPageCount = pRecordset->GetPageCount();

    // close
    pRecordset->Close();

}
catch (_com_error e) {
    m_piResponse->Write(_variant_t(e.Description()));
}

return S_OK;
}
```

Try out this new method with the ASP test page *asp1504.asp.*

Before leaving this section on the ADO Recordset object, I want to point out the technique used in the previous examples to access the returned data. As you have seen, the examples access the data values as variants directly from the Recordset object's Fields collection. However, with Visual C++, there is another approach you can use to access recordset data: using the IADORecordBinding interface.

The IADORecordBinding Interface

The IADORecordBinding interface is a Visual C++ extension to ADO that provides a way for you to bind the recordset data with a C++ class and to access the data as class members. As you traverse the recordset associated with the Recordset object, the data in the class members changes to reflect the current row.

To use this technique, you create a C++ class that's derived from the CADO-RecordsetBinding class and use the BEGIN_ADO_BINDING and END_ADO_BINDING macros to define the bound fields. Within these two macros, the binding is handled through another macro, depending on the type of data in the field. For instance, to bind to VARCHAR data, which is a variable-length character field, use the ADO_VARIABLE_LENGTH_ENTRY macro, providing the information necessary to perform the binding. Other macros are ADO_FIXED_LENGTH_ENTRY and ADO_NUMERIC_ENTRY, and there are variations of the macros based on the number of parameters passed into the macro call. The fields are bound to data members created in the new class.

To try out this data-binding technique, create a new header file for your project and name it *CTypeTable.h*. Add it to the project by right clicking on the Header Files folder in FileView and selecting Add Files to Folder, then add the code shown in Example 15-8 to your header file. The code in the header file creates your data bound class. The query used to create the recordset example is a complete table view that uses the **adCmdTable** command type and passes the name of the table when opening the recordset. In the example, the query is performed against any one of the Weaver database code tables, so the only fields that are returned are the code and the matching description. Your new class, named CTypeTable, has only two data members.

Example 15-8. C++ Class Used for Data Binding

```
#ifndef __TYPE_H_
#define __TYPE_H_

#include "icrsint.h"

#import "C:\Program Files\Common Files\System\ADO\msado15.dll" \
    no_namespace rename("EOF", "EndOfFile")

class CTypeTable : public CADORecordBinding
{
BEGIN_ADO_BINDING(CTypeTable)

    // code
    ADO_VARIABLE_LENGTH_ENTRY2(1, adVarChar, m_code,
        sizeof(m_code),lau_cdStatus, FALSE)

    ADO_VARIABLE_LENGTH_ENTRY2(2, adVarChar, m_description,
        sizeof(m_description), lau_descriptionStatus, FALSE)

END_ADO_BINDING()

public:

    CHAR m_code[4];
    ULONG lau_cdStatus;

    CHAR m_description[51];
    ULONG lau_descriptionStatus;

};
#endif
```

Notice in the example that an include file, *icrsint.h*, is added to the file. This header file adds support for the CADORecordBinding class and the macros discussed previously and prevents compiler errors.

The macro used for binding, ADO_VARIABLE_LENGTH_ENTRY2, takes the following parameters:

- The ordinal position of the field (in the selection list or table if a full table query is made)
- The datatype
- The buffer to hold the data (the class member)
- The size of the buffer
- A status field that can be used to check the status of the data access
- A true/false flag to set whether the value can be modified or not; read-only data is set to FALSE

Once the class is defined, add the following reference to the header file to your *page.cpp* file:

```
#include "CTypeTable.h"
```

Add a new method to the page component and name it showTypes. The only parameter it has is an input BSTR value containing the name of the code table:

```
[in] BSTR bstrTableName
```

The code for the method is shown in Example 15-9. In the method, the table name is passed as the first parameter to the Recordset object's Open method, and the command type is set to adCmdTable. However, after the recordset is opened, the recordset pointer's QueryInterface method is called, passing in a GUID of IADORecordBinding to obtain a reference to the IADORecordBinding interface. The result set is then bound to the C++ class through a call to BindToRecordset on this interface, passing in a reference to the C++ class. As the recordset is traversed, the code and description for each row are accessed through the C++ class data members and output to the web page.

Example 15-9. Using Visual C++ Extensions and Data Binding

```
STDMETHODIMP Cpage::showTypes(BSTR bstrTableName)
{
  _RecordsetPtr pRecordset = NULL;
  IADORecordBinding    *typeRs = NULL;
  CTypeTable tble;

  try {
    pRecordset.CreateInstance(__uuidof(Recordset));

    // open recordset
    pRecordset->Open(bstrTableName,m_bstrConnection,
                    adOpenForwardOnly, adLockReadOnly,adCmdTable);

    pRecordset->QueryInterface(__uuidof(IADORecordBinding),
                        (LPVOID*)&typeRs);
```

Example 15-9. Using Visual C++ Extensions and Data Binding (continued)

```
    typeRs->BindToRecordset(&tble);

    // process rows
    while(!(pRecordset->EndOfFile)) {
        m_piResponse->Write(_variant_t(tble.m_code));
        m_piResponse->Write(_variant_t(" = "));
        m_piResponse->Write(_variant_t(tble.m_description));
        m_piResponse->Write(_variant_t("<br>"));

        pRecordset->MoveNext();
    }
    // close
    pRecordset->Close();

    // release binding
    typeRs->Release();
  }
  catch (_com_error e) {
      m_piResponse->Write(_variant_t(e.Description()));
  }

  return S_OK;
}
```

Once the recordset is processed, it's closed and the binding is released.

Test this new component method against all of the Weaver code tables using the following script, found in *asp1505.asp*:

```
<%
Dim obj
Set obj = Server.CreateObject("asp1502.page")

Response.Write "<h3>PageType</h3>"
obj.showTypes "PageType"

Response.Write "<h3>StyleType</h3>"
obj.showTypes "StyleType"

Response.Write "<h3>MediaType</h3>"
obj.showTypes "MediaType"

Response.Write "<h3>ComponentType</h3>"
obj.showTypes "ComponentType"

Response.Write "<h3>XmlAuxType</h3>"
obj.showTypes "XmlAuxType"
%>
```

The result of running this ASP script is a page similar to that shown in Figure 15-2.

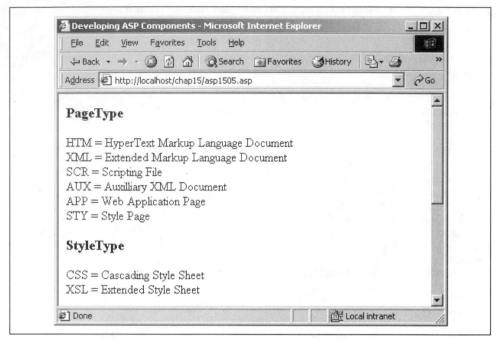

Figure 15-2. Results from accessing Weaver code tables using data binding

The queries used in the examples have not used a WHERE clause, nor have they used parameters. If you want to use parameters with a query or with a data source update, you'll need to use the ADO Command object, discussed next.

The Command Object

The Command object is used to execute a specific data source command—a query, a stored procedure call, or a data source update. As with the Connection object, the Command object's Execute method is used to execute the data command, and any data returned from the command has to be processed through the Recordset object. The Connection object can also execute a command that may or may not return a recordset. However, the Command object differs from the Connection object in allowing you to use parameters.

The Command object has a collection unique to it that consists of Parameter objects. These objects can be set and changed before the command is executed without having to re-create or rebuild the command. Best of all, when used in connection with the Command.Prepared property, the command can be compiled once and then executed many times—improving the performance of the application using the command.

In a more traditional client/server environment, the Command object can be pre-compiled, and different parameter values can be passed to it based on the user's actions. In an ASP environment, the Command object is discarded before the web page with the command results is ever returned to the user. The user's actions result in a second instance of the Command object being created, rather than the first one being reused.

Still, the Command object's Parameters collection and its Prepared property can be handy. For instance, if your application has more than one variation of a query to make, you can use the Command object to optimize the query, run it, and process the results—all before returning the page to the client.

To try out working with the Command object from a Visual C++ component, create a new Visual C++ project using the ATL AppWizard, and name the project **asp1503**. Do not select either MFC or MTS support.

Create a new component using the ATL Object Wizard, and name the component **cmnd**. Add in support for the Response object through the **IObjectControl** interface to access the connection string from the Application object by following the process described previously in Example 15-1. Add the code shown in Example 15-10 to your new *cmnd.cpp* file, and be sure to make the necessary adjustments to add header files and private data members in the *cmnd.h* header file.

Add the ADO import directive to the component, but this time add it to the component's header file, *cmnd.h*, just after the COM+ Services and ASP header files:

```
#import "C:\Program Files\Common Files\System\ADO\msado15.dll" \
    no_namespace rename("EOF", "EndOfFile")
```

Add a new method named showPages to the component that takes a pointer to a VARIANT array, as follows:.

```
VARIANT *pvarTypes
```

This array contains page type codes, each of which is used within a query at separate times.

The code for showPages appears in Example 15-10. In the method, an input parameter for the Command object is defined using the CreateParameter method, and it is added to the Command object's Parameters collection through the Append method. The Command object's Prepared property is set to **true** to pre-compile the Command object's query before the first Execute method call and to use this precompiled command on each subsequent command execution.

The incoming parameter array is copied to a **SAFEARRAY** structure for processing, and each page type code is pulled from the array and passed as a parameter value to the precompiled Command object.

Example 15-10. Using a Precompiled Command and Parameters to Query the Database

```
STDMETHODIMP Ccmnd::showPages(VARIANT *pvarTypes)
{
    HRESULT hr;

    _CommandPtr pCommand = NULL;
    _ParameterPtr pprmPageType = NULL;
    _RecordsetPtr pPages = NULL;

    // set command properties
    pCommand.CreateInstance(__uuidof(Command));
    pCommand->PutPrepared(true);
    pCommand->PutCommandText(
            L"select name from WebPage where page_type_cd = ?");
    pCommand->PutActiveConnection(_variant_t(m_bstrConnection));

    // create parameter
    pprmPageType = pCommand->CreateParameter(L"page_type_cd",
                                        adChar,adParamInput,3);
    pCommand->Parameters->Append(pprmPageType);

    // wrap with _variant_t for resource allocation and
    // deallocation
    _variant_t vtArray (pvarTypes);

    VARTYPE vt = V_VT(&vtArray);

    // if array, process as SAFEARRAY
    if (vt & VT_ARRAY)
        {

        LONG lLBound, lUBound;
        SAFEARRAY * psa;
        _variant_t vtVal;

        // copy variant array to SAFEARRAY
        SafeArrayCopy(*(vtArray.pparray), &psa);

        // get dimensions of array
        // get array bounds
        hr = SafeArrayGetLBound(psa, 1, &lLBound);
        if (FAILED(hr))
            return hr;
        hr = SafeArrayGetUBound(psa, 1, &lUBound);
        if (FAILED(hr))
            return hr;

        // get each value, print out
        for (long l = lLBound; l <= lUBound; l++) {
            hr = SafeArrayGetElement(psa, &l, &vtVal);
            if (FAILED(hr))
                return hr;
```

Example 15-10. Using a Precompiled Command and Parameters to Query the Database (continued)

```
        try {
          // get parameter value and execute command
          pprmPageType->Value = vtVal;

          // process results
          pPages = pCommand->Execute(NULL,NULL,adCmdText);
          showPageInfo(pPages,vtVal);

        }
        catch (_com_error e) {
          m_piResponse->Write(_variant_t(e.Description()));
        }
      }
      // cleanup
      SafeArrayDestroy(psa);
  }
    return S_OK;
}
```

Finally, the results of running the command are passed to another method, show-PageInfo, for output to an HTML table. This method is added manually to the component's header file, *cmnd.h*, to the private section after the ObjectContext and Response objects, as follows:

```
    private:
        CComPtr<IObjectContext> m_spObjectContext;
        CComPtr<IResponse>m_piResponse;
        void showPageInfo(_RecordsetPtr pPages, _variant_t vtVal);
```

The method references the ADO **_RecordsetPtr** smart pointer, which is why the ADO import directive needed to be added to the component's header file.

The new method is not exposed on the interface for external access, which is why you won't use the Class View page to add the method. The only reason the function is created as a class method is to give the method access to the component's private data members. Add the code for the method, shown in Example 15-11, to the *cmnd.cpp* file, just after the code for the showPages method.

Example 15-11. Method to Process the Recordset

```
void Ccmnd::showPageInfo(_RecordsetPtr pPages, _variant_t vtVal) {

    // print out recordset
    m_piResponse->Write(_variant_t("<h3>"));
    m_piResponse->Write(vtVal);
    m_piResponse->Write(_variant_t("</h3>"));
    m_piResponse->Write(_variant_t("<table border='1'
                                    cellpadding='5' cellspacing='0'>"));

    while (!(pPages->EndOfFile)) {
```

Example 15-11. Method to Process the Recordset (continued)

```
    m_piResponse->Write(_variant_t("<tr><td>"));
    m_piResponse->Write(pPages->Fields->GetItem(
                                _variant_t("name"))->GetValue());
    m_piResponse->Write(_variant_t("</td></tr>"));
    pPages->MoveNext();
  }

    m_piResponse->Write(_variant_t("</table>"));
}
```

Test the new component method using *asp1506.asp*, containing the following ASP
script:

```
<%
Dim obj
Set obj = Server.CreateObject("asp1503.cmnd")

Dim ary(2)
ary(0) = "APP"
ary(1) = "HTM"
ary(2) = "STY"

obj.showPages (ary)
%>
```

An array of page type codes is passed as the parameter to the showPages method.
The result of running the page is three HTML tables with WebPage rows that
match the page type codes.

A more common use of Command parameters is to call stored procedures. Stored
procedures can have input, output, and return parameter values, and the only way
to access the output and return parameters is to use the Command object.

To test parameters with stored procedure calls, create a stored procedure in the
SQL Server version of the Weaver database (Access does not support stored procedure calls). This procedure is called *sp_getpages*, and its syntax is:

```
CREATE PROCEDURE [sp_getpages]
(@output integer OUTPUT,
@page_type CHAR(3))
AS
BEGIN
SELECT name, filename
FROM WebPage
WHERE page_type_cd = @page_type
SELECT @output = COUNT(*)
FROM WebPage
WHERE page_type_cd = @page_type
IF (@output > 0)
  RETURN 0
ELSE
```

```
    RETURN 99
  END
  GO
```

This stored procedure takes one input parameter, a page type code, and returns an output parameter with the number of rows in the table that match the query. Additionally, the stored procedure also returns a value signaling whether any rows were found (a value of zero) or not (a value of 99).

Create a new method for `asp1503.cmnd` and name it showPagesWithParm. This method has two parameters, an input BSTR value for the page type code and an output BSTR pointer containing a message about the number of rows found:

```
[in] BSTR bstrType, [out,retval] BSTR* bstrRows
```

In the component method code, which is shown in Example 15-12, three parameters are created for the three parameters associated with the stored procedure call. The first parameter is the return value, defined with the `adParamReturnValue` type code; the second parameter is the output value, defined with the `adParamOutput` type; and the third is the input parameter.

Once the stored procedure call has been made, the showPageInfo method is called to process the results. Afterward, the smart pointer reference wrapping the Recordset object is released with a call to Release. A condition of accessing output parameters is that the recordset results must be processed, and the cursor must be beyond the rowset's end-of-file. A further requirement in Visual C++ is that the recordset must also be released. Once the recordset is released, the output and return parameters are accessed from the Parameter objects and their values processed.

Example 15-12. Using Input, Output, and Return Parameters

```
STDMETHODIMP Ccmnd::showPagesWithParm(BSTR bstrType, BSTR *bstrRows)
{

   _CommandPtr pCommand = NULL;
   _ParameterPtr pprmPageType = NULL;
   _ParameterPtr pReturn = NULL;
   _ParameterPtr pOutput = NULL;
   _RecordsetPtr pPages = NULL;
   ParametersPtr pParms = NULL;

   _variant_t vtConn = m_bstrConnection;
   _bstr_t bstrReturn;
   bstrReturn = L"No rows were found for page type code";

   // set command properties
   pCommand.CreateInstance(__uuidof(Command));
   pCommand->PutPrepared(true);
   pCommand->PutCommandText(L"sp_getpages");
```

Example 15-12. Using Input, Output, and Return Parameters (continued)

```
    pCommand->PutActiveConnection(vtConn);

    try {

       // create parameters
       pReturn = pCommand->CreateParameter(L"return",
                                adInteger,adParamReturnValue,NULL);
       pCommand->Parameters->Append(pReturn);

       pOutput = pCommand->CreateParameter(L"output",
                                adInteger,adParamOutput,NULL);
       pCommand->Parameters->Append(pOutput);

       pprmPageType = pCommand->CreateParameter(L"page_type_cd",
                                adChar,adParamInput,3);
       pCommand->Parameters->Append(pprmPageType);

       //set value
       pprmPageType->Value = _variant_t(bstrType);

       pPages = pCommand->Execute(NULL,NULL,adCmdStoredProc);
       showPageInfo(pPages,_variant_t(bstrType));

       // release recordset to get output paramters
       pPages.Release();

       // get output and return parms
       _variant_t vtReturn;
       _variant_t vtRows;

       vtReturn = pReturn->GetValue();
       vtRows = pOutput->GetValue();

       if (vtReturn.lVal > 0)
          bstrReturn = L"No rows were found for page type code";
       else
          bstrReturn = L"Number of rows found was " + _bstr_t(vtRows);
    }
    catch (_com_error e) {
          m_piResponse->Write(_variant_t(e.Description()));
    }

    *bstrRows = bstrReturn;

    return S_OK;
}
```

Notice in the example code that the parameter values are pulled from Parameter objects and not from the Command object.

To test this last Command object example, access the *asp1507.asp* test page, containing the following ASP script:

```
<%
Dim obj
Set obj = Server.CreateObject("asp1503.cmnd")

Dim code, return

' existing page code
code = "SCR"
return = obj.showPagesWithParm(code)
Response.Write "<P>"
Response.Write return & "</p>"

' nonexistent page code
code = "BRB"
return = obj.showPagesWithParm(code)
Response.Write "<P>"
Response.Write return & "</p>"
%>
```

The test page sends both an existing page code and a non-existent page code to demonstrate what happens when values are found or not. Figure 15-3 shows the result.

I mentioned earlier in the chapter that the ADO object model has two new objects that were introduced with ADO 2.5: the Record and Stream objects. The next, and last, section of this chapter takes a look at how to work with these objects in Visual C++ ASP components.

Stream and Record Objects

Accessing files and messages from folders is a different data access operation than querying data from a relational database, primarily because of the hierarchical nature of filesystems. To support operations on this type of data, Microsoft introduced the Stream and Record objects in ADO Version 3.5. The Record object represents a file or folder in a filesystem. With the new OLE DB Provider for Internet Publishing, you can even reference a file or folder via an URL. The Stream object is used to manipulate the bytes that make up a file, regardless of whether the file is in binary or text format.

You can use the Record and Recordset objects together. For instance, you can obtain a reference to a folder using the Record object and then traverse the folder's files using the Recordset object. You can also use the Record and the Stream objects together. As an example, you can create a reference to an existing file with the Record object and copy it using the Stream object.

To demonstrate the capabilities provided by the Record and Stream objects, you'll create a new Visual C++ component and add two methods to it. The first method results in a listing of files for a given URL and demonstrates using the Recordset

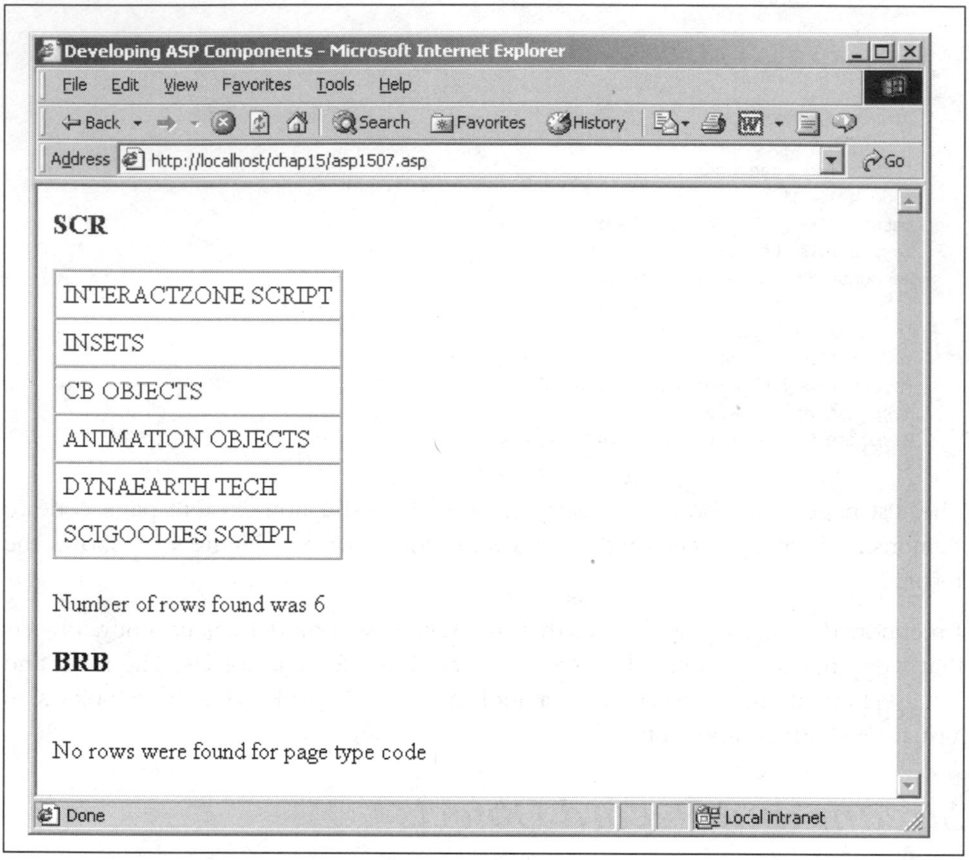

Figure 15-3. Results of component method call that uses input, output, and return parameters with a stored procedure call

object with the Record object. The second method copies a file by opening the source file, reading its contents, and then writing the contents to another file. This method demonstrates using the Record and Stream objects together.

First, create the Visual C++ project and name it `asp1504`. Use the ATL COM App-Wizard, and don't check either the MFC or MTS options. When the project is generated, create a new ATL object named `newguys`, in honor of the new ADO objects. You'll add support for the ASP Response object again to this component, except that you won't set the ADO connection string from the Application object—the connection string used for these examples is not the same as you've used for all the others in this chapter. So add support for `IObjectControl`, but add only the m_piResponse member and alter the Activate method code to that shown in Example 15-13.

Example 15-13. JIT Activate Method sans Application Object Access

```
HRESULT Cnewguys::Activate()
{
   HRESULT hr = S_OK;
   CComVariant vt;
   CComPtr<IGetContextProperties> pProps; //Context Properties

   IDispatch* piDispatch = NULL;

   // get ObjectContext
   hr = CoGetObjectContext(IID_IObjectContext,
                                           (void **)&m_spObjectContext);
   if (FAILED(hr))
      return hr;

   // get context properties
   hr = m_spObjectContext->QueryInterface( IID_IGetContextProperties,
                (void**)&pProps );
   if (FAILED(hr))
       return hr;

   // get Response property
   hr = pProps->GetProperty( L"Response", &vt ) ;

   if (FAILED(hr))
       return hr;

   piDispatch = vt.pdispVal;
   hr = piDispatch->QueryInterface( IID_IResponse,
                   (void**)&m_piResponse );

   return hr;
}
```

Add the `#import` directive to the newly generated C++ file, *newguys.cpp*, just after the include files section. You should also add an inline command that generates a COM error exception if an operation fails (an **HRESULT** value other than zero, signifying failure):

```
#import "C:\Program Files\Common Files\System\ADO\msado15.dll" \
    no_namespace rename("EOF", "EndOfFile")

inline void TESTHR(HRESULT x) {if FAILED(x) _com_issue_error(x);};
```

In all the examples shown so far, when an ADO object is created using CreateInstance, no error handling has been used in case the CreateInstance fails:

```
pCommand.CreateInstance(__uuidof(Command));
```

The CreateInstance method works with the raw ADO interface and therefore doesn't provide support for COM exceptions. To add exception processing for the

CreateInstance methods and any method that doesn't throw a COM error but does return an HRESULT value, surround the function call with the TESTHR macro:

```
TESTHR(pRec.CreateInstance(__uuidof(Record)));
```

Anytime you access the raw ADO interface—that is, anytime you use the dot notation rather than the pointer notation—using TESTHR with the method generates a COM exception when the method fails.

Add a new method to `asp1504.newguys` named displayFileNames. This method lists all of the files and folders contained within the subdirectory specified by an URL that is passed as a BSTR to the method. Add the following to the Parameters text box of the Add Method to Interface dialog:

```
BSTR bstrURL
```

In the method code, which is shown in Example 15-14, instances of both the Record and Recordset objects are created, and the URL passed as an argument to the method is modified to prepend the characters URL=. This syntax triggers the OLE DB provider to process the requested data source as an URL rather than to access a database or other data source.

The Record object's Open method is called, passing in a blank query and the modified URL for the connection parameter. Flags are set in the method to cause the Open method to fail if the folder specified in the URL doesn't exist. The Open method's parameters, all of which are optional, are the following:

Source
> The URL of the entity to be represented by this Record object, or a row of an open Recordset object

Connection
> The connection string or a reference to a Connection object

Mode
> The access mode for the Record object (adModeUnknown by default)

Create
> Whether the method opens or creates the file or folder; set to **adFailIf-Exists** by default

Options
> Options for opening the Record object; set to **adOpenRecordUnspecified** by default

Username
> The user's name, if needed

Password
> The user's password, if needed

The folder you'll be accessing is the Weaver database administration application, included in the examples and installed on your local development machine. Because this URL is installed on a local machine and you have permission to access the folder, you won't need to provide the username and password. The method then calls the Record object's GetChildren method to return a recordset with a list of the files and folders contained in the directory just opened. The method then traverses the recordset and displays the record's first data field, which is its filename.

To access the files in the directory given in the URL, you'll have to change the access permissions for the Weaver virtual directory. Access the properties page for the Weaver application in IIS, and change the access permissions to support directory browsing as well as read access.

Example 15-14. Display Filenames for Given URL

```
STDMETHODIMP Cnewguys::displayFileNames(BSTR bstrURL)
{
    _RecordsetPtr pRecs = NULL;
    _RecordPtr pRec = NULL;

    try {
        // create objects
            TESTHR(pRec.CreateInstance(__uuidof(Record)));

        _bstr_t bURL = L"URL=" + _bstr_t(bstrURL);

        // open URL into record
        pRec->Open("",bURL,adModeUnknown,adFailIfNotExists,
            adOpenRecordUnspecified,"","");

        // get children (files, directories)
        pRecs = pRec->GetChildren();

        // display filenames
        _variant_t vtVal;
        vtVal.lVal = 0;
        vtVal.vt = VT_I4;
        while(!(pRecs->EndOfFile)) {
            m_piResponse->Write(pRecs->Fields->GetItem(vtVal)->GetValue());
            m_piResponse->Write(_variant_t("<br>"));
            pRecs->MoveNext();
        }

        // close record, recordset
        pRec->Close();
```

Example 15-14. Display Filenames for Given URL (continued)

```
    pRecs->Close();

}
catch (_com_error e) {
  m_piResponse->Write(_variant_t(e.Description()));
}

return S_OK;
}
```

To test the new component, the following ASP script, *asp1508.asp*, passes in the URL for the Weaver application, located via the *localhost* host:

```
<%
Dim obj
Set obj = Server.CreateObject("asp1504.newguys")
Dim url
url = "http://localhost/weaver/"
obj.displayFileNames url
%>
```

If you access another URL, such as a web site located on the Internet, you might find that the application won't work because the virtual directory permissions have not been set for directory browsing. If your site has FrontPage support, then this example should work, but you'll most likely (or should) be asked for a username and password in order to access the files, as shown in Figure 15-4. Once you provide the valid username and password, you'll get the list of files and folders.

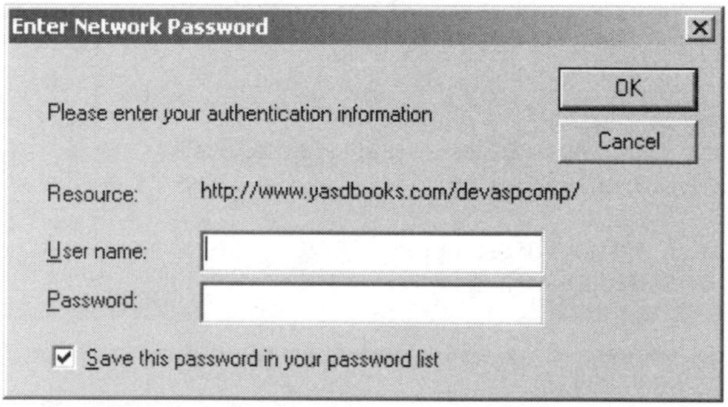

Figure 15-4. Login authentication window to run file display example

You can do more than just list files and folders with the Record object. With a little help from the Stream object, you can also open files, copy them, and remove them from a folder. To illustrate this, add a second method to `asp1504.newguys`, and call this one copyFile. This method takes three parameters: the URL of the folder, the name of an existing file, and a new filename:

```
[in] BSTR bstrURL, BSTR bstrFile, BSTR bstrNewFile
```

The method, which is shown in Example 15-15, creates instances of both the Record and Stream objects. The call to the Record object's Open method this time specifies a filename in the *Source* parameter and changes the creation flag to OR adOpenIfExists with adCreateStructDoc. This combination of enumerated values opens the file if it exists or creates it as a document if not.

The interface pointer to the Record is passed as the first argument of the Stream object's Open method. The Open method opens the file for read or write access— in this case, the file is opened for read access. The copyFile method calls the Stream object's ReadText method after first setting some of the Stream object's properties to account for the type of data being read (in this case, ASCII text). It then calls the Close method for both objects.

To copy the file contents, copyFile again calls the Record object's Open method, except this time it passes the name of the new file and specifies that the file should be overwritten if it already exists. The method then passes the Record object's interface pointer to the Stream object's Open method, which opens the new file for write access. The contents of the previous file are then written to the new file, and then both the Record and Steam objects are closed one last time.

 You could have saved some steps by calling the Stream object's SaveToFile method and providing the name of the new file. But then you wouldn't have had a chance to both read from and write to a file using the Stream object.

Example 15-15. Copying a File with the ADO Record and Stream Objects

```
STDMETHODIMP Cnewguys::copyFile(BSTR bstrURL,
                                BSTR bstrFile, BSTR bstrNewFile)
{
   _RecordPtr pRec = NULL;
   _StreamPtr pStream = NULL;

   try {

      // create objects
      TESTHR(pStream.CreateInstance(__uuidof(Stream)));
      TESTHR(pRec.CreateInstance(__uuidof(Record))) ;

      _bstr_t bURL = L"URL=" + _bstr_t(bstrURL);

      pRec->Open(bstrFile,bURL,adModeRead,
         (RecordCreateOptionsEnum)(adOpenIfExists | adCreateStructDoc),
         adOpenRecordUnspecified,"","");

      // open stream
      pStream->Open(pRec.GetInterfacePtr(),adModeRead,
```

Example 15-15. Copying a File with the ADO Record and Stream Objects (continued)

```
                         adOpenStreamFromRecord,"","");

    pStream->PutCharset(L"ascii");
    pStream->PutType(adTypeText);

    _bstr_t bstrText;
    bstrText = pStream->ReadText(adReadAll);

    // close objects for reuse
    pRec->Close();
    pStream->Close();

    // copy file
    pRec->Open(bstrNewFile,bURL,adModeWrite,
      (RecordCreateOptionsEnum)(adCreateStructDoc | adCreateOverwrite),
             adOpenRecordUnspecified,"","");

    pStream->Open(pRec.GetInterfacePtr(),adModeWrite,
                  adOpenStreamFromRecord,"","");

    pStream->WriteText(bstrText,adWriteChar);

    // clean up
    pRec->Close();
    pStream->Close();

  }

  catch (_com_error e) {

    m_piResponse->Write(_variant_t(e.Description()));
  }

  return S_OK;
}
```

Before you run this example, you must set the directory where the file is being written to have write permission for the web user. In the example script, the file being copied is from the Chapter 15 example directory, so make sure that this directory has both the write and directory browsing access options checked. The example script is found in *asp1509.asp*:

```
<%
Dim obj
Set obj = Server.CreateObject("asp1504.newguys")
Dim url, file, newfile
url = "http://localhost/chap15/"
file = "asp1507.asp"
newfile = "listfiles.asp"
obj.copyFile url, file, newfile

Server.Transfer "listfiles.asp"
%>
```

After running the ASP script, you'll see the newly copied file in the Chapter 15 web directory. This newly copied file is returned to the client using the Server object's Transfer method—and the result of running the ASP page (*asp1507.asp*) is displayed back to the client.

Now that you've had a chance to try out accessing ADO from Visual C++ components, check out the examples in Chapter 9 and convert them to Visual C++.

16

The CDO Interfaces from C++ Components

CDO, or Collaborative Data Objects, is an excellent example of the concept of less is more in software development APIs. The CDO objects support sending and retrieving messages from SMTP or NNTP servers—that's it, no more, no less. Because of the simplicity of the CDO object model, it is one of the simplest of the Microsoft APIs covered in this book.

This chapter takes a look at using CDO—specifically CDO for Windows 2000—from within your ASP components created with C++. Among the features we'll look at will be constructing a message, sending it, and then processing the message for the receiver.

 This chapter does not provide an overview of CDO or explore the concepts of using CDO in an ASP component. For this, you'll want to read Chapter 11, *Take a Message: Accessing CDO from ASP Components*. Once you've read about the concepts of CDO in Chapter 11, try out the CDO examples created in C++ in this chapter.

Accessing CDO Interfaces in C++

There are several C++ header files you can use within your components when working with CDO. The list of CDO-specific files is:

CDOSys.h
   Type information for the interfaces, classes, and enumerations

CDOSys_i.c
   The GUIDs for CDO

CDOSysErr.h

> Custom CDO error codes

CDOSysStr.h

> CDO string constants

The first two header files—*cdosys.h* and *cdosys_i.c*—provide the type information and GUID for CDO. If you use these in your components, you should be aware that there could be naming conflicts between CDO and other technologies. To resolve potential problems, you should consider using namespaces to avoid clashes.

For instance, if you use MAPI and CDO in the same component, then you'll need to reference the CDO-specific version of the **IMessage** interface with the CDO namespace, since both CDO and MAPI have an **IMessage** interface:

```
CDO::IMessage* pMsg;
```

If you're not using other technologies that could conflict with CDO, then you might consider the **using namespace** directive to improve performance:

```
#include "cdosys.h"
#include "cdosys_i.c"
using namespace CDO;
```

You can also specify that no namespaces be used:

```
#define CDO_NO_NAMESPACE
#include "cdosys.h"
#include "cdosys_i.c"
```

The other two CDO headers—*cdosyserr.h* and *cdosysstr.h*—aren't required to work with CDO, but they do provide handy constants you can use in the application in place of lengthy strings. For instance, if you're setting the body part content type of a message (discussed later in the chapter), you could use something like the following:

```
iBPMain->put_ContentMediaType(L"multipart/mixed");
```

Instead of specifying the string to use, you could use the associated constant found in *cdosysstr.h*:

```
iBPMain->put_ContentMediaType(cdoMultipartMixed);
```

This might not seem like much of a savings in typing for this example, but consider the following:

```
Flds->Item["urn:schemas:mailheader:content-transfer-encoding"]->Value =
                                    L"quoted-printable";
```

A preferable and less wordy alternative is:

```
Flds->Item[cdoContentTransferEncoding]->Value = cdoQuotedPrintable;
```

CDO is dependent on ADO (ActiveX Data Objects) for much of its functionality, so you'll also need to include support for ADO. The ADO header files are:

adoint.h
> Provides ADO type information

adoid.ic
> Provides GUIDs

The *adoint.h* header file is actually included within *cdosys.h*, so you won't need to include it directly. However, you would need to include the *adoid.ic* file for the GUIDs.

Instead of using header files, another approach to include type information is to import the information into your components using the C++ #import directive. For instance, to add support for both ADO and CDO, use import statements such as the following:

```
#import <msado15.dll> rename ( "EOF", "adoEOF" ) no_namespace
#import <cdosys.dll> no_namespace
```

The ADO library must be imported first, since it contains definitions used by the CDO type library. Additionally, the ADO and CDO namespaces differ, so you'll need to either redefine the ADO namespace to CDO or use the **no_namespace** option, as the code shows. You'll also need to rename the ADO end-of-file (EOF), since EOF is defined already in most C++ applications to a value of −1. If you don't rename EOF (to **adoEOF** in the example), you'll get compile errors.

If you don't want to use the CDO smart pointers, such as **IMessagePtr**, and would prefer to access the raw CDO interfaces, use the following #import directive:

```
#import <msado15.dll> rename ( "EOF", "adoEOF" ) no_namespace
        raw_interfaces_only
#import <cdosys.dll> no_namespace raw_interfaces_only
```

However, the smart pointers provide so much useful functionality, such as handling all COM AddRef, Release, and QueryInterface method calls, that I recommend that you use them unless you have a specific reason not to.

The examples in this chapter use the #import directive to include type information—primarily because access to smart pointers such as **IMessagePtr** and other functionality simplifies the coding process. When using the #import directive, you need not include any of the header files mentioned in this section—all the constants, type information, and GUIDs are pulled into the component.

The CDO documentation mentions that the `#import` directive does not include header files such as *cdosysstr.h* and that these include files need to be added. However, if you take advantage of the smart pointer functionality, you shouldn't need to include these files.

If you use raw interfaces or if you find that the constants are not working in your environment, include the *cdosyserr.h* and *cdosysstr. h* files in your components.

Creating and Sending a Message

Messages can be very simple, consisting only of a simple text body, or they can be very complex, with hierarchical messages consisting of different content types. Messages can also be forwarded or cc'ed (carbon copied). Regardless of what type of message you send, all messages share a basic functionality: the message is sent from one email address to one or more other email addresses.

We'll take a look at creating and sending a basic text-based message, and then we'll explore more complex messages, such as multipart messages and messages with attachments.

Adding Address and Subject Information

The CDO message is implemented by the **IMessage** interface. This object has properties for defining the email address of the message recipient and sender, as well as the subject and message body and other information. Configuration information about the SMTP service, as well as the user ID and password to access this service, are defined by another CDO interface, **IConfiguration**. In **IConfiguration**, the configuration properties are set into the object's Fields property, itself an ADO Field object (hence the need for ADO in CDO applications). Each configuration property is defined in a separate Field item.

To demonstrate how simple sending an email message can be when using CDO, you'll create your first ASP CDO component of this chapter. Create a new Visual C++ project using the ATL COM AppWizard, and name the project **asp1601**. Don't check any of the options to add support for MTS or MFC.

When the project files are generated, create a new object using the ATL Object Wizard. Select the Simple Object option, and name the new component **message**. Accept all attribute defaults for the component, except change the threading model to Both.

When the C++ and header files are created for the component, add a new method, sendMessage, to the **IMessage** interface. This method takes four **BSTR** input parameters, representing the email addresses of the recipient and sender, the subject, and the message, respectively:

```
[in] BSTR bstrTo, BSTR bstrFrom, BSTR bstrSubject, BSTR bstrMessage
```

Open the *message.cpp* file and add the following import directives to the top of the page, just after the include file section:

```
#import <msado15.dll> rename ( "EOF", "adoEOF" ) no_namespace
#import <cdosys.dll> no_namespace
```

Add the code for the new method next, as shown in Example 16-1. (Make sure you change the user ID and password, as well as the SMTP server, to use settings that work in your own environment.) First, the method creates instances of the **IConfiguration** and **IMessage** interface objects. It then accesses the Fields property of the configuration object and assigns it to an instance of the ADO Fields interface. Next, the method sets the properties necessary for successfully sending the email message. This includes the SMTP server to use, as well as the authentication method, and the SMTP user ID and password, if required by the SMTP service. The port transport technique (indicated by the constant **cdoSendUsingPort**) is used to send the message, meaning that the message is sent over the network (or Internet IP connection). The other option is **cdoSendUsingPickup**, in which case the message is sent to the local SMTP pickup service. Once the properties are set, the Fields collection's Update method is called to save the properties.

After the message configuration properties have been defined and saved, sendMessages attaches the **IConfiguration** object to the **IMessage** interface's Configuration property, and sets the message's To, From, Subject, and TextBody properties. The message is text-based, so its contents can be assigned directly to the **IMessage** interface's TextBody property. Lastly, the message is sent using the Send method.

Example 16-1. Sending a Simple Text-Based Email Message

```
STDMETHODIMP Cmessage::sendMessage(BSTR bstrTo, BSTR bstrFrom,
                               BSTR bstrSubject, BSTR bstrMessage)
{
    HRESULT hr;
    IMessagePtr    iMsg(__uuidof(Message));
    IConfigurationPtr iConf(__uuidof(Configuration));
    FieldsPtr        Flds;

    // set configuration fields
    Flds = iConf->Fields;

    // set configuration properties
    Flds->Item[cdoSendUsingMethod]->Value =
        _variant_t((long)cdoSendUsingPort);
```

Example 16-1. Sending a Simple Text-Based Email Message (continued)

```
Flds->Item[cdoSMTPServer]->Value  =
      _variant_t("mail.company.com");

Flds->Item[cdoSMTPConnectionTimeout]->Value = _variant_t((long)20);
Flds->Item[cdoSMTPAuthenticate]->Value  = _variant_t((long)cdoBasic);
Flds->Item[cdoSendUserName]->Value      = _variant_t("userid");
Flds->Item[cdoSendPassword]->Value      = _variant_t("somepassword");

Flds->Item[cdoURLGetLatestVersion]->Value  =
      _variant_t(VARIANT_TRUE);

// update fields
Flds->Update();

// attach config properties to message
iMsg->Configuration = iConf;
iMsg->To        = bstrTo;
iMsg->From      = bstrFrom;
iMsg->Subject   = bstrSubject;
iMsg->TextBody  = bstrMessage;

// send message
hr=iMsg->Send();

   return hr;
}
```

Because the Configuration object's Field properties are variants, you'll need to use **_variant_t** to encapsulate the values. Using **_variant_t** handles any allocation and deallocation of resources for you. Normally, you need to include *comdef.h* in any application that uses this COM support class, but importing the CDO and ADO libraries also adds access to **_variant_t**, **_com_error**, **_bstr_t**, and other helpful COM objects.

To test the new component method, use the following ASP script, *asp1601.asp*, after first changing the values to email addresses that you can test in your environment (such as your own email address). Just make sure that you're connected to the Internet if your SMTP service isn't local to your machine or accessible via a LAN:

```
<%
Dim obj
Set obj = Server.CreateObject("asp1601.message")

obj.sendMessage "person@company.com","other@company.com", _
            "test message","This is a test message."
Set obj = Nothing
%>
```

If you sent the email to yourself, access your email reader (such as Outlook), and you should find the new email waiting for you.

The SMTP server you'll use in your code is the same one you use with outgoing SMTP mail when setting up an email account for your email reader.

You can also attach a secondary recipient using the **IMessage** interface's CC property:

```
iMsg->CC = bstrCC
```

Or you can set the blind carbon copy recipients with the BCC property.

If you have multiple email addresses, separate the addresses with commas:

```
person1@company.com, person1@company2.com
```

Try changing the code in the example to send a CC to another email address (or to the same address as the original recipient), and also try using multiple recipients.

Sending HTML and Plain Text Messages

The last section sent a plain text email, but many email readers are capable of processing HTML content as well as text content. Sending a message in both formats ensures that the message is processed by the reader properly regardless of whether the reader can process HTML or not.

To send a message in both HTML and text formats, you'll need to set two **IMessage** properties. The first is the HTMLBody property, to which you'll assign the HTML-formatted message content. The second is AutoGenerateTextBody; setting this property to **true** means that when the HTMLBody property is assigned HTML-formatted content, a duplicate of the content—sans HTML formatting—is automatically assigned to the message's TextBody property. You can also set the MimeFormatted property to **true** to indicate that the message is formatted using MIME content, but this property is automatically set when the HTMLBody property is set.

To try sending an HTML/plain text message, add a new method to **asp1601. message** named sendMultiPart. This method takes four parameters, all **BSTR**s, for the email addressee, the sender, the subject, and the HTML-formatted message:

```
[in] BSTR bstrTo, BSTR bstrFrom, BSTR bstrSubject, BSTR bstrMessage
```

The code for the new method, which is shown in Example 16-2, is almost identical to that shown in Example 16-1, except that the message text is assigned to HTMLBody, and the AutoGenerateTextBody property is set to **true**.

Example 16-2. Sending a Message Formatted as Both Plain Text and HTML

```
STDMETHODIMP Cmessage::sendMultiPart(BSTR bstrTo, BSTR bstrFrom, BSTR bstrSubject,
BSTR bstrMessage)
{
    HRESULT hr;
    IMessagePtr     iMsg(__uuidof(Message));
    IConfigurationPtr iConf(__uuidof(Configuration));
    FieldsPtr        Flds;

    // set configuration fields
    Flds = iConf->Fields;

    // set configuration properties
    Flds->Item[cdoSendUsingMethod]->Value =
        _variant_t((long)cdoSendUsingPort);

    Flds->Item[cdoSMTPServer]->Value  =
        _variant_t("mail.company.com");

    Flds->Item[cdoSMTPConnectionTimeout]->Value = _variant_t((long)20);
    Flds->Item[cdoSMTPAuthenticate]->Value  = _variant_t((long)cdoBasic);
    Flds->Item[cdoSendUserName]->Value      = _variant_t("userid");
    Flds->Item[cdoSendPassword]->Value      = _variant_t("somepassword");

    Flds->Item[cdoURLGetLatestVersion]->Value   =
        _variant_t(VARIANT_TRUE);

    // update fields
    Flds->Update();

    // attach config properties to message
    iMsg->Configuration = iConf;
    iMsg->To        = bstrTo;
    iMsg->From       = bstrFrom;
    iMsg->Subject    = bstrSubject;

    // HTML and plain text
    iMsg->AutoGenerateTextBody = true;
    iMsg->HTMLBody = bstrMessage;

    // send message
    hr=iMsg->Send();

    return hr;
}
```

To test this new method, the following ASP script, *asp1602.asp*, generates a message body formatted with HTML:

```
Dim obj
Set obj = Server.CreateObject("asp1601.message")

Dim str
```

```
str ="<h1>Howdy!</h1><p>I hope this finds you <strong>well</strong>!</p>"

obj.sendMultiPart "person@company.com", "from@company.com", _
              "testing multipart", str

Set obj = Nothing
```

Make sure to change the email recipient and sender to fit your environment.

Unlike the text-based message, the HTML-formatted content displays the message with a larger header for the greeting and the word *well* in bold. If your email reader is capable of reading MIME content, you'll see the HTML formatting. If not, then you'll still see the message, but without the HTML formatting.

You can also send HTML content using the CreateMHTMLBody method, passing in the URL of the HTML page. The syntax of the CreateMHTMLBody method is:

> CreateMHTMLBody (BSTR *url*, *cdoMHTMLFlags*, BSTR *userName*,
>   BSTR *password*)

This message creates body parts (discussed next) for all of the page's contents. Additionally, you can suppress the inclusion of certain HTML elements such as images, stylesheets, frames, and sounds using this method.

You can send content type other than HTML and plain text. You can also create fairly complex messages with multiple message bodies, discussed next.

Sending Multipart Messages

Up to this point, the email message content has been added directly to properties on the **IMessage** interface, through the TextBody property for plain text messages and the HTMLBody property for HTML-formatted content. However, if you want more finite control of the message content and to include content other than text or HTML messages, you need to work with the **IBodyPart** interface.

CDO messages consist of a main message body, accessible from the **IMessage** interface's BodyPart property, which returns an **IBodyPart** instance. You can create the message content by working with **IBodyPart** directly. Like **IConfiguration**, it has several properties that you set (or access) through an ADO Fields collection, which is returned when you call the **IBodyPart** interface's GetFields method.

The message body can also consist of multiple body parts, arranged in a hierarchy. The **IBodyPart** interface has a collection called BodyParts, which contains the different parts of the message. To add multiple body parts, call the **IBodyPart** interface's AddBodyPart method to add the new body part to the existing message's body parts collection. Its syntax is:

```
AddBodyPart(long index, IBodyPart ** pVal)
```

Additionally, the new body parts can themselves have additional body parts added to them and so on, in a hierarchical manner.

To add message content to an **IBodyPart** interface, you'll need to use an ADO Stream object to write the content to the message. This Stream object is returned when you call the **IBodyPart** interface's GetDecodedContentStream or GetEncodedContentStream methods (neither of which has parameters). The difference between the two is that one returns the content in an encoded format, the other returns the content already decoded. To add content to the message, you usually use the GetDecodedContentStream method.

To demonstrate sending a mixed-content multipart message, add a new method to `asp1601.message`, and name it sendMixedMultiPart. This new method will send a message consisting of text, HTML, and GIF content.

The sendMixedMultiPart method takes six **BSTR** parameters: the to, from, and subject strings, as well as the plain text and HTML-formatted messages, and the name of a GIF file. Add these parameters to the method with the following parameter string:

```
[in] BSTR bstrTo, BSTR bstrFrom, BSTR bstrSubject, BSTR bstrMessage,
BSTR bstrHTMLMsg, BSTR bstrGIF
```

In the method code, which is shown in Example 16-3, the configuration properties for the message are set in the same way as they were with the previous two methods. (You'll have to change the values of the configuration properties to match your environment.) You can define a global version of **IConfiguration** and store this in the ASP Application object using the *global.asa* file. However, you'll need to add access to the ASP built-in objects to your component or pass it to the methods as a parameter from the ASP script.

Another technique you can use to create the Configuration object is to declare a member object reference for the Configuration object, implement IObjectControl in your ASP component, and instantiate the Configuration object and set its properties in the IObjectControl interface's Activate method. See Chapter 14, *Creating C++ ASP Components*, for information about integrating IObjectControl into your ASP components for just-in-time (JIT) activation.

After setting the message's configuration, the sendMixedMultiPart method accesses the message's main body part object and then sets it to support multipart mixed content. It also creates three body parts, one for each of the associated content types sent with the message (text, HTML, and image). The content type and encoding method for each body part is set using the ADO Fields object, and the Stream object is used to write out the content. Notice in the code that the GIF file is loaded into the message content stream using the Stream object's LoadFromFile method. The Stream object's WriteText method is used to add both the text and the HTML-formatted content. Once all of the body parts are defined and the content loaded, the message is sent.

Example 16-3. Sending a Multipart Mixed Email Message

```
STDMETHODIMP Cmessage::sendMixedMultiPart(BSTR bstrTo, BSTR bstrFrom,
                                 BSTR bstrSubject, BSTR bstrMessage,
                                 BSTR bstrHTMLMsg, BSTR bstrGIF)
{
    HRESULT hr;
    IMessagePtr    iMsg(__uuidof(Message));
    IConfigurationPtr iConf(__uuidof(Configuration));
    FieldsPtr        Flds;

    // set configuration fields
    Flds = iConf->Fields;

    // set configuration properties
    Flds->Item[cdoSendUsingMethod]->Value =
        _variant_t((long)cdoSendUsingPort);

    Flds->Item[cdoSMTPServer]->Value  =
        _variant_t("mail.company.com");

    Flds->Item[cdoSMTPConnectionTimeout]->Value = _variant_t((long)20);
    Flds->Item[cdoSMTPAuthenticate]->Value  = _variant_t((long)cdoBasic);
    Flds->Item[cdoSendUserName]->Value   = _variant_t("userid");
    Flds->Item[cdoSendPassword]->Value   = _variant_t("somepassword");

    Flds->Item[cdoURLGetLatestVersion]->Value   =
        _variant_t(VARIANT_TRUE);

    // update fields
    Flds->Update();

    // attach config properties to message
    iMsg->Configuration = iConf;
    iMsg->To       = bstrTo;
    iMsg->From     = bstrFrom;
    iMsg->Subject  = bstrSubject;


    // **** multi-part **** //
    IBodyPartPtr iBPMain;
    IBodyPartPtr iBPText;
    IBodyPartPtr iBPHTML;
```

Example 16-3. Sending a Multipart Mixed Email Message (continued)

```
    IBodyPartPtr iBPGif;
    _StreamPtr iStm;

    iBPMain = iMsg->BodyPart;
    iBPMain->put_ContentMediaType(cdoMultipartMixed);

    // text
    // properties set directly
    iBPText = iBPMain->AddBodyPart(-1);
    iBPText->put_ContentMediaType(cdoTextPlain);
    iBPText->put_ContentTransferEncoding(cdo8bit);

    // message body
    iStm = iBPText->GetDecodedContentStream();
    iStm->WriteText(bstrMessage,adWriteChar);
    hr=iStm->Flush();

    if (FAILED(hr)) return hr;

    // HTML
    // properties set using Fields
    iBPHTML = iBPMain->AddBodyPart(-1);
    Flds = iBPHTML->GetFields();
    Flds->Item[cdoContentType]->Value = cdoTextHTML;
    Flds->Item[cdoContentTransferEncoding]->Value = cdoQuotedPrintable;
    Flds->Update();

    // message body
    iStm = iBPHTML->GetDecodedContentStream();
    iStm->WriteText(bstrHTMLMsg,adWriteChar);
    hr=iStm->Flush();

    if (FAILED(hr)) return hr;

    // image
    // properties set directly
    iBPGif = iBPMain->AddBodyPart(-1);
    iBPGif->put_ContentMediaType(cdoGif);
    iBPGif->put_ContentTransferEncoding(cdoBase64);

    // message body, GIF loaded from file
    iStm = iBPGif->GetDecodedContentStream();
    iStm->LoadFromFile(bstrGIF);
    hr=iStm->Flush();

    if (FAILED(hr)) return hr;

    // send message
    hr=iMsg->Send();

    return hr;
}
```

Test your new component method by accessing the ASP test page *asp1603.asp*, changing the email addresses of the message's receiver and sender as well as the path to the image file to match your own environment:

```
<%
Dim obj
Set obj = Server.CreateObject("asp1601.message")

Dim strHTML, strMsg, strGif
strHTML="<h1>Howdy!</h1><p>I hope this finds you <em>well</em>!</p>"
strMsg = "Howdy! I hope this finds you well!"
strGif = "c:\mm\image.gif"

obj.sendMixedMultiPart "person@company.com", "from@company.com", _
                       "testing multipart using IBodyPart", _
                       strMsg, strHTML, strGif

Set obj = Nothing
%>
```

In the email reader, the plain text shows in the message, and the HTML and GIF image are added as attachments to the message.

Speaking of attachments, there are actually two different ways you can add attachments to an email message; they are discussed next.

Adding Attachments

Email message attachments have been in the news a lot this last year. The infamous Love virus had a Visual Basic attachment that, when accessed, triggered the virus—generating email messages for everyone in the recipient's email address book, as well as damaging essential files on system (in the case of hybrid versions of the virus). However, email attachments are essential in order to send files, documents, applications, and other content to people. This section demonstrates how to create attachments within your ASP components. Hopefully, your recipients will find that your attachments are useful rather than harmful.

In the last section, you actually created an email attachment for the message when you created a mixed multipart content. However, in the example you created, the attachments are given a generated content name, rather then the name of the actual attachment file.

You don't have to work with **IBodyPart** in order to add an email attachment. You can, instead, use the **IMessage** interface's AddAttachment method, passing in the URL of the object you want to include and a user ID and password if the content is protected:

```
AddAttachment(BSTR url, BSTR userName, BSTR password, IBodyPart ** pVal)
```

All message attachments are added to the Attachments collection within the message's BodyPart object. When you use AddAttachment, the main body part object is returned.

To demonstrate the two techniques for adding attachments, add one last method to **asp1602.message**, calling it sendAttachments. The new method takes seven BSTR parameters, including the URLs for an image and a web page that will form the contents for the attachments:

```
[in] BSTR bstrTo, BSTR bstrFrom, BSTR bstrSubject, BSTR bstrMessage, BSTR
bstrAttachment1, BSTR bstrFile, BSTR bstrAttachment2
```

Add the code for the new method, as shown in Example 16-4. In the code, the web page is added using the AddAttachment method, and the image is added using the BodyPart object returned by the AddAttachment method. This BodyPart object represents the main message body. When the image is added as an attachment, the BodyPart content disposition property is set to an attachment type and the filename is given. This ensures that the image name shows in the attachment, rather than a generated name displayed when the image is sent as part of a multipart mixed message.

Example 16-4. Sending an Email with Attachments

```
STDMETHODIMP Cmessage::sendAttachments(BSTR bstrTo, BSTR bstrFrom,
                                BSTR bstrSubject, BSTR bstrMessage,
                                STR bstrAttachment1, BSTR bstrFile,
                                BSTR bstrAttachment2)
{
    HRESULT hr;
    IMessagePtr    iMsg(__uuidof(Message));
    IConfigurationPtr iConf(__uuidof(Configuration));
    FieldsPtr        Flds;

    // set configuration fields
    Flds = iConf->Fields;

    // set configuration properties
    Flds->Item[cdoSendUsingMethod]->Value =
        _variant_t((long)cdoSendUsingPort);

    Flds->Item[cdoSMTPServer]->Value  =
        _variant_t("mail.company.com");

    Flds->Item[cdoSMTPConnectionTimeout]->Value = _variant_t((long)20);
    Flds->Item[cdoSMTPAuthenticate]->Value  = _variant_t((long)cdoBasic);
    Flds->Item[cdoSendUserName]->Value      = _variant_t("someuser");
    Flds->Item[cdoSendPassword]->Value      = _variant_t("somepassword");

    Flds->Item[cdoURLGetLatestVersion]->Value  =
        _variant_t(VARIANT_TRUE);
```

Example 16-4. Sending an Email with Attachments (continued)

```
    // update fields
    Flds->Update();

    // attach config properties to message
    iMsg->Configuration = iConf;
    iMsg->To        = bstrTo;
    iMsg->From      = bstrFrom;
    iMsg->Subject   = bstrSubject;
    iMsg->TextBody  = bstrMessage;

    // **** attachment **** //
    IBodyPartPtr iBPMain;
    IBodyPartPtr iBPAttach;
    _StreamPtr iStm;

    // Attachment 1
    iBPMain = iMsg->AddAttachment(bstrAttachment1,"","");

    // Attachment 2, from file
    iBPAttach = iBPMain->AddBodyPart(-1);
    iBPAttach->put_ContentMediaType(cdoGif);
    iBPAttach->put_ContentTransferEncoding(cdoBase64);

    Flds = iBPAttach->GetFields();
    Flds->Item[cdoContentDisposition]->Value =
                    _bstr_t("attachment; filename=\"") +
                    _bstr_t(bstrFile) + _bstr_t("\"");
    Flds->Update();

    // message body
    iStm = iBPAttach->GetDecodedContentStream();
    iStm->LoadFromFile(bstrAttachment2);
    hr=iStm->Flush();

    if (FAILED(hr)) return hr;

    // send message
    hr=iMsg->Send();

  return hr;
}
```

Test the new method using the following ASP page, *asp1604.asp*, making sure to adjust both the ASP script and the component code to reflect your environment:

```
<%
On Error Resume Next
Dim obj
Set obj = Server.CreateObject("asp1601.message")

Dim strMsg, strAttachment1, strAttachment2, strFile
strMsg = "Howdy! I hope this finds you well!"
strAttachment1 = "http://www.company.com/some.htm"
```

```
strAttachment2 = "c:\image.gif"
strFile = "image.gif"

obj.sendAttachments "to@company.com", "from@company.com", _
                    "testing attachments", _
                    strMsg, strAttachment1, strFile, strAttachment2
If Err.Number <> 0 Then
   Response.Write "Message not sent due to error"
Else
   Response.Write "Message sent"
End If
Set obj = Nothing
%>
```

The email should show the text message and two attachments, *some.htm* and *image.gif.*

Retrieving and Reading Messages

You can do more than just send messages with CDO—you can read them also. The incoming messages aren't stored in memory or in some obscure virtual storage area of Windows 2000. Instead, the messages are stored physically on the disk where the SMTP service resides, in a folder called the SMTP drop directory. To read the messages, all you have to do is access the SMTP drop directory where the messages are currently stored and process each one in turn. When you read a message, you can also delete it from the directory if you so choose.

Accessing a Drop Directory

The SMTP drop directory is the default folder where messages are stored until they are deliberately deleted. By default, this directory is usually located at *c:\inetpub\ mailroot\drop.* If you open this folder with Windows Explorer (you may have to change the Explorer options to show hidden and system files and folders to see *inetpub*), you should see incoming messages stored as individual files in the folder—each given an encrypted filename and each with an *.eml* extension.

If you open one of these messages using a text editor such as Wordpad, you'll see that the top part of the message contains information about the message recipient, the sender, the MIME type of the message, the time when the message was sent and so on. This is all information you can retrieve from a message when you access it from your C++ ASP components.

To access messages from the drop directory, create an instance of **IDrop-Directory** and then call its GetMessages method, passing in the physical location of the drop directory:

```
iMessages = iDDirectory->GetMessages(L"c:\\inetpub\\mailroot\\drop");
```

The method returns a collection of all available messages, which are then accessible via the **IMessages** interface. The next section uses both the **IDropDirectory** and **IMessages** interfaces to create an online email message reader.

Displaying Message Contents on the Web

You can use CDO to create your own web-based email reader. To start, create a new Visual C++ project using the ATL COM AppWizard, and don't add support for MFC or MTS. Name the project **asp1602**. Once the project files are generated, open the Project Settings dialog and click on the Link tab to view the existing object/library modules defined for the project. Add the COM+ Services library (*comsvcs.lib*) to the end of the module list, since you'll be using COM+ Services to access the built-in ASP objects in your new email reader.

Insert a new ATL object into your project using the MTS object template, and name the component **drop**. Accept the default Dual Interface setting, and check the Support IObjectControl setting, but not the Can Be Pooled setting.

Open the new *drop.h* header file and add the following code just after the reference to the *resources.h* file:

```
#include <comsvcs.h>
#include <asptlb.h>
```

The header files provide support for COM+ as well as the built-in ASP objects. Also add a private label to the **drop** class definition section, move the generated m_spObjectContext object to this section, and add a reference to the ASP Response object interface so that the code appears as follows:

```
private:
    CComPtr<IObjectContext> m_spObjectContext;
    CComPtr<IResponse>m_piResponse;
```

Open the *drop.cpp* file next and add the code for just-in-time activation. In the Activate method, create an instance of the m_spObjectContext and m_piResponse objects. In the Deactivate method, release both of these objects, as shown in Example 16-5.

Example 16-5. Implementing the IObjectControl Methods

```
HRESULT Cdrop::Activate()
{
    HRESULT hr = S_OK;
    CComBSTR bstrObj;
    CComVariant vt;
    CComPtr<IGetContextProperties> pProps; //Context Properties

    IDispatch* piDispatch = NULL;
```

Example 16-5. Implementing the IObjectControl Methods (continued)

```
    // get ObjectContext
    hr = CoGetObjectContext(IID_IObjectContext,
                                (void **)&m_spObjectContext);
    if (FAILED(hr))
        return hr;

    // get Context Properties
    hr = m_spObjectContext->QueryInterface( IID_IGetContextProperties,
                (void**)&pProps );
    if (FAILED(hr))
        return hr;

    // get Response property
    bstrObj = "Response";
    hr = pProps->GetProperty( bstrObj, &vt ) ;

    if (FAILED(hr))
        return hr;

    piDispatch = vt. pdispVal;
    hr = piDispatch->QueryInterface( IID_IResponse,
                    (void**)&m_piResponse );

    return hr;
}

BOOL Cdrop::CanBePooled()
{
    return TRUE;
}

void Cdrop::Deactivate()
{
    m_piResponse.Release();
    m_spObjectContext.Release();
}
```

Finally, add the import directives for the ADO and CDO type libraries to the top of
the *drop.cpp* file, just after the generated include files:

```
#import <msado15.dll> rename ( "EOF", "adoEOF" ) no_namespace
#import <cdosys.dll> no_namespace
```

You're now ready to add your first method for your new component—a method
to display a list of emails to the web page.

Displaying a List of Emails

In an email reader application, you'll want to provide a list of the emails and a
means for the person to read an individual email and delete it from the list once it
is read. Your new component's first method provides the functionality for the first

requirement of your email reader—it displays a list of email message subject lines and email senders.

Use Class View to create a new method called getMessages. It has no parameters. The method, which is shown in Example 16-6, retrieves a reference to the default SMTP drop directory and uses this to get the messages currently in the folder. Once it has the messages, it gets the count of items and uses a **for** loop to access each message (using **IMessage**) and then list each message subject and sender to an HTML table on the web page. The reason a **for** loop is used instead of enumeration (**IMessages** is a collection and therefore has enumeration capability) is to capture the message number associated with each message.

The method encloses the sender's name in a hypertext link and associates the message number with the query string for the link. The message number allows the application to retrieve a specific message if the user clicks on the link to view the message contents.

Example 16-6. Display Unread Messages Contained in SMTP Drop Directory

```
STDMETHODIMP Cdrop::getMessages()
{
  IDropDirectoryPtr    iDDirectory(__uuidof(DropDirectory));
  IMessagesPtr iMessages;

  try {

    // get messages from drop directory
    iMessages = iDDirectory->GetMessages(L"c:\\inetpub\\mailroot\\drop");

    long lCt;
    lCt = iMessages->Count;

    // setup output table
m_piResponse->Write(_variant_t("<table border=2 width='80%'>"));
m_piResponse->Write(_variant_t("<TR><TH>From</TH><TH>Subject</TH></TR>"));


    // process each message
    for (long l = 1; l <=lCt; l++) {
        IMessagePtr pMsg;
        iMessages->get_Item(l,&pMsg);

        // process message info
        m_piResponse->Write(_variant_t("<TR><TD>"));
        m_piResponse->Write(_variant_t("<a href='asp1606.asp?ct="));
        m_piResponse->Write(_variant_t(l));
        m_piResponse->Write(_variant_t("'>"));
        m_piResponse->Write(_variant_t(pMsg->From + "</a></td><td>"));
        m_piResponse->Write(_variant_t(pMsg->Subject + "</td></tr>"));
    }
```

Example 16-6. Display Unread Messages Contained in SMTP Drop Directory (continued)

```
    m_piResponse->Write(_variant_t("</table>"));

  }
  catch (_com_error e) {
      m_piResponse->Write(_variant_t(e.Description()));
  }
  return S_OK;
}
```

Notice that the getMessages method uses exception handling to process any errors that occur with the component. In the last several examples, error handling has either been handled by the default IIS 5.0 error handler or by capturing the Err object's Number property in the ASP script and testing to see if its value is 0. You can't access the error message directly in either of these approaches.

To provide better error processing and print out meaningful error messages, use exception handling in your method and either return a **BSTR** pointer with the error message as a return parameter for your method, or use the ASP built-in Response object to display the message. You could also add the error message to an application log if you wish.

 To support exception handling in the component, you have to modify the Project Settings by accessing the C/C++ tab, selecting the C++ Language Category, and then checking the Enable Exception Handling option.

To display the email list, the ASP test page, *asp1605.asp*, creates an instance of the new component and calls its getMessages method:

```
<%
Dim obj
Set obj = Server.CreateObject("asp1602.drop")

obj.GetMessages
Set obj = Nothing
%>
```

The results of accessing the ASP test page should be similar to that shown in Figure 16-1, except that the messages and subjects should match those of your own emails.

When a particular email is selected for reading, you'll want to access that email from the collection and display its contents. The email reader is text-based only, so only the text-based contents are displayed. We'll create the method to read an email message next.

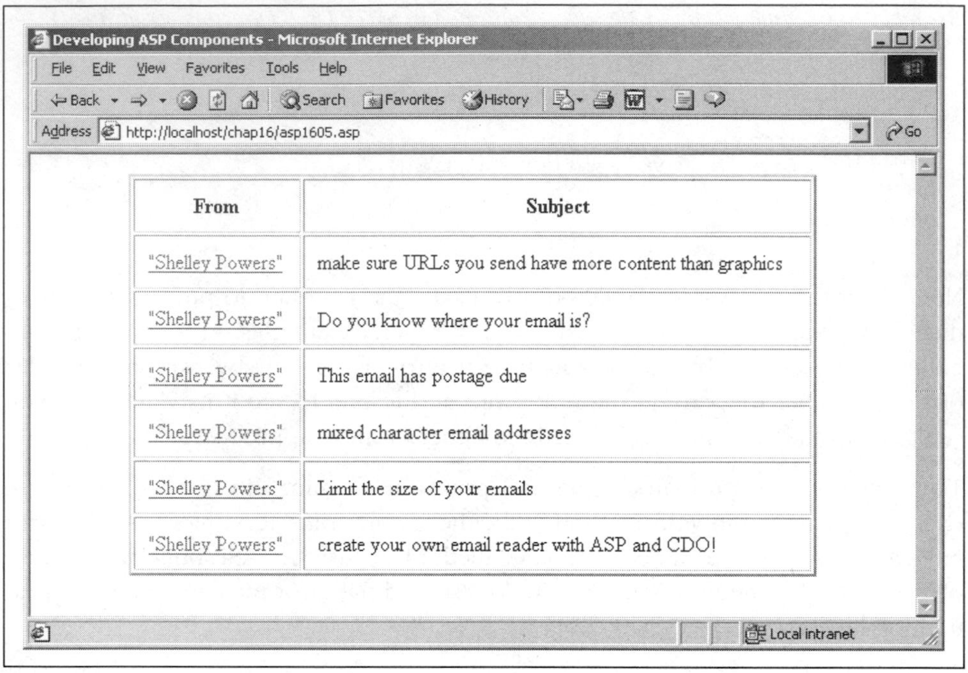

Figure 16-1. Email reader and list of unread emails

Reading the Email

Add a new method to `asp1602.drop` and call it getMessage. This method takes one parameter, a long value containing the item number of the message to read.

The code for the method is shown in Example 16-7. It creates an instance of the drop directory interface and calls GetMessages to get the collection of messages. However, instead of looping through the collection, it accesses a specific message, based on the message number passed into the method. Once it retrieves the message, it displays the message text, sender, and subject to the page. At the end of the method, the message is deleted.

Example 16-7. Read and Delete a Specific Email Message

```
STDMETHODIMP Cdrop::getMessage(long lItem)
{
  IDropDirectoryPtr    iDDirectory(__uuidof(DropDirectory));
  IMessagesPtr iMessages;
  IMessagePtr pMsg;

  try {
    // get messages from drop directory
    iMessages = iDDirectory->GetMessages(L"c:\\inetpub\\mailroot\\drop");

    // get message
```

Example 16-7. Read and Delete a Specific Email Message (continued)

```
    iMessages->get_Item(lItem,&pMsg);

    // process message info
    m_piResponse->Write(_variant_t("<P>From: " + pMsg->From));
    m_piResponse->Write(_variant_t("<P>Subject: " + pMsg->Subject));
    m_piResponse->Write(_variant_t("<p>" + pMsg->TextBody));

    // delete message
    iMessages->Delete(lItem);

}
catch (_com_error e) {
    m_piResponse->Write(_variant_t(e.Description()));
}

return S_OK;
}
```

The following ASP test page, *asp1606.asp*, is called when the user clicks on a message in *asp1605.asp*, and the message number is passed to the new component method:

```
<%
Dim obj
Set obj = Server.CreateObject("asp1602.drop")

Dim imsg
imsg = Request.QueryString("ct")

obj.getMessage imsg
Set obj = Nothing
%>
```

This script retrieves the message number from the Request object's QueryString collection.

Once you've created the email reader, try it yourself by sending several messages to your local SMTP service (see Chapter 11 for details on doing this within a local environment), and then view the messages with your new component. Vary what's displayed by accessing HTML content through the **IMessage** interface's HTML-Body property and attachments through the Attachments collection.

17

Accessing Active Directory from C++ Components

Active Directory is a directory service that provides information about objects of interest within a system. Among the types of objects of interest are groups, users, computer resources, separate machines or nodes, and so on.

Active Directory is primarily used for administrative purposes within a distributed system. However, just because the tasks are administrative in nature does not mean that Active Directory activities are not good candidates for use from within ASP applications. Administrative tasks can be performed by numerous folks, and providing an ASP application to perform these tasks simplifies both maintenance and security. Additionally, allowing people to perform some of their own administrative tasks in a secure environment, rather than channeling these tasks through a few key people, prevents the sort of bottlenecks that have characterized older centralized administrative control.

Active Directory objects are exposed for manipulation by ASP components through the Active Directory Services Interfaces (ADSI). These interfaces provide all access to all Active Directory functionality regardless of the type of programming language used, as long as the language supports access to COM objects.

This chapter demonstrates how you can work with the Active Directory interfaces from within C++ ASP Components.

This chapter does not provide an overview of the Active Directory services or explore the concepts of using ADSI in an ASP component. You'll want to read Chapter 12, *Working with Active Directory from ASP Applications*, first to get an understanding of how ASP components can work with the services. Then apply this understanding to C++ components by trying out the examples in this chapter.

Binding to Active Directory Objects

You don't create instances of Active Directory objects—they already exist. What you do instead is retrieve a reference to the objects that you can then use in your components. The process of attaching a reference to an Active Directory object is known as *binding*.

You can bind to a specific object, such as a single user in a system. Or you can bind to a group or collection of objects, such as all users of a system. The key is that you must specify the path of the object, and you must access the domain controller for your system.

 Chapter 12 has information about setting up a standalone domain controller for your Windows 2000 server environment.

An example of a path used to bind to an Active Directory object is the following, which binds the component code to the Users collection of my system:

```
LDAP://CN=users,DC=development,DC=local
```

This path specifies the ADSI LDAP provider (`LDAP://`), which we'll be using for all of the examples in this chapter, and accesses the users on the **development. local** domain controller. Though the controller is referenced, its physical location is not; this means that the controller could be moved to a physically different machine and the code would still work, as long as the same domain controller name is used.

There are two ADSI helper functions you can use to access specific Active Directory objects. A *helper function* is one that provides easier access to more commonly used functionality, especially when using COM within C++.

The first function, AdsOpenObject, has the following parameters:

LPWSTR
    Pathname

LPWSTR
    Username

LPWSTR
    Password

DWORD
    Member from **ADS_AUTHENTICATION_ENUM**—authentication used

REFIID
> Interface identifier

*VOID FAR * FAR*
> Pointer to object

This method has a user ID and password, used to track the ADSI request with the profile of a user with different authority from the person actually accessing the application:

```
hr = ADsOpenObject(L"LDAP://CN=Users,DC=development,DC=local",
                "someuser",
                "somepassword",
                ADS_SECURE_AUTHENTICATION,
                IID_IADs,
                (void**) &pObject);
```

In this function call, the first parameter is the previously mentioned path of the object, and the second and third parameters are the user's identifier and password, respectively. The fourth parameter is the type of authentication to use with the access, the fifth is the interface identifier for the object, and the last parameter is an indirect pointer to the interface we're accessing.

AdsOpenObject can be used to bind to an object using a specific set of credentials. This should be used only within components, since the password is provided in plain text.

The second function you can use to bind to an Active Directory object is AdsGetObject. The only difference between it and AdsOpenObject is that AdsGetObject does not have parameters to specify user credentials or the security scheme:

```
hr = ADsGetObject(L"LDAP://CN=Users,DC=development,DC=local",
                IID_IADs,
                (void**) &pObject);
```

Once you've bound to a specific object, you can then access information about the object or its children or members if the object is a collection of some form.

Binding to Collections

There are actually three ADSI interfaces that support collections. The core interface is IADsContainer, which contains methods to support enumeration. Two other interfaces can be used to provide access to collection or group members.

One collection interface is IADsCollection, used to access members of a class of objects that all have the same Variant datatype. The IADsCollection interface is usually accessed through some other interface's method. For instance, to access the print jobs from a specific queue, you could call the PrintJobs method on the IADsPrintQueueOperations interface.

The other collection interface is IADsMembers. This interface groups elements based on their membership within a group, such as all users (group or individual) accessible from the main Users collection in the directory service. These elements are grouped by their physical proximity, though they differ in object type. Unlike IADsCollection, IADsMembers can be of differing types.

To demonstrate working with IADsMembers, create a new Visual C++ project using the ATL COM AppWizard and name it asp1701. Don't select support for MTS or MFC when given this option by the wizard.

You'll be using the ASP Response object in this example, so once the project's created, add support for COM+ Services as well as ADSI. Select the Project → Settings menu option and select the Link tab. At the end of the Object/Library modules text box, add the following libraries:

```
comsvcs.lib activeDS.lib adsiid.lib
```

The first library is the COM+ Services library, which is necessary for this component to access the ASP built-in Response object. The other two libraries provide support for ADSI. Figure 17-1 shows the Project Settings dialog once these libraries are added.

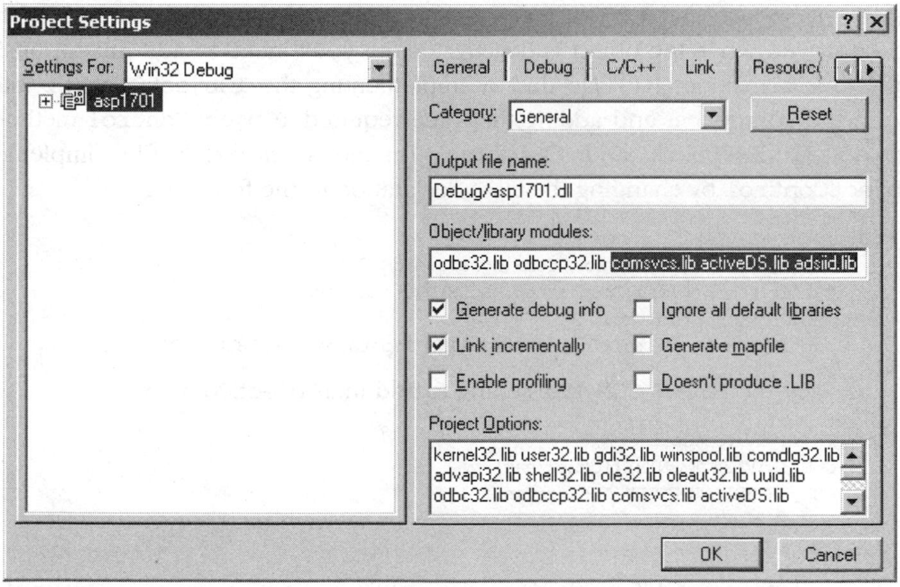

Figure 17-1. Adding support for COM+ Services and ADSI libraries to a Visual C++ project

Next, create a new object in the project by using the ATL Object Wizard to create a Simple Object. Name the object container and select the default Dual Interface and support for Aggregation, but change the Threading Model to Both.

> Instead of using the Simple Object template to create the compo-
> nent, you can also use the MTS template. If you do, you can skip
> much of the following material, which manually adds in support for
> IObjectControl. However, you won't be able to pool the object if
> you use the MTS template. See Chapter 14, *Creating C++ ASP Com-
> ponents*, for more information on pooling.

Once the new C++ object and header files have been generated, open *container.h*
and add the following include statements just below the statement that includes
the *resource.h* file:

```
#include <comsvcs.h>
#include <asptlb.h>
#include <activeds.h>
```

The first header file is for COM+ Services, the second supports the built-in ASP
objects, and the third is for Active Directory.

As I mentioned, the ASP Response object is used to write information from the
component to the web page; you instantiate it by accessing an instance of Object-
Context and then accessing Response from this object's Items collection. Both
objects—Response and ObjectContext—are created when the object is activated
and destroyed when the object is deactivated, so you'll need to add in support for
just-in-time activation (JIT). Do this by implementing the **IObjectControl** interface in the component and adding the three required **IObjectControl** methods:
Activate, CanBePooled, and Deactivate. In the *container.h* file, implement
IObjectControl by changing the class declaration to the following:

```
class ATL_NO_VTABLE Ccontainer :
    public CComObjectRootEx<CComSingleThreadModel>,
    public CComCoClass<Ccontainer, &CLSID_container>,
    public IObjectControl,
    public IDispatchImpl<Icontainer, &IID_Icontainer, &LIBID_ASP1701Lib>
```

Next, modify the **BEGIN_COM_MAP** setting to add in **IObjectControl**:

```
BEGIN_COM_MAP(Ccontainer)
    COM_INTERFACE_ENTRY(Icontainer)
    COM_INTERFACE_ENTRY(IObjectControl)
    COM_INTERFACE_ENTRY(IDispatch)
END_COM_MAP()
```

Finally, add the three JIT methods to the public section of the component class
declaration:

```
public:
    STDMETHOD(Activate)();
    STDMETHOD_(BOOL, CanBePooled)();
    STDMETHOD_(void, Deactivate)();
```

Also add in support for two private data members—a reference to ObjectContext and one to the Response interface:

```
private:
    CComPtr<IObjectContext> m_spObjectContext;
    CComPtr<IResponse>m_piResponse;
```

Finally, all you have to do is implement the **IObjectControl** methods to provide support for just-in-time activation, as well as for instantiating the Response object when the component is activated. Add the code shown in Example 17-1 to the component C++ file.

Example 17-1. Code to Support JIT Activation and Pooling for a Component

```
HRESULT Ccontainer::Activate()
{
    HRESULT hr = S_OK;
    CComBSTR bstrObj;
    CComVariant vt;
    CComPtr<IGetContextProperties> pProps; //Context Properties

    IDispatch* piDispatch = NULL;

    // get ObjectContext
      hr = GetObjectContext(&m_spObjectContext);
    if (FAILED(hr))
       return hr;

    // get Context Properties
    hr = m_spObjectContext->QueryInterface( IID_IGetContextProperties,
                (void**)&pProps );
    if (FAILED(hr))
        return hr;

    // get Response property
    bstrObj = "Response";
    hr = pProps->GetProperty( bstrObj, &vt ) ;

    if (FAILED(hr))
        return hr;

    piDispatch = vt. pdispVal;
    hr = piDispatch->QueryInterface( IID_IResponse,
                    (void**)&m_piResponse );

    return hr;
}

BOOL Ccontainer::CanBePooled()
{
    return TRUE;
}

void Ccontainer::Deactivate()
```

Example 17-1. Code to Support JIT Activation and Pooling for a Component (continued)

```
{
    m_piResponse.Release();
    m_spObjectContext.Release();
}
```

Now that the component support code has been added, you can concentrate on adding the Active Directory–specific code. Use the Visual C++ Class View to add a new method to the component and call it enumObjects. The method takes one input parameter of type BSTR,with the name of the ADSI container:

```
[in] BSTR bstrContainer
```

The method, the source code for which is shown in Example 17-2, calls ADsGet-Object to get a reference to the object specified in the *bstrContainer* parameter, and specifies IID_IADsGroup as the interface reference used in the function. Once it has a reference to the group, the method gets the group members through the Members method, assigning the reference to an instance of the IADsMembers interface. It enumerates each member and queries for each member in the collection, displaying the value of the CN property (which represents the unique name) for each item.

Example 17-2. Method to Enumerate Through Objects in an ADSI Group

```
STDMETHODIMP Ccontainer::enumObjects(BSTR bstrContainer)
{
    HRESULT hr = S_OK;

    IADsGroup *pGroup;
    IADsMembers *   pADsMembers       = NULL;
    IEnumVARIANT *  pEnumVariant      = NULL;
    IUnknown *      pUnknown          = NULL;
    IDispatch *pDisp                  = NULL;
    IADs *pADs                        = NULL;

    CComVariant vtout;
    CComVariant vtEntry;
    ULONG lng;

    // get group
    hr = ADsGetObject(bstrContainer,IID_IADsGroup,
                    (void **) &pGroup);

    // get members
    hr = pGroup->Members(&pADsMembers);
    if (FAILED(hr))
      return hr;
    pGroup->Release();

    // get enumerator
    hr = pADsMembers->get__NewEnum(&pUnknown);
```

Example 17-2. Method to Enumerate Through Objects in an ADSI Group (continued)

```
    if (FAILED(hr))
        return hr;
    pADsMembers->Release();

  hr = pUnknown->QueryInterface(IID_IEnumVARIANT,(void **)&pEnumVariant);
    if (FAILED(hr))
        return hr;
    pUnknown->Release();

    // enumerate through entries, printing out "cn"
    while (S_OK == pEnumVariant->Next(1,&vtEntry,&lng)) {
        pDisp = V_DISPATCH(&vtEntry);
        pDisp->QueryInterface(IID_IADs, (void**)&pADs);
        pADs->Get(L"cn",&vtout);
        m_piResponse->Write(vtout);
        vtout = "<br>";
        m_piResponse->Write(vtout);

    }
    pEnumVariant->Release();

    return hr;
}
```

Comparing the code in Example 17-2 with the Visual Basic code in Example 12-1, you can see that more of the COM implementation of the ADSI interfaces is exposed with Visual C++, but the functionality is basically the same: access the container, get the members, and use the built-in enumeration support to access each member and output a specific property.

To test your new C++ ASP Component, use the ASP test page *asp1701.asp*, which contains the following script:

```
<%
Dim obj
Set obj = Server.CreateObject("asp1701.container")
obj.enumObjects "LDAP://CN=test,CN=Users,DC=development,DC=local"
%>
```

The value passed as a parameter to the component is the complete path for the test group, containing two users. The usernames (their unique CN values) are listed:

```
George Washington
Bryan James
```

The code in Example 17-2 isn't overly complicated, but it is a bit more "wordy" than the Visual Basic code. It would be nice to have a little of the VB simplification and still create the component using C++. Luckily, with ADSI, you have this ability through a group of ADSI helper functions.

ADSI Helper Functions

The functions used to access Active Directory objects, ADsOpenObject or ADsGet-Object, are ADSI helper functions. These functions provide much of the functionality necessary to create the objects, simplifying your coding experience.

There are other ADSI helper functions, including ones to access recent errors, to create strings used with ADSI methods, and to handle much of the complexity of enumerating objects. As you saw in Example 17-2, enumeration is a multistep process, consisting of the following:

1. Call get_NewEnum, passing in a pointer to **IUnknown**.

2. Query the **IUnknown** interface for the **IEnumVariant** interface.

3. Access each member of **IEnumVariant**.

4. Release both the **IEnumVariant** and **IUnknown** interfaces.

The ADSI helper functions ADsBuildEnumerator, ADsEnumerateNext, and ADs-FreeEnumerator can simplify the use of enumeration and make your Active Directory code a whole lot easier to read and maintain.

To demonstrate, add a second method to your existing **asp1701.container** component and call it showUsers. This new method doesn't take any parameters. Its source code is shown in Example 17-3.

The method uses **IADsContainer** to work with the collection of users at the **development.local** domain controller. It also uses the ADSI helper function to handle all enumeration. As you can see in Example 17-3, the use of the helper functions completely eliminates the need to access **IUnknown** for the collection and to query for the enumerator interface.

Example 17-3. Enumeration Code Using ADSI Helper Functions

```
STDMETHODIMP Ccontainer::showUsers()
{
   HRESULT hr = S_OK;
   IADsContainer *pContainer;
   IEnumVARIANT *  pEnumVariant       = NULL;
   ULONG lng;
   IDispatch *pDisp                   = NULL;
   IADs *pADs                         = NULL;
   CComVariant vtout;
   CComVariant vtEntry;

   // get group
   hr = ADsGetObject(L"LDAP://CN=Users,DC=development,DC=local",
                 IID_IADsContainer,
                    (void **) &pContainer);
```

Example 17-3. Enumeration Code Using ADSI Helper Functions (continued)

```
// get enumerator
hr = ADsBuildEnumerator(pContainer,&pEnumVariant);
if (FAILED(hr))
    return hr;

// enumerate through entries, printing out "cn"
while (S_OK == ADsEnumerateNext(pEnumVariant,1,&vtEntry,&lng)) {
    V_DISPATCH(&vtEntry)->QueryInterface(IID_IADs, (void**)&pADs);
    pADs->Get(L"cn",&vtout);
    m_piResponse->Write(vtout);
    vtout = "<br>";
    m_piResponse->Write(vtout);

}
ADsFreeEnumerator(pEnumVariant);

return hr;
}
```

As you can see, although the helper functions don't eliminate all of the code needed to enumerate through a collection (you'll still have to query for each specific object to access its properties), it does cut the number of lines of code—decreasing potential errors and increasing readability.

To test the component, use a script similar to the following, which you can find in *asp1702.asp*:

```
<%
Dim obj
Set obj = Server.CreateObject("asp1701.container")
obj.showUsers
%>
```

As I mentioned earlier, there are other helper functions, including ones to build arrays of values to use in some of the ADSI methods, as you'll see demonstrated in the next section.

The ADsBuildEnumerator helper function works only with the IADsContainer and IADsMembers collections. Using the function with the IADsCollection interface will fail because of the location of get_NewEnum in the IADsCollection vtable. The IADs-Container and IADsMembers collections have get_NewEnum in the ninth vtable position, making them compatible with this helper function. IADsCollection has get_NewEnum in the eighth vtable position.

Filtering Collections

The good thing about collections is that it's very easy to enumerate through the members of the collection for whatever reason. However, the downside of collections is that many times you don't need to access *all* members of the collection—only a select few.

Instead of having to check out each collection member to see if it meets your selection criteria, you can instead filter the collection using the collection interface's put_Filter method. Note, though, that put_Filter is supported only with the **IADsMembers** and **IADsContainer** interfaces.

To demonstrate using filters, create one more method on **asp1701.container** and call this one enumObjectsByFilter. Add a **BSTR** parameter for receiving the specific filter to use:

```
[in] BSTR bstrFilter
```

The code for the method is shown in Example 17-4. It retrieves a reference to the Users collection and assigns it to an **IADsContainer** object. Next, it prepares the filter by building a variant array using the ADsBuildVarArray helper function, passing it the filter string provided as a parameter to enumObjectsByFilter, as well as a variant to hold the results, which are returned as a variant array. This variant array created by ADsBuildVarArray is then passed as a parameter to put_Filter. All that's left at this point is to enumerate through the filtered collection. To make things a little different in Example 17-4, the ADsPath is output instead of the unique name.

Example 17-4. Enumerating a Filtered Collection

```
STDMETHODIMP Ccontainer::enumObjectsByFilter(BSTR bstrFilter)
{
    HRESULT hr = S_OK;
    IADsContainer *pContainer;
    IEnumVARIANT *  pEnumVariant      = NULL;
    ULONG lng;
    IDispatch *pDisp                  = NULL;
    IADs *pADs                        = NULL;
    CComVariant vtout;
    CComVariant vtEntry;
    VARIANT vtArray;
    CComBSTR bstrPath;

    // get users
    hr = ADsGetObject(L"LDAP://CN=Users,DC=development,DC=local",
                    IID_IADsContainer,
                    (void **) &pContainer);
```

Example 17-4. Enumerating a Filtered Collection (continued)

```
//  VariantInit(&vtArray);
  ADsBuildVarArrayStr(&(LPWSTR)bstrFilter,1,&vtArray);

  // filter
  pContainer->put_Filter(vtArray);

  // get enumerator
  hr = ADsBuildEnumerator(pContainer,&pEnumVariant);
  if (FAILED(hr))
      return hr;

  // enumerate through entries, printing out "cn"
  while (S_OK == ADsEnumerateNext(pEnumVariant,1,&vtEntry,&lng)) {
      V_DISPATCH(&vtEntry)->QueryInterface(IID_IADs, (void**)&pADs);
      pADs->get_ADsPath(&bstrPath);
      vtout.bstrVal = bstrPath.Detach();
      m_piResponse->Write(vtout);
      vtout = "<br>";
      m_piResponse->Write(vtout);
  }
  ADsFreeEnumerator(pEnumVariant);

  return hr;
}
```

When you test your new component method using a script like *asp1703.asp*, you'll pass in the class name of the objects you want to include within the collection when your code processes it. For instance, if you only want to show the individual users (objects with User class) in the collection, pass **user** for the filter:

```
<%
Dim obj
Set obj = Server.CreateObject("asp1701.container")
obj.enumObjectsByFilter "user"
%>
```

Running this ASP script results in a list of user object types from the Users collection. If you wanted to see the groups contained in the Users collection, you would use the following:

```
obj.enumObjectsByFilter "group"
```

Try this with your component. Change the class name from **user** to **group** to see the differences in the results.

To this point, all you've had a chance to do is work with collections of objects and display information about the objects. You can also use ADSI to create and remove objects, discussed next.

Creating and Removing Active Directory Objects Using ADSI

To create a new Active Directory object, you first need to retrieve a reference to the object's container. So, to create a new user or group, you first have to access the User collection through **IADsContainer** and then use this interface's Create method to create the object.

Once you create an instance of the object, you can set its individual properties using the method supported for that type of object or using the more generic Put method. For instance, to make a new ADSI user, you create an instance of the **IADsUser** object and set the individual user properties:

```
pUser->put_FullName(bstrName);
pUser->put_EmailAddress(bstrEmail);
```

You could also use Put for these same properties:

```
pUser->Put(L"name",varName);
pGroup->Put(L"emailAddress",varEmail);
```

There are some properties that are required when you create a new object. For users and groups, you must specify the CN property (the unique name), as well as the SAMAccountName property. The latter is the name used by Windows client applications to use the object and is usually the same as the value given for CN.

To demonstrate creating and removing objects, specifically group objects, create a new Visual C++ project using the ATL COM Wizard, and again, don't check either the MFC or MTS option. Name the project **asp1702**. Attach the ADSI libraries (*activeDS.lib* and *adsiid.lib*) to the project's library modules.

Create a new Simple Object using the ATL Object Wizard and name it group. Set its Threading Model to Both, and keep the default settings for Dual Interface and Aggregation support.

Once the object's been created, add the Active Directory header file to the generated *group.h* file. Also add the *comdef.h* file (to provide support for the COM wrapper objects you'll use in your code):

```
#include <activeds.h>
#include <comdef.h>
```

Use the Visual C++ Class View to add a method named createGroup to the project. This method takes as its only parameter the name of the new group object:

```
[in] BSTR bstrGroup
```

The code for the createGroup method is shown in Example 17-5. It retrieves a reference to the group's container, in this case the Users collection. Then it calls the object's Create method, passing in the relative name of the new group. The relative name for the group is created by prepending CN= to the group name. The Create method returns a reference to an IDispatch interface. Calling its Query-Interface method then returns a reference to the IADsGroup object for the new group. Once you have the group, .set the properties that are required for all groups—namely the CN, SAMAccountName, and GroupType properties.

The GroupType property takes a value from the ADS_GROUP_TYPE_ENUM enumeration. Available values are the following:

ADS_GROUP_TYPE_GLOBAL_GROUP
: Contains accounts and other groups from its own domain

ADS_GROUP_TYPE_DOMAIN_LOCAL
: Can contain accounts and groups from any domain (LDAP only)

ADS_GROUP_TYPE_LOCAL_GROUP
: Same as ADS_GROUP_TYPE_DOMAIN_LOCAL but for WinNT

ADS_GROUP_TYPE_UNIVERSAL_GROUP
: Can contain groups and accounts from any domain but the local domain

ADS_GROUP_TYPE_SECURITY_ENABLED
: Security-enabled group

For the example, ADS_GROUP_TYPE_GLOBAL_GROUP and ADS_GROUP_TYPE_ SECURITY_ENABLED are combined with the bitwise OR operator to create a global, security-enabled group.

Once the group's properties have been set, the SetInfo method is called to persist the new group to the directory.

Example 17-5. Creating a New Group

```
STDMETHODIMP Cgroup::createGroup(BSTR bstrGroup)
{
    HRESULT hr = S_OK;
    IADsGroup *pGroup;
    IADsContainer *pContainer;
    IDispatch *pDisp            = NULL;
    IADs *pADs                  = NULL;
    _variant_t varGroup = bstrGroup;
    _variant_t varType;
    _bstr_t bstrGrp = bstrGroup;

    // change group name to a relative, unique name
    bstrGrp = "CN=" + bstrGrp;

    // get group
    hr = ADsGetObject(L"LDAP://CN=Users,DC=development,DC=local",
                    IID_IADsContainer,
                    (void **) &pContainer);
```

Example 17-5. Creating a New Group (continued)

```
    if (FAILED(hr))
        return hr;

    // create group object
    hr = pContainer->Create(L"group",bstrGrp,&pDisp);
    if (FAILED(hr))
        return hr;
    pContainer->Release();

    hr = pDisp->QueryInterface(IID_IADsGroup,(void **)&pGroup);
    if (FAILED(hr))
        return hr;
    pDisp->Release();

    // assign group properties
    pGroup->Put(L"cn",varGroup);
    pGroup->Put(L"sAMAccountName",varGroup);


    varType.lVal = ADS_GROUP_TYPE_GLOBAL_GROUP |
                                    ADS_GROUP_TYPE_SECURITY_ENABLED;
    pGroup->Put(L"groupType",varType);

    // save information
    hr=pGroup->SetInfo();

    return hr;
}
```

The script that tests the new component passes in the name of the new group, **devasp**, as shown in the following ASP test page, *asp1704.asp*:

```
    <%
    Dim obj
    Set obj = Server.CreateObject("asp1702.group")

    obj.createGroup "devasp"
    %>
```

Using the Active Directory Services Viewer (see Chapter 12 for details on using this tool), you can see that the new group has been added to the Users collection, as shown in Figure 17-2, and given a CN and SAMAccountName property value of **devasp**.

You can remove items as easily as you create them. The key to removing an existing item is to again access the item's container and then call the Delete method to delete the specific object.

To remove the new group you just created, add a new method to your **asp1702.group** component and call this method removeGroup. Again, the method takes a BSTR value representing the group name as its only parameter. The method code,

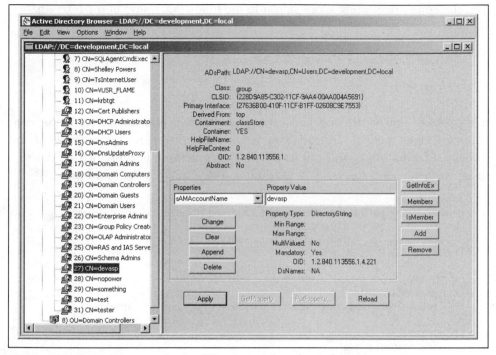

Figure 17-2. Active Directory Services Viewer snapshot of new devasp group

which is shown in Example 17-6, obtains a reference to the group's container and then deletes the object.

Example 17-6. Remove the Group from the Container

```
// could not use removeGroup
STDMETHODIMP Cgroup::removeGrp(BSTR bstrGroup)
{
    HRESULT hr = S_OK;
    IADsContainer *pContainer;
    _bstr_t bstrGrp = bstrGroup;
    bstrGrp = "CN=" + bstrGrp;

    // get group
    hr = ADsGetObject(L"LDAP://CN=Users,DC=development,DC=local",
                    IID_IADsContainer,
                    (void **) &pContainer);
    if (FAILED(hr))
        return hr;

    // delete group, release container
    pContainer->Delete(L"group",bstrGrp);
    pContainer->Release();

    return hr;
}
```

Test the component using script similar to the following, found in *asp1705.asp*:

```
<%
Dim obj
Set obj = Server.CreateObject("asp1702.group")

obj.removeGrp "devasp"
%>
```

If the object you're deleting had contained children, you couldn't use the container's Delete method. Instead, you would have to create an instance of the **IADsDeleteOps** object and call its DeleteObject method. For instance, to delete a group with accounts (users), you would use code similar to the following:

```
// get group
hr = ADsGetObject(L"LDAP://CN=somegrp,CN=Users,DC=development,DC=local",
                  IID_IADsContainer,
                  (void **) &pContainer);
if (FAILED(hr)) return hr;

// delete group
IADsDeleteOps *pDel;
hr = pContainer->QueryInterface(IID_IADsDeleteOps, (void **)&pDel);

if (FAILED(hr)) return hr;
pDel->DeleteObject(0);
```

The parameter used with DeleteObject is reserved for future use—use a value of zero (0) for now.

In all the examples examined so far, you've known the ADS path for the object you wanted to work with. However, in a larger setup, you might not have this information but will instead need to search for a specific item. The next and final section of this chapter discusses how to use the **IDirectoryService** object to search for specific Active Directory objects.

Searching Active Directory with IDirectorySearch

In Chapter 12, the example that demonstrated searching through Active Directory objects used ADO to perform the search. A second technique for searching through Active Directory uses the **IDirectorySearch** interface. The **IDirectorySearch** interface has methods to execute a search and then process its results.

Active Directory searches using the **IDirectorySearch** interface are restricted to selecting objects based on the object class. For instance, to get all objects with a class of **user**, you'd use the following selection criteria:

```
(ObjectClass=user)
```

This type of selection criteria will traverse all subtrees in the directory service, returning a collection of all objects with the class name of user.

With IDirectorySearch, you can also specify what columns, or object properties, to return from the search. The selection list is contained within an array passed with the search.

To try out searching with IDirectorySearch, create a new Visual C++ project using the ATL COM Wizard, and don't add support for MTS or MFC. Name the project asp1703. Once the project files are generated, add the Active Directory libraries to the project's library modules. Also add the COM+ Services library, since you're again going to be using the built-in ASP Response object to print out your results. You should add the following libraries to the end of the Object/Library Modules text box:

```
comsvcs.lib activeDS.lib adsiid.lib
```

Create a new Simple Object using the ATL Object Wizard, name the object search, and set the Threading Model to Both. Leave all other properties at their default values.

Once the *search.h* header file is generated, add in the necessary header files to support Active Directory, COM+ Services, and the ASP built-in objects. You'll also be using COM wrapper classes, so add support for *comdef.h*. The following are the #include statements you should add to the header file:

```
#include <comsvcs.h>
#include <asptlb.h>
#include <activeds.h>
#include <comdef.h>
```

Use Class View to add a new method named doQuery. This method takes one BSTR input parameter—the name of the class you'll be searching for:

```
[in] BSTR bstrClass
```

In the newly generated method, add the code to instantiate the IObjectContext object, which is used to create an instance of the IResponse object, as shown in Example 17-7. The method uses the Response object to display the results of the query.

Example 17-7. Create an Instance of IResponse for Web Page Output

```
HRESULT hr = S_OK;
CComPtr<IObjectContext> spObjectContext;
CComPtr<IResponse> piResponse;
CComBSTR bstrObj;
CComVariant vt;
CComPtr<IGetContextProperties> pProps; //Context Properties

IDispatch* piDispatch = NULL;
```

Example 17-7. Create an Instance of IResponse for Web Page Output (continued)

```
// get ObjectContext
 hr = CoGetObjectContext(IID_IObjectContext,
                              (void **)&spObjectContext);
if (FAILED(hr))
   return hr;

// get Context Properties
hr = spObjectContext->QueryInterface( IID_IGetContextProperties,
            (void**)&pProps );
if (FAILED(hr))
     return hr;

// get Response property
bstrObj = "Response";
hr = pProps->GetProperty( bstrObj, &vt ) ;

if (FAILED(hr))
     return hr;

piDispatch = vt. pdispVal;
hr = piDispatch->QueryInterface( IID_IResponse,
                  (void**)&piResponse );
```

In the same doQuery method, next add the code to create an instance of the
IDirectorySearch interface, as shown in Example 17-8. The path used with the
ADsGetObject method call is the name of the domain controller, since you're
searching throughout the domain's entire directory service for all objects having
the specified search class.

The code instantiates **IDirectorySearch** and calls its ExecuteSearch method,
which has the following parameters:

pszSearchFilter
> A LPWSTR representing the search filter or criteria (the class name in the form
> of a search expression).

pAttributeNames
> A LPWSTR representing an array containing the names of the attributes to
> return.

dwNumberAttributes
> A DWORD representing a count of the number of attributes to return.

phSearchHandle
> A PADS_SEARCH_HANDLE representing the handle to the search context. This
> parameter must be used with all methods when processing the search results.

After the successful search, the method processes the results and displays the values. To display the values, each attribute is accessed using the GetColumn

method, and the contents are assigned to an ADS_SEARCH_COLUMN object. ADS_
SEARCH_COLUMN has the following structure:

```
typedef struct ADS_SEARCH_COLUMN
{
  LPWSTR     pszAttrName;
  ADSTYPE    dwADsType;
  PADSVALUE  pADsValues;
  DWORD      dwNumValues;
  HANDLE     hReserved;
} ADS_SEARCH_COLUMN, *PADS_SEARCH_COLUMN;
```

The attribute name and type are given in *pszAttrName* and *dwADsType*, respectively. The attribute value(s) are retrieved from *pADsValues*, an array of ADSVALUE structures. In the code, the value of each attribute is accessed from the array through the ADSVALUE structure's *CaseIgnoreString* value.

Example 17-8. Using the IDirectorySearch Interface

```
// Active Directory code
IDirectorySearch *pDSearch;

// array with selection list items
LPWSTR pszAttr[] = { L"cn", L"samAccountName",
                            L"distinguishedName", L"ADsPath" };

ADS_SEARCH_HANDLE hSearch;
ADS_SEARCH_COLUMN hCol;
DWORD dwCount= sizeof(pszAttr)/sizeof(LPWSTR);

// create search string for given object class
_bstr_t bstrCls = bstrClass;
_bstr_t bstrSearch = "(objectClass=" + bstrCls + ")";
_variant_t varout;
int i;

// get IDirectorySearch for domain
hr = ADsGetObject(L"LDAP://DC=development,DC=local",
                  IID_IDirectorySearch,
                  (void **) &pDSearch);
if (FAILED(hr))
    return hr;

// execute search
// pass in search string, selection list array, and search handle
hr = pDSearch->ExecuteSearch((LPWSTR)bstrSearch,pszAttr,
                             dwCount,&hSearch);

if (FAILED(hr))
    return hr;

// while more rows
// print out selection list items
```

Example 17-8. Using the IDirectorySearch Interface (continued)

```
// item name on left, value on right
while( pDSearch->GetNextRow(hSearch)  != S_ADS_NOMORE_ROWS ) {
    for (i = 0; i < 4; i++) {
        varout = pszAttr[i];
        piResponse->Write(varout);
        varout = " = ";
        piResponse->Write(varout);

        // set column to column handle
        pDSearch->GetColumn(hSearch,pszAttr[i],&hCol);
        varout = hCol.pADsValues->CaseIgnoreString;
        piResponse->Write(varout);
        varout="<br>";
        piResponse->Write(varout);

        // free column handle
        pDSearch->FreeColumn(&hCol);
    }
}

// clean up
pDSearch->CloseSearchHandle(hSearch);
pDSearch->Release();

return hr;
```

To test the new component, create an ASP test script like the following one, *asp1706.asp*, and pass in the class name of the objects to search for. To look for all User objects, pass in the "user" text string:

```
<%
Dim obj
Set obj = Server.CreateObject("asp1703.search")

obj.doQuery "user"
%>
```

To look for all groups, pass in "group":

```
obj.doQuery "group"
```

Vary the name of the object class you use with each test, and view the results. These are some of the classes you can try:

```
user
group
computer
contact
```

You can specify search criteria using the SetSearchPreference method, which has the following parameters:

pSearchPrefs

    Pointer to an array of ADS_SEARCHPREF_INFO structures with information about search preferences

dwNumPrefs

    A DWORD indicating the number of preferences

Use this to set search preferences such as the page size for the search results. You can also abandon an existing search by calling the AbandonSearch method, passing in the existing search handle.

18

Accessing MSMQ from C++ ASP Components

Microsoft's Message Queue technology, known by the acronym MSMQ, provides a way for applications to communicate with one another literally across time and space. MSMQ crosses time by allowing one application to create messages that are placed in a queue at one time but processed (by the same or another application) at a later time. MSMQ crosses space by being designed to be used in heterogeneous, distributed applications—applications such as ASP applications.

ASP application components can send messages to queues, and the messages can be processed by other non-ASP applications. Conversely, other applications can send messages to queues for pickup by an ASP application (that pickup being initiated via a web page). Or the sender and the receiver of the message can both be ASP application-based.

This chapter looks at working with MSMQ from within C++ components.

 This chapter does not provide an overview of MSMQ or explore the concepts of using MSMQ in an ASP component. For this, you'll want to read Chapter 13, *Working with MSMQ Components*. Once you've read about the concepts of MSMQ, try out the MSMQ examples created in C++ in this chapter.

Adding Support for MSMQ to the C++ Project

MSMQ has three basic components: the MSMQ queue (used to hold and provide access for MSMQ messages), the MSMQ message itself, and transaction support.

In your C++ components, you can programmatically create (and remove) private or public message queues, with or without transaction support. A *public queue* is one accessible by any Active Directory node, such as one on another machine. A *private queue*, on the other hand, is accessible only by the machine where the node resides. Once a queue is created, you can send and retrieve messages from it. You can also add transaction support that is specific to MSMQ only or integrate it with MTS/COM+ transaction support.

MSMQ also supports specialized queues, such as dead-letter queues for messages that can't be delivered, as well as journaling—echoing sent or retrieved messages for historical or recovery purposes.

There are two ways you can access MSMQ objects and functionality from within Visual C++ components. The first way is to use the MSMQ COM objects created specifically for use by applications that support COM. The second way is to use the MSMQ functions.

The MSMQ functions are accessible from C++ only and use a set of structures to pass properties, parameters, and other values to and from function calls. For instance, to create a message queue using MSMQ functions, you create an array of **MQPROPVARIANT** structures to define the queue properties, an array of **QUEUEPROPID** structures to set the property identifiers, and an array of **HRESULT** values to hold the status of each property:

```
MQPROPVARIANT aQueuePropVar[NUMBEROFPROPERTIES];
QUEUEPROPID aQueuePropId[NUMBEROFPROPERTIES];
HRESULT aQueueStatus[NUMBEROFPROPERTIES];
```

Each property then needs to have an entry defined in the queue property and identifier arrays:

```
// set queue name
aQueuePropId[0] = PROPID_Q_PATHNAME;
aQueuePropVar[0].vt = VT_LPWSTR;
aQueuePropVar[0].pwszVal = (LPWSTR)bstrPath;
```

All these structures are then assigned to members in another structure, **MQQUEUEPROPS**:

```
// set queue properties
QueueProps.cProp = NUMBEROFPROPERTIES;
QueueProps.aPropID = aQueuePropId;
QueueProps.aPropVar = aQueuePropVar;
QueueProps.aStatus = aQueueStatus;
```

This structure is then passed as a parameter to the *MQCreateQueue* function to create the queue:

```
hr = MQCreateQueue(pSecurityDescriptor,
            &QueueProps,
```

```
wszFormatNameBuffer,
&dwFormatNameBufferLength);
```

As you can see, working with MSMQ functions can be a lengthy process.

If you want to use MSMQ functions in your Visual C++ components, you'll have to include the MSMQ header file into your component:

```
#include <mq.h>
```

Additionally, you'll also have to add the MSMQ library to your other component library/object modules. Do this by accessing Project → Settings from the main menu, selecting the Link tab of the Project Settings dialog, and adding the following to the end of the list of objects in the Object/Library Modules list:

```
Mqrt.lib
```

A later section in this chapter, "Searching for a Specific Queue," provides a complete example of using MSMQ functions.

As I said, working with MSMQ can be a lengthy process, which is the reason that I prefer using the COM objects to implement MSMQ functionality from within Visual C++ components. The MSMQ COM objects are identical in behavior and functionality regardless of what language is used—Visual Basic, Visual C++, Delphi, or another language. However, the exact syntax used with the objects can differ considerably between languages. In Chapter 13, you had a chance to see how the MSMQ COM objects work within Visual Basic. This chapter shows how many of these same objects work within C++.

First, though, you have to add support for MSMQ COM objects by using the **import** directive to incorporate the MSMQ type library into your component:

```
#import "mqoa.dll" no_namespace
```

The **import** directive is a very handy feature to wrap the raw COM interfaces of MSMQ (or other COM objects) with *smart pointers*, making it almost as easy to work with interfaces in Visual C++ as it is in Visual Basic. The **no_namespace** attribute means that you can access the objects directly without having to precede them with a namespace identifier.

Chapter 14, *Creating C++ ASP Components*, covers the **import** directive and smart pointers in more detail. Most of the C++ chapters use the import directive to simplify the coding.

Another advantage to using the **import** directive is that C++ exception handling is provided for the COM objects, so you don't have to litter your code with tests of the **HRESULT** return value for every method call.

Once you've imported the type library into your C++ component, you're ready to work with MSMQ COM objects. First up: creating the message queue.

Working with Queues

Think of an MSMQ queue as a mailbox. A mailbox shares the same overall physical location with several other mailboxes, but each one has a unique identifier and occupies a unique space within the location. Given a mailbox number, you can easily go to that box and get your mail.

Working with MSMQ queues is just as easy as getting mail from and putting mail into a physical mailbox—but with MSMQ, you have to create the mailbox first.

Creating Queues

As stated earlier, there are two types of queues: private and public. If you don't have Active Directory installed, you can create only private queues—trying to create a public queue results in an error.

 If you're working with MSMQ on a machine that doesn't have Active Directory installed or doesn't have access to a machine with an Active Directory domain controller, you can create only private queues. See Chapter 12, *Working with Active Directory from ASP Applications*, for instructions on how to set up a standalone Active Directory installation.

There are multiple types of queues that you as an MSMQ developer can create, including queues for messages, administrative system messages, and so on. Additionally, there are also system queues that are created by MSMQ, such as the dead-letter and journal queues. You can't create these, but you can access them. This chapter focuses on the type of queue you'll most likely use with your ASP components: the message queues.

To create a new message queue, you must provide a unique pathname for it. This pathname can contain the NetBIOS or DNS machine name or a period for the local computer. The examples in this chapter use the period, since all of the components are created and tested locally on the development machine.

The pathname also includes additional naming information to provide a unique identifier. This additional information is separated by backslashes. When you provide the backslashes (\) for the name, make sure you *escape* it within C++ by preceding the backslash with a second backslash. For example:

```
.\\newqueue
```

Once you create the queue, you can use it to send and receive messages.

To demonstrate how simple it is to create a message queue within your C++ components, create a new Visual C++ project using the ATL COM AppWizard, and name the project **asp1801**. Don't check either the MFC or MTS options when prompted by the wizard.

Once the project files are generated, insert a new ATL object using the ATL Object Wizard, choosing the Simple Object option and naming the new object **msgqueue**. Accept the default attributes for the object, except change the threading model to Both.

Once the new object's C++ and header files have been created, add your first method to the component using the Visual C++ Class View. The new method is named newPublicQueue and takes three **BSTR** parameters, two input and one return value:

```
[in] BSTR bstrQueue, BSTR bstrLabel, [out,retval]BSTR* pbstrMessage
```

The first input parameter is used to derive the queue's pathname, and the second is the queue's label. A *label* is a way of grouping one or more queues for accessibility as a group and provides a descriptive name for the queue. The return parameter is used to pass a status message from the component to the ASP page.

Add the component code shown in Example 18-1 to the new method. The code creates an instance of **IMSQQueueInfoPtr**, the smart pointer that wraps the MSMQQueueInfo object. This object is used to create the queue once the queue properties have been defined. Next, it creates the queue pathname by concatenating the location information to the queue name passed as the first parameter. It assigns this string to the MSMQQueueInfo PathName property, as well as assigning the label to the Label property. Finally, it calls the Create method to create the queue. The Create method takes one parameter, a **true** or **false** value indicating whether the queue is transactional or not. By default, this parameter is set to **false** (don't create a transactional queue) when no parameter is present, as is the case with the example.

Example 18-1. Creating a Public MSMQ Message Queue

```
STDMETHODIMP Cmsgqueue::newPublicQueue(BSTR bstrQueue,
                                       BSTR bstrLabel,
                                       BSTR* pbstrMessage)
{
    CComBSTR bstrMessage;
    bstrMessage = "Queue Created";

    IMSMQQueueInfoPtr qinfo("MSMQ.MSMQQueueInfo");

    // create path
    qinfo->PathName = _bstr_t(".\\") + _bstr_t(bstrQueue);
```

Example 18-1. Creating a Public MSMQ Message Queue (continued)

```
      qinfo->Label = bstrLabel;
      try
      {
        qinfo->Create();
      }
      catch (_com_error comerr)
      {
        HRESULT hr = comerr.Error();
        if (hr == MQ_ERROR_QUEUE_EXISTS)
        {
          bstrMessage = "Queue already exists";
        }
        else
        {
          bstrMessage = "Could not create queue";
        }
      }

      *pbstrMessage = bstrMessage.Detach();

      return S_OK;
}
```

In the component, the call to the Create method is enclosed within a **try** block, so that any error that results is trapped within the associated **catch** block, which assigns the error message to a string that is returned to the calling ASP script.

 Before you compile your new component and method, you'll need to enable C++ exception handling. You can do this by selecting Project → Settings from the menu, clicking on the C/C++ tab, and selecting C++ Language from the Category dropdown list. Check the Enable Exception Handling option.

Try out your new component by creating an instance of it within the following ASP script, *asp1801.asp*, and calling newPublicQueue, passing in the queue's name and label:

```
<%
Dim obj
Set obj = Server.CreateObject("asp1801.msgqueue")

Dim queue, label
queue = "first"
label = "First public queue"

Dim msg
msg = obj.newPublicQueue(queue,label)
Response.Write "<h3>" & msg & "</h3>"
%>
```

Notice that the script displays the message returned from the component, which signals success or failure while creating the queue.

The example just shown creates a public queue that's registered with the directory service. Any machine and any MSMQ application that shares the same domain controller on which the MSMQ queue is created can now send and read messages from this queue.

There are times when you might not want to have a queue be publicly accessible, or you might not have access to an Active Directory domain controller. In these circumstances, you can create a private queue instead of a public one by simply adding the PRIVATE$ token to the pathname.

To try out creating a private queue, create a second method on asp1801. msgqueue, and name this new method newPrivateQueue. It takes three parameters, defined as follows in the Parameters text box of the Add Method to Interface dialog:

```
[in] BSTR bstrQueue, BSTR bstrLabel, [out,retval]BSTR* pbstrMessage
```

Add the code shown in Example 18-2 for the second method. This code is exactly the same as that shown in Example 18-1 except for the addition of the private token.

Example 18-2. Creating a Private MSMQ Message Queue

```
STDMETHODIMP Cmsgqueue::newPrivateQueue(BSTR bstrQueue,
                                        BSTR bstrLabel,
                                        BSTR *pbstrMessage)
{
    CComBSTR bstrMessage;
    bstrMessage = "Queue Created";

    IMSMQQueueInfoPtr qinfo("MSMQ.MSMQQueueInfo");

    qinfo->PathName = _bstr_t(".\\PRIVATE$\\") + _bstr_t(bstrQueue);
    qinfo->Label = bstrLabel;
    try
    {
      qinfo->Create();
    }
    catch (_com_error comerr)
    {
      HRESULT hr = comerr.Error();
      if (hr == MQ_ERROR_QUEUE_EXISTS)
      {
        bstrMessage = "Queue already exists";
      }
      else
      {
        bstrMessage = "Could not create queue";
      }
```

Example 18-2. Creating a Private MSMQ Message Queue (continued)

```
    }

    *pbstrMessage = bstrMessage.Detach();

    return S_OK;
}
```

Try this component method with the following script, *asp1802.asp*:

```
<%
Dim obj
Set obj = Server.CreateObject("asp1801.msgqueue")

Dim queue, label
queue = "second"
label = "First private queue"

Dim msg
msg = obj.newPrivateQueue(queue,label)
Response.Write "<h3>" & msg & "</h3>"
%>
```

You can view queues using the Active Directory Users and Computers administrative tool. Open the tool, and select the "Users, groups, and computers as containers" option from the View menu. Then click on the Advanced Features option in the View menu.

To find a queue, right-click on the DNS and select Find from the menu that opens. In the Find dialog, you can enter the label you used for either the private or public queue, and the queue should show in the list. Or you can leave the search criteria empty, and all MSMQ queues will be listed, as shown in Figure 18-1. Notice in the figure that both the public and private queues are displayed in the list.

You can access any of the queue's properties by right-clicking on the queue, and you can also delete an existing queue. Needless to say, you must have administrative privileges before you can use the Active Directory administrative tools.

Speaking of deleting queues, once you're done with a queue, you can get rid of it programmatically. Removing queues is discussed in the next section.

Removing Queues

What can be created can be destroyed, including MSMQ queues. First, though, you have to obtain a reference to the queue.

There are two ways to search for an active reference to an MSMQ queue. In the next section we'll look at one way, which is to use MSMQQuery and do a lookup for a queue. The second way is to actually create the queue. Wait a second here. To get the queue you have to create the queue? Sounds crazy, doesn't it? However,

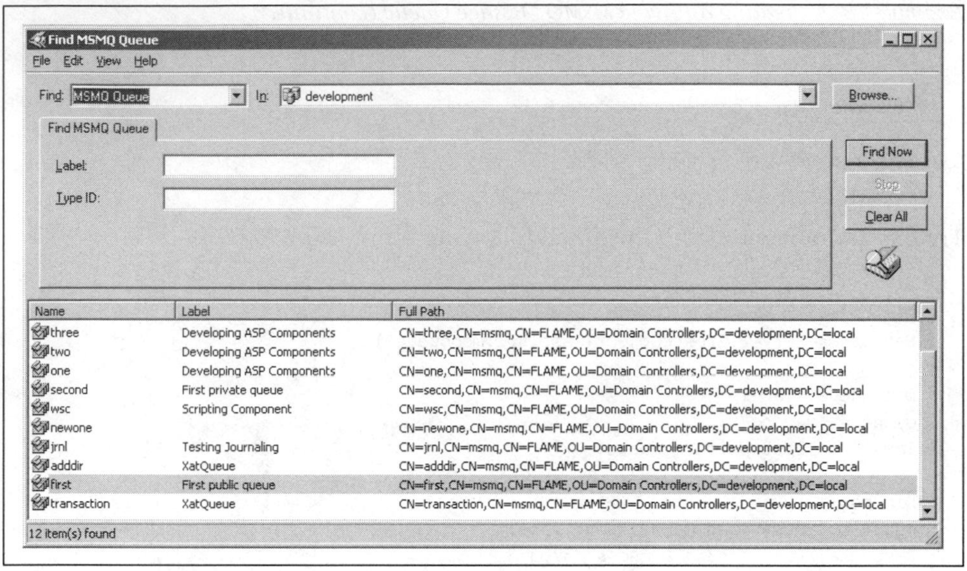

Figure 18-1. Using the Active Directory Users and Computers administrative tools

this isn't as odd as it sounds. Yes, if you use the MSMQQueueInfo object's Create method on an existing queue, you'll get a message that the queue has already been created. However, you'll also get a reference to the queue, and this is the approach that Microsoft uses for many of its own MSMQ examples.

Test this for yourself by removing the public and private queues you created in the last section. First, add a new method to **asp1801**, and name it removeQueue. This method takes three parameters:

```
[in] BSTR bstrQueue, int iType, [out,retval] BSTR* pbstrMessage
```

The first parameter is the queue name used for the path, the second is a value indicating if the queue is private or public, and the third is the status message. The *iType* parameter is used to determine whether the code should concatenate the PRIVATE$ token with the pathname.

Next, add the code for the method, which is shown in Example 18-3. Like Examples 18-1 and 18-2, you'll use the Create method to "create" the queue, but this time you'll trap the method call in its own **try...catch** block. The reason for the separate exception-handling block is that we're expecting the call to generate an error condition, since the queue already exists. In a second **try...catch** block, you'll then use the reference to the queue you obtained from the Create method to delete the queue using the MSMQQueueInfo object's Delete method.

Example 18-3. Removing an MSMQ Queue

```
STDMETHODIMP Cmsgqueue::removeQueue(BSTR bstrQueue,
                      int iType,
```

Example 18-3. Removing an MSMQ Queue (continued)

```
                                     BSTR *pbstrMessage)
{
    CComBSTR bstrMessage;
    bstrMessage = "Queue Removed";

    IMSMQQueueInfoPtr qinfo("MSMQ.MSMQQueueInfo");

    // build path based on type of queue
    if (iType == 1)
        qinfo->PathName = _bstr_t(".\\PRIVATE$\\") + _bstr_t(bstrQueue);
    else
        qinfo->PathName = _bstr_t(".\\") + _bstr_t(bstrQueue);

    // obtain reference to queue
    try
    {
        qinfo->Create();
    }
    catch (_com_error comerr)
    {
        HRESULT hr = comerr.Error();
        if (hr == MQ_ERROR_QUEUE_EXISTS)
        {
            // disregard
        }
        else
        {
            bstrMessage = "Could not create queue";
            *pbstrMessage = bstrMessage.Detach();
            return hr;
        }
    }

    // delete queue
    try {
        qinfo->Delete();
    }

    catch (_com_error comerr)
    {
        bstrMessage = "Could not remove queue";
    }

    *pbstrMessage = bstrMessage.Detach();
    return S_OK;
}
```

To test the new method, the following script, *asp1803.asp*, removes both the public and private queues you created earlier:

```
<%
Dim obj
Set obj = Server.CreateObject("asp1801.msgqueue")
```

```
Dim msg

' remove public queue
msg = obj.removeQueue("first", 0)
Response.Write "<h3>" & msg & "</h3>"

msg= obj.removeQueue("second", 1)
Response.Write "<h3>" & msg & "</h3>"
%>
```

The next section demonstrates how to search for a queue based on the label. Included within the section is a component that uses the MSMQ functions as well as a component using the MSMQ COM objects.

Searching for a Specific Queue

As I said earlier, in this section you'll be able to create queue search functionality using both MSMQ COM objects and the MSMQ functions. We'll start with the COM objects first.

Searching Queues with the MSMQ COM Objects

The MSMQQuery object can be used to search for a queue based on its identifier, service type, creation or modification time, or label.

MSMQQuery has one method, LookUp, with several optional parameters. The first five parameters hold the values used for searching; the last three parameters are used to specify the type of query used. The search parameters are identifier, service type, label, creation time, and modification time, in that order. All queries are based on equality, by default, so the only time you'll need to specify one of the remaining three parameters is to perform a search other than an equality search.

If you search for the label, for example, you'll need to use a placeholder value for all parameters before the one you're listing. The placeholder for C++ smart pointers is **vtMissing**, a predefined value used to indicate a null or missing value.

 One limitation with the MSMQQuery object's LookUp method is that it works only on public queues. You have to use an alternative approach (such as the Create method, used earlier) for finding private queues.

To search using MSMQ COM objects, add a new method to **asp1801.msgqueue** and name it findQueues. The method takes a **BSTR** value with the queue label used for the search:

```
[in] BSTR bstrLabel
```

The results of your search will be displayed directly from the component using the built-in ASP Response object, so you'll need to add support for the ASP intrinsics to your component. First, add the following include statements to the *msgqueue.h* header file:

```
#include <comsvcs.h>
#include <asptlb.h>
```

Additionally, add the COM+ Services library (*comsvcs.lib*) to the project's linked object/library modules list.

Add the code for your new method, beginning with the code to create a reference to the ASP Response object shown in Example 18-4.

Example 18-4. Code to Create Reference to ASP Response Object

```
HRESULT hr = S_OK;

// **** create Response object **** //

CComPtr<IObjectContext> spObjectContext;
CComPtr<IResponse> piResponse;
CComBSTR bstrObj;
CComVariant vt;
CComPtr<IGetContextProperties> pProps; //Context Properties

IDispatch* piDispatch = NULL;

// get ObjectContext
  hr = CoGetObjectContext(IID_IObjectContext,
                              (void **)&spObjectContext);
if (FAILED(hr))
    return hr;

// get context properties
hr = spObjectContext->QueryInterface( IID_IGetContextProperties,
            (void**)&pProps );
if (FAILED(hr))
    return hr;

// get Response property
bstrObj = "Response";
hr = pProps->GetProperty( bstrObj, &vt ) ;

if (FAILED(hr))
    return hr;

piDispatch = vt. pdispVal;
hr = piDispatch->QueryInterface( IID_IResponse,
                    (void**)&piResponse );
```

Next, add the code shown in Example 18-5 for the MSMQ query. Because more than one queue can have the same label, you'll need to process the results of the lookup in a loop. In the loop, the Response object is used to print out two queue properties, the format name and the path, to the returning web page. Notice in the call to LookUpQueue that the **vtMissing** placeholder value is used for every parameter before the one of interest, the label. The placeholder does not need to be used for the parameters that follow.

Example 18-5. Using MSMQQuery to Look Up Queues Based on Queue Label

```
STDMETHODIMP Cmsgqueue::findQueues(BSTR bstrLabel)
{

  /// ... the code to get the Response object fits here...


    // **** MSMQ Functionality **** //

  IMSMQQueryPtr query("MSMQ.MSMQQuery");
  IMSMQQueueInfosPtr qinfos;
  IMSMQQueueInfoPtr qinfo;
  _variant_t vtLabel;

  vtLabel = bstrLabel;

  // lookup based on label
  qinfos = query->LookupQueue(&vtMissing, &vtMissing, &vtLabel);

  // get first
  qinfo = qinfos->Next();

  _bstr_t bstrFormatName;
  _bstr_t bstrPathName;

  // if no queues found
  if (qinfo == NULL) {
     piResponse->Write (_variant_t("no queues matching the label"));
     return S_OK;
  }

  // while queues
  while (qinfo != NULL)
  {
    bstrFormatName = qinfo->GetFormatName();
    bstrPathName = qinfo->GetPathName();
    piResponse->Write(_variant_t(bstrFormatName + L"<br>"));
    piResponse->Write(_variant_t(bstrPathName + L"<p>"));
    qinfo = qinfos->Next();
  }

  return S_OK;
}
```

Once you compile the component, test the page. First, use the following ASP test page, *asp1804.asp*, to create five new public queues, each with the same label (the label is the same, but the queue name has to differ or a query already exists error will be generated):

```
<%
Dim obj
Set obj = Server.CreateObject("asp1801.msgqueue")

Dim queue, label
label = "Developing ASP Components"

Dim msg
msg=obj.newPublicQueue("one", label)
Response.Write "<h3>" & msg & "</h3>"

msg=obj.newPublicQueue("two", label)
Response.Write "<h3>" & msg & "</h3>"

msg=obj.newPublicQueue("three", label)
Response.Write "<h3>" & msg & "</h3>"

msg=obj.newPublicQueue("four", label)
Response.Write "<h3>" & msg & "</h3>"

msg=obj.newPublicQueue("five", label)
Response.Write "<h3>" & msg & "</h3>"
%>
```

Once the public queues are created, test the component's new findQueues method by calling it with the `Developing ASP Components` queue label, as shown in the following ASP test script, *asp1805.asp*:

```
<%
Dim obj
Set obj = Server.CreateObject("asp1801.msgqueue")

obj.findQueues "Developing ASP Components"
%>
```

The result is a page with the format names and paths of the five queues:

```
PUBLIC=69af321f-13f8-49d7-8490-38d864e6f46f
flame\one
PUBLIC=2a570b7d-9d6c-47f4-91c5-9662275bbdb9
flame\two
PUBLIC=09a70a92-4885-49a7-9604-f32a2ae2f1ee
flame\three
PUBLIC=99c56ee6-70ac-44f7-a5e8-610ba8fe4bf9
flame\four
PUBLIC=c6453600-9c77-4e34-a067-6ec727d2c905
flame\five
```

If you've checked out the examples in Chapter 13, the comparable Visual Basic version of this example (Example 13-4) also displayed the full DNS pathname of each queue. Unfortunately, the DNS pathname is not accessible as a property when using the Visual C++ smart pointer objects.

To get output that matches the Visual Basic example, we'll use the MSMQ functions to perform the search and display the results. I'll warn you now, though, that you're in for a significant coding effort just to get this information.

Searching Queues with MSMQ Functions

All the examples to this point have used the MSMQ COM objects to work with MSMQ. As we've just noted, there can be limitations to the COM objects, such as lack of access to the DNS full pathname for the queues from the MSMQQueueInfo object.

In this section, you'll use the MSMQ functions to search for queues based on a label and to display each queue's path, full DNS path, and formatted name.

To use the MSMQ functions, create a new Visual C++ project using the ATL COM AppWizard and name this one `asp1802`. Don't check either the MFC or MTS options when prompted by the wizard.

Once the project files are generated, modify the library modules. As with the component method in Example 18-5, you'll be using COM+ Services to access the ASP Response object for displaying the results of the search. So you'll need to add the COM+ Services library to the list. You'll also need to add the MSMQ library:

```
Mqrt.lib comsvcs.lib
```

Insert a new ATL object into the project, choosing the Simple Object option, and name it `msgqueue` (you can use the same object name within a different project and component). Change the threading model to Both, and leave the other object attributes at their default values.

In the *msgqueue.h* header file, add the COM+ Services and ASP include files. Also add the MSMQ include file and *comdef.h* to access the COM helper functions (for access to `_bstr_t` and `_variant_t`):

```
#include <comsvcs.h>
#include <asptlb.h>
#include <comdef.h>
#include <mq.h>
```

Use Class View to create a method for your component called findQueues. It takes one BSTR, the queue name, as an input parameter:

```
[in] BSTR bstrLabel
```

Add code for accessing the ASP Response object. This code is identical to that shown in 18-4, so I'll omit it for brevity. Next comes the fun part—using the

MSMQ functions to do the queue search and process the results. I'll be splitting the code up into different examples in order to explain the functionality better. If you want to see the component code as a whole, check out the project in the book examples.

Next, add the code in Example 18-6 after the code that accesses the ASP Response object. The first function the code calls is *MQLocateBegin*. This function locates the queue or queues matching the search and returns a query handle. The handle is used in all other functions that process the query results. The MQPROPERTYRESTRICTION structure is used to define the query, and it's assigned to the MQRESTRICTION.paPropRes member to pass to the function. Additionally, the columns (properties of the queue) to return from the query are defined with another structure, PROPID, and are attached to yet another structure, MQCOLUMNSET. Unlike the MSMQ COM objects, your query won't return objects, but rather properties that you specifically request.

Next, if the call to the *MQLocateBegin* function is successful, the code processes the results. It calls the *MQLocateNext* function to retrieve the queue information and passes an array of MQPROPVARIANT structures to receive the properties you queried for.

Example 18-6. Using the MSMQ Functions to Search for Queues

```
// * rirst, search for queues based on label
//    return pathname  * //

MQPROPERTYRESTRICTION PropertyRestriction;
MQRESTRICTION  Restriction;
MQCOLUMNSET    Column;
PROPID     aPropId[2];

// set search string -- search based on label
PropertyRestriction.rel = PREQ;
PropertyRestriction.prop = PROPID_Q_LABEL;
PropertyRestriction.prval.vt = VT_LPWSTR;
PropertyRestriction.prval.pwszVal =(LPWSTR)bstrLabel;

// set restriction
Restriction.cRes = 1;
Restriction.paPropRes = &PropertyRestriction;

// set column list -- pathname and label
aPropId[0] = PROPID_Q_PATHNAME;

Column.cCol = 1;
Column.aCol = aPropId;

// do query
HANDLE         hEnum;
hr=MQLocateBegin( NULL, &Restriction,
                  &Column, NULL,&hEnum);
```

Example 18-6. Using the MSMQ Functions to Search for Queues (continued)

```
if (FAILED(hr)) return hr;
DWORD dwPrpCt = 1;
MQPROPVARIANT aPropVar[1];

hr = MQLocateNext(hEnum,&dwPrpCt,aPropVar);
if (FAILED(hr)) return hr;

// **** process queue results **** //
//     * until props are zero * //
while (dwPrpCt > 0) {

    ... continued in next example
```

The method's final block of code is shown in Example 18-7. Notice the call to *MQLocateNext* to get the next queue in the query and the call to *MQLocateEnd* to close the query. Add this code to your component.

In the loop, the first value the code retrieves is the path, returned from calling *MQLocateNext*. This is needed to find the other two properties. First, the method gets the formatted name using the *MQPathNametoFormatName* function, passing in the queue path. It will display the formatted name, but the formatted name is also needed to find the DNS path.

The *MQGetQueueProperties* function is used to get the full DNS pathname. First, though, the method has to create arrays of the following structures to define the queue property, the DNS path:

```
MQQUEUEPROPS
PROPVARIANT
QUEUEPROPID
HRESULT
```

Then it calls *MQGetQueueProperties*. All that's left at that point is to display the queue properties.

Example 18-7. Looping Through the Queues, Getting the Properties, and Printing the Properties to the Web Page

```
... previous content ...

while (dwPrpCt > 0) {

    // get path
    _bstr_t bstrPath = aPropVar[0].bstrVal;

    // get formatted name
    DWORD dwFormatNameBufferLength = 256;
    WCHAR wszFormatNameBuffer[256];

    // get format name
    hr= MQPathNameToFormatName((LPWSTR)bstrPath,
```

Example 18-7. Looping Through the Queues, Getting the Properties, and Printing the Properties to the Web Page (continued)

```
                              wszFormatNameBuffer,
                              &dwFormatNameBufferLength);

    if (FAILED(hr)) return hr;

    // use formatted name to find DNS path
    // using MQGetQueueProperties
    MQQUEUEPROPS qprops;
    PROPVARIANT aQueuePropVar[1];
    QUEUEPROPID aQueuePropId[1];
    HRESULT aQueueStatus[1];

    // set pathname DNS property
    aQueuePropId[0] = PROPID_Q_PATHNAME_DNS;
    aQueuePropVar[0].vt = VT_NULL;

    qprops.aPropID = aQueuePropId;
    qprops.aPropVar = aQueuePropVar;
    qprops.aStatus = aQueueStatus;
    qprops.cProp = 1;

    // get DNS pathname
    hr = MQGetQueueProperties(wszFormatNameBuffer, &qprops);
    if (FAILED(hr)) return hr;


    // get value of path
    _bstr_t bstrDnsPath = aQueuePropVar[0].bstrVal;

    // now, FINALLY, print out results
    piResponse->Write(_variant_t(wszFormatNameBuffer));
    piResponse->Write(_variant_t("<br>"));
    piResponse->Write(_variant_t(bstrDnsPath + "<br>"));
    piResponse->Write(_variant_t(bstrPath + "<p>"));

    MQLocateNext (hEnum, &dwPrpCt,aPropVar);
  }

  hr=MQLocateEnd(hEnum);

  return hr;
}
```

Compile this component and test it with the following ASP script, *asp1806.asp*:

```
<%
Dim obj
Set obj = Server.CreateObject("asp1802.msgqueue")

obj.findQueues "Developing ASP Components"
%>
```

All told, you've used eight structures and several lines of code to get the following results:

```
PUBLIC=69af321f-13f8-49d7-8490-38d864e6f46f
flame.development.local\one
flame\one
PUBLIC=2a570b7d-9d6c-47f4-91c5-9662275bbdb9
flame.development.local\two
flame\two
PUBLIC=09a70a92-4885-49a7-9604-f32a2ae2f1ee
flame.development.local\three
flame\three
PUBLIC=99c56ee6-70ac-44f7-a5e8-610ba8fe4bf9
flame.development.local\four
flame\four
PUBLIC=c6453600-9c77-4e34-a067-6ec727d2c905
flame.development.local\five
flame\five
```

Now you see why I prefer the MSMQ COM objects. However, when you need access to certain functionality and the COM objects just don't seem to work for you, remember to check out the MSMQ functions.

Now that you're pretty comfortable with creating, removing, and searching MSMQ queues, it's time to try them out by sending them some messages. After all, queues by themselves might be interesting but aren't too useful.

Working with MSMQ Messages

Messages can be used to start or stop processes, to provide feedback, to warn of problems, and to perform a host of other actions. Messages can have objects attached, be plain strings, be read by applications automatically, or, in the case of ASP components, be read by the receiver from a web-based application.

Messages are implemented with the MSMQMessage object, wrapped in the smart pointer IMSMQMessagePtr. You'll need to open the queue that will receive the message and pass the open queue as the first parameter in the Send method. If you have the queue path, you can open it directly using the MSMQQueueInfo object.

To send messages to your queues, create a new Visual C++ project using the ATL COM AppWizard, and name the project asp1803. Once the project files are generated, create a new ATL object, except this time use the MTS option. Name the object message, and check the attribute option to add support for IObject-Control, but do not check the pooling option. You'll be using the ASP Response object again, but this time you'll create the object in the IObjectControl interface's Activate method.

In Windows 2000, pooled components must support aggregation, and the ATL MTS option generates a component that specifically prohibits aggregation. This can be modified, though. See Chapter 14, *Creating C++ ASP Components*, for more information.

Once the C++ and header files are generated, add a private data member, m_piResponse, to the class header file, and move the generated member, m_spObjectContext, to the private section:

```
private:
    CComPtr<IObjectContext> m_spObjectContext;
    CComPtr<IResponse>m_piResponse;
```

Add the code shown in Example 18-8 to implement both the ObjectContext and Response objects in the Activate and Deactivate methods in *message.cpp*.

Example 18-8. Getting ObjectContext and Response in JIT Methods

```
HRESULT Cmessage::Activate()
{
   HRESULT hr = S_OK;
   CComBSTR bstrObj;
   CComVariant vt;
   CComPtr<IGetContextProperties> pProps; //Context Properties

   IDispatch* piDispatch = NULL;

   // get ObjectContext
    hr = CoGetObjectContext(IID_IObjectContext,
                                    (void **)&m_spObjectContext);
   if (FAILED(hr))
      return hr;

   // get context properties
   hr = m_spObjectContext->QueryInterface( IID_IGetContextProperties,
              (void**)&pProps );
   if (FAILED(hr))
       return hr;

   // get Response property
   bstrObj = "Response";
   hr = pProps->GetProperty( bstrObj, &vt ) ;

   if (FAILED(hr))
       return hr;

   piDispatch = vt. pdispVal;
   hr = piDispatch->QueryInterface( IID_IResponse,
                   (void**)&m_piResponse );

   return hr;
```

Example 18-8. Getting ObjectContext and Response in JIT Methods (continued)

```
}

BOOL Cmessage::CanBePooled()
{
    return TRUE;
}

void Cmessage::Deactivate()
{
    m_piResponse.Release();
    m_spObjectContext.Release();
}
```

You also should add the following **import** directive to *message.cpp* to make the MSMQ's enumerated constants available to your code:

```
#import "mqoa.dll" no_namespace
```

Open the *message.h* file and add the following header files:

```
#include <comsvcs.h>
#include <asptlb.h>
```

This adds support for COM+ Services and the ASP built-in objects.

Finally, add support for COM+ Services by adding *comsvcs.lib* to the list of modules in the Object/Library Modules list of the Project Setting's Link tab.

Once you've added the support for ObjectContext and Response, you're ready to add the code to send your messages.

Sending Messages

Create a new method for your component using Class View and name it send-StringMessage. Add two **BSTR** input parameters for the method:

```
[in]BSTR bstrQueue, BSTR bstrMessage
```

The first parameter is the queue name; the second is the message you want to send.

Add the code for the new method, which is shown in Example 18-9. First, it sets the MSMQQueuePath pathname property using the putPathName method (generated through the **import** directive) to identify the queue and then calls the Open method, passing in the information about how the queue is accessed (MQ_SEND_ACCESS) and how the queue is shared once open (MQ_DENY_NONE). For this example, the queue is opened for sending, and the queue can be shared with other applications.

The message string is assigned to the Message object's Body property. This property is a variant, so any variant-compatible message could be attached to the message, including references to objects. The calls to open the queue and send the message are enclosed within exception handling, and if an error occurs, the Response object is used to write out the error message.

The message is sent using the MSMQMessage object's Send method, passing in the open queue as the first parameter. If the message used MSMQ transactions, the second parameter would hold an MSMQ transaction or transaction flag.

Example 18-9. Sending an MSMQ Message

```
STDMETHODIMP Cmessage::sendStringMessage(BSTR bstrQueue,
                                         BSTR bstrMessage)
{
  HRESULT hr = S_OK;
  IMSMQQueueInfoPtr qinfo("MSMQ.MSMQQueueInfo");
  IMSMQQueuePtr qQueue;
  IMSMQMessagePtr msg("MSMQ.MSMQMessage");

  _bstr_t bstrPath = L".\\" + _bstr_t(bstrQueue);

  // open queue, send message
  try {
      // open queue
      qinfo->PutPathName(bstrPath);

      qQueue = qinfo->Open(MQ_SEND_ACCESS, MQ_DENY_NONE);

      // send message
      msg->Body = bstrMessage;
      msg->Send(qQueue);
  }
  catch( _com_error e) {
      m_piResponse->Write(_variant_t(e.Description()+"<P>"));

  }
Return hr;
}
```

Compile the component and add it to an existing COM+ application (or create a new one for the example). The component uses JIT (just-in-time) activation and should be included within a COM+ application, or the ASP test page will hang when you access it.

Try your new component by sending several messages to one of the existing queues created in the last section. The following ASP test script can be found in *asp1807.asp*:

```
<%
Dim obj
Set obj = Server.CreateObject("asp1803.message")

obj.sendStringMessage "five", "This is the first message"
obj.sendStringMessage "five", "This is the second message"
```

```
obj.sendStringMessage "five", "This is the third message"
%>
```

If no error occurs, three messages are sent to the queue named `five`.

Reading Messages

Reading messages using the MSMQ COM objects is just as easy as sending them, with the difference being mainly the code necessary to process all of the messages. To try reading messages, create a new method in `asp1803.message`, calling it readStringMessage. This method takes just one parameter, a `BSTR` for the queue name.

Add the code for the new method, as shown in Example 18-10. The queue is opened and the MSMQQueue object's Receive method is used to access each message in the queue until they're all read. All of the Receive method's parameters are optional. The first parameter holds a transaction, if the message is included in a transaction (discussed in the next section). This value is set to `MQ_MTS_TRANSACTION` by default, which means that MSMQ uses MTS (COM+) transactions. The second parameter holds a `true` or `false` value to specify whether the destination information in the MSMQMessage DestinationQueueInfo property is set (its default value is `false`). The third parameter is a `true` or `false` value indicating whether the message body is returned. This value is set to `true` by default, indicating that the message body is returned. Finally, the last parameter is the receive timeout value. In the example, this is set to a variant holding a value of 100 milliseconds.

You *must* set the receive timeout property when reading an MSMQ message, or the method will block application execution and continue waiting for more messages in the queue—not a behavior you want in an ASP application.

Example 18-10. Reading Messages from the Message Queue

```
STDMETHODIMP Cmessage::readStringMessage(BSTR bstrQueue)
{
   HRESULT hr = S_OK;
   IMSMQQueueInfoPtr qinfo("MSMQ.MSMQQueueInfo");
   IMSMQQueuePtr qQueue;
   IMSMQMessagePtr msg("MSMQ.MSMQMessage");
   _variant_t varMsgBody;

   _variant_t vtReceiveTimeout;
   vtReceiveTimeout = (long)100;

   _bstr_t bstrPath = L".\\" + _bstr_t(bstrQueue);
```

Example 18-10. Reading Messages from the Message Queue (continued)

```
// open queue, send message
try {
    // open queue
    qinfo->PutPathName(bstrPath);
    //qinfo->PutLabel(bstrLabel);
    qQueue = qinfo->Open(MQ_RECEIVE_ACCESS, MQ_DENY_RECEIVE_SHARE);

    // get messages
    msg = qQueue->Receive(&vtMissing, &vtMissing,
                          &vtMissing, &vtReceiveTimeout);
    while (msg != NULL) {
      varMsgBody = msg->GetBody();
      m_piResponse->Write(varMsgBody);
      m_piResponse->Write(_variant_t("<br>"));

      msg = qQueue->Receive(&vtMissing, &vtMissing,
                            &vtMissing, &vtReceiveTimeout);
    }
}
catch( _com_error e) {
    m_piResponse->Write(_variant_t(e.Description()));
}

return hr;
}
```

In the example, the datatype of the message body is not tested before it is written out, primarily because we know we're receiving string messages. However, in your ASP applications, you'll want to test the datatype of the message before processing it.

Try out the component's new method using the following ASP page, *asp1808.asp*:

```
<%
Dim obj
Set obj = Server.CreateObject("asp1803.message")

obj.readStringMessage "five"
%>
```

The result of this ASP script is a page with the three messages sent with the earlier example.

When the message is read using the Receive method, it's removed from the queue. If you want to leave the message on the queue, you use the Peek method instead. However, after the first message, you'll need to use PeekNext to get each message after the first.

Using Transactions

In the last section, I mentioned that transactions could be associated with messages. To use transactions, you first have to add transaction support for the message queue.

To add transaction support for the queue, pass a value of **true** when creating the queue using the MSMQQueueInfo object's Create method. Once the queue is created to support transactions, then your messages themselves must support transactionsn or you could receive an error with some actions.

 From Chapter 13: If the queue is remote (located other than on the local machine), then you can't use a transactional receive against the queue. Additionally, you can't use a transactional receive call against a non-transactional queue. You can, however, use a nontransactional receive call against either a transactional queue or a nontransactional queue, even if the queue is remote. You can perform a transactional send against a remote transactional queue, but you can't send a transactional message against a nontransactional queue, regardless of its location. Neither can you send a nontransactional message against a transactional queue.

To demonstrate transactional messages, you'll need to create a transactional queue first. Open the **asp1801.msgqueue** project and add a new method named createXatQueue. This method takes three **BSTR** parameters; they are the queue name, the label, and a pointer to a **BSTR** message containing the status of the request:

```
[in] BSTR bstrQueue, BSTR bstrLabel, [out,retval] BSTR* pbstrMessage
```

Add the code for the new method next. As you can see in Example 18-11, the code is very similar to that shown in Example 18-1, except a variant holding a **true** value is passed to the MSMQQueueInfo object's Create method.

Example 18-11. Creating a Transactional MSMQ Queue

```
STDMETHODIMP Cmsgqueue::createXatQueue(BSTR bstrQueue, BSTR bstrLabel,
                                       BSTR* pbstrMessage)
{
    CComBSTR bstrMessage;
    bstrMessage = "Queue Created";
    _variant_t varXact((bool)TRUE);

    IMSMQQueueInfoPtr qinfo("MSMQ.MSMQQueueInfo");

    qinfo->PathName = _bstr_t(".\\") + _bstr_t(bstrQueue);
    qinfo->Label = bstrLabel;
```

Example 18-11. Creating a Transactional MSMQ Queue (continued)

```
try
{
  qinfo->Create(&varXact);
}
catch (_com_error comerr)
{
  HRESULT hr = comerr.Error();
  if (hr == MQ_ERROR_QUEUE_EXISTS)
  {
    bstrMessage = "Queue already exists";
  }
  else
  {
    bstrMessage = "Could not create queue";
  }
}
*pbstrMessage = bstrMessage.Detach();

return S_OK;
}
```

The ASP test page *asp1809.asp* contains the ASP script to create the transactional queue using the new method:

```
<%
Dim obj
Set obj = Server.CreateObject("asp1801.msgqueue")

Dim msg
msg=obj.createXatQueue("transaction","XatQueue")
Response.Write "<h3>" & msg & "</h3>"
%>
```

Once you've created a transaction queue, you can send messages to and read messages from the queue—as long as those messages have transaction support.

There are actually two different approaches you can use to add transaction support for MSMQ messages. The first approach is to use MTS/COM+ transactions for your messages, as well as your other resources such as database updates. The second approach is to use MSMQ transactions, valid only for MSMQ messages.

The MSMQTransactionDispenser object provides the transaction management when using MSMQ transactions. You create an instance of this object and then call its BeginTransaction method to return a reference to the MSMQTransaction object. The latter object can be sent as the second parameter in the MSMQMessage object's Send method and can be used as the first parameter in the MSMQQueue object's Receive method.

Calling Commit or Abort with a reference to the MSMQTransaction object commits or aborts the process of sending or reading the message:

```
IMSMQTransactionDispenserPtr disp("MSMQ.MSMQTransactionDispenser")
IMSMQTransactionPtr trans;
trans = disp->BeginTransaction();
...
trans->Commit();
```

Instead of passing in a transaction object, you can also specify a transactional enumerated constant. This is helpful when sending a message to a transactional queue without having to create a formal transaction object. The following are the allowable values to use for the transaction parameter with either the Send or Receive operations:

MQ_MTS_TRANSACTION
Use MTS/COM+ transactions, if any; this is the default value.

MQ_NO_TRANSACTION
No transaction is used.

MQ_SINGLE_MESSAGE
The transaction consists of only the single message.

MQ_XA_TRANSACTION
Part of an externally coordinated transaction.

I prefer using MTS/COM+ transaction support for MSMQ messaging, primarily because it provides better integration into the ASP application environment. That's the approach we'll take with the chapter's last two examples, in which you'll send and receive messages using MTS/COM+ transactions.

First, reopen the **asp1803** project. Add a new method to the **message** component and name it sendXactMessage. This method takes a queue name and the message as parameters, as follows:

```
[in] BSTR bstrQueue, BSTR bstrMessage
```

Add the code for the new method next; it is shown in Example 18-12. Unlike the previous Send method, this time you'll attach transaction information to the Send method if, and only if, the component is not included as part of an MTS/COM+ transaction. You can find this out by calling the IsInTransaction method of the ObjectContext object, referenced as a class member.

The reason for this transaction testing activity is that you can't send a nontransactional message to a transactional queue—you'll receive an error. Since transaction support is set to MTS by default, you'll have to provide some transaction information with the message to allow the message to be successfully sent. In the case of the example, the **MQ_SINGLE_MESSAGE** option is used, as shown in Example 18-12.

Example 18-12. Sending a Transactional Message

```
STDMETHODIMP Cmessage::sendXactMsg(BSTR bstrQueue, BSTR bstrMessage)
{
    IMSMQQueueInfoPtr qinfo("MSMQ.MSMQQueueInfo");
    IMSMQQueuePtr qQueue;
    IMSMQMessagePtr msg("MSMQ.MSMQMessage");

    _bstr_t bstrPath = L".\\" + _bstr_t(bstrQueue);

    try {
        // open queue
        qinfo->PutPathName(bstrPath);
        qQueue = qinfo->Open(MQ_SEND_ACCESS, MQ_DENY_NONE);

        // send message
        msg->Body = bstrMessage;

        _variant_t varType;
        varType.lVal = MQ_SINGLE_MESSAGE;
        varType.vt = VT_I4;

        if (m_spObjectContext->IsInTransaction())
            msg->Send(qQueue);
        else
            msg->Send(qQueue,&varType);

    }
    catch( _com_error e) {
        m_piResponse->Write(_variant_t(e.Description()));
    }

    return S_OK;
}
```

To add transaction support for the component, open the COM+ application where the **asp1803.message** component is currently installed, and right click on the component to access its Properties dialog. In the Transaction sheet, check the Required option for transaction support, as shown in Figure 18-2.

Even if COM+ transaction support was not added for the component, the MSMQ message would still be sent because you added in support for MSMQ transactions when COM+ transaction support is missing.

In the ASP page, add transaction support with the **TRANSACTION** directive as the first line in the page, as follows:

```
<%@ TRANSACTION = required %>
```

Next, send the message, and use COM+ within the ASP script, *asp1810.asp*, to commit the sending of the message:

```
<%
Dim obj
```

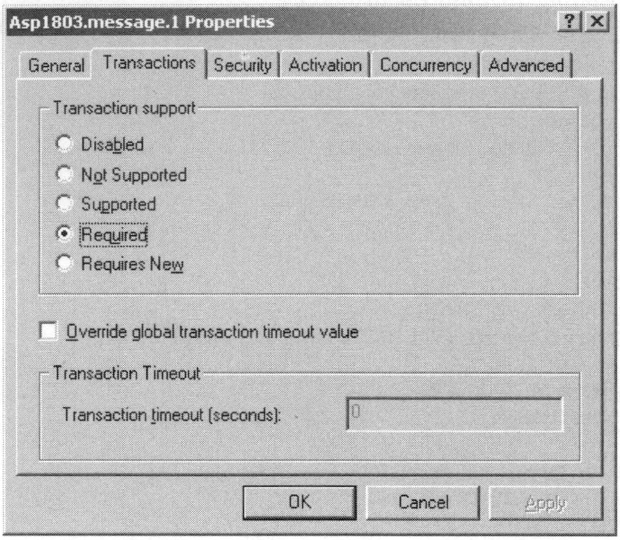

Figure 18-2. Adding transaction support to the asp1803.message component

```
Set obj = Server.CreateObject("asp1803.message")

obj.sendXactMsg "transaction", "This is a transaction message"

ObjectContext.SetComplete()
%>
```

To read the transactional messages, create a new method in **asp1801.message**, and name it readXactMessage. This method takes an input **BSTR** parameter with the queue name.

The code for this new method is identical to that shown in Example 18-10, except that transaction support is added when calling the MSMQQueue object's Receive method. Add the code shown in Example 18-13 to your new method.

Example 18-13. Reading Transactional Messages

```
STDMETHODIMP Cmessage::readXactMsg(BSTR bstrQueue)
{
  IMSMQQueueInfoPtr qinfo("MSMQ.MSMQQueueInfo");
  IMSMQQueuePtr qQueue;
  IMSMQMessagePtr msg("MSMQ.MSMQMessage");
  _variant_t varMsgBody;

  _variant_t vtReceiveTimeout;
  vtReceiveTimeout = (long)100;

  _bstr_t bstrPath = L".\\" + _bstr_t(bstrQueue);

  // open queue, send message
```

Example 18-13. Reading Transactional Messages (continued)

```
try {
    // open queue
    qinfo->PutPathName(bstrPath);
    qQueue = qinfo->Open(MQ_RECEIVE_ACCESS, MQ_DENY_RECEIVE_SHARE);

    _variant_t varType;
    varType.lVal = MQ_SINGLE_MESSAGE;
    varType.vt = VT_I4;

    if (m_spObjectContext->IsInTransaction())
        msg = qQueue->Receive(&vtMissing,&vtMissing,
                              &vtMissing,&vtReceiveTimeout);
    else
        msg = qQueue->Receive(&varType,&vtMissing,
                              &vtMissing,&vtReceiveTimeout);
    // get messages

    while (msg != NULL) {
      varMsgBody = msg->GetBody();
      m_piResponse->Write(varMsgBody);
      m_piResponse->Write(_variant_t("<br>"));

      if (m_spObjectContext->IsInTransaction())
          msg = qQueue->Receive(&vtMissing,&vtMissing,
                                &vtMissing,&vtReceiveTimeout);
      else
          msg = qQueue->Receive(&varType,&vtMissing,
                                &vtMissing,&vtReceiveTimeout);
    }

}
catch( _com_error e) {
    HRESULT hr = e.Error();
    m_piResponse->Write(_variant_t(e.Description()));
    m_spObjectContext->SetAbort();
    return hr;
}

m_spObjectContext->SetComplete();

return S_OK;
}
```

Again, the following ASP test page, *asp1811.asp*, has the TRANSACTION directive as the first line and the following script to read the transactional messages:

```
<%@ TRANSACTION = required %>
<%
Dim obj
Set obj = Server.CreateObject("asp1803.message")

obj.readXactMsg "transaction"
```

```
ObjectContext.SetComplete()
%>
```

To really try out transaction support, instead of using SetComplete when you send the message, change the ObjectContext method call to SetAbort and then try reading the transaction message queue. You'll find that the message is not in the queue.

Do the same with the script to read the messages. If you change the SetComplete method call to SetAbort, you'll be able to access and print out the message, but it won't be removed from the queue.

19

Persistence with ASP Components Using ATL and MFC

Using the ActiveX Template Library (ATL) does not preclude using the Microsoft Foundation Classes (MFC). In fact, for the examples created in this chapter, we'll see that the two technologies blend to create a simple but powerful ASP component.

In earlier chapters, you had a chance to store information into the ASP Session or Application objects, persisting this information for the session or until the ASP application was shut down. What happens, though, when you need information that lasts beyond the application?

This chapter discusses two approaches for maintaining information. The first is to write and read the information to and from a file; the examples use the MFC CFile class for this. The second is to persist an entire object—its structure as well as its data—to a file. This technique uses the MFC CFile, CArchive, and CObject classes to first create a serializable class and then to archive and retrieve this object from a file.

By the end of the chapter you should come away with the realization that file-based I/O and object serialization are not as complicated as you might have originally thought—with a little help from ATL and MFC, of course.

Combining MFC and ATL

Usually you won't want to include a large framework such as MFC when creating small, lightweight components, but there are advantages to using MFC. One such advantage is the built-in class support for objects such as CString and CStdioFile. Another advantage is the built-in macros that do things such as support object serialization. This section demonstrates adding MFC support to an ATL component that's used in the rest of the examples in this chapter.

Create a new Visual C++ project using the ATL COM AppWizard, and name it **asp1901**. The wizard asks whether you want to include support for proxy/stub code merging, MTS, and/or MFC. Select the MFC and MTS options.

You can add MFC support to an existing component by selecting Project → Settings from the main menu and then changing support for MFC in the General tab.

Two header files are included in the generated *StdAfx.h* header file to support the MFC core and automation functionality, *afxwin.h* and *afxdisp.h*. The wizard also automatically alters the DLL support code to include CWinApp as part of the application, as shown in the excerpt from *asp1901.cpp* in Example 19-1.

Example 19-1. Code Generated by ATL COM AppWizard to Provide Support for the MFC Class CWinApp

```
class CAsp1801App : public CWinApp
{
public:

// Overrides
    // ClassWizard-generated virtual function overrides
    //{{AFX_VIRTUAL(CTest2App)
    public:
    virtual BOOL InitInstance();
    virtual int ExitInstance();
    //}}AFX_VIRTUAL

    //{{AFX_MSG(CTest2App)
        // NOTE - the ClassWizard will add and remove member functions here.
        // DO NOT EDIT what you see in these blocks of generated code!
    //}}AFX_MSG
    DECLARE_MESSAGE_MAP()
};
```

The wizard also implements two methods, InitInstance and ExitInstance, within the project's main C++ file.

When MFC is incorporated into a component, the initialization and termination functionality is really invoked within the context of the Microsoft Foundation Framework. This means that the initialization code is included in the CWinApp InitInstance method, and termination code is included in the CWinApp object's ExitInstance method. The code that the wizard generates to handle this is very similar to that shown in the Example 19-2.

Example 19-2. AppWizard-Generated Code to Add MFC Instance Management

```
BOOL CAsp1901App::InitInstance()
{
    _Module.Init(ObjectMap, m_hInstance, &LIBID_ASP1801Lib);
    return CWinApp::InitInstance();
}

int CAsp1901App::ExitInstance()
{
    _Module.Term();
    return CWinApp::ExitInstance();
}
```

The ATL COM AppWizard also generates the following code for every COM method:

```
AFX_MANAGE_STATE(AfxGetStaticModuleState());
```

The **AFX_MANAGE_STATE** macro protects exported methods and is used by MFC when managing the state of data. This is mainly used with DLLs that might do such things such as open a dialog window and that have to manage window resources. Since you don't manage window resources with an ASP component, the statement can be removed, or you can leave it in—there's no harm in its inclusion.

Adding MFC to the DLL does not impact on how ATL components are added to the DLL. Add a new component using the ATL Object Wizard and selecting the MS Transaction Server Component object. Name the component **Advanced**, and select the options for Dual Interface and support of **IObjectControl**, but not the support for Object Pooling. Then generate the component.

Add support for ASP and the built-in ASP objects by including the following in the header file for the component, following the line that includes the *mtx.h* header file:

```
#include <asptlb.h>
```

You can also change the MTX header to the one for COM+ Services if you wish, as discussed in Chapter 14, *Creating C++ ASP Components.*

Add a new private data member, **m_piResponse**, to the class header file to support the ASP Response object:

```
CComPtr<IResponse> m_piResponse;
```

Modify the generated Activate method to add the code shown in Example 19-3 to instantiate the Response object.

Example 19-3. Instantiating Response in the Activate Method

```
HRESULT CAdvanced::Activate()
{
    HRESULT hr = S_OK;
```

Example 19-3. Instantiating Response in the Activate Method (continued)

```
    CComBSTR bstrObj;
    CComVariant vt;
    CComPtr<IGetContextProperties> pProps; //Context Properties

    IDispatch* piDispatch = NULL;

    // generated code
     hr = GetObjectContext(&m_spObjectContext);
    if (FAILED(hr))
       return hr;

    // add in code to get built-in objects

    // get Context Properties
    hr = m_spObjectContext->QueryInterface( IID_IGetContextProperties,
               (void**)&pProps );
    if (FAILED(hr))
        return hr;

    // get Response property
    bstrObj = "Response";
    hr = pProps->GetProperty( bstrObj, &vt ) ;

    if (FAILED(hr))
        return hr;

    piDispatch = vt. pdispVal;
    hr = piDispatch->QueryInterface( IID_IResponse,
                 (void**)&m_piResponse );

    return hr;
}
```

Add the following line of code to the Deactivate method to release the Response object:

```
        m_piResponse.Release();
```

The next section discusses file I/O from the ASP component.

File Access from ASP Components

By adding support for MFC, you also add support for MFC classes such as CFile and the classes derived from CFile: CMemFile, CSocketFile, and CStdioFile. These classes provide methods to control I/O to a file, standard input and output, memory, or even across a network.

Some forms of I/O don't make much sense from an ASP component. As an example, writing to standard input and output such as a Windows console is not very meaningful for a component that does not have access to the console or when communication to the standard input is not monitored. However, file-based I/O does occur frequently from ASP applications.

There are different approaches to file-based I/O. The CFile class supports reading and writing of unbuffered binary data directly to memory or to disk. CStdioFile, a class derived from CFile, is used mainly for text input and output. For writing simple text to a file, either of these classes can be used. The main difference between them is that CStdioFile does not support some of the locking methods implemented in CFile.

To demonstrate file I/O using CStdioFile, add two methods to the CAdvanced component. The first method is called setInfo and contains one input parameter of type **BSTR**:

```
BSTR bstrName
```

This method, the source code for which is shown in Example 19-4, instantiates a new object of type CStdioFile that, by default, opens the associated file as well as creates the object to manipulate the file. The instantiated object is used to write out the **bstrName** value to the file. Standard C++ exception handling is used to catch and process any exceptions that might result from this activity.

Example 19-4. Storing Information in a Disk File with the MFC Class CStdioFile

```cpp
// write out parameter to disk file
STDMETHODIMP CAdvanced::setInfo(BSTR bstrName)
{
AFX_MANAGE_STATE(AfxGetStaticModuleState())

// write object to file
  try {

    // filename
    char* pFileName = "c:\\output\\test1.dat";

    //open file using text type, create/write modes, and exclusive share
    CStdioFile stdFile( pFileName, CFile::modeCreate | CFile::modeWrite |
                    CFile::shareExclusive | CFile::typeText);

    // if successful on opening file, write out parameter
    CString cName = bstrName;
    stdFile.WriteString(cName);
    stdFile.Close();
    }

// error handling
  catch (CFileException *e) {

    // write out error to returned web page
    TCHAR   szError[255];
    e->GetErrorMessage(szError, 255);
```

Example 19-4. Storing Information in a Disk File with the MFC Class CStdioFile (continued)

```
    CComVariant vt = CComVariant(szError);
    m_piResponse->Write(vt);
    }
return S_OK;
}
```

The first parameter to the CStdioFile constructor is the location and name of the file being opened, in this case *c:\output\test1.dat*. Where double backslashes are used in the file string, the first backslash in the text tells the compiler that the second backslash should be read literally.

The second parameter to the CStdioFile constructor specifies the file opening options. These options include **modeCreate**, which will create the file if it does not already exist; **modeWrite**, which opens the file for writing; **typeText**, which sets the output to text mode; and **shareExclusive**, which opens the file for exclusive access and denies other access, whether read or write. This last option prevents another web page access from opening the file until the contents are written out. Once the string is written out to the file, it is closed, releasing the exclusive lock on the file.

If a CFileException occurs, the error message associated with the exception is output to the returned web page.

Since a file in the output directory is being created and written to, the permissions on this directory should be set to allow both read and write access for the users. For nonrestricted Internet access, the **IUSR_MACHINE** (**MACHINE** is your machine's name) user needs to be added to the directory's users list and given read/write permissions, or an error similar to the following will occur when the component is accessed:

```
    Access to c:\output\test1.dat was denied
```

To retrieve the string from the file, add another method, getInfo, to the CAdvanced class. This method takes a pointer to a **BSTR** as a return value:

```
    [out,retval] BSTR *pbstrName
```

Similar to the setInfo method, getInfo creates a CStdioFile object and uses it to read the string from the file and return the string to the requesting web page; its source code appears in Example 19-5. The code to access the file through the CStdioFile object is contained within C++ exception handling. Unlike setInfo, though, this method uses the CException class rather than the derived CFileException class. Using CException captures all exceptions that could occur with the method, not just those that are file-based. When constructing the CStdioFile object in getInfo, the file opening option is set to text output and read mode. After the value in the file is read, it's assigned to the **BSTR** pointer for return to the web page.

Example 19-5. Retrieving Information from a Disk File with the MFC Class CStdioFile

```
// access string in file and return
STDMETHODIMP CAdvanced::getInfo(BSTR *pbstrName)
{
    AFX_MANAGE_STATE(AfxGetStaticModuleState())

    // read object from file
    try {

        // filename
        char* pFileName = "c:\\output\\test1.dat";
        CString strName;

        // create file object and open file for read
        CStdioFile stdFile( pFileName, CFile::modeRead | CFile::typeText);

        // read string, close file and return string
        stdFile.ReadString(strName);
        stdFile.Close();
        CComBSTR bstrName(strName);
        *pbstrName = bstrName.Detach();
    }

    // error handling
    catch (CException *e) {

        // write out error to returned web age
        TCHAR    szError[255];
        e->GetErrorMessage(szError, 255);
        CComVariant vt = CComVariant(szError);
        m_piResponse->Write(vt);
    }
    return S_OK;

}
```

After the component is compiled, register it in a COM+ application (create a new one or use an existing test application). Create the following ASP page, *asp1901. asp*, that tests both setInfo and getInfo by creating an instance of **asp1901. Advanced**, calling setInfo to create the datafile and set its contents, calling getInfo to get the value back from the file, and writing this value to the web page:

```
<%
Dim obj
Set obj = Server.CreateObject("asp1901.Advanced")

'  set value
obj.setInfo "test value"

' get value and print
Dim str
str = obj.getInfo()
```

```
Response.Write str
%>
```

Accessing information from a file within an ASP component is relatively simple, but not without its limitations. If several people request an ASP page that tries to write to the same file at the same time, later users are locked out until the current user releases the lock on the file. Also, as seen earlier, an error can occur because the permissions set for the file or the file folder won't allow the specific activity.

The CStdioFile class is useful for fairly standard text I/O, but other classes, such as CFile, are better suited to tasks other than direct reading and writing of a file. One such task is object serialization, discussed next.

Creating a Serializable Class

Serialization is used to maintain object state. By this I mean that an object, including the object structure and current values, can be written out in some persistent form and used to recover the object at a later time. The persistent form is usually a disk file, but it could also be a memory file for actions such as undoing a change.

To create a serializable object, you first need to create the class that can be serialized. Microsoft has actually provided five easy steps for creating a serializable object, steps which are demonstrated in this section.

A requirement for an object to be serialized is to derive the class for the object from the MFC CObject class or from an object that is itself derived from CObject. In the case of our example, the class that we will create is called CGame, and its purpose is to store information about an online game winner, perhaps to maintain a listing of high scores.

The CObject class has only a few methods. IsSerializable checks whether the object that is derived from CObject is serializable, and Serialize actually performs the serialization. There is also a method, IsKindOf, which allows runtime comparison between an instance of a class and the class type. You can also access a runtime structure describing the class using the GetRuntimeClass method. The returned structure contains the class name, a pointer to the object's constructor, and other information, all necessary to support the serialization and instantiation of an object from the serialized store.

Add a new class to the **asp1901** project by selecting the New Class option from the Insert menu, then selecting the Generic Class option from the Class Type drop-down list box. Name the new class CGame. In the Derived From list box, type the word **CObject**, so that the new class is derived directly from this base class.

Be forewarned that you'll receive a warning about having to manually add in the header files to support the "unknown" CObject class. Disregard this warning, since you won't have any problems working directly with CObject in this project, and you won't need to add any header files.

Once the CGame class has been added to the project, access Class View and add the following four data members by right clicking on the class and choosing Add Member Variable from the pop-up menu:

Name	Type
m_gametime	LONG
m_score	WORD
m_date	CTime
m_name	CString

All of the data members should be defined as public.

Visual C++ generates the following code for the four new data members and places this code in the class header file, *Game.h*:

```
class CGame : public CObject
{
public:
    CString m_name;
    CTime m_date;
    WORD m_score;
    LONG m_gametime;
    CGame();
    virtual ~CGame();

};
```

The next step in creating the object is to override the Serialize method for the CObject base class. The CObject class doesn't provide any implementation for this method, so we have to provide it ourselves in our derived object. Override Serialize by right-clicking on the CGame class in Class View and selecting Add Member Function from the context menu. Give the function a **void** function type, and provide the following function declaration:

```
Serialize (CArchive &ar)
```

Leave the access option set to the default of Public. The CArchive class used as the type for the parameter of the new method is used to store complex objects in a persistent, binary form.

Once the function is added, Visual C++ generates the declaration for the method and adds this to *CGame.cpp*. Open *CGame.cpp* and add the implementation code for the Serialize method, as shown in Example 19-6. The first line calls the Serialize function on the base object, passing in the CArchive parameter. Next, the code tests whether the object information is being stored or retrieved. If stored, then the method serializes the data to the CArchive object. Otherwise, it pulls the data from the persistent store and assigns it to the CGame data members.

Example 19-6. Overridden Serialize Method for New Class

```
void CGame::Serialize( CArchive& ar )
{
    // call base class function first
    CObject::Serialize( ar );

    // now do the stuff for our specific class
    if( ar.IsStoring() )
        ar << m_name << m_date << m_gametime << m_score;

    else
        ar >> m_name >> m_date >> m_gametime >> m_score;
}
```

The IsStoring method of the CArchive class returns 0 if the archive is in a load state; otherwise, it returns a nonzero value. (The archive state is described a bit later.) The double angle bracket operators (<< and >>) are used to store or retrieve the simple datatypes for the object.

The next step to provide for a serializable object is to use the DECLARE_SERIAL macro with the CGame class:

```
    DECLARE_SERIAL( CGame )
```

This macro is called from within the public declaration section of the object in *game.h* and must be the first line of the class definition, just before the Serialize method prototype. The DECLARE_SERIAL macro generates the C++ header code to support serialization of the object.

The next step for making CGame serializable is to have a default constructor for the class that contains no arguments. This is handled for us automatically; when the class is created using the Insert → New Class menu option, it is automatically created with a default constructor (with no parameters) and destructor.

The final step in making CGame serializable is to include another macro, IMPLEMENT_SERIAL, in the *CGame.cpp* file:

```
    IMPLEMENT_SERIAL( CGame, CObject, 1 )
```

This macro generates the C++ code for a dynamic CObject-derived class at runtime. This code is included just before the methods for the default constructor and destructor, as shown in the following block:

```
IMPLEMENT_SERIAL( CGame, CObject, 1 )

CGame::CGame()
{

}

CGame::~CGame()
{

}
```

Once all of the serialization steps have been performed, any object instantiated from the class can be serialized, as demonstrated in the next section.

Just to summarize, here are the steps for serializing the object:

1. Create a new object by inheriting from CObject.

2. Add in the object's data members.

3. Override the CObject's Serialize method in the new object, and provide serialization specific for the object's data members.

4. Include the **DECLARE_SERIAL** macro in the new object's header file.

5. Define a constructor with no parameters, used by default for serialization.

6. Add in the **IMPLEMENT_SERIAL** macro to the C++ file, after the header file section and before the object's methods.

Persistence Through Object Serialization

The key to serialization is the CArchive class passed to the Serialize function of the object class. CArchive has a constructor that takes a pointer to a CFile object for the first parameter, a flag that sets the load or store state as the second parameter, and an optional buffer size and buffer, for an internal buffer used by the CArchive class, as the following prototype illustrates:

```
CArchive (CFile* file, UINT mode, int bufsize, void * lpbuff)
```

Usually the buffer that CArchive creates by default is sufficient, and these two parameters are not used. The file pointer in the first parameter actually references an open file, which is then used for the I/O-specific parts of the serialization process.

The CGame class will be used in the CAdvanced class created earlier in the chapter. Even though both classes are part of the same project and the same DLL, they aren't "aware" of each other. So add the header file for the CGame class to the CAdvanced C++ header file, after the *asptlb.h* file:

```
#include <asptlb.h>

#include "Game.h"
```

To support serialization using the CGame object, you'll need to add two new methods to the CAdvanced class. Add the first method by accessing Class View, right-clicking on the **IAdvanced** interface, and selecting Add Method from the context menu. Name the method setScore, and create three parameters for it: a **BSTR** parameter named **bstrName**, an integer named **iScore**, and another integer named **iTime**, as follows:

```
[in] BSTR bstrName, int iScore, int iTime
```

Add the source code for the setScore method, as shown in Example 19-7. The set-Score method creates a CGame object, sets its data members' values, and then archives it to disk using CFile. No exception handling is required within the method, since the CFile object's Open method actually handles the CFileException exception by returning it as one of the parameters in the method. Error checking occurs by testing the returned value of the Open method, with a **false** return value indicating a failed open condition and a **true** value representing a successful condition.

Why does the Open method for CFile not throw exceptions? Because failure from attempts to open a file are expected failures rather than unexpected failures. Processing is actually meant to continue from the point where the method is called regardless of the return value

---

Example 19-7. Creating an Object of Type CGame, Assigning It Values, and Serializing It to a Disk File

```
// serialize the game object to disk
STDMETHODIMP CAdvanced::setScore(BSTR bstrName, int iScore, int iTime)
{
    AFX_MANAGE_STATE(AfxGetStaticModuleState())

    // create new version of Game class
    CGame *m_game = new CGame();

    // set information
    m_game->m_date = CTime::GetCurrentTime();
    m_game->m_gametime = iTime;
    m_game->m_name = bstrName;
    m_game->m_score = iScore;

    // serialize object to file
```

Example 19-7. Creating an Object of Type CGame, Assigning It Values, and Serializing It to a Disk File (continued)

```
    CFile f;
    CFileException e;
    char* pFileName = "c:\\output\\game.dat";

    // open file, check for error
    if( !f.Open( pFileName, CFile::modeCreate | CFile::modeWrite |
        CFile::shareExclusive, &e ) )
    {
        CComVariant vt(OLESTR("Could not Store Game Results"));
        m_piResponse->Write(vt);
    }
    else {

        // serialize the object
        CArchive archive(&f, CArchive::store);
        m_game->Serialize(archive);
        archive.Close();
        f.Close();
    }
    return S_OK;
}
```

In addition to assigning the values passed in as parameters to the CGame's data members, the time the object was created is also set using the GetCurrentTime method of the CTime class to get the current system time. After the object's data members are set, the CFile object is created and the disk file is opened. If the file is opened successfully, the CArchive object is created and serialization can start.

Notice from the code in Example 19-7 that the instance of the CArchive class is set to a "store state" when created. This will result in a call to the CArchive object's IsStoring method (shown in Example 19-6) returning a **true** value. When this happens, the object is serialized to the file. After the object is serialized, the archive object and then the file are closed.

The second method you'll need to add to CAdvanced is called getScore. This method has three parameters, two of type **VARIANT** and one of type pointer to BSTR. The **VARIANT** datatypes are necessary to return values by reference to VBScript, and ASP components must code to the lowest common denominator—in this case VBScript's reliance on the one datatype. Since the last parameter is a return value from the method, it can be any supported COM datatype. In this case, the value being returned is a string, and the COM-compatible **BSTR** value is used. So add the following to the Parameters text box of the Add Method to Interface dialog:

```
[out] VARIANT* varScore, VARIANT* varTime, [out,retval] BSTR* pbstrName
```

In getScore, the source code for which is shown in Example 19-8, an instance of CGame is created. The serialized object file is opened via the CFile object, and the

CArchive object is created, passing in the CFile object and a state of loading. When the CGame object's Serialize method is called, the data members for the game object are set to the previously persisted values. Once the data members of the CGame object have been set, the appropriate data member values are assigned to the appropriate parameters for return to the calling ASP program.

Example 19-8. Obtaining the Serialized CGame Object from the Disk File

```
STDMETHODIMP CAdvanced::getScore(VARIANT *varScore,
                                 VARIANT *varTime, BSTR *pbstrName)
{

    AFX_MANAGE_STATE(AfxGetStaticModuleState())

    // create new version of CGame class
    CGame *objGame = new CGame();

    CFile f;
    CFileException e;
    char* pFileName = "c:\\output\\game.dat";

    // open file and check for error
    if( !f.Open( pFileName, CFile::modeRead, &e ) )
    {
        CComVariant vt(OLESTR("Could not access Game Results"));
        m_piResponse->Write(vt);
    }
    else {

        // restore object state
        CArchive archive(&f, CArchive::load);
        objGame->Serialize(archive);

        // return values as Variants
        CComVariant *vtScore = new CComVariant(objGame->m_score);
        vtScore->Detach(varScore);
        CComVariant *vtGametime = new CComVariant(objGame->m_gametime);
        vtGametime->Detach(varTime);
        objGame->m_name.AllocSysString();

        // return name as BSTR
        *pbstrName = objGame->m_name.SetSysString(pbstrName);
    }
    return S_OK;
}
```

Again, recompile the project DLL and test the new functionality. The following ASP script, *asp1902.asp*, tests object serialization by first calling setScore and getScore, then displaying the scoring information:

```
<%
Dim authorsObject
```

```
Set authorsObject = Server.CreateObject("asp1901.Advanced")

Dim str
str = "Shelley"
authorsObject.setScore str, 537, 689

Dim int1, int2
Dim str2
str2 = authorsObject.getScore(int1, int2)

Response.Write("<H3>" & str2 & " is the winner with a score of " & _
            CStr(int1) & _
            " and a time of " & Cstr(int2) & "</H3>")
%>
```

Many times, object serialization is used to maintain object state in a distributed environment. As an example, an object may be serialized before being passed as a parameter in a method from one component on one machine to another component on another machine. Then, the object is serialized again and the persisted object on the originating machine is destroyed. Using this approach, if a transaction fails at any point in the application, recovery can begin at the point of failure, rather than at the beginning of the process.

However, there's no reason that object serialization can't be used to maintain persistence for a complex object within an Internet application, as the game example has demonstrated in a simplified manner. It doesn't replace a database for more extensive transactions, but it can be an effective approach for isolated information.

20

*ASP Components
Created with Java*

ASP components are COM objects, but if a particular development environment supports COM, there is no limitation on which tool or programming language can be used to build the component. This includes Java and the Visual J++ programming tool, Microsoft's entry into the Java IDE market.

Being COM objects, though, ASP components must meet certain requirements, such as exposing certain interfaces and requiring the use of pointers to these same interfaces. Since Java does not support pointers, the inference is that Java cannot be used to create ASP components. This logic fails—Java can be used to create ASP components. Not only that, but these same ASP components can also be COM+ components and can take advantage of some COM+ Services.

Java-based ASP components are created as Java code classes or as nonvisual Java-Beans. JavaBeans are separate components that can be incorporated into an application in much the same manner that ActiveX controls can be used within applications. A Java code class is no different than any other language code class: it is included in an application and does not have a beginning *main* routine. The primary purpose of a code class is to provide access to a basic set of functionality, such as the functionality included in an ASP component through the addition of the ASP object library.

Wrappers are used to allow a Java class to access other COM/COM+ objects, including those of COM+ Services and the built-in ASP objects. To facilitate the use of the latter within a Java component, Microsoft has created a set of wrappers for the ASP objects that can be used directly. The purpose of the Java class wrappers is to provide a more Java-like interface to the ASP objects, including the use of more familiar Java datatypes. Microsoft has provided a set of Java wrappers for other libraries, such as the ActiveX Data Objects (ADO).

In this chapter, we'll take a look at accessing standard Java classes from ASP pages and creating Java-based COM/COM+ objects using Visual J++ (and using the JDK with help from some Microsoft utilities). Additionally, you'll have a chance to develop Java components that access the built-in ASP objects, as well as ADO.

 At the time this was written, Microsoft was involved in a legal suit with Sun Microsystems on Microsoft's use of Java. Based on this, Microsoft has been prohibited from most Java development until a decision in the suit with Sun has been made.

Creating Java Components

You can access Java from ASP pages using a couple of different approaches. If you have Java classes that you've used in other applications, you can access these classes directly from an ASP page using Java monikers. If you'd rather, you can create a COM/COM+ wrapper for a Java class and access the object as you would any other component created in a different language, such as Visual Basic or Visual C++. You can create the component using Visual J++ or create a Java class and wrap it using utilities provided by Microsoft in the Microsoft Java SDK.

 Before using the examples in this chapter, you'll want to have the latest version of the Sun Java Development Kit (JDK) installed (access this from *http://www.javasoft.com*); the latest version of the Microsoft Java SDK installed (access from *http://www.microsoft.com/ java/*); and Visual J++ 6.0 installed. If you don't have Visual J++, you can create the components in this chapter using the Java SDK—it's freely available and can be installed on Windows 2000.

Accessing Java Classes through Monikers

The simplest approach to take to include Java classes in your ASP applications is to use monikers to access the Java classes directly. Monikers are used with the GetObject method, passing in the name of the Java package and class, preceded by the **java** moniker text:

```
java:packagename.classname
```

The Java class can be created with the JDK and compiled with the JDK compiler, *javac.exe*. Once compiled, the class must be located in the CLASSPATH in order for it to be found.

To demonstrate using Java monikers, create a file named *test.java*. In the file, add the code shown in Example 20-1. This code defines a class named test (the filename should agree with the class name) and provides the code for a method that prints out a familiar greeting.

Example 20-1. Simple Java Class with One Method

```
public class test {

  public String sayHello(String strName)
    {
    String strMessage;

    strMessage = "Hello " + strName;
    return strMessage;
    }

}
```

Once you've created the Java file, compile it using *javac.exe* and move the compiled class file to your CLASSPATH directory. In Windows 2000, the CLASSPATH directory can usually be found in the Java subdirectory of the Windows directory. Place your Java classes in the Classes subdirectory.

To access the Java class in an ASP file, use the following script, contained in *asp2001.asp*:

```
<%
Dim obj
Set obj = GetObject("java:test")

Dim str
Dim name
name = "World!"
str = obj.sayHello(name)

Response.Write str
%>
```

In this script, the Java class test is accessed with the Java moniker, and the returned object's method is called. If you didn't want to place the Java class in CLASSPATH, you could access the class by providing the full pathname to the compiled class instead:

```
java:c:\class\test.class
```

If your class were part of a package, you would access the package and the class. To demonstrate this, add a folder to the *Classes* directory named *mytest*. Create a copy of *test.java* in this new directory. Open the file and add the following to the top of the class file:

```
package mytest;
```

Compile this version of the Java class, and access it with the following moniker:

```
java:mytest.test
```

Notice that a period is used to separate the package name from the class. Try this yourself using the *asp2002.asp* test page.

A key for the Java moniker to work is that the Java class must have a default constructor that takes no parameters.

If you want to use the more traditional *CreateObject* to create an instance of your Java class, you can wrap the class with a COM interface, discussed next.

Wrapping Existing Java Classes with COM/COM+

You can register a Java class in the Windows Registry or wrap the class within a COM/COM+ wrapper.

Microsoft provides a command-line utility, *javareg.exe*, created specifically for registering a Java class in the Windows registry. This utility can also assign a ProgID to the class, as well as generate a class identifier. The *javareg* switches are shown in Table 20-1.

Table 20-1. Switches for javareg.exe

Switch	Description
/?	Displays utility switches and usage
/class	Java class being registered
/clsid	CLSID for class
/codebase	Used while registering a class, codebase returns base location of the component
/control	Used while registering a class, to designate that the component is an ActiveX control
/progid	COM program ID for class
/q	Suppresses messages
/register	Registers the Java class as an ActiveX component
/remote	For remote access; server where remote component is located
/surrogate	Used when Java class is run as a DCOM server
/typelib	Used while registering a class; generates type library for file
/unregister	Unregisters the Java class

Not all of the switches listed are required. For example, if the clsid switch and a class ID are not present, the utility generates a class identifier for the class. The clsid switch is used only if the class ID was generated outside the utility and is used in registering the class. In addition, the progid switch is needed only if the class is being accessed by its ProgID value, using the *CreateObject* method. The remote and surrogate switches are needed only if the class is accessed through DCOM.

> To generate a class ID outside of the utility, you can use *guidgen. exe.* Both this and *javareg.exe* should be available for download at the Microsoft Java web site at *http://www.microsoft.com/java/.* Look for them to be a part of the Microsoft Java SDK. The *javareg.exe* utility is also installed as part of the IIS sample installation.

To use the *javareg* utility on the Java class created in the last section, use a line similar to the following:

```
javareg /register /class:test /progid:mytest.test.1
```

Additionally, when using the *javareg* utility, the Java class should be moved to a location on the Java CLASSPATH. Unless a problem occurs, a message similar to that shown in Figure 20-1 should pop up, stating that the Java class has been successfully registered and giving the class identifier used with the component.

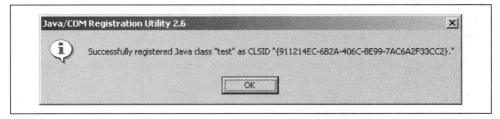

Figure 20-1. Success message after registering Java ASP component using javareg

Now, to access the Java class, you use code similar to the following ASP script, *asp2003.asp,* which creates an instance of the Java class in the same way as it would a COM/COM+ component:

```
<%
Dim obj
Set obj = Server.CreateObject("mytest.test.1")

Dim str
Dim name
name = "World!"
str = obj.sayHello(name)

Response.Write str
%>
```

If you have more than one class file to register, you can use the *vjreg.exe* utility instead. This utility, unlike *javareg.exe,* can register more than one Java class at a time.

The *javareg.exe* registers the component in the Windows Registry but doesn't actually create a DLL to wrap the class as a component. To wrap a Java class in a COM/COM+ DLL, you use the *jexegen.exe* utility. To create the COM wrapper for the Java class, specify the name of the class with the *jexegen* utility. You'll also need to provide information about the class to the tool. One way to do this is to use the @com directive within the Java file (a technique demonstrated in the section "Building a Java Component Using Visual J++"). You can also create an IDL file for the class, providing the JAVACLASS and PROGID entries:

```
JAVACLASS("test")
PROGID("mytest.test.1")
```

You can also provide a CRI file for the utility and specify the /cri option. A CRI file provides COM registration information for the class, such as the class name, the CLSID, the type library unique identifier, the threading model, and so on.

 See the documentation for *jexegen* for the specific details of all the CRI file options.

To wrap your Java class within a COM DLL, create a CRI file with the following text, and name the file *test.cri*:

```
class:test progid:test2.test ThreadingModel:Neutral
```

Add the file to the same directory as your original *test.class* file—the one that *isn't* part of the mytest package. The class entry is required, but the other entries (the threading model and the PROGID) are not. However, they are useful in allowing you to choose which threading model is used and what PROGID to specify when using *CreateObject*.

Enter the following in a Command window:

```
jexegen /d /out:test.dll /cri:test.cri test.class
```

This command uses the *jexegen* utility to create a COM DLL (the /d option) named *test.dll* (the /out:test.dll option), using the CRI file *test.cri* and the source file *test.class*. Once the DLL is generated, register it with *regsvr32.exe*.

Access your new COM-wrapped DLL with the following ASP test script, found in *asp0204.asp*:

```
<%
Dim obj
Set obj = Server.CreateObject("test2.test")

Dim str
```

```
Dim name
name = "World!"
str = obj.sayHello(name)

Response.Write str
%>
```

Your Java class can now be accessed directly as a COM object. In addition, the COM object now uses the neutral-threading model. If you create the object using Visual J++, you'll find that the both-threaded model is used by default.

Speaking of threads, before we take a look at creating objects using Visual J++, let's take a look at Java and threads.

Component Execution and Threads

Java has thread capability built directly into the language, and thread management is actually relatively simple. A class that can run on a separate thread is subclassed from the Java **Thread** class, and the **run** method is overridden to include the thread-specific code.

Creating threads within a Java ASP component is not as much of an issue as is creating thread-safe components. It is up to the component developer to ensure that the Java-based component is thread-safe. One way to ensure this is to protect the component's global data from inadvertent access, such as a both-threaded component accessing and changing global data while another both-threaded component is still processing a method and therefore expects the global data to retain its original value. This problem was demonstrated in Chapter 4, *ASP Components, Threads, and Contexts*.

Another way of ensuring that a method within a Java component is thread-safe is to use the **synchronized** method modifier, which serves to prevent a thread from entering a method currently accessed by another thread.

Access to a component may be marshaled or not, depending on the threading model used for the component and for the client. How COM handles marshaling and Java component instantiation depends on the threading model used with the component. The Microsoft VM determines on which thread to create the component, and this in turn determines if the calls to the component are marshaled.

If the component is designated as both-threaded, the component is instantiated on the calling thread, and all method calls are direct to the object. If the component is designated as single-threaded, the component is created on the application's main thread, and all calls to the component are marshaled if the calling thread is not the main thread. A free-threaded component is created in the client's multithreaded apartment, and calls are marshaled if the client thread is based anywhere else. If the component is designated as neutral-threaded, it is created in the client's neutral-threaded apartment, and calls should not be marshaled. If the component is apartment-threaded, it is instantiated on the calling thread if this thread is capable of hosting an apartment-threaded component. Otherwise the component, and all other apartment-threaded components are instantiated on a special thread that the VM creates. All components must then share this one thread, and all component calls must be marshaled.

Building a Java Component Using Visual J++

If you prefer developing in Java with an IDE, you can use Visual J++ to create your ASP components. Visual J++ takes care of the issues of wrapping your Java classes for access as COM objects.

To try out Visual J++, create a new project named **asp2001**, choosing the Components/COM DLL option when the tool provides the project type options.

> When you create the COM project, you'll most likely get a warning about having to use functionality that isn't standard with the Java SDK. This warning is the direct result of the legal action that Microsoft is involved in with Sun. The reason for the warning is that adding COM functionality to a Java component makes it nonportable—you'll be able to use the component only within a Windows environment.

A default Java class is automatically created for the project, which includes a directive to register the class as a COM object. The class is created simply, with no inheritance implied, as shown in the following code block:

```
public class Class1
```

When developing a Java component, you will most likely change the name of the class and its associated file. In fact, if you rename the class, you *have to* rename the file or an error occurs. For the example, rename the class file to *First.java*, and the class to `First`.

You could also add annotation for the class. For example, the following shows a class that is renamed to **MyConcatenator** with the **final** modifier:

```
final class MyConcatenator
```

The final modifier applies to the class declaration and prevents the class from being overridden or subclassed. Another class modifier, **abstract**, is used with classes that contain abstract functions. An *abstract function* is one that does not have an implementation in the ancestor but must have an implementation in a descendant or an error will result. By default, all classes are defined with the **public** modifier, which means the class is visible to applications that use the class.

Inheritance in Java is through the use of the **extends** clause, and if the class is an extension of an existing Java class, this information is added to the class declaration. When one class is an ancestor, or superclass, of another, it is listed in the **extends** clause of the descendant, or subclass, as shown in the following example:

```
class MyInsertConcatenator extends MyConcatenator
```

Since the original class, **MyConcatenator**, was defined with the **final** modifier, inheriting from the class will result in an error. To inherit from **MyConcatenator**, its class declaration would need to be modified:

```
public class MyConcatenator
class MyInsertConcatenator extends MyConcatenator
```

Once you've renamed the class file and name, you can add its first method.

You can add methods directly to the class file. Additionally, you can add methods through Visual J++ by using the Add Method dialog. For **asp2001.First**, add a new method by right clicking on the First interface in the Class Outline window, and selecting Add Method. In the window that opens, type **sayHello** for the method name, and change the return type to **java.lang.String**. Leave the Access modifier at **Public**, and don't check any of the modifiers. Add a method parameter by clicking the button with the ellipsis (. . .) to the right of the Parameters field. In the dialog that opens, select **java.lang.String** as the parameter type, and name the parameter *strName*. Returning to the main Add Method dialog, you should see a result similar to that shown in Figure 20-2.

Visual J++ generates the method using the properties you defined. All that's left is to add the method code. In the method, concatenating the string message with the name provided as the parameter creates a greeting, which is returned from the method. Example 20-2 has the complete contents of the Java file at this point.

Example 20-2. Simple Java Class with Code for the sayHello Method

```
/**
 * This class is designed to be packaged with a COM DLL output format.
 * The class has no standard entry points, other than the constructor.
 * Public methods will be exposed as methods on the default COM interface.
@com.register ( clsid=49CBA0AB-72D2-4A03-98D5-8FA183CAC217,
 typelib=79CC2A06-A5F5-4BC4-8CEC-86ADC08162C8 )
 */

public class First
{

    public String sayHello(String str)
    {
        String strMessage;

        strMessage = "Hello " + str;
```

Example 20-2. Simple Java Class with Code for the sayHello Method (continued)

```
        return strMessage;
    }
}
```

As you can see, except for the generated COM directive, the class is identical to that shown in Example 20-1. One of the advantages of using Visual J++ is that you can disregard most of the effort necessary to creating COM wrappers for your Java classes and instead concentrate on just creating the class.

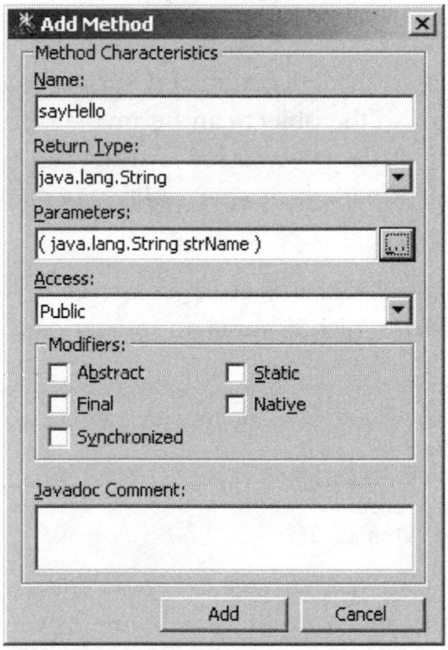

Figure 20-2. Defining a method in Visual J++

Compile the component, which results in the component being registered. You can also add the component to a COM+ application at this time if you wish. Test the component using the following ASP script, *asp2005.asp*:

```
<%
Dim obj
Set obj = Server.CreateObject("asp2001.First")

Dim str, msg
str = "World!"
msg = obj.sayHello(str)

Response.Write msg
%>
```

In this section you've had a chance to access a Java class from ASP using three different techniques. However, this is only half the process of integrating Java components into the ASP environment. The second half of the process is being able to access COM/COM+ objects from within Java components, covered next.

Invoking a COM Object from a Java Component

The component in Example 20-2 could be accessed by any COM application, including ASP. However, to invoke COM methods from a Java class could become complicated and would necessitate creating Java wrappers for the object before you could access it from Java.

Thankfully, Visual J++ has provided automated support to add the necessary Java wrappers to a COM object so the object can be invoked from a Java class. In addition, for older versions of Visual J++ and for Java development products other than Visual J++, Microsoft has provided another utility, *Jactivex*, to assist in creating a Java COM wrapper.

To demonstrate accessing a COM object in Java, create a Visual Basic object that has one method, testObject, which accepts an integer as a parameter and returns a string:

```
Public Function testObject(intValue As Integer) As String
    If intValue = 1 Then
        testObject = "Value is 1"
    ElseIf intValue = 2 Then
        testObject = "Value is 2"
    Else
        testObject = "Some other value"
    End If
End Function
```

Name the VB project **vbtest**, and name the class file **test**. The compiled DLL for the project can be found in the examples. Register it using *regsvr32* (or by accessing the project and compiling it if you have VB). The component is accessed with the PROGID of **vbtest.test**.

The next two sections show how a COM wrapper can be added to a Java class using Visual J++ 6.0, and using the *Jactivex* utility.

Adding a COM Wrapper Class to the Component Using Visual J++

To demonstrate accessing a COM object from within Visual J++, create a new Visual J++ COM DLL project and name it **asp2002**. Name the generated class **access**. Right-click on the class, and from the context menu that opens, select

Add → Add COM Wrapper. A dialog will open listing the available COM objects registered on the machine. Find and check the **vbtest** component in the list.

Adding a COM wrapper to the project generates the Java code to wrap the VB component and attaches this code as a dependency to the project. You can actually view the Java code for the class and the associated interface code by selecting the classes from the Project view window. The code block contained in **test. java** is shown in Example 20-3.

Example 20-3. Adding a COM Wrapper for a VB COM Component

```
//
// Auto-generated using JActiveX.EXE 5.00.3167.1
//    ("C:\Program Files\Microsoft Visual Studio\VJ98\jactivex.exe"
/w /xi /X:rkc /l "C:\DOCUME~1\ADMINI~1\LOCALS~1\Temp\jvc1E8.tmp"
/nologo /d "C:\writing\asp2000\chap20\source\asp0202" "C:\writing\asp2000\chap20\
source\vbtest.dll")
//
// WARNING: Do not remove the comments that include "@com" directives.
// This source file must be compiled by a @com-aware compiler.
// If you are using the Microsoft Visual J++ compiler, you must use
// version 1.02.3920 or later. Previous versions will not issue an error
// but will not generate COM-enabled class files.
//

package vbtest;

import com.ms.com.*;
import com.ms.com.IUnknown;
import com.ms.com.Variant;

/** @com.class(classid=D797F78A-212C-4444-9D0B-E6F74B10215A,DynamicCasts)
    @com.interface(iid=4BD4C0B8-9B03-4789-9176-45EF15DB4C17,
 thread=AUTO, type=DUAL) */
public class test implements IUnknown,com.ms.com.NoAutoScripting,
vbtest._test
{
  /** @com.method(vtoffset=4, dispid=1610809344, type=METHOD,
name="testObject", addFlagsVtable=4)
      @com.parameters([in,out,size=1,elementType=I2,type=ARRAY] intValue,
 [type=STRING] return) */
  public native String testObject(short[] intValue);


  public static final com.ms.com._Guid iid = new
com.ms.com._Guid((int)0x4bd4c0b8, (short)0x9b03, (short)0x4789,
  (byte)0x91, (byte)0x76, (byte)0x45, (byte)0xef, (byte)0x15, (byte)0xdb,
  (byte)0x4c, (byte)0x17);

  public static final com.ms.com._Guid clsid = new
com.ms.com._Guid((int)0xd797f78a, (short)0x212c, (short)0x4444,
  (byte)0x9d, (byte)0xb, (byte)0xe6, (byte)0xf7, (byte)0x4b,
  (byte)0x10, (byte)0x21, (byte)0x5a);
}
```

Notice how the generated class includes imports for the necessary COM interface, IUnknown. Additionally, the class also includes the **Variant** class to handle most unknown or object parameter types. Code that looks very much like Interface Definition Language (IDL) is used to define both the VB component's method and the method parameters.

Once the COM wrapper is added to the class, compiling the class also compiles the COM wrapper for Java. Using the wrapped object is discussed in the section "Using the COM-Wrapped Class." First, though, we'll take a look at how to use *Jactivex* to create the wrapped COM object.

Using Jactivex to Wrap a COM Object

For earlier versions of Visual J++ and for other Java development tools, there is another utility to make your development task much easier—the *Jactivex* utility.

The *Jactivex* tool requires that the Java compiler recognize @com directives in the Java files. Visual J++ should be version 1.02.3920 or higher. Additionally, the Java compiler that comes with the Microsoft Java SDK also recognizes the @com directive. The Java compiler that comes with the JDK does not recognize these directives.

The *Jactivex* tool creates a Java class for each COM object within a type library. A type library is any COM-based object with a *.tlb*, *.olb*, *.ocx*, *.dll*, or *.exe* extension, including the type library included within the Visual Basic test component, mentioned in the last section.

To try *Jactivex* with the VB component, make sure the component is registered, and then run the following command (in the Command window) in the same directory where *vbtest.dll* resides:

```
jactivex /javatlb /xi vbtest.dll
```

This command creates a subdirectory named *vbtest*, located in the Java trusted library (usually located off of the Windows directory, contained in *java/trustlib*). Included in this subdirectory are three generated Java files, *_test.java*, *_testDefault. java*, and *test.java*.

The **/javatlb** option used in the command ensures type library compatibility between the component and the Java class. The **/xi** option duplicates the method and COM declarations in the Java wrapper class so that the methods can be accessed directly and don't have to be cast using an interface pointer (using automation). All of the *Jactivex* options can be seen just by running this command:

```
jactivex /?
```

If you open the *test.java* file generated by *Jactivex*, you'll see that this file is very similar to that shown in Example 20-3.

To use the Jactivex-generated code, compile the classes using Visual J++ or the Java compiler that comes with the Microsoft Java SDK.

Once the COM wrapper classes have been generated and compiled either by using Visual J++ 6.0 directly or by using *Jactivex*, the wrapped class can be used within a Java component, as discussed next.

Using the COM-Wrapped Class

After the COM wrapper classes have been generated and compiled, import the COM wrapper Java classes into your object using the following statement:

```
import vbtest.*;
```

Make sure that this import line (and all others) occurs *before* the COM directive comments. The COM directive comments must be located just before the Java class definition.

To demonstrate, open the **asp2002** project and add a method to the **access** class. Name the method RcturnValue. The method takes a short value as an input parameter and a String as a return value. In the method, create an instance of the VB component and call its method. After adding the method code, your Java component should look similar to that shown in Example 20-4.

Example 20-4. Accessing a VB Component from Within a Visual Java Component

```
import vbtest.test;

/**
 * This class is designed to be packaged with a COM DLL output format.
 * The class has no standard entry points, other than the constructor.
 * Public methods will be exposed as methods on the default COM interface.
@com.register ( clsid=62AF6D7F-5CB2-494F-89CC-ACA26912DE23,
typelib=70626B1F-4A14-4D99-8BD3-E4DAE6098F79 )
 */

public class access
{
   // invoke COM method
   public String ReturnValue (short shrtValue)
   {
    String strTest;
    short x[] = new short[1];
    x[0] = shrtValue;

    // create object
    vbtest.test objTest = new vbtest.test();
```

Example 20-4. Accessing a VB Component from Within a Visual Java Component (continued)

```
    // call method
    strTest = objTest.testObject(x);
    return (strTest);
    }
}
```

In the code, the Integer type from Visual Basic has been mapped to a short type in Java. The reason is that VB's integer is only a 16-bit value, and Java's int type is a 32-bit value. Also, notice that the method uses a one-element array to pass the value to the VB component. The reason for this is that in the original VB component, the parameter is passed by reference because ByVal is not explicitly specified with the parameter. Visual Basic passes parameters by reference by default. However, passing an element by reference involves pointers, something that Java does not support.

A way around the pointer limitation is to pass one-element arrays. Because Java passes arrays by reference, the value becomes passed by reference. For the Visual Basic example, an array of datatype short is created with one element, which is then passed to the VB method.

To avoid having to use arrays, the VB method can be changed and the ByVal modifier added to the parameter, as in the following declaration:

```
    Public Function testObject(ByVal intValue As Integer) As String
```

More on datatypes and mappings between COM and Java are included in the next section.

To test the new Java component, use this ASP script (found in *asp2006.asp*):

```
    <%
    Dim obj
    Set obj = Server.CreateObject("asp2002.access")

    Dim str
    str = obj.ReturnValue(1)

    Response.Write str
    %>
```

Try this script yourself with your own component. A line with "Value is 1" is returned when you access the page.

Java/COM Datatype Mappings

A rule to handle datatype mappings for COM/Java development is to use ODL (Object Description Language) datatypes, which have a default mapping from COM to Java. Other datatypes, and more complex datatypes, can require custom marshaling. For the most part, the available datatypes should match most needs.

The Java SDK, which can be downloaded from *http://www.microsoft.com/java/* and is available on CD if you have a membership in the Microsoft Developer Network, lists the datatype mappings. The mappings work for Visual C++ and Visual Basic components used within Java components, but there are some differences.

For an integer value, as shown earlier, a VB integer is only a 16-bit value, but an int for C++ and Java is a 32-bit value. To map correctly to Visual Basic, the Java component will need to use a **short** value, which is 16-bit.

The Visual Basic Variant datatype maps to a Java ODL **VARIANT** type, which maps in turn to a **com.ms.com.Variant** class. Microsoft documentation also states that any **out** parameters in Java should be of the Variant datatype.

The String datatype maps straight through, though the String class is immutable in Java. An immutable class is one that is never versioned, never revised.

In the examples, a constant string is concatenated with a String passed in as a parameter. What happens behind the scenes is that a StringBuffer object is created to handle the concatenation, and the result is returned as a String. To avoid this behind-the-scenes maneuvering, use StringBuffer directly.

Working with COM+ Services

You can create Java classes that minimize the dependencies on the Windows environment, and the classes should work within ASP and other applications and on different machines. If you want to work with the ASP environment, though, or with COM+, you'll need to use the WFC (Windows Foundation Classes).

Microsoft provides Java-wrapped classes for the most commonly accessed libraries, such as the COM+ and ASP libraries. In this section, we'll take a look at using these Java wrapper classes to access COM+ Services as well as to work with ASP objects.

Using IObjectContext

To access COM+ Services, you must import a package called **com.ms.mtx**. This package contains the Java classes you'll need to create an instance of ObjectContext, to control transactions, or to create instances of the ASP built-in objects. If you want to access COM datatypes, such as the Variant, you'll also need to import the **com.ms.com** package.

In the COM+ Services package, a static class, **MTx**, is used to get access to the **IObjectContext** interface by calling the object's GetObjectContext method. You

can control transactions and test the state of the transaction environment with
`IObjectContext`. To get access to the ObjectContext properties, create a reference to the `IGetContextProperties` interface through the same GetObjectContext method, but cast the return value as `IGetContextProperties`. This latter
interface is what you'll use to access the ASP objects.

We'll cover the ASP objects in more detail later, but for now, if you want to access
these objects, you'll also need to import the **com.ms.asp** package or import each
individual ASP object from this package. So to access `IResponse`, the interface to
the ASP Response object, you would need to import the following three libraries
into your Java component:

```
import com.ms.mtx.*;
import com.ms.com.*;
import com.ms.asp.IResponse;
```

The MTS `IObjectContext` object is used to instantiate instances of other objects
within a transaction, to commit or roll back a transaction, or to check the state of
the object. By *state of the object*, I mean whether the object is participating in a
transaction, which can be determined using the object's IsInTransaction method.
The method returns **True** if the component is executing within a transaction. The
DisableCommit and EnableCommit methods can be used to control whether a
component is in a state that can be successfully committed or not. The IsCallerIn-
Role method checks what role a caller is participating in, and the IsSecurityEnabled method determines whether security is enabled for the object. Security is
enabled for a component by default unless it is running within the client's process. The CreateInstance method can be used to create an instance of an object
that participates in the same transaction as the component creating the instance.

Including the `IObjectContext` interface as part of an ASP component and then
installing that component into a transaction package provides hooks for COM+ to
actually catch all invocations of the component. The transaction server then handles all references to the component. By doing this, when a component marks that
it is finished its processing by calling SetAbort or SetComplete from the
`IObjectContext` interface, COM+ marks the component for unloading even if the
client still has a reference to it. This allows the system to unload the component
and any resources it contains from memory. When the client calls one of the component's methods again using the reference to the pointer the client *thinks* it has,
COM+ either creates and loads a new instance of the ASP component or retrieves
a reference from an available pool of the same component. This on-demand activation of an ASP component is referred to as *just-in-time activation*.

Beginning with Windows 2000, you can also access the `IContextState` interface
through the **MTx** object. This interface provides more detailed control of how the
object is managed. With `IContextState`, you can mark a transaction as successful or not using the SetMyTransactionVote method. There is an enumeration

available to use for this vote in C++ or VB, but unfortunately, it isn't implemented in Java—you'll need to use the actual numeric values instead. Use a value of zero (0) to commit the transaction, a value of one (1) to abort it. You can also mark the component as ready to be discarded through the use of the SetDeactivateOn-Return method, passing in a value of **True** to deactivate the object; a value of **False** signals to leave the object active.

To try out ObjectContext functionality within your Java component, create a new Visual J++ project and name it **asp2003**. Rename the generated class to **ObjCont**. Before the COM directive comment, add the following three **import** statements:

```
import com.ms.mtx.*;
import com.ms.com.*;
import com.ms.asp.IResponse;
```

Create a new method named showStatus, with a Variant input parameter, and add the code in Example 20-5 to your component. In the method, instances of **IObjectContext** and **IGetContextProperties** are referenced through calls to the **MTx** GetObjectContext method. The call is cast to the appropriate instance object type for **IGetContextProperties**. This object is then used to create a Response object by using GetProperty to get the Response object returned as a Variant datatype and then using the Variant object's getDispatch method and casting the value returned to a reference to an **IResponse** interface object type. The Response object's methods can then be invoked.

 The ASP objects are covered in more detail later.

The **IObjectContext** interface's IsInTransaction, IsCallerInRole, and IsSecurityEnabled methods are called, and a message is written out with the results of the function calls. If the component is participating within a transaction, the IsInTransaction method returns **true**; if the component client is within the Developer security group, IsCallerInRole returns **true**; and the IsSecurityEnabled returns **true** if access-level security is enabled for the component. The Variant parameter contains the separator used to separate each message.

Example 20-5. Accessing COM+ State Information and Printing Out Information

```
public class ObjCont
{

  public void showStatus(Variant vtSep)
  {

  IObjectContext objCont = null;
```

Example 20-5. Accessing COM+ State Information and Printing Out Information (continued)

```
IGetContextProperties objProps = null;
IResponse objResponse = null;

Variant v = new Variant();

// get ObjectContext, Props, and Response
objCont = MTx.GetObjectContext();
objProps = (IGetContextProperties)MTx.GetObjectContext();

// get response
v = objProps.GetProperty("Response");
objResponse = (IResponse)v.getDispatch();
v.VariantClear();

// print out state
try {
   if (objCont.IsInTransaction())
       v.putString("In Transaction");
   else
       v.putString("Not in Transaction");
   objResponse.Write(v);
   objResponse.Write(vtSep);
   v.VariantClear();

   if (objCont.IsCallerInRole("Developer"))
       v.putString("In Role");
   else
       v.putString("Not in Role");
   objResponse.Write(v);
   objResponse.Write(vtSep);
   v.VariantClear();

   if (objCont.IsSecurityEnabled())
       v.putString("Security Enabled");
   else
       v.putString("Security not enabled");
   objResponse.Write(v);
   objResponse.Write(vtSep);
   v.VariantClear();
   }
catch(Exception e) {
   v.putString(e.getLocalizedMessage());
   objResponse.Write(v);
   }
  }
}
```

In the component method, the calls to access state information are contained within a Java `try`...`catch` exception-handling block to capture any errors that might occur. If an error occurs, the description is accessed through the Exception object and output to the web page.

Test your component using the following ASP script, found in *asp2007.asp*:

```
<%
Dim obj
Set obj = Server.CreateObject("asp2003.ObjCont")

obj.showStatus "<p>"
%>
```

The result of accessing this ASP page is a web page containing:

```
Not in Transaction
In Role
Security not enabled
```

The component isn't within a transaction, since none was started in the ASP page, and the component is not part of a COM+ application that requires transaction support. To include transaction support for the page, add the following transaction directive as the very first line of the ASP test page:

```
<% @ TRANSACTION = required %>
```

Now when you access the component, you will get a message that it's within a transaction.

IsCallerInRole always returns a value of **True** when it is accessed in the client address, as it is with this component. (The Java component is both-threaded, which means it will be created on the same thread as the client, in this case the thread processing the ASP page.) Security isn't enabled, since the component isn't part of a COM+ application.

To get a better idea of how role-based security will impact these two methods (and the component), create a new COM+ application (name it whatever you prefer) using the Component Services Management tool, and set the activation type to a Server application (runs in a separate server process). Add *asp2003.dll* as a component to the application.

Also, create a new Developer role by right-clicking on the application's Roles folder and selecting New → Role. You'll be asked for the name of the role—give it a name of Developer. Add users for the role by right-clicking on the Users folder contained within the role and selecting New → User. You'll be shown a list of users or groups already defined on your system. Select one or more, then click the Add button to add each user, as shown in Figure 20-3. In the figure, I'm adding the default web user for my system to the Developer role.

After creating the role, right-click on the **asp2003** component and access its Properties dialog. Switch to the Transactions page and check the Supported option for transaction support. Then switch to the Security page. The new Developer role should show in the page. Check the "Enforce component level access checks" option, and check the box next to the Developer role.

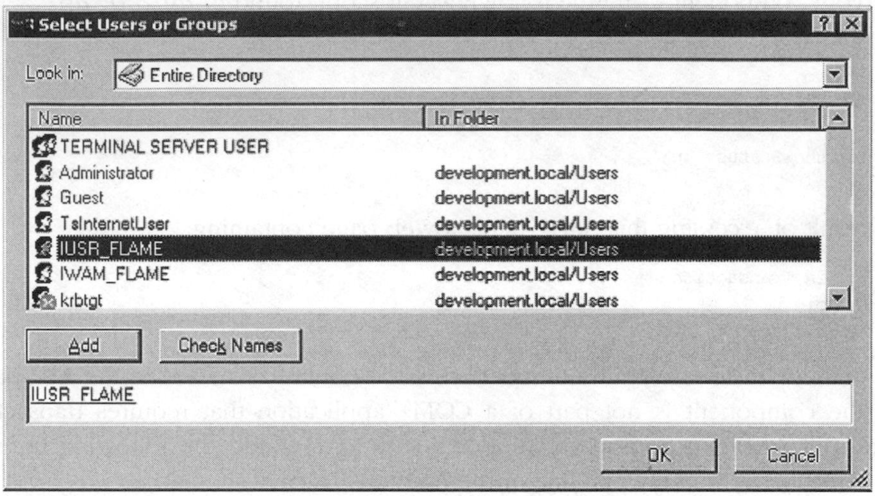

Figure 20-3. Adding users to a new role

You'll also need to add security enforcement at the COM+ application level. Access the application's Properties dialog, switch to the Security tab, and check the "Enforce access checks for this application" option. After making these changes, access the ASP test page *asp2007.asp* again. Now you'll see the following in the web page:

```
In Transaction
In Role
Security Enabled
```

Before you test the page again, you may need to unload the web site you used to run the first page test in order for the changes to take effect.

With the current security settings, if you accessed the web page as someone who is not in the Developer role, you would get a security violation error instead.

Another COM+ service you can take advantage of with COM+ Services is JIT—just-in-time activation.

JIT with IObjectControl

In the last section, when you added the component to a COM+ application, you automatically added support for JIT for your component. If you access the component's properties and switch to the Activation page, you'll see that the Enable Just-In-Time Activation option is checked.

COM+ can control the lifetime of the object based on how the done bit is set when you return from each component's method. If the done bit is set, COM+ can deactivate the component; otherwise COM+ keeps the component active within the ASP page. With JIT, when the component is deactivated, it isn't marked for removal from memory. Instead, it remains in a deactivated state until it is referenced again. Additionally, when an application, such as an ASP application, creates an instance of the component, the component isn't actually created until it's used. Both of these actions combined improve the overall performance of the application by minimizing how long an application holds a live reference to the component. The shorter this time, the less memory used by the application.

You can capture when the component is activated and deactivated by implementing the `IObjectControl` interface within your Java component. `IObjectControl` has three methods—Activate, Deactivate, and CanBePooled—that are called when the component is activated or deactivated. When you implement `IObject-Control`, you implement these three methods and can include code to instantiate objects or create global values when the component is activated and perform cleanup when the component is deactivated. This is particularly helpful if you want to provide global access to valuable resources—you can reference the resource in Activate and release the reference in Deactivate.

To try out JIT with your ASP components, create a new Visual J++ COM DLL project and name it **asp2004**. Rename the generated class **jit**. Add the following **import** statements to the top of the class:

```
import com.ms.mtx.*;
import com.ms.com.*;
import com.ms.asp.IResponse;
```

Modify the generated class to implement the `IObjectControl` interface:

```
public class jit implements IObjectControl
```

In the component, you'll have to provide an implementation of the `IObject-Control` interface's Activate, Deactivate, and CanBePooled methods; these are shown in Example 20-6. The Activate method references the `IResponse` interface and writes out a message that the component is activated. The Deactivate method writes out a message that the component is deactivated, and the CanBePooled function returns a value of **False**. Also add a new method with no parameters named sayHi (also shown in Example 20-6) that writes out a greeting to the web page.

Example 20-6. Processing JIT Events

```
public class jit implements IObjectControl
{
    private IResponse m_objResponse = null;

    public void Activate() {
        IGetContextProperties objProps = null;
        Variant v = new Variant();

        // get Props
```

Example 20-6. Processing JIT Events (continued)

```
        objProps = (IGetContextProperties)MTx.GetObjectContext();

        // get response
        v = objProps.GetProperty("Response");
        m_objResponse = (IResponse)v.getDispatch();
        v.VariantClear();

        v.putString("Activated");
        m_objResponse.Write(v);
    }

    public void Deactivate() {
        Variant v = new Variant();
        v.putString("Deactivated");
        m_objResponse.Write(v);
    }

    public boolean CanBePooled() {
        return false;
    }

    public void sayHi() {
        Variant v = new Variant();
        v.putString("Hi from method");
        m_objResponse.Write(v);
    }
}
```

According to our understanding of JIT, the Activate method is called not when the
component is created, but only when its methods or properties are first accessed.
In addition, the component is not deactivated unless it is released in the script
(setting the component reference to **Nothing** in VBScript) or when the ASP page
script is finished processing.

To test all of this, the following ASP test script, *asp2008.asp*, writes out messages
when the component is first created, before the component's sayHi method is
called, after the method, and after the component reference is set to **Nothing**:

```
    <%
    Dim obj
    Set obj = Server.CreateObject("asp2004.jit")

    Response.Write "Before call to message, after creating object"
    Response.Write "<p>"

    obj.sayHi
    Response.Write "<p>"

    Response.Write "After call to message"
    Response.Write "<p>"
```

```
Set obj = Nothing
Response.Write "<p>"

Response.Write "After setting object to nothing"
%>
```

As expected, the result from accessing this ASP script is the following web page output:

```
Before call to message, after creating object
ActivatedHi from method
After call to message
Deactivated
After setting object to nothing
```

Notice that the component's Activate method is called when the component's method is accessed, not when it is created. Notice also that Deactivate is called when the object is set to **Nothing**.

When using Visual J++ 6.0 SP 3.0 in Windows 2000, I have found that to recompile the object, I have to literally remove the object from the COM+ application—shutting down the application isn't enough. However, once I remove it and recompile it, I just add it back to the application.

The ASP Built-in Object and Helper Interfaces

There are six main built-in ASP objects that can be used for communication between the client and server and between the server component and the server environment. These are the Response, Request, Session, Application, ASPError, and Server objects. Each of these objects except ASPError is discussed and demonstrated in turn in the following sections.

You can find a detailed listing of each object's methods and properties in Appendix A, *ASP Built-in Object Quick Reference*. The ASP-Error object is not detailed in this chapter primarily because it is only used to provide custom error handling—it won't be used very often with business components.

The `com.ms.asp` package provides access to the built-in object interfaces. You've seen `IResponse` in action; the other interfaces are `IApplicationObject`, `ISessionObject`, `IRequest`, and `IServer`. In addition to the ASP built-in objects, the `com.ms.asp` package has other interfaces to facilitate working with the collections returned from several methods. These interfaces are `IVariantDictionary`, `IReadCookie`, `IWriteCookie`, `IStringList`, and `IRequestDictionary`. The `IVariantDictionary` interface provides support for the `IApplicationObject` and `ISessionObject` interfaces; the `IRequestDictionary` interface provides support for the `IRequest` and `IResponse` interfaces; `IReadCookie` and `IWriteCookie` provide support for reading and writing to Netscape-style cookies.

The Application Object and Its Associated Interface, IApplicationObject

The Application object contains application-level information that persists for the life of the ASP application. A variable can be set to a beginning default value when the application starts, and any changes to this value persist until the application is shut down. This makes application-level variables useful for storing values that must persist for the life of the application and must be accessible by all sessions within the application.

Application-level variables are defined either by setting values directly in the Application object or by defining a static variable in the *global.asa* file for the application.

> The *global.asa* file is a single static file located in the root directory of the IIS application. It contains references to application- and session-level variables, as well as some event handlers. This file is discussed in more detail in Appendix A.

The Application object's functionality is accessible from Java components through the `IApplicationObject` interface, defined in `com.ms.asp`. One of this object's methods is getContents, which returns a reference to the `IVariantDictionary` interface's Contents collection (getStaticObjects returns a reference to the Application's StaticObjects collection).

The `IVariantDictionary` interface is an enumerator interface, which means that it has methods to access a single object or methods that can be used to iterate through the entire collection of objects managed by the enumerator.

> An example of using enumeration is provided in the later section covering `IRequest`.

To use **IVariantDictionary** to access a specific value, create a new Visual J++ project named **asp2005** and rename the generated class to **App**. Add the COM+, COM, and ASP packages:

```
import com.ms.mtx.*;
import com.ms.com.*;
import com.ms.asp.*;
```

Add the code for the tstApplication method shown in Example 20-7. The component method does several things. First, it creates a reference to the **IGetContextProperties** interface, which it uses to create a reference to the **IApplicationObject** and **IResponse** interfaces. Next, the **IApplicationObject** interface's getContents method is called to return a reference to **IVariant-Dictionary**. This interface, in turn, contains a reference to the Application object's Contents collection.

To access a specific value in the Contents collection, two Variant objects are used, one for the Contents item key and one for the Contents item value. The new component then outputs the value using the Response object. At the end of the method, the component changes the tstVariable value in the Contents collection item by using the **IVariantDictionary** interface's putItem method.

Example 20-7. Combining IApplicationObject and IVariantDictionary

```
public class App
{

    public void tstApplication() {

        // program variables
        IGetContextProperties objProps = null;
        IApplicationObject iObjApplication = null;
        IVariantDictionary iObjDictionary = null;
        IResponse iObjResponse = null;
        Variant v = new Variant();
        Variant v2 = new Variant();

        // get context properties
        objProps = (IGetContextProperties)MTx.GetObjectContext();

        // Get the Application object
        v = objProps.GetProperty("Application");
        iObjApplication = (IApplicationObject)v.getDispatch();

        // get response object to output info
        v.VariantClear();
        v = objProps.GetProperty("Response");
        iObjResponse = (IResponse)v.getDispatch();
        v.VariantClear();

        // access dictionary interface for Contents collection
```

Example 20-7. Combining IApplicationObject and IVariantDictionary (continued)

```
    try {
        iObjDictionary = iObjApplication.getContents();
        v.VariantClear();

        // get contents item for key "tstVariable"
        v.putString("tstVariable");
        v2 = iObjDictionary.getItem(v);
        iObjResponse.Write(v2);

        // reset value
        v2.VariantClear();
        v2.putString("this is a new value");
        iObjDictionary.putItem(v, v2);
        }
    catch(Exception e) {
        v.putString(e.getLocalizedMessage());
        iObjResponse.Write(v);
    }
    }

}
```

Use the following ASP script, *asp2009.asp,* to test the component. Note that the tstVariable variable in the Application object's Contents collection is set before calling the component method, and its value is displayed after calling the component's method:

```
Dim obj
Set obj = Server.CreateObject("asp2005.App")

Application("tstVariable") = "this is a test item"
obj.tstApplication

Response.Write "<p>"
Response.Write Application("tstVariable")
```

Two other **IApplicationObject** methods are getValue and putValue. These can be used to access variables that are assigned directly to the Application object. For example, the following code block gets the string value for an application-level variable named tstString, displays its value using the **IResponse** interface, and then changes it:

```
    try {

        // get application value
        v = iObjApplication.getValue("tstString");
        iObjResponse.Write(v);
        v.putString("new value");
        iObjApplication.putValue("tstString",v);
        }
    catch(ClassCastException e) {
```

```
      v.VariantClear();
      v.putString(e.toString());
      iObjResponse.Write(v);
      }
```

The final two methods for the `IApplicationInterface` interface are Lock and UnLock. These methods should be used whenever you make a change to the Application object's collections by calling Lock to prevent other changes while making yours, and UnLock to release the lock. However, their use should be limited, and the lock should be released as soon as possible, since no other changes to the Application object can be made while it is locked.

The Session object is similar to the Application object and is discussed in the next section.

The Session Object and Its Associated Interface, ISessionObject

Like the Application object, the Session object persists beyond a specific web page. Unlike the Application object, the Session object persists for the length of time that one person (as a session) is connected to the ASP application.

Session-level variables can be created by direct assignment to the Session object or by declaration in the *global.asa* file. The variables are initialized when a specific user accesses the first page for the ASP application, and they persist until the user's session times out or the user logs out.

The Session object is accessible from within Java components through the `ISessionObject` interface. The Session object's getContents, getStaticObjects, getValue, and putValue methods operate the same with the `ISessionObject` interface as they did with `IApplicationObject`. The main difference is, of course, that the values impacted by these methods persist only through the session of the person currently logged into the application. Session-level variables might be used, for example, to maintain a running total for a catalog system or to provide a user identifier for database entries.

The Session object's getCodePage and getLocale methods are unique and are of interest if you are working with international web page applications. For example, the CodePage value defines the keyboard mapping for a system, allowing for specialized characters based on a country or language character set. The Locale is used to determine regional character settings, such as the use of metrics for numbers or which characters are used with currency. In the United States, currency uses the dollar sign ($), but the United Kingdom uses the symbol for pounds, which I really can't show because I am using a system based on the United States locale. The following code fragment displays the CodePage and Locale currently in use on a system:

```
try {
    // session object
    v = objProps.GetProperty("Session");
    iObjSession = (ISessionObject)v.getDispatch();

    // get application value
    int i;
    i = iObjSession.getCodePage();

    v.putInt(i);

    // response object defined earlier
    iObjResponse.Write(v);
    v.putString("<p>");
    iObjResponse.Write(v)
    i = iObjSession.getLCID();
    v.putInt(i);
    iObjResponse.Write(v);
    }
catch(Exception e) {
    v.putString(e.getLocalizedMessage());
    iObjResponse.Write(v);
    }
```

CodePage and Locale can be changed using the associated putCodePage and put-LCID methods. Both CodePage and Locale can be used to return content based on the settings for the browser accessing the ASP page.

Two other methods that are useful with the Session object are the Abandon and putTimeout methods. The Abandon method can be used to destroy the Session object and free any resources currently in use by the session. The putTimeout method is used to set a new timeout value for the session.

To demonstrate how to work with the `ISessionObject` interface, add a new class to **asp2005** by right-clicking on the project name in the Project Explorer and selecting Add → Add Class from the pop-up menu. When prompted for the type of class, select the standard Class option, and name the class **Sess**.

To add the COM directive to this new class, access Project → Properties from the main menu and switch to the COM Classes page in the Properties dialog. Check the box next to the new class, as shown in Figure 20-4. This adds the COM directive to the top of your new class.

In the new component class, add the three **import** statements, and create a new method named sesnLogout. Add the code in Example 20-8 to your component class. The method accesses the Session object and calls its Abandon method.

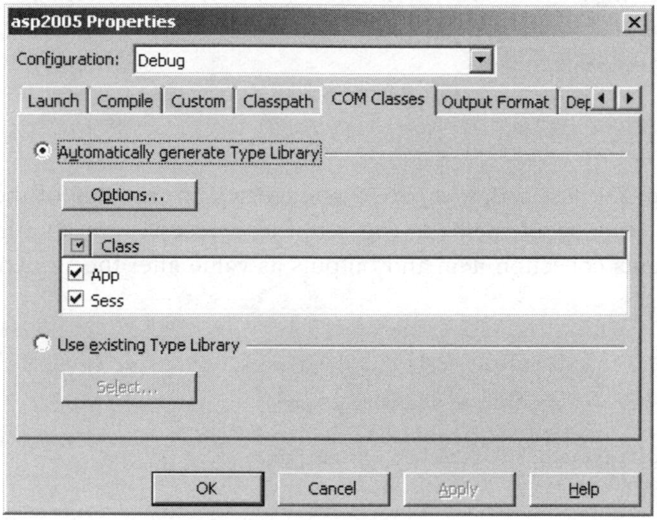

Figure 20-4. Adding COM support for the new class

Example 20-8. Using the ISessionObject Abandon Method to Release Resources When the User Logs Out

```
public class Sess
{
    // test function
    public void sesnLogout() {
        IGetContextProperties objProps = null;
        ISessionObject iObjSession = null;
        IResponse iObjResponse = null;
        Variant v = null;

        // get context properties
        objProps = (IGetContextProperties)MTx.GetObjectContext();

        v = objProps.GetProperty("Response");
        iObjResponse = (IResponse)v.getDispatch();

        try {
            // session object
            v = objProps.GetProperty("Session");
            iObjSession = (ISessionObject)v.getDispatch();

            v.putString("Thanks for stopping by!");
            iObjResponse.Write(v);

            // free Session
            iObjSession.Abandon();
        }
        catch(Exception e) {
            v.putString(e.getLocalizedMessage());
```

Example 20-8. Using the ISessionObject Abandon Method to Release Resources When the User Logs Out (continued)

```
        iObjResponse.Write(v);
    }
  }
}
```

The following ASP test script, *asp2010.asp*, creates an instance of the component and calls the sesnLogout method. The script also accesses an item in the Session object's Contents collection item and outputs its value after the sesnLogout method is called:

```
<%
Dim obj
Set obj = Server.CreateObject("asp2005.Sess")

Session("tstVariable") = "this is a test item"
obj.sesnLogout

Response.Write "<p>"
Response.Write Session("tstVariable")
%>
```

When you access the ASP test page, you might expect that the Session object's Contents collection doesn't have the value set before the call to sesnLogout. However, the value still exists—the Abandon method forces the destruction of the Session object *after* the ASP page is finished and not during the page processing.

Other information specific to the server can be accessed or changed using the IServer object, discussed next.

The Server Object and Its Associated Interface, IServer

The Server object can be used to create new instances of other COM classes by using its CreateObject method and passing in the component's PROGID value. In addition, it can also be used to derive encoded strings using either HTML encoding or URL encoding or to map a relative location to a physical location.

For example, the angle brackets (< and >) are used to delimit HTML tags, such as <p> for a paragraph or <H1></H1> to define a header. To actually output the angle brackets as is, without triggering formatting, special encoding characters are used. The left angle bracket is encoded using the sequence <, and the right angle bracket is >. The IServer object's HTMLEncoding method encodes all

HTML-specific characters into their associated encoded values. So, the following code:

```
str = iServer.HTMLEncode("<h1>test</h1>");
v.putString(str + "<p>");
iObjResponse.Write(v);
```

would output the following string:

```
&lt;h1&gt;test&lt;/h1&gt;
```

which would output the following to the web page that is viewed:

```
<h1>test</h1>
```

rather than create the header.

The URLEncode method maps the URL special characters into their associated encoded character sequences. The following code:

```
str = iServer.URLEncode("% this/is a test % +");
v.putString(str + "<p>");
iObjResponse.Write(v);
```

would result in the following string:

```
%25+this%2Fis+a+test+%25+%2B
```

with the percent sign, space, slash, and plus sign encoded. This is similar to how the URLPathEncode method works, except that it does not try to include the slashes.

The MapPath method doesn't encode any characters, but instead translates whatever string is passed to the method with the actual physical location where the ASP application is running. This is especially helpful when performing any access that depends on a physical location. The following code:

```
str = iServer.MapPath("/test/test2");
v.putString(str);
iObjResponse.Write(v);
```

results in the following string, based on the physical directory location where my ASP component testing occurs:

```
E:\Inetpub\wwwroot\New Folder\test2
```

In addition to methods to create COM instances and encode strings, the getScript-Timeout and putScriptTimeout methods can be used to check the current script run times and modify the time until a script times out. You may want to use put-ScriptTimeout to increase the value for components that may take time, such as those that access a database or perform some other time-consuming operation. The getScriptTimeout method returns an integer, and putScriptTimeout takes an integer, both representing the number of minutes for the timeout.

The Request Object and Its Associated Interface, IRequest

The Request object contains information that the web page reader is sending to the ASP application. Anytime a form is submitted, information is appended to the end of an URL, or a Netscape-style cookie is set, an item is added to one of the Request object's collections. Among the collections that can be accessed through the Request object are the following:

Cookies
> Small, persistent bits of information that can be stored on the client and accessed from the ASP application via an HTTP request

ServerVariables
> A list of environment variables

Form
> The name-value pairs submitted from an HTML form

QueryString
> The name-value pairs appended to the URL of the ASP page

ClientCertificate
> Client certification fields for certification requests

Cookies originated with Netscape and are bits of information stored on the client side and indexed by the URL of the page that set the cookies. They allow an application to maintain information between the client and the application that persists beyond a specific web page. The cookies collection contains the Netscape-style cookies for the page. The ServerVariables collection contains information about the client, the client certification object, the HTTP request, the browser, and other information pertaining to the client, the server, and the communication between the two. The QueryString and Form collections both contain name-value pairs, with the name forming the key that's used to access its associated value. Finally, the ClientCertificate collection contains the fields of the client certificate issued with the request, in support of the SSL3.0/PCT1.0 security protocol.

The Request object's interface is `IRequest`, and most of these methods are used to access collection information. In order to access specific values, the `IRequest-Dictionary` interface is used.

One use of the `IRequest` and `IRequestDictionary` interfaces is to access the information resulting from user interaction with a page. As an example, if an ASP page has a form whose results are submitted using the `POST` method, the form's field/value pairs can be accessed within an ASP component using the `IRequest` interface's getForm method and the `IRequestDictionary` interface's getItem method, as the following code fragment shows:

```
// get session object
v = objProps.GetProperty("Session");
isesnObject = (ISessionObject)v.getDispatch();

// get Request object and form collection
v = objProps.GetProperty("Request");
iRequest = (IRequest)v.getDispatch();
iRqstDict = iRequest.getForm();

// get reader's last name
v.putString("lastname");
v = iRqstDict.getItem(v);

// store in Session object
isesnObject.putValue("name",v);
```

In this code, the web page reader's last name is accessed from the submitted form and stored as an item in the Session object. By doing this, the last name is then available to all session-level ASP pages. The getForm method returns a reference to an **IRequestDictionary** interface, which is used to access the Form collection. The form's **lastname** field is assigned to a Variant object passed to getItem. This method, in turn, returns the value associated with the **lastname** field. The value is stored persistently for the session by using the **ISessionObject** object's putValue method. If the form had been submitted using a **GET** rather than a **POST** request, the QueryString collection would have been populated instead of the Form collection. However, the same approach would work with both collections.

Another use of the **IRequest** and **IRequestDictionary** combination is to access the ServerVariables collection, which contains environment information about the browser, the server, and the connection between the two. This collection can be accessed using the getServerVariables method. The ServerVariables collection contains information such as the URL of the requesting page, the request method (**GET** or **POST**), the IP address of the requester, the protocol used, even the NT user account the reader is logged in as. An individual item can be accessed by using the getItem method, or the get_NewEnum method can be used to access the Java enumerator interface, **IEnumVariant**.

One handy use of the **IEnumVariant** enumerator and the ServerVariables collection is to list all of the variables and their associated values. This allows the developer to have a better idea of what variables are available, the format the values take, and how changes in the environment can impact on the variables. To see the server variables in your own environment, add a new class to **asp2005** and name it **Req**. Make sure to mark it as a COM class in the Project Properties dialog. Also add the following **import** statements:

```
import com.ms.mtx.*;
import com.ms.com.*;
import com.ms.asp.*;
```

Example 20-9 shows the code for the Req method, which lists all of the environment variables and their associated values. In the example, once the `IRequest`
interface is accessed, the getServerVariables method is called to return the
`IRequestDictionary` interface. The get_NewEnum method is then used to return
an `IEnumVariant` interface. To enumerate through the items in the collection, a
count is obtained of the number of items in the collection and the Next method is
called. This method takes three parameters: an integer that indicates the number of
items to return, an open-ended Variant array to hold the items, and an integer
array to indicate the number of items returned. Once the Variant array is populated, a **for** loop is used to display the environment variable names and their
associated values using HTML table cell and row elements, with each label and its
associated value output in a separate table row.

Example 20-9. Output All the Environment Variables from the Request

```java
public class Req
{
    // test function
    public void showVariables() {
      IGetContextProperties objProps;
      IRequest iRequest;
      IRequestDictionary iRqstDict;
      IResponse iObjResponse;
      Variant v = null;

      // get Context Properties
      objProps = (IGetContextProperties)MTx.GetObjectContext();

      v = objProps.GetProperty("Response");
      iObjResponse = (IResponse)v.getDispatch();
      try {

          // get Request object and environment variables collection
          v = objProps.GetProperty("Request");
          iRequest = (IRequest)v.getDispatch();
          iRqstDict = iRequest.getServerVariables();

          // get enumerator
          IEnumVariant ienum;
          ienum = (IEnumVariant) iRqstDict.get_NewEnum();

          // set up enumeration
          int[] iItems = new int[1];
          iItems[0] = 0;

          int iCount = iRqstDict.getCount();
          Variant[] vt = new Variant[iCount];
          ienum.Next(iCount,vt,iItems);

          // print out environment variables
          v.putString("<table>");
          iObjResponse.Write(v);
```

Example 20-9. Output All the Environment Variables from the Request (continued)

```
            for (int i = 0; i < iCount; i++) {
                v.putString("<TR><TD>");
                iObjResponse.Write(v);
                iObjResponse.Write(vt[i]);
                v.putString("</TD><TD>");
                iObjResponse.Write(v);
                iObjResponse.Write(iRqstDict.getItem(vt[i]));
                v.putString("</TD></TR>");
                iObjResponse.Write(v);
                }
            v.putString("</table>");
            iObjResponse.Write(v);
            }
        catch(Exception e) {
            v.putString(e.toString());
            iObjResponse.Write(v);
            }
        }
    }
}
```

To test the component, use the following ASP script, found in *asp2011.asp*:

```
<%
Dim obj
Set obj = Server.CreateObject("asp2005.Req")

obj.showVariables
%>
```

The same techniques to individually access a collection item or to enumerate through a collection can be used with all of the collections obtained using `IRequestDictionary`.

The Request object has information about a request being submitted to the server. The Response object, on the other hand, contains information to be returned to the client and is discussed next.

The Response Object and Its Associated Interface, IResponse

The Response object and the Java `IResponse` interface have been used throughout this chapter to write information to a web page returned to the client browser. However, the Write method is not the `IResponse` interface's only useful function. The Response object can also control how content is buffered before being sent to the browser and whether ASP pages are cached. The object can also determine if the client is still connected, control what status to return to the client, and define what type of content is being returned. This is in addition to directing the browser to another location, altering the header for the HTML output, and appending information to the IIS log file.

The Response object's control of output can be manipulated by several of the IResponse methods, such as Clear, End, and Flush. Using these methods in conjunction with transaction management can be particularly effective. Consider the scenario of an ASP application consisting of several different actions, all performed within one transaction. If any one of the actions fails and the transaction is rolled back, how much of the output that is already generated can be controlled with Response buffering. For example, the following code turns buffering off:

```
iObjResponse.putBuffer(false);
```

Since the putBuffer method controls how output is returned to the client, any component calling this method must be instantiated in the ASP page and must call the method before any other output is returned to the client, or an error will result.

With buffering enabled, as it is with IIS 5.0 by default, output can be returned or not, based on the success or failure of any one of the component actions, as the following code demonstrates:

```
try {

    //...other code
    iObjResponse.Flush();
    objContext.SetComplete();
    }
catch(Exception e) {

    // clear existing output
    iObjResponse.Clear();

    v.putString(e.getLocalizedMessage());
    iObjResponse.Write(v);
    objContext.SetAbort();
    }
```

The IResponse object can also be used to set whether an ASP page is cached or not. If content is unlikely to change within the same ASP application session, the caching expiration time should be set to a high value by using code such as the following, so that the page is retrieved from the client cache rather than the server:

```
iObjResponse.putExpires(300);
```

In addition to controlling caching and buffering, the IResponse interface can also be used to change the status of the HTTP response, such as setting the status or redirecting the output, as the following code demonstrates:

```
iObjResponse.Redirect("http://www.somewhere.com/someother.htm")
```

The advantage of using redirection is that the component can query for information, such as browser type and version, and then direct the client to a set of pages created specifically for the browser/version.

Another method of the **IResponse** interface that can be particularly handy is putContentType. One example of its use is for web pages that provide buttons for people to see the actual HTML source. When a user chooses this option, the page is returned as **text/plain** rather than **text/HTML**, as the following demonstrates:

```
if (type == 0) {
    v.putString("HTML");
    iObjResponse.Write(v);
    iObjResponse.putContentType("text/HTML");
    }
else {
    v.putString("plain");
    iObjResponse.putContentType("text/plain");
    iObjResponse.Write(v);
    }
```

To display the page as HTML, a value of zero (0) is sent with the component method call. Otherwise, a value other than zero is sent with the method, and the HTML is returned as plain text without any processing of the HTML tags.

Accessing ADO from Java Components

The use of ADO within Visual J++ has been facilitated by a set of classes included within the Windows Framework Classes (WFC). This section demonstrates how to use WFC to connect to a data source and create several types of result sets using different types of queries.

Connecting to a Data Source with ADO

To add support for ADO to a Java component, an **import** statement is added to the component that pulls in the WFC classes for ADO:

```
import com.ms.wfc.data.*;
```

An ADO Connection object encapsulates a specific database session. Within an ASP application, the connection can be either a direct database connection or a network connection if the data source is remote to the ASP component. The ADO connection may or may not be represented by a specific instantiation of a Connection object. A connection to the database can be created without having to specifically create a Connection object. However, if the connection is used for more than one recordset, it is more efficient to create a separate Connection object that is usable for all queries and database commands.

A Connection object has several methods and properties. For instance, the Open method is used to create the database connection and can optionally take a connection string, a user ID, a password, and an open option, as shown in the following prototypes, taken from the Microsoft Connection class documentation:

```
public void open()
public void open(String connectionString)
public void open(String connectionString, String userID)
public void open(String connectionString, String userID, String password)
public void open(String connectionString, String userID, String password,
int options)
```

The connection string itself consists of a set of key/value pairs, each separated by a semicolon (;). All connection strings, regardless of the OLE DB provider, require that certain information be in the connection string, such as the server and the database or the DSN for the data source, the user ID, and the password. An example of a connection string is the following:

```
Provider=SQLOLEDB;DSN=pubs;uid=sa;pwd=;database=pubs;
pwd=somepassword;Driver={SQL Server}
```

The first keyword shown in the string defines the OLE DB provider for the database. The provider listed in the example is for the Microsoft SQL Server database. If no provider is given, the default is a generic OLE DB for ODBC Provider, MSDASQL. The following connection string uses this default provider to connect to an Access database:

```
DSN=books;uid=sa;Driver={Microsoft Access Driver(*.mdb)}
```

In addition to the provider, the connection string can also contain a driver name, which is a reference to the database server, such as {SQL Server} for Microsoft SQL Server, and {Microsoft Access Driver (*.mdb)} for Access. You can take this information from the ODBC Data Source Administrator. Instead of, or in addition to, the server, you can also specify a Data Source Name (DSN) or a File Data Source Name (FileDSN). The DSN references data sources installed on the computer, and the FileDSN represents data sources installed and configured in such a way as to be accessible by all users that have access to the installed driver. For ASP components, the data source can be configured using either the DSN or FileDSN. If the DSN is provided in the connection string, the database source does not need to be provided, though this is a good technique to ensure you can connect to the correct database.

The user identifier and password can be specified separately within the connection string as optional Open method parameters. In addition, other keyword/value pairs may be required for each OLE DB provider; if so, they should be documented by the provider.

In addition to the connection string and the user identifier and password, the Connection object's Open method can establish an asynchronous database connection by specifying a value of `AdoEnums.ConnectOption.ASYNCCONNECT` as an argument to the optional *options* parameter. (By setting the connection to be asynchronous, processing can continue while the connection is being made.) This value is accessible by adding the `import` statement for the WFC ADO classes, accessing the `AdoEnums` package, and then accessing the enumeration and its specific constant. Visual J++'s autofill capability will provide a listing of enumerated members.

Other Connection object methods are used specifically to control database access and transaction management, two issues critical for a multiuser system such as an Internet or intranet application. Database access can be controlled by using the setMode method to control whether the access is read/write, read-only, or write-only and whether the database is opened in such a way as to deny other connections. The following code prevents others from opening a connection to the database while the existing connection is active (open):

```
conn.setMode(AdoEnums.ConnectMode.SHAREEXCLUSIVE);
conn.open(str,"sa","");
```

Another property of the Connection object that can impact database access is the isolation level. By default, database transactions supported by ADO default to a type of `AdoEnums.IsolationLevel.CHAOS` and `AdoEnums.Isolationlevel.CURSORSTABILITY`. The CHAOS isolation level means that pending changes from isolated transactions cannot be overwritten by actions of the component. The CURSORSTABILITY isolation level setting means that other ADO transactions operating on the same server-side database can view changes in this specific transaction only after these changes have been committed. The ADO provider determines the types of isolation level supported, and trying to use unsupported types can result in a different level of isolation being set or in an error.

Transactions can be controlled directly for a connection with the use of the Connection object's beginTrans, commitTrans, and rollbackTrans methods. This is an effective approach to take to fine-tune transaction control for a specific set of database activities, as opposed to controlling the transaction for several components using MTS transaction control. Using beginTrans creates a new transaction on the Connection, and using commitTrans or rollbackTrans impacts the activity for the specific connection only.

To begin a new transaction, use the following code:

```
conn.beginTrans();
```

After creating changes on the database, the transaction can be committed using the following command:

```
conn.commitTrans();
```

The transaction can be rolled back by using the following:

```
conn.rollbackTrans();
```

The rollbackTrans method ends the transaction without committing any pending changes to the database for the specific database connection. Each of the transaction methods also has associated event handlers: onBeginTransComplete, onCommitTransComplete, and onRollbackTransComplete. These event handlers can be used to return a message with the transaction status to the ASP application user.

One last method to mention is the Connection object's Close method. You will want to close every connection as soon as possible, since there are a finite number of database connections available. Creating a connection and then not closing it locks out other users when they access the application and the application attempts to create a new connection.

Querying the Data

Database queries can fall into several categories:

- Simple one-table queries, such as

  ```
  select au_lname from authors
  ```

- More complex multiple-table join queries, such as

  ```
  select authors.au_lname, titles.title from authors, titles, titleauthor where
  titles.title_id = titleauthor.title_id and authors.au_id = titleauthor.au_id
  ```

- Simple or complex queries using parameters

- Data retrieval for updates

- Calls to stored procedures

You might think that a simple, one-table query to return information and output it to an ASP page would have no real effect on any other transaction activity. However, any data action impacts on all other actions, even one as simple as the following:

```
Recordset rs = new Recordset();
Variant vtSource = new Variant("select * from WebPages");
rs.open(vtSource, (Connection)conn, AdoEnums.CursorType.FORWARDONLY,
          AdoEnums.LockType.READONLY, AdoEnums.CommandType.TEXT);
```

This query selects all the fields from the Authors table using an existing Connection object and a forward-only cursor—meaning that the cursor is read from the first record to the last. In addition, a read-only lock is applied with the query, which prevents any modifications to the retrieved information. This is probably the simplest type of query to make: no joined tables or stored procedure calls, no passed parameters, and no updates on the returned data. What possible impact can something like this have on any other transactions?

One possible impact is the use of resources to fulfill the command. There is only so much CPU and memory to handle all database transactions, and this small one does take its own piece. It also impacts the network traffic to support the query. This query returns a small number of rows, but querying a table with a thousand or even a million rows without any form of selection criteria can consume all system resources as well as much of the available server bandwidth to return the query. This is in addition to a possible timeout of the existing ASP request, as well as a very slow response time for the web page reader.

To control the number of rows returned, criteria are usually applied to database retrieval. In addition, the Recordset object's setMaxRecords method controls the number of records that are returned for a particular result set, regardless of any other criteria.

Adding Selection Criteria

The next simplest data query adds a selection criteria, otherwise known as a **WHERE** clause, to the SQL **SELECT** statement. Again, this can be used with a single table query or with a more complex, multitable join.

To try this type of query, create a new Visual J++ project and name it **asp2006**. Name the generated class **query**. Add the following **import** statements to the class:

```
import com.ms.mtx.*;
import com.ms.com.*;
import com.ms.asp.IResponse;
import com.ms.wfc.data.*;
```

In the component, add a method called simpleQuery that takes a String input parameter. This parameter contains the page type code that will be used in the simple query.

In the component method, which is shown in Example 20-10, an instance of the **IResponse** object is created, as well as instances of the ADO Recordset and Connection objects. The Connection object is used to establish a connection to the database, in this case the SQL Server version of the Weaver database. A SQL statement is created using a StringBuffer object, and the page type code is added to the query. Once finished, the Recordset object's Open method is called, passing in the query and the open connection. Once the recordset is returned, the results are processed in a loop and displayed.

Example 20-10. A SQL Query Using the WHERE Clause

```
public class query
{
    public void simpleQuery (String strPageType) {
```

Example 20-10. A SQL Query Using the WHERE Clause (continued)

```java
IGetContextProperties objProps = null;
IResponse iObjResponse = null;
Variant v = new Variant();

// get ObjectContext, Props, and Response
objProps = (IGetContextProperties)MTx.GetObjectContext();

// get response
v = objProps.GetProperty("Response");
iObjResponse = (IResponse)v.getDispatch();
v.VariantClear();

try {
// create recordset and select
Recordset rs = new Recordset();
Connection conn = new Connection();

// open connection
conn.open("Provider=SQLOLEDB;server=FLAME;database=weaver;uid=sa;pwd=");

// set select statement
StringBuffer strBuff = new StringBuffer();
strBuff.append("select name from WebPage where ");
strBuff.append("page_type_cd = '");
strBuff.append(strPageType);
strBuff.append("' order by name");
Variant vtSource = new Variant(strBuff.toString());

// open recordset
rs.open(vtSource, (Connection)conn, AdoEnums.CursorType.FORWARDONLY,
                AdoEnums.LockType.READONLY, AdoEnums.CommandType.TEXT);

// print out name
Variant vtOutput = new Variant();
rs.moveFirst();
while (!rs.getEOF()) {
   String str;
   str = rs.getFields().getItem("name").getValue().toString();
   vtOutput.putString(str + "<br>");
   iObjResponse.Write(vtOutput);
   rs.moveNext();
   }
rs.close();
conn.close();
}
catch (Exception e) {
   v.putString(e.getLocalizedMessage());
   iObjResponse.Write(v);
}
}
}
```

Compile the new component and test it with the following ASP script, contained in *asp2012.asp*:

```
<%
Dim obj
Set obj = Server.CreateObject("asp2006.query")

obj.simpleQuery "HTM"
%>
```

All entries in WebPage with a page type code of **HTM** are returned to the web page.

Using the Command Object and Parameters

For most ASP components, database queries will be based on selection criteria that are all or in part provided by the web page reader's interaction with the ASP application. The criteria can be accessed using the built-in ASP Request object. The criteria are then retrieved from the form or query string collection, depending on the method of submitting the form or whether the values are submitted using a query string.

If more than one parameter is provided, or if the recordset retrieval procedure is run multiple times with different names each time, using parameters with a Command object is a better approach than using a Recordset object and dynamically generating a query string. Using a command caches the query for reuse, allowing you to change the parameter value rather than having to reissue the query directly. When using a Command object instead of adding the query values to the query string, you can create parameters for the command and use the search values to set these parameters.

To demonstrate how to use the Command object and its associated Parameters collection, add a new method to **asp2006.query** named cmndQuery. The method has one String input parameter, the page type code. Its source code is shown in Example 20-11. In this example, the Command object's properties are set first: the CommandText property is assigned a SQL **SELECT** statement containing the query by calling the setCommandText method, and the CommandType property, which contains a command type specifier, is assigned by using the setCommandType method. To add the parameter for the query, the Parameters collection is accessed from the Command object. Next, a new Parameter object is created, and its datatype, size, and value are set using the setType, setSize, and setString methods, respectively. The new parameter is then appended to the Parameters collection. (For more than one query criteria, more than one parameter can be created and appended to the Parameters collection.) Finally, the query is run via the Command object's execute method. The result of the operation returns a Recordset object, which is then used to process the returned records in a manner similar to that shown in Example 20-11.

Example 20-11. Using the ADO Command Object and the Parameters Collection

```java
public void cmndQuery (String strPageType) {

    IGetContextProperties objProps = null;
    IResponse iObjResponse = null;
    Variant v = new Variant();

    // get ObjectContext, Props, and Response
    objProps = (IGetContextProperties)MTx.GetObjectContext();

    // get response
    v = objProps.GetProperty("Response");
    iObjResponse = (IResponse)v.getDispatch();
    v.VariantClear();

    try {
        // create recordset and select
        Recordset rs = null;
        Connection conn = new Connection();
        Command cmd = new Command();

        // open connection
        conn.open("Provider=SQLOLEDB;server=FLAME;
                                    database=weaver;uid=sa;pwd=");

        // set select statement
        StringBuffer strBuff = new StringBuffer();
        strBuff.append("select name from WebPage where ");
        strBuff.append("page_type_cd = ?");
        strBuff.append(" order by name");

        cmd.setActiveConnection(conn);
        cmd.setCommandText(strBuff.toString());
        cmd.setPrepared(true);
        cmd.setCommandType(AdoEnums.CommandType.TEXT);

        // parameter
        Parameters parms = cmd.getParameters();
        Parameter parm = new Parameter();
        parm.setType(AdoEnums.DataType.VARCHAR);
        parm.setSize(3);
        parm.setString(strPageType);
        parms.append(parm);

        rs = cmd.execute();

        // print out name
        Variant vtOutput = new Variant();
        rs.moveFirst();
        while (!rs.getEOF()) {
```

Example 20-11. Using the ADO Command Object and the Parameters Collection (continued)

```
        String str;
        str = rs.getFields().getItem("name").getValue().toString();
        vtOutput.putString(str + "<br>");
        iObjResponse.Write(vtOutput);
        rs.moveNext();
      }
      rs.close();
      conn.close();
      }
    catch (Exception e) {
      v.putString(e.getLocalizedMessage());
      iObjResponse.Write(v);
      }
    }
  }
}
```

To test this second query, the ASP test script found in *asp2013.asp* creates an instance of the component and calls cmndQuery:

```
<%
Dim obj
Set obj = Server.CreateObject("asp2006.query")

obj.cmndQuery "APP"
%>
```

This time all WebPage entries with a page type code of **APP** show in the page.

These two examples demonstrate how much of the ADO functionality works with Java and the WFC. Try this out with other examples shown in Chapter 8, *Creating ASP/ADO Components*, and Chapter 9, *Creating an ASP Middle Tier with ADO*. Though these database chapters use Visual Basic to demonstrate how to work with ADO, you should be able to convert the examples to Java by comparing them with the examples you've seen in this chapter. The functionality may change, but the Java syntax is the same.

21

Creating ASP Components with Delphi

Delphi is a Pascal-based development tool and environment that has one of the more sophisticated IDEs that I've ever used. It's also one that hasn't received much coverage (along with Perl, covered in the next chapter) when it comes to creating ASP components. However, not only is Delphi an excellent tool for creating most applications, it's also a very good choice when creating your ASP components.

As I've stated, Delphi is a sophisticated tool, and I won't be able to cover all the nuances of using the tool in this chapter, so you'll need to have experience with the IDE before reading this chapter. What you won't need, though, is experience working with COM-based applications in order to work with the examples and to understand the concepts.

In this chapter, we'll look at the different types of COM objects you can create with Delphi using COM wizards, and we'll also look at building ASP components by manually importing the necessary COM+ and ASP libraries. We'll also cover using ADO to access data sources from within your components.

 If you've not worked with COM or COM+ previously, you should first read Chapter 3, *ASP Components and COM*; Chapter 4, *ASP Components, Threads, and Contexts*; and Chapter 5, *COM+ Services and ASP Components and Applications*.

Using the COM Wizards to Create ASP Components

There are several COM wizards you can use to create components, but you should only use the wizards that add in support for the dual interface when creating your

ASP components. The dual interface adds support for access of the component using automation—necessary from ASP script—as well as early binding through vtable (table lookup) access.

When you use the dual interface option, all component methods are defined automatically with the **safecall** calling convention. This calling convention maps COM error methods into exception handling and converts the returned **HRESULT** values into exceptions. This calling convention is required for all methods for dual interface components.

Before we take a look at the different COM wizards and see what they provide for ASP component development, you'll first need to create a component project that you'll use for all of the wizard-based examples.

After opening Delphi, select File → New. In the dialog that opens, switch to the ActiveX tab. Click on the ActiveX library option. When you do this, the form that's automatically created for Delphi applications is removed and is replaced by a library project page. Name the project **asp2101** and save it. You're now set to create your first ASP component.

This chapter's examples were created using Delphi Enterprise 5.0. If your version and edition of Delphi doesn't have some of the COM wizard support mentioned in this section, see the later section "Manually Adding Support for COM+/ASP."

Using the ASP COM Wizard

For your first component, you'll use the ASP COM Wizard. Select File → New and switch to the ActiveX tab when the dialog opens. Select the Active Server Object option. In the dialog that opens, type in the component name, in this case First. Also change the threading model to Both. In addition, select the Object Context Active Server Type option, since you're working with IIS. Accessing the ASP objects through the ScriptingContext is deprecated in Windows 2000 (though it's still supported for backward compatibility). You can have Delphi generate a test ASP page, but one is provided with the examples for this book, so uncheck this option. The dialog should look like that shown in Figure 21-1.

Delphi creates the component Pascal file and also adds in the necessary support libraries for this type of component.

The Type Library Editor should show when the component files are generated. In this editor, you can do such things as add a reference to a help file or provide a better name than "asp2101 Library" for the component. You can also use the editor to add component methods and properties.

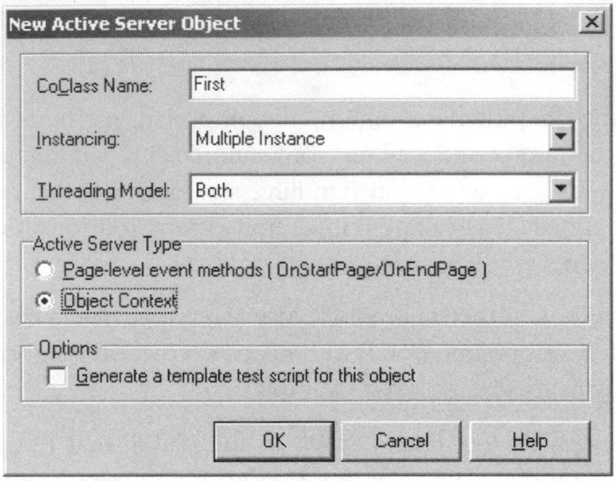

Figure 21-1. Using the ASP COM Wizard to generate component

Create a new method by right-clicking on the **IFirst** component interface and selecting New → Method. A method is added to the interface, and its properties are displayed.

 Use the Type Library Editor whenever you add any new publicly exposed methods to your components.

Rename the method sayHello and then switch to the Parameters tab. In this tab, leave the return type as is—COM objects always have an **HRESULT** return type. Add an input **BSTR** name, as well as a pointer to a **VARIANT** return value, as shown in Figure 21-2.

The method prototype is automatically added to the component's Pascal file when you click the Refresh Implementation button in the editor. This button looks similar to the recycle symbol and is located in the toolbar at the top of the Type Library Editor. Once the prototype is added to the component, complete it by adding in code, shown in bold, to create the greeting message using the name passed in to the component and returning the result to the ASP script, as shown in Example 21-1.

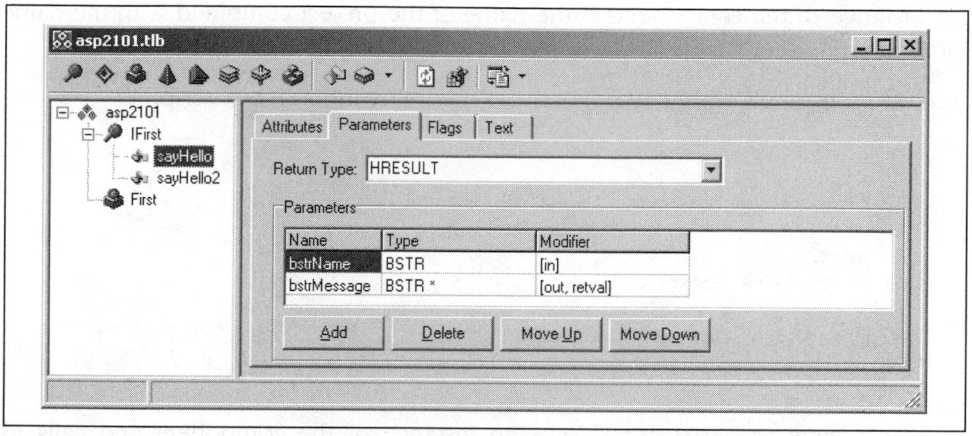

Figure 21-2. Defining the method parameters for the new ASP component

Example 21-1. First Delphi Component Code

```
unit First;

interface

uses
  ComObj, ActiveX, AspTlb, asp2101_TLB, StdVcl;

type
  TFirst = class(TASPMTSObject, IFirst)
  protected
    function sayHello(const bstrName: WideString): WideString; safecall;
  end;

implementation

uses ComServ;

function TFirst.sayHello(const bstrName: WideString): WideString;
var
tmpString: WideString;
begin
tmpString := 'Hello ' + bstrName;
Result := tmpString;
end;

initialization
  TAutoObjectFactory.Create(ComServer, TFirst, Class_First,
    ciMultiInstance, tmBoth);
end.
```

Before compiling the component, rename the Pascal file to *First* by selecting File → Save As from the main menu and naming the file *First.pas*. This also renames the unit within the code. The component's PROGID (the identifier used to create an instance of the component) is the name of the project combined with the name of the component Pascal file—asp2101.First. Compile the object.

To test your new Delphi component, use the following ASP test script:

```
<%
Dim obj
Set obj = Server.CreateObject("asp2101.First")

Dim msg
msg = obj.sayHello("World!")

Response.Write "<h3>" & msg & "</h3>"
Set obj = Nothing
%>
```

This test page, *asp2101.asp*, creates an instance of the component and calls its only method. The results that are returned are displayed to the web page. In the case of this script, the following results:

```
Hello World!
```

Any of the COM object wizards that provide dual interface support will work for creating your ASP components. What makes the ASP option unique is the ASP library that Inprise has created for use with Delphi and that is installed with Delphi 5.0. This library, **AspTlb**, is automatically added, as you can see in the **uses** section of the code. In this library, the ASP built-in objects are created as properties of the new object through the use of the ancestor class **TASPMTSObject**. To access the objects, you just have to refer to them by name:

```
Response.Write...
```

The ASP objects are created using the MTS/COM+ ObjectContext when the property is first accessed. If you had selected the ScriptingContext option when creating the component, the class name would have been **TASPObject**, and the objects would be created using ScriptingContext.

With access to the ASP objects, to print out the greetings created in sayHello, you can use the ASP Response object's Write method instead of returning the string to the ASP script. To demonstrate this, add a second function to your component and name it sayHello2. This parameter has an input **BSTR** value, but no return or output values. The code for the function uses the Response object to write out the greeting, as shown in Example 21-2.

Example 21-2. Using the ASP Objects Created with the ASP COM Wizard

```
procedure TFirst.sayHello2(const bstrName: WideString);
var
vtOut: OleVariant;
begin
vtOut := '<h3>Hello ' + bstrName + '</h3>';
```

Example 21-2. Using the ASP Objects Created with the ASP COM Wizard (continued)

```
Response.Write(vtOut);
end;
```

Recompile the component (after first unloading the ASP application through IIS) and test the second method with the following ASP script, found in *asp2102.asp*:

```
<% Dim obj
Set obj = Server.CreateObject("asp2101.First")

obj.sayHello2("World!")

Set obj = Nothing %>
```

The Active Server Page COM Wizard option isn't the only one that works with ASP objects. Another is the MTS option, discussed next.

 After installing Delphi 5.0, you must install the Update pack available from Inprise/Borland (*http://www.borland.com*) before trying the ASP wizard option. If you don't install this package, the examples just shown will not work—you'll get an error when you try to access the ASP Response object.

Using the MTS COM Wizard

Another COM wizard you can use to create an ASP component is the MTS Object option. This option provides automated access to the component's ObjectContext to control transactions or to test the ASP component environment.

To demonstrate how to work with the MTS Object option, add a new component to the existing **asp2101** project by selecting File → New and switching to the Multitier tab when the Application Option dialog opens. In this tab, double-click the MTS Object option.

In the dialog that opens, name the new component **FirstMts**, and select the Supports Transactions option. Also change the threading model to Both, and don't check the "Generate Event support code" option—you won't want to add event handling to your ASP component. The dialog should look like that shown in Figure 21-3 when you're done.

As I said, the MTS Object option adds support for accessing the ObjectContext for the component; specifically, it creates an instance of the **IObjectContext** interface that you can then access directly in your code.

The **IObjectContext** interface provides methods to abort or commit the current transaction or to mark the component as ready for deactivation if you're using JIT

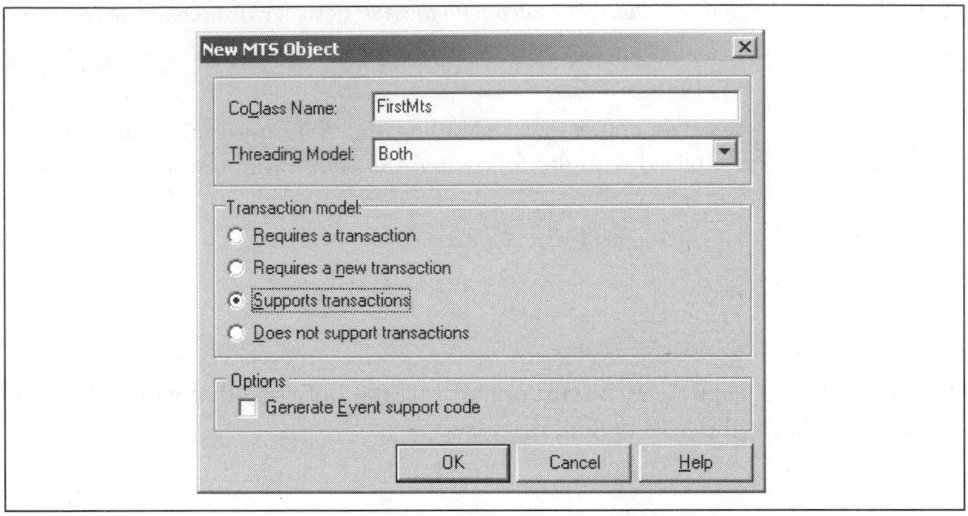

Figure 21-3. Creating an ASP component using the MTS Object option

activation with your component. JIT is used to increase the efficiency of your component access by not creating a reference to the component until it is actually used and not discarding the component until it's actually no longer needed. The `IObjectContext` interface also has methods that can be used to test for role-based security. Both the role-based security and the support for JIT are COM+ Services.

To try out the interface's methods, create a method named tstEnvironment that has three output parameters, all pointers to **VARIANTS**, as shown in Figure 21-4. Because VBScript supports only the Variant data type, you must use **VARIANT** for any output values. You can use other COM-compatible data types for the input parameter and the return values because COM/COM+ does the translation between the data type and the VBScript Variant.

Chapter 3 discusses COM/COM+ data types in more detail.

Once the prototype for the method has been generated, save the Pascal file as *FirstMts.pas*, which also renames the file unit. Next, you'll add the code shown in Example 21-3 to access the `IObjectContext` methods in your component method. In the code, the `IObjectContext` IsInTransaction method is called to see if the component is participating within a COM+ transaction. The result is output to a message string. The same process occurs with the IsCallerInRole method to see if the user is part of the Developer role and the IsSecurityEnabled method (to determine if access-level security is enabled).

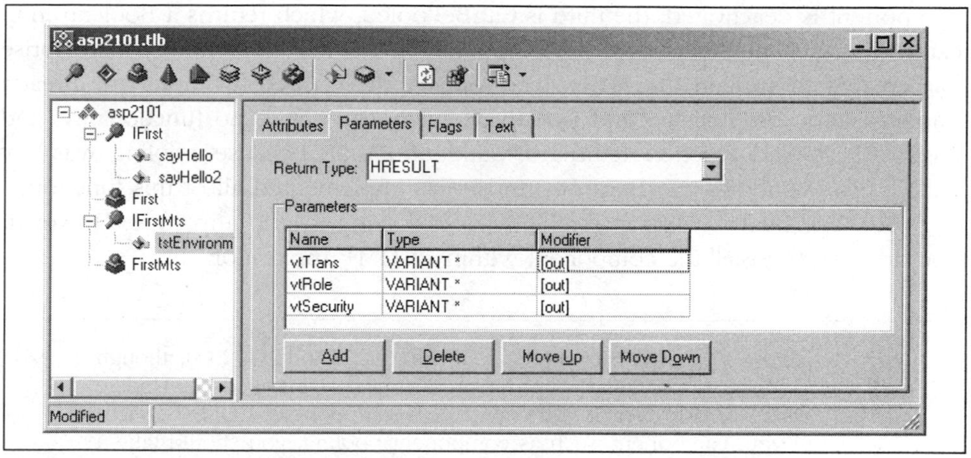

Figure 21-4. Defining the new ObjectContext associated method

Example 21-3. Testing the Component Environment with the IObjectContext Environment

```
procedure TFirstMts.tstEnvironment(out vtTrans, vtRole,
  vtSecurity: OleVariant);
begin

// test transaction
if ObjectContext.IsInTransaction Then
   vtTrans := 'Component is in Transaction'
else
   vtTrans := 'Component is not in Transaction';

// test role
if ObjectContext.IsCallerInRole('Developer') Then
   vtRole := 'Component is within role'
else
   vtRole := 'Component is not within role';

// test security
if ObjectContext.IsSecurityEnabled Then
   vtSecurity := 'Security is enabled'
else
   vtSecurity := 'Security is not enabled';
end;
```

Once you compile the component, you'll need to install it into a COM+ application. The reason for this is that the MTS Object option automatically adds in support for the **IObjectControl** interface in the component. This interface is used with JIT to provide processing for the component when it's activated or deactivated and if the component supports object pooling.

When a component implements **IObjectControl**, it must provide an implementation of three functions. The first is Activate, which is called when the component is first activated; the second is Deactivate, which is called when the component is deactivated; the third is CanBePooled, which returns a Boolean indicating whether the component can be pooled. In the MTS type library that Inprise has created to support the MTS Object option, these three functions are already implemented. The Activate and Deactivate methods contain no functionality, and the CanBePooled function returns a value of FALSE because pooling was not enabled for Windows NT. Because Inprise has implemented all of this functionality, you have built-in support for JIT without having to add any code. However, you do have to install the component within a COM+ application.

 Delphi 5.0 is not guaranteed to work with Windows 2000, though I've had no problems with the product once I installed the Update pack 1.0. However, if you want to have support for COM+ Services in your component, such as component pooling, you should take a look at how to manually add support for COM+ services in your component, covered in the next section.

To do this, access the Administrative tools, and open Component Services. If you don't have a test COM+ application, create one (get details on this in Chapter 3). Once the application is created, add the *asp2101.dll* to it by right-clicking on the application's components folder and selecting New → Component. From the wizard that opens, select the Install New Component option, and in the page that opens, browse for and select *asp2101.dll*. Support for JIT is automatically added for all components.

After adding the component to the COM+ application, test it with the following script, *asp2103.asp*, which displays each string returned from the component:

```
<%
Dim obj
Set obj = Server.CreateObject("asp2101.FirstMts")

Dim trans, role, security
obj.tstEnvironment trans, role, security

Response.Write trans & "<p>"
Response.Write role & "<p>"
Response.Write security & "<p>"

Set obj = Nothing
%>
```

You should get the following results:

```
Component is not in Transaction
Component is within role
Security is not enabled
```

The component isn't within a transaction, since no transaction was started before the component was called. If you try the component using the ASP test page *asp2104.asp*, you'll get a positive answer for the transaction test, because this ASP page has the following transaction directive placed in it (in the first line) to start a transaction:

```
<% @ TRANSACTION = required %>
<HTML>
<HEAD>
<TITLE>Developing ASP Components</TITLE>
</HEAD>
<BODY>
<%
Dim obj
Set obj = Server.CreateObject("asp2101.FirstMts")

Dim trans, role, security
obj.tstEnvironment trans, role, security

Response.Write trans & "<p>"
Response.Write role & "<p>"
Response.Write security & "<p>"

Set obj = Nothing
%>
</BODY>
</HTML>
```

When you try this page, you'll see that the component is now within a transaction.

The IsCallerInRole function always returns **True** when the component runs within the client process—as it is within the COM+ application (or accessed directly from an ASP page and declared using the apartment- or both-threaded models). To actually enable role-based security, you'll need to add a new role for the COM+ application you just created.

Create the role by right-clicking on the Roles folder within the application and selecting New → Role from the menu that opens. In the role window that opens, type in **Developer** as the name of the role. Once the role is created, add users by right clicking on the Users folder within the role and selecting New → User from the menu. A dialog opens that lists users and groups within the system. Click the user that matches IUSR_*machinename*, where *machinename* is the name of your machine. (IUSR_*machinename* is the generic IIS client used for most of your external IIS access.) Figure 21-5 shows the page on my development machine (named **FLAME**) once I select the user IUSR_FLAME.

After adding the user to the group, you'll need to enable role-based security for the tstEnvironment method. Open the asp2101.FirstMts component in Component Services until you see the Methods folder, and right-click on the tstEnvironment method. From the menu that opens, select Properties. Switch to the Security

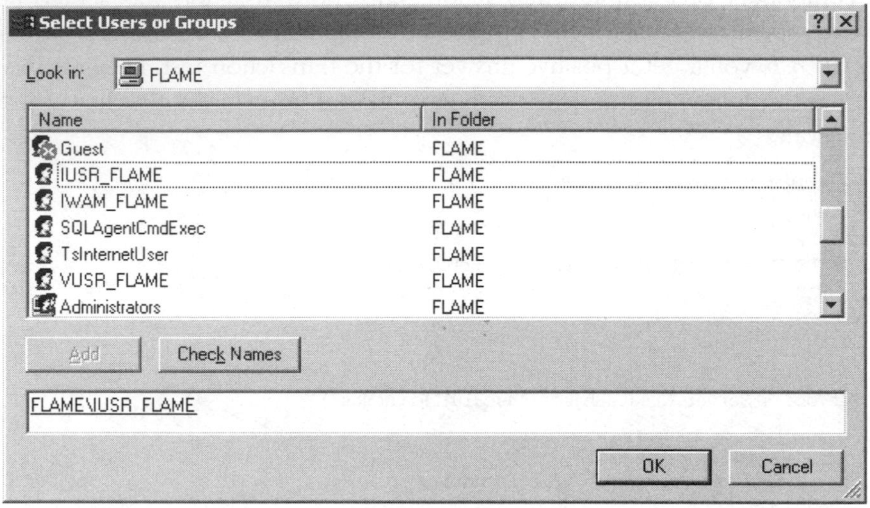

Figure 21-5. Adding a user to the Developer group

page and check the box next to the Developer role. This enables role-based security for this specific method.

Next, add role-based security for the COM+ application by right clicking on the application name and selecting Properties. Switch to the Security tab and check the "Enforce access checks for this application" box.

Access the *asp2104.asp* page one more time (after unloading the ASP application through IIS) to make sure the page isn't cached. This time, all three functions should return a positive result.

As I mentioned, Inprise provides an implementation of the `IObjectControl` JIT methods. You can, however, access virtual functions created by Inprise that allow you to capture the Activate and Deactivate events to provide your own components. These methods are OnActivate and OnDeactivate, and you can override the methods:

```
procedure OnActivate; override;
```

and provide your own implementation; or you can hide the function and, again, provide your own implementation of the function. (See the Delphi 5.0 documentation for more information on function overriding and hiding.) The only method that doesn't have a virtual function that you can use to hook into JIT is the CanBe-Pooled method—Delphi 5.0 was created before the release of Windows 2000, and object pooling wasn't support until Windows 2000 was released.

The examples in this section and the last have used wizard support to access COM+ or ASP technologies and type libraries. Because of this, you won't have access to specific functionality, such as the new COM+ interfaces. You can add support for this functionality by adding references to COM+ and ASP manually, discussed in the next section.

Manually Adding Support for COM+/ASP

The ASP and MTS COM wizards provide excellent methods for getting quick and easy access to the ASP built-in objects and MTS/COM+ transaction support, respectively. However, if you want additional functionality outside of what's provided automatically, you'll need to add references to the ASP and COM+ Services type libraries manually. You can do this by importing these type libraries.

When you import a type library, Delphi wraps the contents in Pascal, giving you access to the library interfaces and their associated properties and methods. However, you'll have to manually create the references to the objects, such as `IObjectContext` when accessing COM+ Services or `IResponse` when accessing the ASP objects.

To demonstrate how to manually import support for both COM+ and the ASP objects, in this section you'll create a new component and add support for the object context as well as JIT through `IObjectControl`. We'll also discuss how you can use the same techniques to access newer COM+ Services interfaces, such as `IContextState` and `IObjectContextInfo`.

Once you've set up your component for JIT support, you'll create references to the main ASP objects—Application, Session, Request, Response, and Server—within the Activate method. You'll use these objects within several ASP pages, where you'll have a chance to try out several of their methods and properties. You'll then release the references to the objects within the component's Deactivate method.

To begin, create a new Delphi project using the ActiveX Library option, as you did with `asp2101`. Name the new project `asp2102`. Add a new component to the project, but this time, use the Automation object option. In the dialog that opens, enter the name of the component, `Manual`, and change the threading model to Both. When the component Pascal file is generated, name the file *Manual.pas*, which also renames the unit to `Manual`.

You're now ready to start adding COM+ and ASP support.

Importing COM+ Services

To add support for COM+ Services, select Project → Import Type Library from the main menu. A list of available type libraries is displayed. From the list, select COM+ Services Type Library. In the dialog, you can specify which palette page the library is added to, and you can check an option to have Delphi wrap the library. You can also specify the location where the library will be placed once it is wrapped. Delphi also lists the wrapped names it's providing for the classes the tool finds within the library. Unless these names conflict with other, already imported class names, you can leave them as is; otherwise, you can change the names. You can also choose not to create component wrappers by unchecking the Generate Component Wrapper option. Since you won't be using component wrappers in the examples in this chapter, uncheck this option. Figure 21-6 shows the Import Type Library dialog after adding support for COM+ Services.

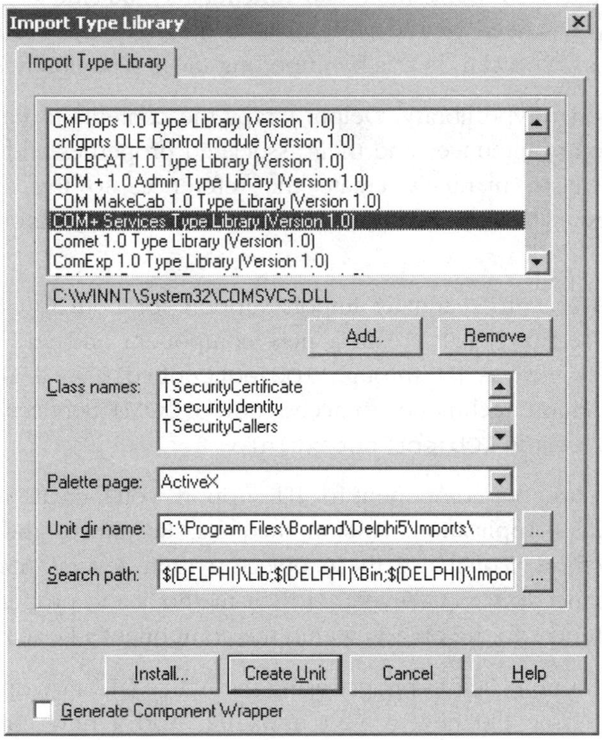

Figure 21-6. Importing the COM+ Services type library

You can choose either the Install or Create Unit option to add support for the library. The Install option adds the library file to a new or existing package, and the Create Unit option adds the file to your existing project. Use the Create Unit option with your component.

Delphi creates a project file named *COMSVCSLib_TLB*. You'll want to add a reference to this file to your *Manual.pas* uses section, as follows:

```
uses
  ComObj, ActiveX, COMSVCSLib_TLB, asp2102_TLB, StdVcl;
```

Next, you'll add the implementation of IObjectControl and its methods to your component. Modify the component's class definition to add a reference to Object-Control:

```
type
   TManual = class(TAutoObject, IManual, ObjectControl)
```

COM components can implement more than one interface. In this case, both the ObjectControl and the IManual interfaces are implemented by the component.

You'll need to add the prototypes and implementations for the three Object-Control methods. Add the following prototypes first, using the exact declarations used within the generated *COMSVCSLib_TLB* file (the declarations must match or an error results):

```
protected
   function  Activate: HResult; stdcall;
   function  Deactivate: HResult; stdcall;
   function  CanBePooled(out pbPoolable: WordBool): HResult; stdcall;
```

Don't add the prototypes using the Type Library Editor, since you're implementing the IObjectControl interface, not creating the methods directly on your new interface.

In addition, add a private global variable of type ObjectContext to the component. You'll be instantiating this member within the Activate method:

```
private
   m_piObjContext : ObjectContext;
```

Next, add the code for the three methods. All methods return the **HRESULT** value of **S_OK**. To have access to the predefined **HRESULT** values, you'll also have to add the Windows type library to your component's **uses** section:

```
uses
   ComObj, Windows, ActiveX, COMSVCSLib_TLB, asp2102_TLB, StdVcl;
```

The code for the three methods is shown in Example 21-4. The Activate method assigns a reference to ObjectContext to the private data member. In Visual Basic or Visual C++, you'd instantiate the ObjectContext object through a call to GetObject-Context (or CoGetObjectContext). In Java, you would call GetObjectContext on a predefined class named **Mtx**. However, trying either of these techniques with Delphi will generate an error when we compile the component. Instead, taking a look at the Pascal wrapper for the component, we find the GetObjectContext method on an interface named **IMTxAS**. So you'll want to access this interface in order to get a reference to the ObjectContext object.

Further investigation of the Pascal-wrapped MTS type library also shows that **IMTxAS** will be returned when the Create method of the implemented class CoAppServer is called. So we can use CoAppServer.Create to get a reference to the

IMTxAS interface and then call the GetObjectContext method on this interface to retrieve the reference to the ObjectContext object we need.

The CanBePooled method returns a value of **False**, since the component won't be pooled.

Example 21-4. Implementing JIT Methods

```
function TManual.Activate: HRESULT;
var
    mtx: IMTxAS;
begin
mtx := CoAppServer.Create;
m_piObjContext := mtx.GetObjectContext;
Activate := S_OK;
end;

function TManual.Deactivate: HRESULT;
begin
Deactivate := S_OK;
end;

function TManual.CanBePooled(out pbPoolable: WordBool): HResult; stdcall;
begin
  pbPoolable := False;
  CanBePooled := S_OK;
end;
```

To test our success in retrieving the reference to the ObjectContext object, add a new method to the component using the Type Library Editor and name it testObj-Context. The method returns a **BSTR** value. In the method, add the code shown in Example 21-5 that calls the IsInTransaction method to test if the component is within a transaction.

Example 21-5. Testing Existence of ObjectContext Variable

```
function TManual.testObjContext: WideString;
var
tmpStr : WideString;
begin
if m_piObjContext.IsInTransaction Then
    tmpStr := 'In Transaction'
else
    tmpStr := 'Not in Transaction';

testObjContext := tmpStr;
m_piObjContext.SetComplete;
end;
```

The ObjectContext.SetComplete method is called at the end of the method, primarily to signal that the component is finished processing.

To test the component, you'll have to add the component to a COM+ application—if you don't, the component will hang when you access the ASP test script. When you add it, change the transaction support for the component to Requires transactions. Then, access the component with the following script, *asp2105.asp*:

```
<% @ TRANSACTION = required %>
<%
Dim obj
Set obj = Server.CreateObject("asp2102.Manual")

Dim msg
msg = obj.testObjContext

Response.Write "<h3>" & msg & "</h3>"
Set obj = Nothing
%>
```

When you access the page, the web page shows a message that the component is in a transaction.

Beginning with Windows 2000, there are new interfaces to provide support for context state and accessing ObjectContext properties. For instance, ObjectContext has the SetAbort and SetCommit methods to abort or commit a transaction, respectively. Both of these methods also signal that a component is finished processing by setting the ObjectContext done bit. If you want to control these actions separately, you can use the `IContextState` interface.

`IContextState` has a SetMyTransactionVote method, which allows you to signal the success of the transaction, and a SetDeactivateOnReturn method, which signals that the component is finished processing. You can access this interface using the following:

```
m_piCntxtState := mtx.GetObjectContext As IContextState;
```

Then call this object's methods:

```
m_piCntxtState.SetDeactivateOnReturn(True);
```

Chapter 5 has more information on the new COM+ interfaces. Next up: adding support for ASP.

Adding Support for ASP

The ASP built-in objects are accessible as properties from ObjectContext, and you can access the properties by calling the ObjectContext's Get_Item method. First, though, you'll have to add a reference to the ASP objects to your component.

In `asp2102`, import Version 3.0 of the Microsoft Active Server Pages library.

When you import a type library, the Pascal file for the library is automatically placed in the *Imports* subdirectory for Delphi. You can then use this library from all of your components without having to reimport the libraries again.

The examples with this book do *not* include the imported libraries— you should create these within your own system.

Again, uncheck the option to create component wrappers, since they are not used in the examples in this book. Even with the option unchecked, you'll get an error when you try to create the imported library, because a TSession object already exists. To work around this problem, just rename TSession to TASPSession.

Once the type library is wrapped, add a reference to the Pascal file to your component's **uses** section, as follows:

```
uses
   ComObj, Windows, ActiveX, COMSVCSLib_TLB, ASPTypeLibrary_TLB,
   asp2102_TLB, StdVcl;
```

Now you're ready to create instances of the ASP objects. First, add private data members for each of the following intrinsic objects:

```
private
   m_piObjContext   : ObjectContext;
   m_piResponse     : Response;
   m_piRequest      : Request;
   m_piSession      : Session;
   m_piServer       : Server;
   m_piApplication  : Application;
```

Next, modify the Activate method to implement each of the objects, as shown in Example 21-6. When you access the ObjectContext.Get_Item method, you'll actually receive a pointer to the **IDispatch** interface. In order to access an ASP object, such as the Response object, as an **IResponse** interface, the **IDispatch** interface will need to be queried for the particular interface. With C++, you could use something like the COM *QueryInterface* method to query for and access the interface. However, with Pascal you use the **As** operator. The **As** operator calls *QueryInterface* for you, and the dynamic binding it provides allows you to assign a value originally accessed from ObjectContext to a specific interface reference. Then, once you have the reference to the **IResponse** interface, you can invoke this interface's methods.

Example 21-6. Creating Instances of the ASP Objects

```
function TManual.Activate: HRESULT;
var
   mtx: IMTxAS;
```

Example 21-6. Creating Instances of the ASP Objects (continued)

```
    piIdisp: IDispatch;
begin
mtx := CoAppServer.Create;
m_piObjContext := mtx.GetObjectContext;

// get response
piIdisp := m_piObjContext.Get_Item('Response');
m_piResponse := piIdisp As IResponse;

// get request
piIdisp := m_piObjContext.Get_Item('Request');
m_piRequest := piIdisp As IRequest;

// get session
piIdisp := m_piObjContext.Get_Item('Session');
m_piSession := piIdisp As ISessionObject;

// get application
piIdisp := m_piObjContext.Get_Item('Application');
m_piApplication := piIdisp As IApplicationObject;

// get response
piIdisp := m_piObjContext.Get_Item('Server');
m_piServer := piIdisp As IServer;

Activate := S_OK;
end;
```

To provide cleanup, you can release the references to the ASP objects in the Deactivate method:

```
    function TManual.Deactivate: HRESULT;
    begin
      m_piResponse._Release;
      m_piRequest._Release;
      m_piSession._Release;
      m_piApplication._Release;
      m_piServer._Release;
      Deactivate := S_OK;
    end;
```

To test your new object references, add a method to the component using the Type Library Editor. Name the method sayHi, and give it an input **BSTR** parameter (*bstrName*). In the method's implementation, create a greeting, but this time, output the greeting using the m_piResponse object, as shown in Example 21-7.

Example 21-7. Using Response Object Reference to Write Out a Message

```
procedure TManual.sayHi(const bstrName: WideString);
var
tmpString : WideString;
tmpVt : OleVariant;
```

Example 21-7. Using Response Object Reference to Write Out a Message (continued)

```
begin
  tmpString := 'Hello ' + bstrName;
  tmpVt := tmpString;
  m_piResponse.Write(tmpVt);
  m_piObjContext.SetComplete;
end;
```

Testing the component with the following script (contained in *asp2106.asp*) results in the greeting being displayed on the web page:

```
<%
Dim obj
Set obj = Server.CreateObject("asp2102.Manual")

obj.sayHi "World!"

Set obj = Nothing
%>
```

Now that you have references to each of the ASP objects, you'll have a chance to try them out in the next section.

 Should you use the libraries created by Inprise or import the type libraries directly? Well, the answer is, it depends. If the functionality that Inprise provides is what you need for your component, use the built-in functionality; otherwise, import the libraries.

Working with the ASP Objects

In this section, you'll get a chance to work with the individual ASP objects. The examples that follow assume that you created the `asp2102.manual` component, discussed in the last section. If not, then you can create an ASP component using the Active Server Pages COM Wizard and just modify the examples to use the Application, Request, Response, Server, and Session references directly.

The examples in this chapter don't demonstrate every property, collection, and method of the ASP objects. Instead, you'll have a chance to work with some of the more common methods, as well as with the ASP helper interfaces and enumeration. For more details on each of the object's methods and properties, see Appendix A, *ASP Built-in Object Quick Reference*. You might also want to check out Chapter 7, *Creating a Simple Visual Basic ASP Component*, for more detailed information about using the ASP objects from within your custom components— regardless of the language used.

The Response Object

The Response object is used to control the output returned to the client browser. It's been used to this point to write output to the client, and it can also be used to control buffering.

When buffering is turned on, as it is with IIS 5.0, all of the page contents must be generated before the page is returned. You can control this by using the buffering methods to control the output.

For instance, if you have buffering turned on, and you want to flush the buffer (return the output to the browser before finishing the remaining processing), you can call the Response object's Flush method:

```
m_piResponse.Flush;
```

If an error occurs, and you want to eliminate the buffered output, use the Clear method instead:

```
m_piResponse.Clear;
```

You can also access the Cookies collection to update or add cookies through the **IRequestDictionary** collection. **IRequestDictionary** is also used to access other Request-specific collections and is demonstrated later in the section describing the Request object.

Another Response object member is the Redirect method, which redirects the browser to another page and sends an HTTP response with the 302 Object Moved status. When you use Redirect, the current state (such as any form or query string information or any transaction) is lost. To send the browser to a different page without losing state, use the Server.Transfer method.

You can manually send a specific HTTP status value to the browser using the put_ Status method. For instance, to send a value of 401 Unauthorized, use the following:

```
m_piResponse.put_Status('401 Unauthorized');
```

This triggers a login window to open. Other Response methods and properties are detailed in Appendix A.

The Application Object

The Application object is created when an ASP application is first referenced and lasts until the application is shut down or until the last session to access the ASP application is terminated. This object can be used to store information that needs to be accessible by all sessions that access the ASP application.

The Application object has two collections with application-level information. The first is StaticObjects, with data that's set through the *global.asa* file. The second is the Contents collection, with data that can be set at runtime. Both collections can be read by ASP components, but only the Contents collection can be set by components.

 Due to memory constraints, avoid adding objects to either the Application or Session objects. If you must add an object to the Application collections, the object must be both- or neutral-apartment-threaded, or you'll receive an error.

To demonstrate how to access the Contents collection, add a new method to your component using the Type Library Editor, and name it OnAccessValue, as shown in Example 21-8. The method has no parameters. It accesses the value of the intCounter variable from the Application object, increments its value, and reassigns it back to the Application object.

Example 21-8. Increment the Application Contents Value

```
procedure TManual.OnAccessValue;
var
iCounter : Integer;
begin
 iCounter := m_piApplication.Contents.Get_Item('intCounter');
 iCounter := iCounter + 1;
 m_piApplication.Contents.Set_Item('intCounter',iCounter);
end;
```

In a multiuser environment, you would call the Application's Lock method before accessing and incrementing the application-wide value and call the UnLock method afterward.

To test the component, use the script contained in *asp2107.asp*:

```
<%
Application("intCounter") = 0

Dim obj
Set obj = Server.CreateObject("asp2102.Manual")

obj.OnAccessValue

Dim i
i = Application("intCounter")

Response.Write "Value is " + CStr(i)
Set obj = Nothing
%>
```

In the script, the counter value is accessed and displayed after calling the component's new method. If the value had not been incremented, you would see a zero

(0) on the web page. However, what you see is a value of one (1), because the component incremented the counter.

The Session Object

The Application object lasts for the lifetime of the ASP application, but an instance of the Session object is created for each unique user session. The session starts when a person first accesses the ASP application and lasts until the user closes his browser or terminates the session (if this functionality is provided) or until the session times out.

As with the Application object, the Session object also has both a StaticObjects and a Contents collection, but unlike the Application object, you can't lock the Session object down when it's accessed—only one person has access to the Session object at a time, and locking isn't necessary.

In the previous section, you saw code that accessed one specific value in the Contents collection. You can also access all collection items by getting a count of items in the collection and then iterating through them. To demonstrate, add a new method to asp2102.**Manual** named getContents. This method does not have parameters.

The method, which is shown in Example 21-9, gets a count of items in the Session object's Contents collection by accessing the collection through the **IVariantDictionary** helper interface. This interface is used to obtain information about the collection, access the collection contents, and even enumerate through the collection, if you wish. Once the method has a reference to **IVariantDictionary**, it uses a **for** loop to access each item and list both its key name and its value.

Example 21-9. Iterating Through the Session's Contents Collection and Printing the Key-Value Pairs

```
procedure TManual.OnAccessValue;
var
iCounter : Integer;
begin
 iCounter := m_piApplication.Contents.Get_Item('intCounter');
 iCounter := iCounter + 1;
 m_piApplication.Contents.Set_Item('intCounter',iCounter);
end;

procedure TManual.getContents;
var
piDict: IVariantDictionary;
iCount: Integer;
iTotal: Integer;
ovName: OleVariant;
```

Example 21-9. Iterating Through the Session's Contents Collection and Printing the Key-Value Pairs (continued)

```
ovValue: OleVariant;
begin

// get contents
piDict := m_piSession.Get_Contents;
iTotal := piDict.Count;

for iCount := 1 to iTotal do
begin
  // get name
  ovName := piDict.Get_Key(iCount);
  m_piResponse.Write(ovName);
  m_piResponse.Write(' = ');

  // print value
  ovValue := m_piSession.Get_Value(ovName);
  m_piResponse.Write(ovValue);
  m_piResponse.Write('<p>');
end;

end;
```

To test this component method, the ASP script *asp2108.asp* loads several values into the Session object's Contents collection before it calls the getContents method:

```
Dim obj
Set obj = Server.CreateObject("asp2102.Manual")

Session("one") = 1
Session("two") = 2
Session("three") = 3
Session("four") = 4
Session("five") = 5

obj.getContents
```

The result of accessing this ASP test page is a web page with the five Contents items listed.

Instead of accessing a count of items in the collection, you could have used enumeration to list the collection contents. The use of enumeration is demonstrated in the next section, covering the Request object.

The Request Object

The Request object has information about the environment, as well as information provided by the ASP application user. It is unique among all of the ASP objects because of the larger number of collections it supports, including the following:

Forms

    Contains information posted from HTML forms

QueryString

    Contains information posted using the **GET** method or appended to the query string

Cookies (read-only)

    Contains cookies included with the client request

ClientCertificate

    Contains information contained in any client certificates attached with the request

ServerVariables

    Contains information about the environment

As with other collections already demonstrated, you can access individual items in any of the collections directly from the Request object. However, you can also use the **IRequestDictionary** object to access the collection, particularly if you want to use enumeration to process the collection contents.

To demonstrate how to work with **IRequestDictionary**, as well as how to use enumeration with the ASP collections, add a new method to **asp2102.Manual** named showVariables. The method doesn't have parameters.

In the code for showVariables, which is shown in Example 21-10, the Request object's Get_ServerVariables method is called to obtain a reference to the **IRequestDictionary** interface encapsulating the ServerVariables collection. Since it is enumerating the members of the collection, it needs to call the Get_ NewEnum method on this collection interface. This latter method returns a reference to an **IUnknown** object.

 Microsoft collections that support enumeration always support the Get__NewEnum method when the interface is exposed in Delphi.

A C++ component would then call the QueryInterface method on **IUnknown** to obtain a reference to **IEnumVariant**, the interface that's accessed when using enumeration. However, Delphi Pascal uses the shortcut **As** keyword to perform checked type interface access—a nice touch that simplifies interface access. Once the method obtains the **IEnumVariant** interface, it uses its methods to enumerate through the entire collection, listing the ServerVariable key/value pairs.

Example 21-10. Enumerating Through ServerVariables to Print Out Key/Value Pairs

```
procedure TManual.showVariables;
var
  piReqDict: IRequestDictionary;
  piIEnum: IEnumVariant;
  piIUnknown: IUnknown;
  liReturn: LongWord;
  ovName: OleVariant;
  ovValue: OleVariant;
begin

  // get ServerVariables and enum for variables
  piReqDict := m_piRequest.Get_ServerVariables;
  piIUnknown := piReqDict.Get__NewEnum;
  piIEnum := piIUnknown As IEnumVariant;

  // while S_OK get name and value, print
  while piIEnum.Next(1,ovName,liReturn) = S_OK do
    begin;
      m_piResponse.Write(ovName);
      m_piResponse.Write(' = ');

      ovValue := piReqDict.Get_Item(ovName);

      m_piResponse.Write(ovValue);
      m_piResponse.Write('<br>');
    end;

end;
```

The ServerVariables collection provides information such as the user agent used to access the ASP page, the hostname, the IP address, the physical path, the username and password if authentication is used, and so on. Test the new component method using the ASP test page, *asp2109.asp*, to see these values in your environment:

```
<%
Dim obj
Set obj = Server.CreateObject("asp2102.Manual")

obj.showVariables

Set obj = Nothing
%>
```

Of course, you can access a value directly from the ServerVariables collection, using code such as the following:

```
m_piRequest.ServerVariables.Get_Item('HTTP_USER_AGENT');
```

The Server Object

In ASP script, the Server object's CreateObject method is used to create all of the custom components you've made in this chapter. However, this object has several methods you can use to provide encoding of special characters. For instance, if you want some HTML to appear as is (including brackets) within a web page, you could use the Server object's HTMLEncode method to encode the string so that the HTML isn't interpreted by the user agent (the browser).

You can also use the MapPath method to map an existing filename to the current literal path—helpful when opening files on the server.

To demonstrate the Server encoding methods, add a new method to **asp2102. Manual** named encodeValues, as shown in Example 21-11. This method takes four input parameters, all of type BSTR: *bstrHTML*, *bstrURL*, *bstrPath*, and *bstrMap*. The method passes each input string to its associated encoding method and lists each encoded string using the Response object.

Example 21-11. Using the Server Object to Encode Strings

```
procedure TManual.encodeValues(const bstrHTML, bstrURL, bstrPath,
  bstrMap: WideString);
var
strHTML : WideString;
strURL  : WideString;
strPath : WideString;
strMap  : WideString;
begin

// encode values
strHTML := m_piServer.HTMLEncode(bstrHTML);
strURL  := m_piServer.URLEncode(bstrURL);
strPath := m_piServer.URLPathEncode(bstrPath);
strMap  := m_piServer.MapPath(bstrMap);

// print values
m_piResponse.Write(strHTML);
m_piResponse.Write('<br>');
m_piResponse.Write(strURL);
m_piResponse.Write('<br>');
m_piResponse.Write(strPath);
m_piResponse.Write('<br>');
m_piResponse.Write(strMap);

end;
```

Once you've compiled the component, test it with the following ASP script (found in *asp2110.asp*):

```
<%
Dim obj
Set obj = Server.CreateObject("asp2102.Manual")

Dim strHTML, strURL, strPath, strMap
strHTML = "<H1>This is a test</H1>"
strURL = "% this is a test % ++"
```

```
strPath = "test/test2/this is a test"
strMap = "/test/test2/"

obj.encodeValues strHTML, strURL, strPath, strMap
Set obj = Nothing
%>
```

When you access the page, the following values are displayed:

```
<H1>This is a test</H1>
%25+this+is+a+test+%25+%2B%2B
test/test2/this%20is%20a%20test
c:\inetpub\wwwroot\test\test2
```

In this section, you've had a chance to try out the ASP objects in your Delphi components. Another common library that's accessed from ASP components is the ActiveX Data Objects (ADO) library, discussed next.

Working with ADO

The Enterprise version of Delphi 5.0 has a set of ADO class wrappers you can use in your applications. I won't cover these, since they are covered in the Delphi 5.0 documentation. Instead, I'll demonstrate how to add ADO functionality to your component by importing the ADO type library.

The examples in this section use the downloadable Weaver database. Read more on this in Appendix B, *The Weaver Database*. Read a more thorough overview of working with ADO from ASP components in Chapter 8, *Creating ASP/ADO Components*, and Chapter 9, *Creating an ASP Middle Tier with ADO*.

First, you'll need to create another Delphi project using the ActiveX Library Option. After the project is created, generate the project's component using the Active Server Pages COM Wizard option. If you don't have access to this option, see the previous section for information about adding support for ObjectContext and the ASP Response object using **import**, since you'll be using the Response object in these examples. Name the new project file **asp2103** and the component **Data**.

Once you've created the component project, import the latest Microsoft ActiveX Data Objects library on your system. This creates a wrapped type library called ADODB_TLB. Add a reference to the type library to your component's **uses** statement:

```
uses
    ComObj, ActiveX, ADODB_TLB,AspTlb, asp2103_TLB, StdVcl;
```

We won't provide an exhaustive overview of working with ADO, but I do want to provide two examples of using ADO to perform queries. The first example is a simple query—a full table scan of the WebPage table. The second query example also accesses the WebPage table, but it uses parameters.

A Simple Query Using the Connection and Recordset Objects

In the first example, you'll establish a connection to the Access version of the Weaver database using the ADO Connection interface. You'll then create a new ADO Recordset object and use this to run the actual query: a full table scan of the WebPage table. Once you have the result set, you'll iterate through it and list the table's name field value for each record.

To create the example, add a method to asp2103.Data named showWebPages. The method has no parameters. In the method's variable declaration section, add a reference to the Recordset and Connection default interfaces:

```
cn: Connection;
rs: Recordset;
```

In the code, create instances of both interfaces, using the CoConnection and CoRecordset classes (created by Delphi). These classes can be used to create references to the ADO objects without having to specify either the GUID for the interfaces or the CLSID values (values you would need if you created instances of the components using the object creation functionality provided by Delphi):

```
cn := CoConnection.Create;
rs := CoRecordset.Create;
```

The showWebPages method, which is shown in Example 21-12, queries the database and processes the results. The records associated with the result set are traversed and the name field is listed for each record.

Example 21-12. A Simple Query Using the ADO Connection and Recordset Objects

```
procedure TData.showWebPages;
var
cn: Connection;
rs: Recordset;
vtVal: OleVariant;
begin
// open connection
cn := CoConnection.Create;
cn.Open('DSN=weaver;uid=sa;pwd=',
        '','',-1);
// create query
rs := CoRecordset.Create;
rs.Open('select name from WebPage',cn,
        adOpenForwardOnly,adLockReadOnly,adCmdUnknown);
```

Example 21-12. A Simple Query Using the ADO Connection and Recordset Objects (continued)

```
rs.MoveFirst;
while Not rs.EOF do
begin
  vtVal := rs.Fields.Get_Item('name');
  Response.Write(vtVal);
  Response.Write('<br>');
  rs.MoveNext;
end;

rs.Close;
cn.Close;

end;
```

After compiling and registering the component (or adding the component to a COM+ application), try it with *asp2111.asp*, the ASP test page:

```
<%
Dim obj
Set obj = Server.CreateObject("asp2103.Data")

obj.showWebPages
Set obj = Nothing
%>
```

The result is a web page showing the names of all of the web pages contained in the WebPage table of the Weaver database.

In some applications, parameters are used to limit queries, and the next ADO example uses parameters and the Command object to perform a query against the same table.

Using Parameters with a Query

You can modify a query to use a SQL WHERE clause to limit the number of rows you get back. In web applications, you won't want to do full table scans unless the table has only a few rows.

One technique you can use to limit the query is to concatenate the WHERE clause parameters to the end of the SQL used for the query. However, a better approach is to use the ADO Command object and add the parameters to the query using the Command object's Parameters collection.

To demonstrate how to use the Command object, add a new method to asp2103. Data and name it showSpecificPages. The method has one BSTR input parameter named *bstrType*. In the method, you'll search on WebPage again, but this time you look only for records matching a specific page type code, such as HTM for HTML pages or APP for ASP and other application pages.

As Example 21-13 shows, the method creates an instance of the Connection object, but this time the example connects to the SQL Server version of Weaver using the OLE DB Provider for SQL Server. After creating and opening the connection, it instantiates the Command object through the CoCommand class's Create method and sets the Command object's active connection to the newly created Connection object. The Command's Prepared property is set to **True**. By doing this, the command is compiled and stored in memory, which increases the performance of additional accesses. Normally, you would want to do this only with commands that are accessed more than once, but I wanted to give you a feel for setting Command properties.

After setting the Command's query, the method accesses its Parameters collection next and creates a new Parameter. After the Parameter information is set, it's appended to the Parameters collection, and then the command is executed. The query results are then displayed on the web page.

Example 21-13. Creating a Parameterized Query Using the Command Object

```
procedure TData.showSpecificPages(const bstrType: WideString);
var
cn: Connection;
rs: Recordset;
cmnd: Command;
vtVal: OleVariant;
parms: Parameters;
parm: Parameter;
vtRecs, vtPlace, params: OleVariant;
begin
// open connection
cn := CoConnection.Create;
cn.Open('Provider=SQLOLEDB;server=FLAME;database=weaver;uid=sa;pwd=',
       '','',-1);

// create command
cmnd := CoCommand.Create;
cmnd.Set_ActiveConnection(cn);
cmnd.Set_Prepared(True);
cmnd.Set_CommandText('select * from WebPage where page_type_cd = ?');

// set parameter
parms := cmnd.Get_Parameters;
parm := cmnd.CreateParameter('page_type_cd',adChar,adParamInput,3,null);
parms.Append(parm);

// execute query
vtPlace := null;
params := VarArrayCreate([0,0], varVariant);
params[0] := bstrType;
rs := cmnd.Execute(vtRecs,params,adCmdText);

while Not rs.EOF do
```

Example 21-13. Creating a Parameterized Query Using the Command Object (continued)

```
begin
  vtVal := rs.Fields.Get_Item('name');
  Response.Write(vtVal);
  Response.Write(' ');
  vtVal := rs.Fields.Get_Item('filename');
  Response.Write(vtVal);
  Response.Write('<br>');
  rs.MoveNext;
end;

rs.Close;
cn.Close;

end;
```

Test this component method using the following ASP script, *asp2112.asp*:

```
<%
Dim obj
Set obj = Server.CreateObject("asp2103.Data")

obj.showSpecificPages "APP"
Set obj = Nothing
%>
```

Change the page type and rerun it to see how the results differ.

Though this introduction to working directly with ADO from Delphi components is brief, it should provide you enough in the way of examples so that you can extrapolate the other information you'll need when working with ADO.

ADO isn't the only service you can access from your Delphi components. Other Windows 2000 services, such as Collaborative Data Objects (CDO), discussed next, are also accessible when you import the associated type libraries.

Working with Windows 2000 Functionality: CDO

Windows 2000 has a wealth of technology you may want to take advantage of when creating Delphi ASP components. You had a chance to work with data access using ADO in the last section. In this section, you'll have a chance to work with email by using Collaborative Data Objects (CDO) for Windows 2000.

CDO is used to provide access to SMTP (email) and NNTP (newsgroup) services. With it, you can easily create email to send to people from your ASP applications. For instance, if your ASP application is an online store, you can send an email to people to confirm their orders, to provide copies of their passwords if they've forgotten them, or for any of a dozen other reasons. You can even create your own email and newsgroup readers, if you so choose.

CDO has been around for some time, but a new and very different version of the objects was released with Windows 2000, and it's CDO for Windows 2000 that we'll look at in this section.

To try out CDO, create a new Delphi project using the ActiveX Library option and name the project **asp2104**. Add a new Automation object to the project and name it **msg**. Next, import the CDO type library by selecting Project → Import Type Library from the main menu and selecting the Microsoft CDO for Windows 2000 Library. Use the Create Unit option and uncheck the option to create Pascal wrappers for the classes.

CDO is dependent on ADO for much of its functionality, so you'll also have to add a reference to the ADO type library to your project. You can use the Pascal wrapped library you created in the last section.

Once the Pascal-based wrapper is created for the CDO type library, add a reference to it and the ADO library within your new component's **uses** statement:

```
uses
    ComObj, ActiveX, asp2104_TLB, ADODB_TLB, CDO_TLB, StdVcl;
```

You can now access the CDO objects within the Delphi component.

For details on working with CDO from within ASP components, read Chapter 11, *Take a Message: Accessing CDO from ASP Components*.

Your component will send a plain text email message to an email address of your choice. The message will include an image added as an attachment. Add a method to your component named sendImage, which is shown in Example 21-14. This component has five input BSTR parameters: *bstrTo*, *bstrFrom*, *bstrSubject*, *bstrMessage*, and *bstrImage* (the last is the filename of the image).

CDO message properties, such as the SMTP server to use, are attached as configuration properties using the **IConfiguration** interface. The message itself is defined within the **IMessage** interface, and attachments can be added using the **IBodyPart** interface. As with the ADO objects, the showImage method generates classes for the CDO objects that make it easier to access the individual type library interfaces.

The component method creates the message configuration properties first using a Microsoft naming schema to name the individual properties. In Visual Basic, there are predefined constants you can use for these property names, but they aren't available when you import the CDO type library into your Delphi component. If you wish, you could create constants in your Delphi code for the different property names. The properties are actually contained within an ADO Fields collection, and the ones set are the SMTP server, the method of sending the message, the authentication type, and the connection timeout. You can also add the username and password if your SMTP server requires this information. Make sure to use your own SMTP server for this example.

> What is the value you should use for your SMTP server? It's the same value you use when you set up your email account using Outlook or whatever email reader you use.

Once the sendImage method defines the message configuration properties, it sets other message information, such as to whom the email goes, whom it's from, and the subject line. These values are set directly on the Message object.

Next, the method adds the image attachment and the text message. Email messages can be hierarchical in nature, which means that emails can contain body parts that contain other body parts, and so on. This hierarchy is managed through the IBodyPart interface. Instead of attaching a message to the message directly, you can attach various versions of the message (in different formats) to a series of body parts.

The code in Example 21-14 attaches an image to the message through the IBodyPart interface. First, it obtains the main body part from the message using the IMessage.Get_BodyPart method. Then it provides formatting information for the message contents, in this case for an image. To read in the image, it uses the ADO Stream object (another case of the connection between ADO and CDO). Once the image file is loaded, calling the stream's Flush method writes the contents to the CDO body part. After the attachment is added to the message, the plain text that accompanies it is added directly to the message and it's sent.

Example 21-14. Using CDO to Send a Message with an Image Attachment

```
procedure Tmsg.sendImage(const bstrTo, bstrFrom, bstrSubject,
  bstrMessage, bstrImage: WideString);
var
cdomsg: IMessage;
config: IConfiguration;
bodypart: IBodyPart;
strm: Stream;
begin
cdomsg := CoMessage.Create;
config := CoConfiguration.Create;

// set configuration
with config.Fields do
```

Example 21-14. Using CDO to Send a Message with an Image Attachment (continued)

```
begin
Item['http://schemas.microsoft.com/cdo/configuration/sendusing'].
                                        Set_Value(cdoSendUsingPort);
Item['http://schemas.microsoft.com/cdo/configuration/smtpauthenticate'].
                                        Set_Value(cdoBasic);
Item['http://schemas.microsoft.com/cdo/configuration/smtpserver'].
                                        Set_Value('mail.someco.com');
Item['http://schemas.microsoft.com/cdo/configuration/
                        smtpconnectiontimeout'].Set_Value(20);
end;
config.Fields.Update;

// set message properties
cdomsg.Set_Configuration(config);
cdomsg.Set_Sender(bstrFrom);
cdomsg.Set_To_(bstrTo);
cdomsg.Set_Subject(bstrSubject);

// add image attachment
bodypart := cdomsg.Get_BodyPart;
bodypart.Set_ContentMediaType('image/gif');
bodypart.Set_ContentTransferEncoding('base64');
strm := bodypart.GetDecodedContentStream;
strm.LoadFromFile(bstrImage);
strm.Flush;

// message to go with image
cdomsg.Set_TextBody(bstrMessage);

// send
cdomsg.Send;

end;
```

To test the new component, use the following ASP script, *asp2113.asp*, after first modifying the email address and sender to ones that work within your environment. If your SMTP server is located on the Internet, make sure you're connected before accessing the ASP page.

```
<%
On Error Resume Next
Dim obj
Set obj = Server.CreateObject("asp2104.msg")

' get values
Dim strSubject, strImage, strTo, strFrom, strMessage
strSubject = "Image"
strImage = "c:\web\mm\some.gif"
strTo = "person@someco.com"
strFrom = "person@someco.com"
strMessage = "Here's the image"
```

```
' send url
obj.sendImage strTo, strFrom, strSubject, strMessage, strImage
If Err.Number <> 0 Then
    Response.Write "<h3>The Image could not be emailed</h3>"
    Response.Write "<p>" & Err.Description & "</p>"
Else
 Response.Write "<h3 style='color: blue'>
                                   The image is off and running</h3>"
End If

Set obj = Nothing
%>
```

Notice in the example that I've added error handling to process any errors that might occur. The `safecall` calling method used with dual interface components automatically provides the `HRESULT` value used within the script.

Instead of manually creating the attachment, you could also use the `IMessage` AddAttachment method. You can also send a web page using the createMHTML-Body method.

 Methods such as createMTHML and AddAttachment generate an error of unknown interface when accessed in Delphi. This is most likely due to namespace conflicts between ADO and CDO and to not being able to turn off namespacing when importing the type libraries into Delphi. However, you can work around the problem by using the `IBodyPart` interface, as demonstrated in this example.

Hopefully, this chapter has provided you enough demonstrations of the mechanics of accessing the Windows 2000, COM+, ASP, and other technologies from Delphi components, that you can take the examples shown in the Visual Basic or C++ chapters earlier in the book and apply them to your components.

22

Perl-Based Components Using ActiveState's PDK

ASP components can be created with any programming language, as long as the language provides support for the COM/COM+ architecture. This held true for Delphi, covered in the last chapter. This also holds true for Perl through the help of ActiveState's Perl Dev Kit (PDK).

At one time, the only web server development technique was CGI, or the Common Gateway Interface, and the programming language of choice for it was Perl. Now there are a number of different techniques you can use for your web application development and a number of programming languages. However, Perl is still a popular programming language—not the least reason being that Perl is truly an open source programming language that is not controlled by any one group or any one company.

ActiveState is a company formed in 1997 to provide professional Perl development tools. Among some of the products the company provides is ActivePerl, the de facto standard for Perl for the Win32 environment.

In addition to ActivePerl, ActiveState also provides the Perl Dev Kit (PDK), a commercial product that provides, among other things, the ability to invoke Perl modules and objects within ASP pages through the use of PerlCOM and the ability to create completely independent COM/COM+ components written in Perl through the use of PerlCtrl.

This chapter takes a look at PDK and demonstrates how to use both PerlCOM and PerlCtrl. In addition, we'll also look at how you can access the built-in ASP objects from Perl ASP components and how to incorporate other technologies—specifically ADSI—into your Perl components.

This chapter assumes familiarity with the Perl programming language. If you're interested in working with Perl in an ASP environment and have never worked with the language, I suggest you get a copy of the classic "camel book," *Programming Perl*, by Larry Wall, Tom Christiansen, and Randal Schwartz, published by O'Reilly. In particular, review *The Gory Details*, the chapter on functions, and *Packages, Objects, and Model Classes*, the chapter on objects.

Setting Up PDK

First, be aware that PDK works only within a Windows NT or Windows 2000 environment—this product will not work with Windows 95 or 98. However, you can create Perl ASP components using PerlCtrl that will work within the Win9x environments.

You can download a copy of the Perl Dev Kit from ActiveState's web site at *http://www.activestate.com*. The software comes with a free, seven-day trial. At the end of the trial period, you will have to purchase PDK to continue using it

Before installing PDK, you must download and install ActivePerl for the Win32 environment. ActivePerl is a free product, available for download at the ActiveState web site. The use of ActivePerl was demonstrated in Chapter 6, *ASP Interaction: Scripting and ASP Components*—the product was installed to access PerlScript, the Perl-based Windows scripting language.

Installation of PDK is relatively simple: download the product, click on the installation program, and provide a location for the installation. However, to use the product, you will need an activation key. You can get a seven-day free trial key from ActiveState, or you can purchase the key directly. Note that when you request the key, you'll be asked whether you wish to license PDK by username or by machine name. To use PDK within an ASP environment, you should choose the machine name option—accessing PDK from ASP uses a different "user" (on my machine, the ASP user is IUSR_FLAME, since my machine is named FLAME) than the user licensed to develop with PDK.

PDK comes with several tools, such as a Perl debugger and PerlApp, a tool that creates standalone Perl executables that aren't dependent on Perl being installed within the runtime environment. However, the two products we'll look at in this chapter are PerlCOM and PerlCtrl. First, though, we'll create a basic Perl object.

Once you've installed PDK in Windows 2000, register PerlCOM with Component Services, unless the version of PDK you've accessed was built specifically for the Win2K environment.

Building a Basic Perl Component

Perl has long been known as a superior language when it comes to pattern matching and working with regular expressions. If you haven't worked with Perl (or Unix) previously, regular expressions use a combination of wildcard and literal characters in order to search for a specific pattern within a given context, such as a string or even a file or group of files. The expression can be used to find occurrences of the pattern or to replace content matching the pattern with other content.

As a first Perl component, create a Perl object named `prlcomp` with one method, replaceHTML, as shown in Example 22-1. This method has three parameters: a string containing the name of an HTML file, a string with an HTML tag that the module will search for in the file, and a string used as replacement for the HTML tag being sought. Create the object in a Perl module file named *prlcomp.pm.*

The replaceHTML method tests whether the application can open the input file and, if so, opens it. It also opens a matching output file with the same name as the input file but with the substring "new" appended to the filename. Once both files are opened, each line of the input file is accessed, any instances of the target HTML tag are replaced, and the line is written to the newly created output file.

Because an HTML tag can be an opening or closing tag, the method performs two pattern match and substitute operations on each string: one to replace the opening tag and one to replace the closing tag, if any.

Example 22-1. Perl Object Containing Method to Replace Target HTML Tags

```
package prlcomp;

# create object using anonymous hash
# create object using anonymous hash
sub new {

    # get the name of the class, always passed as first paren
    my $class = shift;

    # get object reference
    my $self = {};

    # bless object and return
```

Example 22-1. Perl Object Containing Method to Replace Target HTML Tags (continued)

```
    return bless $self, ref($class) || $class;
}

# method to replace HTML tag
sub replaceHTML {
  local($class, $file, $target, $replace) = @_;

  # build old filename
  my $extfile = $file . ".htm";

  # if can open HTM file
  if (-r $extfile) {
    open (OLDFILE, $extfile);

    # open new htm file
    my $newfile = $file . "new.htm";
    if (open NEWFILE, ">$newfile") {

        # read through old file
        # substituting HTML tag
        while (<OLDFILE>) {
            s/<$target>/<$replace>/ig;
            s/<\/$target>/<\/$replace>/ig;
            printf NEWFILE;
            }
        close(NEWFILE);
        }
    close (OLDFILE);
    }
}

1;
```

Since this component is a Perl object, the new method is necessary because it acts as a constructor for the object. In the code, the substitution pattern matches all instances of the target HTML tag (specified by the global or g modifier) regardless of case (specified by the i modifier).

Once the Perl module is moved to the Perl library path (usually a path such as *c:\ perl\lib*, if Perl is installed on the C drive), it is accessible by Perl scripts and applications. To test the new Perl object in an ASP-less environment, you'll create a Perl file that generates an instance of the new object and calls its replaceHTML method, passing in the name of a file that exists locally to the code being executed:

```
use prlcomp;

$tst = new prlcomp;

$tst->replaceHTML("test","H1","P");
```

Save the code in a file named *prltest.pl*. Create the test file named *test.htm* in the same location as *prltest.pl* and give it the following content:

```
<HTML>
<HEAD>
<BODY>
<h1>test</H1>
h1 test /h1
<p>test</h1>
<H!>test</h1>
</BODY>
</HTML>
```

When the Perl program is executed within a Command window, as follows:

```
perl prltest.pl
```

any instances of an `<H1>` header in the target file are replaced by paragraph (`<P>`) elements.

Now that you have created and tested the Perl component code, you'll use this new object with PerlCOM in an ASP environment, a topic we'll discuss next.

 All Perl modules (files ending in *.pm*) created in this chapter must be moved to the Perl *lib* directory for the examples to run.

Accessing Perl Modules Using PerlCOM

PerlCOM is a COM-compliant object that actually exposes a Perl interpreter within the environment in which the object is created. Once created, the PerlCOM object can then evaluate Perl code, create Perl objects, and import Perl packages for use within the application.

PerlCOM can be used in any environment that supports instantiation of ActiveX components, and this includes the ASP environment. It comes with three methods—EvalScript, CreateObject, and UsePackage—that allow you to evaluate any valid Perl script, create a Perl object, or import a Perl module, respectively. We'll demonstrate all three of these methods within an ASP page.

First, the EvalScript method takes whatever valid Perl script is passed to the method and passes this on to the Perl interpreter that the PerlCOM object is wrapping. The interpreter evaluates the script (executes it) and returns a string with any errors that may occur.

To demonstrate the use of EvalScript, create an ASP page named *asp2201.asp* that displays the classic software development message "Hello World!" as shown in

Example 22-2. The page uses VBScript as the scripting language, primarily to demonstrate that you can use PerlCOM within a non-Perl language environment.

The ASP script in Example 22-2, *asp2201.asp*, creates an instance of PerlCOM and a string variable containing the text "<H1>Hello Wordl!</H1>". (Notice that the word *world* is misspelled.) The ASP page then uses Perl's pattern-matching capability to replace the incorrect spelling of world with the correct one by using EvalScript and the Perl substitute operator (**s**). The results of this substitution are then assigned to a variable and displayed in the web page.

All PerlScript-based variable assignment processed through EvalScript is attached to the PerlCOM object as a property. This property can then be accessed directly by the ASP script.

Example 22-2. Calling EvalScript on PerlCOM Object to Apply Perl Substitution to a String

```
<HTML>
<HEAD>
<BODY>
<%
  ' create PerlCOM object
  Dim objPerlCOM
  Dim tstPerl
  Set objPerlCOM = CreateObject("PerlCOM.Script")

  ' use EvalScript to substitute within a string
  Dim strng
  strng = "<H1>Hello Wordl!</H1>"

  objPerlCOM.EvalScript "$result = '" & strng & "';"
  objPerlCOM.EvalScript "$result =~ s/Wordl/World/g;"
  strng = objPerlCom.result

  ' write out string
  Response.Write strng
%>
</BODY>
</HTML>
```

Depending on the version of PDK you're using, you might have to install *perlcom.dll* into a Component Services application in order for this component to work within the Windows 2000 environment—registering it with *regsvr32* won't be enough.

In addition to using EvalScript to evaluate Perl script, you can also import an existing Perl package into the ASP page and then use the package's functions and variables directly from script. This provides access to some very powerful Perl code without necessarily having to be very familiar with Perl.

For instance, VBScript has access to some mathematical functions such as *Log* for returning the logarithm of a number, *Sqr* to return a square root, and *Sin* to return the sine of a number. However, the language does not have access to built-in functions for all trigonometric functions such as finding the arcus (arc) tangent of a number. There is, however, a Perl package called Math::Trig that does provide a number of trigonometric functions.

To import Math::Trig for use in an ASP page, you can use the UsePackage method on PerlCOM to import and assign the module to a local variable and then call functions on the variable. To demonstrate this, create an ASP page named *asp2202.asp*, as shown in Example 22-3. The ASP script creates an instance of PerlCOM and then uses UsePackage to assign the Math::Trig module to a local variable. It then calls several of the trigonometric functions from the module and outputs their results to the web page.

Example 22-3. Using the PerlCOM Method UsePackage to Import the Math::Trig Perl Module into an ASP Page

```
<HTML>
<HEAD>
<BODY>
<%
  ' create PerlCOM object
  Dim objPerlCOM
  Dim tstPerl
  Set objPerlCOM = CreateObject("PerlCOM.Script")

  ' import in the Math::Trig package
  Dim mathObject
  Set mathObject = objPerlCOM.UsePackage("Math::Trig")

  ' write out values
  Response.Write("value of PI is " & mathObject.pi & "<P>")
  Response.Write("tan of 0.9 is " & mathObject.tan(0.9) & "<P>")
  Response.Write("sec of 0.9 is " & mathObject.sec(0.9) & "<P>")
  Response.Write("arc tan of 0.1 is " & mathObject.atan(0.1))
%>
</BODY>
</HTML>
```

The results of accessing this ASP page are shown in Figure 22-1.

Returning to the original Perl object created in Example 22-1, an instance of this object can also be created within an ASP page using PerlCOM and the PerlCOM CreateObject method. To see how to do this, create a new ASP page, *asp2203.asp*, as shown in Example 22-4. The script creates an instance of PerlCOM and calls CreateObject to create an instance of the `prlcomp` object, then invokes the object's

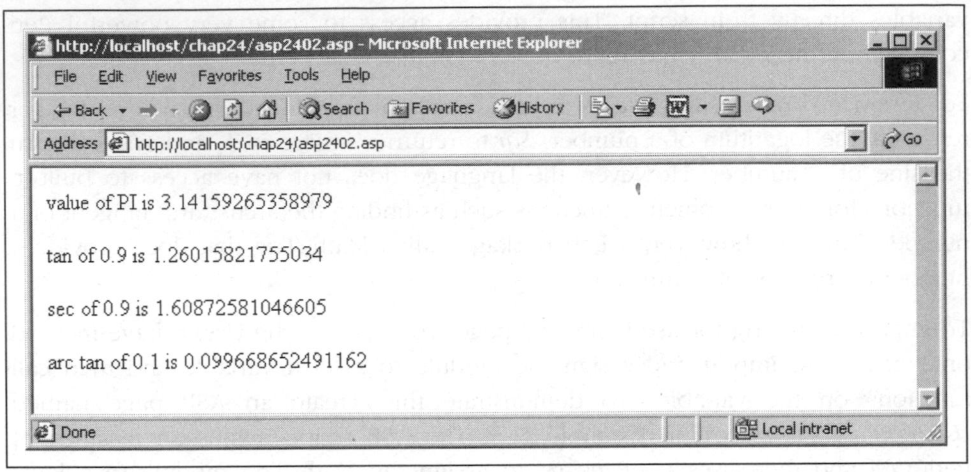

Figure 22-1. Results of accessing and using several Math::Trig functions within an ASP page

replaceHTML method. A complete path to the HTML file is passed as the first parameter.

Example 22-4. Creating an Instance of prlcomp in an ASP Page Using PerlCOM and the CreateObject Method

```
<HTML>
<HEAD>
<BODY>
<%
  Dim objPerlCOM
  Dim tstPerl
  Set objPerlCOM = CreateObject("PerlCOM.Script.1")

  Response.Write "<h3>Replacing H1 with P in test file</h3>"

  Set tstPerl = objPerlCOM.CreateObject("prlcomp", "new")
  tstPerl.replaceHTML "c:\testweb\test","H1","P"
%>

</BODY>
</HTML>
```

Try this yourself after modifying the path to fit your environment. After accessing the ASP page, a new HTML file, *testnew.htm*, is created in the same location as *test.htm*.

Make sure to set the file I/O permissions to allow for read/write of the directory where the test file is being accessed.

Instead of providing a specific directory location for the input file, you could use the ASP built-in Server object and its MapPath method, which maps the physical location of the ASP page to the file:

```
tstPerl.replaceHTML Server.MapPath("test"), "H1", "P"
```

One limitation of PerlCOM, as well as of objects created with Perl-Ctrl, is that you can't pass parameters by reference, only by value. Note, though, that ActiveState is planning to address this limitation in a future release of PDK. Also note that the version of PDK used for the examples in this chapter is PDK 1.2.4.

As has been demonstrated, PerlCOM is a very powerful object for use within ASP applications, but what if you don't want to provide a copy of your Perl code or expose a Perl interpreter in your code? After all, one reason to use ASP components is to hide the code used for the component, regardless of the language used.

You don't have to provide a Perl object or module to deliver ASP components written in Perl, nor do you have to use PerlCOM to create a Perl interpreter in your ASP script. Instead you can use the PerlCtrl application to create standalone COM automation components written in Perl.

Building a Perl DLL Using PerlCtrl

PerlCtrl is a utility that provides a COM wrapper for Perl code, allowing the code then to be accessed as you would a COM object built in any other language.

To create a Perl component using PerlCtrl, you'll use the PerlCtrl utility to generate a template, including type library information, to which you then add the component methods and properties. To demonstrate how to use PerlCtrl, you'll duplicate the functionality used to create *prlcomp.pm* within a new Perl component.

First, create a template named *asp2201.ctrl* using a command line (in the Command window) similar to the following:

```
perlctrl.pl -t > asp2201.ctrl
```

The generated template contains example object, method, and property information that is then replaced with information about the real component. The template also contains the following three lines that must not be edited or altered in any way, or the component can't be compiled:

```
TypeLibGUID     => '{95A2E584-47B5-4E45-9D11-E97CC6933B49}',
                            # do NOT edit this line
ControlGUID     => '{635C2E4C-0797-4AD0-B049-717B872EF954}',
                            # do NOT edit this line either
```

```
    DispInterfaceIID=> '{720C7557-3825-4ED1-A465-2F5ADDDE20F9}',
                                # or this one
```

However, the rest of the generated template information can be altered so that it resembles the source code shown in Example 22-5. Add the `Package` definition and the code for the component method before the =POD line. Additionally, change the package name to `asp2201`, the Control name to "Test of Perl Automation," and the ProgId to `asp2201.test`. Also remove all of the generated properties and the second method from the template. Finally, rename the first method to replaceHTML, and change the method parameters to reflect the component method—three parameters of type `VT_BSTR`, returning a value of `VT_BSTR`.

Example 22-5. The Completed Template File for the tstperl Component

```perl
package asp2201;

# method to replace HTML tag
sub replaceHTML {
  local($file, $target, $replace) = @_;

  # build old filename
  my $extfile = $file . ".htm";

  #
  my $strng = "No errors occurred";

  # if can open HTM file
  if (-r $extfile) {
    open (OLDFILE, $extfile);

    # open new htm file
    my $newfile = $file . "new.htm";
    if (open NEWFILE, ">$newfile") {

        # read through old file
        # substituting HTML tag
        while (<OLDFILE>) {
            s/<$target>/<$replace>/ig;
            s/<\/$target>/<\/$replace>/ig;
            printf NEWFILE;
            }
        close(NEWFILE);
        }
    else {
        $strng = "Could not open output file";
        }
    close (OLDFILE);
    }
  else {
    $strng = "Could not open input file";
    }

  return $strng;
```

Example 22-5. The Completed Template File for the tstperl Component (continued)

```
}

=POD
=BEGIN PerlCtrl
    %TypeLib = (
    PackageName       => 'asp2201',
    TypeLibGUID       => '{1A1EA5C1-ABCE-4198-8D99-2F3C82001D26}',
    ControlGUID       => '{099A259F-817A-414D-9BDA-6955218AAB0E}',
    DispInterfaceIID=> '{52030242-08E9-40FB-A6DB-8998EBB5F69E}',
        ControlName       => 'Test of Perl Automation',
        ControlVer        => 1,
        ProgID            => 'asp2201.test',
        DefaultMethod     => 'replaceHTML',
        Methods           => {
            'replaceHTML' => {
                    RetType             =>  VT_BSTR,
                    TotalParams         =>  3,
                    NumOptionalParams   =>  0,
                    ParamList           =>[ 'file' => VT_BSTR,
                                            'target' => VT_BSTR,
                                            'replace' => VT_BSTR ]
                }
            }, # end of 'Methods'
        Properties        => {

            }, # end of 'Properties'
        ); # end of %TypeLib
=END PerlCtrl
=cut
```

The component code is different from the original Perl module. First, in the replaceHTML method, no reference to `$class` or `$self` is made when accessing the method arguments, since the component is not a Perl object and the class name is not passed as the first parameter. An additional change is that the method returns a string containing information about whether the component method was successful or failed because one of the input or output files could not be opened.

Once the PerlCtrl template for the new COM-based Perl component is complete, generate a COM-wrapper DLL for the component by again calling PerlCtrl and passing it the control filename:

```
perlctrl.pl asp2201.ctrl
```

PerlCtrl checks the syntax of the new component and, if no problems occur, creates a DLL with the same name as the control file, in this case *asp2201.dll*.

The newly generated component can be registered like any other ActiveX component, using either *regsvr32* or preferably registering the component using the Windows 2000 Component Services and adding the component to an applicable package.

Once you've registered the component, access it in an ASP page in the same way that you would instantiate and access any other component, using the built-in ASP Server object. Example 22-6 contains an ASP page, *asp2204.asp*, which instantiates the new component and calls replaceHTML, passing in a filename, target, and replacement HTML tags.

Example 22-6. Creating an Instance of the Perl Component and Calling Its One Method

```
<HTML>
<HEAD>
<BODY>
<%

Dim tstPerl
Set tstPerl = Server.CreateObject("tstperl.test")
Dim str
Dim filename
filename = Server.mappath("test")
str = tstPerl.replaceHTML(filename, "H1", "P")
Response.Write str
%>

</BODY>
</HTML>
```

If no error occurs, a message with "No errors occurred" is output to the web page, and the new HTML file with replaced HTML tags is created.

PerlCtrl has several flags that impact the utility's output. You've seen the -t option to generate a template file, but other options include the following:

-d

　　Dependent option, generates a component that is dependent on the Perl runtime

-f

　　Freestanding option, generates a component that does not require a Perl installation

-rb

　　Builds a DCOM registry binary

-a

　　Provides a list of modules to be added (separated by semicolons)

-c

　　Deletes runtime temp files on exit

-I

　　Adds a list of name-value pairs, with names from the following list:

　　　　comments
　　　　companyname

```
filedescription
filenumber
fileversion
internalname
legalcopyright
legaltrademarks
originalfilename
productname
productnumber
productversion
```

By compiling the component DLL with the `-f` switch, you're creating a component that can be used on any server regardless of whether Perl is installed on the machine. Because all of the Perl functionality to run the component is included, the resulting DLL is much larger than one that is compiled without any switches or with the `-d` switch (the default). For instance, *asp2201.dll* compiled with `-d` ends up 15KB in size; when compiled with `-f`, the component ends up 1,107KB.

All the Perl components compiled as DLLs in this chapter are compiled with the `-f` flag, so they are usable regardless of whether Perl is installed. However, all the components used with PerlCOM or as Perl scripts do require an Active Perl installation in addition to PDK.

Accessing the ASP Built-in Objects

Most ASP components provide business processing, including data access. Because these components do not normally access any ASP-specific functionality (including the ASP built-in objects), they can be used within other environments. However, there can be times when you'll want to access the primary built-in ASP objects—Server, Response, Request, Session, and Application—within your component code. This holds true if the component is created using Visual Basic or Visual C++. This also holds true if you build your ASP components with Perl.

To access the built-in ASP objects from Perl, you need to use the Win32::OLE package that is included with ActivePerl. This package can be used to create an instance of the **MTxAS.AppServer** object, which provides access to the GetObjectContext method when used in an environment that doesn't provide built-in support for the GetObjectContext method.

You don't need to create an instance of **MTxAS.AppServer** in VB or Visual C++, since both of these tools provide access to GetObjectContext. However, you do use a similar technique in Delphi in order to access ObjectContext.

An instance of ObjectContext is returned from calling GetObjectContext, and this object is then used to instantiate each of the ASP objects. We'll look at how to use each of the ASP built-in objects in the following sections.

 Be aware that the ObjectContext object returned from calling Get-ObjectContext within the ASP component does not participate in any transaction that the ASP page is participating in, and calling SetAbort or SetComplete on this object won't impact the transaction in any way.

The Application Object

The Application object has information that is available to all pages that participate within the specific ASP application. The object is instantiated when the ASP application is started and persists until the ASP application is terminated or the last session attached to the application is terminated.

Information can be stored in the Application object in two different collections: the StaticObjects collection, with values set in the *global.asa* file, and the Contents collection, with values set at runtime. The Application object also has two methods: Lock, to lock the object while making a change, and UnLock, to unlock the Application object. Additionally, the Contents collection of the Application object also has two methods: Remove, to remove an item from the collection, and RemoveAll, to clear the Contents collection.

To test setting and getting values from the Application object's Contents collection, create a new Perl file, *perlasp.pm*, containing two methods: setApp, to set a value into the Contents collection, and getApp, to retrieve the value and return it to the ASP page. The component's source code is shown in Example 22-7.

 All of the examples in this and the next sections covering the ASP built-in objects use the same Perl module, *perlasp.pm*. We'll be adding to this module as we advance through the sections.

PerlCOM is not as efficient as PerlCtrl for creating a component, but it is much simpler to use and doesn't require unloading from memory through the Component Services each time a change must be made to the code.

When developing your own Perl components, you might develop them using PerlCOM and then port the code over into a COM component using PerlCtrl once the Perl code has been tested.

The setApp method creates a reference to ObjectContext first and calls the Set-Property method on the Application object's collection to set the application value. In getApp, the code references the Contents collection for the value set in the other method.

Example 22-7. Accessing the Application Object Within a Perl Module Using Win32::OLE and the MTxAS.AppServer Library

```
package perlasp;

# create object using anonymous hash
sub new {

    # get the name of the class
    my $class = shift;

    # get object reference
    my $self = {};

    # bless object and return
    return bless $self, ref($class) || $class;
}

# method to set Application object
sub setApp {
  local($self, $name, $value) = @_;

  $mtx = Win32::OLE->new("MTxAS.AppServer.1");
  $obj = $mtx->GetObjectContext();
  $app = $obj->Item('Application');
  $app->Contents->SetProperty('Item',$name,$value);
}

sub getApp {
  local($self, $name) = @_;
  $mtx = Win32::OLE->new("MTxAS.AppServer.1");
  $obj = $mtx->GetObjectContext();
  $app = $obj->Item('Application');
  $value = $app->Contents($name);

  return $value;
  }

1;
```

To explain this code a little more fully, one difference between working with the ASP built-in objects from Perl and working with the same objects using a tool/language such as Visual Basic or VBScript is that with VB and VBScript, you have access to a shorthand technique to set the Contents collection:

```
Application.Contents("name") = "value"
```

However, this technique is not available within Perl. Instead you have to set the collection property using SetProperty, as shown in the example, or you have to use *hash dereferencing* (demonstrated in the next section on the Session object).

Test this example using PerlCOM to create the object. Example 22-8 shows an ASP page, *asp2205.asp,* used to test the *perlasp.pm* module's two methods. The first method, setApp, is called to set the Application Contents value. The value is then retrieved directly in the script and displayed. Finally, the second method, getApp, is called and the returned string is displayed. Before trying out the ASP test page from your web server, make sure that the *perlasp.pm* module is located in the Perl library path. When the page is accessed, the name passed to the first method should be displayed twice.

Example 22-8. Using PerlCOM to Access perlasp, Calling Its Two Methods

```
<HTML>
<HEAD>
<BODY>
<%
  Dim objPerlCOM
  Dim tstPerl
  Set objPerlCOM = CreateObject("PerlCOM.Script")

  Set tstPerl = objPerlCOM.CreateObject("perlasp", "new")
  tstPerl.setApp "name","Shelley"

  Dim strng
  strng = Application.Contents("name")
  Response.Write strng

  strng = tstPerl.getApp("name")
  Response.Write strng
%>

</BODY>
</HTML>
```

You can't set a value directly into the Application object's StaticObjects collection at runtime. Values can be set in this collection only through the *global.asa* file; at runtime, the collection is read-only. You can retrieve values from the collection using the same technique shown in Example 22-8, but referencing the Static-Objects collection instead:

```
$value = $app->StaticObjects($name);
```

The Application object isn't the only ASP object that has a StaticObjects and Contents collection. The Session object also has these collections, and we'll take a look at this object next.

Example 22-8 doesn't use the Lock or UnLock method, since I have found that using these methods within a Perl component causes the ASP application to freeze up. The methods do work within PerlScript, but I don't recommend their use within Perl components, at least with PDK 1.2.4.

The Session Object

The Session object persists for the life of a particular user session. It begins when a user first accesses the ASP application and lasts until the session is terminated, the user logs off, or some other event occurs to end it.

The Session object has the same two collections as the Application object: Static-Objects, for values set in the *global.asa* file, and Contents, for values set at run-time. Unlike the Application object, the Session object does not have Lock and UnLock methods—only one person can generate a change to this object at a time, so locks aren't necessary—but it does have four properties and one other method.

The Session properties are Timeout, to change the script timeout for the session; SessionID, a unique identifier generated for the session; LCID; and CodePage. The latter two properties have to do with internationalization: the LCID property holds the locale identifier, and CodePage holds the code determining the keyboard mapping.

In addition to the properties, Session also has a method, Abandon, used to terminate the Session and destroy the Session object and all its contents. Additionally, the Session object's Contents collection has the same Remove and RemoveAll methods as the Application object's Contents collection.

I just mentioned that Session has two internationalization properties, LCID and CodePage. The LCID property references an identifier of a locale (a locale is used to determine, among other things, how currency is displayed). The CodePage is also a code value, this one used to determine keyboard mappings. For instance, a CodePage value of 932 represents Japanese Kanji, and the characters associated with keyboard keys reflect the punctuation and characters for this language rather than a codepage value of 1252, which represents American English.

To display both of these internationalization properties for the current ASP environment, create a new method in the existing *perlasp.pm* Perl module. The new method is called getInternational, and the function retrieves the two internationalization code values from the Session object, embeds them in a string, and returns the string to the calling ASP page. Example 22-9 shows the code for this new method.

Example 22-9. Get and Return International Locale Identifier and CodePage Values from Session

```
# method to get internationalization codes
# from Session object
sub getInternational {

  # get Session
  $mtx = Win32::OLE->new("MTxAS.AppServer.1");
  $obj = $mtx->GetObjectContext();
  $session = $obj->Item('Session');

  # get codes
  $locale = $session->LCID;
  $code = $session->CodePage;

  # add to string and return
  $strng = "LCID is $locale and CodePage is $code";

  return $strng;
  }
```

Create the ASP page shown in Example 22-10 to test this new method, and name it *asp2206.asp*. This page creates an instance of PerlCOM and instantiates the **perlasp** object. Once instantiated, the getInternational method is called and the resulting string is displayed.

Example 22-10. ASP Page to Test the New perlasp Object Method, getInternational

```
<HTML>
<HEAD>
<BODY>
<%
  Dim objPerlCOM
  Dim tstPerl
  Set objPerlCOM = CreateObject("PerlCOM.Script")

  Set tstPerl = objPerlCOM.CreateObject("perlasp", "new")

  Dim strng
  strng = tstPerl.getInternational()
  Response.Write strng
%>

</BODY>
</HTML>
```

The result of running this ASP page in my environment is a web page with the following line:

```
    LCID is 2048 and CodePage is 1252
```

The LCID of 2048 is the identifier for the English language, and the CodePage is 1252, for an English language keyboard mapping. The results when you run the example should reflect your own environment.

Earlier, I mentioned that the Session object has the same two collections as the Application object. I also mentioned that there are two methods associated with the Contents collection. These methods, Remove and RemoveAll, allow the ASP developer to clear out one or all of the Session object's Contents collection without having to destroy the Session object—an effective way to "undo" any persisted information.

To demonstrate using Remove and RemoveAll, add three new methods to *perlasp. pm*: setContents, removeSessItem, and removeAllSessItems. Their source code is shown in Example 22-11. The first method, setContents, adds three new items to the Session object's Contents collection. The second method, removeSessItem, removes the item identified with a name passed as a parameter to the method. The third method, removeAllSessItems, clears the Contents collection by calling the Session object's Contents collection's RemoveAll method.

Example 22-11. Three Methods to Set and Remove Session Contents Items

```perl
# set Contents collection items
sub setContents {
    local($self, $item1, $value1, $item2, $value2, $item3, $value3) = @_;

    # get Session object
    $mtx = Win32::OLE->new("MTxAS.AppServer.1");
    $obj = $mtx->GetObjectContext();
    $session = $obj->Item('Session');

    # set contents
    $session->Contents->SetProperty('Item',$item1,$value1);
    $session->Contents->SetProperty('Item',$item2,$value2);

    # you can also use hash dereference to set item
    $session->Contents->{$item3} = $value3;
}

# clear item from Contents
sub removeSessItem {
    local($self, $item) = @_;

    # get Session object
    $mtx = Win32::OLE->new("MTxAS.AppServer.1");
    $obj = $mtx->GetObjectContext();
    $session = $obj->Item('Session');

    $session->Contents->Remove($item);
}
```

Example 22-11. Three Methods to Set and Remove Session Contents Items (continued)

```
# clear all Session Contents items
sub removeAllSessItems {

  # get Session object
  $mtx = Win32::OLE->new("MTxAS.AppServer.1");
  $obj = $mtx->GetObjectContext();
  $session = $obj->Item('Session');

  $session->Contents->RemoveAll();
  }
```

Notice from the code that a different technique is used in setContents to set one of the Contents items. The third Contents item is set using Perl *hash dereferencing*. The two techniques to set properties on an ASP object—using SetProperty or hash dereferencing—work equally well and are used interchangeably in the rest of the examples for this chapter.

To test these new *perlasp.pm* methods, create a new ASP test page, *asp2207.asp*, as shown in Example 22-12. The ASP script calls setContents with three different name-value pairs. Once the Contents items are set, the first is retrieved within the ASP page and displayed to show that the values have, indeed, been set. Next, the removeSessItem method is called to remove the first item from the collection. Once this method finishes, the first item is again retrieved and its value is displayed. Unlike the first time the value is accessed, this time no value for the item is found and no value is displayed, since the Contents item has been cleared. Finally, the third method, removeAllSessItems, is called to clear all of the Contents collection. In the ASP page, the second item of the collection is accessed and its value is displayed. However, since the contents collection has been cleared, once again no value is found, and no value is displayed.

Example 22-12. Calling the perlasp.pm Methods to Set and Clear Contents Items

```
<HTML>
<HEAD>
<BODY>
<%
  Dim objPerlCOM
  Dim tstPerl
  Set objPerlCOM = CreateObject("PerlCOM.Script")

  Set tstPerl = objPerlCOM.CreateObject("perlasp", "new")

  ' set contents items
  tstPerl.setContents "item1", 100, "item2", "test", "item3", 33

  ' get first item from contents and print
  Dim val
  val = Session.Contents("item1")
```

Example 22-12. Calling the perlasp.pm Methods to Set and Clear Contents Items (continued)

```
Response.Write ("item1 value is " & val & "<p>")

' clear item and try again to retrieve
tstPerl.removeSessItem "item1"
val = Session.Contents("item1")
Response.Write ("item1 value is " & val & "<p>")

' clear all items, try for second item
tstPerl.removeAllSessItems
val = Session.Contents("item2")
Response.Write ("item2 value is " & val & "<p>")
%>

</BODY>
</HTML>
```

Note that no error occurs when the nonexistent Contents items are accessed. The only result is that no values are found, and this is reflected in the string—no value is printed out because the string's value is set to null (nothing found).

Up to now, all reporting to the browser has occurred in the ASP pages using the built-in ASP Response object. This object can also be accessed in Perl components, demonstrated next.

The Response Object

The Response object handles all communication from the web server back to the client. This includes, as we've seen in previous examples, sending output to the client browser using the Response object's Write method.

The Response object also has one collection, the Cookies collection, used to set web cookies. The Cookies collection is really a set of objects with the same properties: the cookie name and value, the cookie expiration date, the domain, the lowest-level path, and security. To set cookies using the Response object's Cookies collection, you need, at a minimum, to provide the cookie name and value—all other cookie properties can be set by default.

To demonstrate creating a cookie, add a new method to *perlasp.pm* named setCookies; its source code is shown in Example 22-13. The method has three parameters: the cookie name, value, and expiration date. Notice that only the cookie expiration property, Expires, is set in addition to the cookie name and value. The other properties, Path and Domain, are set to their default values: Path is set to a forward slash (/), and domain is set to the domain from which the cookie is accessed. If the expiration date had not been provided in the Perl method, the cookie would have expired when the browser was closed.

Example 22-13. Setting a Web Cookie Using the Response Object

```perl
# setting web cookies
sub setCookies {
  local($self, $cookie, $value, $expires) = @_;

  # get Response object
  $mtx = Win32::OLE->new("MTxAS.AppServer.1");
  $obj = $mtx->GetObjectContext();
  $response = $obj->Item('Response');

  # set cookie
  $response->Cookies->SetProperty('Item', $cookie, $value);
  $response->Cookies($cookie)->{Expires} = $expires;
}
```

To test the new method, create a new test page, *asp2208.asp*, as shown in
Example 22-14. This ASP page instantiates the *perlasp.pm* component using Perl-
COM and then calls the setCookies method, passing in the cookie name, value,
and an expiration of March 1, 2001.

Example 22-14. Calling setCookies Method to Set a New Web Cookie

```
<HTML>
<HEAD>
<BODY>
<%
  Dim objPerlCOM
  Dim tstPerl
  Set objPerlCOM = CreateObject("PerlCOM.Script")

  Set tstPerl = objPerlCOM.CreateObject("perlasp", "new")

  tstPerl.setCookies "cookie1", "hello", "March 1, 2001"
%>

</BODY>
</HTML>
```

To visually see the cookie being set, you can modify your browser's properties to
prompt you when setting a cookie. This way, when the cookie is set by the set-
Cookies method, you'll get a message to verify whether the cookie should be set,
as well as be able to see the cookie value.

In addition to working with the Response object's Cookies collection, the object
also has several properties:

Buffer
> Determines whether web contents are buffered and sent back to the browser
> all at once or sent back as they are generated

CacheControl
> Determines whether proxy servers can cache generated output

ContentType

Sets the HTTP type for the contents being returned

Expires

Determines how long a page is cached on a browser

ExpiresAbsolute

The same as the Expires property, but allows the developer to specify an exact time rather than a relative number of minutes

IsClientConnected

Tests whether the client browser is still connected with the server

Pics

Indicates the Pics content rating

Status

Determines the status of the page request

Several of these properties make modifications to the HTML header returned with the page. For instance, the Status property can be set to any valid HTTP request status, such as 404 File Not Found or 401 Forbidden by setting the Status property using syntax similar to the following:

```
$response->{Status} = "401 Unauthorized";
```

Setting the Status to the given value within a Perl component will generate a message about the login being forbidden. Setting the status within the ASP page can generate a login page, though canceling the dialog still allows a person to view the page (the status is changed, but you need additional security to actually prevent people from accessing pages).

The Response object also has several methods and one collection in addition to its properties. You've seen Write demonstrated, but there are also the following methods:

AddHeader

Adds an HTML header name-value pair to the returning content

AppendToLog

Writes a string to the web server log

BinaryWrite

Writes content in a raw state, without any character conversion

Clear

Clears any buffered HTML output

End

Stops processing the ASP file and returns any buffered content immediately

Flush

　　Sends buffered content immediately but continues processing the ASP file

Redirect

　　Redirects the client browser to a new URL

Using the Redirect method actually generates an HTTP status of 302 Temporary URL Relocation as it redirects the browser to the new URL. Instead of using Redirect—which loses state information during the redirection and requires a round trip to the client browser and back—you might want to use the Server object's Transfer method, discussed later in the section "The Server Object."

Several of the methods are used only when the Buffer property is set to **True** to determine when and what content is actually returned to the browser. Calling the Clear method will clear the existing buffered content before it's sent back to the browser, but processing the ASP page continues. On the other hand, the End method returns the buffered contents immediately, but no other ASP processing is performed. Flush will also return the content immediately, as well as turn off buffering, but as with Clear, it continues processing the ASP page.

To demonstrate the use of Buffer with the Clear and End methods, add a new method to *perlasp.pm*, as shown in Example 22-15. The method, named testBuffer, generates output using Response.Write method calls. However, the Clear method is called after three Write calls, and the End method is called last.

Example 22-15. Using Clear and End to Process ASP Buffered Content

```
# working with buffered output
sub testBuffer {

  # get Response object
  $mtx = Win32::OLE->new("MTxAS.AppServer.1");
  $obj = $mtx->GetObjectContext();
  $response = $obj->Item('Response');

  # start generating output
  $response->Write("<h1>First header</H1>");
  $response->Write("<h1>Second header</H1>");
  $response->Write("<h1>Third header</H1>");

  # now clear the buffer
  $response->Clear;

  # start generating output, again
  $response->Write("<h1>Fourth header</H1>");
  $response->Write("<h1>Fifth header</H1>");

  # now end processing
  $response->End;

}
```

Since ASP buffering is turned on by default for ASP applications in IIS 5.0, no content is returned to the client until the page is finished processing—unless Clear, End, or Flush is called. The testBuffer method calls the Clear method after the first three Response.Write statements. Doing this clears the existing buffer, which means that the headers labeled first, second, and third header won't print. The fourth and fifth headers print even though the End method is called after they are generated, because End stops ASP page script processing and flushes but doesn't clear the buffer.

Create an ASP page that calls testBuffer, and name it *asp2209.asp*; the page is shown in Example 22-16. The page also calls the Response.Write method to create a sixth header after calling testBuffer. However, since the last statement in testBuffer is a call to the Response object's End method, any further ASP script processing is ended, and whatever content is in the buffer is returned at that point. In the case of the example method and ASP page, the only headers that end up being returned to the browser are the fourth and fifth headers—the headers written after the Clear method and before the End method has terminated script processing.

Example 22-16. Testing Buffering with the testBuffer Method

```
<% Response.Buffer = True %>
<HTML>
<HEAD>
<BODY>
<%
  Dim objPerlCOM
  Dim tstPerl
  Set objPerlCOM = CreateObject("PerlCOM.Script")

  Set tstPerl = objPerlCOM.CreateObject("perlasp", "new")

  tstPerl.testBuffer
  Response.Write "<h1>Sixth Header</H1>"
%>

</BODY>
</HTML>
```

The Response object is used to handle communication from the server to the browser, but another built-in ASP object, the Request object, handles all communication from the client to the server, and this object is discussed next.

The Request Object

The Request object encapsulates any communication from the client to the server. In addition, information about the environment is contained in one of this object's collections.

The Request object has only one method, BinaryRead, used to get information sent from the client as raw data. In addition, the object also has only one property, TotalBytes, which provides the byte size for the raw data. In this section we'll focus on the Request object's collections.

 BinaryRead is used to process form data as a SafeArray. An example of using this method for this technique can be found in Chapter 8, *Creating ASP/ADO Components.*

The Request object has more collections than any other ASP built-in object. One collection is Cookies, but unlike the Response object's Cookies collection, the Request object's Cookies collection allows the ASP developer to read the cookies that are sent with the HTTP request. Another collection is ClientCertificate, which allows fields from a requested client certificate to be retrieved.

Of particular interest in the Request object collections are the QueryString and Form collections. The QueryString collection contains name-value pairs attached to the URL of the processing page or posted using the HTML GET form method. The following is an example of attaching name-value pairs to an URL:

```
<a href="http://www.someco.com/process.asp?item1=value1&item2=value2">...
```

The HTML GET method is the default posting method for HTML forms and results in the form elements being appended to the URL targeted by the form. You've most likely seen this used anytime you submit a form and the URL has an unusually long string with pairs of values similar to those shown in the preceding code.

The Form collection contains name-value pairs posted from an HTML form using the POST method. You must specify POST as a method for values to be placed in the Form collection rather than the QueryString collection:

```
<form ACTION="testreq.asp" METHOD="POST">
```

Regardless of which collection contains the name-value pairs, the same techniques can be used to get information. To demonstrate this, create an HTML page containing an HTML form with three elements: a text element for a first name, a test element for a last name, and a submit button. Example 22-17 shows this page, contained in a file named *asp2210.asp.*

Example 22-17. Web Page with an HTML Form

```
<HTML>
<BODY>
<form ACTION="asp2212.asp" METHOD="POST">
<table width=60% align=center cellpadding=10
    style="border-width: 5px; border-style: groove;
                            border-color: #990000">
```

Example 22-17. Web Page with an HTML Form (continued)

```
<tr>
<td><strong>First Name:</strong></td>
<td>
<input type="text" name="firstname" >
</td></tr>
<tr>
<td><strong>Last Name:</strong></td>
<td>
<input type="text" name="lastname" >
</td></tr>
<tr><td colspan=2 align=center>
<input type="submit" value="submit">
</td></tr></table>
</FORM>
</BODY>
</HTML>
```

Notice that the ASP page called to process the form contents is called *asp2212.asp*. You'll create this page in a little bit, but first you'll want to create the Perl method to handle the form contents.

In *perlasp.pm*, create a new method named getFormValues that creates an instance of both the Request and the Response objects. Its source code is shown in Example 22-18. The form elements are pulled from the Form collection, but the actual values are retrieved from the Form collection *item* associated with each form element. Once the first and last names have been retrieved from the collection, they are concatenated into a message and output using the Response object.

Example 22-18. Retrieve Form Elements Using the Request Object

```
# process form values for POSTed form
sub getFormValues {

  # get Response and Request objects
  $mtx = Win32::OLE->new("MTxAS.AppServer.1");
  $obj = $mtx->GetObjectContext();
  $response = $obj->Item('Response');
  $request = $obj->Item('Request');

  # get the two form values
  $firstname = $request->Form('firstname')->item;
  $lastname = $request->Form('lastname')->item;

  # output friendly message back to client
  $response->Write("<h1>Hello $firstname $lastname!</h1>");
}
```

If you've seen ASP with VBScript or Visual Basic, then you might be used to seeing a collection item accessed directly using syntax similar to the following:

```
    val = Request.Form('value')
```

However, with Perl, you must *dereference* the collection item in order to get the item's value, and that's where the second arrow (the *dereference* operator) comes from in the example.

 You would use the same syntax to access a cookie value from the Cookies collection.

To tie the two components, the form page and the Perl ASP component method, together, create one more ASP test page, *asp2211.asp*, that invokes the new component method, as shown in Example 22-19.

Example 22-19. ASP Page to Call Method to Process Form Contents

```
<HTML>
<HEAD>
<BODY>
<%
  Dim objPerlCOM
  Dim tstPerl
  Set objPerlCOM = CreateObject("PerlCOM.Script")

  Set tstPerl = objPerlCOM.CreateObject("perlasp", "new")

  ' get form values
  tstPerl.getFormValues
%>

</BODY>
</HTML>
```

Open the form page, *asp2210.asp*, in your browser, fill in the fields, and submit the form. The resulting page should show the words:

```
Hello (first name) (last name)!
```

based on whatever first name and last name you provide.

The last Request object collection we'll look at is the ServerVariables collection. This collection contains a lot of information about the client, the server, and the connection between the two. If you've worked with Perl and CGI in the past, the ServerVariables collection is similar to %ENV%.

To demonstrate the Request object's ServerVariables collection, create a new method in *perlasp.pm* named prntServerVariables, as shown in Example 22-20. The method accesses the ServerVariables collection and lists each item and its associated value. To assist you with this process, the method uses the Win32::OLE module's enum method to pull the collection into a Perl list, which you can then process using the Perl *foreach* statement. The individual server variables are output to an HTML table, with the server variable name in one column and the value in the other. The Response object is used to output both the HTML table and the server variable values.

Example 22-20. Access ServerVariables from Request, Printing Out with Assist from Win32:: OLE::Enum

```perl
# printing out each of the ServerVariables items
sub prntServerVariables {

  # get Request and Response
  $mtx = Win32::OLE->new("MTxAS.AppServer.1");
  $obj = $mtx->GetObjectContext();
  $response = $obj->Item('Response');
  $request = $obj->Item('Request');

  # access ServerVariables collection as a list
  @lst = Win32::OLE::Enum->All($request->ServerVariables);

  # iterate through each list item, printing out
  # item name and its value
  $response->Write("<table border=2 cellspacing=0 cellpadding=10>");
  foreach my $item(@lst) {

    $response->Write("<tr>");
    $response->Write("<td valign=top>$item</td><td>" .
              $request->ServerVariables($item)->item . "</td>");
    $response->Write("</tr>");
  }
  $response->Write("</table>");
}
```

This is an example of using the ActivePerl Win32 package's classes in order to simplify processing of COM/COM+ objects. Other objects of interest in this package are the following:

Win32::OLE::Variant

Creates variant objects to pass to other objects or to return from their methods

Win32::OLE::Const

Extracts type library constant value definitions (this is demonstrated later in the ADO section)

Create the ASP page to run this example and name it *asp2212.asp*; the page is shown in Example 22-21. The script again uses PerlCOM to create an instance of **perlasp**, then calls the new prntServerVariables method. A portion of the page generated from running the *asp2212.asp* page is shown in Figure 22-2.

Example 22-21. ASP Page That Calls prntServerVariables to Output All Server Variables

```
<HTML>
<HEAD>
<BODY>
<%
  Dim objPerlCOM
  Dim tstPerl
  Set objPerlCOM = CreateObject("PerlCOM.Script")

  Set tstPerl = objPerlCOM.CreateObject("perlasp", "new")

  ' print out Server Variables
  tstPerl.prntServerVariables
%>


</BODY>
</HTML>
```

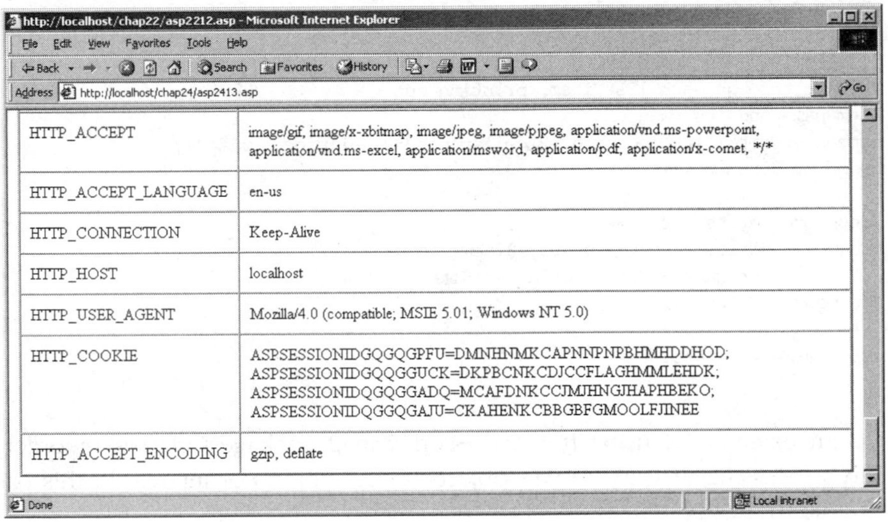

Figure 22-2. Result of running asp2212.asp listing the ServerVariables collection

You've been through a lot of code examples and are probably reeling about now. However, we have only one object left to examine, the Server object, and then we'll be able to leave the world of the built-in ASP objects and take a quick look at data.

The Server Object

The Server object is the only ASP built-in object that doesn't have a collection. Instead, it has one property, ScriptTimeout, and several methods. The Script-Timeout property is used to adjust how long an ASP script will process before it times out. When the script does time out, a message is returned to the client to that effect. You can set this property in Perl using syntax similar to the following:

```
$server->{ScriptTimeout} = 30;
```

The Server object also has several methods, some of which are new with ASP Version 3.0. For instance, there is a new method called Transfer that transfers control from one ASP page to another. However, the existing state for the server, including any Request information and any set Application or Session object values, is also transferred with this method. In addition, the Transfer method does not require a round trip to the client to load the new page.

A second new method is Execute, which executes an ASP page as if the page contents are included within the existing ASP page. This is a rather nice technique to break up larger ASP pages into smaller sizes or to reuse existing ASP code in more than one page without having to create ASP components. (Though why would you not want to use components?)

Another new Server method, GetLastError, actually returns a new ASP object, ASPError. The ASPError object has several properties with information about the last ASP error that occurred. You can't use the method in your ASP pages (or your ASP components)—it's used in a custom (500;100) error page to provide useful information about an ASP error.

As nice as the new Transfer, Execute, and GetLastError methods and the ASPError object are, it is unlikely that one would want to use them within ASP components, so I won't demonstrate these methods in this chapter.

The MapPath method is used to map a filename to an absolute directory location and is helpful when attempting to open a file relative to the web location. This was used with the earlier example that modified an HTML file by replacing HTML tags in the *asp2203.asp* ASP page.

The HTMLEncode and URLEncode methods are used to encode a text string so that the HTML- or URL-specific characters are treated as literals rather than as processing information. For instance, to display an HTML header as is, you can't use the following in an HTML page, since the browser will process the tags and display an HTML header:

```
<H1>Hello</H1>
```

Instead, you can pass the string containing this HTML to HTMLEncode, and the following encoded value is output:

```
&lt;H1&gt;Hello World&lt;/H1&gt;
```

This code displays the literal interpretation of the header, rather than processing it.

To demonstrate these encoding methods, create a last method on our handy *perlasp.pm* module and name it encodeLine. Its source code is shown in Example 22-22. This method takes one parameter, a string to be encoded. Both the Server and Response objects are created, the Server object to access the encoding methods and the Response object to output the results.

Example 22-22. Encoding and Printing a String

```
# try out different encodings
sub encodeLine {
  local($self,$testline) = @_;

  # get Server and Response
  $mtx = Win32::OLE->new("MTxAS.AppServer.1");
  $obj = $mtx->GetObjectContext();
  $response = $obj->Item('Response');
  $server = $obj->Item('Server');

  # encode and print out
  $strng = $server->HTMLEncode($testline);
  $response->Write("HTMLEncode results: $strng<p>");

  # encode and print out
  $strng = $server->URLEncode($testline);
  $response->Write("URLEncode is $strng<p>");

}
```

Create the ASP test page and name it *asp2213.asp*. Example 22-23 shows the page contents you'll add to the test page. Two different strings are passed to encodeLine, one containing HTML characters, the other containing URL characters.

Example 22-23. Calling the encodeLine Method to Encode the Strings

```
<HTML>
<HEAD>
<BODY>
<%
  Dim objPerlCOM
  Dim tstPerl
  Set objPerlCOM = CreateObject("PerlCOM.Script")

  Set tstPerl = objPerlCOM.CreateObject("perlasp", "new")

  ' print out encodings
  tstPerl.encodeLine "<H1>Hello World</H1>"
  tstPerl.encodeLine "http://www.somecompany.com/"
%>

</BODY>
</HTML>
```

The results of accessing this page are:

```
HTMLEncode results: <H1>Hello World</H1>
URLEncode is %3CH1%3EHello+World%3C%2FH1%3E
HTMLEncode results: http://www.somecompany.com/
URLEncode is http%3A%2F%2Fwww%2Esomecompany%2Ecom%2F
```

There is one other Server method of interest to ASP developers. It is CreateObject, and this method has been used in all of the ASP test pages to create versions of PerlCOM or of the component created with PerlCtrl. However, instead of demonstrating this method in this section on the built-in ASP objects, we'll see it in use in the next section, on using ADO within Perl components.

Working with Data

This section on working with ADO from ASP components created in Perl isn't going to be extensive. Instead, we'll look at representative uses of ADO to demonstrate key aspects of working with the ADO objects. Hopefully with this introduction, you should be able to look at the ADO examples in the Visual Basic section in Chapter 8 and interpolate how the examples can be modified to work with Perl.

ADO objects can be created within Perl ASP components using two techniques. First, the Win32::OLE class can be used to create the objects, as was demonstrated in the ASP built-in object sections. However, an approach I prefer is to create the ASP Server object and then create the ADO objects using the Server object's CreateObject method. Doing this, the ADO objects are more tightly integrated into the ASP application, including participating in any transactions that might be aborted or committed outside of the Perl component.

To create ADO objects, you use syntax similar to the following:

```
# create Connection and Recordset objects
$mtx = Win32::OLE->new("MTxAS.AppServer.1");
$obj = $mtx->GetObjectContext();
$server = $obj->Item('Server');

# create ADO Connection object
$conn = $server->CreateObject("ADODB.Connection");
```

In this example, the Server object is created using Win32::OLE, and it, in turn, is used to create any ADO (or other COM/COM+) components needed by the Perl component.

As you had a chance to explore in the last section, there are certain things to be aware of when working with the ADO objects. First of all, you can't use the shorthand technique to set or get ADO object properties as you can with Visual Basic:

```
' set Recordset's ActiveConnection property
set rs.ActiveConnection = conn
```

Instead, you must set a property using the SetProperty method:

```
$rs->SetProperty('CursorLocation', 3);  #adUseClient
```

Or you must use a hash dereference to set or access the property:

```
$rs->{Source} = "select au_lname from authors";
```

Accessing the Type Library Constants

When you create the ADO objects using automation (which is what happens when you use the *CreateObject* function), you aren't including the ADO type library in the component, which means you don't have access to the ADO enumerated constants. These enumerated constants—such as **adUseClient** or **adOpenForward-Only**—are useful in that you can use the named representation of the value rather than the actual numeric value, making your code a lot easier to read.

There is a Perl module that contains all of the ADO enumerated definitions, Win32::ADO, which can be accessed from any CPAN site. (CPAN—Comprehensive Perl Network—is the repository for Perl libraries and code and is mirrored on many different sites. You can locate it at *http://www.cpan.org*.) However, checking the values currently in the most recent release of this Perl module against those defined for ADO 2.6, I did find discrepancies in code values.

 The version of Win32::ADO that I checked while writing this book was Version 0.03. If you find a more recent version, you should download it and compare the values with those provided by Microsoft for their enumerated constants. Newer versions of the Perl module may reflect newer versions of the ADO constants.

However, you can import typelib constant definitions using Win32::OLE::Const. This module actually extracts all of the constant definitions within a given type library and exposes them for access from Perl code. You can use two techniques to extract the definitions. One approach is to load the definitions into a hash with the Load method:

```
$defs = Win32::OLE::Const->Load('Microsoft ActiveX Data Objects 2.5 Library');
```

The values for the definitions can then be accessed from the hash. However, an approach I use in the examples for this section is to import the definitions using the use statement, which then allows the definitions to be used as they are in Visual Basic—directly by the definition name:

```
use Win32::OLE::Const ('Microsoft ActiveX Data Objects 2.5 Library');
...
$rs->SetProperty('CursorLocation', adUseClient);
```

Another approach—though a less readable one—is to use the literal value directly in the code, rather than pulling in any constant definitions:

```
$rs->SetProperty('CursorLocation', 3);
```

Creating ASP/ADO Components in Perl

The best way to show how ADO is accessed from Perl components is to try out a couple of examples.

Create a new Perl object module and name it *aspado.pm*, moving it to the Perl library path; its source code is shown in Example 22-24. Once you've created the object file and the object's new method, create your first ADO method, named getWebPages. The getWebPages method accesses the Weaver SQL Server sample database (see Appendix B), and retrieves all of the web page names. Once the names are returned, they are sorted and then filtered. The method creates both Connection and Recordset objects, opens a connection to the database, and then assigns this open connection to the Recordset object's ActiveConnection property. In addition, several other recordset properties are set: CursorLocation is set to a value of 3, or **adUseClient**, and CursorType is set to a value of 0, or **adOpenForwardOnly**. In addition, the Source property is assigned the following SQL **SELECT** statement:

```
"select name from WebPage"
```

Once the recordset properties are set, the recordset is opened, and the rows are retrieved.

After the rows are retrieved, the Recordset object's Filter property is set to filter the rowset on the name, and the recordset is sorted with the Sort property. A row count is also used to prevent accessing an empty rowset. Finally, the rows are traversed; the returned name column is accessed from the Recordset object's Fields collection and is appended to a string, which is returned to the calling ASP program.

Example 22-24. Complete Code for aspado.pm, with Only the getAuthors Method

```
package aspado;

use Win32::OLE::Const ('Microsoft ActiveX Data Objects 2.5 Library');

# create object using anonymous hash
sub new {

    # get the name of the class, always passed as first paren
    my $class = shift;

    # get object reference
    my $self = {};
```

Example 22-24. Complete Code for aspado.pm, with Only the getAuthors Method (continued)

```perl
        # bless object and return
        return bless $self, ref($class) || $class;
}

# get authors' last names and print
sub getWebPages {

  # create Connection and Recordset objects
  $mtx = Win32::OLE->new("MTxAS.AppServer.1");
  $obj = $mtx->GetObjectContext();
  $server = $obj->Item('Server');

  # create connection and recordset objects
  $conn = $server->CreateObject("ADODB.Connection");
  $rs = $server->CreateObject("ADODB.Recordset");

  # open connection to database
  $conn->Open("provider=SQLOLEDB;server=FLAME;uid=sa;pwd=;
              database=weaver");

  # set Recordset properties
  # two ways to set COM/COM+ object properties
  $rs->{ActiveConnection} = $conn;
  $rs->SetProperty('CursorLocation', adUseClient);
  $rs->{CursorType} = adOpenForwardOnly;
  $rs->{Source} = "select name from WebPage";

  # open recordset
  $rs->Open();

  # filter and sort recordset
  $rs->{Sort} = "name asc";
  $rs->SetProperty('Filter',"name > 'ARTICLES'");

  # get recordcount
  $val = $rs->{RecordCount};

  # move through recordset and print out field value
  if ($val > 0) {
     $rs->MoveFirst;

     until ($rs->EOF) {
        $strResult = $strResult . $rs->Fields(0)->value . "<br>";
        $rs->MoveNext;
        }
  }

  # disconnect from database
  $conn->Close;
  return $strResult;
}
1;
```

Create the ASP page shown in Example 22-25 to test the new component, and name it *asp2214.asp*. The page creates an instance of PerlCOM and then uses this object to create an instance of the *aspado.pm* Perl module using PerlCOM's CreateObject method. Once created, the component's getWebPages method is called, and the string returned from the method is displayed.

Example 22-25. Accessing aspado Perl Module and Calling getWebPages Method

```
<HTML>
<HEAD>
<BODY>
<%
  Dim objPerlCOM
  Dim tstPerl
  Set objPerlCOM = CreateObject("PerlCOM.Script")

  Set tstPerl = objPerlCOM.CreateObject("aspado", "new")
  Dim strng
  strng = tstPerl.getWebPages
  Response.Write(strng)
%>

</BODY>
</HTML>
```

This example demonstrated certain fundamental uses of ADO within Perl, including setting ADO object properties. In addition, the example also demonstrated how to traverse a collection—the Fields collection of the Recordset object—and access values from this collection.

The Command object is another widely used ADO object. Unlike the Connection or Recordset objects, the Command object has a Parameters collection that can be used to provide values for a SQL statement. Using parameters means that the same common object can be used again and again, changing the parameter values each time.

To illustrate the Command object and its Parameters collection, add another method to *aspado.pm*, this one named getHtmlWebPageInfo, as shown in Example 22-26. As you can see from the code, a Connection object is created to open a database connection. The method then uses a Command object to search for all HTML web pages in the Weaver database that share the same directory identifier, which is passed as a parameter to the method. A Parameter object is used to pass the value with the Command query.

A stored procedure is used to wrap the SQL query used for this example. The procedure is named *sp_htmlwebpageinfo*, and its source code is:

```
CREATE PROCEDURE [sp_gethtmlwebpageinfo]
(@directory_id Integer)
AS
BEGIN
```

```
SELECT name, filename, html_version
FROM WebPage, HtmlWebPage
WHERE directory_id = @directory_id and
webpage_id = id
END
```

This procedure joins the WebPage and HtmlWebPage tables based on web page identifier and limits the rows returned to only those in which the WebPage `directory_id` value matches that passed in as a parameter to the stored procedure.

The Connection object isn't necessary—the connection information could be set directly into the ActiveConnection property of the Command object.

Once the command is executed, the result set is passed to a Recordset object. This object is traversed and the returned column values are pulled from each row. The information is then output to an HTML table using the ASP Response object. At the end of the method, the Connection object's database connection is closed.

Example 22-26. Method to Execute Stored Procedure with Parameter Using the Command Object

```
# get web page info
sub getHtmlWebPageInfo {
  local($self, $dirid) = @_;

  # create Connection and Recordset objects
  $mtx = Win32::OLE->new("MTxAS.AppServer.1");
  $obj = $mtx->GetObjectContext();
  $server = $obj->Item('Server');
  $response = $obj->Item('Response');

  # create Connection and Recordset objects
  $cmnd = $server->CreateObject("ADODB.Command");
  $conn = $server->CreateObject("ADODB.Connection");
  $rs = $server->CreateObject("ADODB.Recordset");

  # open connection to database
  $conn->Open("provider=SQLOLEDB;server=FLAME;uid=sa;pwd=;
                                        database=weaver");

  $cmnd->{ActiveConnection} = $conn;
  $cmnd->{CommandType} = adCmdStoredProc;
  $cmnd->{CommandText} = "sp_gethtmlwebpageinfo";

  $param = $cmnd->CreateParameter("type", adInteger,adParamInput);

  $cmnd->Parameters->Append($param);
  $cmnd->Parameters->Item(0)->{value} = $dirid;
```

Example 22-26. Method to Execute Stored Procedure with Parameter Using the Command Object (continued)

```
$rs = $cmnd->Execute;

$val = $rs->{RecordCount};

# move through recordset and print out field value
$rs->MoveFirst;

# values are printed out to an HTML table
$response->Write("<table align=center cellpadding=10 border=2>");
$response->Write("<TR><TH align=left>Page Name</TH>");
$response->Write("<TH align=left>File Name</TH>");
$response->Write("<TH align=left>HTML Version</TH></TR>");
until ($rs->EOF) {
  $name = $rs->Fields('name')->value;
  $filename = $rs->Fields('filename')->value;
  $html_version = $rs->Fields('html_version')->value;

  $response->Write("<TR>");
  $response->Write("<TD>$name</TD><TD>$filename</TD>");
  $response->Write("<TD>$html_version</TD>");
  $response->Write("</TR>");

  $rs->MoveNext;
  }
$response->Write("</TABLE>");

# close connection
$conn->Close;
}
```

The ASP test page for this new method is called *asp2216.asp*, and it performs the usual task of creating an instance of PerlCOM and creating an instance of the aspado Perl object. It then has code that calls the getHtmlWebPageInfo method. Passed to the method is a directory identifier—a value of 16 for this example:

```
<HTML>
<HEAD>
<BODY>
<%
  Dim objPerlCOM
  Dim tstPerl
  Set objPerlCOM = CreateObject("PerlCOM.Script")

  Set tstPerl = objPerlCOM.CreateObject("aspado", "new")

  tstPerl.getHtmlWebPageInfo 16
%>
</BODY>
</HTML>
</HTML>
```

Accessing this page from the test web server results in a page that looks similar to that shown in Figure 22-3, with a list of web page names, filenames, and HTML versions.

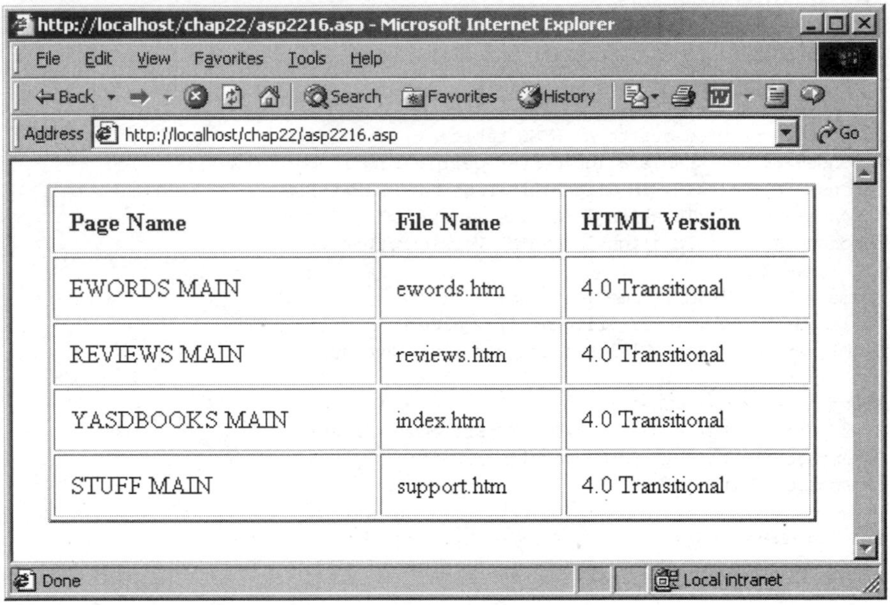
http://localhost/chap22/asp2216.asp - Microsoft Internet Explorer
File Edit View Favorites Tools Help
Back Search Favorites History
Address http://localhost/chap22/asp2216.asp
Go
Page Name
File Name
HTML Version
EWORDS MAIN
ewords.htm
4.0 Transitional
REVIEWS MAIN
reviews.htm
4.0 Transitional
YASDBOOKS MAIN
index.htm
4.0 Transitional
STUFF MAIN
support.htm
4.0 Transitional
Done
Local intranet

Figure 22-3. Results from accessing the asp2216.asp page and printing title information based on directory ID

Working with the Win2K Environment

So far, I've demonstrated how Perl can be used to create Perl ASP components and how these components can then access the built-in ASP objects as well as the ADO objects. This last section of the chapter will demonstrate how Perl can be used for all ASP development needs by trying out other Windows 2000 features. In this case, we'll try access ADSI with Perl.

> To try the example in this section, you'll need to remove anonymous directory access from the virtual directory or site hosting the test page—you can access administrative functions only from a secure web site.

Chapter 2, *Setting Up the ASP Development Environment*, demonstrated how to use ADSI to manipulate the Internet setup for a specific virtual web directory. For instance, Example 2-4 showed a Visual Basic component using ADSI to access the default scripting language for the *chap2* virtual directory. I've repeated the code for this component here, in Example 22-27.

Example 22-27. Using the ADSI Get Method to Access the Property Value for AspScriptLanguage for the chap2 Virtual Directory

```
Function adminScriptLanguage() As String
    Dim myObject
    Set myObject = GetObject("IIS://localhost/W3SVC/1/root/chap2")

    adminScriptLanguage = myObject.Get("AspScriptLanguage")
End Function
```

This VB component is using functionality not previously demonstrated in this chapter; it uses the *GetObject* automation function to retrieve a COM object given a *moniker*—a pathname rather than a program identifier (*progid*). Though this functionality is new, it isn't complicated. In fact, it's very simple to re-create.

First, create a new Perl module, this time named *aspmisc.pm*. In the module, create the necessary new method, and we'll also create a method called *tstADSI*. This method uses the Win32::OLE method *GetObject* to retrieve a COM object given a path—for this example the ADSI object for the *chap22* virtual directory. (Modify the reference to access a Virtual Directory on your server.) Once the ADSI object is obtained, it's queried for the AspScriptLanguage property, which holds the default scripting language for the directory's ASP application. The scripting language string is then returned from the component, as shown in Example 22-28 (note that the Perl object's new function has been omitted for clarity).

Example 22-28. Retrieving the ADSI Object for a Virtual Directory Using the GetObject Method of Win32::OLE

```
package aspmisc;

# new method omitted

$myObject = Win32::OLE >GetObject("IIS://localhost/W3SVC/1/root/chap22");
$adminScriptLanguage = $myObject->Get('AspScriptLanguage');

return $adminScriptLanguage;

1;
```

Now, compare this component written in Perl to the one written in Visual Basic. You should be able to see how similar the two functions are once you understand how to handle the differences between the two languages. In this case, *GetObject* for the Perl component was accessed from the Win32::OLE package instead of being accessed directly, and the *dereferencing* operator is used with the method rather than the VB dot notation (myObject.Get).

More importantly, the behavior of the two components is identical—they both identify the default scripting language for a specific virtual directory.

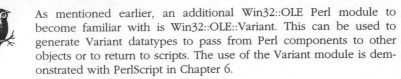

As mentioned earlier, an additional Win32::OLE Perl module to become familiar with is Win32::OLE::Variant. This can be used to generate Variant datatypes to pass from Perl components to other objects or to return to scripts. The use of the Variant module is demonstrated with PerlScript in Chapter 6.

This chapter also has a discussion on error handling within the Perl environment using Win32::OLE->LastError.

To test the component, create an ASP test page and name it *asp2216.asp*; it is shown in Example 22-29. The page uses PerlCOM to access the new **aspmisc** Perl module and call its tstADSI method.

Example 22-29. Accessing aspmisc and Calling Its tstADSI Method

```
<HTML>
<HEAD>
<BODY>
<%
  Dim objPerlCOM
  Dim tstPerl
  Set objPerlCOM = CreateObject("PerlCOM.Script")

  Set tstPerl = objPerlCOM.CreateObject("aspmisc", "new")
  Dim strng
  strng = tstPerl.tstADSI
  Response.Write(strng)
%>

</BODY>
</HTML>
```

Now that you've had a chance to try out PDK and create several different types of Perl ASP components, take a look at the Visual Basic chapters in the earlier sections of the book. You should be able to convert most, if not all, of the VB examples to Perl using the notation demonstrated throughout this chapter.

23

Creating Scripting Language Components

In this book, you've had a chance to look at ASP components created in Visual Basic, Visual C++, Java, Delphi, and Perl. However, you don't have to use a separate programming language or tool to create components—you can use the same scripting language you employ when building your ASP script. The technology that allows you to build ASP components using scripting languages is Microsoft's Windows Script Components (WSC).

We'll end the book with a chapter on creating script-based components and demonstrate this technique with two of the more widely used ASP scripting languages: VBScript and JScript. But first, we'll take a closer look at the WSC architecture.

 Examples throughout this chapter are in VBScript; however, the next to last section of the chapter provides coverage of script components created using JScript/JavaScript.

The Windows Script Components Architecture

Script component files are created using XML with a predefined WCS object model for the XML elements. The active agent to the WSC architecture is a single component, *scrobj.dll*, which acts as the host for the script-based component. Not only does this component act as an in process server for the script component, it also includes prebuilt support for COM automation, ASP, and DHTML behaviors, all of which are supplied through interface handlers. These handlers take care of the necessary details involved in implementing the component's functionality, such as handling COM automation for components that implement the automation handler, or providing access to the ASP built-in objects for those components implementing the ASP handler, as shown with the following `<implements>` tag::

```
<implements type="ASP" id="ASP"/>
```

The script components are created in files and given a *.wsc* extension. In these files, XML is used to provide information about the component, such as what properties and methods are exposed or whether a specialized interface handle is being used. The following XML, for instance, defines a public method named vbTest that has a single parameter:

```
<public>
    <method name="vbTest">
        <PARAMETER name="strName"/>
    </method>
</public>
```

Also contained in the file is a script section, which contains the actual script for the component.

Once the component file is created, right-clicking on this file from Windows Explorer opens a menu that contains options to register the component, unregister the component, or generate a type library. Choosing the option to register the component installs and registers the new component with *scrobj.dll.*

---

regsvr32.exe, included in the *bin* directory of the Platform SDK, can be used to register WSC components. You can download the Platform SDK from the Microsoft developer web site at *http://msdn. microsoft.com.*

Once registered, the component can then be accessed from ASP pages as one would access a component built in any other scripting language—using the CreateObject method of the Server object:

```
Dim obj
Set obj = Server.CreateObject("mycomp.comp")
```

To demonstrate script components, create a file named *asp2301.wsc* using Wordpad or your favorite text editor, and add the code shown in Example 23-1 to it. The example shows a VBScript script component that implements the ASP interface and has one exposed method, vbTest, with one parameter, *strName*. The built-in ASP Response object is used to write out a string containing a concatenated message and the name passed as the parameter to the method.

Example 23-1. VBScript-based WSC Component with One Method

```
<?xml version="1.0"?>
<component>

<registration
     description="vbcomp"
     progid="vbcomp.comp"
     version="1.00"
     classid="{51d99eb3-664f-4e00-a52c-5b81c88f5402}"
>
</registration>

<public>
     <method name="vbTest">
          <PARAMETER name="strName"/>
     </method>
</public>

<implements type="ASP"/>

<script language="VBScript">
<![CDATA[

sub vbTest(strName)

  Response.Write("Hello, " & strName & "!")

end sub

]]>
</script>

</component>
```

Once you save the component as *asp2301.wsc*, register it by right-clicking on the file from Windows Explorer and choosing Register from the pop-up menu. An information window opens, providing information about whether the component was successfully registered or not. If successful, registering *asp2301.wsc* should generate a message similar to that shown in Figure 23-1.

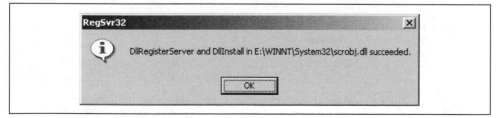

Figure 23-1. Message of success when registering WSC component

Notice that unlike registering a component created using a language or tool such as Delphi or using PerlCtrl and Perl, the script component is actually registered and installed with the in-process server, *scrobj.dll.*

Create the page to test the new component and name it *asp2301.asp.* In the ASP script, create an instance of the component and call its method, passing a string containing a name as the parameter, as shown in Example 23-2.

Example 23-2. ASP Page That Creates an Instance of a WSC Component and Calls Its Method

```
<HTML>
<HEAD>
<BODY>
<%
Dim obj
Set obj = Server.CreateObject("asp2301.vbcomp")

Dim str
str = obj.vbTest("Shelley")
%>
</BODY>
</HTML>
```

The result of accessing the test page is a web browser page containing the message:

```
Hello, Shelley!
```

You've had a chance to see an example of a script component; now it's time to take a more detailed look at the XML used for the component file.

Elements of a WSC File

As stated earlier, WSC files are XML files that are compliant with the Version 1.0 XML recommendation released by the World Wide Web Consortium (the W3C). Compliance means, among other things, that all elements have matching begin and end element tags or are formatted as empty tags.

For instance, in Example 23-1, the **METHOD** element, as it is used in this file, has beginning and ending tags:

```
<method name="vbTest">
    <PARAMETER name="strName"/>
</method>
```

 The WSC elements are shown in capital letters in this chapter to make them easier to spot. However, when you use the WSC elements in your scripting component, use lowercase letters only, or registering your component will generate an error.

The IMPLEMENTS element, though, is an empty tag or an element that doesn't have an ending tag, at least in the current file (an element can be defined with beginning and ending tags in one file but as an empty tag in another):

```
<implements type="ASP" id="ASP"/>
```

Element attributes are specified as name-value pairs, such as type="ASP" or name="vbTest". In addition, the scripting portion of the component is surrounded by a CDATA section, which prevents the enclosed text from being treated as XML. XML parsers ignore whatever text is enclosed between beginning and ending CDATA elements.

The elements, their relationship to one another, and the element attributes all syntactically define the object model used with WSC to wrap the ASP script within a scripting component. The first tag in the file is the XML tag, specifying that the file contains data that should be parsed as XML and containing the version of the XML specification the page adheres too, as well as whether the file has a reference to a DTD (Documentation Type Definition) file. Another optional attribute for the tag is the character set encoding used for the document. WSC component files do not have external DTD files and usually use the default encoding, so the tag should look like this:

```
<?xml version="1.0"?>
```

Other tags are described in the next sections.

Not all of the Windows Scripting Components elements are described in this chapter, just the ones I thought would be of the most interest to ASP developers. You can get more information on the WSC and the elements by accessing Microsoft's Scripting web site at *http://msdn.microsoft.com/scripting/*.

The Package and Component Elements

A script component is enclosed within beginning and ending COMPONENT tags. A file can actually contain more than one component, as long as each component's script and XML elements are enclosed within separate beginning and ending COMPONENT tags.

The only attribute the COMPONENT element has is id, providing a unique way of identifying each individual component when multiple components are being defined in the file

If you do have more than one component within a single WSC file, you must enclose all of the components within beginning and ending PACKAGE element tags. Each component can be given a separate progid to access it (discussed later), or you can provide a component identifier and then use *GetObject* to get the component using a *moniker*—a string containing the location of the object.

To demonstrate using the PACKAGE and COMPONENT elements together, copy the component file created in Example 23-1 and save it into a new file named *asp2302.wsc*. Modify the file by enclosing the existing component within PACKAGE element tags, and then add a new component to the file, as shown in Example 23-3. Give the first component an ID of comp1 and the second component an ID of comp2. Additionally, remove the classid attribute from the first component's registration, as you don't want two separate components to have the same class identifier, and change the progid attributes of both components to match those of their component IDs, with the addition of the filename (i.e., *asp2302.comp1* and *asp2302.comp2*).

The registration properties for the second component are the same as for the first. In fact, the new component is a copy of the old one, except that the component's method's name is changed to vbGetSrvVar, and the name of the method parameter is changed to *strSrvVar*. Instead of a name, the parameter for the new method now holds the name of a member of the Request object's ServerVariables collection.

The code for the new component takes the parameter passed to the component *function* (not subroutine as is defined for the first component), uses it to look up the value in the ServerVariables collection, and then returns that value.

Example 23-3. Altered WSC File, Now Containing Two Component Definitions

```
<?xml version="1.0"?>
<package>
<component id="comp1">

<registration
    description="vbcomp"
    progid="asp2302.comp1"
    version="1.00"
/>

<public>
    <method name="vbTest">
        <PARAMETER name="strName"/>
    </method>
</public>

<implements type="ASP"/>

<script language="VBScript">
<![CDATA[
```

Example 23-3. Altered WSC File, Now Containing Two Component Definitions (continued)

```
sub vbTest(strName)

  Response.Write("Hello, " & strName & "!")

end sub

]]>
</script>

</component>
<component id="comp2">

<registration
    description="vbcomp"
    progid="asp2302.comp2"
    version="1.00"
/>

<public>
    <method name="vbGetSrvVar">
        <PARAMETER name="strSrvVar"/>
    </method>
</public>

<implements type="ASP"/>

<script language="VBScript">
<![CDATA[
function vbGetSrvVar(strSrvVar)

  vbGetSrvVar = Request.ServerVariables(strSrvVar)

end function

]]>
</script>

</component>
</package>
```

After saving the changes to the file, register the new component.

Create a new test page and name it *asp2302.asp*. Add the code shown in Example 23-4 to the file (modified for your own directory location). The *GetObject* function is used to access the component via the component's moniker, passed as an argument to the function call. In the ASP script, the moniker is the script component file's directory location concatenated with a pound sign (#) and then the component identifier.

Example 23-4. ASP Page to Test Scripting Components with Different Component Identifiers

```
<HTML>
<HEAD>
<BODY>
<%
Dim obj
Set obj = _
        GetObject("script:e:\devaspcomp\source\asp2301.wsc#comp1")

obj.vbTest("Shelley")
Response.Write("<p>")

Dim obj2
Set obj2 = _
        GetObject("script:e:\devaspcomp\source\asp2302.wsc#comp2")

Dim str
str = obj2.vbGetSrvVar("ALL_HTTP")
Response.Write str
%>
</BODY>
</HTML>
```

Instead of using component identifiers, the *GetObject* function, and monikers to identify each component, you can also specify a different **progid** for each, and use the CreateObject method to instantiate the components. The progid for the components is discussed in the next section.

The Registration Element

Following the beginning **COMPONENT** tag in Example 23-1 or 23-3 is the registration section, defined with an empty **REGISTRATION** element (one that doesn't have both beginning and ending element tags). The **REGISTRATION** tag contains optional attributes with information about the component, such as the **progid**, used to provide the program identifier used by applications to access the component; the **classid**, used to hold a component **GUID** (Globally Unique Identifier); the text **description** for the component; and the component's **version**, if more than one version of the component can exist within the same system. Additionally, if the component is going to be accessed remotely, another registration attribute is a remote flag specifying that the component can be accessed remotely:

```
<registration ... remotable=true/>
```

The components developed in previous examples in this chapter specified both the progid and the classid, or the progid alone, but neither of these attributes is necessary if the components are accessed using a moniker. If the progid but no classid is given, the latter is automatically generated for the component when it is registered. When a progid is provided, the component can be accessed by this value, as shown in Example 23-2. If the `classid` attribute is specified without the `progid` attribute, the component then needs to be accessed by the `classid`.

Create another component to try out instantiating a component using only the classid. First, you'll need to generate the GUID for the attribute. There is a utility named *uuidgen.exe*, installed with the Platform SDK as well as with Visual Studio (in the Tools subdirectory), that generates this GUID from a Command prompt:

```
C:\> uuidgen.exe
```

Name the new component file *asp2303.wsc* and add the code shown in Example 23-5, except use the GUID you just generated in place of the one shown in the example. Unlike the component in Example 23-3 that displays the Server-Variables value for one given name, this component displays all of the ServerVariables collection. In the component file, the registration section—located just after the first component tag, though there is no required order for WSC elements—sets the description and classid attributes, but no other attributes. Following the registration section is the definition for the method, the interface handler for ASP, and the actual script.

Example 23-5. Script Component with Method to Print Out All Server Variables, Identified by Classid Only

```
<?xml version="1.0"?>
<component>

<registration
    description="vbcomp2"
    classid="{d730573e-9a74-48f7-99f1-c065eef4803d}"
/>

<public>
    <method name="prntAllSrvVars" />
</public>

<implements type="ASP"/>

<script language="VBScript">
<![CDATA[
sub prntAllSrvVars()

  For Each elem In Request.ServerVariables
    Response.Write elem & " = " & Request.ServerVariables(elem) & "<br>"
  Next
end sub
]]>
</script>

</component>
```

When you create the component, instead of instantiating the object using the CreateObject method and passing in a progid or using *GetObject* and a moniker, create the component within the *global.asa* file, as a Session object:

```
<OBJECT RUNAT=Server SCOPE=Session ID="scriptcomp"
    CLASSID="clsid:d730573e-9a74-48f7-99f1-c065eef4803d">
</OBJECT>
```

> The scripting component is running within the in-process server, *scrobj.dll*, which is apartment-threaded. Normally, you wouldn't want to add an apartment-threaded object to any of the Session object's collections (see Chapter 4, *ASP Components, Threads, and Contexts*, for details). We are doing so in Examples 23-5 and 23-6 for demonstration purposes only.

The object will be instantiated when you access it the first time within the session, and it lasts until the session is destroyed.

Create the ASP test page and name it *asp2303.asp*, as shown in Example 23-6. The script in the page accesses the object from the Session object's StaticObjects collection and invokes the component's prntAllSrvVars method.

Example 23-6. ASP Page That Accesses Component from Session's StaticObjects Collection

```
<HTML>
<HEAD>
<BODY>
<%
Dim obj
Set obj = Session.StaticObjects("scriptcomp")

obj.prntAllSrvVars
%>
</BODY>
</HTML>
```

As has been demonstrated with several examples, a component's methods, properties, and events are exposed with the PUBLIC element, and we'll take a look at this next.

The Method, Public, Property, and Event Elements

The PUBLIC element by itself doesn't have any interesting attributes, but it does act as a parent to a set of elements that are critical when defining the component: the PROPERTY, METHOD, and EVENT elements. We won't look at the EVENT element in this chapter, but we will take a closer look at METHOD and introduce the PROPERTY element.

You've seen the METHOD element used in earlier examples to define publicly exposed component methods. These are the methods that can be accessed by the component client, such as by the script within ASP pages. The external name for the method is given in the name attribute. In addition to name, other attributes are internalName, if the method is has a different internal name in the script, and dispid, used to hold dispatch identifiers used for event notification.

The METHOD element has an optional child element, PARAMETER, that can be used to define the parameters for the method. These parameter definitions aren't required, but they are useful if you generate a type library for your component.

The PROPERTY element is used to define publicly exposed component properties. What the element really does is map a component property to a set of Get and Put methods, defined as child elements, which is the way properties are set and accessed from a COM/COM+ component.

To become familiar with the PROPERTY element, create a new script component. Save the new component in a file named *asp2304.wsc*, and give the component a progid of asp2304.vbcomp3. Example 23-7 has the code you'll need to add to the component file. The component has one method, externally named applyFactor but internally named multiplyFactor, and a property named mfactor. The method has one parameter, an incoming value, which the method multiplies by the value of the mfactor property. The method then returns this result.

mfactor is defined as a property, but two methods are created to actually set and retrieve the property. Instead of specifying the methods individually, a shorthand technique is used to specify that the component is using default naming for these methods. In this case, the default set method is named put_mfactor, and the default get method is named get_mfactor.

Example 23-7. Component That Uses PROPERTY to Define a Component Property

```
<?xml version="1.0"?>
<component>

<registration
    description="vbcomp3"
    progid="asp2304.vbcomp3" />

<public>
    <method name="applyFactor" internalName="multiplyFactor" >
        <parameter name="lInValue" />
    </method>
        <property name="mfactor" get put/>
</public>

<implements type="ASP"/>

<script language="VBScript">
```

Example 23-7. Component That Uses PROPERTY to Define a Component Property (continued)

```
<![CDATA[

' global property
Dim gMFactor

' multiply incoming value by factor
Function multiplyFactor(lInValue)
  Dim val
  multiplyFactor = CDbl(lInValue) * gMFactor
End Function

' return factor
Function get_mfactor()
   get_mfactor = gMFactor
End Function

' set factor
Function put_mfactor(val)
  gMFactor = CDbl(val)
End Function

]]>
</script>
</component>
```

To test the new component once you've registered it, create a new ASP page as shown in Example 23-8 and name it *asp2304.asp*. This page creates the new component and then sets the component's mfactor property to 23.55. It then calls applyFactor with a value of 20. The page displays the component method's return value and calls applyFactor one more time, this time passing in a value of 3.5. Again, the page displays the returned value. Finally, the page script accesses and displays the value of the mfactor property itself.

Example 23-8. Seting a Script Component Property and Calling a Method That Uses This Property Value

```
<HTML>
<HEAD>
<BODY>
<%
Dim obj
Set obj = Server.CreateObject("asp2304.vbcomp3")

' set property
obj.mfactor = 23.55

' apply factor
Dim val
val = obj.applyFactor(20)
Response.Write("For value of 20, applying factor results in " & CStr(val))
Response.WRite("<P>")
```

Example 23-8. Setting a Script Component Property and Calling a Method That Uses This Property Value (continued)

```
' apply factor
val = obj.applyFactor(3.5)
Response.Write("For value of 3.5,applying factor results in " & CStr(val))
Response.WRite("<P>")

' get factor
val = obj.mfactor
Response.Write("And the factor is " & CStr(val))

%>
</BODY>
</HTML>
```

The resulting web page generated by this ASP has three lines that look like this:

```
For value of 20, applying factor results in 471
For value of 3.5, applying factor results in 82.425
And the factor is 23.55
```

We'll look at two other WSC elements, and then we'll take a look at working with ADO from script components.

The Implements, Script, Comment, and Object Elements

Throughout the examples, we've used the following line to be able to reference the ASP built-in objects from the script component code:

```
<implements type="ASP"/>
```

The **IMPLEMENTS** element has three attributes: the **type** attribute, which we've used in all of the examples to designate the ASP interface handler, the **id** attribute, and the **assumed** flag. Normally, all you need to specify is the **type** attribute. However, you could use the **id** attribute if you want to preface the events, methods, and properties inherited from the interface handler with an identifier to prevent any name collisions between your script and the handler. By default, when you use the **id** attribute, the **assumed** flag is set to **True** by default, which means that the interface handler methods are added to the script namespace and you can access these methods directly without prefacing the method with the ID. If you wish different behavior, set the **assumed** flag to **false**.

Unlike the **IMPLEMENTS** element, the **SCRIPT** element has only one attribute, **language**, which is used to specify the scripting language. In the examples so far, we've used VBScript as the scripting language—but other languages such as JScript could also be specified in the language attribute and used for the code.

You can add commenting to the code without having to enclose it within CDATA sections by using the COMMENT element to wrap the comment:

```
<COMMENT>
Add your script component comments here
</COMMENT>
```

You might want to include a COMMENT section right after the first COMPONENT tag to include general information about the component, such as the component creator, the date, and a brief description of the component. Other comments can be used within the script itself to document your code.

In addition to IMPLEMENTS, SCRIPT, and COMMENT, you can also add a reference to an object to the component file with the OBJECT element, and the object will be instantiated when your component is accessed. The OBJECT element has an id attribute used to identify the object in your script. In addition, the progid and classid attributes are used to provide some way of specifying the object you want to access within your script component.

Earlier, in Example 23-5, you created a script component that provided only a classid in its registration section. That component iterates through the ServerVariables collection from the Request object and lists each of the name-value pairs in the collection. In Example 23-9, we'll instantiate this component from within a new script component.

Create a new script component in a file named *asp2305.wsc* that uses the OBJECT element to instantiate the component from Example 23-5 and call its one method; its source code is shown in Example 23-9. This component, unlike earlier examples, does not include the IMPLEMENTS element, since none of the ASP built-in objects are being accessed. As you can see in Example 23-9, your new component has a progid of asp2305.vbcomp4 and only one method, callObject. All this method does is call the prntAllSrvVars method of the external component.

Example 23-9. Component That Instantiates Another Component Using OBJECT and the Component's Classid

```
<?xml version="1.0"?>
<component>

<registration progid="asp2305.vbcomp4"/>

<object id="obj" classid="clsid:d730573e-9a74-48f7-99f1-c065eef4803d" />

<public>
    <method name="callObject" />
</public>

<script language="VBScript">
<![CDATA[
```

Example 23-9. Component That Instantiates Another Component Using OBJECT and the Component's Classid (continued)

```
Sub callObject()

    obj.prntAllSrvVars

End Sub

]]>
</script>
</component>
```

When this new component is called from an ASP page, *asp2305.asp*, it calls the method on the external component, and the results are printed out to the page:

```
<HTML>
<HEAD>
<BODY>
<%
Dim obj
Set obj = Server.CreateObject("asp2305.vbcomp4")

' call method
obj.callObject
%>
</BODY>
</HTML>
```

> Though the component in Example 23-9 didn't implement the ASP interface handler, the included external object from Example 23-5 did, which is why the Request and Response ASP objects are available for the external component.

There is a last WSC element to examine, which we'll look at in the context of working with data (using ADO).

Script Components and ADO

Most ASP components provide some form of data manipulation, and script components are no exception. It's fairly simple to use ADO within script components—you can always use the OBJECT element to instantiate the ADO objects, or use a variation of CreateObject in the script. However, one problem that remains is that using automation does not provide access to the type library and, more importantly, to the type library constants defined for use with the ADO objects.

To provide support for type libraries, the WSC has another element, the REFERENCE element, used to include a reference to a type library from the script component.

To reference a type library, you can specify a progid for a component that can then be used to derive the type library, or you can specify the type library GUID. If more than one version of the type library exists in the system, you can even specify the version of the library that you want to access, with the **version** attribute.

To demonstrate how to include the ADO type library within a scripting component, create another script component in a file named *asp2306.wsc;* its source code is shown in Example 23-10. This component has a progid of `asp2306.dacad` and includes one method, displayFiles. The method has one parameter, named *strDirectoryId.* The new component accesses the Weaver database and finds all script web pages that are contained within a directory identified by a given directory identifier. A join is made on two tables, WebPage and ScrptWebPage, to return the page's name, filename, scripting language, and version.

The script for the component creates ADO Connection and Recordset objects using the *CreateObject* automation function. Next, it sets the Connection's ConnectionString string to use the SQL Server OLE DB Provider to connect to the Weaver database on the local server. Once this connection string is defined, the connection is opened.

The Weaver database is discussed in more detail in Appendix B. You can also modify the connection string to use the OLE DB Provider for ODBC and to connect to the Access version of Weaver if you prefer.

The Recordset object has several properties that are set in the script, including the ActiveConnection property (set to the Connection object just opened), as well as the CursorType, CursorLocation, and Source properties. The CursorType holds the type of cursor and is set to the ADO constant `adOpenForwardOnly` for a forward-only result set that can be traversed once. The CursorLocation value is set to use the client-side cursor, indicated with the `adUseClient` constant. The Source property is set to an embedded SQL string.

Without the ability to reference the type library with the **REFERENCE** element, values for the ADO constants would have to be used within the script component—something to avoid, since these underlying values may change in the future. However, as can be see in Example 23-10, the use of the **REFERENCE** tag allows you to use the constants directly.

Example 23-10. Referencing the ADO Type Library and Performing a Query Against a Database

```
<?xml version="1.0"?>
<component>
```

*Example 23-10. Referencing the ADO Type Library and Performing a Query Against a
Database (continued)*

```
<registration
    description="Developing ASP Components -- adocomp"
    progid="asp2306.dacado"
/>

<public>
    <method name="displayFiles">
        <parameter name="strAuname" />
    </method>
</public>

<implements type="ASP"/>

<reference object="ADODB.Connection.2.6" />

<script language="VBScript">
<![CDATA[


Sub displayFiles(strDirectoryId)

  ' create and open connection
  Set cnn = CreateObject("ADODB.Connection")
  cnn.ConnectionString = "provider=SQLOLEDB;server=FLAME;uid=sa;
                                            pwd=;database=weaver"


  cnn.Open

  ' create and open recordset
  Set rs = CreateObject("ADODB.Recordset")
  Set rs.ActiveConnection = cnn
  rs.CursorLocation = adUseClient
  rs.CursorType = adOpenForwardOnly
  rs.Source = "select name, filename, script_language, script_version " _
              & "from Webpage, ScrptWebPage " _
              & "where webpage_id = id and  " _
              & " directory_id =  " & strDirectoryId & " " _
              & " order by script_language, script_version, name"

  rs.Open

  ' process results
  Dim strResult

  If rs.RecordCount > 0 Then
     Do Until rs.EOF
        strResult = strResult & rs.Fields.Item("name") & " -- " _
                    & rs.Fields.Item("filename") & " -- " _
                    & rs.Fields.Item("script_language") & ", " _
                    & rs.Fields.Item("script_version") & "<P>"
        rs.MoveNext
```

Example 23-10. Referencing the ADO Type Library and Performing a Query Against a Database (continued)

```
    Loop
  Else
      strResult = "No Records Found"
  End If


  ' print out using Response
  Response.Write("<H3>Results of query are:</H3>")
  Response.Write(strResult)

End Sub

]]>
</script>

</component>
```

The ASP page that uses the new component is relatively simple. It creates an instance of the component and calls the component method, passing to it the identifier of a specific directory, as defined in *asp2306.asp* and shown in Example 23-11.

Example 23-11. ASP Page That Tests ADO Script Component

```
<HTML>
<HEAD>
<BODY>
<%
Dim obj
Set obj = Server.CreateObject("asp2306.dacado")

' call method
obj.displayFiles 30
%>
</BODY>
</HTML>
```

If you're interested in working with ADO in script components, check out Chapter 8, *Creating ASP/ADO Components*, and Chapter 9, *Creating an ASP Middle Tier with ADO*. In fact, the code for most of the Visual Basic examples in the book should work almost as well with script components using VBScript, except that VBScript has only one datatype—Variant.

The WSC Wizard

You've built all of the examples in this chapter by hand (or you've copied them from the downloaded source code). However, an easier approach to building a script component can be to use the Windows Script Components Wizard to generate the WSC file, complete with preset WSC element specifications, and then add your own script.

The wizard can be downloaded from Microsoft's Scripting web site at *http://msdn. Microsoft.com/scripting/*. Once downloaded and installed, it's very easy to use the tool to generate a component. For instance, let's use the wizard to create a component in a file named *asp2307.wsc*, with a progid of `asp2307.comp`. When you start the Wizard and add the information, it should look similar to the image shown in Figure 23-2.

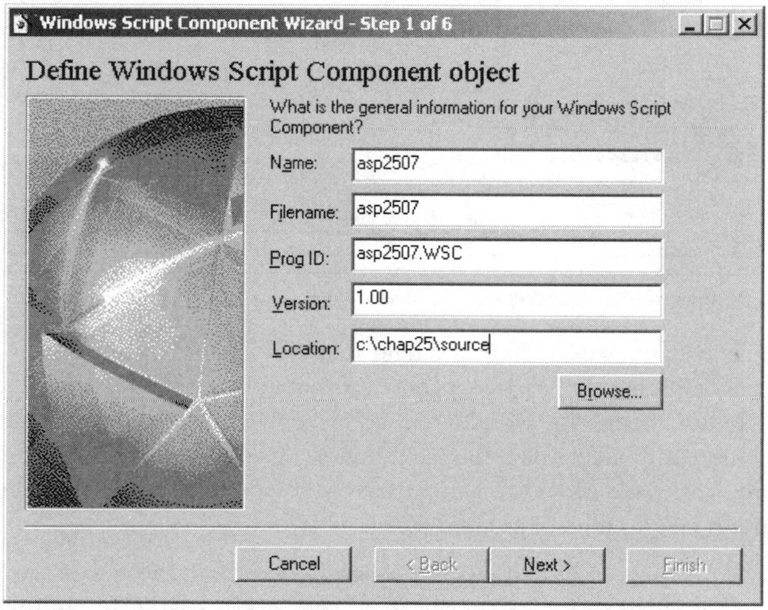

Figure 23-2. First page of WSC Wizard, creating a new script component

On the next page of the wizard, provide the characteristics of the component. For the example, set the component's scripting language to VBScript, check the Support Active Server Pages option, and enable Error Checking.

The third page allows you to define properties for the component. In the case of our example component, the component will perform either HTML or URL encoding of any string passed to it, depending on the value of a flag that determines the type of encoding to be used. To implement this functionality, create a property to hold the current type of encoding, name the property m_encode, set it to Read/Write, and set its default value to "HTML," for HTML encoding by default. Figure 23-3 shows the wizard page with the property defined.

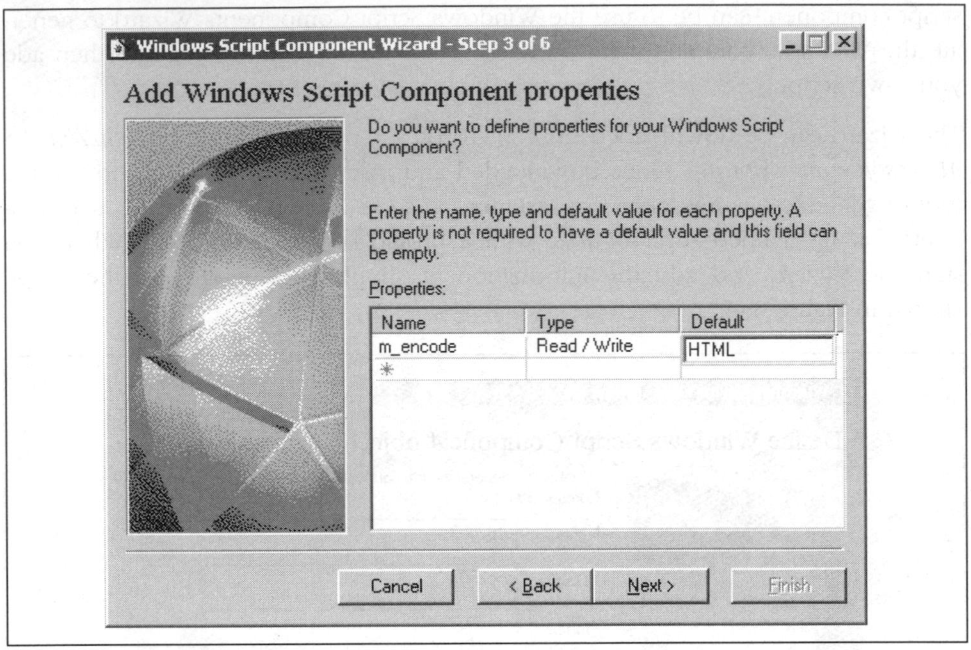

Figure 23-3. Wizard with one property defined

In the next wizard page, define a single method for the component. Name the method encodeString. It has one parameter, named **strEncString**. Clicking on the Next button opens the window to add events; since you aren't adding any events to the component, click the Next button again to bring up the last page of the wizard. This page provides a summary of the component, and clicking on the Finish button creates the component file.

The new file, shown in Example 23-12, is created with all the necessary WSC elements, such as COMPONENT, REGISTRATION, IMPLEMENTS, PUBLIC, and SCRIPT, in place. In addition, the file already contains the definitions for the component's method and property, as well as a progid and a generated classid for registration. Within the Script block, the get and put methods have been created to handle the property, and the property has been defined. Finally, as shown in Example 23-12, a prototype for the encodeString method has also been added to the component.

Example 23-12. Component Shell Generated by WSC Wizard

```
<?xml version="1.0"?>
<component>

<?component error="true" debug="false"?>

<registration
    description="asp2307"
    progid="asp2307.comp"
    version="1.00"
```

Example 23-12. Component Shell Generated by WSC Wizard (continued)

```
    classid="{03daa5ce-e7a4-47cf-9e32-72d224526965}"
>
</registration>

<public>
    <property name="m_encode">
        <get/>
        <put/>
    </property>
    <method name="encodeString">
        <PARAMETER name="strEncString"/>
    </method>
</public>

<implements type="ASP" id="ASP"/>

<script language="VBScript">
<![CDATA[

dim m_encode
m_encode = "HTML"

function get_m_encode()
    get_m_encode = m_encode
end function

function put_m_encode(newValue)
    m_encode = newValue
end function

function encodeString(strEncString)
    encodeString = "Temporary Value"
end function

]]>
</script>

</component>
```

Notice the <? component ?> processing instruction in the example. This is used to turn on error checking or script debugging within the component. In this example, we turned on error checking but left off debugging.

 Read more about and access the script debugger at Microsoft's Scripting site, *http://msdn.microsoft.com/scripting/.*

All that's left to do with the component is to add the actual code for this method.

Replace the current functionality (assigning a return string value), with the new code. This code checks the m_encode property: if the value is HTML, your code uses the HTMLEncode method of the ASP Server object to encode the string; if URL, your code uses URLEncode:

```
Dim str
If m_encode = "HTML" Then
    str = Server.HTMLEncode(strEncString)
Else
    str = Server.URLEncode(strEncString)
End If

encodeString = str
```

Once the body of the component method has been replaced with the new code, register the component and then create the test page.

The ASP test page *asp2307.asp*, which is shown in Example 23-13, creates the new component and calls the encodeString method, passing it a string with HTML tags. The value returned by the method is then displayed. The page then sets the component's m_encode property to URL and calls the method again, this time passing the method a string containing URL characters. Again, the string returned by the method is displayed.

Example 23-13. ASP Page Testing Wizard-Generated Component

```
<HTML>
<HEAD>
<BODY>
<%
Dim obj
Set obj = Server.CreateObject("asp2307.comp")

' call method
Dim str
str = obj.encodeString("<h1>Hello</h1>")
Response.Write str
Response.Write("<P>")

' change encode
obj.m_encode = "URL"
str = obj.encodeString("http://www.somecompany.com?test=value")
Response.Write str
%>
</BODY>
</HTML>
```

The result of running this example is a page with two encoded strings, similar to the following:

```
<h1>Hello</h1>
http%3A%2F%2Fwww%2Esomecompany%2Ecom%3Ftest%3Dvalue
```

So far, all of the examples we have looked at have used VBScript for the scripting language. However, script components can use other scripting languages such as JScript, demonstrated next.

Creating Script Components with JScript

Scripting components can be written in other ASP scripting languages such as JScript. The WSC elements are exactly the same, only the scripting language is changed with the SCRIPT element, and the script itself is written in the new language.

There is one difference between VBScript components and those created using JScript. With JScript, you must define a new JavaScript object and assign the methods defined for the component to this new object. To better understand this, use the WSC Wizard to create a new component named *asp2308.wsc*, with a progid set to asp2308.jscomp. In the second page of the wizard, instead of picking VBScript, click on the JScript radio button, as shown in Figure 23-4.

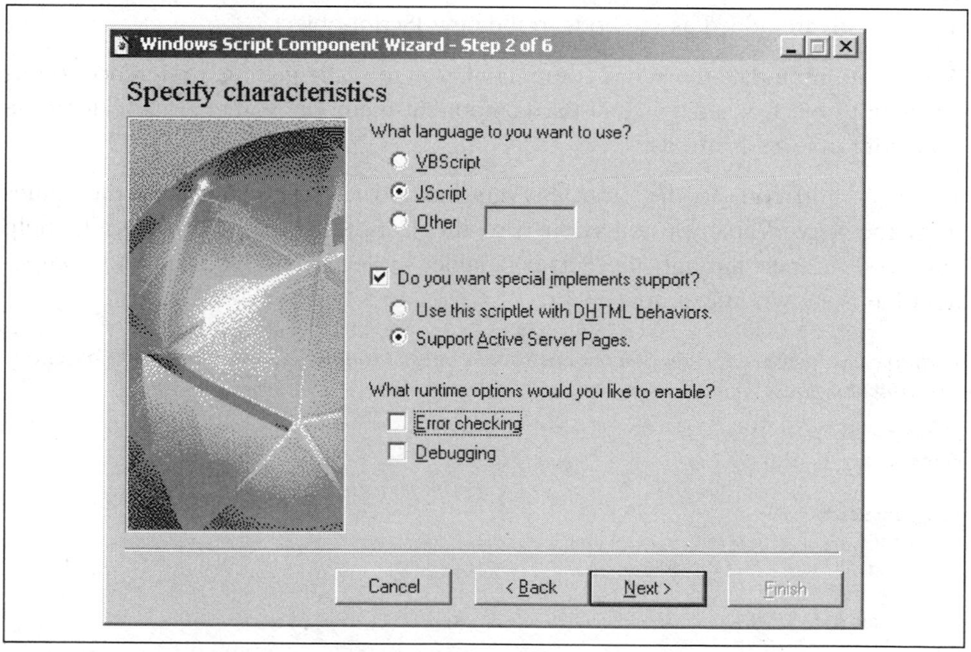

Figure 23-4. WSC Wizard page defining characteristics of a new component

The new component that we're creating will have one method that lists the name-value pairs in the Request object's ServerVariables collection. However, how the values are listed differs from earlier examples—a component property holds a value that determines which HTML tag is used to separate the values. This property could be set to the HTML break tag (<br>) or to the HTML paragraph tag (<P>).

In the property definition page of the wizard, name the new property m_break, set it to be read/write, and give it a default value of **
**. In the method definition page of the wizard, name the new method prntAllSrvVars; it takes no parameters.

The file that's generated is very similar to the one we generated earlier for Example 23-12, but this time a new method is added to the file: a constructor for the object with the same name as the ASP component itself, in this case **asp2308**. This JavaScript object is necessary to access the component and its methods and properties as an object; without this constructor the component wouldn't work:

```
var description = new asp2308;

function jscomp()
{
    this.get_m_break = get_m_break;
    this.put_m_break = put_m_break;

    this.prntAllSrvVars = prntAllSrvVars;
}
```

The component property get and set methods, as well as the component's external method, are added as methods to the new JScript object.

When you instantiate the script component, you're really getting a reference to this JavaScript object; when you call the component methods, you're really calling the JavaScript object's methods.

To finish, add code to the prntAllSrvVars method to access and print the values from the ServerVariables collection. Use the JScript **Enumerator** object to help your code iterate through the ServerVariables collections. The complete component file is shown in Example 23-14.

Example 23-14. JScript Script Component That Iterates Through the ServerVariables Collection, Printing Out Each Value

```
<?xml version="1.0"?>
<component>

<registration
    description="jscomp"
    progid="asp2308.jscomp"
    version="1.00"
    classid="{135e517d-ccd3-4270-a589-e6e8cd9c5204}"
>
</registration>

<public>
    <property name="m_break">
        <get/>
        <put/>
    </property>
```

Example 23-14. JScript Script Component That Iterates Through the ServerVariables Collection, Printing Out Each Value (continued)

```
    <method name="prntAllSrvVars">
    </method>
</public>

<implements type="ASP" id="ASP"/>

<script language="JScript">
<![CDATA[

var description = new asp2308;

function asp2308()
{
    this.get_m_break = get_m_break;
    this.put_m_break = put_m_break;

    this.prntAllSrvVars = prntAllSrvVars;
}

var m_break = "<BR>";

function get_m_break()
{
    return m_break;
}

function put_m_break(newValue)
{
    m_break = newValue;
}

function prntAllSrvVars()
{

  //Create an Enumerator object.
  var myvars = new Enumerator(Request.ServerVariables);

  //Iterate
  while (!myvars.atEnd())
  {
    var x  = myvars.item();
    Response.Write(x + " = " + Request.ServerVariables(x) + m_break);
    myvars.moveNext();
  }
}

]]>
</script>

</component>
```

To test the new JScript component, create a new ASP test page in a file named *asp2308.asp*, as shown in Example 23-15. In the page, the JScript object is instantiated, and the prntAllSrvVars method is called. The component's m_break property is changed to the HTML paragraph tag (<P>) and prntAllSrvVars is called again.

Example 23-15. Creating a JScript Script Component, Setting Its Properties, and Calling Its Methods

```
<HTML>
<HEAD>
<BODY>
<%
Dim obj
Set obj = Server.CreateObject("asp2308.jscomp")

obj.prntAllSrvVars

obj.m_break = "<p>"

obj.prntAllSrvVars
%>
</BODY>
</HTML>
```

The web page returned from the test page contains two listings of the Request object's ServerVariables collection: the first listing shows the values separated by line breaks (through the use of <BR>); the second shows the values separated by paragraphs (through the use of <P>).

Accessing Windows 2000 Functionality

Scripting component access isn't limited to just ADO and the built-in ASP objects—you can access much of the Windows 2000 functionality, such as Active Directory and MSMQ.

Chapter 13, *Working with MSMQ Components*, has a component written in Visual Basic that has a method that wrote three messages to a specific MSMQ message queue. The method was shown in Example 13-5 and is repeated here in Example 23-16 for ease of comparison.

Example 23-16. Original VB Component—Sending a String Message to a Queue

```
Sub sendStringMessage(ByVal strQueue As String, _
                ByVal strLabel As String, _
                ByVal strMessage As String)

Dim qInfo As New MSMQQueueInfo
Dim qQueue As MSMQQueue
Dim qMessage As New MSMQMessage
```

Example 23-16. Original VB Component—Sending a String Message to a Queue (continued)

```
' open queue for sending
qInfo.PathName = ".\" & strQueue
qInfo.Label = strLabel
Set qQueue = qInfo.Open(MQ_SEND_ACCESS, MQ_DENY_NONE)

If qQueue.IsOpen = 1 Then
  ' define message
  qMessage.Body = strMessage

  ' now send it
  qMessage.Send qQueue

  ' close queue
  qQueue.Close
End If

End Sub
```

The component also had a method that then accessed the message queue and wrote the messages to the web page. This method was shown in Example 13-6, and is repeated here in Example 23-17.

Example 23-17. Original VB Component—Method to Get All Messages on a Specific Queue and Print the Message If It's a String Type

```
Sub readStringMessage(ByVal strQueue As String, _
                      ByVal strLabel As String)

' get response object from objectcontext
Dim objContext As ObjectContext
Dim objResponse As Response

Set objContext = GetObjectContext()
Set objResponse = objContext("Response")

Dim qInfo As New MSMQQueueInfo
Dim qQueue As MSMQQueue
Dim qMessage As MSMQMessage
Dim varObject As Variant

' open queue for reading
qInfo.PathName = ".\" & strQueue
qInfo.Label = strLabel
Set qQueue = qInfo.Open(MQ_RECEIVE_ACCESS, MQ_DENY_RECEIVE_SHARE)

' check to see if queue is open
' if it is, receive first message which removes message from queue
If qQueue.IsOpen = 1 Then
  Set qMessage = qQueue.Receive(ReceiveTimeout:=500)

  ' loop through messages
  While Not (qMessage Is Nothing)
    varObject = qMessage.Body
```

*Example 23-17. Original VB Component—Method to Get All Messages on a Specific Queue and
Print the Message If It's a String Type (continued)*

```
      If TypeName(varObject) = "String" Then
         objResponse.Write varObject
      End If
      objResponse.Write "<br>"
      Set qMessage = qQueue.Receive(ReceiveTimeout:=500)
   Wend

   ' close queue
   qQueue.Close
End If

End Sub
```

To see for yourself that most Visual Basic ASP components can port to VBScript
scripting components, you'll port this component from Visual Basic to a new
scripting component—with no change in functionality.

First, create a new file named *asp2309.wsc* and add the registration section, providing a progid of `asp2309.msmq`. Following this, add two **METHOD** definitions:
one for a method called sendStringMessages that has three **PARAMETER** elements,
and one for a method named readStringMessages with two **PARAMETER** elements.

The scripting component implements ASP and also includes a reference to the
`MSMQ.MSMQMessage` object to have access to the MSMQ type library constants.

As shown in Example 23-18, the scripting component subroutines are virtually
identical to those created in Visual Basic. In fact, the subroutines are direct copies
of the VB methods, except for three key differences. First, all data types are
removed, since VBScript supports only the Variant data type. Second, the instances
of `MSMQQueueInfo` and `MSMQMessage` that were created using the **New** operator in
VB must be created using the *CreateObject* automation method in VBScript.
Finally, the technique of assigning a specific optional argument in VB using a
named argument, as in:

```
   qQueue.Receive(ReceiveTimeout:=500)
```

is not supported in VBScript. Instead, leave the optional parameters blank until
you get to the parameter you want to utilize:

```
      Set qMessage = qQueue.Receive(, , ,500)
```

Other than handling these three differences and providing the WSC framework,
there are no other code modifications necessary to port the VB component to a
scripting component.

Example 23-18. Scripting Component Ported from Existing VB Component

```
<?xml version="1.0"?>
<component>
```

Example 23-18. Scripting Component Ported from Existing VB Component (continued)

```
<registration
    description="Developing ASP Components -- MSMQ"
    progid="asp2309.msmq"/>

<public>
    <method name="sendStringMessage">
        <parameter name="strQueue" />
        <parameter name="strLabel" />
        <parameter name="strMessage" />
    </method>
    <method name="readStringMessage">
        <parameter name="strQueue" />
        <parameter name="strLabel" />
    </method>
</public>

<implements type="ASP"/>

<reference object="MSMQ.MSMQMessage" />

<script language="VBScript">
<![CDATA[

' send messages
Sub sendStringMessage(ByVal strQueue, _
                ByVal strLabel, _
                ByVal strMessage)

Dim qInfo
Dim qQueue
Dim qMessage

Set qInfo = CreateObject("MSMQ.MSMQQueueInfo")
Set qMessage = CreateObject("MSMQ.MSMQMessage")


' open queue for sending
qInfo.PathName = ".\" & strQueue
qInfo.Label = strLabel
Set qQueue = qInfo.Open(MQ_SEND_ACCESS, MQ_DENY_NONE)

If qQueue.IsOpen = 1 Then
  ' define message
  qMessage.Body = strMessage

  ' now send it
  qMessage.Send qQueue

  ' close queue
  qQueue.Close
End If

End Sub
```

Example 23-18. Scripting Component Ported from Existing VB Component (continued)

```
' read messages
Sub readStringMessage(ByVal strQueue, _
                      ByVal strLabel)
Dim qInfo
Dim qQueue
Dim qMessage
Dim varObject

Set qInfo = CreateObject("MSMQ.MSMQQueueInfo")
Set qMessage = CreateObject("MSMQ.MSMQMessage")

' open queue for reading
qInfo.PathName = ".\" & strQueue
qInfo.Label = strLabel
Set qQueue = qInfo.Open(MQ_RECEIVE_ACCESS, MQ_DENY_NONE)

' check to see if queue is open
' if it is receive first message which removes message from queue
If qQueue.IsOpen = 1 Then
   Set qMessage = qQueue.Receive(, , ,500)

   ' loop through messages
   While Not (qMessage Is Nothing)
      varObject = qMessage.Body
      If TypeName(varObject) = "String" Then
         Response.Write varObject
      End If
      Response.Write "<br>"
      Set qMessage = qQueue.Receive(, , ,500)
   Wend

   ' close queue
   qQueue.Close
End If

End Sub
]]>
</script>

</component>
```

After you've added the code in Example 23-18 to *asp2309.wsc*, register it.

To test the scripting component, first create a test queue to use. You'll use the existing component created in Chapter 13, `asp1301.msgqueue`, to create the component. It can be accessed using the following ASP page, *asp2309.asp*:

```
<%
Dim obj
Set obj = Server.CreateObject("asp1301.msgqueue")
obj.newPublicQueue "wsc", "Scripting Component"

%>
```

Next, to add messages to the new queue, call the scripting component's send-StringMessages method from the following ASP page, *asp2310.asp*:

```
<%
Dim obj
Set obj = Server.CreateObject("asp2309.msmq")

obj.sendStringMessage "wsc", "Scripting Component", _
                                    "This is the first message"
obj.sendStringMessage "wsc", "Scripting Component", _
                                    "This is the second message"
obj.sendStringMessage "wsc", "Scripting Component", _
                                    "This is the third message"
%>
```

Finally, call the scripting component's readStringMessages method from a third ASP test page, *asp2311.asp*:

```
<%
Dim obj
Set obj = Server.CreateObject("asp2309.msmq")

obj.readStringMessage "wsc", "Scripting Component"

%>
```

When you access *asp2311.asp*, three lines should print to the web page:

```
This is the first message
This is the second message
This is the third message
```

Once you've ported the MSMQ VB component to a scripting component, take a look at the other Visual Basic components shown in Chapters 7 through 13. You'll find that many of these examples should port, with similar, minor modifications, to scripting components written in VBScript, and even other supported scripting languages.

A

ASP Built-in Object Quick Reference

The built-in ASP objects provide the interaction between the server application and the client and with the environment. Normally, the objects are accessed from within script instead of within components, but there might be times—such as when a component processes a form's contents—when you'll want to access the ASP objects from within your components.

This appendix covers the basic ASP objects you'd access from within components, including demonstrations of the objects' methods and properties using VBScript and JScript.

The Application Object

The Application object is used to create variables and values that are accessible by all sessions and all users of a common ASP application. Remember that an ASP application consists of all the ASP files within a virtual ASP directory and all subdirectories contained within this same directory. An Application object is created when the first page of the ASP application is accessed by a client after the web server for the application is started. The Application object lasts until the web server is shut down. As the Application object's sole purpose is to provide a common area for sharing information, it has two methods, Lock and Unlock, which are used to lock the Application object while one of the object's data values is being modified and to free it so that it can be accessed by other processes. The Application object also has two collections, Contents and StaticObjects, which contain values that are declared within server-side scripts and within the *Global.asa* file, respectively.*

---

* If you are not familiar with the term *collection*, it is a predefined array structure used to hold known types of data structures, both complex and simple.

The Application object also has two events, Application_OnEnd and Application_OnStart. Code can be created to provide event handling whenever the ASP application is started or at the application's end. Again, these events can be coded using script within the *Global.asa* file.

The Global.asa File and StaticObjects

Each ASP application has one, and only one, *Global.asa* file, and it is located in the root directory for the application. Your application can use it to add scripted events at the application or session level and to add application- and session-level component instances to the ASP application.

An *application component* is an instance of an ASP object that exists for the life of the application and is shared by all sessions accessing the same application. An example of such a component is a counter, which is incremented each time a particular page is accessed or some other activity occurs. This component is not reset for each person, but once for the application itself or for some other significant event. When all pages within the application access the component, they are accessing the same component and the same value. Additionally, the component can be persisted, with the value periodically saved to a file in case some problem occurs and the ASP application or the web server hosting the application is stopped. When the application is restarted, the saved value is accessed and the counting process begins from that point.

Note that an ASP application is started when a page within the application is accessed, not when the web server hosting the application is started.

To follow through on the counter example and to demonstrate how to create an application-level component, Microsoft has created a Counters ASP component that can be used anytime some form of counter is needed. The syntax to add this component to the application is the following:

```
<OBJECT RUNAT=Server Scope=Application ID=PgCounter PROGID="MSWC.Counters">
</OBJECT>
```

The `Scope` attribute can take two values, Application or Session, depending on whether the component is available for the entire application or only the specific session. The `ID` is the identifier for the component instance and is the name used to access the component from the Application object at runtime. The `PROGID` is the program ID for the component class. Either a program ID or a specific CLSID must be specified for the component. The format for the program ID is *vendor.component.version*, with the vendor and version parts being optional, as long as the values correspond to the registry entry for the component. A class ID follows the format for an OLE class identifier, explained in more detail in Chapter 3, *ASP Components and COM*. The value for RUNAT is fixed at this time and only takes the value of Server.

Once a component, in this case the Counter object instance, has been created within the *Global.asa* file, any page within the entire ASP application can access it using syntax similar to the following:

```
<% PgCounter.Set("ItemRF45",0) %>
There have been <%= PgCounter.Increment("ItemRF45") %>
copies of Item RF45 sold
```

In the example, the first line of server-side script sets the value of the counter to zero (0). The second line increments the existing counter and then prints out the results. Regardless of which ASP application page accessed the *PgCounter* counter, the value set for the counter item ItemRF45 will be the same for all the pages.

The StaticObjects collection of the Application object contains references to all object instances created using the <OBJECT> tag within the *Global.asa* file. It is provided as a means to iterate through all component instances created within *Global.asa* and check for the existence of component instances, perhaps in an application administration page that lets an administrator quickly see what component instances have been added. Code for this display might be similar to the following:

```
<%
Dim obj
For Each obj in Application.StaticObjects %>
   Object Instance : <%= obj %> <p>
<% Next %>
```

In this example, each object is printed out to the web page returned to the client.

With ASP 3.0, you can remove items from a collection using the Remove method to remove a specific item or the RemoveAll method to remove all members of the Contents collection:

```
Application.Contents.RemoveAll
```

The advantage of using the <OBJECT> tag to create application-level components is that all of the components are declared and maintained in one place. Also, the component instance can be referenced directly, rather than having to be prefaced with the Session or Application object, as will be demonstrated in the next section. Finally, there is an improvement in application performance when a component instance is defined with the <OBJECT> tag, since this type of component is not instantiated until it is accessed. A component instance created using the CreateObject method, discussed next, is created instantly. This has little impact on an application-level component, but it can make a difference with session-level components.

Application Variables and Objects and the Contents Collection

To create a variable that is available to all sessions of a specific application, you can also use the following syntax:

```
<% Application("counter1") = 0 %>
<% Set Application("PageCounter") = Server.CreateObject("MSWC.PageCounter") %>
```

The first line of code shows how to create a scalar variable that is available throughout the application. The second line of code creates a reference to an object instance that is available for application-wide access. Both statements create an entry within the Application object's Contents collection, unlike objects created in the *Global.asa* file, which adds entries to the StaticObjects collection. However, code can access the values in this collection in the same manner as values are accessed in StaticObjects, as the following code demonstrates:

```
The counter is <%= Application.Contents("counter1") %>
<% Set tmp = Application.Contents("PageCounter") %>
The page has been visited <%= tmp %> times
```

Application components created using CreateObject can also be accessed directly from the Application object, as the following demonstrates:

```
The counter is <%= Application("counter1") %>
<% Set tmp = Application("PageCounter") %>
The page has been visited <%= tmp %> times
```

The Application object reference must be used with objects created using CreateObject.

A handy technique to use to set initial values when an application starts is to code for the Application_OnStart event within *Global.asa* and then access the application global values throughout the application, as shown in the following short scripting block:

```
<SCRIPT LANGUAGE=VBscript RUNAT=Server>
Sub Application_OnStart
    Application("tst") = "value1"
    Application("second") = "value2"
End Sub

</SCRIPT>
```

The Application object's Application_OnEnd event can also be trapped to code for handling of application-level values, perhaps by storing the values in files in order to maintain some form of persistence for the item.

Using the Lock and Unlock Methods

One problem with variables or objects that can be modified by different people at the same time is that one person may access a variable and modify the variable at exactly the same time another person accesses the same variable and performs the same modification. The following scenario demonstrates the unexpected results:

1. Person A accesses the page with Application counter `itemRF8`, which tracks the number of RF8 items that have been ordered. There are only 9 of these items for sale, and 8 have been sold, so Person A can safely order item RF8. The person places an order for the item.

2. In the meantime, Person B accesses the same page and wants to order the same item. As the Application counter is not locked, she accesses this counter and sees, as did Person A, that there is still one RF8 item for sale. This person, too, places an order for the item.

3. Person A's order has incremented the RF8 item counter as a part of the order process, effectively blocking any other order from going through for the item, since the total available is compared to the total sold for any item before an order is allowed. However, Person B's order has been allowed, since the number of items sold when Person B accessed the data was 8.

4. During order processing for Person B, the item counter is incremented, meaning that the item counter is now set to a value of 10, and Person B has effectively ordered something that doesn't exist. Person B is not happy when she doesn't receive her item, needless to say.

An ASP developer does not want an updateable value to be accessed at the same time that an update occurs. To prevent this, the Application methods Lock and Unlock are used to lock out all access to the Application item until the update has occurred. For the scenario just demonstrated, the code to perform this action is the following:

```
<%
If (Application("itemRF8") < 9 Then
  Application.Lock
  Application("itemRF8") = Application("itemRF8") + 1
  Application.Unlock
End If
%>
```

A note of warning with the use of Lock and Unlock: when you lock the Application object, you lock the object for all Application variables for all sessions. You will want to lock and unlock the Application object quickly and minimize the amount of code to run while the Application object is locked. Ideally, the only code that should be run while the Application object is locked is the code to modify the Application variable value.

As stated earlier, Application components and variables last the lifetime of the Application object. Session components and variables last for a specific session; they are detailed next.

The Session Object

If the Application object manages object instances and variables at the ASP application level, the Session object manages object instances and variables at the session level. Session-level variables can be created for such uses as maintaining a running balance for an online store, maintaining a connection to a client through many ASP application pages, or even tracking the flow of a transaction to determine if all the transaction's actions have completed successfully or not.

Unlike the Application object, a Session object is unique to a session and thus is uniquely accessed by one client. Because of this, the Session object does not need to be locked and unlocked during updates: only one client accesses any one session variable or object at a time. Instead of the Lock and Unlock methods, the Session object has a method called Abandon which can be used to destroy all Session objects and release Session resources. Normally, the Session objects would be freed when the session timed out, but if the ASP developer has an explicit logout page, the Abandon method could be called to free up Session resources prior to a timeout.

Another difference between the Session object and the Application object is how object information is maintained. Application information is maintained by the application web server and is not affected by any client-side setting. Session state, however, is maintained using client-side cookies and works only if the client accessing the ASP application supports cookies and allows cookies to be set.[*] The SessionID that identifies the particular session is stored as a cookie and maintains a connection between the client and the session variables stored on the web server. If cookies are not supported or allowed, this SessionID property cannot be maintained.

---

[*] If you haven't worked with web development, a *cookie* is a small bit of information that is stored for a set period of time on the client machine and is stored as a named value and keyed by the ASP application path.

ASP server-side scripting sets certain properties, such as the CODEPAGE property (which is discussed in this section), using directives. Directives begin with an at sign (@) and are usually the first line within the ASP page or the first line of a server-side scripting block. An example of setting a directive that changes the scripting language is the following, which changes the scripting language from the default VBScript to JScript:

```
<%LANGUAGE=Jscript …%>
```

Properties that can be set with directives are CODEPAGE, ENABLESESSIONSTATE, LANGUAGE, LCID, and TRANSACTION. If the directive is not set, a default value is provided.

In addition to the SessionID property, other Session properties are the following:

CodePage

Sets the codepage to be used for the ASP file. A code page is for support of internationalization and includes characters and glyphs specific to a language and a locale. A default code page can be set in the @CODEPAGE directive.

LCID

The locale identifier. This identifier is a standard locale identifier used to display locale-specific content.

Timeout

The specific time period that determines when the session ends. If the client has not accessed a page within the ASP application before the time period ends, the session is ended. The default time period is 20 minutes.

Internationalization

As you can see, two of the Session properties have to do with support for internationalization, a concept to keep in mind when creating your own components. Consider whether they are to be accessed by English-speaking people only or whether they must support a broader audience. If they must support a multilingual audience, check out the internationalization topics for ASP applications at Microsoft's Developer Network pages, at *http://msdn.microsoft.com.*

Like the Application object, the Session object has both a StaticObjects collection, containing all objects defined using the <OBJECT> tag in *Global.asa*, and a Contents collection. As both collections behave identically for the Session object as for the Application object, and the only difference is application scope, I won't go into detail on these objects, except to demonstrate how the Session object variables and object instances are created.

To create a Session-level component in the *Global.asa* file, use the following syntax:

```
<OBJECT RUNAT=Server Scope=Session ID=PgCounter PROGID="MSWC.Counters">
</OBJECT>
```

This actually creates a counter that is available for the session only.

To create a Session variable using a script block, use syntax like this:

```
<% Session("variable1") = "somevalue" %>
<% Set Session("object1") = Server.CreateObject("MSWC.Counters") %>
```

Finally, to access objects created using the <OBJECT> tag, the ASP web developer can use the StaticObjects collection. To access objects and variables created using scripts, the ASP web developer can use the Contents collection or access the value directly from the Session object, as shown in the following code block:

```
<%
Dim obj
For Each obj in Session.StaticObjects %>
  Object Instance : <%= obj %> <p>
<% Next %>
...

<% Session("itemRF8") = 1 %>
<% Session.Contents("itemRF8") = 1 %>
...
There have been <%= Session("itemRF8") %> items sold
```

As with the Application object, there are restrictions on which threading model can be used with Session-level variables; you can read about this in Chapter 4, *ASP Components, Threads, and Contexts.*

 Again, whether to create session component instances using <OBJECT> tags or CreateObject is up to the ASP developer, but there is a performance improvement to using the <OBJECT> tags when creating session-level components. Additionally, application maintenance can be easier, since all application and session component instances are created in the same place. A good choice is to use the <OBJECT> tags to create both application and session component instances.

The Server Object

The Server object is used to create instances of server component objects, which can then be used within another component or within an ASP page. This includes any of the ASP components demonstrated in this book. Components must be instantiated before any of the component's properties or methods are accessed.

There are actually two different techniques that can be used to create an ASP component instance, as was demonstrated in the previous two sections. The first is to use the <OBJECT> tag in the *Global.asa* file. The second uses the CreateObject method of the Server object and assigns the results to a variable, as the following code demonstrates:

```
<% Set PageCounter = Server.CreateObject("MSWC.PageCounter") %>
```

The ASP PageCounter component counts the number of times a web page is accessed. This count is maintained within a file, and the file path and name are stored as part of a Registry key. Once a local *page-level* reference to the Page-Counter object is created, it can then be used to access the methods for this object, in this case Hits, to access the number of page hits, and Reset, to set the counter back to zero. The value returned from the Hits method can then be displayed within the page, as the following code shows, or used for other purposes:

```
You are visitor <strong>#<%= PageCounter.Hits %></strong> to
access this web page. I bet you really wanted to know this,
didn't you?
```

When the PageCounter component instance was created, it was defined to be of local page scope only, meaning that the variable is destroyed when the web page is unloaded.

The other methods for the Server object, in addition to CreateObject, are the following:

HTMLEncode

Takes a string as a parameter and returns the same string with HTML encoding

MapPath

Maps a virtual or relative path to a path relative to the directory of the ASP file being accessed

URLEncode

Takes a string as a parameter and returns the same string with URL encoding

If you have worked much with web applications, you are probably familiar with URL and HTML encoding, and may want to skip the next few paragraphs.

Both HTTP and HTML have reserved characters, such as the angle brackets for HTML and the plus sign (+) for HTTP. When these characters are used in a text stream, such as name-value pairs appended to an URL to be sent to an application, or within a web page, the reserved characters need to be encoded. This ensures that the web server does not process the characters in the URL stream, and the browser does not process the HTML reserved characters contained within the web document. The characters are encoded as their hexadecimal equivalent, or they can be encoded using predefined alias values. For instance, the HTMLEncode method applied to a string such as:

```
<%= Server.HTMLEncode("<H1>This is a header</H1>") %>
```

would print out a line in the web document as follows:

```
&lt;H1&gt;This is a header&lt;/H1&gt;
```

but it would appear to the user viewing the web page in a browser as:

```
<H1>This is a header</H1>
```

rather than being processed as a header element and displaying the text as larger, bolder script.

URL encoding relates to the text appended to an URL. Certain characters in the text string have special meaning, such as the ampersand (&), which indicates an additional name-value pair, or the equals sign (=), which separates the name-value pair. Even spaces are encoded using the plus sign (+), meaning that a literal plus sign within the text must itself be encoded.

An example of using the Server object URLEncode method to encode a string to attach to an URL is shown in Example A-1. This small ASP page uses URLEncode to create a set of name-value pairs, which are then attached to an URL within a link in the page.

Example A-1. Using the Server Object's URLEncode Method

```
<%@ LANGUAGE = javascript %>
<HTML>
<HEAD>
<TITLE>URL Encoding</TITLE>
</HEAD>
<BODY>
<%
value = Server.URLEncode("last name") + "=powers&" +
        Server.URLEncode("special characters")+"=" +
        Server.URLEncode("+% &/!=#") + "&address=" +
        Server.URLEncode("1243 Some Avenue North, Some City, VT, 00000") +
        "&" +
        Server.URLEncode("Some other special characters:")+"=" +
        Server.URLEncode("%/.. . ! = && .. \/#");
%>

<a href="asp_d02.asp?<% = value %>">Test</a>
</BODY>
</HTML>
```

This URL-encoded string contains four name-value pairs, as you can see when you view the source for this page. The target page, *asp_d02.asp*, then takes the name-value pairs and displays them to the client.

The only property that the Server object has is ScriptTimeout. This property can be set to the number of seconds that any one script can run within the application page, a useful technique to handle overly long scripting runs. If the script runs longer than the allocated time, it is terminated and an error message is written to the log file.

The IIS Metabase Values

A general attribute, `AspScriptTimeout`, is used to set the script timeouts generally for the web server. This attribute is one of the IIS Metabase values, which replace the need for registry entries. Metabase values, unlike Registry values, are preloaded into memory and have faster access times. To read more about the Metabase, consult the documentation that comes with IIS 4.0/5.0.

The Request Object

When a web page returns information to the server by appending it to a link or posting it from a form, the information is collected in the Request object. The only method the Request object has at this time is BinaryRead, which accesses the data passed with the Request object as bytes and stores the value in a SafeArray—an array that includes dimension information, such as bounds and the number of dimensions of an array. The only property for the Request object, aside from several collections which will be detailed in a moment, is TotalBytes. This property gives the total number of bytes sent in the client request.

The Request object includes references to the query string, form field values, digital certificate information, and predefined environment variables; each of these values can be accessed as a collection. Which type of collection to access depends on what type of information is needed within the ASP application and how the information was sent from the client. The following are the collections that have been defined for the Request object:

ClientCertificate
> Contains information about the client certificate, if a client certificate is requested by the server.

Cookies
> Contains Netscape-style cookies sent as part of the HTTP request. A cookie can contain multiple keys, each of which can be accessed as a group or individually.

Form

> Contains name-value pairs sent from a form using the POST form posting method. Each form element becomes one entry in the Form collection.

QueryString

> Contains name-value pairs sent using the form's GET posting method or appended to the end of the URL used to reference the ASP page. Each name-value pair becomes one entry in the QueryString collection.

ServerVariables

> Contains certain preselected environment variables, such as QUERY_STRING, REMOTE_ADDR, and REQUEST_METHOD.

The collections are stored as name-value pairs, and to access the value, you enter the name. For example, the following code will set a variable to a query string value with a given name of "lastname":

```
Dim Lastname
Lastname = Request.QueryString("lastname");
```

If the ASP page is opened using a hypertext link similar to the following, the value of "lastname" would be set to "Powers":

```
<A href="file.asp?lastname=powers&firstname=shelley">Open</a>
```

Each of the collections is discussed and demonstrated in detail in the following sections.

The ClientCertificate Collection

Server digital certificates are used to verify that a server application being accessed is from the originating server, that it has not been improperly modified, and that it is safe. Client certificates verify that the client is who the client claims to be. When a client accesses a secure application located on a secure server, the web server may then transmit the server digital certificate and request that the client submit the client's digital certificate. Once the client's certificate information is transmitted back to the server, a secure communication channel is established between the client and the server.

When the server requests a digital certificate, the Request object returns digital certificate information in the ClientCertificate collection. Instead of generic data, the ClientCertificate contains very specific information, detailed in the following list:

Certificate

> Contains all of the certificate as a binary string.

Flags

> Contain additional certificate information.

Issuer

Contains subject values for the digital certificate issuer that can be accessed independently, just as with the Subject collection item.

SerialNumber

Specifies the certificate serial number.

Subject

Contains subject values that can be accessed independently using the different subject field names. Among these subject field names are C for company name and L for locality.

ValidFrom

Specifies the start date for the certificate.

ValidUntil

Specifies the date when the certificate ends.

Before working with digital certificates, I suggest that you read the information on the certificate process at the Microsoft Developer Network web site, at *http://msdn.microsoft.com*.

The Cookies Collection

As stated earlier, the ASP Session object makes use of client-side cookies. In addition, the ASP developer can use client-side cookies to store persistent information that relates to the specific client. The information can then be accessed the next time the client accesses the ASP application.

Cookie information is accessed by the browser and by using the path of the document being loaded as a key to finding whether any cookies exist for the specific page within the client's cookie file or directory. If so, the cookie name-value pairs are added to the HTTP request for the page.

This same cookie information can be pulled from an HTTP request using the Cookies collection. The cookie can be a scalar value, accessible by name for the name-value cookie pair. Or the cookie can be part of a more complex cookie dictionary, with the value itself being another name-value pair.

To access a cookie, use the following syntax:

```
<% tmp = Request.Cookies("first") %>
```

In this example, if the cookie named **first** existed, the value for **first** would be returned; otherwise, an empty string would be returned. If the cookie itself contained a name-value pair, or *key*, the key value can be accessed using the following syntax:

```
<% tmp = Request.Cookies("first")("second") %>
```

Unlike array elements in the other collections, the Cookies collection assumes a named index for the second level of values. In addition, no other levels of values are supported. An attribute, 'HasKeys, can be used to determine if a cookie is a dictionary object or a scalar value. A value of **True** is returned if the cookie is a more complex object; a value of **False** is returned if the cookie is not a complex object.

Cookies can be created using client-side scripting, and this technique is explained in detail at both Netscape's and Microsoft's web sites. Cookies can also be created using server-side scripting and the Response object, discussed later in this chapter.

The Form Collection

If a form is posted using the **POST** method, the form field name-value pairs are added to the Form collection rather than the QueryString collection. Usually, an ASP developer will want to use the **POST** method rather than the **GET** method because there is a limitation on the length of the string that can be appended to an URL in a **GET** request. This length can easily be exceeded with a larger form. Additionally, it can be a bit intimidating to the client to see the long, encoded string attached to the URL.

There is absolutely no difference in how the Form name-value pairs are accessed compared to the QueryString pairs. The following code is how the values used in Example A-2 would be accessed if the form had been posted instead of submitted with **GET**:

```
<% name = Request.Form("name");
    address = Request.Form("address");
%>
```

A form field that can return multiple values can also have each value accessed individually using the index value, just as with QueryString:

```
<% street_address1 = Request.Form("streetaddr")(1) %>
```

Additionally, the entire form contents can be accessed by reference to the Form collection without providing a name with the Form collection. For collection arrays, the entire array can be returned as a comma-delimited string by referencing the array name without providing an array index:

```
<% street_address1 = Request.Form("streetaddr") %>
```

The QueryString Collection

The QueryString collection is an array containing name-value pairs and is parsed from the **QUERY_STRING** environment variable. Each specific entry within the collection is accessible by its position as it occurs in the collection or by its name.

This collection has entries only if the ASP page is opened as a result of a form request sent using the default **GET** method or if name-value pairs have been added to the URL to access the page.

 To add name-value pairs to an URL, the values must be URL encoded, as discussed earlier in the section "The Server Object."

As an example of accessing a value from the QueryString collection, if one page in the ASP application contains a form with a field named **name** and the form was posted using the **GET** method, accessing the specific field values can be done using the following:

```
<% name = Request.QueryString("name");
   address = Request.QueryString("address");
%>
```

As stated, another way that the QueryString collection gets name-value pairs is if the values are appended to the end of an URL, as was demonstrated in Example A-1. That example showed how to encode strings to append to the URL. The code in Example A-2 shows how the name-value pairs are accessed using the QueryString collection and then displayed in an HTML table.

Example A-2. Using the Request Object QueryString Collection

```
<HTML>
<HEAD>
<TITLE>QueryString</TITLE>
<STYLE type="text/css">
    BODY { margin: 0.5in }
</STYLE>
<BODY>
<H1> QueryString name-value pairs </H1>
<TABLE border=0 width=90% cellspacing=5>

   <% For Each name In Request.QueryString %>
   <TR><TD> <% = name %></TD><TD> <% =Request.QueryString(name) %></TD></TR>
   <% Next %>

</TABLE>
</BODY>
</HTML>
```

In this example, the page returned displays both the name of the name-value pair and its associated value.

If the same name is given more than one value within a query string, the ASP application creates an array of objects for a specific name within the QueryString collection. So if I use the following string within a hypertext link URL, I end up with a named array instead of a scalar value for the name test:

```
<a href="test.asp?test=one&test=two&test=three">Test</a>
```

To access the individual values for **test** requires code similar to the following:

```
<%
  test1 = Request.QueryString("test")(1);
  test2 = Request.QueryString("test")(2);
  test3 = Request.QueryString("test")(3);
%>
```

Notice that, unlike JavaScript arrays, the first index for a collection array begins with the value 1 instead of 0. Also, the QueryString collection object and array index references use parentheses instead of square brackets regardless of the scripting language used. The same holds true for all built-in object collections.

To find out if a specific element within the QueryString collection is an array object, you can access the Count property for the element, which returns the number of elements that make up the object. In the previous example, the following would print out the value 3:

```
The number of text objects is <%= Request.QueryString("test").Count %>
```

You can also access all of the values for a collection array element at once by accessing it without using an index. The value returned is a list of the values separated by commas. Additionally, if you want to access all of the QueryString data without parsing it, access the QueryString collection name directly without specifying a name:

```
The data sent is <%= Request.QueryString %>
```

Again, the result returned is the name-value pairs as sent with the original request.

The ServerVariables Collection

There are certain environment variables available with any HTTP client-server transaction. Some of the variables—such as QUERY_STRING, which contains the query string sent with an HTTP request—have been discussed already. Other values include cookies, the type of browser making the request, client certificate information, information about the remote connection, the client language, and a host of other information. All of these environment variables can be accessed via the ServerVariables collection.

Example A-3 has the code for an ASP page that displays the contents of the Server-Variables collection. Try this page in your own environment to see what information you have access to in your development effort.

Example A-3. Using the Request Object ServerVariables Collection

```
<HTML>
<HEAD>
<TITLE>Server Variables</TITLE>
<STYLE type="text/css">
    BODY { margin: 0.5in }
</STYLE>
<BODY>
<H1> Server Variables </H1>
<TABLE border=0 width=90% align=center cellspacing=5>
<% For Each name In Request.ServerVariables %>
<TR><TD> <% = name %></TD><TD> <% =Request.ServerVariables(name) %></TD></TR>
<% Next %>
</TABLE>
</BODY>
</HTML>
```

The environment variables accessible via the Request object are shown in Table A-1.

Table A-1. Members of the Request Object's ServerVariables Collection

Variable	Description
ALL_HTTP - HTTP	All HTTP headers sent by the client
ALL_RAW	All data sent in raw form by the client
APPL_MD_PATH	Metabase path for the application
APPL_PHYSICAL_PATH	Actual physical pathname for the application
AUTH_PASSWORD	Contains the password if Basic authentication is used
AUTH_TYPE	Authentication type
AUTH_USER	Authenticated user
CERT_COOKIE	Unique ID for a client certificate
CERT_FLAGS	Flags to determine if a certificate is present and valid
CERT_ISSUER	Client certificate issuer field
CERT_KEYSIZE	Secure Sockets Layer bit key size
CERT_SECRETKEYSIZE	Server certificate private bit key size
CERT_SERIALNUMBER	Certificate serial number
CERT_SERVER_ISSUER	Server certificate issuer
CERT_SERVER_SUBJECT	Server certificate subject
CERT_SUBJECT	Client certificate subject
CONTENT_LENGTH	Client content length, defined by the client
CONTENT_TYPE	Content data type, used with attached data only
GATEWAY_INTERFACE	The CGI revision
HTTPS	Set to on if request is from a secure server; otherwise set to off
HTTPS_KEYSIZE	SSL connection key size

Table A-1. Members of the Request Object's ServerVariables Collection (continued)

Variable	Description
HTTPS_SECRETKEYSIZE	Size of secure server certificate key size
HTTPS_SERVER_ISSUER	Secure server certificate issuer
HTTPS_SERVER_SUBJECT	Secure server certificate subject
INSTANCE_ID	IIS instance ID
INSTANCE_META_PATH	IIS instance Metabase path
LOCAL_ADDR	Server address of request
LOGON_USER	NT account user is logged into
PATH_INFO	Path information of ASP application page
PATH_TRANSLATED	A virtual to physical path translation
QUERY_STRING	The query string
REMOTE_ADDR	IP address of remote host
REMOTE_USER	Name supplied by user and without any filter being applied
REQUEST_METHOD	Method of request, such as GET or POST
SCRIPT_NAME	Virtual path of script
SERVER_NAME	IP or DNS alias of server; localhost is the loopback address of 127.0.0.1
SERVER_PORT	Name and revision of request port
SERVER_PORT_SECURE	Set to 0 if request is not through secure port, otherwise set to 1
SERVER_PROTOCOL	Request information protocol, such as HTTP/1.0
SERVER_SOFTWARE	The web server; the examples in this book were run against Microsoft-IIS/4.0 Beta 2, which is the second beta release for IIS, version 4.0
URL	Base URL

There are several variables that appear in the ServerVariables collection when the code from Example A-3 is run, but that are not documented in the ASP documentation. These all have to do with the HTTP request, such as the HTTP cookie, HTTP host, and language. As undocumented variables can be dropped or altered without advance notice from Microsoft, I won't document them here.

Accessing a Value Without a Collection

Values can be accessed directly from the Request object, rather than having to use any of the collections. The web server searches through the collections in a specific order and returns the first value for the given name that it finds. So, if the ASP developer enters a name request as follows:

```
<% tmp = Request("temp") %>
```

the server first searches through the QueryString collection, then the Form collection, the Cookies collection, the ClientCertificate collection, and finally through ServerVariables. As the same name can be used for an object listed in more than one collection, it might be safer to use the collection name whenever the duplicate use of a name is possible.

The Response Object

If a *request* is information sent from the client to the server, a *response* is output to a client from the server, and the Response object is used to send this information. This can include HTTP header information, as well as output used to create the HTML web page. Because some of this information is part of the document header, some calls to Response object methods have to be made before any other HTML is written for the document page, unless Response buffering (discussed in the next section) is enabled.

Unlike the Request object, the Response object has only one collection, the Cookies collection. This collection allows for creating and setting the value of cookies on the client machine.

The following are the Response object properties:

Buffer
> A flag to determine whether Response output is buffered until the server script is finished processing or until a buffer output is forced

CacheControl
> A flag to determine whether proxy servers can cache ASP-generated output

Charset
> HTTP response character set

ContentType
> The HTTP content type; `text/HTML` by default

Expires
> Minutes before the ASP page content is expired

ExpiresAbsolute
> A specific date and time when the cached page contents are expired

IsClientConnected
> Whether the client is still connected after the last Response.Write method call

PICS
> PICS label field; PICS is a rating system used voluntarily by sites to rate the adult nature of content within the site

Status
> Three digit status line, such as 404 for file not found, returned by the server

The Response object methods are the following:

AddHeader
> Adds an HTML header to the response

AppendToLog
> Appends a string of up to 80 characters, not including any commas, to the log file for the response

BinaryWrite
> Writes data to output without any character conversion

Clear
> Clears the current buffered contents

End
> Ends server script processing and forces output of buffered contents

Flush
> Forces output of buffered contents and ends keep-alive requests for the page

Redirect
> Redirects the connection to a different URL

Write
> Writes output to the HTTP output; can be used within server scripting blocks

The following sections take a closer look at some of the more interesting properties and methods. The Cookies collection is also detailed in its own section.

Redirection

An HTTP header is always written first for any web page returned to a browser. Certain object methods can be used to alter this HTTP header, such as the Response object's Redirect method. The method takes an URL as a parameter and redirects the browser to another page:

```
Response.Redirect "http://www.yasd.com/plus.htm"
```

In addition to redirecting the browser to a different page, an HTTP status of 302 is also returned, which tells the browser that redirection is occurring since the object has moved.

When altering the header response, the code that makes the modification must be included before any other HTML for the ASP page, or an error occurs. This includes calling an ASP component that itself contains a method call that makes the modification. The only exception to this is through the use of buffering, discussed in the next section.

The Buffer Property and the Use of End, Clear, and Flush

One of the more important Response object properties is Buffer. The Buffer property is set to **True** when no response is sent to the client until all of the server-side scripting has been processed or until either the Flush or End methods have been called to output the buffer. Buffering output offers a number of advantages:

- Based on some script activity, different content can be displayed, or even an entirely different page can be opened, without any perceptible page flickering that can occur with normal page redirection.

- Buffering maintains a keep-alive connection between the server and the client, which means that any client requests are made in the same connection, thus eliminating the overhead from the server having to create multiple connections. Keep-alive requests are basically pings between the two ends of the connection that keep the connection open.

- Buffering allows modifications to the HTTP header from script blocks that are located throughout the page, without having to place the script blocks as the first content of the page. As stated earlier, modifications to the HTTP response must be made before the response is sent or an error occurs.

The disadvantage of page buffering is that no contents are displayed until the scripts are finished processing—and if the script processing takes a considerable amount of time, the client is going to be faced with a blank browser for longer than might be considered wise.

The buffer property must be set before any other output is sent to the client, so it should be the first line within the HTML document:

```
<% Response.Buffer = True %>
```

The buffer contents can be controlled by using three methods:]End, Clear, and Flush. The End method forces the web server to stop processing the server script and output the buffered results immediately. This is effective if the ASP developer wants to display the results up to a point in the script, but no further. The Clear method, on the other hand, does not force an end to buffering but will clear whatever contents are in the buffer at the time the method is called. The Flush method does not prevent scripts from processing, but it does force an output of the buffer contents, and the server no longer maintains keep-alive requests for the page.

A handy use of these buffer control methods is to process a script until an error occurs, clear the buffer contents so that they do not output to the page, and then call End to stop script processing. The Response headers, but not the Response body, are output:

```
<% Response.Clear
   Response.End
%>
```

Altering Output Using ContentType and Status

The simplest change to output can be setting the ContentType property to a different value. For example, if an HTML document normally has a ContentType of `text/html`, setting this value to `text/plain` causes most browsers to display HTML as text, including the markup tags, rather than interpreting the tags directly. This is a handy technique to use for links labeled "show source." The link would contain the following:

```
<a href="test.asp?source=1">Show Source</a>
```

The top of the document being opened could have logic to test whether source should be shown, and the content type set accordingly:

```
<%
If Request.QueryString("source") = 1 Then
    Response.ContentType = "text/plain"
Else
    Response.ContentType = "text/html"
End If
%>
```

Since the content type is part of the header, this block of server code must precede any other block, unless the Buffer property is set to **True** to allow for output buffering.

The Status property can be used to return any HTTP response status code, such as 404 File Not Found or 302 for File Redirected. Using a value of 401 Unauthorized can literally trigger a dialog for the user to enter a username and password. However, canceling the dialog allows access to the page, since security really has not been implemented; only the status returned to the browser has been modified.

The Response.Write Method and IsClientConnected Property

Probably one of the most effective Response methods is Write. In previous examples within this chapter, document output is created by using a combination of script blocks interspersed with regular HTML output. The advantage of the Write method is that the ASP developer does not have to "chop" up the scripting block in such a way that the code is difficult to read.

To demonstrate the improvement to readability that Write can make, the document shown in Example A-3 is rewritten to use the Write method and is shown in Example A-4.

Example A-4. Using the Request Object ServerVariables Collection

```
<HTML>
<HEAD>
<TITLE>Server Variables</TITLE>
<STYLE type="text/css">
    BODY { margin: 0.5in }
</STYLE>
<BODY>
<H1> Server Variables </H1>
<TABLE border=0 width=90% align=center cellspacing=5>
<%
For Each name In Request.ServerVariables
    Response.Write "<TR><TD>"
    Response.Write name
    Response.Write "</TD><TD>"
    Response.Write Request.ServerVariables(name)
    Response.Write "</TD></TR>"
Next
%>
</TABLE>
</BODY>
</HTML>
```

The page output is less choppy, with distinct separation between direct HTML output and server script-generated output. Additionally, the FOR loop is more distinct, making it clear what output is controlled by the loop and what output is located outside the loop. An improvement—and this is only a simple case.

A good rule of thumb to use when determining whether to use embedded script output or the Response object's Write method is, if the output must be controlled by some conditional or looping statement or traverses multiple lines, use the Write method. For simple variable assignment and one-statement outputs, use embedded script instead.

One last note before leaving the Response.Write method: if the script that is generating the output is time consuming, the client may actually disconnect between one Response.Write method call and another. In order to prevent a write to a disconnected client, use the IsClientConnected property to test if the client is still connected and then issue the Write method call if the property is set to True:

```
<%
If Response.IsClientConnected Then
    Response.Write ...
```

The Response Cookies Collection

The Response object's Cookies collection is used to send a cookie to the client, rather than pull cookie information from the client request. Cookies can be created to be scalar values, consisting only of one name-value pair, or the cookie can be a dictionary, with the value component being made up of other name-value pairs. If the cookie does not exist when it is set with the Response object, it is created.

As an example, the following sets the value of a cookie called test to be 1. In addition, it uses several Cookies collection attributes to determine how the cookie is created:

```
<%
Response.Cookies("test") = 1
Response.Cookies("test").Expires = "March 1, 2001"
Response.Cookies("test").Path = "/book/"
Response.Cookies("test").HasKeys = FALSE
%>
```

This code creates a cookie named test that has an initial value of 1. It expires on March 1, 2001, and has a relative path of */book/*, which means that it is sent with the HTTP request only when a page is accessed on this particular path. The cookie is a simple scalar value and does not have a key, so the HasKeys attribute is set to **FALSE**. Other properties that could have been used with this cookie are Domain, which sets the domain (such as *yasd.com*) of the cookie, and Secure, which sets whether this cookie is secure.

To create a more complex cookie, one that has keys, I could use the following:

```
<%
Response.Cookies("test")("value1") = 1
Response.Cookies("test")("value2") = 2
%>
```

In this case, the expiration is set to the default, which means the cookie will expire when the client closes the browser. The cookie attribute HasKeys is set to a value of **TRUE** by the fact that the cookie is created with key values.

New for ASP 3.0: Transfer and Execute

Starting with ASP 3.0, the Server object has two new methods: Transfer and Execute.

Transfer is used to transfer a current ASP page's state information to a second page. Unlike the Redirect method, control is not returned to the client first before the second page is displayed, and current state information—such as form or environment information—is also passed to the second page.

The Transfer method has one parameter, the path for the second ASP page:

```
Server.Transfer("/second.asp")
```

The Execute method is used to execute a second ASP, providing an ability to split a larger ASP application page into smaller pages and execute each ASP page in turn. This method, as with Transfer, takes one parameter, the path for the second ASP page:

```
Server.Execute("/second.asp")
```

Why haven't I covered ASPError? The primary reason is the specialized use of ASPError. You use this object to get error information within a specialized error-handling page. Because of its limited use, the ASPError is unlikely to be used within a component—components are usually used from more than one ASP page.

B

The Weaver Database

The first edition of this book used the SQL Server Pubs database for all data access examples, such as working with ActiveX Data Objects (ADO). However, there were a lot of readers who had Access on their development (and production) machines and didn't have SQL Server. So with this new edition, I've created a database for use with the examples in the book: the Weaver database.

The Weaver database stores information about web sites: web pages, images, scripting files, application pages, and so on. The database is based on the relational data model, and constraints have been added to both the Access and the SQL Server versions in order to enforce basic data integrity and relational constraints. I then preloaded test data from my own web sites into the database. Additionally, I also provided a simple ASP-based administrative application that you can use to stage your own data.

Installing Weaver

In the *Weaver* subdirectory of the book examples, there is an Access 2000 version of the database ready for you to use. Just move the file to your preferred location. For Access installations, you'll need to set up an ODBC DSN connection for the Access database using the ODBC Administration tool.

 See Microsoft documentation for how to use the ODBC Administration tool to create an ODBC DSN.

When you create the ODBC connection, set the DSN name to **weaver**. The username for the database should be set to **sa**, and no password should be required for either the Access or the SQL Server database for the Weaver administrative application to work.

If you want to use the SQL Server version of the database, then you'll need to install it. First, create a new, empty database and call it **Weaver**. Then, in the *Source* subdirectory of the *Weaver* directory, there is a file called *weavertables.sql* that has the SQL code necessary to create the Weaver database tables. Use the *isql.exe* application located in the *bin* directory of SQL Server (or whatever SQL tool you prefer) to open and execute this file within the Weaver database, to build the database tables. Don't worry if you receive errors when the table drops occur in the script—the errors don't impact the rest of the script execution, which then creates the tables just dropped.

Once the tables have been built, click on the new database in the SQL Server Enterprise tool and select Data Transformation Services → Import Data from the Tools menu.

When the DTS Import Wizard opens, set the data source to be a Microsoft Access database and select the Access version of Weaver to use. Leave the username and password blank, as shown in Figure B-1.

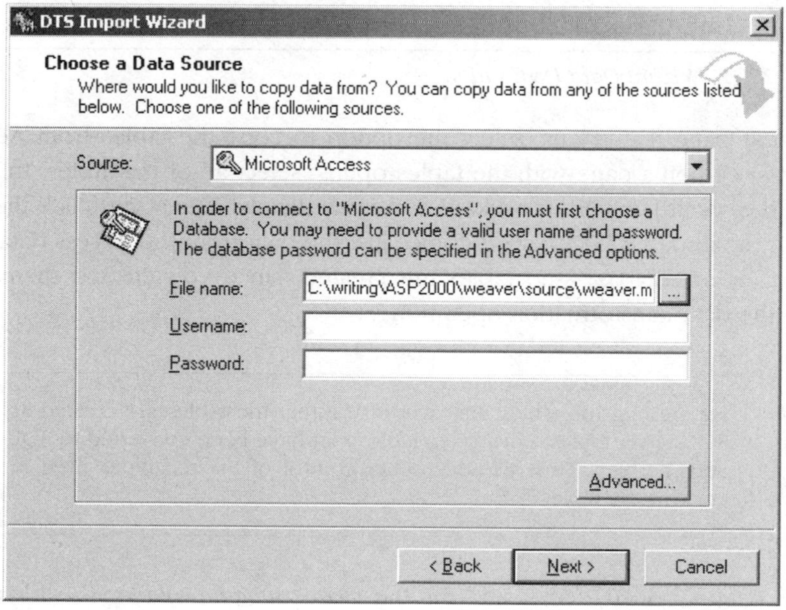

Figure B-1. DTS Wizard Data Source

For the destination of the data transfer, pick the OLE DB Provider for SQL Server and select your new Weaver database. Set the wizard to use SQL Server authentication, set the username to be **sa**, and leave the password blank, as shown in Figure B-2.

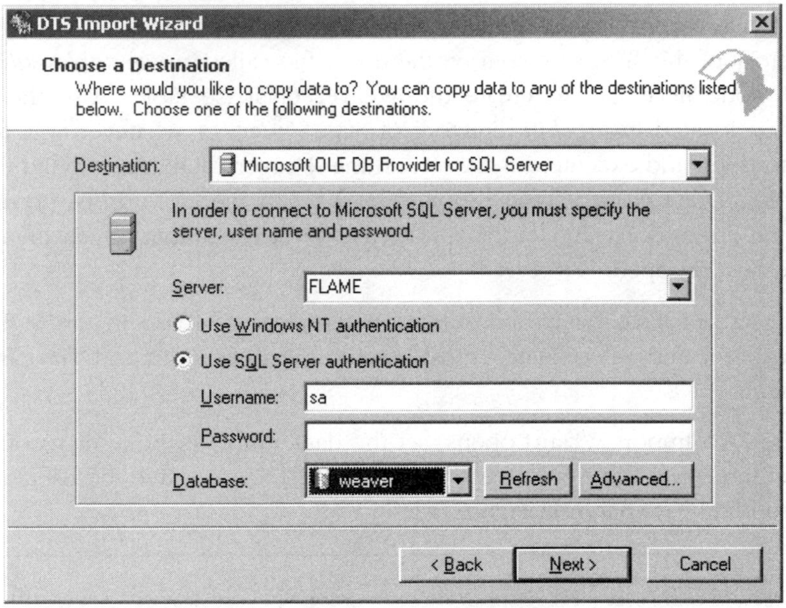

Figure B-2. DTS Wizard Data Destination

In the next page that opens, select the option to copy the tables from Access to SQL Server. When a page with the tables opens, select all of the tables. In the last page of the wizard, have the package run immediately. When you click the Finish button at the end, the DTS wizard copies just the data from the Access database to the SQL Server database—no tables are created, since you created them before running the data transformation operation.

> By creating the tables first, we ensure that the tables are created as SQL Server tables, not Access tables that have been converted to SQL Server tables. This provides better control of the datatypes used in creating the tables.

After the data is loaded, access and run the *weaverschema.sql* file. This file adds all of the relational and data constraints for the new database. These can't be added until after the data is loaded, or errors will occur during the data load process.

The Weaver Administration Application

The Weaver administration application ASP pages and the associated Visual Basic components are found in the *Weaver* subdirectory in the book examples. These pages make use of Visual Basic components in order to perform all data updates and queries, and the database connection strings used in the components are set to the ODBC version of Weaver:

```
m_connString = "DSN=weaver;uid=sa;pwd="
```

You can set the ODBC version to point to either the Access or the SQL Server Weaver database version. The only requirement is that the DSN (**weaver**), username (**sa**), and password (none) must match that of the connection string just shown.

If you're using the SQL Server database, you want to use the OLE DB Provider for SQL Server. If you have Visual Basic, you can open each of the Visual Basic component projects and change the connection string. Each component's ObjectControl_Activate method has the following commented-out SQL Server OLE DB connection string you can uncomment and adjust for your own environment:

```
m_connString="Provider=SQLOLEDB;server=FLAME;database=weaver;uid=sa;pwd="
```

If you don't have Visual Basic and are using SQL Server, set up an ODBC DSN for the SQL Server database so that the administration pages will work as is in your environment.

To use the Weaver administration application, you'll first need to create a new COM+ application in the Component Services administration tool. The VB components used in the application do use just-in-time activation, which means they must be used within the context of a COM+ application.

Chapter 5, *COM+ Services and ASP Components and Applications* has information about setting up and working with a COM+ application.

After creating the COM+ application, install each of the following Visual Basic component DLLs into this application:

Page.dll
Types.dll
Web.dll
WebPage.dll

After creating the COM+ application and adding the components, you'll next need to create an IIS virtual directory for the Weaver application. Do this by accessing the IIS management console and right-clicking on the Default Web Site. Select New → Virtual Directory from the menu. In the wizard that opens, name the web site *weaver* and have it point to the location where the ASP pages are stored (these can be found in the *Web* subdirectory of the *Weaver* directory). Accept the defaults for everything else.

After you've created the Weaver application web site, you can access it in your browser with the following URL if you're using *localhost* to access your web development environment:

```
http://localhost/weaver/
```

Before accessing the Weaver application, make sure that the database is running and accessible—an entry in the *global.asa* file for the Weaver application accesses the database to set an application variable as soon as the application is first started.

The main page of the application opens into a multicolored page with options to view, add, delete, or update most of the Weaver tables. Again, you don't have to use the Weaver administration application unless you want to add your own test data—the database that comes with the examples has test data already loaded.

The Weaver Database

Figure B-3 shows the Weaver database as captured by the SQL Server diagram tool.

As you can see in the diagram, the central table in the database is the WebPage table. This table is a category table, which means that it has a one-to-one association with several other tables: HtmlWebPage, StyleWebPage, AppWebPage, XmlWebPage, XmlAuxWebPage, and ScrptWebPage.

Every page in the database is a variation of a web page, but each type of page could have different data associated with it. For instance, a style page could have information about what type of style is used (XSL or CSS), and a script page could have a scripting language associated with it. To avoid having one large table with a whole lot of nullable fields, I created the WebPage table and associated it with the others.

So to add a new HTML page, you'd add the WebPage first and then add the associated HtmlWebPage entry. Again, there's always a one-to-one correspondence between the category and its associated dependent tables, and referential integrity requires that you insert records into the parent (WebPage) table first.

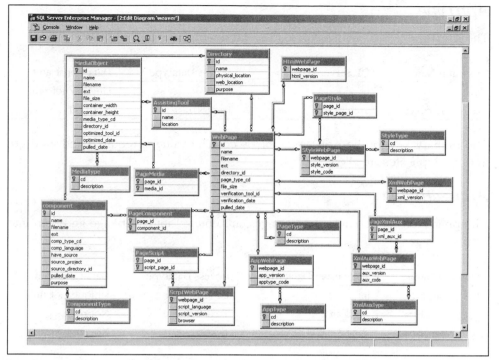

Figure B-3. Diagram of the Weaver database

To differentiate what type of page is in a particular WebPage row, a type field, `page_type_cd`, is set to reflect the type of page: HTM for an HTML page, STY for style page, SCR for scripting page, and so on.

Multimedia such as images can also be stored in the Weaver database in the MediaObject table. Multimedia is associated with a specific page through the Page-Media table, and the media types are found in the MediaType table.

Both pages and multimedia can be optimized, evaluated for compliance to standards, or both. This type of information is stored in the AssistingTool table, which has a foreign key relationship with both WebPage and MediaObject. Additionally, component information can be stored in the database in the Component table and associated with pages through the PageComponent association table.

Pages, multimedia objects, and components all have a physical and a web location, and this is found in the Directory table.

The sections that follow provide a detailed description of each table in the Weaver database.

AppType

The AppType table contains type codes and descriptions for application types.

Column Name	SQL Server Datatype	Access Datatype	Data Constraint
cd	char(3)	Text(3)	Unique/not null
description	varchar(50)	Text(50)	Not null

The primary key for the AppType table is cd. The value is required and indexed, and no duplicates are allowed.

AppWebPage

All application pages, such as ASP pages, are entered into WebPage and then into AppWebPage.

Column Name	SQL Server Datatype	Access Datatype	Data Constraint
webpage_id	int	Long Integer	Unique/not null
app_version	varchar(20)	Text(20)	Not null
apptype_code	char(3)	Text(3)	Not null

- The primary key for AppWebPage is webpage_id. The value is required and indexed, and no duplicates are allowed.

- There is a mandatory one-to-one foreign key relationship from the WebPage table to AppWebPage, reflected in webpage_id.

- There is a mandatory one-to-many foreign key relationship from the AppType table to AppWebPage, reflected in apptype_code. This column is indexed and duplicates are allowed.

AssistingTool

The AssistingTool table contains the names and locations of tools used to optimize or validate web content.

Column Name	SQL Server Datatype	Access Datatype	Data Constraint
id	int	Long Integer	Identity/AutoNumber Unique, not null
name	varchar(20)	Text(20)	Not null
location	varchar(50)	Text(50)	Not null

The primary key for the AssistingTool table is id. The value is an identify column in SQL Server and an AutoNumber column in Access—the value is automatically incremented when a new row is inserted.

Component

The Component table contains information about the components used within the web pages. This includes Java classes, applets, and COM-based objects.

Column Name	SQL Server Datatype	Access Datatype	Data Constraint
id	int	Long Integer	Identity/AutoNumber unique, not null
name	varchar(20)	Text(20)	Not null
filename	varchar(20)	Text(20)	Not null
ext	char(4)	Text(4)	Not null
comp_type_code	char(3)	Text(3)	Not null
comp_language	varchar(20)	Text(20)	Not null
have_source	bit	Yes/No	Not null, set to (1)/Yes by default
source_project	varchar(50)	Text(50)	Nulls allowed
source_directory_id	int	Long Integer	Nulls allowed
pulled_date	datetime	Date/Time	Nulls allowed
purpose	text	memo	Not null

- The primary key for the Component table is id. The value is an identify column in SQL Server and an AutoNumber column in Access—the value is automatically incremented when a new row is inserted.

- There is a mandatory one-to-many foreign key relationship from Component-Type to Component, reflected in comp_type_code. This column is indexed.

- There is a nonmandatory one-to-many foreign key relationship from Directory to Component, reflected in source_directory_id. This column is indexed.

ComponentType

The ComponentType table contains component type codes and descriptions.

Column Name	SQL Server Datatype	Access Datatype	Data Constraint
cd	char(3)	Text(3)	Unique/not null
description	varchar(50)	Text(50)	Not null

The primary key for the ComponentType table is cd. The value is required and indexed, and no duplicates are allowed.

Directory

The Directory table contains physical and web locations, as well as the purpose for each directory.

Column Name	SQL Server Datatype	Access Datatype	Data Constraint
id	int	Long Integer	Identity/AutoNumber Unique, not null
name	varchar(20)	Text(20)	Not null
physical_location	varchar(50)	Text(20)	Not null
web_location	varchar(50)	Text(20)	Not null
purpose	varchar(50)	Text(50)	Not null

The primary key for the Directory table is id. The value is an identify column in SQL Server and an AutoNumber column in Access—the value is automatically incremented when a new row is inserted.

HtmlWebPage

All web site HTML pages are entered into WebPage and then into HtmlWebPage.

Column Name	SQL Server Datatype	Access Datatype	Data Constraint
webpage_id	int	Long Integer	Unique/not null
html_version	varchar(20)	Text(20)	Not null

- The primary key for the HtmlWebPage table is webpage_id. The value is required and indexed, and no duplicates are allowed.
- There is a mandatory one-to-one foreign key relationship from the WebPage table to HtmlWebPage, reflected in webpage_id.

MediaObject

This table holds information about the multimedia objects used in the web sites, including all graphics.

Column Name	SQL Server Datatype	Access Datatype	Data Constraint
id	int	Long Integer	Identity/AutoNumber Unique, not null
name	varchar(20)	Text(20)	Not null
filename	varchar(20)	Text(20)	Not null
ext	char(4)	Text(4)	Not null

Column Name	SQL Server Datatype	Access Datatype	Data Constraint
file_size	decimal	decimal	Not null
container_width	int	Long Integer	Nulls allowed
container_height	int	Long Integer	Nulls allowed
media_type_cd	char(3)	Text(3)	Not null
directory_id	int	Long Integer	Not null
optimized_tool_id	int	Long Integer	Nulls allowed
optimized_date	datetime	Date/Time	Nulls allowed
pulled_date	datetime	Date/Time	Nulls allowed

- The primary key for the MediaObject table is **id**. The value is an identify column in SQL Server and an AutoNumber column in Access—the value is automatically incremented when a new row is inserted.

- There is a mandatory one-to-many foreign key relationship from MediaType to MediaObject, reflected in **media_type_code**. This column is indexed.

- There is a mandatory one-to-many foreign key relationship from Directory to MediaObject, reflected in **directory_id**. This column is indexed.

- There is a nonmandatory one-to-many foreign key relationship from Assisting-Tool to MediaObject, reflected in **optimized_tool_id**. The column is indexed.

MediaType

The MediaType table contains media type codes and descriptions.

Column Name	SQL Server Datatype	Access Datatype	Data Constraint
cd	char(3)	Text(3)	Unique/not null
description	varchar(50)	Text(50)	Not null

The primary key for the MediaType table is **cd**. The value is required and indexed, and no duplicates are allowed.

PageComponent

The PageComponent table is an associative table joining the WebPage and Component tables.

Column Name	SQL Server Datatype	Access Datatype	Data Constraint
page_id	int	Long Integer	Not null
component_id	int	Long Integer	Not null

- The primary key for PageComponent is a concatenated key consisting of both page_id and component_id.

- There is a mandatory one-to-many foreign key relationship from WebPage to PageComponent, reflected in page_id. This column is indexed.

- There is a mandatory one-to-many foreign key relationship from Component to PageComponent, reflected in component_id. This column is indexed.

PageMedia

The PageMedia table is an associative table joining the WebPage and MediaObject tables.

Column Name	SQL Server Datatype	Access Datatype	Data Constraint
page_id	int	Long Integer	Not null
media_id	int	Long Integer	Not null

- The primary key for PageMedia is a concatenated key, consisting of both page_id and media_id.

- There is a mandatory one-to-many foreign key relationship from WebPage to PageComponent, reflected in page_id. This column is indexed.

- There is a mandatory one-to-many foreign key relationship from MediaObject to PageMedia, reflected in media_id. This column is indexed.

PageScript

The PageScript table is an associative table joining the WebPage and ScrptWebPage tables.

Column Name	SQL Server Datatype	Access Datatype	Data Constraint
page_id	int	Long Integer	Not null
script_page_id	int	Long Integer	Not null

- The primary key for PageScript is a concatenated key, consisting of both page_id and script_page_id.

- There is a mandatory one-to-many foreign key relationship from WebPage to PageScript, reflected in page_id. This column is indexed.

- There is a mandatory one-to-many foreign key relationship from ScrptWebPage to PageScript, reflected in script_page_id. This column is indexed.

PageStyle

The PageStyle table is an associative table joining the WebPage and StyleWebPage tables.

Column Name	SQL Server Datatype	Access Datatype	Data Constraint
page_id	int	Long Integer	Not null
style_page_id	int	Long Integer	Not null

- The primary key for PageStyle is a concatenated key, consisting of both page_id and style_page_id.
- There is a mandatory one-to-many foreign key relationship from WebPage to PageStyle, reflected in page_id. This column is indexed.
- There is a mandatory one-to-many foreign key relationship from StyleWebPage to PageStyle, reflected in style_page_id. This column is indexed.

PageType

The PageType table contains web page type codes and descriptions.

Column Name	SQL Server Datatype	Access Datatype	Data Constraint
cd	char(3)	Text(3)	Unique/not null
description	varchar(50)	Text(50)	Not null

The primary key for the PageType table is cd. The value is required and indexed, and no duplicates are allowed.

PageXmlAux

The PageXmlAux table is an associative table joining the WebPage and XmlAux-WebPage tables.

Column Name	SQL Server Datatype	Access Datatype	Data Constraint
page_id	int	Long Integer	Not null
xml_aux_id	int	Long Integer	Not null

- The primary key for PageXmlAux is a concatenated key, consisting of both page_id and xml_aux_id.
- There is a mandatory one-to-many foreign key relationship from WebPage to PageXmlAux, reflected in xml_aux_id. This column is indexed.
- There is a mandatory one-to-many foreign key relationship from WebPage to PageXmlAux, reflected in page_id. This column is indexed.

ScrptWebPage

All scripting files, such as JavaScript/JScript, VBScript, and Perlscript files, are entered into WebPage first and then into ScrptWebPage.

Column Name	SQL Server Datatype	Access Datatype	Data Constraint
webpage_id	int	Long Integer	Unique/not null
script_language	varchar(20)	Text(20)	Not null
script_version	varchar(20)	Text(20)	Not null
browser	varchar(20)	Text(20)	Not null

- The primary key for ScrptWebPage is **webpage_id**. The value is required and indexed, and no duplicates are allowed.

- There is a mandatory one-to-one foreign key relationship from the WebPage table to ScrptWebPage, reflected in **webpage_id**.

StyleType

The StyleType table contains style type codes and descriptions.

Column Name	SQL Server Datatype	Access Datatype	Data Constraint
cd	char(3)	Text(3)	Unique/not null
description	varchar(50)	Text(50)	Not null

The primary key for the StyleType table is **cd**. The value is required and indexed, and no duplicates are allowed.

StyleWebPage

All files containing style information, such as CSS or XSLT files, are added into WebPage first and then into StyleWebPage.

Column Name	SQL Server Datatype	Access Datatype	Data Constraint
webpage_id	int	Long Integer	Unique/not null
style_version	varchar(20)	Text(20)	Not null
style_code	char(3)	Text(3)	Not null

- The primary key for StyleWebPage is **webpage_id**. The value is required and indexed, and no duplicates are allowed.

- There is a mandatory one-to-one foreign key relationship from the WebPage table to StyleWebPage, reflected in **webpage_id**.

- There is a mandatory one-to-many foreign key relationship from the Style-Type table to StyleWebPage, reflected in `style_code`. This column is indexed and duplicates are allowed.

WebPage

All web site pages (HTML, ASP, other) are entered into this table.

Column Name	SQL Server Datatype	Access Datatype	Data Constraint
id	int	Long Integer	Unique/not null
name	varchar(20)	Text(20)	Not null
filename	varchar(20)	Text(20)	Not null
ext	char(4)	Text(4)	Not null
directory_id	int	Long Integer	Not null
page_type_cd	char(3)	Text(3)	Not null
file_size	decimal	decimal	Not null
verification_tool_id	int	Long Integer	Nulls allowed
verification_date	datetime	Date/Time	Nulls allowed
pulled_date	datetime	Date/Time	Nulls allowed

- The primary key for the WebPage table is `id`. This value is manually set, is indexed, with no duplicates allowed.

- There is a mandatory one-to-many foreign key relationship from the Directory table to the WebPage table, reflected in `directory_id`. This column is indexed, and duplicates are allowed.

- There is a mandatory one-to-many foreign key relationship from the Page-Type table to the WebPage table, reflected in `page_type_cd`. This column is indexed, and duplicates are allowed.

- There is a nonmandatory one-to-many foreign key relationship from the Assisting Tool table to WebPage, reflected in `verification_tool_id`. This column is not indexed.

XmlAuxType

The XmlAuxType table contains XML auxiliary type codes and descriptions.

Column Name	SQL Server Datatype	Access Datatype	Data Constraint
cd	char(3)	Text(3)	Unique/not null
description	varchar(50)	Text(50)	Not null

The primary key for the XmlAuxType table is **cd**. The value is required and indexed, and no duplicates are allowed.

XmlAuxWebPage

All XML auxiliary pages, such as DTD files, are entered into WebPage first and then into XmlAuxWebPage.

Column Name	SQL Server Datatype	Access Datatype	Data Constraint
webpage_id	int	Long Integer	Unique/not null
aux_version	varchar(20)	Text(20)	Not null
aux_code	char(3)	Text(3)	Not null

- The primary key for XmlAuxWebPage is **webpage_id**. The value is required, indexed, and no duplicates are allowed.
- There is a mandatory one-to-one foreign key relationship from WebPage to XmlAuxWebPage, reflected in **webpage_id**.
- There is a mandatory one-to-many foreign key relationship from XmlAuxType to XmlAuxWebPage, reflected in **aux_code**. This column is indexed, and duplicates are allowed.

XmlWebPage

All XML files are entered into WebPage first and then into XmlWebPage.

Column Name	SQL Server Datatype	Access Datatype	Data Constraint
webpage_id	int	Long Integer	Unique/not null
xml_version	varchar(20)	Text(20)	Not null

- The primary key for XmlWebPage is **webpage_id**. The value is required, indexed, and no duplicates are allowed.
- There is a mandatory one-to-one foreign key relationship from the WebPage table to XmlWebPage, reflected in **webpage_id**.

Index

We'd like to hear your suggestions for improving our indexes. Send email to *index@oreilly.com*.

I

About the Author

Shelley Powers is a consultant/author with her own company, Burning Bird Enterprises. In the last several years, she has worked with a variety of distributed, Internet, and Web development applications, for different platforms and using a variety of tools. Shelley has authored or coauthored books on Dynamic HTML, JavaScript, Java, CGI, Perl, P2P, general Web technologies, and more. Shelley can be reached at *shelleyp@yasd.com*, and her book support site can be found at *http://www.burningbirdenterprises.com.*

Colophon

Our look is the result of reader comments, our own experimentation, and feedback from distribution channels. Distinctive covers complement our distinctive approach to technical topics, breathing personality and life into potentially dry subjects.

The animal on the cover of *Developing ASP Components, Second Edition*, is an asp, which is a term applied to various venomous snakes, including the depicted asp viper (*Vipera aspis*) of Europe as well as the Egyptian cobra (*Naja haje*), thought to have been the means of Cleopatra's suicide.

Needing to eat at least 50–60% of their body weight in food per week, European asp vipers hunt by lying in wait for approaching prey. After grabbing and biting a small rodent or other prey, they release it and wait several minutes for it to stop moving; the generally sluggish viper rarely chases prey. Vipers know their home territory very well, which allows quick escape from their asp-kicking natural enemies, serpent eagles, and hedgehogs. This trick hasn't helped them escape from their greatest threat, the expansion of human civilization, which frequently wipes out large sections of their territory.

The chemical composition of asp viper venom can vary from one population to the next, hampering initial antivenin development until 1896, but few viper bite fatalities occur in Europe today.

Leanne Soylemez was the production editor and proofreader for *Developing ASP Components, Second Edition*. Norma Emory was the copyeditor, Mary Anne Weeks Mayo and Colleen Gorman provided quality control, and John Bickelhaupt wrote the index.

Hanna Dyer designed the cover of this book, based on a series design by Edie Freedman. The cover image is a 19th-century engraving from the Dover Pictorial

Archive. Emma Colby produced the cover layout with QuarkXPress 4.1 using Adobe's ITC Garamond font.

David Futato designed the interior layout based on a series design by Nancy Priest. Clifford Dyer converted the files from Microsoft Word to FrameMaker 5.5.6 using tools created by Mike Sierra. The text and heading fonts are ITC Garamond Light and Garamond Book; the code font is Constant Willison. The illustrations that appear in the book were produced by Robert Romano using Macromedia Free-Hand 8 and Adobe Photoshop 5. This colophon was written by Nancy Wolfe Kotary.

Whenever possible, our books use a durable and flexible lay-flat binding. If the page count exceeds this binding's limit, perfect binding is used.

O'REILLY®

O'Reilly & Associates, Inc.
101 Morris Street
Sebastopol, CA 95472-9902
1-800-998-9938

Visit us online at:
www.oreilly.com

O'REILLY WOULD LIKE TO HEAR FROM YOU

Which book did this card come from?

_____

Where did you buy this book?
- ❏ Bookstore
- ❏ Direct from O'Reilly
- ❏ Bundled with hardware/software
- ❏ Other _____
- ❏ Computer Store
- ❏ Class/seminar

What operating system do you use?
- ❏ UNIX
- ❏ Windows NT
- ❏ Other _____
- ❏ Macintosh
- ❏ PC(Windows/DOS)

What is your job description?
- ❏ System Administrator
- ❏ Network Administrator
- ❏ Web Developer
- ❏ Other _____
- ❏ Programmer
- ❏ Educator/Teacher

❏ Please send me O'Reilly's catalog, containing a complete listing of O'Reilly books and software.

Name _____ Company/Organization _____

Address _____

City _____ State _____ Zip/Postal Code _____ Country _____

Telephone _____ Internet or other email address (specify network) _____

Nineteenth century wood engraving
of a bear from the O'Reilly &
Associates Nutshell Handbook®
Using & Managing UUCP.

POST CARD

NO POSTAGE
NECESSARY IF
MAILED IN THE
UNITED STATES

BUSINESS REPLY MAIL
FIRST CLASS MAIL   PERMIT NO. 80   SEBASTOPOL, CA

Postage will be paid by addressee

O'Reilly & Associates, Inc.
101 Morris Street
Sebastopol, CA 95472-9902